Hoover Institution Publications 126

The Stalinist Terror in the Thirties

THE STALINIST TERROR IN THE THIRTIES

Documentation from the Soviet Press

Compiled, with Preface and Introduction, by

Borys Levytsky

Hoover Institution Press
Stanford University
Stanford, California

Hoover Institution Publications 126
International Standard Book Number 0-8179-1261-4
Library of Congress Card Number 72-137404
© 1974 by the Board of Trustees of the
    Leland Stanford Junior University
All rights reserved
Printed in the United States of America

CONTENTS

List of Illustrations xiii
Preface xv
Statement on Transliteration and Dates xix
Select Terminology xxi
Abbreviations xxv

INTRODUCTION 3

1. LEADERS IN REVOLT AGAINST STALIN:
   KIROV AND ORDZHONIKIDZE 37
   Sergei Mironovich Kirov* 37
   Grigorii Konstantinovich (Sergo) Ordzhonikidze* 43

2. THE DESTRUCTION OF MILITARY CADRES ... 45
   General Facts about the Purge 45
   The "Tukhachevsky Affair" 48
   Khrushchev's Remarks 48
   Mikhail Nikolaevich Tukhachevsky* 51
   Officers Shot with Tukhachevsky 61
   Robert Petrovich Eideman* 61
   Boris Mironovich Fel'dman 65
   Iona Emmanuilovich Iakir* 66
   Avgust Ivanovich Kork 73
   Vitalii Markovich Primakov 75
   Vitovt Kazimirovich Putna 76
   Ieronim Petrovich Uborevich* 79
   Other Cadres 84
   Iakov Ivanovich Alksnis 84
   Mikhail Petrovich Amelin 87
   Vladimir Aleksandrovich Antonov-Ovseenko* 88
   Ernest Frantsevich Appoga 92
   Ivan Panfilovich Belov 93
   Ian Karlovich Berzin* 96

*Photograph included

v

Vol'demar Aleksandrovich Biuler 103
Georgii Ivanovich Blagonravov 103
Iosif Frantsevich Blazhevich 103
Vasilii Konstantinovich Bliukher* 105
Boris Iosifovich Bobrov 113
Gustav Gustavovich Bokis 114
Anton Stepanovich Bulin 115
Ivan Naumovich Dubovoi 117
Pavel Efimovich Dybenko* 118
Aleksandr Il'ich Egorov 121
Ivan Fedorovich Fed'ko 122
Gaia Dimitrievich Gai (Bzhishkian)* 125
Ian Petrovich Gailit 126
Ian Borisovich Gamarnik 126
Markiian Iakovlevich Germanovich 130
Vladimir Mikhailovich Gittis 113
Vladimir Davidovich Grendal' 113
Nikolai Evgen'evich Kakurin 133
Valentin Aleksandrovich Kangelari 134
Nikolai Dimitrievich Kashirin 135
Grigorii Davidovich Khakhan'ian 136
Dimitrii Iosifovich Kosich 139
Epifan Iovich Kovtiukh 140
Dimitrii Aleksandrovich Kuchinsky 143
Nikolai Vladimirovich Kuibishev* 145
Aleksandr Ivanovich Kuk 145
Ivan Semenovich Kutiakov 146
Nikolai Nikolaevich Kuz'min 146
Al'bert Ianovich Lapin 148
Ian Ianovich Latsis 149
Mikhail Karlovich Levandovsky 149
Mikhail Evgen'evich Medvedev 151
Konstantin Aleksandrovich Mekhonoshin 151
Sergei Aleksandrovich Mezheninov 152
Mikramid Mirsharapov 152
Nikolai Nikolaevich Movchin 153
Romual'd Adamovich Muklevich 153
Shamir Arakelovich Osenian 155
Gaik Aleksandrovich Osepian 157
Petr Matveevich Oshlei 159
Aleksandr Vasil'evich Pavlov 159
Lev Filippovich Pechersky 159
Aleksei Makarovich Peremytov 160

Evgenii Leonidovich Perfil'ev 160
Iakov Khristoforovich Peters 161
Rudol'f Avgustovich Peterson 161
Sergei Adreevich Piontkovsky 163
Semen Andreevich Pugachev 164
Iurii Vladimirovich Sablin 164
Aleksandr Ignat'evich Sediakin 169
Evgenii Nikolaevich Sergeev 169
Ernest Genrikhovich Shakht 169
Iosif Eremeevich Slavin 172
Andrei Evgen'evich Snesarev 173
Ivan Iakovlevich Strod 173
Nikolai Aleksandrovich Suleiman 175
Aleksandr Andreevich Svechin 175
Vladimir Khristoforovich Tairov (Ter-Grigor'ian) 175
Benedikt Ustinovich Troianker 178
Iosif Stanislavovich Unshlikht* 181
Semen Petrovich Uritsky* 185
Pavel Ivanovich Vakulich 187
Matvei Ivanovich Vasilenko 188
Ioakim Ioakimovich Vatsetis 188
Mikhail Dimitrievich Velikanov 188
Aleksandr Ivanovich Verkhovsky 191
Iakov Il'ich Vesnik 191
Ian Matisovich Zhigur 192
Dimitrii Petrovich Zhloba 192
    Rehabilitated Writers of Military Theory 193

3. PROMINENT LEADERS OF THE CPSU 197

Iakov Andreevich Andreev 197
Nikolai Kirillovich Antipov 197
Eremiia Saiadovich Bakunts 198
Karl Ianovich Bauman 198
Andrei Sergeevich Bubnov 199
Vladimir Aleksandrovich Degot' 203
Naum Ignat'ovich Dubovoi 211
Evgeniia Nikolaevna Egorova (Ella-Marta Lepin') 212
Robert Indrikovich Eikhe 214
Avel' Safronovich Enukidze* 220
Artemii Grigor'evich Geurkov 223
Nikolai Fedorovich Gikalo 225
Levan Davidovich Gogoberidze 225
Filipp Isaevich Goloshchekin 228

Grigorii Fedorovich Grin'ko 229
Mirza Davud Bagir-ogly Guseinov 229
Akmal' Ikramov 231
Aleksandr Fedorovich Il'in-Zhenevsky 233
U. D. Isaev 234
V. I. Ivanov 234
Astur Kakhoian 235
Betal Edygovich Kalmykov 236
Aligeidar Agakerim-ogly Karaev 239
Lavrentii Iosipovich Kartvelishvili 242
Mendel' Markovich Khataevich 243
Vil'gel'm Georgievich Knorin 247
Aleksandr Vasil'evich Kosarev 249
Stanislav Vikent'evich Kosior* 252
Aikaz Arkad'evich Kostanian 255
Aleksandr Ivanovich Krinitsky 257
Mikhail Maksimovich Kul'kov 259
U. D. Kulumbetov 265
Bela Kun 265
Petr Mikhailovich Kuznetsov (Darbinian) 267
Emmanuil Ionovich Kviring 268
Vasilii Dimitrievich Lakoba 270
Dimitrii Zakharovich Lebed' 271
Nikolai Mikhailovich Lukin 273
Aleksei Vasil'evich Medvedev 274
Aram Mikhailovich Mirzabekian 275
Levon Isaevich Mirzoian 276
Muzaffar Akper-ogly Narimanov 279
Amaiak Markarovich Nazaretian 282
N. N. Nurmakov 284
Mamiia Dimitrievich Orakhelashvili 285
Mariia Platonovna Oradhelashvili-Mikeladze 287
Sergei Porfir'evich Petrov 288
Iosif (Osip) Aronovich Piatnitsky* 288
Ol'ga Vladimirovna Pilatskaia 290
Mikhail Georgievich Pleshakov 291
Vladimir Ivanovich Polonsky 292
Ian Vasil'evich Poluian 294
Iakov Abramovich Popok 295
Pavel Petrovich Postyshev 296
Sharif Radzhabov 300
Dzhainak Sadeevich Sadaev 301
Sakhibgarei Said-Galiev 302

Shirinsho Shotemore 303
Elena Kirillovna Sokolovskaia 306
Karl Petrovich Soms (Kaufman) 307
Vladimir Gordeevich Sorin 308
Alesha Svanidze 313
Nikolai Samsonovich Svanidze* 315
Iosif Mikhailovich Vareikis 316
Evgenii Il'ich Veger 323
I. A. Zelensky 323
Tengiz Gigoevich Zhgenti 324

4. LEADERS OF THE NATIONAL COMMUNIST
PARTIES 327
The Destruction of Cadres in the Republics: Overview 327
Zigmas Ionovich Angaretis 340
Ian Ianovich Anvel't 341
Semen Bantke (Ruban) 343
Aleksandr Grigor'evich Cherviakov 347
Vlas Iakovlevich Chubar' 348
Petr Iur'evich Diatlov 349
Butabai Dodobaev 350
Mikhei Nikolaevich Erbanov 351
Nikolai Matveevich Goloded 353
Grigorii Vasil'evich Ivanenko (Baraba) 354
Faizulla Khodzhaev 355
Iurii Mikhailovich Kotsiubinsky 360
Ivan Iulianovich Kulik 361
Ian Davidovich Lentsman 361
Avis Sogomonovich Nuridzhanian 362
Sadyk Nurpeisov 365
Aga Gusein Rasulzade 367
Turar Ryskulov 369
Boris Petrovich Sheboldaev 373
Nikolai Alekseevich Skripnik 374
Grigorii Ivanovich Staryi (Borisov) 376
Gamid Sultanov 379
Saak Mirzoevich Ter-Gabrielian 382
Daniil Ivanovich Volkovich 386
Vladimir Petrovich Zatonsky 387

5. STATESMEN
.... 389
Kaigysyz Serdarovich Atabaev 389
Mazhid Mukhamedzhanovich Chumbalov 390

Aramais Artemovich Erznkian 391
Iakov Arkad'evich Iakovlev (Epstein) 393
Grigorii Naumovich Kaminsky 394
Sarkis Oganesovich Kas'ian (Ter-Kasparian) 398
Aleksei Semenovich Kiselev 402
Ivan Evdokimovich Klimenko 402
Nikolai Vasil'evich Krylenko* 405
Nestor Apollonovich Lakoba 412
Mikhail Moiseevich Maiorov 412
Vardan Aleksandrovich Mamikonian 413
Pavel Nikolaevich Mostovenko 414
Aleksandr Ivanovich Muralov 414
Gazanfar Makhmud-ogly Musabekov 416
Aleksandr Vasil'evich Odintsov 416
Ovsep Ambartsumovich Pogosian 417
K. Sarymuldaev 418
Vasilii Ivanovich Toksin 419

6. CAPTAINS OF INDUSTRY 421

General Comments on the Purge of Economic Executives and
Its Effects on Industrialization 421
Teimur Makhmud-ogly Aliev 423
Mikhail Vasil'evich Barinov 425
Karl Mikelevich Begge 427
David Samuelovich Beika 429
Nikolai Pavlovich Briukhanov 432
Karl Iulii Khristianovich Danishevsky 433
Gabib Pirdzhan-ogly Dzhabiev 434
Shalva Zurabovich Eliava 436
Nikolai Pavlovich Glebov-Avilov 438
Nikolai Afanas'evich Kubiak 439
Georgii Ippolitovich Lomov-Oppokov 439
Valerii Ivanovich Mezhlauk 442
Vladimir Pavlovich Miliutin 445
N. Osinsky 447
Andrei Fedorovich Radchenko 448
Ian Ernestovich Rudzutak* 451
M. S. Samatov 461
Aleksandr Pavlovich Serebrovsky 461
Ashot Sarkisovich Shakhmuradov 463
Kirill Vasil'evich Sukhomlin 465
Panteleimon Ivanovich Svistun 466
S. I. Syrtsov 467

    Valentin Andreevich Trifonov 467
    Il'ia Venidiktovich Tsivtsivadze 469
    I. I. Zheltov 471

7. DIPLOMATS 473
    Lev Mikhailovich Karakhan 473
    Nikolai Nikolaevich Krestinsky 473

8. CHEKISTS 475
    Ivan Alekseevich Akulov 475
    Terentii Dimitrievich Deribas 475
    Tarichan Mikhailovich D'iakov 476
    Serikgali Dzhakupov 479
    Ionas Gruodis 481
    Ivan Dimitrievich Kashirin 482
    Mikhail Sergeevich Kedrov 485
    Martyn Ivanovich Latsis 489
    Sergei Luk'ianovich Lukashin (Sarkis Sradionian) 490
    Magaza Masanchin 493
    Aleksandr Nestorovich Mikeladze 495

APPENDIX A: Fate of Lenin's First Government 499
APPENDIX B: Fate of Full Members
Elected at 17th Congress 501
Notes.. 505
List of Document Sources 519

LIST OF ILLUSTRATIONS

Sergei Mironovich Kirov 36
Grigorii Konstantinovich (Sergo) Ordzhonikidze 42
Marshal Mikhail Nikolaevich Tukhachevsky 50
Corps Commander Robert Petrovich Eideman 60
Army Commander First Class Iona Emmanuilovich Iakir 67
Army Commander First Class Ieronim Petrovich Uborevich 78
Vladimir Aleksandrovich Antonov-Ovseenko 89
Army Commisser 2nd Class Ian Karlovich Berzin 97
Marshal Vasilii Konstantinovich Bliukher 104
Pavel Efimovich Dybenko 119
Corps Commander Gaia Dimitrievich Gai (Bzhishkian) 124
Corps Commander Nikolai Vladimirovich Kuibishev 144
Iosif Stanislavovich Unshkikht 180
Semen Petrovich Uritsky 184
Avel' Safronovich Enukidze 221
Stanislav Vikent'evich Kosior 253
Iosif (Osip) Aronovich Piatnitsky 289
Nikolai Samsonovich Svanidze 314
Nikolai Vasil'evich Krylenko 404
Ian Ernestovich Rudzutak 450

PREFACE

While the fiftieth anniversary of the Soviet State was being celebrated with great fanfare in 1967, the government went to considerable length to divert attention from another milestone—the thirtieth anniversary of the Ezhovshchina. In September 1936, when Nikolai Ezhov succeeded G. G. Iagoda as the chief of the Soviet security organization, the intensifying terror of the 1930s was approaching its culmination. At the February–March 1937 plenum of the Central Committee of the All-Union Communist Party (Bolsheviks) (AUCP[B]), Stalin and Ezhov reported that a large spy ring had been unmasked. It was at that plenum that Stalin proposed his thesis that class struggle is inevitably intensified as socialism approaches its ultimate victory. This claim served to justify the ever-increasing terror and also gave the official green light to the Ezhovshchina. Thousands of Party, government, and business and industry functionaries, as well as scientists, writers, and artists, were arrested and shot. Although this terror wave continued through 1938, the Soviet equivalent of the "Bartholomew night"—the destruction of the entire elite of Soviet society—was achieved in 1937.

Many of the events that took place in the Soviet Union during the thirties are still not entirely clear, for obvious reasons. Stalin and his accomplices were successful in creating a façade for their actions by staging the Moscow showcase trials. There were three major trials—the so-called "Case of the Trot-skyite–Zinovievite Terrorist Center," held August 19–24, 1936; the "Anti-Soviet Trotskyite Center" case which took place January 23-30, 1937; and the "Case of the Anti-Soviet Bloc of Rights and Trotskyites," which took place March 2-13, 1938. In these trials many of Lenin's old Bolshevik comrades (G. I. Zinoviev, N.I. Bukharin, L. B. Kamenev, A. I. Rykov, and others) were sentenced to death as enemies of the people, and Stalinist propaganda used the trials to divert the attention of the Western world and of the Soviet citizenry from the much more far-reaching events of the Ezhov terror. During the Ezhovshchina there were only a few Trotskyists or followers of Bukharin and Zinoviev who fell victim to the executioners. Most of the terror was directed against Stalin's co-workers, against those cadres who had accepted Stalinism and who in many cases had helped Stalin to defeat his opposition.

Thus we know today that experts who in the past have compared the Moscow trials to an iceberg with only the tip showing the bulk submerged below surface, were making a somewhat valid comparison. The visible tip in fact helped Stalin to obscure the most important objective of the trials, an objective which had nothing to do with those who stood accused. The following documentation of Stalin's terror in the 1930s should provide a better understanding of the events of those years. It consists entirely of Soviet documents, particularly those published around the time of the Twenty-second Congress of the Communist Party of the Soviet Union (1961).

For reasons that are discussed in greater detail in the introduction to this work, the CPSU leadership decided to open the archives a crack after Khrushchev came to power. Biographies of victims of Stalin's terror began to appear, scattered and unsystematically, in magazines, newspapers, and reference books. We have classified all these documents, and what emerges is a picture which not only reveals new facets of Stalin and his regime but, more particularly, enriches our understanding of the history of the Soviet Union and of the larger social processes in operation during the 1930s within the Communist Party and the Soviet system.

These documents also represent a slice of the cultural history of our century. They demonstrate how a despotic system can destroy the most basic norms of man's existence in a society. This was one of the most important goals the compiler set for himself. The leitmotif for this work was George Santayana's admonishment: "Those who are not informed of the past are condemned to repeat it."

After Khrushchev's fall in 1964, the rehabilitation of Stalin's victims slowed down considerably. This tendency became particulary pronounced after the Soviet intervention in Czechoslovakia in 1968. Neostalinism and chauvinism became the new main ideological tenets of the Party. The leaders attempted to impress on the Soviet citizenry that the mass murders of the 1930s were unimportant and that, in any case, they had not interfered in the slightest with the development of socialism. Biographies of Stalin's victims continue to appear occasionally, but the phrase frequently used during Khrushchev's regime, "... he became a victim of arbitrary use of power during the years of the personality cult," today is seldom used.

The rehabilitated victims of the Stalinist terror belonged to the political elite of their day: Party leaders, high government functionaries, leaders of commerce and industry, scientists, writers, artists, and top military commanders. They were mostly Party members and they had contributed, both physically and intellectually, to the buildup of the Soviet State. The academician Professor A. D. Sakharov claimed in his now world-famous treatise of 1968 that more than half of all the Party members, more than 1.2 million, were arrested between 1936 and 1939 alone, and that of these only fifty thousand were freed. The reader of this book will be justified in wondering what happened to all those millions of Soviet citizens who did not belong to the Party and who disappeared into the night without a trace.

I wish to thank all who assisted me in this work, particularly Mrs. E. Sprogis, the head of my archive, and Mrs. L. Skimel, who copied the Russian texts. I am deeply grateful for the numerous contributions made by members of the Hoover Institution staff and their associates, especially for the Russian translation by Paul Stevenson, the German translation by Gary Gerard, and the final editing by Mrs. E. Dewar.

I acknowledge the particularly useful ideas for the study suggested by the analysis entitled *Die Ezhovshchina,* which was supported by the Bundesinstitut für ostwissenschaftliche internationale Studien in Cologne.

Munich, January 1973   Borys Levytsky

STATEMENT ON TRANSLITERATION AND DATES

The transliteration in these translations follows the system used by the U.S. Library of Congress. Exceptions are made for the spelling of some proper names in the text, thus: Tukhachevsky, not Tukhachevskii; Beria, not Beriia; Mikoyan, nor Mikoian. Russian titles and authors' names in source citations are all in Library of Congress transliteration.

Names of Ukrainian, Turkic, Caucasian, or other non-Russian origin are shown for the most part in their Russified form.

Dates generally are given according to the Gregorian calendar, which was adopted in the Soviet state in 1918; however, although under the Gregorian calendar the Bolshevik seizure of power took place in November 1917, the more familiar "October Revolution" is retained here in reference to that event and is the term commonly used in Soviet sources.

SELECT TERMINOLOGY

Alash-orda — Kazakh national party formed in March 1917 to unify Kazakh plainsmen, check Russian and Ukrainian colonization in the area, and effect a gradual settlement of nomads. During the Civil War this party at first tried to establish alliance with local anti-Bolshevik forces. After all such attempts proved abortive, Alash-orda leaders were won over to cooperation with the Bolsheviks (1918) with assurances that regional autonomy would be granted. Subsequently, Alash-orda leaders played a major role as members of the revolutionary committee that set up the political and administrative organization of the plains of Central Asia, and Alash-orda constituted the main indigenous political force during the first five years of the Kazakh Autonomous Socialist Republic (created in August 1920).

ataman — Russian word meaning a Cossack leader. *See* hetman.

Basmachi — members of an anti-Bolshevik resistance movement active in Turkestan after the October Revolution. They began simply as a band of brigands, but were organized as guerrillas by some of the adherents of the anti-Bolshevik government of Kokand after that government was suppressed in 1918. The movement spread throughout Turkestan, and at the peak of their effectiveness the Basmachi controlled the entire Turkestan countryside and effectively limited Soviet authority to the principal cities and railway lines. Eventually the movement became anti-Russian as well as anti-Bolshevik. By 1924 it was functioning only in the more mountainous areas, where it was intermittently active during the 1930s and again during World War II.

Borot'ba faction, Borot'bists — a group of Ukrainian nationalists who generally supported the Bolsheviks but opposed their policy of centralized control from Moscow. Declared counterrevolutionary by Lenin, this faction was dissolved in 1920.

Dashnak — a member of Dashnaktsutiun, the national revolutionary party of Armenia, founded in 1890. After the October Revolution this became the chief party in the independent Armenian Republic of 1918-20.

gubernia — a province.

Great Patriotic War — World War II.

Gummet ("Energy") — a Moslem social-democratic party established in Baku in 1904. It was an autonomous party, but was operating effectively as a branch of the Bolshevik faction of the RSDWP in 1905, was repressed by the tsarist government and went underground. It surfaced in 1918, went undergound again during the Turkish invasion that year. In 1920 Gummet merged with the Azerbaidzhan CP.

hetman — Ukrainian word meaning a Cossack leader. *See* ataman.

kolkhoz — collective farm.

krai — territorial unit in the Russian Soviet Federated Socialist Republic (RSFSR), virtually equivalent to an oblast (*q.v.*).

kulak — wealthy peasant, commonly characterized by Communists as oppressor of less fortunate peasants.

Mezhraiontsy — a group of Russian social democrats organized in 1913 to seek unification of all social-democratic factions into one party. This group (headed by Trotsky, D. Riazanov, A. Lunacharsky, and S. Uritsky) also organized and agitated effectively among workers in St. Petersburg and Moscow and carried propaganda to the armed forces. In August 1917 the Mezhraiontsy joined the RSDWP(B).

Musavat — pan-Islamic social-democratic party formed in Baku in 1911-12 by young intellectuals, many of whom had cooperated with local Bolshevik groups during the revolution of 1905. It was forced underground during World War I because of its pro-Turkish stance, but resurfaced after the February 1917 revolution and became the most influential part among Moslems in Transcaucasia and later in the Azerbaidzhan SSR.

oblast — an administrative region, usually economic, within a constituent republic.

Osoaviakhim — a paramilitary organization first established in 1927 solely to provide military training for civilians, but subsequently (probably after 1934) extended to virtually every area of Soviet life to bolster reserves of trained manpower.

Rada — a Ukrainian word meaning council; refers to the Ukrainian Central Rada, which was the governing body granted authority over the central Ukraine by the Provisional Government of 1917.

raion — a district or region.

solkhoz — a state farm.

uezd — a county.

volost — a rural district.

ABBREVIATIONS

agitprop — agitation and propaganda department.

AUCCTU — All-Union Central Council of Trade Unions.

CC — central committee.

CCC — central control committee.

CEC — central executive committee.

Cheka — Russian abbreviation for All-Russian Extraordinary Commission for Combating Counterrevolution, Speculation, and Delinquency in Office, the security police organization established in December 1917 under the leadership of Feliks Dzerzhinsky. The Cheka was abolished in 1922 and replaced by the GPU *(q.v.)*.

CP — Communist Party.

CPC — council of people's commissars.

CPSU — Communist Party of the Soviet Union. The official name adopted by the All-Union Communist Party (Bolsheviks) *(see under* RCP[B]) at its Nineteenth Congress in October 1952. This is currently the official name of the ruling party of the U.S.S.R. *See also* RSDWP.

GPU — State Political Administration, the security police agency established in February 1922 as a branch of the People's Commissariat of Internal Affairs (NKVD). Became the OGPU *(q.v.)* in 1923 as a result of an organizational and administrative change.

Komsomol — Young Communist League.

LSDP — Latvian Social Democratic Party or Lithuanian Social Democratic Party.

MD — military district.

NKVD — People's Commissariat of Internal Affairs. *See under* GPU, OGPU.

OGPU — Unified State Political Administration, the title taken by the GPU *(q.v.)* in 1923 when it was taken out of the Commissariat of Internal Affairs and attached to the Council of People's Commissars of the newly formed U.S.S.R. The OGPU, like the Cheka and the GPU before it, was headed by Feliks Dzerzhinsky until his death in 1926. He was succeeded by Viacheslav Menzhinsky, who died in 1934 and was in turn succeeded by Genrikh G. Iagoda. By a decree of July 10, 1934, the OGPU was abolished, its functions were transferred back to the Commissariat of Internal Affairs (NKVD), and it became the GUGB (Main Administration of State Security). In September 1936 Iagoda was replaced by Nikolai I. Ezhov, who carried out Stalin's great purge (hence this period is sometimes known as the "Ezhovshchina" or "Ezhov terror"). After two years of purges, the NKVD was accused of "excesses" owing to the activities of "wreckers and saboteurs" who allegedly had infiltrated its ranks. A bloody purge of the NKVD ensued, and Ezhov was replaced by Lavrentii Beria in December 1938. In February 1941 the GUGB was transformed into a separate commissariat—the People's Commissariat of State Security (NKGB)—headed by V. N. Merkulov; Beria remained head of the NKVD. The two commissariats were reunited under Beria after the German invasion of the U.S.S.R., but in April 1943 they were again separated. In 1946, when the people's commissariats became ministries, the NKGB became the MGB, the NKVD became the MVD. After Stalin's death in 1953, the MGB was merged with the MVD, but in March 1954 it was transformed into a new agency directly subordinate to the Council of Ministers—the Committee of State Security (KGB).

orgburo — organization bureau.

PC — people's commissar or people's commissariat.

politburo — political bureau.

raikom — district committee.

RCP(B) — Russian Communist Party (Bolsheviks). The official title adopted by the Bolsheviks at the Seventh Party Congress in Petrograd, March 1918. This title was changed to All-Union Communist Party (Bolsheviks) at the Fourteenth Congress in Moscow in December 1925, and the new designation was retained until 1952, when it became the CPSU *(q.v.)*. However, to minimize confusion, the abbreviation CPSU is used in these translations to designate the Party after 1925.

RMC — revolutionary military committee.

RSDWP — Russian Social Democratic Workers' Party. Founded at a congress in Minsk in March 1898. At its Second Congress (Brussels-London, July-August 1903) it split into Bolshevik and Menshevik factions. At its sixth conference (Prague, January 1912) the Bolshevik faction decided to form a separate party, which at the next conference (Petrograd, May 1917) took the name Russian Social Democratic Workers' Party (Bolsheviks). *See* RSDWP(B).

RSDWP(B) — Russian Social Democratic Workers' Party (Bolsheviks). The official name of the Russian Bolsheviks' party from the time of their seventh conference (May 1917) until their Seventh Congress (Petrograd, March 1918). *See* RCP(B).

SCNE — supreme council of the national economy.

SDPLR — Social Democratic Party of the Lettish Region.

SR — socialist revolutionary.

The Stalinist Terror in the Thirties

INTRODUCTION

In his secret speech at the Twentieth Congress of the Communist Party of the Soviet Union (1956) Khrushchev revealed that in 1954 a special commission had been given the task of rehabilitating Stalin's purge victims. Since that time, the Military Collegium of the Supreme Court had reviewed many rehabilitation cases, and in 1954 concentration camp gates had opened for many convicts. Included among them were some survivors of the terror in the 1930s.

It became apparent soon after Stalin's death that the problem of rehabilitation was extremely complex. To be sure, the Party bureaucracy was happy about the elimination of arbitrariness and of terroristic excesses, but it was also aware that it had a tiger by the tail. The Party functionaries had no trouble agreeing on the so-called literary rehabilitations. The victims here were artists and writers who either had been liquidated or labeled "bourgeois nationalists" in the various republics and whose works had then been withdrawn. Apparently A. I. Mikoyan was one of the Soviet leaders advocating such rehabilitation as early as 1954.[1] Political rehabilitations were of course a different matter. The problem was complicated by the fact that the entire leadership of Poland's Communist Party and many leading Communists from Yugoslavia, Hungary, and other countries were among the victims of Stalin's repressions. Without waiting for instructions from Moscow, the Polish United Workers' Party published as early as May 1, 1955, the photographs of liquidated Polish Communist leaders. The official rehabilitation of the Polish Communist Party (dissolved by the Comintern in 1938) was announced only later, on February 19, 1956, in a joint resolution of the central committees (CCs) of the Communist parties of the Soviet Union, Italy, Bulgaria, Finland, and Poland.[2] The rehabilitation of the Hungarian Béla Kun, at one time one of the most prominent members of the Comintern, also came about as late as February 1956.

The movement for rehabilitation of the Soviet terror victims started outside the Party apparatus. Certain historians in Moscow and Leningrad particularly deserve credit for their insistent demands that Soviet nationals also be rehabilitated. These historians centered around the journal *Voprosy istorii*, Madame A. M. Pankratova, editor-in-chief; and E. N. Burdzhalov, deputy editor. On the eve of the Twentieth CPSU Congress this journal sponsored a reader conference, an unheard-of political event in those days and one that could not be ignored. At the time some Soviet historians, Burdzhalov prominently among them, criticized charges brought by Beria and Bagirov and declared

3

that the evidence on which the charges were based was forged. They demanded a new look at the events of the 1920s and 1930s. Burdzhalov criticized articles in *Voprosy istorii* that had given the impression that "the Party fought in the 1920s not against anti-Party and anti-Leninist movements and groups, but against a bunch of insidious spies and saboteurs."[1]

One must keep in mind the political situation prevailing at that time in the Soviet Union. The leadership in the immediate post-Stalin period apparently entertained no thought of abolishing Stalin's personality cult. On the occasion of the first anniversary of Stalin's death, in March 1954, commemorative articles appeared in a number of newspapers and journals praising Stalin as an "authority on Marxism" and as "leader of the working people of the entire world."[4] On the occasion of Stalin's seventy-sixth birthday, December 21, 1955, the press again released a flood of praise, complete with hundreds of pictures recording milestones in the dead leader's career and honoring him as "a great revolutionary and a deep thinker." At the nineteenth congress of the Communist Party of the Ukraine, a giant portrait of Stalin hung behind the speakers' platform and the then first secretary of the central committee (CC) of the Ukrainian Party, Kirichenko (a former confidant and protege of Khrushchev), finished his speech with this statement: "The Ukrainian Communists will close ranks even more firmly around the Central Committee of the Communist Party of the Soviet Union and will be in the forefront of the struggle for the ultimate victory of the Marx-Engels-Lenin-Stalin cause."[5]

All this took place before the CPSU Twentieth Congress but after a number of large trials in which security functionaries held responsible for the arbitrariness and terror during Stalin's regime had been indicted and in some cases even shot. In addition to the Beria trial in December 1953,[6] a number of other prominent trials, had taken place: in July 1954, for example, there had been the trial against M. D. Riumin; and in December 1954 former minister of state security V. S. Abakumov and five of his associates had been tried.[7] Thus even as the executors of Stalin's orders were sentenced to death in trials frequently attended by numerous representatives of the Party bureaucracy, Stalin continued to be praised as a great leader not only of the Soviet Union but of "all the progressive peoples of the world."

The Twentieth Congress of the CPSU was held February 14–25, 1956, in this tension-laden and discordant political climate. On February 25, Khrushchev delivered his now famous "secret speech." (It was published on June 4, 1956, by the U. S. Department of State, and the authenticity of the document is beyond any doubt.) The Twentieth Party Congress has historical significance because it took on Stalinism. But in the official proceedings of the congress only Mikoyan dared to criticize Stalin and to attack his *History of the CPSU (B). A Short Course*. The rehabilitation of Stalin's victims was never so much as mentioned, although in the course of a polemic Mikoyan referred to Antonov-Ovseenko and Kosior as "comrades" even though their rehabilitation had not yet been officially announced.

What was the most significant aspect of Khrushchev's secret speech? It revealed a number of details, carefully concealed until then, of the great purges of the 1930s and during the post-World War II years. Khrushchev described the findings of the special investigative commission of the CC and even quoted verbatim from some of the commission's interrogations of surviving functionaries of the security apparatus—interrogations concerning the methods used to secure convictions during the purges, with particular emphasis on the methods used in extracting "confessions."

Another highlight of the speech was the mention by name of numerous famous Bolsheviks liquidated by Stalin. Khrushchev spoke of Postyshev, of Rudzutak, of Rozenblum. He also mentioned Kirov's co-workers in Leningrad who were shot during Beria's terror reign: Chudov, Ungarov, Smorodin, Pozern, Shaposhnikova (Chudov's wife), Kabakov, Kosior, Chubar, Kosarev, and Eikhe. He disclosed that Kedrov also was ordered shot by Beria. Finally, he identified the four main victims of the "Leningrad affair": Voznesensky, Kuznetsov, Rodionov, and Popkov.

While Khrushchev described vividly Stalin's brutality as well as the overall mechanism of the mass liquidations, he painstakingly avoided talking about Stalin's motives. Instead he talked at length about Stalin's character flaws and his pathological distrust of people. He forfeited some credibility by relating obvious absurdities, however. He claimed, for example, that Beria had collaborated during the Civil War with the intelligence service of an Azerbaidzhan organization, the anti-Communist Musavat movement. Here is a sample of Khrushchev's argument:

> In staging a number of dirty and shameful cases, Beria, this rabid enemy of our Party and agent of a foreign espionage service who had succeeded in worming his way into Stalin's confidence, played a very odious role. ... It has been established that this scoundrel rose to the highest government positions by stepping over innumerable corpses.

The makeup of the Party leadership was of course a very important factor at that time. Because of a need to compromise, Khrushchev resorted to tricks that are only now coming to light. For example, he called on Molotov and Kaganovich to attest to Stalin's weaknesses and crimes, and at Khrushchev's request Kaganovich became the star witness against Beria. Yet a few years later Khrushchev charged that both Molotov and Kaganovich had been Stalin's accomplices and were therefore equally responsible for his crimes. Moreover even Voroshilov, who was widely known to have participated in the liquidation of the military cadres in the 1930s and to have distorted the history of the Civil War, now attempted to portray Khrushchev as a victim of Stalin's arbitrary repression ("Stalin suspected him of being a British spy").

It thus becomes apparent that the rehabilitation of Stalin's victims was motivated not so much by moral considerations as by tactical, power-political ones. This *tactical-utilitarian aspect of the rehabilitations survives to this day.* In fact, political considerations of this sort have been the major factor controlling the pace of the rehabilitation program.

The Twentieth Party Congress unleashed a number of contradictory processes in the Soviet Union, with the result that public attitudes suddenly began changing. This development was further promoted by measures to restore "socialist laws." Active forces emerged from society demanding a drastic acceleration of the rehabilitations. Some of the surviving old-guard Bolsheviks were particularly active in this movement, demanding courageously and effectively that the rehabilitations of their victimized comrades be speeded up.[8]

The Party bureaucracy regarded with particular alarm the emergence of historians pressing for a broadening of the rehabilitations as well as an acceleration. Several articles appeared in *Voprosy istorii* in 1956 and 1957 in which the role of the Mensheviks in the Russian revolutionary movement was reexamined; historians were also urged to take a fresh look at the various revolutionary opposition movements within the Party.[9] Attempts were made in the Ukraine to rehabilitate the "Borotbist" movement, a leftist splinter group of the Social Revolutionary Party that united with the Communist Party in 1919 as a result of Lenin's prodding.[10] In Central Asia attempts were made as early as 1955 to rehabilitate Dzhadidism, a progressive populist movement active around the turn of the century. Both of these movements were labeled "reactionary" and "nationalistic" during Stalin's time.[11]

The pro-Stalinist forces did not give up easily. They were very influential in Georgia, as one might expect, because of primitive nationalistic feelings ("Stalin as the big brother"). Even so, in August 1956 the CC plenum of the Georgian CP had to admit, among other things, that:

> The CC of the CP Georgia is aware of the fact that the Stalin personality cult is deeply rooted in the consciousness of Georgia's population, that it has reached excessive proportions here, and that it has assumed a nationalistic coloring.[12]

Pro-Stalinist forces unleashed propaganda in all the important Party organs. The July 1956 issue of *Partiinaia zhizn'* carried an article that may be called the platform of the "moderate Stalinists." Its main target was an article that had appeared in the March 1956 issue of *Voprosy istorii,* "The Twentieth Party Congress and the Task of Re-examining Party History," in which historians well known in the 1920s (Knorin, Bubnov, Popov, and others) had been forgotten. *Partiinaia zhizn'* reacted as follows to this article:

> It is possible, naturally, to discover some interesting things even in these texts, and it is useful to compare them with the *History of the CPSU(B). A Short Course.* Admittedly, the latter does in fact suffer from many errors and shortcomings. ...[13]

However, even though Khrushchev had said that the terror against opposition factions was intolerable and the evidence against Stalin's political rivals fabricated, *Partiinaia zhizn'* tried to justify the repressions:

> ...one must not hush up the fact that some leaders of anti-Leninist groups had overstepped not only the limits of Party loyalty but also those of Soviet legality. Every fifty-year-old member of our society is fully aware, even if he is not thoroughly familiar with Party history and theory, that the annihilation of the anti-Leninist ideology of the Trotskyites, Bukharin Rights and national deviationists; the separation of the misguided members of the anti-Leninist groups from their ringleaders; the fight for the monolithic unity of the Party were all important prerequisites for the ultimate victory of socialism in the Soviet Union.

Similar articles appeared in various other newspapers and journals. Protagonists claiming that Stalin was one of the most important theoreticians of Marxism-Leninism were particularly abundant. The theoretical Party organ *Kommunist* (no. 4, July 1956), for example, published an article listing those of Stalin's works claimed to have "eternal value."

The Party leadership tried to straddle the line between the reformist and pro-Stalinist forces. On July 30, 1956, a resolution of the CC of CPSU was published, entitled "Overcoming the Personality Cult and Its Consequences." This was obviously an attempt to regain control over the new situation and to channel the de-Stalinization tendencies. This document praised Stalin as a "superb theoretician and organizer"; however, it also mentioned his "negative personality traits" and stated that he "vastly overestimated his role and his accomplishments," that he "considered himself infallible," and that he "had begun to demand glorification of his person."[14] This resolution also attempted to make Beria principally responsible for the reign of terror, which of course is at variance with historical facts. The Party cadres were purged before Beria was appointed people's commissar of internal affairs in December 1938. In fact, the terror began to ebb under Beria.

The Party leadership was not homogeneous in the mid-1950s and its pragmatic need to consolidate delayed the rehabilitation of Stalin's victims. Khrushchev and his followers were hard pressed by the pro-Stalinist elements in the Party, particularly around the turn of 1956-57. For this reason, Khrushchev attempted to strike a few bargains. His speech at the New Year's party in the Kremlin on December 31, 1956, was significant:

> When it comes to fighting imperialism, I can assure you that we all are Stalinists. We are proud that we participated in the struggle against our enemies to ensure progress of our great cause. In this respect, I'm proud that we are Stalinists.

A few days later, on the occasion of a reception for Chou En-lai (January 17, 1957), he made the following remarks:

Not only do I fail to see a difference between Stalinism and communism but I am also of the opinion that Stalin, who as a Communist struggled for the welfare of a certain class, namely the working class, was an exemplary Communist.[15]

On March 10, 1957, the Party leadership decided to strike a blow against *Voprosy istorii*. In a resolution of the CC, Madame Pankratova, editor-in-chief, was given a stern reprimand and Burdzhalov was fired from his position as deputy editor.

In those days, the Stalinist forces worked determinedly to depose Khrushchev. The well informed Italian Communist journalist Giuseppe Boffa has claimed that Molotov was the political instigator and chief ideologist and Malenkov the organizer of a plot against Khrushchev.[16] In June 1957 events came to a critical point. Available documents reveal that Khrushchev and his followers suddenly decided, again for pragmatic reasons, to accelerate the rehabilitation of the victims of Stalin's terror. It was then decided to re-investigate the "Leningrad affair," a terrorist action against Party cadres after World War II. The chairman of the Committee of Party Control, N.M. Shvernik, was given the task of re-examining the Leningrad affair. He found that Malenkov, Kaganovich, and Molotov shared responsibility for the mass repressions.[17] According to existing reports, these Party leaders had attempted through some of their connections to lay their hands on the compromising documents in order to destroy them. The director of the Ukrainian branch of the Institute for Marxism-Leninism, I. Nazarenko, claimed, for example, that "Kaganovich tried to destroy a number of important Party documents and it is only thanks to Nikita Sergeevich Khrushchev that these documents were saved."[18]

A plenum of the CC of the CPSU was convened June 22-29, 1957, to take up the matter of the "anti-Party group." Involved were Malenkov, Kaganovich, Molotov, and Shepilov. Details of this meeting were released only during the Twenty-second Party Congress. It turned out that shortly before the plenum a dramatic meeting of the Presidium had been held during which a majority voted to expel Khrushchev. The controversy surrounding Stalin's purges was largely responsible for this. Madame E.A. Furtseva later related the events as follows:

A meeting of the Presidium of the CC was held shortly before the June plenum of the CC. It was attended by many members and candidates of the present Presidium. I believe they can all remember the mood prevailing during that meeting. The item under discussion was the complete rehabilitation — including Party membership — of erstwhile prominent leaders of our army: Tukhachevsky, Iakir, Uborevich, Egorov, Eideman, Kork, and others. Their innocence was so obvious that even Molotov, Malenkov, Kaganovich, and others were in favor of rehabilitating them, even though they had had a hand in their tragic deaths. In the course of the debate, Nikita Sergeevich challenged them quietly but directly: "When did you act in good faith? Years ago when you voted to send them to their tragic deaths or now when you vote to rehabilitate them fully? Tell me, when did you act in good faith?" This direct and honest question threw them into a rage and confusion. It was obvious from their behavior that they were afraid that the truth might come out, that the Party and people would find out about their gross violations of Soviet law. It was then that these wreckers hatched their plot to divert the Party from its new course, namely one that would return it to Lenin's ideas of Party life. They wanted to recapture their old positions, those they held during the days of the personality cult. It was this common goal that united them.[19]

All the documents available on the June 1957 plenum of the CC show clearly that Khrushchev deftly introduced rehabilitation politics into the power struggle, and that this facilitated his victory. Also, it was not until the Twenty-second Party Congress that it became known that K.E. Voroshilov was a prominent member of the "anti-Party" group and that he had been personally involved in the repressions of the Ezhovshchina. Polansky reported at the Twenty-second Congress that Voroshilov had come to Kaganovich's defense, and when Polansky enumerated Kaganovich's crimes Voroshilov had jumped up from his chair, waved his fists, and shouted: "You are young and we can still beat some sense into you!"[20]

The tug of war about Stalin's despotism continued after the June 1957 plenum. This was the start of a new era in post-Stalin society. Khrushchev and his supporters proposed a number of reforms in an attempt to portray themselves as "constructive" politicians, and in all the excitement the rehabilitation of the Stalin victims receded somewhat from the limelight. In the public forum, however, the rehabilitation debate became more heated.

The end of 1958 saw the publication of the last volume (vol. 51) of the second edition of *Bol'shaia sovetskaia entsiklopediia* (Large Soviet Encyclopedia). It contained the biographies of some of the Communist leaders who had been subjected to repressions during Stalin's regime. This was the first official document reporting the rehabilitation in some detail, and with its publication the Soviet public found out for the first time that a number of military leaders had finally been rehabilitated. Isolated victims of the "Leningrad affair," liquidated Jewish writers, and "forgotten" scientists were also mentioned in this volume. Then, in 1959, the much anticipated *Istoriia Kommunisticheskoi partii Sovetskogo Soyuza* (History of the CPSU) was published. This volume confirmed the cautiousness of the Party leadership in releasing information about the events in the 1930s. The mass repressions were described in a few noncommittal sentences and another attempt was made to blame the "scoundrel and political adventurer" Beria for all the crimes.

The Twenty-first Party Congress, at which the Seven Year Plan (1959-1965) was adopted, was held in Moscow from January 27 to February 5, 1959. The "anti-party" group (Malenkov, Kaganovich, Molotov, Bulganin, and Shepilov) again came under attack at this meeting, this time not because of their past activities but because of their opposition to Khrushchev, and were again labeled "divisive forces" and "conspirators."

The events at the Twenty-second Party Congress, held October 17-31, 1961, took an entirely different course, during which the rehabilitation of the Stalin victims took a giant step forward. Khrushchev and his followers had decided, not because of ideological motives but because of pure pragmatism and political expediency, to move rehabilitation back into the limelight. At that time relations between Moscow and Peking were already strained, and there was danger that the Stalinist forces within the Soviet Union would again become active. Not for truth's sake, then, but in an effort to compromise his opponents, Khrushchev decided to document Kaganovich's, Malenkov's, Molotov's, and Voroshilov's participation in the repressions of the 1930s. At the Twenty-second Congress Shvernik accused Molotov of "providing the theoretical basis for the need to intensify the mass repressions in 1937." He was also accused of arranging the arrest of G. I. Lomov-oppokov, who was subsequently liquidated. Shelepin accused Molotov of concurring in the arrests of Kabakov, first secretary of the CPSU in the Ural area; of Krutov, chairman of the Far Eastern executive committee of the Supreme Soviet; of Uchanov, people's commissar of light industry; and of others. Finally, Serdiuk accused Molotov of cosigning (with Stalin) the liquidation lists.

Kaganovich was portrayed as one of the main perpetrators of the repressions. He was accused by Podgornyi of having prepared the ground for the mass terror in the Ukraine in 1947, and by Shvernik of instigating the arrest of a series of functionaries in Chelyabinsk, Ivanovo, Iaroslave and other places; of using blackmail and provocations in enforcing the arrest of numerous Party and government functionaries; of proclaiming at a meeting (March 10, 1937) of railroad activists: "I can't think of a single railroad administrative body, of a single communications network that is not infiltrated by Trotskyite-Japanese saboteurs"; and according to Shvernik of being personally responsible for the arrest of 83 leading co-workers in the Railroad Ministry (32 incriminating letters were produced to substantiate these charges).

Malenkov was accused by Spiridonov and Shelepin of participation in the "Leningrad affair"; by Masurov and Shvernik of personally participating in acts of terror and unlawful interrogations, particularly in Belorussia in the years 1935 and 1936; and by Shvernik of purges in Armenia and Tiflis, in close cooperation with Beria.

Voroshilov was accused of complicity in the murder of Iakir. According to Shelepin, Voroshilov is supposed to have written on June 9, 1937, the eve of Iakir's execution, "I have doubts about the honesty of a man who is generally dishonest."

In his two speeches at the Twenty-second Party Congress, Khrushchev made public some details of Kirov's murder, of G.K.(Sergo) Ordzhonikidze's suicide, and of the execution of Alesha Svanidze, the brother of Stalin's first wife. On this occasion the world also learned for the first time about some of the circumstances surrounding the execution by firing squad of P. A. Voznesensky.

It is interesting to note that the representatives of the Party Control Committee (Shvernik, Serdiuk) and of the security forces (Shelepin) in addition to Khrushchev himself were in possession of a great deal of documentary evidence about the terror of the Stalin era. Only a few Party leaders from the republics said anything about the terror in their own areas while nothing at all was said, save for a few general accusations made by Mukhitdinov, about Stalin's reign of terror in Central Asia. It is also interesting to note that while Mikoyan expressed himself as favoring rehabilitation in principle, he made few concrete proposals and accused no one in particular, even though he must have been better informed than Khrushchev was about the events in the 1930s. Malinovsky, the late minister of defense, carefully avoided even mentioning the liquidation of the military cadres in the thirties.

The Twenty-second Congress passed a resolution on "Vladimir Il'ich Lenin's Mausoleum." It was resolved that Stalin's bier would be removed from the "sanctuary of the Soviet people and of the workers of the whole world." Khrushchev also proposed erecting a monument in Moscow in memory of the victims of Stalin's terror.

The Soviet Union was again enveloped in an anti-Stalinist wave, over which the Party once more lost control. In November and December 1961, at Party meetings held in all the republics, Stalin's terror was reported in great detail. The Soviet leaders in the Caucasian republics were particularly bold: there the populace was told of the most gruesome events, some forgotten and others until then unknown. All of this shook the Soviet society in the Caucasus to its foundations. Young writers and students particularly asked for assurance that this would never happen again in the Soviet Union and demanded a "return to the truth."[21] Even the concept of "justice" was relegated to a secondary position. The young people brazenly declared their distrust of the Party leadership and made it clear that Khrushchev's entire rehabilitation scheme did not satisfy them. A few lines by a young poet, Evgen Letiuk, symbolize this distrust:

I don't believe them.... The untruth has remained in their hearts and I know that they pray all night before their idol, Stalin's gypsum bust.[22]

The publishing houses were virtually overwhelmed with memoirs recalling the events in the 1930s. Stories about Stalin's terror began to appear in magazines, and the first books were published on the subject. This put Khrushchev and his followers in a defensive position. In an attempt to regain control of public opinion, Khrushchev called two meetings of leading Party and government leaders with writers and artists. The meeting on March 8, 1963, was particularly important because of a new tack taken by Khrushchev. He now upgraded Stalin, especially his contribution in the fight against the opposition:

> One trusted him and supported him. It couldn't have been different because in the past, in the history of our Party we had many cases of treason. ... Stalin was then in charge of the Party struggle against the enemies of the Revolution and of the socialist society.[23]

Khrushchev spoke of Stalin as a Marxist theoretician who was "fully dedicated to communism." He further said:

> When Stalin was being buried, many of the onlookers, including myself, had tears in their eyes. Even though we knew of some flaws in Stalin's character, we trusted him.[24]

Khrushchev again attempted to blame "the blemishes in Stalin's character" for all the trouble: "In the last years of his life Stalin was a very sick man, suffering from suspicion and a persecution complex."

During the last years of Khrushchev's regime the Party leadership stepped up its efforts to hold off the demands of an aroused public opinion, again particularly among the young people, for intensified de-Stalinization. Publishing houses and newspapers were cautioned to refrain from publishing accounts of the Stalin terror. This tendency became even more pronounced after Khrushchev was toppled from power. His successors stressed that objectivity was needed in dealing with the personality cult, and some leaders even went so far as to say that Khrushchev had indulged in "subjectivism and sensationalism" in describing Stalin's terror. A quote from the Party magazine *Voprosy istorii KPSS* illustrates this new attitude:

> One of the signs of the subjectivistic influence is the strident sensationalist tone used in some articles dealing with Party historical themes. Based on a few quotations cited out of context or some arbitrarily interpreted facts, the authors attempted to proclaim a "new view" of history and to revise the actual course of historical events.[25]

Since October 1964, the time of Khrushchev's fall, the rehabilitation drive has slowed considerably. Biographies of purge victims have become rarer and even in those that have appeared there is scarcely a mention of the Stalinist terror. The phrase "he was a victim of the personality cult" is now very seldom used. The Twenty-third Party Congress (1966) produced a particular glaring demonstration of this reactionary trend: at no time during the Congress were past problems of the Party mentioned. The present Party leadership does not wish to be reminded of its past. In this respect it is not unlike some Nazi remnants in the Federal Republic of Germany.

THE THREE KINDS OF REHABILITATION

The so-called rehabilitations transcended completely the strong ideological currents of the twenties—Trotskyism, Bukharinism, workers' opposition, etc. While it is admitted officially that not all of these enemies of the Party were traitors and spies, the general attitude is that the Party was justified in fighting its enemies. Even Khrushchev's viewpoint in these matters did not prevail. For he had declared at the Twentieth Congress that "there were no sufficient grounds for the physical destruction of all those persons who at one time or another had held different views than the official Party line. The label 'enemy of the people' was introduced for the sole purpose of murdering these people."[26] Khrushchev emphasized that many former Trotskyists had "returned to Leninism." He then posed the question:

> Was it necessary to destroy these people? We are thoroughly convinced that had Lenin been alive, such extreme measures would not have been used.[27]

With the many pressures for rehabilitation, one might have thought that the Soviet Party leadership after Stalin's death would muster enough moral strength to divorce itself from its past and restore the honor of its innocent victims. However, that is not what happened. In addition to the prominent opposition leaders, hundreds of thousands of concentration camp inmates, mostly peasants and workers, were not rehabilitated. The first ones to be rehabilitated were former Stalinists and they were followed by persons in nonpolitical categories: scientists, industrial managers, and members of the intelligentsia.

Immediately following Stalin's death, a Party commission reporting directly to the Presidium of the Central Committee was given the task of rehabilitating innocent victims. This commission had the power to inspect material in the NKVD archives and in other places, and to collect and classify many documents. The first rehabilitation recommendations were passed on, after clearance by the CC, to the proper courts. In his secret speech Khrushchev reported that the Military Collegium of the Supreme Court had rehabilitated 7,679 persons since 1954. There is indirect evidence that after the Twenty-second Party Congress the function of this Party commission was transferred to the Committee of Party Control.

The first group of survivors of the Stalin terror were released from concentration camps in early 1954. Nothing was found in official Soviet sources that would shed light on the mechanics of their discharge. Some information became available from private sources, mostly from former concentration camp inmates who later succeeded in leaving the Soviet Union. After regaining freedom, most of the former convicts found themselves in extremely precarious economic conditions. A lump-sum payment of 5,000 rubles (old currency) that was paid each of them on receipt of an application was of little help. However, the freed and rehabilitated prisoners theoretically were not forced to settle in the vicinity of the concentration camps, as were many other discharged convicts (such as active resistance fighters from World War II and former Vlasov supporters); those rehabilitated regained all of their civil rights; and the time spent in detention was fully applicable to an old-age pension.

No literature could be found about any legal basis for the rehabilitations. However, a study of rehabilitation documents reveals three categories of posthumously rehabilitated prisoners.

The fully rehabilitated make up the *first category*. Their names appear in all reference books in the political literature with no reservations attached. Their publications—articles, books, and scientific works—may appear individually or in collected works. In the *second category* are those rehabilitated victims whose historical contributions are acknowledged but who remain accused of having committed certain political errors. This category is very large. It harbors mainly the liquidated leaders of the national republics who were not always in agreement with the nationality policies of the Party and also former members of the opposition who returned to the official fold prior to the onset of the Great Purge. Their biographical sketches show them as only slightly tainted, but difficulties set in when it comes to republishing their works. The works of the Ukrainian Party leader Skrypnik and the Moslem Communist leaders Khodzhaev and Ryskulov, for example, are subjects of great controversy. Specifically, the debate revolves around which works are considered "correct" and therefore worthy of being published and which ones contain "errors" that make them unsuitable for publication.

Finally, the *third category* includes rehabilitated victims who have undergone what the Soviet press refers to as *grazhdanskaia reabilitatsiia* (civilian rehabilitation). This category consists of Party leaders and particularly of writers and artists who were liquidated during the Stalin era on contrived charges (espionage, treason, diversion) and who, though subsequently cleared of these charges, remain politically unrehabilitated. These were mostly low-level Party functionaries or well-known artists and intellectuals whom the Party continues to regard with suspicion, either because of their opposition to the Party or because of their "social origin."

It is known from private sources that Soviet Party historians are currently engaged in a heated discussion on the desirability of introducing still another category, *istoricheskaia lichnost* (historical personality). Pressure to do this comes primarily from Communists in the various People's Republics (particularly Rumania) but also from other countries. Advocates believe that such personalities as Trotsky and Bukharin, persons who played leading roles in the October Revolution, should be mentioned in reference and history books even though they may not be rehabilitated. This should be done, they claim, for the sake of historical accuracy. Such pressures have placed Soviet Party theoreticians and historians in an extremely difficult position, and they are currently searching for a formula that might help alleviate this sensitive condition.

A few words are in order about the punishment meted out to the organizers of the mass executions. Soviet law has no such provisions as has the law of the Federal Republic of Germany, for example, for "crimes against humanity." The number of security officers who were punished for these crimes is extremely small and all kinds of transgressions have been excused save those committed during the *Ezhovshchina*. The most important cases are the following.

In December 1953, a special tribunal presided over by Marshal Konev heard the case against Beria and his codefendants. Sentenced to death by shooting were L. P. Beria, V. N. Merkulov, B. Z. Kobulov, V. G. Dekanozov, S. A. Goglidze, P. Ia. Meshik, and L. E. Vlodzimirsky. Of these seven defendants, only Beria was active in Stalin's Great Purge. The others were involved chiefly in the power struggle following Stalin's death.

In July 1954, M. D. Riumin was sentenced to death and executed. He had been head of the section for investigating specially important cases in the Ministry of State Security and was active in the purges following World War II.

A public trial before the military collegium of the Supreme Court was held in Leningrad December 14–19, 1954. The accused were a former minister of state security, V. S. Abakumov, and five of his associates: A. G. Leonov, former head of the section for investigating specially important cases of the Ministry of State Security; V. I. Komarov and M. T. Likhachov, former deputy chiefs of this section; and I. A. Chernov and Y. M. Broverman. Abakumov, Leonov, Komarov, and Likhachov were sentenced to death; Broverman and Chernov were sentenced to twenty-five and fifteen years of hard labor, respectively.

Tiflis was the site in November 1955 of a trial against another former minister of state security, A. N. Rapava; and against the former minister for state security of the Georgian SSR, N. M. Rukhadze; a former deputy minister of the interior in Georgia, Tsereteli; and two Georgian public prosecutors. All those mentioned were sentenced to death, and two others were sentenced to twenty-five years in a penitentiary. The events of the 1930s did not rate as highly in this trial as did the repressions after 1950 (the so-called "Mingrelian affair").

In the Bagirov trial in April 1956, the defendants were actually organizers of Stalin's reign of terror. Bagirov and his codefendants were sentenced to death by firing squad. According to the March 23, 1956, issue of *Bakinskii rabochii*, Bagirov and his associates were accused of participating in the physical liquidation of Party cadres.

These are the only trials about which the public was informed. It is probable that a few secret trials also were held against those responsible for the terror in Stalin's time (this assumption is in fact corroborated by private sources), but any such trials appear to have been exceptional cases. There never was in the Soviet Union a general, orderly approach to court action against all the participants in the repressions.

Some Soviet press reports support the assumption that a small number of Party functionaries were expelled from the Party or, in "milder" cases, relieved of their Party duties because of participation in the Purge.

It is important to remember that all these measures were directed only against the organizers of the mass murders and not against those who were politically responsible. The latter not only favored the liquidations but also became indirectly involved in them (for example, as initiators of defamation and denunciation campaigns). They were kept out of all rehabilitation actions, and in most cases they retained their jobs in Party, government, or social organizations.

The present leaders of the Soviet Union are certainly aware that the complex rehabilitation problem cannot be ignored at a time when they themselves are preaching objectivity and temperance, particularly when the youth of the country is pressing for more information concerning activities in the Party and in society at large. They would like to continue this slightly embarrassing, though appeasing, business of occasional rehabilitations for as long as they can. It is doubtful that this approach can be successful in the long run, however, mostly because of growing pressures from abroad to clear the air about the events in the thirties. The pressures exerted by Rumania in 1966, for example, were even stronger than those applied by Poland and Hungary in 1956.

WHAT THE MOST RECENT DOCUMENTS REVEAL

The documents available to us today about the events in the Soviet Union in the 1930s are interesting primarily because they clearly reveal for the first time Stalin's motives for the bloody purge in 1937. They show, for example, that those who chose Stalin's side in the power struggle following Lenin's death became increasingly disenchanted with Stalin's policies in the early 1930s, and that one of the principal causes of this disenchantment was the continuing expansion of Stalin's terror. As the terror expanded, the security forces inevitably became an inportant *political* factor and were used in the "common struggle" against the great opposition of the 1930s. Indeed the secret police became Stalin's main support, his personal instrument of power.

Party cadres were particularly shocked by events in the Caucasus. In Georgia, L. P. Beria occupied a number of important positions in the security system and had gained Stalin's confidence as early as in the 1920s; along with Kirov and Ordzhonikidze, he deserves much credit for eliminating the opposition. In October 1931, the Central Committee of the Russian Party having uncovered "serious political errors and distortions" in the leading trans-Caucasian Party organizations, the "deserving Chekist" Beria was ordered to work for the Party. In November of that year he was elected first secretary of the CC of the Georgian CP; subsequently he became secretary of the Transcaucasian provincial committee of the RCP(B) and in 1932 first secretary of that committee.[28]

Events in Azerbaidzhan followed essentially the same course. Mir Dzhafar Abbakovich Bagirov, whose role in the purges was no less fateful than that of

Beria, had a similarly meteoric career. Between 1921 and 1930 he was chief of the security organs in Azerbaidzhan, commissar of internal affairs and, simultaneously, deputy chairman of the Azerbaidzhan council of people's commissars. After successfully finishing a course on Marxism-Leninism in 1932 in Moscow, he became chairman of the council. From 1933 on he was first secretary of the CC of the CP of Azerbaidzhan and then held the same position in the CP of Baku.[29]

These two cases are indicative of the trend then prevailing in the Soviet Union. The security organs not only gained supremacy in the Party but began to bring the Party under control. The terms "political leaders" and "supporters" underwent a profound change in the early thirties. The entire generation of Party and military leaders who had fought alongside Stalin first in the October Revolution and then in the struggle against the opposition, and who together with Stalin were now in a position to determine the fate of the Party and of the entire country, felt increasingly insecure and threatened.

The second area of discontent involved Stalin's policy of collectivization of farming. All Stalin's associates in those days agreed in principle with the notion of enforced collectivization, but some soon began to recognize the more serious errors and excesses of the program that was implemented. The accelerated rate of collectivization by force brought about a serious agricultural crisis in 1930. This led to discontent in all strata of the population, including the poor farmers. Stalin did attempt to alleviate the situation by retreating somewhat from his original plans (he did this by means of an article entitled "Golovokruzhenie ot uspekhov" [Giddiness Due to Success] which appeared in *Pravda* March 2, 1930), but at the same time he began to blame the Party cadres and organizations in the countryside for the crisis. In 1961 voluminous documentation was published in the Soviet Union revealing that a number of prominent persons who had gone with Stalin through thick and thin (such as Kaminsky, Kosior, Vareikis, and Bauman) became increasingly rebellious against his agricultural policies. Even some writers joined this opposition. In the previously mentioned meeting between Party luminaries and artists and writers in March 1963, Khrushchev cited a letter to Stalin written by M. A. Sholokhov (dated April 16, 1933) in which the writer protested the tyranny unleashed in the spring of 1933 in the area of the River Don. Khrushchev indicated that two such letters from Sholokhov to Stalin, and Stalin's replies, had been "recently found." He remarked:

> "One is deeply moved by Sholokhov's letters, written in blood, in which he described the shocking and criminal mistreatment of people in the Veshenskaia and other raions in the Don region."[30]

Sholokhov had given details of the happenings in the countryside and asked that an investigation be ordered:

> If you should decide that all this of which I write deserves the attention of the CC, I beg you to send real Communists to Veshenskaia raion who would be

courageous enough to unmask, regardless of their position, all those responsible for killing the collectivization effort in this country, Communists who would investigate not only those who are using torture, beatings, and insults in dealing with kolkhoz farmers but also all those persons who put them up to it.[31]

One may conclude on the basis of the published materials, which unfortunately is still sparse, that a relatively strong group in the Party preferred and advocated a "rational" and "measured" approach to collectivization, and that Stalin, Molotov, Kaganovich, and Postyshev (who was loyal and devoted to Stalin in those days) must be blamed for most of the excesses perpetrated during the collectivization. The dissatisfaction with Stalin's approach to collectivization was certainly not ideological; it was merely pragmatic.

Party cadres also became increasingly dissatisfied with Stalin's nationalities policies. At the Sixteenth Congress of the CPSU, in 1930, Stalin flirted with the national cadres from the republics, who were loyally devoted to him. The Belorussian contingent in particular had distinguished itself by crushing the "national deviationists" and various other similar opposition movements in that republic. The national Party cadres were hoping Stalin would channel the national relations onto what they felt to be the right track. In his report to the congress, Stalin criticized severely those who espoused Russian chauvinism and labeled them foes of Lenin's policy. He condemned their thesis proposing "melting" of national languages and the creation of a "national" socialist culture. By contrast, his criticism of nationalism in the national republics was much weaker and in essence followed Lenin's views. However, many changes in the realm of nationality politics occurred between this and the Seventeenth Party Congress in 1934. Centralist abuses in the interim chipped away at the rights of the Union republics. Industrialization led to many conflicts between the indigenous populations and the rapidly growing numbers of immigrant Russian technocrats and bureaucrats. These conflicts increasingly annoyed the Party cadres of non-Russian origin. The reactions took different forms, the most extreme being the suicide in 1933 of N. A. Skrypnik, a man who had been a companion-in-arms of Lenin and was a co-founder of the Ukrainian Communist Party. At the time of his death Skrypnik was deputy chairman of the council of people's commissars in the Ukrainian SSR and chairman of the Gosplan State Planning Commission of that republic. His credits in fighting the "leftist" Communists, Trotskyist, rightist-deviationists, and even "national deviationists" in the Ukraine were beyond question.[32] But though he was a loyal follower of Stalin, he opposed his nationality policies. His sensational suicide served to publicize his opposition.

The list of areas of strain is long. Military leaders, for example, felt annoyance at the official exaggeration of Stalin's contributions to the Civil War and to the shaping of the Red Army. What one can say in general is that discontent among Party members widened as Stalin's personality cult grew. It is not surprising that Stalin's old colleagues would be most offended by this development, and most critical. It was the behavior of the Party cadres (not of the Trotskyists and other members of the great oppositions) that turned out to be the biggest obstacle in Stalin's drive toward one-man dictatorship.

The Seventeenth Party Congress of the CPSU was a turning point in the history of the Soviet system. As one can see from the documents comprising this volume, even Soviet reference books admitted after Stalin's death that disenchanted Stalinists attempted at that time to remove Stalin from his position as general secretary of the Party and to replace him with Kirov. These reports have been confirmed by several Western observers living in Moscow who had occasion to establish contact with some of the old Bolsheviks released from concentration camps. The Communist journalist Giuseppe Boffa dealt in his book *Dopo Krusciov* with the rumors surrounding the events at the Seventeenth Congress. Although this was the first Party congress at which not a single voice was raised against Stalin, Boffa wrote,

> ... one knows from subsequent disclosures that most of the delegates and most of the members then elected to the CC were later purged by Stalin. The year 1934 was officially designated as the beginning of the worst despotic acts.... Rumors about these events started circulating in 1956. The most reliable of these has it that an informal meeting was held at the time of the Seventeenth Party Congress; that this was attended by delegates concerned about the state of affairs in the country, particularly agriculture; that in the secret balloting, Stalin's name was crossed out more often than any other person's. ... Some even claim that he was never elected and that he barely made it only because the number of CC members was increased at the last moment.[33]

Other private sources report that such rumors circulate predominantly among the old Bolsheviks and that it is they who exert the strongest pressure on the proper Party organs to clarify once and for all the events of the thirties. Thus far, the Party has reacted neither positively nor negatively, and Boffa believes that the available documents neither deny nor confirm the rumors. Khrushchev's hint that Stalin may well have staged Kirov's death merely contributes to the murkiness of the whole affair.

Because the official documents of the Seventeenth Party Congress were subject to Stalin's censorship, they of course do not reveal the extent and depth of the unhappiness among the Party cadres. However, one fact is not easily overlooked, and that is that Kirov scored an extraordinary personal triumph at the Congress. He was the last speaker to comment on Stalin's state-of-the-Union report. In the transcript of this meeting, he was praised as "the eminent and tested leader of the Leningrad Bolsheviks" and as the "laureate Party speaker" *narodnyi tribun*. He reportedly spoke "with clarity and color," and he was in fact the only speaker to be continually interrupted by applause. At the end of his speech "the Congress gave him a round of ovations. The applause and such shouts as 'long live the Leningrad proletariat' went on for several minutes."[34] It became apparent at the Seventeenth Party Congress that the Party bureaucracy was made up of two kinds of functionaries. Both were committed to the program associated with Stalin. But Kirov represented the revolutionary type committed fanatically and enthusiastically to the realization of communism, whereas Molotov, Kaganovich, and Voroshilov were typical *apparatchiki*—totally, unconditionally, and uncritically devoted to the despot Stalin.

December 1, 1934, marked the beginning of a new chapter in the chronicle of terror in the 1930s. It was on that day that S. M. Kirov was killed at the Smolnyi Institute in Leningrad. The shot that took his life triggered the bloodiest purges in the history of the Soviet Union. There are documents that seem to suggest that Stalin ordered the assassination. Khrushchev reported at the Twenty-second Congress that on the day of Kirov's murder the following directive, issued at Stalin's request without sanction by the Politburo (whose members were only casually informed of it two days later) was signed by Abel Enukidze, secretary of the Presidium of the Central Executive Committee:

1. Judicial bodies are directed to speed up bringing to trial those accused of plotting or carrying out terroristic acts.
2. The Courts are directed not to postpone the execution of death sentences for crimes in this category because of the possibility of a pardon. The Presidium of the Central Executive Committee of the U.S.S.R. will not consider appeals for pardon in these cases.
3. The People's Commissariat of Internal Security [NKVD] is instructed to carry out the execution of those sentenced to death for crimes in this category immediately following the sentencing.[35].

Khrushchev's comments about the effects of this directive, which came to be known in Western literature as the "Lex Kirov," were as follows:

This directive became the basis for the massive misuse of socialist laws. In numerous staged trials the defendants were accused of *preparing* terroristic acts. This precluded any possibility of a successful defense, even when they claimed in court that their "confessions" had been extracted by force or when they were able to refute convincingly the charges against them.[36]

A decision had been made even before Kirov's death to inspect the old Party membership cards and to issue new ones. This process for "cleansing" the Party of "foreign elements" was used by Stalin to collect the needed material for the Great Purge that followed. Ezhov was responsible for the cleansing operation. The examination of documents was completed in 1936, and on October 1 of that year the Party again began to accept new members. On September 25, 1936, Stalin and Zhdanov sent the following telegram from Sochi to Kaganovich, Molotov, and other members of the Politburo:

We believe it is absolutely necessary and urgent that Comrade Ezhov be appointed people's commissar of internal security. Iagoda is obviously incapable of unmasking the bloc of Trotskyites and Zinovievites. The GPU [State Political Administration] is at least four years behind in this matter. This is being recognized by all Party functionaries and most NKVD workers.[37]

On February 18, 1937, Sergo Ordzhonikidze committed suicide. Khrushchev had this to say at the Twenty-second Party Congress about the events leading to the suicide:

> Let us turn to Sergo Ordzhonikidze. I was present at his funeral. I believed the official announcement that he had died suddenly because we all knew he had a weak heart. It was not until years later, in fact only after the War, that I learned quite by chance that he had committed suicide. Before that, his brother had been arrested and shot, and Sergo realized that he could not go on working with Stalin even though he had been one of his closest friends. Ordzhonikidze held a high position in the Party—Lenin had known and valued his merits—but conditions became such that he could no longer work in a normal manner and, in order to avoid a collision with Stalin or the responsibility of contributing to Stalin's abuses of power, he decided to commit suicide.[38]

The available documents show clearly that Kirov and Ordzhonikidze were not only close political friends but also the main spokesmen for the dissatisfied Stalinists. They counted among their close friends F. F. Raskol'nikov, who defected abroad in protest against Stalin's policies, and Marshal Tukhachevsky.

The next important event in the chronicle of Stalin's terror was the 1937 February-March plenum of the CC of the CPSU. At that plenum, Stalin advanced the thesis that the class struggle would intensify as socialist development in the Soviet Union became more successful. He claimed the Party still harbored conspiring groups of Japanese, German, and Trotskyist agents. This claim was supported by Molotov, who criticized particularly the military establishment. Following a report by Ezhov entitled "Lessons from the Sabotage, Diversion, and Espionage Activities of Japanese, German, and Trotskyite agents," the plenum passed a resolution which said in part:

> The Plenum is of the opinion that all facts that emerged in the course of the investigation of the anti-Soviet Trotskyite Center and its followers in the provinces prove that the People's Commissariat of Internal Affairs is at least four years behind schedule in unmasking these most inexorable enemies of the people.[39]

During this plenum a new nebulous term was added to the already established designations "wrecker," "agent," and "traitor." From then on the term "double dealer" (*dvuruzhnik*) was used extensively in actions leading to the liquidation of Party cadres.

Soon after the plenum finished its deliberations, the NKVD machinery went into high gear. The first blow was directed against the Central Committee elected at the Seventeenth Party Congress. Khrushchev had this to say about the mass liquidation that ensued:

It was established that of the 139 members and candidates of the Party Central Committee elected at the Seventeenth Congress, a total of 98 persons, i. e. 70 percent, were arrested in 1937-1938 and liquidated.

This figure was confirmed in a *Pravda* article by Shaumian.[41] More than half (1,108) of the 1,996 delegates to the Congress were subsequently arrested for "counterrevolutionary activities."[42]

The delegates from Georgia were particularly hard hit by this purge: 70 percent were imprisoned or shot.[43] We are also in possession of a long list of CC members elected at the Seventeenth Party Congress who were eventually executed.

Among the victims of Stalin's terror, the military establishment led by Marshal Tukhachevsky occupies a special place. In the fall of 1936 the Soviet military attaché in Great Britain, V. K. Putna, was suddenly recalled from London and arrested.[44] Under torture Putna said some incriminating things about Marshal Tukhachevsky and certain other military leaders. Simultaneously, other preparations for the liquidation of military cadres were under way in various departments of the commissariats of Transportation and Heavy Industry, the latter headed by Sergo Ordzhonikidze.[45] The arrested functionaries, primarily from the defense industry, included a number of works managers who were accused of committing sabotage at the behest of foreign intelligence services. Ordzhonikidze's suicide of February 18, 1937, is related to these arrests.

At the 1937 February-March plenum Molotov demanded that the military cadres be purged because they had refused to eradicate the "enemies of the people" within the armed forces.[46] Between February and May the Soviet security apparatus worked feverishly at building up a case for the existence of a "secret organization in the employ of foreign intelligence services," a case based on "confessions" extracted from arrested officers. Tukhachevsky was arrested on May 26, 1937. Mass arrests of other military leaders throughout the entire country followed. Ia. B. Gamarnik, deputy people's commissar for defense and chief of the political administration of the Red Army, was branded as one of the main organizers of the *counterrevolutsionnaia voennaia fashistkaia organizatsiia* (counterrevolutionary military fascist organization). Apparently informed of his imminent arrest, he committed suicide.[47] In June 1937 Stalin gave a speech at a meeting of the Military soviet in which he reported that a counterrevolutionary military fascist organization had been uncovered; he demanded that this "conspiracy" within the armed forces be squashed. Grave accusations were raised at this meeting also against a number of military leaders and political functionaries who had not yet been arrested. These accusations of course led to a new wave of arrests. One of Stalin's closest collaborators in carrying out these arbitrary repressions was L. S. Mekhlis, who in 1937 became chief of the political administration of the Red Army.[48]

On June 11, 1937, Marshal Tukhachevsky was shot, along with I. E. Iakir, I. P. Uborevich, R. P. Eideman, B. M. Fel'dman, A. I. Kork, V. M. Primakov, and V. K. Putna.[49] Since Tukhachevsky was the most prominent military leader among those executed, the case is frequently referred to, both in the Soviet and Western literature, as the "Tukhachevsky affair."

Stalin's strikes against the political personnel in the army deserve special mention. In meetings with these military functionaries, Stalin demanded stronger vigilance against the "enemies of the people" within the army. When a participant in one of these conferences asked Stalin, "Can we talk freely about the enemies of the people?" Stalin replied: "Yes, definitely ... and we must proclaim it to the whole world."[50]

Party functionaries constituted another group of Stalin's victims. It is surprising that the biographies published since Stalin's death concern not only the central Party elite; there are also biographies of some of the so-called "national deviationists," i.e., leaders of the Communist movement among non-Russian nationalities. The rehabilitation of the Moslem Communist leader T. Ryskulov is particularly interesting. In *Ocherki istorii Kommunisticheskoi partii Kazakhstana* (Outlines of the history of the Kazakhstan CP), published in 1963, Ryskulov's program was described as follows:

1. Formation of a national army;
2. Formation of a national party;
3. Expatriation of the colonizers or at least limitation of their rights in using the land;
4. Creation of a union of all the oriental provinces, free of both West European capitalism and Soviet political influence.[51]

Ryskulov's rehabilitation is particularly intriguing because he, along with Khodzhaev, Ikramov, and others, had had a falling out with Lenin, and in the eyes of the judges concerned with rehabilitation that is a severe demerit. Ryskulov's biographies emphasize, however, that Lenin showed "great patience" in dealing with him, that Lenin attempted to convert him to his own views and in fact succeeded. Ryskulov was deputy chairman of the council of people's commissars of the RSFSR from 1926 to 1937 and simultaneously held a position in the Orient department of the Comintern. In 1925 he became the official Comintern representative in Mongolia.[52]

Among the state functionaries and managers of the economy who were victims of the repressions, the Soviet "captains of industry" represent the strongest and most interesting group. This group consists of hard-working, talented functionaries who helped Stalin fulfill the First Five Year Plan. The documents available to us unfortunately give a far from complete picture of this important segment of Soviet society. It is safe to say, however, that the liquidated plant managers were not vestiges of the old order or of Tsarist Russia, but belonged to the post revolutionary generation of Communists. And although accurate figures of the number of liquidated industrial managers are not available, it is estimated that 50 to 75 percent of the middle and top management echelons fell victim to the repressions in the 1930s and that many of these subsequently perished. It is characteristic of Stalin's insanity that he concentrated on those branches of industry which at the time contributed more than any others to the political power of the Soviet Union: the armaments industry and the chemical industry. Among those liquidated in the 1930s were the following capable and well-known managers of chemical plants: P. G. Arutiuniants (Bobr Combine), M. Granovsky (Beresna Combine), V. E. Zifrinovich (Solikamsk Combine) and L. Stresh (SK-1 plant). Others who suffered the same fate were E. L. Brodov (manager of Glavazot trust) and I. I. Todorsky (manager of Glavkhimprom trust). Deputy Commissar for Heavy Industry O. P. Osipov-Shmidt, who was responsible for the chemical industry, also was liquidated during the Ezhovshchina. Moreover Stalin ordered the liquidation of a number of scientists active in chemical research. Prominent victims in this field included Prof. N. F. Iushkevich and Professor S. R. Tsintsadze.[53] It should be noted that the managers of the chemical industry were preponderantly dedicated Communists. In 1929, for example, 88.5 percent of the 52 trust managers and 97.1 percent of the 106 managers of the largest chemical plants were Party members.[54]

Another industry that was particularly hard hit was the machine-building industry. Among the victims in this segment of the economy was the nationally known manager of the Kharkov tractor plant, P. I. Svistun. He had made the Kharkov facility a model plant: its output of 200 tractors per day in December of 1935 exceeded by far the daily norm of 144 specified in the Plan. Svistun was an old Bolshevik and Party member since 1909. When the Supreme Council of the National Economy of the U.S.S.R. decided in the fall of 1929 to build a tractor plant at Kharkov, Svistun was picked as the project manager. Nineteen months after construction began the plant was finished, and Svistun was celebrated as the exemplary model of a Communist plant manager. In 1937 he was executed, along with the manager of the Kharkov locomotive plant, L. P. Bodnarenko (Party member since 1917); the manager of another factory in Kharkov, I. I. Lisin (Party member since 1913); and others. Accused of being "co-conspirators" and executed with them were N. N. Demchenko, then first provincial secretary of the Ukrainian Communist Party in Kharkov, and a number of other high Party functionaries.[55]

Among the managers of metallurgical plants liquidated during the Ezhovshchina was G. V. Gvachariia of the Makeevsky plant, a man who became famous in the days of the Second Five Year Plan (1933–1937). He was accused of working with the Trotskyists in the 1920s, an activity for which he was actually arrested in 1929. However, he was soon released, broke off his association with the Trotskyists and became a trusted associate of Ordzhonikidze.[56] Another victim was I. I. Sheltov, manager of *Tsentroruda* (iron ore industry trust in Central U.S.S.R.), who had earned his reputation in the construction of the Cheliabinsk metallurgical combine.[54] Another famous industrial manager was Ia. I. Vesnik, who came to the armaments industry from the Red Army, where he had made a name for himself as a materials supply expert. Vesnik subsequently built the Magnitogorsk and Kuznetsk metallurgical plants and was construction manager of *Krivorozhstal* at the time of his execution. He had been awarded the Order of Lenin.[58]

A. P. Serebrovsky[59] distinguished himself in the coal mining industry, even though his specialties were the petroleum and the nonferrous metals industries. K. I. Rumiantsev also made important contributions in the coal mining industry.[60]

The purge was particularly sweeping in the armaments industry because the Stalinists claimed it was infested with enemy organizations; consequently the number of rehabilitated managers from this industry has been very small. Among the few rehabilitated is S. I. Syrtsov, who opposed Stalin in the late twenties and was expelled from the Party in 1930. It is now known that Syrtsov became manager of the military-chemical works at Noginsk in 1936, only to be arrested and liquidated two years later.[61] Another well-known specialist in the armaments industry was the Georgian I. V. Tsivtsivadze. In 1934 he became chief of the Technical Special bureau, which concerned itself exclusively with armaments projects. He then became manager of an unidentified armaments plant, and in 1937 he was arrested and liquidated.[62]

As already mentioned, attempts at rehabilitating writers and artists have encountered the least opposition from the Party apparatus. However, anyone attempting to construct a list of the names of the victims in this field will soon be disappointed. Although a large number of encyclopedias have appeared in recent years, as well as reference works about the literature and culture of minority nationalities in the Soviet Union, the names of liquidated writers and artists are mentioned only casually. One gains the impression that the Government either is ashamed of what has happened or does not itself know how many representatives of the intellectual elite were killed in Stalin's dungeons in the 1930s. The same is true of scientists. And although some historians spoke in 1962 of "mass executions of historians," here also even those who today condemn Stalin's crimes seem afraid to speak the whole truth or to give names and dates. However, even from the few available documents, which allow only a few glimpses into the Great Purge of 1937, one can gain some insight into the events of 1937: the purge of the Party leadership was part and parcel of a conscious destruction of the social elite of the Soviet Union. We have already seen that among those liquidated were representatives from every social segment, starting with Party functionaries and extending to industrial experts, scientists, artists, plant managers, and even representatives of youth organizations.

Before we come to the question of what it was that Stalin hoped to achieve by this liquidation, it is necessary to consider at least two erroneous interpretations of the Ezhovshchina.

The first misinterpretation has already been corrected. A number of Western experts believe that Stalin liquidated only those bureaucracies which no longer fitted into his industrialization plans because they had little to offer by way of help or up-to-date experience. Indeed, some experts claim that Stalin was virtually forced to get rid of the entire generation of "useless" professional revolutionaries. This interpretation, however, does not fit the facts. Actually the victims were the best specimens of Soviet society. These were no professional revolutionaries, unable to cope with new problems, but experienced organizers of the First Five Year Plan. These were people who had thoroughly modernized the Red Army and many were scientists and intellectuals enjoying worldwide reputations. Moreover how can one compare Tukhachevsky and his colleagues with the semiliterate Voroshilov and Budennyi. Stalin did not replace inept people with knowledgable ones; the only qualifications he expected in his new associates were servility and blind submissiveness.

The latest documents on Stalin's terror force a second correction of an earlier misconception about the Ezhovshchina. Some experts have made it sound as though the liquidated Party cadres were exclusively Trotskyists, Bukharin followers, or anti-Stalinists of one variety or another, and that the events of the 1930s were nothing more than intra-Party squabbles not unlike those known from the 1920s. We have already shown how misleading this interpretation is. However, this version refuses to die in the West, and partially also in the East, because Stalin and his helpers succeeded so well in perpetuating an enormous deception in staging the Moscow "showcase" trials. While Stalin's staging artists were focusing world attention on these trials, Stalin was able to decimate his erstwhile followers almost unnoticed, unhampered by any troublesome public opinion. However, the new documents on the Stalin terror in 1937 reveal clearly that the Moscow trials cannot be considered representative of the Ezhovshchina. They served merely as a façade behind which the real terror could proceed.

Still, the Moscow trials deserve a few words. The first trial in the series took place Augest 19–24, 1936. The defendants in this so-called "Case of the Trotskyite-Zinovievite Terrorist Center" were G. E. Zinoviev, L. B. Kamenev, G. E. Evdokimov, I. N. Smirnov, I. P. Bakaev, V. A. Ter-Vaganian, S. V. Mrachkovsky, E. A. Dreitzer, E. S. Goltsman, I. I. Reingold, R. V. Pikel, V. P. Olberg, K. B. Berman-Iurin, Fritz David (I. I. Krugliantsky), M. E. Lurie, and N. Lurie. All sixteen defendants were sentenced to death, the sentence was carried out immediately, and all the possessions of the condemned were confiscated.

The second trial, the so-called "Case of the Anti-Soviet Trotskyite Center," took place on January 23–30, 1937. The defendants were E. L. Piatakov, K. S. Radek, G. Ia. Sokolnikov, L. P. Serebriakov, N. I. Muralov, Ia. A. Livshits, Ia. N. Drobnis, M. S. Boguslavsky, I. A. Kniasev, S. A. Rataichak, B. O. Nerkin, A. A. Shestov, M. S. Stroilov, I. D. Turok, I. I. Hrasche, G. E. Pushin, and V. V. Arnold. Of the seventeen defendants, only Arnold and Stroilov were given ten-and eight-year jail terms, respectively; all the others were sentenced to death by shooting.

The third trial, known as the "Anti-Soviet Bloc of Rights and Trotskyites" case, was held March 2–13, 1938. The defendants were N. I. Bukharin, A. I. Rykov, G. G. Iagoda, N. N. Krestinsky, K. G. Rakovsky, A. P. Rozengolts, V. I. Ivanov, M. A. Chernov, G. F. Grin'ko, I. A. Zelensky, S. A. Bessonov, A. Ikramov, F. Khodzhaev, V. F. Sharangovich, P. T. Zubarev, P. P. Bulanov, L. G. Levin, D. D. Pletnev, I. N. Kazakov, V. A. Maksimov-Dikovsky, and P. P. Kriuchkov. All defendants were sentenced to death with the exception of Pletnev, who was given twenty-five years, and Rakovsky and Bessonov, who each received a fifteen year jail sentence.

The charges were so absurd and threadbare that it is really surprising they found such credence, not only among Communists but in some middle-class circles as well. At worst, Stalin was believed to have staged the trials against groups of conspirators. To be sure, certain prestige considerations affected Stalin's decision to hold the trials: with the exception of Trotsky, all the Communist leaders who would be found guilty of treason and spying were mentioned in Lenin's testament as the most prominent personalities in the Party—Zinoviev, Kamenev, Piatakov, and Bukharin. Trotsky was in exile, and these other legendary figures from Lenin's days no longer held any de facto power. Hence they provided an excellent decoy for Stalin's deceptive maneuver, and Stalin would become the only surviving Bolshevik of any stature. But what is more important, while the public, both in the Soviet Union and in the West, watched with fascination as the showcase trials progressed, Stalin was able to pursue, practically unnoticed, the real liquidation, which was directed with entirely different motives against an entirely different circle of enemies.

After Stalin's death, the Moscow trials were only indirectly labeled arbitrary and illegal. It is not known whether any actions were taken prior to 1967 to review all the sentences and rehabilitate all the victims of these consciously perpetrated judicial crimes. However, the entire framework of the trials has collapsed because several of the defendants who were sentenced to death have been fully rehabilitated and returned to honorable status, among them N. N. Krestinsky, V. I. Ivanov, A. Ikramov, and F. Khodzhaev.

Some of the more recent documents contain considerable detail about the techniques used in Ezhov's purges and about Stalin's personal responsibility for them. This aspect of the Ezhovshchina is treated only slightly in the documents contained in this volume; however, it is implied in several of the biographies given here.

The special laws passed following Kirov's assassination, the rules of procedure generally known as the Lex Kirov, opened the door to the most flagrant arbitrariness. With these laws in force the security forces had no need to bother about evidence or charges in making an arrest, knowing full well that suitably incriminating material would somehow follow. The first provincial secretary of the Georgian CP in the Abkhazian ASSR, M.T. Bgazhba, gave a detailed account of these techniques at a Party meeting in Tiflis, on November 17,

1961.[63] In some cases those arrested signed prefabricated confessions only after being subjected to incredibly cruel torture. That is what happened to Ia. E. Rudzutak, a former comrade of Lenin. At the Twentieth Party plenum, Khrushchev quoted from a letter Rudzutak had written to the central committee of his Party: "The examination procedures are such that the accused are forced to lie and to incriminate not only themselves but also other innocent persons."[64]

Another legendary Bolshevik leader, R. I. Eikhe, declared at his trial:

> In all my so-called confessions, which were extracted from me, there is not a single word written by me except my signature. I have made a number of depositions under pressure from the examining magistrate, who began torturing me immediately after my arrest. After that I began writing all that nonsense. ... The most important thing is for me to let the Court, the Party, and Stalin know that I am innocent.[65]

One can find in Khrushchev's secret speech a whole series of concrete examples from which one can derive a good picture of the techniques used during the Ezhovshchina. We shall restrict ourselves here to only one example, because it illustrates a technique that was also employed during Stalin's later terror. Khrushchev reported at the Twentieth Party Congress that an old-guard Bolshevik named Rosenblum was arrested in 1937 and subjected to terrible torture. He soon agreed to "cooperate" in the pretrial examinations of other victims. Rosenblum declared after Stalin's death that his examining magistrate, one Zakovsky, enumerated "several possible variants of the organization of [a] Center and of its branches. After going into a detailed description of the organization, Zakovsky told me that the NKVD would take over the case and that the trials would be public."[66] This technique was used in fabricating a number of "anti-Soviet Centers" and "blocs," which were then used to incriminate and to liquidate Party cadres. Examining magistrates like Zakovsky—and there were thousands like him in those days—would tell the prisoners that "they need not be concerned about anything, that the NKVD would see to it that detailed evidence of the activities of these hostile organizations would be made available promptly." The prisoner who had agreed to "cooperate" would then be given four to five months to familiarize himself with the "evidence" and to rehearse his role in the forthcoming trial. (This, by the way, is exactly what happened in the "Leningrad affair.") The prisoner was also told that his own fate would depend on how well he played his role. Rosenblum was told, for example (and this is now available in documentary form):

> If we should catch you lying or giving false testimony, you'll have no one to blame for the consequences but yourself. However, if you are good, you not only save your neck but we'll see to it that the Government will take care of you to the end of your days.[67]

Having established a pattern, the examining magistrates found it increasingly easy to concoct new cases. The just-completed trials served as models for new ones; the testimony of witnesses, affidavits, and the gathering of all kinds of other "evidence" fell into a pattern. All that was needed was to find the first link in a chain and after that the course of the trial was essentially predictable. In order to liquidate a well-known Party leader, for example, the NKVD might arrest distant or even close relatives of the marked man and extract "confessions" from them; after that, the liquidation of the leader was practically automatic. The biography of G. I. Petrovsky, an old-guard Bolshevik who died after Stalin's death, reveals how the technique was used in one case. Petrovsky himself was not purged in 1937, although he had been marked for liquidation. His sons were arrested first and accused of belonging to some conspiratorial organization; this of course also incriminated their father and set him up to be arrested and tried.[68]

The examining magistrates were assured that their activities were not unlawful. One of Stalin's most "meritorious" henchmen, the then chief prosecuter of the U.S.S.R. A. Ia. Vyshinsky, made sure there would be no qualms. At a meeting of public prosecutors in March 1937 he declared: "Everyone should remember Comrade Stalin's remark that there are phases, moments in the life of a society and in our own, when the laws are outdated and should be set aside."

Vyshinsky provided scientific backing for the premise that in crimes against the State, the confession of the accused constitutes the most important and decisive evidence. This is why the NKVD would go to any length to extract "confessions."[69]

Liquidation lists provided an important basis for the arrests. The security forces were asked to prepare lists of "suspicious persons" and to classify them by certain criteria. In most cases (according to documents made public at the Twenty-second Congress), these lists were submitted personally to Stalin, and either he or his closest collaborators, such as Kaganovich, Molotov, Malenkov, or Voroshilov, would decide on life or death for those on the lists.[70] Khrushchev reported at the Twentieth Party Congress that in 1937-38 Stalin was shown 383 such lists, containing thousands of names.[71]

The Ezhovshchina did not limit itself to the extermination of supposed enemies. The entire Soviet society was infected by a "spy mania." Everyone was asked to report to authorities anything suspicious. Informers became heroes of the socialist society, and Stalin considered assiduous informing one of the main virtues of a loyal Communist. The campaign against the Komsomol (Young Communists League), for example, was started after Stalin and Ezhov decided that the leadership of the Komsomol (Kosarev and others) was not sufficiently zealous in promoting among its members the practice of informing on one another.

At the November 1962 plenum of the CC of the CPSU, S. P. Pavlov, first secretary of the Komsomol CC, reminded his listeners that at the Eleventh plenum of the Komsomol CC Stalin had urged the Komsomol members "to spy out the enemy, identify him, and to remove him forcefully, physically, and permanently."[72] As is well known, the liquidation of P. P. Postyshev was due in large measure to a conflict he had with a girl turned informer.

The purges became particularly cruel when, at Stalin's instigation, the security forces began to arrest not only "principals" but also members of their families—a kind of "guilt by kinship" justice. Examples of this practice abound. Along with V. K. Bliukher were arrested his brother Pavel and his first wife Galina Pavlovna; it was in her honor that he had assumed the Chinese cover name Ga Lin.[73]

Marshal Tukhachevsky's wife Nina Yevgen'evna, and his brothers Aleksandr and Nikolai were arrested with him and shot. Three sisters and his mother were sent to a concentration camp where the mother and one of the sisters died. Tukhachevsky's daughter, who was under age at the time of his arrest, was arrested soon after she reached majority.[74] After Vareikis's arrest, Stalin ordered the arrest of his wife, Liubov' Grigor'evna, mother of three children, who also was killed in the fall of 1939. She had been a Party member since 1919.[75] Mirzoian's wife, Zhulia Teodorovna Tevosian, was arrested and shot at the same time as her husband. She had joined the Party in 1918 and by the time of her arrest was director of the Institute for Marxism-Leninism in Kazakhstan.[76] The wife of M. D. Drakhelashvili, Maria, was minister of education of the Georgian Republic when she was arrested and shot along with her husband.[77] S. Z. Eliava and his entire family were arrested and liquidated.[78] These examples can be multiplied at will. However, we are not so much interested in listing the victims as in giving examples of the large variety of Stalin's criminal extermination methods.

We shall also limit ourselves no more than a brief mention of what new light the most recent documents shed on the personality of Stalin. They confirm beyond any doubt that Stalin was the instigator of the Ezhovshchina. Any attempts by current Party leaders to transfer a portion of the blame to henchmen such as Beria and the "anti-Party group" are not justified by the facts. Various documents reveal, for example, that Stalin personally encouraged security officers to fabricate certain "cases." Moreover Stalin not only suffered from such character flaws as pathological distrust, vanity, and pride; he also identified himself with the "idea of communism" to the extent that he virtually considered himself its incarnation. Just as Hitler was convinced that the German people would perish after his death, so apparently did Stalin believe that he was insolubly and indispensably tied to communism. At the November 1962 plenum of the CC of the CPSU, Khrushchev recalled some of his personal encounters with Stalin:

Stalin ... talked like this: If I die, you too will perish. The imperialists will suffocate you.[79]

Previously, at the Twentieth Congress, in talking about the second wave of terror after World War II, Khrushchev had related other, similar remarks by Stalin:

> "You are just as blind as young kittens; what will you do without me? Our country will fall apart because you don't understand how to recognize enemies."[80]

We finally arrive at a problem of great import. To what extent do the events in 1937 reflect on the Soviet leaders and the system of today? The Soviet society today must be considered essentially "postdespotic." In spite of some important structural changes and the recent incorporation of individual agencies (particularly security) into the over-all system, there is a certain continuity between Stalin's despotism and the government of his heirs. This is evidenced by the continued existence of the same apparatuses and institutions; by manifestations of a mentality and behavioral pattern that had been molded for years; and by the fact that the generation that consciously and unreservedly served the despot Stalin, thus becoming morally responsible for the decimation of the "Leninist Party cadres," remains in power.

One must remember that the current leaders grew up during Stalin's reign. Many Party functionaries and particularly many military leaders were able to advance rapidly only because the Ezhovshchina created many vacancies. The entire elite in the Party, the government, the economy, and particularly in the army belongs to this generation. As we already know, the Eighteenth Party Congress (1939) was designated officially as the beginning of a new cycle in the history of the CPSU. The CC members and candidates elected at that time were a group of subservient henchmen who had nothing in common with "Lenin's cadres." And yet many of them (more than 25 percent) continued to serve in important positions long after Stalin was gone, as shown in the following table:

Elected at Eighteenth
CPSU Congress (1939)

Members	Last posititian as of February 1, 1970, (Stand v. 1.II. 1970 unless otherwise specified)
V. M. Andrianov	Until 1953, first secretary of the CPSU in Leningrad
I. A. Benediktov	Soviet ambassador to Yugoslavia
G. A. Borkov	Party and state functionary
S. M. Budennyi	Member of the Presidium of the Supreme Soviet of the U.S.S.R.
I. Iu. Iusupov	Director of Khalkabad industrial combine in area of Tashkent (died May 7, 1966)
L. R. Korniets	Chairman of the State Committee for Procurement, member of the Council of Ministers of the U.S.S.R. (died May 29, 1969)

D. S. Korotchenko	Chairman of the presidium of the supreme soviet of the Ukrainian SSR and a member of the politburo of the CC of the Ukrainian CP (died April 7, 1969)
A. N. Kosygin	Chairman of the Council of Ministers of the U.S.S.R., member of the Politburo of the CC of the CPSU
G. M. Malenkov	Until 1957, minister for electrical power plants, deputy chairman of the Council of Ministers of the U.S.S.R.
N. A. Mikhailov	Chairman of the committee for printing and publishing, Council of Ministers of the U.S.S.R.
M. B. Mitin	Until 1968, editor-in-chief of *Voprosy filosofii*
N. M. Pegov	Soviet ambassador to India
M. G. Pervukhin	Until 1962, Soviet ambassador to the German Democratic Republic; currently active in Gosplan.
P. K. Ponomarenko	Until 1964, Soviet representative to the International Atomic Energy Commission in Vienna
P. N. Pospelov	Director of the Institute for Marxism-Leninism
A. I. Shakhurin	Deputy Chairman of the state committee for economic relations with foreign countries, Council of Ministers of the U.S.S.R.
S. K. Timoshenko	Marshal of the Soviet Union, Chairman of the Soviet committee of war veterans (died March 31, 1970)
A. G. Zverev	Until 1960, finance minister of the U.S.S.R. (died July 27, 1969)

Candidates

I. P. Boitsov	Until 1961, deputy chairman of the Committee of Party Control of the CC of the CPSU
P. I. Doronin	Until 1961, first provincial secretary of CPSU in Smolensk
A. F. Gorkin	Chairman of the Supreme Court of the U.S.S.R.
N. I. Gusarov	Until 1957, first provincial secretary of the CPSU in Tula
S. D. Ignatev	Until 1960, first provincial secretary of the CPSU in the Tatar ASSR
N. G. Ignatov	Chairman of the presidium of the supreme soviet of the RSFSR (died November 14, 1966)
S. V. Kaftanov	Rector of the Mendeleyev Chemical-Technical Institute, Moscow
P. T. Komarov	Until 1961, first deputy chairman of the Committee of Party Control of the CC of the CPSU
I. S. Konev	Marshal of the Soviet Union, inspector-general for the U.S.S.R. Ministry of Defense
S. N. Kruglov	Until 1956, minister of the interior of the U.S.S.R.

K. A. Meretskov	Marshal of the Soviet Union (died December 30, 1968)
N. S. Patolichev	Minister of foreign trade of the U.S.S.R.
G. M. Popov	Until 1962, director of various factories in Moscow; pensioned as of 1962 (died January 14, 1968)
Z. T. Seredyuk	Until 1966, deputy chairman of the Committee of Party Control of the CC of the C.P.S.U.
Ia. V. Storozhev	Until 1956, deputy chief of the department of Party organization, RSFSR
V. G. Zhavoronkov	Until 1962, deputy chairman of the Commission of State Control, Council of Ministers, U.S.S.R.
V. P. Zotov	Until 1970, minister of the food industry of the U.S.S.R.; pensioned as of January 1970

Among the members and candidates elected to the Central Committee at the Twenty-third Party Congress of the CPSU in 1966 are the following persons who had also been elected to the CC at the Eighteenth Party Congress held in 1939, shortly after the Ezhovshchina:

Members	Candidates
I. A. Benediktov	S. M. Budennyi
N. G. Ignatov	L. R. Korniets
I. S. Konev	S. K. Timoshenko
D. S. Korotchenko	V. P. Zotov
A. N. Kosygin	
N. A. Mikhailov	
A. I. Mikoyan	
N. M. Pegov	
N. S. Patolichev	
P. N. Pospelov	
N. M. Shvernik	
K. E. Voroshilov	

These lists of course, include only the more prominent Party functionaries. A study of the origins and ages of Party functionaries at the provincial and krai levels confirms that they too tend to belong to the Stalin generation, and that they continue to set the tone for activities at their own levels.[81] This generation has succeeded not only in dissociating itself from Stalin and his system but also in containing de-Stalinization within certain bounds.

The effects of Ezhovshchina are visible in other important spheres of current Soviet society. We have in mind the conscience problem. Many works published in the last few years have insistently asked how the Ezhovshchina could have gone so far, and particularly what were the reasons for Stalin's terrorism. Not unexpectedly, the Party leaders are not eager to answer these questions—and according to the Communist journalist Boffa, many Soviet citizens, particularly the younger ones, are not likely to be satisfied with flimsy explanations. The Party anxiously avoids releasing any information about the "social roots of the Stalin cult"; it keeps the relevant material carefully locked up in its archives. By so doing, it unwittingly encourages thoughtful Soviet citizens to develop their own theories about Stalinism. These theories, according to Boffa, range from the conclusion that the leadership fears a "bourgeois counterrevolution" to the accusation that Stalinism has "violated history."

Noteworthy in this connection is the fact that the hierarchic structure of the Stalinist government system has survived in spite of some changes in recent years. This structure does allow for communication between the leadership and the people, but in only one direction: vertically down. No provisions exist for a reverse flow. Such a system inevitably is conducive to popular lethargy, even among the most enlightened segments of the population. An apathetic society acquires a great deal of inertia, and its citizens are unlikely to develop much initiative. They grow used to acting on orders from above, and this in turn reinforces the one-way vertical communication structure of the society. Horizontal channels are not encouraged for fear the government and the Party might lose control of them. This system has been practiced in the Soviet Union for decades and has become so ingrained that nobody questions it any more. Thus while leaders might accuse Stalin, they do so from perspectives within a structure that remains essentially as Stalin created it. Their basic thinking style and leadership pattern have changed very little. Their mentality fits into the framework of Stalin's model.

Only future generations with upgraded notions of political responsiveness will be able to look at their past without shame. Only future generations will be able to change the system in such a way that terror can never again become an instrument of government. Only then will Ezhovshchina be a thing of the past. The current generation not only lacks the will power to break with Stalinism; it is incapable of doing so.

Sergei Mironovich Kirov

I. LEADERS IN REVOLT AGAINST STALIN: KIROV AND ORDZHONIKIDZE

SERGEI MIRONOVICH KIROV

The last hours of Kirov's life

November 30, [1934] was an ordinary working day for Kirov. He spent the morning at the Smolnyi Institute checking preparations for the meeting of Party activists to be held next day at the Uritsky (Tavrida) Palace. On the day after that there was to be a joint plenum of the organization committee of the Leningrad city committee of the CPSU to discuss: "practical measures for carrying out the decisions of the November plenum of the CC of the CPSU" and "the position as regards flax and timber procurement." These important questions called for hard work on the part of the entire staff of the Smolnyi Institute. The collective of the oblast committee and city committee worked smoothly, it was true, but there might be oversights due to haste. It was necessary for Kirov himself to check everything and to acquaint himself with the draft resolutions.

Having done so, he summoned by telephone Ivan Fedorovich Kodatsky and Petr Ivanovich Struppe, the chairmen of the Leningrad oblast soviet and the Leningrad soviet, for a conference in which it was decided to place on the executive committees the main burden of the task of preparing for the abolition of the ration system. Having dealt with these matters, Kirov went with the two chairmen to the vestibule, where they encountered a canteen waitress carrying a tray on which stood a glass of strong tea. Kirov exclaimed: "What, is it twelve o'clock already? Thanks, I'll have tea at home."

Having entered his car at the main entrance, Kirov drove first to Avtovo to see how the bridgebuilders at the Pushchin intersection were getting on, and then to the workers housing estate under construction on Kamennyi Ostrov and the building site at Lesnoe in the Vyborg quarter. It was evening when he finally returned to his home in the Petrograd district.

December 1 likewise began as usual. The dawn broke late and sullen; curls of smoke rose from factory chimneys; children ran to school and housewives hurried toward the shops. The people of Leningrad, as elsewhere in the Soviet Union, had no suspicion that a jarring chord was about to mar the peaceful harmony of their everyday lives, with far-reaching consequences that would bring tragedy to many.

Kirov finished preparing his report at four in the afternoon. As he thrust his scribbled notes into the breastpocket of his tunic, he reflected that the regional

leaders would already be on their way to the Tavrida Palace to take part in
the discussion of Party activists on the results of the November plenum of
the CC of the CPSU. His wife and the maid offered to serve lunch in the
diningroom, but he sat down at the kitchen table and ate a quick snack, then
put on a light overcoat and khaki cap he always wore and telephoned to the
Smolnyi to say he was on his way. As he left the house, he leafed through
a calendar and said jokingly to his wife: "Say, Mary, when did I last have
a 'birthday'?"

"All right, you shall have cabbage dumplings tonight, and some specially
strong tea; I'll brew it myself."

Kirov kissed her and said with a smile, "You know, my dear, great things
are afoot. Bread rationing is coming to an end, and then we can have a 'birthday'
every day."

At the front door he greeted his chauffeur Iudin and the security guard
and got into his car. They drove over the Troitsky bridge, the handsomest
of those that cross the Neva. The secretary of the oblast committee and the
CC could not guess that on the following day a mourning procession would
line the route across this bridge from the Petrograd quarter to the Tavrida Palace,
the pediment of which would be covered by a huge portrait of himself, wreathed
in black and red ribbons. For thirty years Sergei Mironovich Kirov had rendered
wholehearted service to the working people and to the Party's fight for a brighter
future. He could remember every year of the hard struggle for socialism—its
events were etched into his memory and were mirrored in his wrinkles and
gray hair. But the best, he thought to himself, was yet to come. How many
adventures lay ahead, and with what zest he looked forward to life! He little
knew what was to happen in barely a quarter of an hour's time, at half-past
four. If he had, he might have got out of the car to take a last look at Leningrad,
the city he loved so well.

As it was, he sat and watched the wet asphalt and crushed snow disappearing
under the radiator as the car sped along. Gazing forward, he made calculations
as to the productivity of bread-baking plants that would be necessary to keep
the population fed adequately and without interruption. Data on this subject
had been prepared by the Leningrad soviet for the purpose of his report and
submitted to a special section of the oblast committee. But first he had to
call on Chudov, who was holding an important meeting—what would be its
result?

... As he stepped inside the Smolnyi, Kirov realized he no longer heard
the steps of the security guard behind him. He thought with amusement "So
he's left me!" and without waiting began to climb to the third floor, where
he made for the office of the second secretary of the oblast committee. As
he paused to open the door, there was a muffled explosion: he had been shot
at close quarters in the neck. He staggered, half-turning as he did so, and
crashed headfirst against the parquet floor. His peaked cap was pushed half-way
off and lay across his neck, where it stirred as the warm blood gushed forth.

That evening Leningrad was plunged in deep mourning. The radio emitted doleful music. The inhabitants of the city lay awake, smitten by sorrow. People wept openly in the factories, in the streets, and at home.[1]

Accounts of Kirov's murder in the History of the CPSU

1959 edition: On December 1, 1934, one of the chief leaders of the Communist Party and the Soviet state, S. M. Kirov, was treacherously shot dead at the Smolnyi Institute in Leningrad. The murderer, who was arrested on the spot, was imbued with hatred toward the Party leaders who had stoutly defended the policy leading to the victory of socialism in the USSR: he was an embittered renegade, an associate of former members of the Zinov'evite anti-Party group. He was a Party member and carried on him a Party card, thanks to which he was able to commit his heinous crime.

The murder of Kirov showed that a Party card could be used as a cover for revolting anti-Soviet acts. It was necessary to protect the Party from alien elements and thus render impossible the commission of acts hostile to socialism and the interest of the Soviet state by individuals enjoying cover of any kind.[2]

1962 edition: On December 1, 1934, one of the chief leaders of the Communist Party and the Soviet state, S. M. Kirov—a member of the Politstat and secretary of the CC and of the Leningrad Oblast Committee of the CPSU—was treacherously shot dead at the Smolnyi Institute in Leningrad. His death was a severe blow to the Party and the nation. The murderer, who was arrested on the spot, was imbued with hatred toward the Party and its leaders who had stoutly defended the Leninist policy leading to the victory of socialism in the USSR. He was an embittered renegade who had been expelled from the Party but used his Party card in order to commit his heinous crime.

The crime was a premeditated one and, as N. S. Khrushchev declared at the Twenty-second Congress of the CPSU, its circumstances are still the subject of investigation.[3]

Khrushchev's denunciation of Kirov's murder

Kirov's murder marked the beginning of the period of mass repressions. It is still no easy matter to determine who was responsible for the deed. The more closely we study the evidence, the more questions arise. It is noteworthy that the murderer had twice before been arrested by NKVD agents near the Smolnyi and had been found to be carrying weapons, but had been released on both occasions on the instructions of someone unknown. Now the same man was allowed to penetrate, gun in hand, to the corridor in the Smolnyi along which Kirov was in the habit of passing. And for some reason, at the moment of the crime Kirov's chief security guard was, contrary to instructions, a considerable distance behind him.

There is another strange circumstance. When the security guard was being driven to the place where he was to be interrogated by Stalin, Molotov, and Voroshilov, his escort, according to the driver's subsequent story, deliberately caused an accident and declared that the guard had been killed as a result, although in actual fact he was shot by them. Thus Kirov's official protector was killed, and those who killed him were executed in their turn. The deed was clearly no accident, but a premeditated crime. Who could have been responsible? The circumstances of this obscure affair are being carefully investigated.

It turns out that the driver of the truck in which Kirov's chief security guard was taken to be interrogated is still alive. He has declared that, on the way, an NKVD man sat in the cab beside him and two others were in the back of the vehicle with the guard. (It is of course very strange that a truck was used for the purpose, as though an ordinary car was not available. Clearly everything had been planned in detail beforehand.) The driver goes on to say that the man beside him suddenly wrenched the wheel from his hands and headed the vehicle toward a house. The driver seized the wheel once more and righted the vehicle's course so that it only struck the building sidelong; and he was told afterward that when this happened the security guard was killed.

Why was this man killed when none of those with him were injured? And why were the two NKVD men who had been in charge of him subsequently shot? Someone clearly had an interest in covering up the traces by making away with them.

There are many, very many circumstances of this and similar incidents which are still unexplained.

It is our duty, comrades, to investigate thoroughly and from every angle such episodes connected with the abuse of power. Time will pass and we shall die—we are all mortal—but as long as we are able to work, we can and must clear up many things and tell the truth to the Party and the people. We must do our utmost to establish the truth without delay, for the more time elapses since these events, the harder it will be to ascertain the truth. Even now, as the saying goes, you can't bring the dead back to life. But in the history of the Party the truth must be told about all these things so that such deeds can never again occur.[4]

The extermination of Kirov's staff

The murder of S. M. Kirov had grave consequences for the Soviet Union. The murderer, Nikolaev, an embittered renegade who had been expelled from the Party, was caught on the scene of his crime. The investigation of the circumstances took place in the atmosphere of the cult of Stalin's personality, which set in about that time. Stalin then began to depart further and further from Leninist principles and the norms of Party life, to violate the principles of collective leadership and to abuse his position. He seldom visited Leningrad, but he went there on this occasion and took charge of the investigation of the circumstances of Kirov's murder, which he used as a pretext to settle accounts with persons inconvenient to him. First in Leningrad and then throughout the country, mass arrests were carried out and many honest Communists were subjected to unjust repression. The checking and renewal of Party documents which took place in 1935-36, a measure which was certainly necessary and on the whole justified, was also used to expel from the Party many who were devoted to the cause of socialism. The Leningrad Party organization in particular suffered severely from these lawless measures.

In spite of the grievous conditions created at this time by Stalin's gross violations of the Party statutes and socialist legality, the Leningrad Party organization and the working population of the city, along with the whole Party and the rest of the Soviet people, continued their confident and unfaltering struggle for the realization of the Party's general line and achieved new successes in all fields of socialist construction.

After Kirov's death, A. A. Zhdanov was elected secretary of the Leningrad oblast and city committees of the Party ....

The mass repressions which began after Kirov's murder took their most monstrous form in 1937-38. The victims of arbitrary power in Leningrad in those years included hundreds of the most active Party and Soviet workers in the city and oblast, including the secretaries of the oblast and city committees of the Party, M. S. Chudov, A. I. Ugarov, P. I. Smorodin, and B. P. Pozern; the chairmen of the oblast and city executive committees, P. I. Struppe, I. F. Kodatsky, and A. N. Petrovsky; the chairman of the oblast soviet of trade unions, P. A. Alekseev; the secretary of the oblast committee of the All-Union Lenin's Young Communist League, I. S. Vaishlia; the senior members in the organization of the oblast and city committees of the CPSU, I. I. Alekseev, S. M. Sobolev, M. V. Bogdanov and P. L. Nizovtsev; and many secretaries of raion committees of the Party and important local Party organizations.

I. V. Spiridonov, the delegate of the Leningrad Party organization at the Twenty-second Congress of the CPSU, said in his speech at the congress that after Kirov's murder "for four years there took place in Leningrad an uninterrupted series of repressions against honest people who had committed no misdemeanor whatsoever. Promotion to an important job often meant a step towards the abyss. Many people were ruined without trial or investigation on the strength of false charges concocted in haste."

Leningrad was deprived in this way of many talented economists, organizers, and leaders of Soviet production. This dealt a heavy blow to Leningrad industry, which played a major part in the fulfillment of the economic tasks of the Five Year Plans.

After the trumped-up "Tukhachevsky affair," the ablest military and political officers of the Leningrad Military District and the Red Banner Baltic Fleet were arrested and liquidated, including the commander of the Leningrad military district, P. E. Dybenko; the commander of the Baltic Fleet, A. K. Sivkov; many members of the staff and political administration of the district, commanders of units and ships. All this had its effect on the military operations of the troops of the district and the ships and units of the Baltic Fleet during the Soviet-Finnish War and the first phase of the Great Patriotic War.[5]

Grigorii Konstantinovich
(Sergo) Ordzhonikidze

GRIGORII KONSTANTINOVICH (SERGO) ORDZHONIKIDZE

Khrushchev on Ordzhonikidze's suicide

Let us turn to Sergo Ordzhonikidze. I was present at his funeral. I believed the official announcement that he had died suddenly of natural causes because we knew he had a weak heart. It was not until years later, in fact only after the war, that I learned quite by chance that he had committed suicide. Before that, his brother had been arrested and shot, and Sergo realized that he could not go on working with Stalin even though he had been one of his closest friends. Ordzhonikidze held a high position in the Party—Lenin had known him and valued his merits—but conditions became such that he could no longer work in a normal manner and, in order to avoid a collision with Stalin or the responsibility of contributing to Stalin's abuses of power, he decided to commit suidice.[6]

Ordzhonikidze and Kirov

S. M. Kirov's closest friend and comrade was Sergo Ordzhonikidze. Their friendship of many years lasted until the last day of Kirov's life, and was never marred by the slightest disagreement. Sergo told his wife Zinaida Gavrilovna that in spite of his own impulsiveness he had never raised his voice to Kirov. The latter had on his writing desk at home a signed photograph of Sergo, who himself kept a large picture of Kirov on top of a bookcase containing the works of Lenin.

When Kirov visited Moscow he stayed at Sergo's home. He would usually let him know (of his impending arrival) the evening before by telephone, and Zinaida Gavrilovna remembers how impatiently Sergo awaited his friend. In the morning, before getting dressed, he would telephone to make sure that a car had been sent, and sometimes he himself would go to the station. If a plenum or a congress was being held, [the two friends] would lunch at Sergo's home during the midday break; if Kirov came on other business they would usually meet in the evening. After dinner they would sit and talk in the study or diningroom. After a while Sergo would lie down and Kirov would ensconce himself nearby. At about two or three o'clock in the morning Zinaida Gavrilovna would peep around the door:

"Really, you two are inseparable, like a pair of twins. It's time to go to bed."

"All right, we shan't be long," Sergo would answer. And Kirov would add: "Don't be cross with us, Zina."

In the early twenties Kirov and Sergo usually took their holidays together. Later, when Sergo's health declined, he used to go south while Kirov spent his vacations and sometimes his free days hunting.[7]

II. THE DESTRUCTION OF MILITARY CADRES

GENERAL FACTS ABOUT THE PURGE

The first repressions began at the end of 1934, immediately after the assassination of S. M. Kirov. They were sharply intensified in the autumn of 1936, when on Stalin's direct orders Ezhov became people's commissar for internal affairs.

By 1937 the repressions had taken on a mass character, especially against Party and government workers and the cadres of the main branches of national economy such as heavy industry and transport, as well as against political workers in the armed forces, especially in the higher ranks. After the CC plenum in February-March 1937 Stalin, in order to justify his illegal treatment of honest Communists, advanced the thesis, which was indefensible on theoretical and practical grounds, that the class struggle was bound to become more acute as the Soviet Union advanced toward socialism. The term "double dealer," which Stalin launched at the plenum, like its predecessor "enemy of the people," was used to disarm members of the Party and condemn them to unjustified persecutions. Stalin also insisted on the rule that "double dealers" and "enemies of the people" might be denounced several years after their alleged offenses. This directive practically obliged the agents of the NKVD to carry out mass repressions. In his speech at the plenum Molotov called for an onslaught on the military cadres, whom he accused of reluctance to combat "enemies of the people."

Soon after the plenum, the careerists and provocateurs who had wormed their way into the NKVD concocted the story of a "counterrevolutionary military fascist organization" within the armed forces. The charge of leadership in this organization was leveled against distinguished military leaders of the Soviet Union, able theoreticians and practical soldiers who had passed through the furnace of war against the interventionists and White Guards and had borne on their shoulders the whole burden of organizing the armed forces. Among these were the deputy people's commissar for defense, M. N. Tukhachevsky; the commander of the Kiev military district, I. E. Iakir; the commander of the Belorussian military district, I. P. Uborevich; and the head of the Frunze Military Academy, A. I. Kork, who also commanded the Moscow district. One of the alleged organizers of the "counterrevolutionary military fascist organization" and "enemies of the people" was the first deputy people's commissar for defense and head of the Red Army political administration, Ia. B. Gamarnik, an able officer who had done much for the creation and strengthening of the Red Army and the Red Fleet. On the eve of his expected arrest he shot himself.

At the beginning of June 1937 Stalin addressed an enlarged session of the military council, at which the only question on the agenda was the unmasking of the "counterrevolutionary military fascist organization." In this speech and in various subsequent utterances he referred to the bogus confessions of the disgraced military leaders, demanded the complete liquidation of the nonexistent "conspiracy" in the armed forces and, in effect, called for the destruction of the military cadres. At the council session itself, unfounded charges were made against several commanders and political officers, such as D. A. Kuchinsky, the head of the academy of the General Staff, formerly chief of staff of the Kiev military district; A. I. Sediakin, the head of the department of antiaircraft defense; and I. E. Slavin, the head of the political administration of the Leningrad military district.

After this session of the Military Council, mass repressions against military and political cadres in the armed forces were greatly intensified. They were especially disastrous for the central apparatus of the People's Commissariat for Defense; the political administration of the Red Army; the Moscow, Leningrad, Kiev, and Belorussian districts; the special Far Eastern force (decorated with the Red Banner); the Baltic and Black Sea fleets; the academies; and the corps and division cadres. The services which suffered most were the air arm and the armored and mechanized forces, to which, as is well known, the best Party workers were appointed. For example: only two months before the council, held at the beginning of June 25, commanders and political officers were dismissed from Fifth Mechanized Brigade of the Belorussian military district, and as many more were listed for dismissal. Of the former, nine were arrested, including five out of the brigade's six battalion commissars. All of these five were expelled from the Party, and the sixth received by way of Party discipline a severe reprimand and warning. In addition, the brigade's political commissar and the head of the political department were expelled from the Party and arrested.

Repressions in the army and navy reached an even higher pitch after Stalin's speech at a conference of political workers at the beginning of August 1937. Here as at the military council in June, Stalin displayed spy mania, calling for the eradication of "enemies of the people" and for denunciations of their activities. When one of those present asked "Are we to speak openly about 'enemies of the people'?" Stalin replied, "Yes, definitely ... and we must proclaim it to the whole world."

The number of members of the armed forces subjected to unjust repression grew steadily.

The situation was to some extent rectified by the January plenum of the CPSU, but the repressions did not stop. In the armed forces, and especially as far as political officers were concerned, the repressions were largely associated with the change of leadership in the political administration of the Red Army, and also the unjust and misguided decisions imposed on the all-army conference of political officers held, with the participation of commanders, in April 1938. On Stalin's instructions, this meeting adopted as a directive a letter by him entitled "Deficiencies in Party Political Work in the Red Army, and Measures to Eliminate Them." This set as the main task for Communists in the armed forces the "bolshevization of the whole Red Army." Communists in the army and navy were called on to work hard to strengthen Party organizations, to acquire a thorough command of Marxist-Leninist theory, to attract the best soldiers, sailors, and officers into the Party, to improve liaison with the rank and file and strengthen military discipline and the efficiency of units at all levels. However, this directive contradicted the Party's wholly correct position according to which the victory of socialism in the Soviet Union had brought about moral and political unity, while with the defeat of the exploiting classes the brunt of the class struggle had shifted from the national to the international arena. The directive was also at variance with the true state of the armed forces and their Party organization, in that it demanded a "purge of enemies of the people" within the army, the "liquidation of the consequences of sabotage," and attention to the problem of "silent individuals without political principles." This highly erroneous picture, based on Stalin's false theory that the class struggle would become more acute as the country progressed toward socialism, led to the spread of general distrust toward commanders and political officers and served as a ground for the violation of socialist legality.

At the Twentieth Party Congress it was pointed out that the arbitrary behavior of a single man had permitted and encouraged such behavior in others. Mekhlis, who in December 1937 was appointed head of the Red Army political administration used his high position to persecute in accordance with Stalin's directive all those who had had any connection whatever with the "opposition group within the army" which had been ideologically shattered ten years earlier and now presented no threat whatsoever to the Party or the armed forces. All the leaders of this group had acknowledged their mistakes and had worked hard and conscientiously to put the Party's military policy into effect. But Mekhlis demanded that all who had in any degree shared the views of the "opposition within the army" should be treated as adherents of the "anti-Party Belorussian-Tolmachevsky group within the army".* Any political officer who might be declared a member of this group was, as a rule, expelled from the Party. On

---

*This refers to two centers of opposition to the Party military policy: (1) the N. G. Tolmachev Military-Political Academy in Leningrad for the training of political commissars in the armed forces, and (2) a group of highly placed political workers in the Belorussian military district. In 1927 these groups opposed the principle of single command *(edinonachalie)* urged by Tukhachevsky, Bubnov, Unshlikht, and others. In 1928 these "deviationists" were condemned and admitted their errors. However, the "dual command," with the powers of political commissars greatly increased, was restored by a decree of May 8, 1973. —ED.

the pretext of eradicating this group from the army and navy, many former members of the military and political academy were dismissed from the services, as were political officers of the Belorussian, Leningrad, Kiev, and Kharkov military districts ....

As a result of the cult of personality, in 1937-38 unjust repressions were meted out to thousands of senior personnel in the army and navy, including a large number of political officers. Among those affected were the deputy heads of the political administration of the Red Army, A. S. Bulin and G. A. Osepian; nearly all members of the military district soviets (M. P. Amelin, L. N. Aronshtam, G. I. Veklichev, and G. D. Khakhan'ian); and the heads of political departments (A. M. Bitte, T. K. Govorukhin, S. I. Zemskov, M. G. Isaenko and A. V. Tarutinsky). All of these men were devoted servants of the Party who had done much to strengthen the army and navy.

Others who underwent repression at this time were the chief of the general Staff, A. I. Egorov; the commander of the air force; Ia. I. Alksnis; the commander of armored units, I. A. Khalepsky; the commander of the special Far Eastern Army, V. K. Bliukher; the district commanders I. P. Belov, P. E. Dybenko, I. F. Fed'ko; and many others.

The repressions dealt a severe blow to the armed forces. They took place at a time when the threat of armed attack on the Soviet Union was growing, and were directed against the most highly qualified senior officers of the army and navy, men who possessed wide theoretical knowledge and profound experience of the Soviet military machine. This had a catastrophic effect on the country's preparations to resist aggression, and helped to bring about grave defeats of the Soviet forces in the first phase of the Great Patriotic War.[1]

The "Tukhachevsky Affair"

KHRUSHCHEV'S REMARKS

Among the victims of repression were such eminent commanders as Tukhachevsky, Iakir, Uborevich, Kork, Egorov, Eideman and others. These were senior officers of note who had rendered good service to the army, especially Tukhachevsky, Iakir, and Uborevich. Subsequently Bliukher and other prominent commanders met the same fate.

A curious report appeared briefly in the foreign press to the effect that Hitler, when preparing his attack on the Soviet Union, had planted a forged document purporting to show that Iakir, Tukhachevsky and others were of the German general staff. This alleged document is said to have reached the hands of President Benes of Czechoslovakia, who with the best intentions forwarded it to Stalin, with the result that Iakir, Tukhachevsky, and other comrades were arrested and liquidated.

Among those liquidated were many noted commanders and political officers of the Red Army. Among the delegates present here there are comrades—I will not mention their names, so as not to cause them pain—who lay in prison for many years. During that time they were subjected to "persuasion" by methods of a certain kind, in order to prove that they were German or British or some kind of spies. Some of them actually "confessed." Even in cases when they were told that the charge of espionage was withdrawn, they insisted on standing by their previous statements, believing that in this way their torments would end and they would be put to death all the sooner.

That is what the cult of personality led to! And that is the meaning of the acts of Molotov and others who sought to re-establish the depraved conditions of the period of the personality cult. The anti-Party group set out to restore such conditions within the Party, and that is why the fight against them was so sharp and strenuous. Everyone knew what was at stake.

I knew Comrade Iakir well, and Tukhachevsky to some extent. This year, during a conference at Alma-Ata, Tukhachevsky's son, who was working in Kazakhstan, came to me and asked about his father. What could I reply? When, in the Presidium of the Central Committee, we examined these cases and were told that neither Tukhachevsky nor Iakir nor Uborevich had committed any crimes against the Party or State, we asked Molotov, Kaganovich, and Voroshilov whether they approved of rehabilitating them. They said they did. "But," we replied with amazement, "you yourselves sentenced these people. Were you acting in accordance with conscience then, or are you now?" They made no answer, and are not likely to do so. You have heard what sort of things they inscribed on letters to Stalin. What can they possibly say?[2]

Marshal Mikhail Nikolaevich Tukhachevsky

MIKHAIL NIKOLAEVICH TUKHACHEVSKY

Biographical data

February 15, 1893: born on the estate of Aleksandrovskoe, Dorogobuzh district, Smolensk province. 1904: family moves to the village of Vrazhskoe, Penza province. 1909: moves to Moscow. 1911: T. leaves high school and enters First Moscow Cadet Corps. 1912-14: studies at the Aleksandrovsky Military Academy. July 14, 1914: promoted to second lieutenant. Enters Semenovsky Regiment of life guards. September 1914: leaves with his regiment for the front. September 1914-February 1915: decorated six times for valor. February 19, 1915: taken prisoner. 1916: having made several attempts to escape, he is transferred to Fort no. 9 of the Ingolstadt Fortress. August-October 1917: successful escape, return to Russia. December 1917: elected company commander of the Semenovsky regiment. April 5, 1918: joins Bolshevik party. May 27, 1918: appointed military commissar for defense of Moscow region. June 19, 1918: ordered to eastern front. June 26, 1918: appointed commander of the First Army. July 4, 1918: together with I.M. Vareikis, chairman of the Simbirsk gubernia committee of the RCP(B), Tukhachevsky carries out first mobilization of former Tsarist officers for service in Red Army. July 11, 1918: arrested by Murav'ev. Suppression of Murav'ev revolt. July-August 1918: prepares First Revolutionary Army to attack. Breaks encirclement of the Sengileev group under G.D. Gai, and carries out first attack on Simbirsk. August 25-September 11, 1918: Simbirsk operation. September 12, 1918: capture of Simbirsk. September 9-October 2, 1918: Melekess and Syzran' operations. October 3, 1918: capture of Syzran'. October 7, 1918: capture of Samara. November 28, 1918: capture of Belebei. December 28, 1918: appointed deputy commander of southern front. January 20, 1919: appointed commander of Eighth Army on southern front. March 23, 1919: appointed commander of Fifth Army on eastern front. April 28-May 3, 1919: Buguruslan operation. May 4, 1919: capture of Buguruslan. May 9-12, 1919: Bugul'ma operation. May 13, 1919: capture of Bugul'ma. May 25-June 19, 1919: Ufa operation. June 25-July 12, 1919: Zlatoust operation. July 13, 1919: Zlatoust captured. July 19-29, 1919: Cheliabinsk operation. August 7, 1919: T. receives Order of the Red Banner. November 4, 1919: capture of Omsk. December 2, 1919: Fifth Army receives Order of the Red Banner. December 22, 1919: T. appointed commander of Thirteenth Army on southernfront. December 28, 1919: receives "Honary Golden Sword". January 31, 1920: appointed temporary commander of Caucasus front. February 16-March 27, 1920: north Caucasus operation. April 29, 1920: appointed commander of western front. May 22, 1920: Tukhachevsky receives title of General Staff Officer. July 1920: Igumen-Minsk operation. July 23-August 14: Warsaw operation. February 2, 1921: while remaining commander of the western front, becomes member of Academic Council of Advanced War Studies. March 5,

1921: appointed temporary commander of Seventh Army while remaining commander of western front. March 8, 1921: first assault on Kronshtadt. March 17, 1921: second assault and capture of Kronshtadt. April 1921: appointed commander for Tambov gubernia while remaining commander of western front. April-May 1921: defeat of Antonov revolt. August 5, 1921: appointed head of Red Army Military Academy. January 24, 1922: appointed commander of armies on western front. 1922-23: elected member of CEC of Belorussian SSR and CC of CP(B) of Belorussia. April 1, 1924: appointed assistant chief of staff of Red Army. May 27, 1924: appointed, in addition, member of commission for normalization of work in People's Commissariat for the Army and Navy. February 17, 1925: appointed member of Revolutionary Military Council of the U.S.S.R. and commander of the Western Military District. November 13, 1925: appointed chief of staff of Red Army. 1926: publishes book on *Problems of Modern Strategy*. January 29, 1927: also appointed member of senior certifying commission of People's Commissariat for the Army and Navy. December 1927: addresses letter to Stalin on rearming of Red Army. May 5, 1928: appointed commander of Leningrad military district. 1929-30: construction of Karelian fortified area; district maneuvers; publishes book on problems of tactical training, *Nashi uchebno-takticheskie zadachi;* edits volume 3 of *Istoriia grazhdanskoi voiny v SSSR* (History of the Civil War in the U.S.S.R.). June 19, 1931: appointed vice-chairman of Revolutionary Military Council of the U.S.S.R. and director of supplies for Red Army. Starts on his basic work *Novye voprosy voiny* (Problems of Modern War). February 21, 1933: receives Order of Lenin. November 7, 1933: receives salute at Red Army parade on Red Square in Moscow. February 1934: elected, at the Seventeenth Party Congress, a candidate member of the CC of the CPSU. June 21, 1934: appointed deputy people's commissar for defense of the U.S.S.R. November 20, 1935: by decision of CEC and CPC of the U.S.S.R., M.N. Tukhachevsky receives supreme military title of Marshal of the Soviet Union. January 15, 1936: presents report on national defense at second session of CEC of the U.S.S.R. February 1936: visits Britain and France. April 9, 1936: appointed first deputy people's commissar for defense and head of re-established Red Army department of battle training. May 11, 1937: released from duties as deputy commissar for defense and appointed commander of Volga Military District. May 27, 1937: dismissed from Red Army and arrested. June 11, 1937: together with I. E. Iakir, I. P. Uborevich, R. P. Eideman, B. M. Fel'dman, A. I. Kork, V. M. Primakov, and V. K. Putna, Tukhachevsky is condemned on infamous and slanderous charge of high treason and shot.[3]

Conflicts with Stalin

Two days previously, on August 1, 1920, the Red Army in its headlong and victorious advance to the west had liberated Brest-Litovsk. The next day the CC confirmed its decision on the uniting of the fronts.

Stalin, who was a member of the revolutionary military council on the southwestern front, received a telegram from Lenin: "Politburo has just decided on division of fronts so that you should be concerned only with Wrangel. Latter presents serious threat in connection with uprisings especially in the Kuban area but also in Siberia. View is gaining ground in CC that we should at once conclude peace with bourgeois Poland. Please consider Wrangel situation most carefully and report your views. I have agreed with commander in chief that he will give you more ammunition, reinforcements, and aircraft."

This plan to split up the southwestern front was not to Stalin's liking. The First Cavalry Army had taken Brody, and the ancient city of L'vov was beckoning—a prize no less tempting than Warsaw, and so close at hand that it was a pity not to seize it. The troops on the western front were determined to take Warsaw, and why should not the southwestern take L'vov? The First Cavalry Army had advanced toward the city and expected to take it by July 29, but both the men and horses were tired; the city had not fallen as planned. Now, when it was proposed to move the First Cavalry Army away from the southwestern front, Stalin grew restive. Frowning, he paced up and down the room and thought angrily: "This is all Kamenev's doing—Sergei Sergeevich, colonel of the General Staff! Il'ich is altogether too trustful toward these chaps with their gold epaulettes!"

Stalin had no faith in the "military specialists," Kamenev, Shorin, and their ilk. It was true, Aleksandr Il'ich Egorov had also been a Tsarist officer, but not for long; moreover, he was the son of a railroadman and had himself been a blacksmith's assistant. But Kamenev was an engineer's son, a petty bourgeois.

Stalin grabbed his cap, pushed it back over his head as usual and hurried to the front commander's office, where he found Egorov standing thoughtfully in front of a wallmap. After greeting him Stalin pulled a pipe out of his pocket, lit up in silence and began pacing about the room.

"Well, what's the news?" he said at last in a hoarse voice. "What else have the Moscow strategists dreamed up?"

"I've had this telegram from the commander in chief," replied Egorov, handing it over. Stalin read the telegram, drawing deeply at his pipe. It said: "Now that western front armies have crossed the Narev and taken Brest-Litovsk, time has come to unite under commander of western front all armies advancing toward the Vistula. Twelfth and First Cavalry armies should therefore be transferred to his command from southwestern front in the next few days."

"Transfer the cavalry to Tukhachevsky!" exclaimed Stalin. "Does Kamenev realize how that will weaken us against Wrangel'?"

* * *

Tukhachevsky felt somewhat abashed when he met Lenin after the termination of the Polish campaign, although it was no more his fault than others' that the Red Army had been forced to retreat from Warsaw.

"Tell me, Mikhail Nikolaevich," said Lenin, "do you think it would have been better to make a halt on some line or other and reinforce the armies before advancing farther?"

"No, I don't think so. The troops were in such a state of enthusiasm that to halt would have spoiled everything."

Lenin thought for a moment and then said with a smile: "Do you play chess by any chance?"

"Yes, a little."

"Well, you know how it is there. You may advance and lose a piece or two, but does that mean you should stop and leave the initiative to the enemy?"

"Yes, but we weren't strong enough," replied Tukhachevsky.

"Exactly so. We weren't strong enough to follow up the attack. One of the chief reasons we failed was that we did not get far enough to reach the Polish industrial proletariat."

"The men were very tired, Vladimir Il'ich."

"I should think they were, after that tremendous march from Polotsk to Warsaw."

"Besides, we were short of everything; food, shells, cartridges."

"I know. The Red Army fought in conditions such as no other army in the world has had to put up with."

"Another thing that did us a lot of harm was the lack of coordination between the fronts. The southwestern front insisted that the main objective was L'vov," remarked Tukhachevsky.

"Yes, they were childishly obstinate," laughed Lenin. "Who would think of going to Warsaw by way of L'vov? But never mind: I am convinced that the red flag will fly over Warsaw, hoisted by the Polish workers and peasants themselves."[4]

On January 11, 1930, M. N. Tukhachevsky, then commanding the Leningrad military district, presented to the People's Commissariat of the Army and Navy a report on the reorganization of the armed forces, in which he said:

> "The successes of our socialist construction . . . place before us in full urgency the task of reconstructing the armed forces in the light of all the latest technical factors and the possibility of mass production of technical military requirements, as well as the progress which has been achieved in rural life. . . . The quantitative and qualitative advance in various kinds of arms involves a re-thinking of proportions and new structural changes. . . . A reconstructed army will lead to new departures in the field of operations.

The main feature of Tukhachevsky's report was the proposal to increase the number of divisions and develop the artillery, aviation, and armored troops. His approach to these matters was correct and timely; specific proposals were to follow in the light of further study. However, Voroshilov and Stalin not only failed to give them their due weight but even took up a hostile attitude. Stalin's conclusion, which Voroshilov fully endorsed, was that the adoption of this program would mean the liquidation of socialist construction and its replacement by some kind of "red militarism." This view was announced by Voroshilov at an enlarged session of the Revolutionary Military Council of the U.S.S.R. Subsequently, Tukhachevsky more than once asked Stalin to re-examine his proposals for the reconstruction of the Red Army. In so doing he emphasized that the Soviet Union must not only win the next war but must preserve its economic power and not undermine the achievements of the building of socialism.

On December 30, 1930, Tukhachevsky was obliged to write to Stalin as follows:

> The formulation of your letter as read by Comrade Voroshilov to the enlarged session of the Revolutionary Military Council of the U.S.S.R. makes it impossible for me to propose for wide discussion a number of questions concerning the development of our defense potential. For instance, I am no longer able to give instruction in strategy at the Red Army Military Academy, where I lectured on this subject for six years. Altogether, my position in these matters has become completely false. However, I declare as emphatically as ever that the Red Army staff has willfully distorted the proposals in my memorandum.

This vehement complaint met with no response. Not until May 1932 did Stalin write to Tukhachevsky a letter admitting that he had adopted a sharp and incorrect approach to the latter's proposals, and apologizing for the delay in acknowledging his mistake.

*   *   *

In February 1934 Tukhachevsky, together with Uborevich, wrote a letter to Voroshilov discussing the modern role of the air force and its military possibilities in the light of experience gained in training and maneuvers. This contained the passage: "A modern air force can interrupt rail transport for a considerable period, destroy stocks of war supplies, prevent mobilization and the concentration of troops. . . . Either adversary risks defeat if he is not in a position to destroy the enemy's air bases, disorganize his railroad transport by means of systematic air attacks, impede his mobilization and concentration by frequent raids, destroy his supplies of fuel and ammunition, and annihilate his garrisons and troop trains by the rapid action of mechanized units supported by cavalry and motorized infantry." On this basis, Tukhachevsky and Uborevich considered that the rapid numerical development of aircraft should be a key factor in the Red Army's development over the next few years. Taking into account practical possibilities, they reckoned that by the end of 1935 the Red Army might have up to 15,000 operational aircraft. Apart from this, they pointed to the important role of armored troops in the strengthening of national defense.

At the same time, Tukhachevsky continued to display constant concern for the improvement of infantry, artillery, antiaircraft, and other specialized troops. In particular he saw to the planning and introduction of new establishments for infantry divisions and corps which greatly improved the infantry's organizational structure, technical equipment, mobility, and maneuverability. He also took the initiative in reducing the number of types of artillery formations in the Red Army, which had an important effect on artillery development by simplifying production and the use of artillery in battle and facilitating the task of rear organizations. Furthermore, he was active in suggesting and putting into effect many important measures for the development of the navy and airborne forces.

* * *

Tukhachevsky was responsible for the development of airborne units in the Red Army. In September 1934, commenting on the maneuvers in the Leningrad Military District, he wrote: "Particular attention was given to the use of airborne troops, which took place on a greater scale than anywhere else in the Red Army." Forseeing the future of this new type of formation, he added in brackets: "We should accustom ourselves to the idea of many thousands of troops landing at once." His prediction soon came true, and in 1936 mass airborne landings figured in the maneuvers of the Kiev and Belorussian military districts.

* * *

As new kinds of troops developed, it became possible to destroy the enemy by simultaneous action against the whole of his tactical rear area. Recognizing this possibility, Tukhachevsky worked out a theory of action in depth* and devoted much effort to incorporating it into training methods. He devised special instructions in accordance with which experimental training was carried out in the armed forces....

It should be noted that the nature and significance of action in depth were not at once recognized and appreciated on all sides. Tukhachevsky had to struggle hard to ensure that his experiment was accorded its proper place in the system of troop training. Some misunderstanding of the basis of his theory was displayed by Voroshilov, who sharply criticized Tukhachevsky at the plenum of the Revolutionary Military Council of the U.S.S.R.

On November 20, 1933, Tukhachevsky was obliged to write to Voroshilov: "Your speech at the plenum of the Council left many with the impression

---

*According to this theory victory is achieved through a coordinated action of all branches of the armed forces, with tanks playing a leading role. Thus the outcome depends on the proper support of tanks by artillery, and of infantry by tanks. This theory became the basis for the tactical preparation of the Soviet armed forces. See M. N. Tukhachevskii, *Izbrannye proizvedeniia* (Moscow, 1964), vol. I, pp. 16-18.—ED.

that in spite of the Army's possession of a new arm, its tactics are to remain the same." The letter ended: "I have decided to write to you because commanders have been in a state of bewilderment since the plenum. There is talk of a refusal to understand or develop new kinds of tactics, and since, I repeat, the general feeling is at variance with the views you have put forward more than once, I have decided that I must bring these discontents to your notice."

At the meeting of the RMC of the U.S.S.R. in 1934 Kamenev declared: "Action in depth is not a method but a form of military action. As advocated by Tukhachevsky, it consists of striking simultaneously, or as nearly so as possible, against the enemy's forward area, his artillery, and his rear. That is the problem—to hit simultaneously everywhere, so that the enemy cannot use his reserves."

Experience has abundantly shown that Tukhachevsky was right.[5]

Tukhachevsky's last days

In May 1937 Tukhachevsky was supposed to go to London to attend the coronation of King George VI. However, it was announced that he would not go because of illness, and that V. M. Orlov, the commander in chief of the navy, would attend the ceremonies in his stead.

Tukhachevsky was then appointed commander of the Volga Military District, and was due to go to Kuibyshev in June to take over from P. E. Dybenko. At this time he felt that Stalin's attitude toward him had changed sharply and openly for the worse. He realized that something unusual had happened, but could not think of any fault of which he had been guilty, and did his best to keep calm. He had accepted the appointment to the Volga District although it was a manifest demotion, which gave rise to all manner of rumors and suspicions. Those close to him were disturbed, and even his chauffeur, who had been with him since 1918, asked him as an intimate why he had been so depressed for the past few days. Tukhachevsky replied that all sorts of stories were being invented against him. The chauffeur, whose name was Ivan Fedorovich Kudriavtsev, advised him to write to Stalin. Tukhachevsky replied that he had already done so. No doubt the letter, which was then in Stalin's possession, asked for an explanation of the change in attitude toward him.

Kudriavtsev drove his master to the Kazan railroad station for the last time. As he said goodbye, Tukhachevsky promised to send for Kudriavtsev as soon as he had settled down in Kuibyshev. "That was the last time," Kudriavtsev relates, "that I saw my old comrade in arms, with whom I shared the joys and sorrows of military life for nineteen years."

One of those who saw the marshal off was Evgenii Vasil'evich Shilov, who thought his friend seemed somewhat calmer after the upsets he had undergone. He imagined Tukhachevsky must have been promised that he would soon return to Moscow. If such a promise was given, it can only have been to dispel Tukha-chevsky's suspicions of the fate in store for him.

The cancelling of his visit to London was explained to him unofficially on the ground that an attempt on his life was being plotted in Warsaw. This was clearly an implausible reason, since he might have gone to London in a warship.

Soon after reaching Kuibyshev with his wife Nina Evgen'evna, he attended a conference of political officers of the Volga military district. One of the commanders, who had known him previously, noticed that in the last two months or so his hair had turned completely grey. He appeared very tired at the conference, but spoke clearly and precisely, as always, about problems of military training and the work that lay ahead.

His wife waited a long time, but he did not return home. At last Pavel Efimovich Dybenko appeared, deathly pale, and said that Tukhachevsky had been arrested.

Nina Evgen'evna returned to Moscow, where she too was soon arrested, together with her husband's mother and sisters and his brothers Aleksandr and Nikolai.

The press reported the arrest of Marshal Tukhachevsky as well as military district commanders Iakir and Uborevich; Primakov, deputy commander of a military district; Kork, head of the military academy; Fel'dman, head of cadres administration; and the corps commanders Eideman and Putna. It also stated that Gamarnik had committed suicide.

After the trial, held behind closed doors, it was announced that all the accused had pleaded guilty. According to several reports, Tukhachevsky had declared: "I feel as if I were in a dream."

The accusation was based on slanders and on such facts as the official journeys abroad by the marshal and his comrades, which were of a purely professional nature. The accused were brave, resolute men who had looked death in the face more than once. We may imagine the sorrow with which these patriotic commanders, full of devotion to the Party, heard the false charges against them, and the fury with which they rejected the court's slanders.

All the accused were sentenced to be shot, and the sentence was carried out at once.

Thus began the period of unbridled arbitrary action against many tried and faithful commanders of the Red Army. Of the judges who took part in the trial of Tukhachevsky and the other principal leaders, six were soon to share their fate.

Tukhachevsky's wife and two brothers were later put to death on Stalin's orders. His three sisters were sent to prison camps and his daughter, when she came of age, was likewise arrested. His mother and his sister Sof'ia died in exile.[6]

Corps Commander
Robert Petrovich Eideman

Officers Shot With Tukhachevsky

ROBERT PETROVICH EIDEMAN

Biographical data

[Corps Commander.] Born, 1895, in the small town of Leiastsems in Latvia; died 1937. Enrolled in the RCP(B) in 1918; however, after the Sixteenth Party Congress the CC, taking into account his services to the revolution and active participation in decisive events on the Bolshevik side, predated his membership to 1917. He entered the Petrograd Forestry Institute in 1914 and was called up six months later. In 1916 he became an ensign in the Sixteenth Siberian reserve infantry regiment. In April 1917 he was elected chairman of the Kansk soviet of soldiers deputies and vice chairman of the combined Kansk soviet of workers, peasants' and soldiers' deputies. On the eve of the October Revolution the Kansk workers and soldiers of the Kansk garrison sent him as the head of the delegation to the first All-Siberian Congress of Soviets, which opened at Irkutsk on October 10, 1917. At this congress he was elected vice chairman of Tsentrosibir', the executive committee for Siberia. He remained at Kansk during the revolution and in December took part in the suppression of the White Guard revolt at Irkutsk. In 1918 he was a delegate to the third all-russian congress of soviets, where he was elected to the All-Russian CEC. In spring 1918, he set out for the Far East as a member of a government commission to organize operations against the ataman Semenov, but was detained at Omsk by the revolt of the White Czechs. There he became a leading member of the West Siberian staff for the suppression of the revolt, and later commanded the First Siberian (Partisan) Army. He remained on the eastern front until the end of 1918, commanding the Second and then the Third Ural divisions. In 1919-21 he commanded the Sixteenth (Kikvidze), Forty-first and Forty-sixth divisions, the Fourteenth and Thirteenth armies and the Right Bank group of armies. In 1921-24 he was deputy commander of troops in the Ukraine and Crimea, and in 1924-25 he commanded the Siberian military district. In 1925-32 he was director and commissar of the Frunze Military Academy of the Red Army, and in 1932-37 chairman of the Union of Soviet Writers and head of its Latvian section. On June 11, 1937 he was shot together with Marshal Tukhachevsky.[7]

A soldier of the revolution

R. Eideman was born on May 9, 1895, in the Latvian township of Leias-tsiems, the son of a progressive-minded teacher. In 1914, after finishing high school in Valki, he entered the Petrograd Forestry Institute. However, he did not graduate there; after eighteen months he was called up and sent to the Kiev infantry school. In October 1916, as an ensign, he was appointed to

the Sixteenth Siberian infantry reserve regiment, stationed at Kansk in the
Eniseisk gubernia.

*   *   *

Eideman was at Kansk when the October Revolution broke out. The change
of regime took place without incident, as the Kansk soviet, the great majority
of which belonged to the Bolshevik-maximalist bloc, had as early as May declared
itself to be the sole authority in the city and surrounding district. However,
a counterrevolutionary rebellion of cadets took place at Irkutsk on December
8. In response to a request for help from his comrades who at that time were
directing the Irkutsk RMC, Eideman, on the day after receiving their telegram,
set out with a detachment of 400 men and took part in the suppression of
the revolt.

In January 1918 he was a delegate to the third all-Russian congress of
soviets, where he heard with emotion Lenin's report on the activity of the
Council of People's Commissars. His sympathy and understanding were aroused
by the views of the leader of the proletarian revolution on the need to create
a socialist army to defend Soviet power. His poem *Petrograd* on the October
Revolution contains the lines:

> If only my soul were no other than a poet's ...
> But my destiny is that of a fighter,
> Bound for the Civil War ....

And indeed, while remaining a poet, Eideman devoted himself more and
more to his military career.

*   *   *

Eideman remained on the eastern front until the end of 1918, commanding
first the Second and then the Third Ural divisions. Here, during the period
of creation of the Red Army and in the fierce fire of battle, he gained the
military and political experience necessary to a commander. The Soviet government more than once recognized his services as a skillful and politically mature
leader of the military masses and a fearless fighting man.

From January 1919 he served on the southern and southwestern fronts,
commanding the Sixteenth (Kikvidze), the Forty-first and Forty-sixth divisions,
and then taking part in the defeat of Denikin and Wrangel by the Fourteenth
and Thirteenth Armies and the Right Bank group of armies. He was the hero
of Kakhovka, celebrated in song. For his able leadership and personal heroism
in the fight against interventionists, White Guardists and the Makhno bands,
he twice received the Order of the Red Banner, as well as gold watches and
other rewards.

*   *   *

Along with other important military figures, Eideman was concerned with the training of highly qualified cadres, the technical equipment of the Red Army, questions of Soviet military science, the theoretical interpretation of the experience of the Civil War, and the study of urgent problems regarding a future war. As head of the Military-Scientific Society, he was responsible for getting many talented researchers to participate in its activity.

Eideman had a high reputation as a Marxist historian and took a prominent part in the activity of the section of the Communist Academy that was set up in 1929 for the study of war problems and included among its members both civilian and military historians. Eideman was a member of its presidium and head of the historical subsection. Being rich in experience of the Civil War and possessing a wide Marxist and military education (he had attended a course at the senior military academy of the German general staff), Eideman was a model to young Soviet war students. He strongly favored creative cooperation between the older and younger military-historical research cadres. While training young Marxist historians to study painstakingly the rich heritage of the past, he criticized experts of the old school for their neglect of Marxist methods. He posed the problem of creating a Marxist school of scientific criticism which would enable Soviet cadres to assess and use bourgeois writings on war and military history that were rich in factual material. This, he believed, was the best way to strengthen the Party's ideological position in regard to military science.

* * *

Eideman wrote more than a hundred works on military science and technology. He also took an active part in editing newspapers and journals, and in the compilation of such major works as the three-volume *History of the Civil War, 1918-21,* the *Soviet Military Encyclopedia,* etc. During the years when the cult of Stalin's personality was taking shape and the consequent attribution to the latter of all credit in regard to the Civil War, Eideman, in his works, correctly brought out the decisive role of the CC of the Party, headed by Lenin, in organizing victory over the nation's enemies. In an article on the tenth anniversary of the battle of Orel against Denikin's forces, he wrote: "In the Civil War, as never before, politics and strategy joined forces in all major questions."

* * *

In 1932 the Party appointed Eideman to work in Osoaviakhim, which he directed for more than five years. As chairman of its central council he displayed his best qualities as a Bolshevik organizer. On the basis of his forecast of the nature of a future war, he considered it necessary "to prepare the population from the political and military points of view to meet the test of war which may be inflicted on us, with all its hardships and sacrifices." For, as he explained in a speech at the tenth congress of the All-Union Lenin's Young Communist League, national defense in the modern sense depends not only on the state and equipment of the armed forces "but on the ability of the broad masses to meet the enemy fully armed."

Under Eideman's direction, Osoaviakhim became a powerful mass organization with over thirteen million members. The main feature of its activity, as required by the Party, consisted of voluntary unpaid work by its members in cells and organizations, with emphasis on the spread of practical knowledge of the training of pilots, glider pilots, riflemen, and organizers of defense against air attack, chemical warfare, etc. In the years before the war, many clubs and groups belonging to Osoaviakhim prepared the civilian population of our country for defense tasks. When young people were called up for service they already possessed a store of military knowledge, were physically fit, and knew how to handle weapons and military equipment. More than one generation of young people educated their fellow citizens in the spirit of ardent Soviet patriotism, ready at every moment to defend the socialist motherland. In all this, no small service was rendered by Eideman, a true son of the Communist Party and soldier of the revolution as he called himself and his comrades.

The Party greatly appreciated Eideman's devotion to the fight for socialism. He was a delegate to the Fourteenth, Sixteenth and Seventeeth congresses and to the fifteenth and sixteenth conferences of the CPSU. Proud of his membership in the great Leninist Party, in a poem entitled *Bolshevik* he depicted the Communist as a tireless fighter for the people's happiness:

We know neither rest nor peace ...
We blaze like torches with fiery thoughts.
The new flourishes as we sweep away the old—
Some of us may fall, but the rest press on.

Eideman was a member of the Union of Soviet Writers, and head of its Latvian section.

This man, to whom all dissembling and double-dealing were foreign, could not imagine that he might fall victim to a base slander. Once, after a Party meeting in the spring of 1937, as he and I were driving home, I was struck by his air of disquiet. He slowly said, "Last night another of our comrades was arrested—a decent fellow as far as I could see. I don't understand it."

A month later, after the arrest of A. I. Kork, whom he had sponsored for membership of the Party, and other eminent military leaders, Eideman himself was arrested. His life was tragically cut short on June 12, 1937. His name lives in the memory of the Soviet people as that of an able and devoted fighter for communism, whose services earned him the gratitude of Party and the people.[8]

Eideman's death

Eideman worked tirelessly to strengthen the country's defense potential. His whole activity was inspired by sincere love of the mother country and by a lofty patriotism. Yet it was not granted to him to take part directly in his country's defense: his heart ceased to beat a few years before the fascist invaders attacked the Soviet Union.

While serving on the Don in the Sixteenth Infantry Division during the Civil War, he became friendly with Brigade Commander F. I. Nyrnenko, whom he had met in unusual circumstances. At a meeting of the command personnel of the division held on the occasion of Eideman's arrival, Nyrnenko had made a hostile speech which, as S. P. Medvedovsky later wrote, "brought tears to the eyes of many of us." Nyrnenko was "unwilling" to accept the new division commander. Ten years later, Eideman had not forgotten this rough-spoken but honest soldier, whose short span of life after the revolution was spent in uninterrupted fighting. In a sketch entitled *O smerti* (On Death), printed in 1930, he wrote:

> I do not wish to die in my bed. That would be too solemn .... As an old partisan, no doubt I would be buried with military music. My friends would see to that. They would stand solemnly around my coffin, whispering softly as if afraid to awaken me .... To the devil with all such ceremony! I wish to die as my friend Nyrnenko did, the unforgettable Donetsk miner who brought his native village of Titovka into the revolution with him and who laid down his ardent and glorious life in the battle for Warsaw.

Eideman was not fated to die in his bed; he met death in an unexpected, unthinkable way, such as no one could have wished for him.

On May 22, 1937, an all-Moscow Party conference was held in the Hall of Columns in the Trade Unions building. Eideman was summoned as he sat there with the rest of the presidium, and did not return. A ban was placed on his name. He died at the height of his creative powers, aged only forty-two. But the mother country does not forget her sons. Eideman's name was restored to honor by a decision of the Twentieth Congress of the CPSU. In the past few years selected literary works of his have been published, as well as writings on military history from newspapers and journals, and articles and sketches on his life and activity. In the town of Valki, where he was educated, a memorial plaque has been affixed to the building of the secondary school, which has been renamed the Robert Eideman school and in which a museum has been opened; in addition, one of the town's streets has been named after him.[9]

BORIS MIRONOVICH FEL'DMAN

Biographical data

[Corps commander.] Born 1890, died 1937. Corps commander, member of the Bolshevik Party from 1919. During the Civil War he was chief of staff of a brigade and then of a division. In 1921 he graduated from the Red Army

Army Military Academy and was subsequently chief of staff of a number of military districts and head of the central administration of the Red Army. He was condemned on a false charge and shot together with M. N. Tukhachevsky.[10]

IONA EMMANUILOVICH IAKIR

Biographical data

[Army commander, first class.] Born 1896 at Kishenev, the son of a druggist; died 1937. Member of the Bolshevik Party from 1917. From the age of fifteen he worked while continuing to study at a secondary modern school. In 1915, having completed his secondary schooling, he entered the Kharkov Technological Institute. From this time on he took part in the revolutionary movement. At the end of 1915 he was called up and sent to the Gen ammunition factory at Odessa, where he worked as a metal lathe operator and continued his revolutionary activity under the direction of the factory's Bolshevik organization. In March 1917, suffering from lung disease, he was moved to Kishenev, where he contacted the local Bolshevik organization and on its orders carried out propaganda activities among the garrison. In April 1917 the Bolshevik military organization of the Fifth Trans-Amur Cavalry Regiment issued him a Party card. In May 1917 he was elected to the Bessarabian soviet of workers' and soldiers' deputies, and shortly afterward to the revolutionary committee of the Bessarabia gubernia. In 1918 he became a member of the RMC of the Eighth Army, and in 1919 commander of the Forty-fifth Infantry Divsion; subsequently he became commander of troops in the Crimea and of the Kiev military district. He received the Order of the Red Banner three times and the Golden Sword. After the Civil War he became head of the main administration of the Red Army military schools. On June 17, 1937, he was condemned and shot together with Marshal Tukhachevsky.[11]

Iakir's activity as a commander and military organizer

I. E. Iakir began his military service at the end of 1917 as a member of the Red Guard in the city of Kishenev. He took part in the fighting against the troops of feudal Rumania which were attempting to occupy Bessarabia. At the beginning of 1918 the Red Guard detachment in which he was serving retreated behind the Dniester under the pressure of superior German forces which had treacherously violated the armistice. Here, in the Odessa area, the most revolutionary units of the former Rumanian front—the Fifth Trans-Amur, First Bessarabian, and Second Dniester regiments and certain Red Guard units —were formed in a somewhat improvised manner into a military force known as the Special Army, and Iakir was appointed commander of a composite unit of this army.

Army Commander First Class
Iona Emmanuilovich Iakir

In difficult conditions, carrying on a desperate fight against all kinds of counterrevolutionary and German forces, the Special Army was forced to retreat in the direction of Ekaterinoslav (Dnepropetrovsk) and, later, Voronezh. Iakir was wounded in the battle for Ekaterinoslav and was out of action for five weeks. After rejoining his unit in the Kalach-Voronezhsky area, he was one of several Bolsheviks who devoted themselves to the task of restoring the Special Army to battle worthiness after the heavy losses it had suffered in combat with General Krasnov's White Cossacks. The units and detachments of the army which had retreated to Voronezh were attached to the forces of the Southern Screen.

In autumn 1918 the position became critical in the south of the country, where Krasnov's White Cossack army was operating. The CC of the RCP (B) resolved upon measures to strengthen the southern front, and on its orders Party organizations mobilized Communists on this front. As many as 1,110 joined the front in the short period from October 20 to December 1. The new Communist detachments appreciably strengthened the Party organization within the armed forces. This was seen in the Eighth Army on the southern front, in which Iakir was a member of the RMC from October onward. The number of Party cells of the RCP(B) in this army grew from eight on November 28, 1918, to eighty-eight on January 1, 1919, when they comprised 1,833 Party members and 2,621 sympathizers.

In the area of the Eighth Army's advance at this time, particular importance attached to capturing the railroad junction at Liski—a task assigned to the Twelfth Infantry Division operating on the army's right flank. Iakir, who took a direct part in the fighting for Liski, showed immense energy and selfless courage, in recognition of which he was promoted to command the Twelfth Division.

* * *

Under the pressure of Denikin's superior forces, the troops of the Fourteenth Army retreated north and northwest. As a result of this and of attacks from Petliura's forces, the position of the Twelfth Army, consisting of the Forty-fourth, Forty-fifth, Forty-seventh and Fifty-eighth divisions, took a sharp turn for the worse. In July 1919 Iakir was appointed to command the Forty-fifth Division. In a short time, he created, out of scattered units and detachments in the Odessa area, a battle-worthy formation of the Red Army.

For skill in commanding troops of the southern group, I. E. Iakir, I. F. Fed'ko (commander of the Fifty-eighth Division), and A. B. Nemitts were decorated with the Order of the Red Banner. Both the Forty-fifth and Fifty-eighth infantry divisions were awarded the Revolutionary Red Banner of Honor. All ranks received an extra month's pay by way of reward.

After this operation, Iakir, commanding the Forty-fifth Division, was transferred to the Petrograd front opposing Iudenich. In December 1919 the division returned to the Ukraine, where it formed part of the Fourteenth Army under I. P. Uborevich.

* * *

In April 1920, despite repeated peace overtures from the Soviet government, the forces of feudal Poland began their advance toward Kiev. The Forty-fourth and Forty-fifth divisions of the Twelfth Army, which were exhausted by their battles with Denikin's forces and were at not more than half strength, received the first onslaught of the White Polish forces in the Ukraine. The Poles attacked at the point of junction of the two divisions, broke through the front and attempted to surround the Forty-fifth Division. At this point Iakir once again displayed masterly generalship and insight into the situation. Using one brigade as cover, he withdrew two other, as well as the staff and administrative units of the division, thus escaping the trap prepared for it. Finally, under the cover of light rearguard forces, he withdrew the whole division.

* * *

From August 9 to the end of the Polish campaign Iakir was again in command of army units, first opposite Zolochev (the Forty-fifth and Forty-seventh Infantry and Eighth Cavalry divisions) and then opposite Lvov (the Forty-fifth and Forty-seventh divisions). After the removal of the First Cavalry Army from the Lvov sector, the remainder of the forces in that area came under the operational command of the Fourteenth Army. In the course of stubborn fighting on the Bug, this army repulsed several determined attacks of the White Poles who had gone over to the offensive at Lvov.

Having broken through to the north of the Forty-fifth Division, the Poles advanced southwest by forced marches in order to cut off the division's retreat and to surround and destroy it. By a successful maneuver, Iakir once more led his division out of the trap. Despite a hasty retreat, its forces and equipment were preserved intact.

For his skillful command of operations on the Polish front, Iakir subsequently received the Order of the Red Banner for the third time.

In November 1920, after the conclusion of the armistice with the White Poles, the Forty-fifth Division, under Iakir's command, took part in the destruction of the forces of the "supreme ataman" Petliura and units of Wrangel's so-called Third Army.

* * *

After the Civil War, Iakir served for a considerable time under the eminent proletarian commander Mikhail Vasil'evich Frunze. During Frunze's command of the Ukraine and Crimea forces, Iakir successively served as commander of troops in the Crimea and Kiev raions and deputy commander of troops in the Ukraine military district.

Frunze valued Iakir's military qualities highly, as is shown by personal reports of his which have been preserved in the achives, and which read, e.g.:

"Worthy of his present appointment." "Being promoted to Army Commander." "Shows undoubted military talent."

In April 1924 Iakir was appointed director and commissar of the Red Army College and chief editor of the *Voennyi vestnik* (Military Gazette). He held this appointment until November 1925, working directly under Frunze, whom the Party had appointed head of the People's Commissariat for Military and Naval Affairs.

* * *

Iakir was active and thorough in his execution of the Party directives regarding army reorganization which were carried out in 1924-25. Considerable interest attaches to his views and practical steps as head of the Administration of Military Schools in regard to training of officer cadres, unity of command, and military discipline. On June 4, 1924, he delivered a report to the RMC of the U.S.S.R. on basic questions concerning the reorganization of military training establishments to accord with general military reforms. This report and the well-argued proposals put before the RMC of the U.S.S.R. were the result of immense preparatory work on the part of the Administration of Military Schools and Iakir personally. In the course of preparing his report Iakir had carried out an extensive investigation of the state of military schools in Leningrad, the Ukraine, the Volga region, and Turkestan. In conversation with the directors of schools and courses, the political staff, lecturers, and students, he had explored every detail of the training process. Not content with investigation on the spot, he had consulted by correspondence with many of the most experienced directors of schools and instructors.

Iakir's proposals, as set out in his report to the RMC, concerning the syllabuses of military educational establishments, the organization of military and preparatory schools, their number, etc., were approved. The RMC resolution stated: "To give a clear notion of the purpose of the various kinds of military educational establishments, it will be convenient to adopt the following nomenclature: (a) preparatory military school; (b) military school; (c) district refresher courses; (d) advanced courses; (e) military academies."

Throughout 1924, intensive efforts were devoted to the reorganization of these establishments, the choosing of teaching staffs, and the establishment of uniform requirements for the organization of the training process in all types of schools and courses. This promoted a clearer understanding of the problems of cooperation between different branches of the armed forces. "It is clearly essential," Iakir wrote, "that the infantry and artillery, which always go into action together, would speak a common language, so that the artillery commander and observer can quickly identify the targets pointed out by the infantry and vice versa."

On November 26, 1924, Iakir once again reported on his work to the plenum of the RMC of the U.S.S.R. The plenum's resolution stated that it regarded "the work of the Administration of Military Schools, after its reorganization, as entirely satisfactory."

Iakir devoted much attention to the training of cadres for the mechanized forces, which were then in an early stage of development. Neither the U.S.S.R. nor any other country at that time possessed special schools for the training of tank commanders and officers of mechanized units. In Leningrad there was a motor-tractor school, part of whose function was to produce technicians in the field of motor transport, from ordinary drivers to the commanders of motorized formations. Iakir pressed hard for the reorganization of this institution. On several occasions he advised the council on Red Army training, of which he was a member, that it was a mark of bad organization to attempt to turn out drivers, mechanics, and commanders by one and the same process. Drivers and mechanics could be turned out by means of short-term courses, while the school should produce specialized commanders of armored units. The council accepted Iakir's proposals, and in 1925 a school of mechanized transport was set up within the Red Army.

* * *

During the last twelve years of his life, from 1925 to 1937, Iakir commanded the Ukraine and Kiev military districts, and from July 3, 1930, he was also a member of the RMC of the U.S.S.R. In those years his organizing ability came especially to the fore. He was one of the outstanding commanders of the time, showing great energy, initiative, and inventiveness in carrying out the decisions of the Party and government, the People's Commissariat for Defense, and the General Staff.

As a pupil of Frunze, Iakir zealously put into practice [his mentor's] scientific doctrine concerning the nature of the coming war. He was a close collaborator of such eminent soldiers as Tukhachevsky, Egorov, Unshlikht, and Bubnov. Drawing on his extensive war experience, he took an active part in the formulation of uniform concepts which became the basis for preparing the armed forces for battle.

* * *

All those who served with Iakir recall that his salient characteristic as a commander of large units was that after much time spent in active service he knew well not only the composition of forces but the personal qualities of all corps and division commanders and the entire senior staff of each military district, as well as the commanders of regiments and frequently even of battalions and companies. He had an extraordinary memory for people.

His success in commanding district forces owed in large measure to the fact that he enjoyed the complete confidence and respect of his staff and immediate collaborators, and knew how to find the way to the hearts of all those associated with him. His deputies were such prominent Soviet commanders as V. K. Bliukher, N. D. Kashirin, G. D. Khakhan'ian, M. P. Amelin, and I. N. Dubovoi, while his immediate subordinates also possessed exceptional skill in the training of troops and staffs. In the Great Patriotic War these men were to become front and army commanders, chiefs of staff on various fronts, and key members of general staffs.

* * *

Iakir was one of the initiators of the policy of creating, on the national borders, a system of fortified areas arranged in depth. He regarded this as one of the most important tasks of his district, and kept a close watch on its execution. The Military Council of the People's Commissariat of Defense of the U.S.S.R. noted several times that thanks to the personal attention paid to the work of construction by I. E. Iakir, head of the political department M. P. Amelin, and other senior officers of the district, preparations were going ahead well and plans were being successfully executed.[12]

How I. E. Iakir was liquidated

The inhuman attitude shown toward leading comrades and other persons under investigation is attested by a number of cynical comments by Stalin, Kaganovich, Molotov, Malenkov, and Voroshilov on letters and statements by those under arrest. For example, Iakir—the former commander of a military district—on one occasion wrote a letter to Stalin assuring him of his complete innocence. This said in part:

> I am and have been for many years an honest soldier, devoted to our Party and state. My whole conscious life has been spent in self-denying, honest work in full view of the Party and its leaders.... I am honest in every word that I speak, and I shall die uttering words of love for you, the Party, and our country, with unbounded faith in the victory of communism.

On this letter Stalin wrote the words "A scoundrel and a whore"; Voroshilov added "Quite right," Molotov signed his name below, and Kaganovich joined in with "Death is the only penalty for such traitors, riffraff, and [here follows a vulgar and unprintable expression]."

On the eve of his execution, Iakir wrote as follows to Voroshilov:

> In memory of my years of honest work for the Red Army I beg you to see that my family is looked after. They are helpless and innocent. I have made the same request to Ezhov. Iakir, June 9, 1937.

On this letter from a man with whom he had served for many years and whom he knew to have often looked death in the face in defending the Soviet Union, Voroshilov wrote: "I have doubts about the honesty of a man who is generally dishonest. K. Voroshilov, June 10, 1937."[13]

Khrushschev speaks of Iakir

In his speech comrade Shelepin has told you how these men, the flower of the Communist Party and the Red Army, were destroyed. He has quoted Iakir's letter to Stalin and the leaders' remarks on it. Yet Iakir at one time actually enjoyed Stalin's confidence.

I may add that at the moment of his execution, Iakir exclaimed: "Long live the Party! Long live Stalin!" Such was his trust in the Party and Stalin that he could not admit the idea that illegality was being deliberately committed. He thought that enemies of some kind had wormed their way into the NKVD.

When Stalin was told how Iakir had behaved at his death, his only reaction was to break into a storm of abuse against the dead man.[14]

AVGUST IVANOVICH KORK

Biographical data

[Army commander, second class.] Born July 22, 1887; died June 2, 1937. Member of the Communist Party from 1927. Born in the village of Ardlan, Iur'ev uezd, Lifliand gubernia, in an Estonian peasant family. Graduated from Chuguev infantry school, 1908, and Nikolaev military academy, 1914. In the First World War he performed staff duties and rose to be a lieutenant colonel. Joined the Red Army in 1918 and served on the staff of the Ninth Army at the beginning of 1919; chief of staff of the Army of Estonia, then deputy commander of the Seventh Army. From June 1919 he commanded the Fifteenth Army, and in 1919-20 successfully directed military operations against the White Poles. From October 1920 he commanded the Sixth Army, which broke through the fortified positions of the White guards at Perekop and Iushun. From May 1921 he commanded the Khar'kov Military District and was later deputy commander of the armed forces in the Ukraine and Crimea, commander of the Turkestan front and of the Red Banner Caucasian army, deputy commander and then commander of the Western, Leningrad, and Moscow military districts. In 1935 he became head of the Frunze Military Academy. Received the order of the Red Banner three times. Subjected to illegal repression at the time of the Stalin personality cult; rehabilitated posthumously.[15]

The Army Commander

Avgust Ivanovich Kork, who was born 80 years ago today, occupies a distinguished place in the list of commanders who built up our army. His career is well known to the older generation of Soviet people.

Born in a poor Estonian family, he attended the city school at Tartu (then known as Yur'ev) and in 1905 entered the infantry cadet's school. Beginning service in the rank of sub-lieutenant in the Ninety-eighth Iur'ev Infantry Regiment at Dvinsk (now Daugavpils), he showed exceptional military ability. In

1914 he graduated in the top category from the Nikolaev Military Academy. His military knowledge and experience were perfected in the First World War, and he became a major war specialist serving with the general staff. After the October victory the young Red Army badly needed such talents, and Kork had no hesitation in joining the people's side. His Red Army service began in June 1918; on February 26, 1925, he became a candidate member of the CP, and in 1927 a full member. He played a prominent part in defending the conquests of the October Revolution and in building up the armed forces of the Soviet Union. He first served in the operational department of the All-Russian General Staff, and was then sent to the southern front by a decision of the collegium of the RMC of the republic. He also took an active part in the heroic defense of Petrograd against Iudenich. His services against the White Poles and as commander of the Fifteenth Army on the western front were highly appreciated by the Party and government. He received the Military Order of the Red Banner in November 1919 and again on July 15, 1920, for "skillful and energetic leadership." His talents were still further displayed in command of the Sixth Army against Wrangle on the southern front, when he received a Revolutionary Sword of Honor together with the Military Order of the Red Banner. The operations in which troops under his command took by storm positions at Perekop and Iushun are inscribed with golden letters in the annals of the Soviet armed forces.

After the Civil War he occupied successively a number of important posts as commander of MDs and deputy commander of armed forces in the Ukraine and Crimea; later he led troops in Turkestan and commanded the Western MD and the Red Banner Army of the Caucasus. In all these posts Kork showed an outstanding grasp of military organization and the political training of troops, adhering strictly to the CP's decisions in regard to the development of military forces. We who served in those years well remember his activity. At all times and with all people he was a model of military bearing, exceptionally tidy and well-groomed, setting high standards for himself and others and winning respect by his organizing powers and many-sided knowledge of military affairs.

He wrote many articles for the press on the development and strengthening of the armed forces, on battle training of commanders and troops, and also military history. In an article on the Seventh anniversary of the October Revolution, published in 1924 in the journal *Prisiaga* (The Oath), he wrote: "The history of the Civil War has shown to the broad working masses the rightness of the teachings of Lenin, leader of the revolution. Indeed, our leader taught us many things, and it was by following his directions that the workers and peasantry of the Soviet Union were victorious in the battle with capitalism." In the same article, he declared that the strength of the Red Army lay "in its high degree of awareness owing to political training, its good organization and military skill brought to a level which ensured us victory." We have also good reason to remember the words he wrote forty-five years ago, in 1922, about the analysis of various problems of military history. He said: "It is clear to every commander that research into military history is of value only in so far as it comprises an exact and careful reconstruction of the circumstances of a given fight or operation and an objective account of events with full attention to their causal relationships. Only in this way can a given battle or operation be correctly appreciated and criticized, and useful deductions drawn for the present and future. ... The military historian must know how to choose his sources and estimate their importance and reliability, and he must have a wide and thorough knowledge of military affairs. We military historians are guided to this day by the criteria here set forth in assessing operations of the Second World War and more recent conflicts. Kork himself strictly observed them in his accounts of the Civil War. This was clearly shown in a lecture he gave in 1921 to the Ekaterinoslav garrison on his brilliant assault on the Perekop-Iushun positions on November 7-11, 1920. Not long ago, this lecture was deservedly reprinted almost in full in a collection published by the Military Printing Works of the Ministry of Defense.

Kork was a man of great gifts and sterling character. His career, though short, was a brilliant one, and he remained devoted until death to the Party and the people. Older people well remember his striking perseverance and determination. He was especially successful as director of the Frunze Military Academy, where he achieved a great deal in less than two years, transforming and improving the teaching process. Greater attention was devoted to the attachment of pupils to units for probationary training, and decisive steps were taken to develop tactical and operational research. Kork's lectures at the academy were distinguished by the clarity of their exposition of the course of former wars and the thoroughness of their analyses and conclusions. More than one class of those who studied under him in the 1930s passed with credit through the furnace of the Great Patriotic War. His pupils and all of the Soviet people remember his services in defense of the conquests of the October Revolution. His life was tragically cut short in 1937 as a result of unjust repression.[16]

VITALLII MARKOVICH PRIMAKOV

Biographical data

Born 1897, died 1937. Born in Semenovka village, Novgorod Seversk uezd, Chernigov gubernia, the son of a village teacher. Spent his childhood in Shumaki village, Polesia. In 1909 he left village school to attend high school at Chernigov, where he met Iurii Mikhailovich Kotsiubinsky and the latter's sister Oksana, whom he later married. In 1912 he joined a revolutionary youth group which in 1913 declared for the Social Democrats (Bolsheviks). In that year, when he was still a fifth-year high school pupil, the Bolshevik organization put him in charge of a local group of shoemakers and tobacco workers. He joined the CP in January 1914 and, together with Kotsiubinsky, took an active part in producing an underground journal for youth. During the First World War he adhered to Lenin's position and took part in the production and distribution of proclamations to the soldiers of the Chernigov garrison. He was arrested on February 15, 1915, and spent four months in solitary confinement. In May 1915 all of the Chernigov prisoners were transferred to the Luk'ianov jail at Kiev, and in July the Kiev military district court condemned Primakov to eight years exile in Siberia. After the February revolution of 1917 he returned to Chernigov and then to Kiev, where he became a member of the Bolshevik committee and worked as a propagandist and editor of the newspaper *Golos sotsial-demokrata*. In August 1917, on the Party's instructions, he became a private in the Thirteenth Reserve Infantry Regiment, then stationed at Chernigov, in order to establish a Bolshevik organization within it. His fellow soldiers made him their delegate to the second all-Russian congress of soviets. During the October Revolution he organized a detachment composed of workers of the Rechkov railroad-car repair works and the Skorohod factory, which repulsed General Krasnov's Cossack regiments at Pulkovo. At the second all-Russian congress of soviets [sic] he was elected a member of the All-Union Central Committee. Not long afterward he was at Kharkov, where in December 1917, on the instructions of the Ukraine Soviet government, he formed and commanded a Red Cossack regiment, the first regular unit of the Ukrainian Red Army. In the Civil War he commanded a regiment, a brigade, a division, and a corps of Red Cossacks. After the war the Red Cossacks under his command took part with other Red Army units in destroying the Petliura-Makhno bands.

In 1925 he was one of a group of Soviet advisers headed by V. K. Bliukher who went to China at the invitation of the Sun Yat-sen government to help in the formation of a revolutionary army. He returned home in May 1926 and was appointed commander of the first Rifle Corps, whose staff was stationed at Leningrad. In 1927-30 he did diplomatic work as a military attaché in Afghanistan and then Japan. In 1930-34 he was commander and commissar of the Thirteenth Rifle Corps at Sverdlovsk and deputy commander of the North Caucasus military district, later of the Leningrad military district. From the end of 1934 he was deputy inspector of advanced education of the Red Army. In January 1936, by a decision of the Party bureau of the CC of the CPSU, he became a member of the military council of the PC of Defense of the U.S.S.R. and in the same year was promoted to the rank of corps commander. For his military exploits he received the Order of the Red Banner three times. His life was tragically cut short in summer 1937.[17]

VITOVT KAZIMIROVICH PUTNA

Biographical data

Born April 24, 1893; died June 11, 1937. Corps commander, 1935. Joined the CP in February 1917. Born at Matskantsy village, Vilna gubernia, the son of a Lithuanian peasant. Attended commercial, handicrafts, and art schools at Riga. Arrested in 1913 for spreading revolutionary propaganda. Called up in 1915; in 1917, finished cadet school, commanded a battalion, and carried on revolutionary propaganda among the soldiers of the Twelfth Army. In April 1918 he volunteered for the Red Army, organized the Vitebsk military section and from May was in charge of the Vitebsk military commissariat. From September 1918 to May 1919 he was commissar of the First Smolensk (later the Twenty-sixth) Rifle Division; from May 1919 he commanded the 228th Karelian Regiment, and from July the Second Brigade of that division. From December 1919 he commanded the Twenty-seventh Rifle Division, fought on the eastern and western fronts, and took part in the suppression of the Kronshtadt mutiny of 1921 and of banditry on the lower Volga. Received the Order of the Red Banner three times. In 1923, after completing the military academy course for senior command personnel, he became commander and commissar of the Second Moscow Infantry School. Joined the Trotskyist opposition in 1923, but subsequently left it. In 1924-27 he served on the staff and central administration of the Red Army and then commanded a corps. In 1927-31 he was military attaché in Japan, Finland, and Germany, and in 1931-34 commanded first a corps and then the maritime group of forces in the Far East. Military attaché in Great Britain, 1934-36. Subjected to illegal repression; posthumously rehabilitated.[18]

Army Commander First Class
Ieronim Petrovich Uborevich

IERONIM PETROVICH UBOREVICH

Biographical data

[Army commander, first class.] Born 1896, died 1937. Joined the Bolshevik Party in 1917. Member of the CEC of the U.S.S.R. at all convocations, and candidate for the CC of the CPSU. During the Civil War he was commander of the Eighteenth Infantry Division and of the Fourteenth and Thirteenth armies, deputy commander in the Ukraine and Crimea and in the Tambov gubernia, then commander in the Minsk gubernia; war minister of the Far Eastern Republic and commander in chief of the people's revolutionary army. Received the Order of the Red Banner three times, also the Sword of Honor. After the war he was commander of troops in the North Caucasian, Moscow, and Belorussian military districts. On June 11, 1937, he was condemned on a false charge and shot together with M. N. Tukhachevsky.[19]

Review of Uborevich's career

In January 1896 a son named Ieronim was born in the peasant family of Piatras Uborevich. The boy's ability soon attracted the attention of his village teachers, and on their advice his father sent him to the technical high school at Dvinsk (now Daugavpils). As a youth, he justified his family's hopes. His relatives helped him through secondary school and encouraged him in his intention to enter the polytechnical institute at St. Petersburg. Owing to the outbreak of the First World War he was unable to take his engineer's degree: in 1915, when a second-year student, he was enrolled as a cadet in the Constantine artillery school, and in summer 1916 he was serving as a second lieutenant on the Rumanian front.

While at Petersburg, Uborevich began to take an interest in Marxist literature and joined a students' revolutionary group. At the front he came into contact with officers and men of Bolshevik sympathies, and under their influence joined the Russian Social-Democratic Workers' Party (Bolshevik) in March 1917. "I would not say," he wrote subsequently, "that at that time I acquired a rapid and exact grasp of the whole subject; but I understood the main principles—antagonism to the war and the bourgeoisie, support for Soviet power—and took active steps to put them into practice."

A man of decision and forthright character, Uborevich once and for all defined his position in the revolutionary struggle: he became a true fighter for Leninism and never swerved from his chosen path. In October 1917 he was one of the organizers and leaders of the Red Guard in Bessarabia, and it fell to him, at the head of one of the detachments he had formed, to defend the young Soviet Republic against the Austro-German interventionists. The detachment was defeated in an unequal struggle and Uborevich, badly wounded, was taken prisoner. In August 1918 he escaped and returned to Petrograd. The Soviet high command appointed him to the northern front, the scene of action against the Anglo-American interventionists.

*   *   *

At the end of November [1918], recognizing Uborevich's bravery and skill as a commander, his wholehearted devotion to the Communist Party and Soviet power, and his remarkable ability as a trainer of Red Army recruits, the high command, on the proposal of N. N. Kuz'min, promoted him to commander of the Eighteenth Division, which had just been formed. His advancement was strongly supported by R. S. Zemliachka, a member of the CC of the RCP(B) who was then on the northern front. Together with the division commissar I. F. Kupriianov and the head of the political department A. A. Aleshin, Uborevich created a unit of the Red Army distinguished for its superior fighting ability, a unit which played a major part in the defeat of the Anglo-American interventionists and the liberation of the north. He remained on the northern front until the late summer of 1919, when he was appointed to command the Fourteenth Army on the southern front.

At this time, Denikin's advance on Moscow was in full swing. The party had sent its best forces to the southern front, where the [Soviet] Republic's fate was being decided. G. K. Ordzhonikidze, a prominent member of Lenin's party, was serving on the RMC of the Fourteenth Army. The troops were engaged in a fierce and bloody battle at Orel, where, as Lenin put it, "the enemy is throwing in his best regiments, the 'Kornilov troops,' a third of whom consist of the most counterrevolutionary and best-trained officers, the most rabid in their hatred of the workers and peasants, those who are fighting for the direct restitution of their power and privileges as landlords." Uborevich and Ordzhonikidze performed wonders in strengthening military units, establishing revolutionary order in the staff and base organizations, and transforming the morale of the troops under the former's command. This cooperation with a fervent Bolshevik, whom Lenin had called the ablest and most trustworthy of revolutionaries, played a great part in Uborevich's whole development and his education as a Leninist commander. He always spoke of Ordzhonikidze with much warmth and gratitude as his old Party comrade and a brilliant organizer of the masses. "We young members of the party," he used to say, "learned from Sergo the foundations of Bolshevism: it was he who forged us into a weapon fit to continue the struggle against the enemy."

The Fourteenth Army, operating on the crucial sector of the southern front under the command of Uborevich and Ordzhonikidze, acquitted itself brilliantly.

Thanks to a bold maneuver, it inflicted a decisive defeat on the flower of Denikin's army.

Uborevich commanded the Fourteenth Army up to the time of Denikin's final defeat, after which, in February 1920, he took over the Ninth Army which was expelling the White Guardists from the northern Caucasus. In the summer and autumn of 1920 he commanded the Thirteenth Army on the south-western front, which, until peace was concluded with the Poland of the landlords and bourgeoisie, bore the brunt of the fight against Wrangel's troops. For his skillful conduct of operations against the White Guardists, Uborevich received the order of the Red Banner for the second time and also the Golden Sword of Honor.

In the spring of 1921 the Soviet government appointed him to the Tambov gubernia as deputy commander of the forces engaged in suppressing the Antonov rebellion.* His superior, M. N. Tukhachevsky, reported: "Comrade Uborevich, commanding the combined unit whose task was to defeat the Antonov army, rendered invaluable service in the fight against lawlessness."

                    *   *   *

By the end of the Civil War Uborevich had become one of the Red Army's chief commanders, distinguished by his mastery of the military art and his power to analyze and use the experience of the Red Army and its opponents, devising and applying new ways of fighting the enemy. These qualities were shown to full advantage in his organization of the conquest of the last important center of White Guard and interventionist activity on Soviet territory, in the Far Eastern maritime area. In summer 1922 Uborevich became commander in chief of the people's revolutionary army of the Far Eastern Republic; under his bold leadership, the Soviet forces overcame the Spassk fortifications and, having inflicted a crushing blow on the enemy, entered Vladivostok on October 25.

                    *   *   *

On October 31, 1922, at the fourth session of the ninth convocation of the All-Union CEC, Lenin referred to the liberation of the [Far Eastern] maritime area as follows: "I am sure that I am expressing the general feeling when I say that all of us here salute this latest exploit of the Red Army and the fact

---

*A spontaneous uprising under the leadership of Aleksandr Antonov, a guerrilla chief who called himself a socialist revolutionary. It is estimated that at least 20,000 peasants took up arms in protest against compulsory requisitions. The uprising began in the fall of 1919, reached its height in August 1920, and was suppressed by autumn 1921 by reliable cavalry units and military trainees. Antonov escaped but was caught by the GPU and shot June 24, 1922, in the village of Nizhni Shibriai. See P. A. Borisov, *Chernym letom* (Black Summer) (Moscow, 1965).—ED.

that a decisive step has been taken to end the war by casting into the sea
the last remnants of the White Guard forces.''

As a reward for expelling the White Guardists and interventionists from
the maritime area, Uborevich received the Order of the Red Banner for the
third time.

After the Civil War was over, he took a prominent part in building up
the armed forces of the first proletariat state in the world and informing and
developing Soviet military theory. He commanded in succession the troops
of the North Caucasus, Moscow, and Belorussian military districts, was a member
of the RMC of the U.S.S.R., directed the battle training of command personnel,
took an active part in the drafting of military manuals and regulations, and
composed works on military theory. He was one of the first Soviet commanders
to analyze and apply the experience of the Civil War to problems of troop
training and education. He realized that army training must be based on the
possible character of a future war. The instruction manuals he composed became
widely used in the Red Army and played a large part in spreading the knowledge
of advanced methods of training command personnel during the period of technical reconstruction of the Soviet armed forces.

Uborevich was a particularly gifted teacher of commanders and political
cadres. "It is difficult to overrate the importance he attached to the training
and preparation of command personnel. He personally instructed corps and
division commanders in the art of commanding military units at a time of rapidly
evolving military techniques"—such were the words of Marshal of the Soviet
Union K. A. Meretskov in his memoirs. "It was his constant endeavor to
ensure that the fruits of training and field work were immediately made available
to the forces to improve their readiness for battle, and that the experiences
of individual units or detachments were made known to all, as soon as possible."
As Marshal of the Soviet Union M. V. Zakharov declared, "Uborevich's constant interest in the officer cadres was of benefit to the careers of many of
us. Many of the commanders who served under him proved to be well prepared
to hold responsible posts in the fearful days of the Great Patriotic War: Generals
R. Ia. Malinovsky, K. A. Meretskov and I. S. Konev commanded fronts,
while A. P. Pokrovsky, V. V. Kurasov, F. P. Ozerov, and I became chiefs
of staff of entire fronts. V. Ia. Kolpakchi commanded an army. All of us
profited from the military training we had received under Commander of the
First Rank Ieronim Petrovich Uborevich."

Uborevich devoted no less attention to the training of junior officers and
the rank and file, as well as military-economic units. He insisted that every
officer and man, no matter in what branch he was serving, should be a thoroughly
trained fighting man. He initiated the practice of discussing tactical methods
not only with commanders but with the rank and file. As he said, "we are
getting a new type of literate fighting man, and we must adapt our methods
to him."

As a commander of the Leninist school, Uborevich always attached the greatest importance to creating the best conditions for party-political work among the troops. He rightly considered the Communists and Komsomols to be the leading element in the fulfillment of the tasks confronting the Party and government in respect of the military training of the armed forces.

It is difficult to enumerate all the problems of military science that were touched upon in Uborevich's articles and speeches. In his view, the steady creative development of military theory and a practical and purposeful approach to training problems were among the most important ways of keeping up to date in military affairs. For this reason he appealed to our military cadres to "regard tactical training in peacetime as a field of research," and rightly maintained that the saying "live and learn" was pre-eminently applicable in the military field. Many of his utterances, despite the military revolution of the last few years, retain their validity to the present day.

Uborevich was not only an eminent commander; he also played an important role in public life. In 1922-24 he was a member of the Far Eastern bureau of the CC of the CPSU, from 1925 a member of the bureau of the North Caucasian regional committee of the CPSU, and from 1931 a member of the bureau of the CC of the Belorussian CP(B). At the Sixteenth and Seventeenth Party Congresses he was elected a candidate member of the CC of the CPSU; from 1922 he was a member of the CEC of the U.S.S.R.

*   *   *

In the last years of his life Uborevich commanded the Belorussian military district, in which post he did much to protect the frontiers of the U.S.S.R. and to promote the development of the Belorussian SSR. He was just over forty-one and at the height of his powers and talent when his life was cut short. Together with such eminent military leaders as M. N. Tukhachevsky, R. P. Eideman, I.E. Iakir and others, he became a victim of unjustified repression and perished in June 1937.

In February 1937, shortly before his tragic end, he spoke as follows at a Komsomol meeting of the Belorussian Military District. "We must regard ourselves and our own lives as a part of the life of our homeland.... Day by day, we must instill into the minds of Red Army men the basic conception of increasing military danger. Much work is necessary in order to make ourselves and all Red Army men more courageous and politically conscious, which is at present our chief task." To achieve this task Uborevich never spared his strength and energy. He was distinguished by a high sense of duty and responsibility to the Party, and he truly made his own life a "part of the life of his homeland." In the hearts of all those who knew him and in the memory of the Soviet people, Uborevich remains as an example of wholehearted devotion to his duty as a soldier, to the communist Party and the socialist motherland.[20]

Other Cadres

IAKOV IVANOVICH ALKSNIS

Biographical data

[Army Commander, Second Class.] Born 1897, died 1938. Army Commander of the Second Class; formerly an ensign in the Tsarist Army, member of the Bolshevik Party from 1916. In the Civil War he was military commissar for the Orel gubernia, then for the Fifty-fifth Infantry Division, later for the Don oblast; and then deputy military commissar for the Orel military district. After the war he occupied senior posts in the general staff of the Red Army and commanded the Red Air Force.[21]

The chief pilot of the Soviet Union

Alksnis joined the Red Air Force after exercising an ordinary military command. A man of strong will, energy, courage, and profound knowledge of military and political affairs, he soon made a place for himself in the new service. He understood at once that to exercise effective command he must himself learn to fly.

One day he sent for a test pilot named V. Pisarenko and asked him: "How long does it take to learn to fly?"

The other replied "At least two or three years."

"Could I do it in three months?"

"I doubt it," said the pilot skeptically.

"I'll be the most hard-working pupil you ever had," Alksnis insisted. "I'll fly every morning and afternoon and spend the evenings studying theory. Will you teach me?"

So, in July 1929, the press carried the headline "New Achievement of Soviet Aviation" over a paragraph which ran:

> On July 21 the deputy commander of the Red Air Force, Comrade Alksnis, and the senior pilot of the Technical Research Institute, Comrade Pisarenko, made a flight in an aircraft of new design. Taking off at 2:32 a.m. from Moscow Central Airports, they flew nonstop to Sevastopol and landed there at 8 a.m. The plane was piloted by Comrade Alksnis.

Although Alksnis thus acted as his own pilot, he was not yet officially qualified to do so. He therefore applied to the People's Commissariat [of Defense?] to be transferred for a few months to the flying school at Kacha near Sevastopol, one of the best in the Red Air Force. Here, instructed by A. Levin, he learned to fly a P-I combat plane, and in November 1929 he received his military pilot's licence from the RMC of the U.S.S.R.

On June 28, 1931, the CEC of the U.S.S.R. appointed him Red Air Force Commander and a member of the RMC of the U.S.S.R. He was only thirty-four years old when the major task of military organization thus fell upon his shoulders. At that time accidents and crashes were not unusual in the air force, owing mainly to lack of discipline among pilots and mechanics and inadequate supervision of their training.

Alksnis set his face firmly against wrong principles which the air force had inherited from Tsarist days. According to a deep-rooted tradition, any pilot who had passed through flying school and obtained his licence was thenceforth treated as a specialist with absolute authority. No one could teach him anything more, and any attempt to test his skill in the air was of course regarded as an insult.

While Alksnis was still at Kacha, and as soon as the news of his pilot's licence was answered, he transformed himself from student into deputy commander of the Red Air Force and set about testing the flying technique of the school's instructors. The story goes that, having flown with a certain experienced squadron commander, Alksnis discussed the flight in detail and pointed out a number of mistakes and acts of carelessness. We may imagine the instructor's face when he was thus taken to task by yesterday's pupil.

"I consider your remarks insulting," he declared, "and I ask you to dismiss me."

"You will be dismissed if necessary," Alksnis replied quietly, "but I warn you that until you correct your mistakes you will not be allowed to train pilots."

The story spread around Kacha like wildfire, and was not long in reaching the ranks.

When Alksnis became head of the Red Air Force, he did much to strengthen this branch of the armed forces. A strong-minded and exacting commander and an excellent pilot, he instilled order with a firm hand, bringing military preparedness to a high level and ensuring the rapid adaptation of the flying personnel to new techniques. Pilots and mechanics spoke with respect of the high standards he demanded. Stories passed from mouth to mouth of how, after trials at one station or another, Alksnis had summarily dismissed the Commander for laxity of discipline and the low state of battleworthiness of his command. I myself had an early opportunity to appreciate his justice and severity.

On a cold autumn morning in 1931 Alksnis flew to our airfield, where routine combat training was going on. Having heard my report, he asked to see some pilots tested on a P-I. The plane was promptly prepared, and three pilots were tested. Two of them did well and were rewarded for their skill and technique, while the third, who was careless in his calculations and in the actual landing, received a reprimand. On the whole, Alksnis was satisfied with the station's performance.

On one occasion I was present at a meeting to investigate a serious breakdown in the delivery of airplane engines by one of our factories. It appeared that the factory had had trouble with the manufacture of certain valve springs without which the M-17 engine, could not be assembled. The director promised to put things right. Alksnis spoke and reminded all concerned of their moral duty as Bolsheviks—it was not only a matter of fulfilling a production plan, but of realizing that such things threatened the military potential of the air force. His trenchant intervention had its effect, and the factory was soon able to report that it was turning out the quantity of engines required by the state.

Later I met Alksnis at meetings of commanders of brigades and other units, held by the commander of the Moscow Military District to test the state of our operational and tactical preparedness. Flights and parachute jumps were carried out, as well as special training exercises; many of these were directed by Alksnis in person. At that time he had introduced a system of drill relating to the technical preparation of flights. The practical demonstration of this by the head of the air force was most instructive, and we followed all the details with interest. At the end of the meetings the people's commissar for defense, K. E. Voroshilov, came to Monino with representatives of the General Staff, who paid close attention to the new system and expressed appreciation of it.

Alksnis devoted the same exacting attention to all aspects of the life and training of flying personnel. He often directly supervised battle training and taught his men personally. All were inspired by his enthusiasm, exceptional energy, and capacity for work. He was ubiquitous. Many will remember his favorite saying: "Trust people, but test them too." His great merit was that he always formed his own judgment on the basis of personal knowledge and observation. He expected much of subordinates, but he gave them the opportunity to analyze their own mistakes and correct them.

I had occasion several times to take part in tactical and map exercises under his direction. They were always instructive and left a deep impression. Once he was in charge of air force training exercises in the Belorussian and Leningrad military districts. His instructions were that we must fly by day and night and in all kinds of weather—in those days a difficult assignment, to say the least. The planes did not have exact instruments and the pilots' skills left much to be desired. Nevertheless the exercises were a success. We prepared each flight carefully and worked out problems on a map beforehand. The commander expected us to make quick decisions and act energetically, with due regard to prevailing conditions.

Another noteworthy characteristic of Alksnis was his concern for human beings. I remember a conference in 1935 on battle training in the Air Force and the avoidance of technical breakdowns. The commanders of military districts and of their air forces were present, as well as those of some air brigades. Alksnis raised various questions of principle concerning the value of new aviation techniques, shortcomings in battle training, etc., and also put forward several important ideas concerning pilots' conditions of life and work, particularly housing, clothing, and food.

At the end of 1936 I happened to meet Alksnis and his wife at the theater. He came up to me and asked questions about the service. I had just finished a course at the operational faculty of the academy and was awaiting my next appointment. He told me that B. M. Shaposhnikov had recommended me for a job involving the latest equipment: I was to command a squadron of high-speed bombers in the Leningrad military district. This was good news. He told me to report next day to the personnel department to confirm the appointment, and spoke in detail of my future work and its difficulties.

That, alas, was our last meeting. I remember it for its intimate and sincere quality. Such is the memory I have preserved of Ia. I. Alksnis—a wise and strict teacher, a good comrade and an outstanding man.[22]

MIKHAIL PETROVICH AMELIN

Biographical data

Born 1896, died 1937. Member of the Communist Party from 1917. Born in the village of Solomina, Zlobnikov uezd, Kursk gubernia, in a poor peasant family. Worked in the Donbass mines, 1909-15. Called up in 1915, served in a training detachment of the Sixty-eighth Riazan' Regiment and became a noncommissioned officer. Member of the Federalist-Anarchist Party, 1916-17. Transferred to a penal company for active agitation among the troops; escaped and worked in Donbass, then in the Urals, where he was in close contact with old-guard Bolsheviks and took an active part in the February revolution. During the period of preparation for the October Revolution he joined the Bolshevik Party and became an active member. At the beginning of 1918 he volunteered for the Kursk revolutionary regiment, and on the orders of the Party committee for the Kursk gubernia he organized a Party committee within that regiment, of which he was deputy chairman. In autumn 1918 he attended a course for military commissars under the All-Russian Bureau for Military Commissars, after which he was assigned for duty under the revolutionary military committee of the Ukraine and became special commissar for supplies in the Ekaterinoslav sector. After the liberation of Odessa from the White Guardists, Amelin, as vice president of the Odessa revolutionary court, took an active part in stamping out the counterrevolution. He was twice appointed special plenipotentiary of the RMC of the Third Army. During the Civil War he was commissar of the Thirtieth Soviet Rifle Regiment and the Fourth Special Brigade on the southern front. In September 1919 he suffered serious wounds and shell shock at the battle of Bobrinsk. After leaving the hospital he was appointed agent of the revolutionary committees of the political administration of the Thirteenth Army. He then contracted typhus and, after recovery, was assigned to set up the Circassian military commissariat. He then became agent for food supplies for the Twelfth Army. During the White Polish invasion he was in charge of the evacuation of military property to Poltava, after which he attended the Twenty-ninth Infantry course there. In April 1920 he and other members of the course took part in the destruction of kulak bands. From September 1920 to March 1921 he was successively a private, company sergeant, political instructor, and battalion commissar during the fighting against Wrangel. After the latter's defeat he returned to Poltava and continued his studies. In May 1921 a detachment was organized from among the students for operations against the bands of Makhno, Maslov, Brov', and Ivniuk, and Amelin was appointed its commissar. After the destruction of those bands he became military commissar of the Sixty-eighth Infantry Training course (Poltava). In 1922-23 he studied at the Institute of Advanced Military Science at Moscow. In 1923-28 he was military commissar at the Kiev Infantry School. From 1928 to 1931 [he was] assistant political adviser to the commander of the Fourteenth Infantry Corps. From 1931 to 1935 he served as head of political administration of the Ukraine military district, and subsequently as its head. From 1934 to 1937 he was a member of the CC and of the organization bureau of the CC of the Ukrainian, and from 1935 to 1937, he was head of political administration of the Kiev military district and a member of the RMC of the U.S.S.R. He was arrested on June 19, 1937, and shot on September 8 of that year.[23]

VLADIMIR ALEKSANDROVICH ANTONOV-OVSEENKO

Biographical data

Born 1884, died 1939. Party pseudonym Shtyk (Bayonet), literary pseudonym A. Gal'sky. Took an active part in the October Revolution and became a Soviet soldier and diplomat. Born at Chernigov, a lieutenant's son. Belonged to the revolutionary movement from 1901 to 1903 as a member of the RSDWP. Finished cadet school at Petersburg in 1904. In 1905-6 he helped to organize a military revolt at Novo-Aleksandriia (Poland), and in 1906 at Sevastopol. For this he received a death sentence, which was commuted to twenty years of hard labor. He escaped and was active in Finland and Petersburg, then in Moscow. In 1910, after being arrested several times, he emigrated to France, where he joined the Mensheviks. He returned to Russia in May 1917 and became a Bolshevik. During the October armed uprising he was secretary of the Petrograd RMC and took an active part in several operations, including the capture of the Winter Palace and the arrest of the Provisional Government. At the second all-Russian congress of soviets (1917) he was elected to the CPC and became a member of the collegium of the PC for Military and Naval Affairs; he also became commander in chief of the Petrograd military district. During the Civil War in 1918-20 he commanded the Ukrainian front and was

Vladimir Aleksandrovich Antonov-Ovseenko

people's commissar for military affairs of the Ukraine. In 1920 he became a member of the collegium of the PC for Labor, and later deputy chairman of the Inner CPC and a member of the collegium of the NKVD. From 1922 to 1924 he was, head of the political section of the administration of the Republican RMC. He sided with the Trotskyist opposition in 1923-27, but broke with it in 1928. He was Soviet ambassador in Czechoslovakia in 1925, in Lithuania in 1928, and in Poland in 1930.[24]

A professional revolutionary

Petrograd, on a historic October night: the Winter Palace is lit up by searchlights; columns of the Red Guard move in to the attack and burst through the palace gates. Bewildered groups of cadets huddle in the half-lit rooms. In a small corner room, the members of the Provisional Government sit as though petrified.

> And one of the attackers, fingering his spectacles, declared in a matter-of-fact way: "I am Antonov, representative of the RMC; I declare the Provisional Government deposed."

Such is Maiakovsky's description of the successful assault on the Winter Palace, in which an active part was taken by the professional revolutionary and underground worker V. A. Antonov-Ovseenko. It was he who, on the orders of the CC of the Party, sent out the coded radio signal for the attack: "Tsentrobalt. Dybenko. Send articles of war. Antonov." Acting on the orders of Lenin, who personally directed the armed uprising, Antonov arrested the members of the last Russian bourgeois government.

V. A. Antonov-Ovseenko was born in 1883, the son of an officer. From his early youth he was a revolutionary, carrying on social-democratic propaganda in the most dangerous sector of the fight against autocracy, namely in the ranks of the Tsarist Army. When supplying autobiographical details for Party purposes, he wrote in reply to the question "Social status?" the words "Professional revolutionary." His right to do so was attested by the events of his entire life.

In 1905 he helped to organize the soldiers' revolt at Novo-Aleksandriia, and was arrested. Having escaped, he worked actively for the Party in Petrograd and then in Kronstadt.

In March 1906 the all-Russian conference of military organizations of the RSDWP was meeting in Moscow. Antonov was one of its members, was arrested and again escaped. The Tsarist government sentenced him to death, but he eluded his executioners.

For many years he was obliged to live in exile in Paris. When war broke out he took an active part in press work, denouncing in his articles the criminal nature of the imperialist slaughter. In June 1917 he was in Petrograd, where on the instructions of the CC he took an active part in preparations for the armed uprising in the capital and in Helsinki. At the beginning of October the northern council of soviets was held, an event whose importance as a major step in the revolution was emphasized by Lenin. Antonov made his mark as the thorough organizer and director of this meeting. In October he joined the RMC of the Petrograd soviet—the general staff of the Revolution—and after the victory of the armed uprising he and N. Krylenko and P. Dybenko were elected to the committee on military and naval affairs of the first CPC.

The Party dispatched its faithful son to the most difficult sectors of the fight for Soviet power. When Kerensky's troops were nearing the capital, [Antonov] became commander of the Petrograd Military District, and in December 1917 he was sent to fight the counterrevolutionaries in the south, where he conducted operations in the Ukraine. Lenin sent him a telegram praising his decisive action.

It fell my lot to take part in talks with the German command after the November revolution in Germany. These took place at Kursk, where Antonov's staff was then located. He took a close interest in the morale of the German officers and men, and showed himself an outstanding diplomat and true internationalist.

In autumn 1919, after the conclusion of operations on the Ukrainian front, Antonov went to Tambov as an agent of the All-Union CEC and of the chairman of the gubernia executive committee. In the difficult conditions created by economic collapse and kulak revolts, he displayed immense energy and perseverance in organizing supplies for the Red Army. His arrival in Tambov brought about many changes. His strength of will and sense of purpose showed themselves above all in a new attitude toward work. The front was close at hand, and he demanded of everyone a state of military efficiency, the ability to make responsible decisions and carry them out immediately. "We must put a stop to chattering and red tape," he declared; and when he had finished going through the agenda of this or that meeting, fifty-odd questions would have been reduced to four or five.

After the Civil War he was appointed deputy chairman of the PC for Labor, where he was again in a job of first-rate importance. In 1921 he headed the plenipotentiary commission of the All-Union CEC for the suppression of the kulak-SR revolt in the Tambov area.

In 1922-24 he headed the political administration of the Republican RMC. In the interests of historical truth it must be recorded that at that time he showed hesitation in conforming to the Party line and joined the Trotskyist opposition. Sometime afterward, having discerned the true nature of the oppositionists' policy, he broke with them and became an active opponent of Trotskyism.

After Lenin's death, Antonov was assigned to diplomatic work from 1925 and thereafter he represented the world's first proletarian state in Czechoslovakia, Lithuania, Poland, and finally Spain. In 1936 he was consul general in Barcelona when Spain was engulfed by civil war. But he was far from being a mere diplomat. The Spanish people well know and remember his energetic activity during the grim years of the fascist insurrection.

At the end of 1937 he became PC for justice of the U.S.S.R. This was his last post, the last page in his glorious life, which was tragically cut short during the period of the personality cult.

A fiery tribune of the revolution, a gifted organizer and a man of iron will, in ordinary life he was exceptionally kind and modest. He was extremely well informed, had a passion for books, was a fine chess player and mountaineer. Everything he did was done with youthful enthusiasm.

He wrote hundreds of articles, verses, original works of criticism, and books. His four-volume *Zapiski o grazhdanskoi voine* (Memoirs of the Civil War) and his *Semnadtsatyi god* (The Year 1917) are among the most vivid and reliable accounts of the October Revolution, and breathe a spirit of ardent devotion to Lenin.[25]

ERNEST FRANTSEVICH APPOGA

Biographical data

[Corps Commander.] Born 1898, died 1937. A working man and member of the Bolshevik Party from 1917. In the Civil War he was commissar on the staff of the Ural military district, and afterward he held important posts on the Red Army staff. Received Order of the Red Banner.[26]

A life devoted to his country

Among the outstanding members of the Red Army who devoted their lives to the defense of the revolution and the building up of its armed forces, a high place is rightfully occupied by the talented corps commander Ernest Frantsevich Appoga.

The son of a metalworker who belonged to the RSDWP, he followed in his father's footsteps and joined the revolutionary movement at an early age. Soon after the October Revolution he became a member of the Red Guard. During the Civil War he showed great talent as a military-political and staff worker. For courage and daring in battle he received the Order of the Red Banner. After the storms of war died down, he remained in the thick of army life. In the responsible posts to which the Party appointed him he worked with selfless ardor, first on the staff of a military district, then as division chief of staff and commander.

After passing through senior command courses and the Frunze Military Academy, he worked on the Council for Labor and Defense. In 1930 he was appointed head of military communications of the Red Army, and then became a member of the military council of the PC for Defense.

Remaining in charge of military communications for eight years, he did much to improve this service and prepare it to undertake large-scale military transport. I well remember his insistence on practical solutions of the problems of developing and constructing highways and railroads and the great importance he attached to the training of cadres.

Appoga was a man of broad outlook, ebullient energy, and great capacity for work. Under his direction theoretical studies were carried out on the main problems of organizing and using transport. An expert organizer, he also did much work in the field of military theory, seeking solutions for new long-term problems. Author and editor of several books, he was responsible for radical changes in the organization and planning of troop transport.

His brilliant military career was cut short in 1937. In the fullness of his powers and energy, he became a victim of unjustified repressions during the cult of personality.

The veterans of the army and navy remember him with respect as one whose whole life was an example of honest service to his country, Party, and fellow citizens.[27]

IVAN PANFILOVICH BELOV

Biographical data

[Army Commander.] Born 1893, died 1938. In 1917 he was a noncommissioned officer of the Tsarist Army in Tashkent. From the outset of the revolution he took an active part in fighting to defend Soviet power. In 1920 he commanded the Third Turkestan Division. After the Civil War he passed the Red Army staff course and commanded a division and then a corps; he was deputy commander and then commander of the Turkestan, North Caucasus, Leningrad, Moscow, and Belorussian military districts. In 1935 he became Army Commander of the First Class. His life was tragically cut short in 1938 during the period of the cult of personality.[28]

The career of an army commander

All who have read Furman's *Miatezh* (The Revolt) doubtless remember the figure of the intrepid division commander Panfilov. But not everyone knows that this character was inspired by one of the most glorious real-life heroes of the Civil War, a man who took an active part in the events of the summer of 1920 in Semirech'e (Kazakhstan): namely the commander of the Third Turkestan Division, Ivan Panfilovich Belov, who with a handful of communists succeeded in suppressing an uprising of several thousand counterrevolutionaries in the town of Vernyi (now Alma-Ata). Belov and his companions distinguished themselves by exceptional courage, coolness, endurance, and readiness to sacrifice their lives for the triumph of the revolution.

Veterans of the Civil War in Turkestan well remember this gifted commander and great organizer, profoundly versed in military affairs.

When the revolution broke out [Belov] was in Tashkent, and he at once took an active part in fighting to establish Soviet power. The First Siberian Infantry Regiment, which he was chosen to command, fought for several days against insurgent cadets and Cossacks. On November 14 the counterrevolutionary forces laid down their arms.

Belov was immensely popular with the revolutionary troops, and was soon appointed commander of the garrison of the Tashkent fortress. At that time the situation in Soviet Turkestan was a difficult one. The young republic, surrounded by a ring of White Guardist forces, was cut off from the center of Soviet Russia. In Tashkent, its capital, secret counterrevolutionary organizations were at work, linked with British and American intelligence groups. Realizing the danger of a counterrevolutionary outbreak, Belov worked intensively to strengthen the Red Army units of the Tashkent garrison. He created a school to train the junior command, and organized workshops for the manufacture of shells, cartridges, etc. The garrison under his command was the only unit to remain loyal to the Soviet power when, on a cold night in January 1919, the traitor Osipov, formerly military commissar for Turkestan, led an uprising to overthrow the soviets. For four days bloody fighting took place in the streets of Tashkent. Finally the rebellion was crushed and its ringleaders fled the town and took refuge in the hills.

This counterrevolutionary revolt organized by the leaders of the "left-wing" SRs plainly showed the true colors of the SR party. Belov, who had formerly been a left-wing SR, broke once and for all with the lackeys of the bourgeoisie. He joined the CP and remained its faithful son to the end of his days.

Despite the prompt crushing of the Tashkent revolt, the position of the Soviet Republic of Turkestan remained precarious. To rescue the Turkestan Army, now under Belov's command, it was necessary for that force to break through a steel ring of enemies and join with the main forces of the Red Army. Belov succeeded brilliantly in directing this effort, and in September 1919 the forces of the Turkestan Republic joined the army headed by M. V. Frunze.

In the complicated breakthrough operation Belov showed his exceptional talents as a commander and organizer.

The Soviet command appointed him to the most critical sectors of the battle to free Central Asia. He commanded troops in Semirech'e, where General Annenkov's bands were finally destroyed, and liberated the working population of Bukhara from oppression by the Emir.

After the victorious conclusion of the Civil War, Belov devoted all his energy, knowledge, and experience to strengthening the Red Army. Having passed the Red Army staff course he commanded a division and then a corps, after which he became deputy commander and then commander of a military district. The military districts he successively commanded were those of the North Caucasus, Leningrad, Moscow, and Belorussia.

In these responsible posts he fully displayed his active and energetic temperament, losing himself wholly in the tasks of training and organizing courses and maneuvers. Spending weeks on end in the field with the troops or staff, he never ceased to seek and to introduce new, progressive methods of warfare. He was distinguished at all times by his flair for new ideas and his detestation of empty routine. He paid much attention to training troops for operations in difficult forest and marshy terrain, especially in winter.

Belov made no small contribution to the defense preparations of our country, and in 1935 he became an Army Commander of the First Class. The comrades with whom he served remember that in all circumstances he succeeded in learning something new, in improving his knowledge. All about him were struck by his vast knowledge of all aspects of army life.

When in summer 1931 he took up his appointment in the Leningrad military district, he began by becoming thoroughly acquainted with his staff. Having listened to the account of its members furnished by the chief and deputy chief of staff, he surprised his audience by giving an exact description of each of his future collaborators, emphasizing their chief characteristics.

His human qualities should on no account be passed over. He combined an exigence verging on severity with tact and extraordinary humanity. The commander of a detachment under him recalls an episode that took place in 1927 in the Caucasus. The detachment, which Belov was accompanying on the march, had lost its way during a sudden snow storm. The troops did their best to find the way until nightfall, but when the darkness closed in the exhausted men began to improvise shelter for the night. Someone took care to lay a felt cloak over the detachment commander and his companions and in the morning it turned out that the officer who had parted with his cloak for this purpose was the deputy commander of the military district, I. P. Belov.

A self-taught man and the son of a peasant, a man who had known hardships and heavy toil since childhood, Belov rose from commanding a Red Guard detachment to the position of Army Commander of the First Class, commanding a military district. His life was tragically cut short at the height of his creative powers, during the cult of personality.

The above is only a brief outline of his carrer, a sketch of the personality of a great Soviet commander, a brilliant organizer, a communist, and a fighting man.[29]

IAN KARLOVICH BERZIN

Biographical data

[Army commissar, second class.] Born 1890, died 1938. Member of the Bolshevik Party from 1905. Served with the Red Army from 1919. In the Civil War he commanded the political department of a division and was later deputy chief, chief, and military commissar of the intelligence administration of the Red Army staff.[30]

The man who sent Sorge on his errand

The dry crackling of rifle fire resounded through the forest, out of which rode a troop of Cossacks, whooping loudly as they pursued a Latvian workers' detachment. The latter's retreat was being covered by a few men, including a youth of tender age. Firing a shot from his Colt, the young man took to flight but soon tripped and fell. When he regained awareness he was in a prison hospital, his head and shoulders bandaged and aching furiously. Later he was interrogated:

"Who are you?" demanded a captain of gendarmes. "What is your surname?"

"Kiusis," was the reply.

"He's an old friend, sir," the captain reported obsequiously to his colonel. "Ian Berzin, party nickname Kiusis—we gave him fifty of the best last year for handing out revolutionary pamphlets."

"Well, my friend, you're pretty young to be a socialist. You'll be tried, and don't expect any mercy from us."

A few weeks later Ian Berzin was duly sentenced to death for active participation in illegal workers' detachments and armed resistance to the forces of law and order. However, on grounds of age the sentence was commuted to imprisonment. That was in 1906.

Who was this sixteen-year-old who had received a death sentence? Ian Karlovich Berzin was born on November 13, 1890, in the Vol'gov volost of Fridrikhshtat uezd, Kurland gubernia, the son of a landless Latvian peasant. He

Army Commissar 2nd Class
Ian Karlovich Berzin

was acquainted with poverty from childhood, and was still a pupil in a teachers' seminary when he began active work as a revolutionary. In 1905 he joined the RSDWP. The seminary having been closed for involvement in the demonstrations of October 25, 1905, Ian joined the partisan force known as the "forest brothers" and took part in armed combat as well as distributing revolutionary literature, for which he was arrested. In 1906 he took an active part in propaganda work for the Bolshevik organization at Riga, was again arrested and this time condemned to death; the sentence was commuted to imprisonment. In 1909 he was arrested for the third time for belonging to the RSDWP, and was exiled to Siberia with deprivation of civil rights.

In the spring of 1914 he escaped and returned to his home territory, where he was called up a year later. While Tsarist Russia waged war, Ian carried on the work of propaganda in the trenches. In 1916 he escaped to Petrograd, where he worked as a mechanic, taking an active part in promoting stoppages and strikes.

When the revolution of February 1917 broke out, he took part in the fighting against the Whites and worked as an organizer and propagandist, a member of local committees in Petersburg. When in October 1917 the Petersburg workers stormed the Winter Palace, Berzin was in the front rank of the assailants.

During the Civil War he was in Soviet Latvia, first as head of a department in the Commissariat of Internal Affairs and then, from March 1919, as deputy PC for internal affairs of the Latvian Republic. After the overthrow of Soviet power in Latvia, in May 1919, he followed the retreating workers' detachments to Petrograd, and from that time on he remained a member of the Red Army. In June-August 1919 he was head of the political department of the Second Petrograd Infantry Division, and from August 1919 to November 1920 he was head of the special department of the All-Russian Cheka in the Fifteenth Army. In December 1920, on the orders of F. E. Dzerzhinsky, he was transferred to the staff of the intelligence department of the Red Army. On this occasion he was given a warm send-off by his fellow Chekists on the staff of the Fifteenth Army, who composed an address full of appreciation and gratitude: "Your humane attitude to one and all, your knowledge, experience, sincerity, simplicity, and firmness have been an example to us all not only in our everyday life but also in our work for the Party."

Berzin's new intelligence work was full of responsibility and anxiety. From 1924 he headed the intelligence department of the Red Army. He was always to be found, full of strength and energy, among his comrades and fellow workers, who sometimes called him "Pavel Ivanovich" but more often "the Old Man." Those who served under him then remember him affectionately. "He had young, lively eyes, an almost childishly good-humored expression, and firm lips. When he greeted anyone, his eyes would shine even more brightly and his smile created a straightforward, easy atmosphere." As to his style of work, "everything about him was extraordinarily tidy and gave an impression of quiet efficiency.

He never shouted or even gave orders, but would simply say 'this ought to be done,' and that sufficed." He was a tactful, considerate man who understood people and knew how to size them up.

It was Berzin who entrusted to Richard Sorge his most responsible missions in China and then Japan. Berzin was not mistaken in his choice.*

A true Leninist and Communist, he commanded authority thanks to his knowledge and personal example. In 1928 he received the Order of the Red Banner. In April 1935, at his own request, he was relieved of his current functions and became first assistant then deputy commander of the Special Far Eastern Army. On this occasion the PC for defense wrote in an order of April 15: "A devoted fighter for Bolshevism, extremely modest, deeply respected and loved by all his working associates, Comrade Berzin has devoted all his time, strength, and rich revolutionary experience to his arduous and responsible duties.... I am certain that in his future work he will fully justify the authority he enjoys as one of the ablest members of the Red Army staff."

However, Berzin was not to remain long in the Far East. The Spanish fascists rebelled against the republic, and Berzin was called to the front line. The Party and government sent him as a senior adviser to republican Spain, where again he earned unquestioned respect and authority.

In 1937 he was recalled from Spain and once more became head of the intelligence department of the Red Army. At the end of 1937, during the cult of personality, he was slandered and arrested, and he met his death in a tragic manner.

Such is the life history of the man who entrusted Sorge with the honorable duties of a Soviet military intelligence agent.[31]

*Richard Sorge (1895-1944) was the head of a highly effective Soviet spy ring operating in Japan during World War II. Born October 4, 1895, near Baku, the son of a German engineer and a Russian mother, he received his education in Germany and fought in the German army in World War I. In the early 1920s he joined the German Communist Party and in 1925 became a member of the RCP(B) and began working as an agitator for the Comintern. Probably in 1929 he was enlisted by General Berzin, then head of the Fourth Bureau of Red Army Intelligence, and after spending some years in China was assigned to Japan in 1933. He became a close and trusted friend and adviser of the German ambassador in Tokyo, Major General Eugen Ott, and gradually succeeded in infiltrating the highest Japanese circles, including those of Prince Kanoye. Sorge is said to have warned Stalin three months ahead of the impending German attack on the Soviet Union, and to have assured him of Japanese neutrality. On the strength of this report, Stalin moved several divisions from the Far East to the western front and thus Moscow was saved from the Germans.

Sorge was arrested in October 1941 with other members of his spy ring. He was tried, convicted, and executed November 2, 1944. In November 1964, after a series of Soviet press releases on him, Sorge was posthumously declared a Hero of the Soviet Union.—ED.

Berzin's meetings with Sorge

It was of course an act of great daring for a Communist newly arrived from Moscow to approach the editor of a respectable bourgeois newspaper and offer his services as a foreign correspondent. But this very audacity seemed to the "Old Man" to guarantee the success of the operation. By the "Old Man" we mean Ian Karlovich Berzin, also known as Pavel Ivanovich—the legendary figure who for years had been at the head of Soviet counter espionage.

Richard remembered exactly how it had all taken place. Berzin had met him in a narrow corridor in an old private house on Znamensky Street and had said, "Come along, let's have a talk." When they reached his office, he went on:

"What do you think about Hitler?"

Richard had thought a great deal about Hitler. The advent of the Nazis to power meant a step toward a war that would be directed first and foremost against the Soviet Union. He had no patience with the view that fascism was an ephemeral, short-term phenomenon. As a Party worker, sociologist, and close student of German affairs, Sorge had closely analyzed the situation and come to the conclusion that events were tending in the direction of an alliance between the forces of worldwide reaction, especially Germany, Japan, and Italy. It could be taken as a foregone conclusion that the fascist forces were preparing for a full-scale attack on democracy.

"I think," said Sorge, "that fascism is growing stronger and more aggressive, and that the threat of war against our country has greatly increased."

Berzin agreed, and added: "That means—don't you agree?—that we must know the plans of our probable opponents and penetrate their organizations. That is our contribution to national defense. If we know what is in the enemy's mind, we can foil his aggressive plans or at any rate anticipate them. The great thing is to avert the risk of war."

"Of course it is!" exclaimed Sorge. "And I beg you, Ian Karlovich, to give me this assignment. I can give reasons why I believe I am the right man for it."

"That is why I asked you to come and see me," replied Berzin. "Let's discuss it further." So they went on discussing—the head of Soviet Intelligence and Richard Sorge, hero of the invisible front.

Many further meetings took place in Berzin's office. Like two chess players, he and Sorge tried out numerous variations, rejecting and returning to them and evolving new ones, until finally the plan known as "Operation Ramsay" came into being.

Time was short, and Hitler's seizure of power had vastly complicated their task. Long before the Reichstag fire, the fascist watchdogs of German imperialism had dreamed of a treacherous attack on the Soviet Union, as their leader had made clear in his writings.

One day, in conversation with Sorge, Berzin went to a bookcase, took down a brown-covered volume and began to leaf through it. It was a translation of Hitler's infamous *Mein Kampf*. Having found the place, he began to read:

> We must embark on the policy of conquering fresh lands in Europe; and if we are to do so, these can only be acquired at the expense of Russia. All conditions are now ripe for this.

Tossing the book onto his desk, Berzin exclaimed: "There, that's what they're up to! And history will not forgive us if we waste time and relax our vigilance. I believe our plan is the right one: to penetrate Japan by way of Germany and get our information there about German plans for aggression. Japan is the place!" Then, thumping his open palm with his fist, he stopped in front of Sorge and added: "In our business, we have to combine calculation with extreme boldness, sober risk-taking with the utmost caution. That's our dialectic—do you understand?"

Yes, Richard understood this man, whom he respected, loved, and regarded as his teacher. He revered Ian Karlovich as a representative of the older generation of revolutionary Russia.

Ian Berzin, the man with the young face and the restless character, was endowed with a wealth of experience of life and revolutionary affairs. Beaten by Cossacks with ramrods at sixteen years of age, wounded three times in fights with gendarmes, sentenced to death and then to lifelong hard labor—as a result of all these trials, Peter Kiusis's hair had turned quite gray. When he had escaped from distant Yakutia and returned home secretly by night, his own mother had not recognized him. He had smiled and said: "That's as it should be. I am Berzin now, Ian Berzin, and Peter is no more. He died somewhere in the Siberian forests. You see, Mother, I've taken Father's name; and I shall never disgrace it, never!"

Ian Berzin kept his oath. In February, July, and October 1917 he was to be found at his revolutionary post, fighting the cadet forces, taking part in the armed uprising in Petrograd and later in Latvia.

"That's how I got my gray hairs!" [he said later.] "The gendarmes and the Tsarist police gave me my lessons in life. Six years at school and another six in prison. Luckily I was able to shorten the stint by running away."

When Sorge and Berzin grew tired, the latter used to suggest a game of chess "to clear our brains." They drank strong tea, brownish-black in color, and went on thinking aloud about Operation Ramsay. Every now and then, Ian Karlovich would speak of the character and aims of Soviet counterintelligence and the qualities required of its agents. Sorge particularly remembered some remarks made during a game of chess: "You know, Richard, I must tell you this: we must always be on the watch and think of the enemy not as stupid or backward...but as a subtle and clever opponent. We must conquer him by courage, boldness, ingenuity, and quickwittedness. Forgive me for saying all this, but you must remember you're going to Berlin."

Then the chessboard was put aside and the tea left to grow cold on the table. The plan of operations had already been worked out: only the details remained to be settled—any one of which might be the cause of success or failure.

"In the Soviet intelligence service you need patriotic ardor, a cool head, and iron nerves," said Berzin. "We bear a heavy responsibility and must do all we can to avert a war, especially one between the Soviet Union and Japan. That will be the chief task of your group. But of course you must also do everything possible to find out the plans of our No. 1 enemy—fascist Germany. All this will be difficult, damnably difficult, but it must be done. Do you understand?" It was a habit of Berzin's to ask in this way whether his collaborators and comrades understood what he was telling them.

When the concept of Operation Ramsay had become clear they began to consider the operational side. The first objective was to penetrate not Berlin but Tokyo, but to do so via Germany, thus striking on two fronts. Nazi phraseology was to serve as a cover and a means of gaining the enemy's confidence. Sorge was to use his old contacts with the business world, made while still in China. How was this to be done in practice? Berzin relied on Sorge's personality: he had the grasp and experience of a true Party man, and the intuition of a born intelligence agent.

It would be best of all if the opportunity should arise for Sorge to go to Japan as the correspondent of a well-known German newspaper. Berzin agreed with Sorge's proposal to aim for the *Frankfurter Zeitung,* where he had some contacts. This decided, Berzin asked Sorge to keep him constantly informed. When they parted, he took two five-dollar bills out of a safe and handed one to Sorge, saying: "You'll get the other in exchange when I send our liaison man to you. You can trust him as though he were myself—be sure that I will send someone absolutely reliable."

It was now over two months since Sorge had left Moscow. Berzin had sent his liaison, and Sorge had told the man what he had so far succeeded in doing. They were climbing a steep path up the northern side of a mountain covered by dense forest. The sun's rays seldom penetrated to the ground, which was covered with a darkgreen moss like malachite. There was not a soul about. They sat on a rough wooden bench at the edge of a slope leading steeply down to a river. Sorge said: "Tell the Old Man that I've managed to get a letter of recommendation to the German ambassador in Tokyo, von Dircksen, from a distant relative of his who is head of the I.G. Farben chemical works at Ludwigshafen. This man can pull a lot of strings and has also telephoned to my editor's office. All sorts of doors will be open to me."[32]

VOL'DEMAR ALEKSANDROVICH BIULER

Biographical data

[Brigade commander.] Born 1896, died 1938. Member of the Communist Party from 1915; took an active part in the revolution at Kazan and was first PC for posts and telegraph of the Tatar Republic. Served as a political officer in the Civil War. Later graduated from the Advanced School of Aerial Observation and occupied a number of senior posts in the air force and antiaircraft defense.[33]

GEORGII IVANOVICH BLAGONRAVOV

Biographical data

Born 1896, died 1938. Member of the Bolshevik Party from 1917 and member of the first convocation of the All-Union CEC. As an ensign, he joined the military organization under the CC of the RSDWP. During the October uprising he was commissar for the Peter and Paul Fortress and took part in the storming of the Winter Palace. In 1918 he became a member of the RMC for the eastern front. After the Civil War he served in the All-Union Cheka, the GPU and the OGPU, and became deputy PC for communications.[34]

IOSIF FRANTSEVICH BLAZHEVICH

Biographical data

Born 1891, died 1938. A lieutenant colonel in the Tsarist Army; served with the Red Army from 1918. In the Civil War he commanded a regiment, then a brigade, then the Fifty-ninth Division, the Semipalatinsk group of forces and the First Army on the Turkestan front. After the war he commanded the Sixteenth Rifle Corps, headed the Sixth Department of the Red Army staff, and was an inspector of Red Army antiaircraft defense.[35]

Marshal Vasilii Konstantinovich Bliukher

VASILII KONSTANTINOVICH BLIUKHER

Biographical data

[Marshal.] Born November 19, 1889, died November 9, 1938. Hero of the Civil War; Marshal of the Soviet Union, 1935. Member of the CP from 1916 and candidate member of the CC of the CPSU from 1934. Born in the village of Barshchinka near Rybinsk, the son of a peasant. Worked until 1910 as a mechanic at the Mytishchi factory, where he was arrested for inciting workers to strike and was imprisoned for two years and eight months. Served as a private and noncommissioned officer in the First World War. Seriously wounded in 1915, he was discharged from the army and worked at the Sormovo shipbuilding yards and the Osterman power station at Kazan. In February 1917, on the orders of the RSDWP, he returned to the army and served in the 102d Reserve Regiment at Samara; he was elected to the regimental committee and the city soviet of soldiers' deputies, and from October 1917 served on the Samara RMC. In November he was sent as commissar with expeditionary force to assist the workers of the town of Cheliabinsk, who elected him chairman of their revolutionary committee. In the spring of 1918 he was in command of the Red Guard detachments which destroyed the bands of the ataman Polkovnikov and General A. I. Dutov and liberated the towns of Troitsk, Miass, and later Orenburg. After the retreat from Orenburg in 1918 as a result of the capture of Ufa by the Whites, the Southern Ural Partisan Army under his command made a heroic forty-day march, fighting as they went, from the Beloretsk raion along the Urals until they joined up with the troops of the eastern front. In September 1918 Bliukher became the first person in the Soviet Republic to receive the Order of the Red Banner. He commanded the Fifty-first Rifle Division (known as the Perekop Division after 1920) in combat against Kolchak's forces in 1919 and, in the following year, on the south-western front in the fight for Perekop and the Kakhovka bridgehead. In 1921-22 he was commander in chief, war minister, and chairman of the military council of the Far Eastern Republic. For his martial prowess and skill in command during the Civil War he received the Order of the Red Banner five times. After the war he was commander of the First Corps and of the Leningrad fortified area, entrusted with highly responsible tasks by the RMC of the U.S.S.R. In 1924-27 he was chief military adviser to the Revolutionary Government of China at Canton, headed until 1925 by Sun Yat-sen. In 1927-29 he was deputy commander of the Ukrainian military district; from 1929, commander of the Special Red Banner Army of the Far East. He became a victim of slander and repressions during the period of the cult of Stalin's personality. Posthumously rehabilitated.[36]

A proletarian commander

The name of Vasilii Konstantinovich Bliukher occupies a place of honor among those commanders who were forged in the furnace of civil war under the leadership of the great Leninist Party. Himself a Leninist and the son of a poor peasant in the Yaroslav oblast, he did much to strengthen the young Soviet state and to build up the armed forces which defended the honor and independence of the socialist motherland against the imperialist and fascist invaders. Treacherously slandered during the time of the cult of Stalin's personality, he died tragically in the fullness of his powers.

Today he would be seventy-five years old. His career was that of a working man who knew from his childhood the nature of heavy work and who stood up fearlessly for all who were deprived and oppressed. He was by turns an errand boy, a laborer, and a mechanic. Dismissed from employment for incitement to strike, he was imprisoned, and was still in exile when the First World War broke out. He was called up and sent to the front, and was seriously wounded early in January 1915. Returned from the front, he worked as a mechanic at the Sormovo shipbuilding works and then at a machinery plant in Kazan. Here he met Bolsheviks, carried out Party tasks, and in 1916 threw in his lot once and for all with that of the Leninist Party.

After the revolution of February 1917 he moved to Samara, where on Party orders he carried on revolutionary work among the soldiers of the 102d Reserve Infantry Regiment. During the October Revolution he took an active part in establishing Soviet power in Samara, where he was elected to the presidium of the revolutionary committee. In November, at the head of a revolutionary detachment, he broke through White Guard covering detachments at Cheliabinsk, where he soon became chief of staff of the Red Guard for the Cheliabinsk raion.

When this industrial center in the southern Urals was threatened with capture by White Cossack bands under ataman Dutov, Bliukher united the Red Guard detachments of the southern Ural factories, and the workers' and peasants' forces under his command marched more than 600 miles through the Ural area and Bashkiria. In heavy fighting they defeated large White Guard bands, broke through the encircling enemy, and joined forces with the Red Army.

Bliukher's iron will power, military talent, and outstanding personal bravery earned him the respect and love of all Soviet people. In a telegram to Lenin and Sverdlov, the Party committee for the Ural oblast once stated that "in Bliukher and his troops we have real heroes, who have accomplished an exploit without precedent in the history of the revolution." About this time the statute creating the Order of the Red Banner was being drawn up. When the question arose as to who should be first to be honored with this supreme military distinction, Bliukher's claim was unanimously supported by all members of the All-Union CEC.

Bliukher continued his military career in Siberia and the Far East. Commanding the Fifty-first Rifle Division, he decisively defeated Kolchak's bands in the Irtysh basin near Tobolsk and advanced to the Novosibirsk raion. This was a significant contribution to the rout of the White Guards on the eastern front.

In summer 1920 Bliukher and the Fifty-first Rifle Division, transferred to northern Tauris, defended the Kakhovka base against Baron Wrangel's soldiery, and saved it from capture in bloody battles in which they were helped by other Red Army units. Later, in November 1920, Bliukher stormed Perekop. The troops under his command defeated the enemy at Perekop and Iuman', and then advanced into the Crimea by way of the isthmus and Sivash.

In the middle of 1921 the Party dispatched him to the Far East, where White Guard bands were still operating with the support of Japanese forces. His great exploit at this time was the renowned battle at Volochaevka, at which the Red troops finally routed the Whites.

A commander of the Leninist school, Bliukher combined the qualities of intrepid Bolshevik, gifted organizer, and military leader. He possessed personal courage and daring and the gift of bold operational and tactical thinking. The operations and battles he conducted during the Civil War are regarded even today as classic examples of skillful choice of time and place for attack and firm determination in the pursuit of objectives.

After the victorious conclusion of the Civil War, Bliukher took an active part in building up our armed forces. For a time he commanded the First Infantry Corps, and later the Petrograd fortified area. In 1924, when the first civil revolutionary war broke out in China, Bliukher was sent there as chief adviser to Sun Yat-sen's revolutionary government. With his help the Chinese national revolutionary army was created and plans were worked out for the eastern and northern campaigns.

In 1929, when military conflict broke out in the Far East, the Party and the Soviet government appointed him commander of the Special Far Eastern Army and entrusted him with the task of defending our frontiers against the White Chinese reactionaries.

For nine years, until the last days of his life, Bliukher commanded the Special Red Banner Army of the Far East. The author of these lines had the good fortune to serve for a long time under his direct command. He was a man of strong mind and sincerity, a gifted commander, simple and charming in his relations with others. All his powers and experience were devoted to strengthening our armed forces. He performed every task to the utmost, whether it was stamping out provocation on the frontier or training troops.

One remembers many episodes which were characteristic of him not only as a strict, just, and wise commander but as a man of great humanity. In field exercises he gave many examples of his concern for the ordinary fighting man. He often spent his leisure in the clubs, where he met officers and their families. I remember the warmth with which he spoke of some American workers who had saved up to buy an automobile as a gift to the proletarian commander.

The Soviet government showed its high appreciation of his services to the motherland by conferring on him the Order of Lenin twice, the Order of the Red Banner five times, and other orders. In November 1935, together with other Red Army leaders, he was raised to the dignity of Marshal of the Soviet Union.

Despite the burden of his command, he found time for political and social work. He was elected a member of Party committees, a candidate member of the Party CC, a member of the CEC, and a deputy to the Supreme Soviet of the U.S.S.R. He often lectured to army Communists and workers and was glad to share his experience and knowledge with junior commanders and political workers.[37]

A legendary career as a commander

The career of Vasilii Konstantinovich Bliukher reads like a legend. He was the first man in the Soviet Union to be decorated with the Order of the Red Banner, and among the first group to be made Marshals of the Soviet Union. But at the time when this story begins he was a simple soldier of the revolution with no dreams of ever receiving a marshal's baton.

The towns and villages of the southern Urals, where the Soviets had only recently come to power, were threatened by ataman Dutov's plans to restore Tsarist rule. His Cossacks, officers, and cadets seized Orenburg, Troitsk, and Verkhne-Uralsk, and surrounded Cheliabinsk; but [at Cheliabinsk] his designs misfired. A detachment of workers and soldiers from Samara met the White Guardists with overwhelming force. Its commander was Bliukher, Red Guard chief of staff.

The bitter struggle against Dutov went on for more than six months while towns in the southern Urals constantly changed hands. Day and night the Red force withstood the pressure of superior enemy forces, until finally Orenburg was lost. What was to be done next? At a short conference, Bliukher rejected the proposal to take to the steppes around Orenburg. "We would lose half our force there," he said, and proposed instead a difficult and dangerous march through the enemy's rear area to the industrial region farther north, where they could join the main Red Army forces. This plan was adopted, and Bliukher was unanimously chosen as leader of the partisan force.

Even the most embittered enemies of the Soviets recognized and feared Bliukher as a great commander. They spread the story that he was descended from a Prussian marshal who fought against Napoleon. Once some of Bliukher's men asked him if this was so. "No, I'm not a German," he replied good-humoredly, "I'm a simple peasant from Barshchinsk village, Yaroslav gubernia. But I do have a certain connection with a German marshal. My grandfather Medvedev, who won the St. George's Cross twice, was a serf, and his master named him Bliukher in the German's honor. The name stuck to him and remained in our family."

In 1919, when the Whites were being pursued in Siberia, the hardened Ural warriors were formed into a new division, the Fifty-first, under Bliukher's command. Along the banks of the Irtysh, swollen by autumn rains, across the taiga and the marshes he led his troops in a new and difficult campaign. Pressing hard at the enemy's heels the division entered Tobolsk, and doggedly continued the pursuit of Kolchak's army as far as Irkutsk.

Later the storm of civil war swept the Fifty-first Division to the southern front, where it performed legendary deeds at Kakhovka, creating a base for the decisive attack against Wrangel. Tremendous work was done to fortify the Kakhovka base and to perfect its artillery and anti-tank defenses. This was a completely new aspect of military science at that time.

Lenin had decreed that by the end of the winter Wrangel must be dislodged from his last sanctuary in the Crimea. Accordingly, Bliukher's troops, aided by other Red Army forces, stormed the supposedly impregnable enemy stronghold of Perekop. Under a hail of fire they hurled themselves on the barbed wire, cut it and tore out the posts, then withdrew and once more threw themselves into the attack. On November 9, after the third and final assault, the Reds reached the Turkish rampart, scaled it, and began to eject the Whites from their firing points. Then, having joined forces with the heroes from Sivash, they hurled themselves on the Iushun fortifications.

In recognition of its immortal Crimean exploit the Fifty-first Division received the title "Perekop Division" and the Order of the Red Banner, while its commander was awarded this order for the third time.

In the early years of Soviet power, on Lenin's proposal, the Far Eastern Republic (FER) was set up in the vast territory between Lake Baikal and the Pacific. In June 1921 Bliukher became war minister of this republic and commander in chief of its national revolutionary army. The times were troubled: the Japanese interventionists and White Guards had occupied Vladivostok and Khabarovsk and were holding sway on the banks of the Amur while they planned further expansion. Meanwhile, to lull the vigilance of the FER government, the Japanese proposed negotiations to stabilize the situation. These talks took place in the Chinese city of Dairen. The FER delegation was led by the deputy prime minister, an old Bolshevik named F.N. Petrov, with Bliukher as a member of his team. They both firmly rejected the insolent Japanese demands, which would have turned the FER into a Japanese colony. After some months of fruitless negotiation, Petrov said to the head of the Japanese delegation: "Your military personnel do not want to negotiate; they prefer to fight. Very well, our commander in chief will give them a chance to do so."

The following "six days of Volochaevka" are famous in song. For six days, without shelter or hot food and in [temperatures below zero], Bliukher's troops attacked the enemy positions without respite.

Two years later the Party sent Bliukher to aid the brother nation of China, as chief adviser to the national revolutionary government of Sun Yat-sen, at Canton in the south. The Soviet officer helped the Chinese to create a revolutionary army, and accompanied it on the famous campaign from Canton to Hankow.

For this he was rewarded with his fourth Order of the Red Banner.

Sun Yat-sen's death and the treason of Chiang Kai-shek and the right-wing Kuomintang prevented the People's Army from consolidating its successes. Reaction once more held sway in China, and the militarists in power took up a hostile attitude toward the Soviet Union. In 1929 they tore up the agreement for joint administration of the Chinese Eastern Railroad and dismissed its Soviet employees, arresting some of them. At the same time they concentrated military forces on our frontiers, including remnants of Russian White Guardists who raided border posts and settlements. The Chinese government's refusal to settle these incidents peacefully led to the formation of the Special Far Eastern Army, commanded by the heroic Bliukher. In November 1929 this army destroyed the Manchurian group of militarists. Bliukher received the Order of Lenin, and on the second anniversary of the formation of the Far Eastern Army he was awarded the newly decreed Order of the Red Star, the supreme Soviet order.

In 1935 he was one of the first to be appointed Marshal of the Soviet Union. His last military operation—as brilliant as its predecessors—was to defeat the Japanese invaders at Lake Khasan.

November 19, 1938, would have been Bliukher's seventy-fifth birthday. He was not fated to see this day or to live until the Great Patriotic War, where his generalship would have been of immense value. Slandered by the enemies of our country, he died in the fullness of his powers, a victim of Stalin's arbitrary rule, sharing the fate of many thousands of the best sons of the Party, to which he remained true until his last breath.[38]

The Marshal's last days

On the night before his departure for Moscow, Bliukher could not sleep for wondering why he was being summoned to the capital so soon after his last visit. Could it be to report on the Khasan operation? But he had already sent full details; besides, Mekhlis had been present and knew all about it.

At dawn he slipped quietly out of doors, hoping that the fresh air in the park would cure his headache. Luckily everyone was still asleep, and he was free to think about the recent past, about tomorrow and what he should take to Moscow, about urgent and important matters—how many there were and always would be! Not long ago, the well-known geologist Vasilii Zakharovich Skorokhod had come into his office and told him there were oil deposits in the Khabarovsk territory. Think of it, their own oil, no farther off than the Tyllar Rifer! Skorokhod had produced a small bottle full of thick, dark liquid and said triumphantly: "There you are—oil from the Tyllar. And there's more in the Aldai and the Lena basin. The whole Far East is a storehouse of nature's treasures; all you have to do is to find them and take what you want. We should send out a proper expedition."

How could he neglect such advice? He had detailed military topographers and provided uniforms, equipment, arms, and rations. All they had to do was look! He had already assigned air transport to take the explorers to the Maia area; if they looked properly they would find what they wanted.

But meanwhile he felt heavy of heart. Men were being arrested on every hand. Many of his comrades in arms were in jail as "enemies of the people." He felt guilty that he could do nothing to stop the repressions. His back ached with the pain of old wounds, a premonition of dire events to come. What he ought to do was to put in for leave at once, take his wife and children and go off for a holiday to Barshchinka. But there was nobody left there any more. His mother had died here, in Khabarovsk, and his father was buried in the cemetery in Georgievskoye village. He greatly missed his mother. How many times he had gone to see her when on the brink of collapse, and she had come to his aid and set him on his feet.

He got up wearily and walked slowly home. His wife met him, anxious and in tears.

"Where on earth have you been? I couldn't imagine what had happened to you."

"Don't you worry, dear, everything will be all right. I'll send you a telegram as soon as I can. Help Vsevolod with his lessons and send Zoia some money to buy a winter coat. Take good care of little Vasilii—he's a handsome fellow, the image of you."

"He's only six months old—how can anyone tell who he's like? He's got your eyes—a deep, deep blue. So you must leave today?

"Yes, Don't come to see me off—it's depressing enough without that."

"Be sure to telegraph at once. I'll be counting the minutes."

"Of course I will. Don't worry yourself unnecessarily."

Throughout the journey Bliukher hardly slept. He sat by the carriage window and stared at familiar villages, stations, and towns, mentally saying farewell to his beloved Far East. He remained in his seat at most of the stops until the train had passed Lake Baikal, when he felt a longing to breathe the scent of pine forests. Then he stepped out of the train and was suddenly surrounded by a crowd—people he had never seen before, yet they all knew him.

"Vasilii Konstantinovich! How are things in the border area?"

"Where are you off to, Comrade Marshal? Is it a long trip?"

A bearded man with the Order of the Red Banner pinned to his jacket came up and said, shaking his head mournfully: "You don't look well; they've been driving you too hard. You look all gray somehow. Be sure to take care of yourself, now."

When he got to Moscow, Bliukher made a full and detailed report to the Supreme Military Council on the military operations at Khasan. The criticism was sharp and biased. Voroshilov, the PC for defense, told him that he had been placed at the disposal of the council, and that until an appointment suited to his rank had been decided on, he should go to Sochi to recuperate. Accordingly he telegraphed to his wife: "Not returning Khabarovsk. Bring family soonest Moscow. Telegraph departure time. Health very poor. Greetings Pavel." After much thought he decided to send also for Pavel, his only brother, of whom he was very fond and who was serving in the air force on the Far Eastern front. When their mother was dying she had said to him: "Vasilii, you're strong. Look after Pavel—see that no harm comes to him." Since then, Pavel had passed through flying school and become one of the ablest officers in the Far Eastern Air Force. The Marshal had always helped his brother, and now he felt a desire to see him and spend a holiday in his company. In addition, he was anxious about his new family. He had married his present wife six years before and was now waiting for her, Vsevolod, Vaira, little Vasilii, and Nina, the daughter of his late sister Aleksandra.

At last the family arrived and they were able to leave for Sochi. Before they did so, Bliukher produced two packets of banknotes, his savings over many years, and said: "Rafushka, go and put these in the savings bank, in your own name."

"What for?"

"Just in case. Listen, you're not to get upset or worried, but my last report was badly received. Stalin always stood up for me in the past, but this time he said nothing. If anything should happen, remember one thing—to tell the children I was always an honest man, a Leninist and a Bolshevik. A Leninist, don't forget. And whatever becomes of me, history will show that I was in the right."

Pavel took his family to Sochi, where they all stayed a month. Bliukher was arrested on October 22. In the morning he had gone into the kitchen, where his wife had just finished feeding little Vasilii. The child was laughing happily and showing four strong teeth. The Marshal went up to his son, tickled his firm belly with two fingers and said, smiling: "He's well fed and happy, and wearing his first pair of pants. What a handsome little fellow he is with his blue eyes!"

"You don't look at all well," said his wife. "You really ought to rest a little."

"All right, I'll just admire you two a little longer and then go and lie down."

No sooner had he left the room than four plainclothesmen dressed in black came and arrested him, his wife, Pavel, and the latter's family. They were taken to the Lefortavo prison in Moscow, where Beria himself conducted the investigation. Two officers questioned them by turns. At the first interrogation they informed Bliukher that he had been a Japanese spy since 1921 (the time of the Dairen Conference), that his sabotage activities in the Far East had been confirmed by his "former henchmen" and that only the intervention of the NKVD had prevented the "arch-enemy and traitor" from flying to Japan with the aid of his brother. Bliukher listened to all this in silence and, having read the record which was already prepared, said sorrowfully: "So that was the best you could think up! What filth, what despicable villainy!"

"So you refuse to sign the record, do you?"

"You can put your papers away. I will never sign such a monstrous slander. I was and remain a Bolshevik and a Leninist."

In the hands of the investigators, the case soon took on wider dimensions. To his deep sorrow Bliukher heard that his first wife, Galina Pavlovna, had been arrested in Leningrad. Zoia, who had remained with her, was old enough to be in danger, being just over fifteen. What would happen to Vsevolod? All doors would be closed to the son of an "enemy of the people"—and the boy had dreamed of being a soldier like his father. Who would look after Vaira and little Vasilii, who might never hear anything about their father? The investigators said: "If you confess, your life will be saved. You'll get a ten-year sentence and then be free." But how was he to confess to crimes he had never committed?

Vasilii Konstantinovich Bliukher, Bolshevik and Leninist, was executed in the Lefortavo prison on November 9, 1938, a victim of arbitrary rule during the cult of Stalin's personality. The good name of this legendary hero and true son of the Communist Party was restored at the Party's Congress in 1956.

A metal worker and the son of a Yaroslav'l peasant, Vasilii Bliukher went through the entire career of a soldier from private to marshal. The Soviet people remember and will always remember this self-taught commander with deep affection and gratitude. The heroic deeds of the southern Ural partisans, the fierce fighting in Siberia, the tenacious defense of Kakhovka, the unparalleled courage and determination of the assault on Perekop, the famous "six days of Volochaevka," the exemplary defeat of the White Chinese on the Chinese Eastern Railroad and the Japanese at Khasan—all these are golden pages inscribed by Bliukher in the history of the Red Army.

Books about Bliukher have sold in hundreds of thousands of copies, and his speeches and articles have been published. His glorious name had been given to streets and schools, as well as to the first major fish-canning plant constructed by men of the Admiralty works where he was employed as a youth. The plant is a mobile one, located in the Pacific Ocean and attached to the port of Vladivostok, a city which preserves as a sacred trust the glorious memory of the immortal Marshal.[39]

BORIS IOSIFOVICH BOBROV

Biographical data

Born 1896, died 1937. Member of the Bolshevik Party from 1919; served in the Red Army from 1918. In the Civil War he was deputy commander and commander of the operational department of army staffs. After the war, chief of staff of the Second Caucasian Rifle Division, deputy commander of the Azerbaidzhan Rifle Division, head of the Twenty-first Tiflis Infantry School, deputy head of the Operations Administration of the Red Army staff, head of the Fourth department of the staff of the Moscow military district, and deputy chief of staff of the Belorussian military district.[40]

GUSTAV GUSTAVOVICH BOKIS

Biographical data

Born 1896, died 1937. Member of the Bolshevik Party from 1913. In 1918, joined the Red Army as a private. After the war he became a leader in the field of tank warfare. In 1924, having graduated from the Military-Economic Academy, he served in the central administration of the Red Army and was then deputy head of administration for mechanization and motorization. In the 1930s he organized the production of tanks, armored cars, and artillery tractors and was head of the Red Army administration for motorized and armored vehicles, with the rank of corps commander. In 1937 he became a victim of unjustified repressions during the cult of personality.[41]

The life of a Bolshevik

There are people who decide on their careers once and for all and devote all their strength and knowledge to them from the outset. One of these, beyond doubt, was Gustav Gustavovich Bokis, a member of the Party from 1913, the son of a simple Latvian peasant.

In 1918, at the age of twenty-two, Bokis formed a group of partisans in German-occupied Latvia. From that time on, his whole life was connected with the Red Army. He began as a private and, having passed through the furnace of the Civil War, became a major expert on tank warfare. Wherever he fought—against the Kaiser's troops or the White Poles, against Denikin's or Wrangel's forces—he aroused enthusiasm by his bravery, and for his services in the Civil War he received the Order of the Red Banner.

After the war the Party sent him to study at the Military-Economic Academy, which he left in 1924. He then worked in the central administration of the Red Army, and later as deputy head of the reorganized mechanization and motorization department. In the 1930s he and his colleagues organized the production of tanks, armored cars, and artillery tractors and trained troops in the new handling techniques. Many new problems had to be solved and new paths trodden. He had to acquire a grasp not only of the work of factories and design offices but also of the technical and operational aspects of troop training. Bokis was one of the Communist commanders who acquitted themselves honorably of these tasks and enhanced the strength of our army. His work was thus assessed by A. Todorsky, a noted commander and old Bolshevik who later became a lieutenant general of the reserve:

> Bokis worked tirelessly to equip the Red Army with new weapons of war and new techniques. The Red Army possessed in him an eminent political and military worker who strove diligently and successfully to enhance its readiness for battle and to strengthen the defenses of our socialist motherland.

It fell my lot to work under Comrade Bokis in those years. All who met him remember the authority this charming man exercised over those around him. A man of strong principles and a convinced Communist and Leninist, he paid close attention to his colleagues' opinions, backed them up, and was careful to encourage the younger cadres. Having discerned in the young engineer and tank officer Zh. Kotin a man of exceptional technical ability and design skill, he boldly promoted him to the post of chief designer and head of one of the chief tank factory design offices. In time Kotin became one of the leading Soviet designers of tanks and self-propelled gun mounts.

Bokis vigorously supported work on the construction of a powerful Diesel engine which was clearly superior to the carburetor-gasoline type. During the Great Patriotic War the new type of engine was fitted to medium and heavy tanks and gun mounts—a major technical achievement. Also during the war, the famous Soviet T-34 tank struck terror into the Nazis; but few know that work on this model was initiated with the active support of Comrade Bokis. During the prewar years, numerous highly skilled cadres of tankmen were created both in the Red Army and in industry. Thanks to the foundations thus laid, our country rapidly outstripped all others in the production and military use of tanks.

Gustav Bokis was soon appointed head of one of the most important central departments of the Red Army—that concerned with motorized and armored vehicles, where he was given the rank of corps commander. But his career was cut short in its prime in 1937, when he became a victim of unjustified repression during the cult of personality. We shall always remember this true son of the Latvian people and staunch Bolshevik-Leninist.[42]

ANTON STEPANOVICH BULIN

Biographical data

Born 1894, died 1937. In 1914 he carried on propaganda work in the army and joined the Bolshevik Party. During the Civil War he was military commissioner of the Sixth, Fifty-sixth, and Sixteenth rifle divisions. Later he was secretary of the raion committee of the CPSU for Vasilii Ostrov and then for Kronshtadt. In 1923 he returned to military service. In summer 1924 he became head of the political administration of the Moscow military district, then deputy head of political administration for the Red Army. From the end of October 1935 he was deputy commander and head of political administration of the Belorussian military district. He soon rose to the rank of army commissar, first class. In June 1937 he became head of the central cadres administration of the PC for Defense and at the same time acting head of political administration of the Red Army. He was arrested and perished tragically in 1937.[43]

A fearless commissar

The Leningrad Museum of the Great October Socialist Revolution contains a gold watch with the inscription: "To a true soldier of the Red Army, from the Petrograd Soviet of Workers' and Peasants' Deputies." This watch belonged to Anton Stepanovich Bulin.

At the beginning of November 1919 the Red Army forces operating against Iudenich in the Narva sector met with determined resistance from the Whites. A. S. Bulin, the commissar of the Sixth Rifle Division, put forward the bold plan of sending to the enemy's rear a small detachment which could strike a sudden blow in support of the frontal attack of the division's main forces. This plan was adopted. After careful preparation, thirty Communist fighting men with two light machine guns set off in the dead of night across the Luga River, on which the ice was not yet firm. Bulin himself led the intrepid band, which succeeded in penetrating the enemy's rear unobserved and cutting off his line of retreat.

A red rocket soared into the air and the general attack began. The White Guardists defended themselves desperately, but, hearing the rattle of machine-gun fire from behind, they wavered and began to retreat. The fight went on for seven hours, and for all that time the handful of brave men led by their commissar held the river crossing and prevented the retreating enemy from gaining access to it. The operation was a complete success, and Bulin, along with eleven others who had especially distinguished themselves, received the Order of the Red Banner, as well as a gold watch from the Petrograd Soviet.

At that time, Bulin had not had special military training; but he already had plenty of experience as a professional revolutionary and Leninist. Ever since he joined the Party in 1914 he had prepared himself for the revolutionary tasks of the future. In the days before the October Revolution he carried on intensive propaganda among the army rank and file. During the armed uprising he became commissar of the Petergof garrison and took part in the fighting against Kerensky's forces.

Throughout the Civil War, when he occupied important political posts in the Red Army military commissar of the Sixth, Fifty-sixth, and Sixteenth rifle divisions, he showed himself a courageous fighter for the people's cause and a fiery Bolshevik leader. By personal example he taught political officers to be always on the spot where the toughest problems needed to be solved. A political officer, he used to say, is above all an organizer and educator of troops.

His great experience in organization was also brought into play on the economic front, when he was secretary of the CPSU raion committees for Vasilii Ostrov and later Kronshtadt.

In 1923 the Party recalled him to service with the army. In the summer of 1924 he became head of political administration of the Moscow military district, at the time when the Party was conducting an active struggle against Trotskyites. Speaking at rallies, meetings, and conferences, Bulin denounced the subversive activity of the factionalists and defended the Leninist line of the CC of the Party. He worked tirelessly to strengthen the Red Army and improve discipline and order among the troops. "All ranks and categories of the service," he would say, "must regard discipline as a military requisite of the first order."

Bulin's exceptional abilities were given even wider scope by his appointment as head of political administration of the Red Army. Working with such eminent Party men as A. S. Bubnov and later Ia. B. Gamarnik, he devoted great energy to the task of strengthening political groups and Party organizations and improving educational work among the troops.

At the end of October 1935 he was sent to the Belorussian military district as deputy commander and head of political administration. Here he was soon promoted to the rank of Army Commissar First Class. Together with Uborevich, the district commander, he devoted all his energies to strengthening the western borders of our country. He played an active part in preparations for the autumn maneuvers of 1936, which demonstrated the technical progress of our army and the unquenchable fighting spirit of its soldiers.

In June 1937 he became head of the central cadres administration of the PC for Defense, and at the same time acting head of political administration of the Red Army. In autumn of that year he was arrested. Thus, at the height of his powers, in his forty-fourth year, death came tragically to this experienced political officer, a delightful man and a true member of the Leninist old guard.

The Party, having once and for all rejected the cult of personality, has restored the good name of Army Commissar First Class A. S. Bulin, which will live forever in the nation's memory.[44]

IVAN NAUMOVICH DUBOVOI

Biographical data

[Army commander, Second Class.] Born 1896, died 1939. Joined the CP in 1917. Born on the farm of Chmirovka, Chigirin uezd, Kiev gubernia (now Cherkasskaia oblast), the son of a miner. Served in the First World War. In 1917, having passed through cadet school, he took an active part in the October

Revolution and organized in the Donbass, Red Guard detachments which he commanded against Krasnov's troops. In 1918 he was deputy chief of staff of the Tenth Army at Tsaritsyn; in 1919, chief of staff of the Kiev sector of the Ukrainian front, then chief of staff and subsequently commander of the First Ukrainian Army. From June 28, after the reorganization of the Ukrainian armies, he commanded the legendary Forty-fourth Division. He handed over command of this unit to Shchors, but after the latter's death commanded it again. Received the Order of the Red Banner for his services in defeating Denikin's forces in the Kiev sector and for his part in the liberation of Kiev. From 1924 he commanded the Fourteenth Rifle Corps, and from 1929 was deputy commander of the Ukrainian military district. From 1935 he commanded the Kharkov military district, and in 1937 was a deputy to the Supreme Soviet of the U.S.S.R., first convocation. On August 30, 1939, he fell victim of the cult of Stalin's personality.[45]

PAVEL EFIMOVICH DYBENKO

Biographical data

Born February 16, 1889; died July 29, 1938. Soviet military and political leader. Joined the CP in 1912. Born the son of a peasant in Liudkov village, Chernigov gubernia. Entered the revolutionary movement in 1907. Served in the Baltic Fleet from 1911. In 1915 he was one of the leaders of the revolt on the battleship *Imperator Pavel I*. After six months imprisonment he was sent to join the land forces in 1916. Arrested once more for anti-war propaganda and set free during the February revolution, 1917. Member of the Helsinki soviet, and from April 1917 chairman of Tsentrobalt (Central Committee of the Baltic Fleet); in prison from the beginning of July to September 4, then again chairman of the Tsentrobalt. During the October Revolution he was in charge of organizing and dispatching to Petrograd revolutionary sailors' detachments; commanded these and workers' detachments in the Krasnoe Selo-Gatchina area at the time of the defeat of the Kerensky-Krasnov march on Petrograd. PC for naval affairs from October 26, 1917, to March 1918. In summer 1918 he carried on underground work in the Ukraine and the Crimea; in August 1918 he was arrested at Sevastopol and in October exchanged for captured German officers. Commanded the Soviet group of forces in the Ekaterinoslav sector and the First Trans-Dnieper Rifle Division, which became the Army of the Crimea after the peninsula was captured in spring 1919. At the same time he was appointed PC for naval affairs of the Crimean Soviet Republic. In 1919-20 he took part in the fighting for Tsaritsyn and the defeat of the White Guardists in the Caucasus, and in 1921 he aided the suppression of the Kronshtadt mutiny. Received the Order of the Red Banner three times

Pavel Efimovich Dybenko

for war services. Graduated from the Red Army Military Academy, 1922. From 1928 to 1938, commanded the Central Asian, Volga, and Leningrad military districts. Did much to build up and strengthen the Soviet armed forces and served on various committees and commissions (chemical committee from 1925, senior attestations commission from 1927, mobilization committee from 1928, etc.) was member of the Central Asian bureau of the CC of the CPSU, also of the CCs of the CPs of the Uzbekistan and Tadzhikistan, and of the RMC of the U.S.S.R.; deputy to the Supreme Council of the U.S.S.R., first convocation. Subjected to illegal repression during the cult of Stalin's personality; rehabilitated posthumously.[46]

A true son of the Leninist Party

Among the glorious fighters of the October Revolution and prominent military leaders of the Soviet state, an important place belongs to Pavel Efimovich Dybenko, a member of the Party from 1912, who rose from a humble seaman to the rank of People's Commissar.

Dybenko was born seventy-five years ago, on February 16, 1889, in the Gomel region, the son of a poor peasant. After working on the landowner's estate, at the age of seventeen he went to Riga and worked for some years as a dock laborer. He was called up for service in the Baltic Fleet, where in 1912 he joined the Party and carried on active propaganda work among the sailors.

After the February revolution of 1917 he was elected chairman of Tsentrobalt, in which post he took an active part in the October Revolution. On the orders of Tsentrobalt, during the tumultuous days of October, warships from Helsinki and Kronstadt brought help to the Petrograd proletariat and transported to the capital more than 15,000 revolutionary soldiers and sailors.

Immediately before and during the Revolution Dybenko had several meetings with V. I. Lenin. His tense account of one of these is as follows:

Leaving Comrade Podvoisky's office, I found Vladimir Il'ich in the next room. He was calm and smiling as usual. When he saw me, he asked: "Well, how are things at the front?" I replied: "I am on my way to the Revolutionary Naval Committee and will see to it that the sailors' detachments arrive from Helsinki today; otherwise we may have Kerensky in Petrograd." Lenin nodded in silent approval.

Commanding Red Guard detachments against the counterrevolutionaries at Tsarskoe Selo and Gatchina, Dybenko personally arrested the White Guard General Krasnov.

When Lenin formed the first Soviet government, Dybenko became PC for naval affairs. At the all-Russian congress of sailors held soon afterward, at which Lenin was present, the delegates proposed to reward Dybenko for his services to the new Soviet power by conferring on him a high military rank.

He replied: "Comrades, I wish to thank you for your esteem and to make a request. I began this fight in the rank of a sailor under the regime of oppression and have been promoted to that of a free Soviet citizen, which is to me one of the greatest in the world. Please allow me to continue the fight in that same rank." A reply worthy of a true Bolshevik and Leninist!

From the beginning of the Civil War Dybenko was at the front. A member of one of the first units of the young Soviet army, whose forty-sixth anniversary our people will be celebrating in a few days, he fought the enemy at Narva; then, on the Party's orders, he was despatched to the Ukraine and the Crimea for underground work. At the end of 1918 he distinguished himself during the liberation of Kharkov and Ekaterinoslav from the Whites. He took part in the fight for the Crimea commanding the Trans-Dnieper Division; then he commanded the Crimean Army and became PC for naval affairs of the Crimean Soviet Republic. In 1919-20, still as a division commander, he took part in the battle for Tsaritsyn and the defeat of Denikin's bands in the Caucasus. In March 1921, commanding a composite rifle division, he suppressed the Kronstadt mutineers, and a few months later, at the head of the legendary Perekop Division, he fought the bandits in the Odessa area. For his signal services during the Civil War he received the Order of the Red Banner three times.

After the defeat of the foreign interventionists and the Whites, this talented commander completed a course at the military adacemy and occupied responsible posts in the Red Army: commander of a rifle corps, head of artillery administration and of supply, and commander of the Central Asian, Volga, and Leningrad military districts.

Many commanders and political officers of the Red Army who enjoyed direct contact with Dybenko remember him as a man of great humanity, devoted heart and soul to the Communist Party and to the Soviet motherland and people. He was greatly respected in army circles and Party organizations. He was elected delegate to a number of Party congresses, was a member of the CEC of the U.S.S.R., and afterwards deputy to the Supreme Soviet of the U.S.S.R. at its first convocation.

This eminent Party and political worker did not escape illegal repression during the cult of Stalin's personality. He was treacherously slandered and arrested in February 1938, and soon thereafter he perished tragically.

A true son of our Party and the Soviet people, Pavel Efimovich Dybenko had a remarkable career, from ordinary seaman to the eminent rank of Soviet Commander. His life of intense revolutionary activity is a shining example of enthusiastic devotion to the Communist Party and our motherland.[47]

ALEKSANDR IL'ICH EGOROV

Biographical data

Born October 22, 1883; died February 22, 1939. Marshal of the Soviet

Union, 1935. Joined the CP in July 1918. Born at Buzuluk, Samara gubernia, the son of a workman. Worked in youth as a loader and blacksmith, and at the same time studied and passed examinations at high school level. Joined the revolutionary movement as an SR in 1904. Volunteered for army service and graduated from Kazan Infantry School in 1905, but soon left the army and became an actor. Called up in 1914, he served in the First World War and distinguished himself by personal bravery; he was wounded five times. By 1917 he had risen to the rank of sublieutenant and was acting commander of a regiment. Joined the Left SRs in 1917, but broke with them in summer 1918. For an anti-war speech on May Day 1917, he was stripped of his command, court-martialed and sentenced to confinement in a fortress. Later he was a delegate to the second all-Russian congress of soviets and a member of the All-Russian CEC. In 1918 he was chairman of the central administration of prisoners and refugees, commissar of the All-Russian General Staff, and chairman of the senior certifying commission for the selection of officers for the Red Army. From August 1918 he commanded the Ninth Army which repulsed Krasnov's forces in the Balashov-Novokhopersk-Kamyshin sector. From December 1918 he commanded the Tenth Army, defending Tsaritsyn. He was one of the initiators in the formation of Budennyi's Cavalry Division, later Cavalry Corps. From August 1919 he commanded the Fourteenth Army in the Kiev and Briansk sectors. In October 1919 he was appointed commander of the southern front and organized the rout of Denikin's forces. From January to December 1920 he commanded the troops of the south-western front which defeated the White Poles in the Ukraine and carried the fighting into Galician territory. After the Civil War he commanded the Kiev and Petrograd military districts and the Caucasian Red Banner Army, then the troops in the Ukraine and the Crimea and, from 1927, the Belorussian Military District. In 1925-26 he was military attaché in China. In 1931-37 he was chief of the general staff of the Red Army, and from 1937 first deputy PC of defense. He took a prominent part in the reorganization and re-equipment of the Red Army and the creation of powerful antitank formations. Received the Order of the Red Banner four times. From 1934 he was a candidate member of the CC of the CPSU. Slandered and subjected to repression during the cult of Stalin's personality, he was posthumously rehabilitated.[48]

IVAN FEDOROVICH FED'KO

Biographical data

Born 1897, died 1937. Army commander, first class. Joined the Bolshevik Party in 1917; deputy to the Supreme Soviet of the U.S.S.R., first convocation.

From January 1918, chairman of the revolutionary committee at Feodosiia; then commanded Second Army, Fifty-eighth, Forty-sixth, and Third divisions. Received Order of the Red Banner four times. After the Civil War he commanded the Caucasian Red Army and the Volga and Kiev military districts and was deputy PC for defense.[49]

Corps Commander Gaia Dimitrievich Gai
(Bzhishkian)

GAIA DIMITRIEVICH GAI (BZHISHKIAN)

Biographical data

[Corps Commander.] Born 1887, died 1937. Joined the Bolshevik Party in 1918. Served in the First World War and was promoted to officer's rank for bravery. In 1918 he commanded and organized the Twenty-fourth "Iron" Division and commanded the First Army on the eastern front. Commanded cavalry corps on the northern Caucasus and western fronts. Graduated from the Frunze Military Academy in 1927. Lecturer and subsequently professor of military history.[50]

Budennyi's opinion of Gai

In the dark days of the Civil War the name of that glorious son of the Armenian people and eminent Soviet commander, Gaia Dimitrievich Gai shone like a bright star. In the summer of 1918, during the fight with Kolchak's forces and the White Czechs, Gai was active in organizing the famous Twenty-fourth Simbirsk Infantry Division, known for its firmness as the "Iron" Division, which fought valiantly under his command for Lenin's native town of Simbirsk. In the fall of that year Gai was appointed commander of the First Army, which took part in the liberation of Buguruslan, Buzuluk, Orenburg, Ufa, Orsk, and other towns.

I met G. D. Gai in February 1920, during the liquidation of Denikin's forces in the northern Caucasus. He was then commanding the First Cavalry Army. Gai's bold cavalrymen were relentlessly pursuing the Denikin forces. After the defeat of the second Entente campaign, he became commander of the Third Cavalry Corps on the western front. Under his skilled command the corps, advancing toward Warsaw, took the towns of Vilna, Grodno, Lomzha, and Osovets and reached the Vistula at Wloclawek, where they captured thousands of enemy officers and men.

In these battles Gai not only showed himself a gifted commander and skilled organizer but displayed personal courage and extreme daring which earned the affection and admiration of his troops.

After the Civil War he remained a cavalry commander and devoted much effort to the training and education of junior officers and fighting men. He became a warm advocate and an active participant in the development and improvement of the cavalry, the strengthening of its firing and offensive power.

Having completed his post-graduate work at the Frunze Academy, Gai became a lecturer. I attended some of his courses, which were distinguished by profound and many-sided analyses bearing witness to his first-class knowledge of tactics and military operations. In a short time, he wrote about a dozen works and became a professor. As a military historian he considered that those who studied history merely for its own sake were hopelessly dead to the present. "The watchword of the Red Army commander who is also historian," he used to say, "is to preserve the heroic traditions of the Civil War, to study its rich experience from all sides and to analyze it critically." These words still have a message for us in the present day.

G. D. Gai died at the age of fifty, at the zenith of his powers, a victim of arbitrary rule and the violation of socialist legality during the cult of Stalin's personality. Gai is no more, but his exploits will live in the people's memory forever. The amazing life and military carreer of this Leninist Communist and hero of the Civil War, twice decorated with the Order of the Red Banner, deserve the widest possible publicity.[51]

IAN PETROVICH GAILIT

Biographical data

Born 1894, died 1938. Sublieutenant in the Tsarist Army. Joined the Bolshevik Party in 1918. In the Civil War he commanded the Penza group, was deputy commander and then commander of the Fifth Division. After the war he commanded the Tenth Corps and was deputy commander of the Siberian, North Caucasian, and Moscow military districts, then deputy head of the administration department of the Red Army.[52]

IAN BORISOVICH GAMARNIK

Biographical data

Born June 2, 1894; died May 31, 1937. Soviet Party and military leader. Joined the Communist Party in 1916. Born at Zhitomir, the son of an official. Began revolutionary work in 1914 in students' organizations at Kiev. Until October 1917 he was a member, and for a time secretary, of the Kiev committee of the RSDWP(B). Took part in preparations for the October Revolution at Kiev and on October 27 became a member of the revolutionary committee. In spring 1918 he attended a conference of activists of the Ukrainian Bolshevik Party. At Taganrog, elected a member of the organization bureau which prepared the First Congress of the Ukrainian CP. In 1918-20 he belonged to the all-Ukrainian underground center (the "Nine") and was a leader of the Odessa, Kharkov, and Crimean Party organizations. In 1919 he was member of the RMC of the southern group of forces of the Twelfth Army, and later commissar of the Fifty-eighth Infantry Division; took part in the liberation of Kiev. In 1920-23, chairman of the Odessa and Kiev gubernia committees of the Ukrainian

CP, and chairman of the CEC for the Kiev gubernia. In 1923-28, chairman of the Far Eastern revolutionary committee and of the regional executive committee, also secretary of the Party's Far Eastern regional committee. In 1928, secretary of the CC of the Belorussian CP. He occupied a number of senior posts in the Red Army: he became a member of the RMC of the Siberian military district in April 1927 and of the Belorussian military district in December 1928, head of the political administration of the Red Army and member of the RMC of the U.S.S.R. in October 1929, editor in chief of the journal *Krasnaia zvezda* (Red Star). From June 1930, deputy PC for defense and deputy chairman of the RMC of the U.S.S.R. Member of the CC of the CPSU from 1927. In an atmosphere of slander and unfounded accusations during the cult of Stalin's personality, he committed suicide. Has been fully rehabilitated since his death.[53]

A commissar of the Leninist school

As the years and decades roll on, many ideas that once seemed inseparable from life itself cease to interest any but historians. But the phrase "commissar during the Civil War," and the images it conjures up, remain alive in popular memory. Each new generation seeks and finds in it something fresh and relevant to the concerns of today. Again and again, people's minds turn back to that stormy epoch when the hard, steely figure of the Communist commissar first appeared above the revolutionary horizon.

Ian Borisovich Gamarnik was one of the glorious band of commissars to whom our Party gave birth in those great days. He began his revolutionary career while still a student, and when he joined the Party in 1918 he at once became one of its most active members.

The October Revolution in Kiev, the creation of the Ukrainian CP, the armed struggle with the White Cossacks, Petliura's bands, and the foreign interventionists—in all these events he took a direct and immediate part, organizing underground work in Odessa, Kharkov, and the Crimea.

In July 1918 he was a member of the delegation of the first congress of the Ukrainian CP which was received by V. I. Lenin. Our great leader conversed with the delegates for about two hours, imparting guidance on all the major problems of Party organization and revolutionary work for the liberation of the Ukraine.

In summer 1919 Gamarnik became a member of the RMC of the southern group of forces of the Twelfth Army. This group, commanded by I. E. Iakir, was surrounded by Petliura's and Denikin's forces and effected a heroic march from Odessa to Zhitomir, breaking through the ring of its opponents. The twenty-five-year-old Commissar Gamarnik was among the members of the group who received the Order of the Red Banner for this exploit.

After the Civil War, the Party assigned to Gamarnik the task of restoring the national economy. Again he was active in the most crucial sectors: first as chairman of the Odessa CEC, then [as chairman] of the Far Eastern [RMC], then secretary of the Party's Far Eastern regional committee, then first secretary of the CC of the Belorussian CP.

In the fall of 1929, after important maneuvers in the Belorussian military district, Gamarnik was appointed head of the political administration of the Red Army, and shortly afterward, first deputy PC for defense for the U.S.S.R. This was a period of important changes in the development of the armed forces of the Soviet Union. The general reconstruction of the economy made it possible to begin the rearmament of the army and navy. The CC of the CPSU, in its resolutions on military problems, called for the further strengthening of the Red Army, better training of its officers and political staff, and the improvement of the political and military education of both the army and navy. Gamarnik brought to the fulfillment of these tasks all his fervid energy and talents as a brilliant organizer and inspirational Party tribune. He received active help from the entire staff of the political administration of the Red Army, including his deputies, the old Communists A. S. Bulin and G. A. Osepian.

The vast majority of commanders and political officers of the army and navy correctly understood what was required of them and set about energetically reorganizing their work. But there were a few comrades who preferred to rest on their laurels, pluming themselves for past services, refusing to learn and therefore unable to teach others. It fell my lot, as a brigade commissar and instructor in the political administration of the Red Army, to direct a group whose duty was to check the state of Party political work and the teaching of social and economic subjects in one of the Moscow military academies. This investigation revealed serious shortcomings, due in the main to incompetent and superficial direction of Party-political work on the part of the deputy head of the academy. This comrade had done good service during the Civil War but had gotten above himself and fallen down on his task. He used antiquated methods and made others do so too. When I explained to him as tactfully as possible the conclusions I had come to, he exploded with rage.

"What!" he shouted. "Do you presume to instruct *me*? We'll soon see who's right—I or that fellow Gamarnik."

It was, of course, not a question of personalities but of principle: here was a deputy political officer setting himself up against the whole political administration of the Red Army. Gamarnik listened carefully to my report and promised to have a talk with the comrade in question. I do not know what passed at their talk, but I well remember its result. At a conference soon afterward at the political administration office, reports were heard on the results of the investigations into various academies; and the officer in question made a speech in which he not only admitted his shortcomings but expressed thanks for having been made aware of them.

In those years, considerable use was made of the practice of seconding organizational and propaganda groups to military units and formations. These included members of various sections of the political administration of the Red Army, and also lecturers from military academies. Gamarnik often talked to the comrades who were sent out in this way. "You should always begin with the human element," he would say. "Study carefully their needs and demands, their politico-moral state, their discipline and political and military training." Only after we had done this and carefully analyzed the results of our investigations were we to draw up a plan of activity, and in doing this Gamarnik strongly advised us to consult as fully as possible with the commanders and political officers of the units in question. "Remember," he would say, "that you are not there to inspect but to help people, and whether they succeed in the future or not will depend on how skillfully and tactfully you are able to do this."

Gamarnik demanded much of himself as well as of others. In 1933 our organizational and propaganda group worked for a considerable time among units of the Special Far Eastern Army. When we had finished our work and were preparing to leave, Gamarnik, who happened also to be in the Far East at that time, summoned us and gave us a further task. It appeared that the joint training of the land forces and the recently created Pacific Fleet had revealed many deficiencies in preparation for war, especially in the area of [interforce] cooperation. So we were sent off again, this time to warships and coastal defense units. Some time afterward, on Gamarnik's orders, further joint exercises were carried out, and showed some improvement.

In the general sphere of Party-political work, Gamarnik laid great weight on socialist emulation. "Party organizations," he said at a Party conference of the Moscow military district, "must be in the forefront of new types of socialist emulation and must see to it that every Party and Komsomol member is a shock worker who sets a personal example of achievement and incites his unit, platoon, or company to do likewise." Sure enough, the "shock worker" movement soon came to embrace the whole army and front, down to the smallest unit, and as a result the combat readiness and efficiency of the armed forces as a whole markedly increased. All forms and methods of Party-political work were aimed at educating the troops in the spirit of unreserved devotion to the Leninist Party, the socialist motherland, and proletarian internationalism. Great importance was attached to the political education of the rank and file, and Gamarnik, who had an excellent memory, would criticize sharply and accurately those comrades who failed to make these lessons interesting and entertaining. He demanded that those officers of the political administration who were attached to units should set an example by themselves giving lectures and conducting tests and political exercises. In those years the Party was at grips with various opposition factions, and it was necessary to help the men, (many of whom were illiterate, to understand the nature of the problems and why this or that solution was required by circumstances.

Gamarnik devoted much time to the military press. In 1929-30 he was editor in chief of *Krasnaia zvezda*. He also took a personal part in launching the journals *Partiacheika* (Party Cell)—later *Kommunist RKKA* (The Red Army Communist)—and *Propagandist RKKA* (The Red Army Propagandist), and in organizing the regular issue of a political manual.

In line with the Party doctrine of unity between the political and military sectors, he constantly encouraged the military to take an interest in the political [sector] and vice versa. On his initiative, courses aimed at instilling all-around knowledge were organized at the Military-Political Academy of the Red Army; while on the other hand, greater emphasis was laid on military discipline in the faculties of that academy.

Gamarnik engaged in many-sided activities as a member of the RMC and first deputy PC for defense. He frequently reported to meetings of the RMC on important questions of military development. Thus, in the year 1930 alone he spoke on the subjects of unity of command, the training of junior commanders, work on military science, the politico-moral state of the Red Army, etc.

Gamarnik was chairman of a special commission of the CC of the CPSU to strengthen the defense efficiency of the Soviet Far East. Under his direction a beginning was made in the formation of the Pacific Fleet, defensive zones were created, and the Special Far Eastern Army was strengthened.

Gamarnik combined the qualities of a first-class Party, political, and military leader of the Leninist type, and for this the Party highly respected him. At its Fourteenth Congress he was elected a candidate member of the CC and at the Fifteenth, Sixteenth, and Seventeenth congresses he was elected a full member of that body. He received the Order of Lenin and was the first Red Army officer to be raised to the rank of Army Commissar First Class.

In 1937 Gamarnik shot himself, being unable to endure any longer the atmosphere of persecution, mass repression, and destruction of many devoted sons of the Party during the period of the cult of Stalin's personality.

Those members of the older generation who knew him personally will always remember his extraordinary simplicity, modesty, and warmth, his transparent honesty, and his passionate love of Soviet life. As he used to say, "When one looks at all that is being built in areas which only yesterday were waste and empty, one realizes... what gigantic strength is inherent in the working class, in our Soviet revolution."

Today, these inspired words are brilliantly confirmed by the constructive work of the Soviet people, building for itself the motherland of justice which is called communism.[54]

MARKIIAN IAKOVLEVICH GERMANOVICH

Biographical data

[Corps commander.] Born 1895, died 1937. Born in the village of Demenichi, Brest-Litovsk district, Grodno gubernia, the son of a poor peasant.

Attended village school and a four-class secondary school at Brest-Litovsk. Called up in 1915 and sent to cadet school at Gatchina. In 1916, appointed junior officer in an infantry company on the northern front. Later commanded a machine-gun detachment and was adjutant of the Seventy-eighth Siberian Rifle Regiment. Rose to be staff captain in the Tsarist Army. Joined the CP in November 1918. In the Civil War he commanded a brigade, then a division. After the war he commanded the Fifth Rifle Corps and was deputy commander of the Belorussian, Central Asian, and Moscow military districts, then head of the Red Army Military Academy for Motorization and Mechanization.[55]

The career of a corps commander

The eminent Red Army commander Markiian Iakovlevich Germanovich, a member of the military council of the PC for Defense, was one of the organizers of the academy for armored forces. He volunteered for the Red Army in April 1918 and commanded a platoon on the northern front, then was deputy commander of the Fifteenth Iur'ev Communist Regiment and took part in the fighting against the British interventionists at Arkhangelsk, later against the White Estonians and White Finns. From June 1919 he commanded the 138th Brigade of the Forty-sixth Division, with which he campaigned from Orel to Perekop. For his bold organization of a raid on enemy positions in the region of the Chongarsky bridge he received the Order of the Red Banner. The order of Republican RMC No. 260 of May 28, 1920 said:

> The planning of the raid was entrusted to Comrade Germanovich, under whose direct and decisive leadership it achieved brilliant results.... Thanks to careful preparation and skillful execution involving secrecy, thorough preliminary reconnaissance, rapidity and decisiveness of action, the glorious warriors of the 138th Brigade took the enemy almost completely by surprise and dislodged him from his positions after a short but fierce battle. As a result they captured: 617 prisoners of the Kerch-Ienikalsk Regiment, the Crimean Battalion, the German volunteer detachment, the First, Fourth, Sixth batteries, and a British platoon. Twenty machine guns and fourteen other guns [were seized], of which fourteen were taken with their horses, etc., complete, and two were sunk as our troops returned across the bay; four others were too heavy to transport, but their panoramic sights were removed and delivered to brigade headquarters. In addition, part of a baggage train was captured with horses, cartridges, and other military equipment. Nearly all of the enemy officers shot themselves at the time of surrender.
>
> Apart from this rich booty seized, this brilliant exploit enhanced the aggressive spirit and initiative of our troops and correspondingly diminished the enemy's as shown by his panic and inertia on the following days. Interrogation of prisoners revealed that on the night in question the enemy had intended to concentrate up to 1,500 men armed with bayonets near the farm of Tiup-Dzhanka in order to attack the Sivash bridge. This design was foiled by our raid, which also produced valuable detailed information about the enemy's numbers, grouping, and fortifications.

When in command of the 138th Brigade Comrade Germanovich was distinguished by his skill, boldness, resolution, efficiency, and devotion to the
revolutionary cause. Later he received the Order of the Red Banner for the second
time, and a gold watch.

During the fierce fighting with Wrangel's forces in the Ukraine and Crimea,
Germanovich successfully commanded the Fifty-second Rifle Division. After
the Civil War he took part in operations against the Makhno bands until these
were finally liquidated. In 1921, when only twenty-six years of age, he became
deputy commander of the Kharkov Military District. The commander of the
district, A. Kork, reported on him as follows at the end of 1921:

> Comrade Germanovich has shown himself an energetic and resolute commander
> with plenty of initiative and understanding of military conditions; he has always
> shown great personal discipline, and despite his relative youth has exerted a strong
> influence over his subordinates by his firmness and self-control.... His
> education (local and cadet school) has been inadequate, but thanks to his lively
> mind and common sense he has been equal to his duties in the service.

In 1922, having completed a senior academy course, he became commander
of the Twenty-third Division. Frunze, then commanding the Ukrainian and
Crimean troops, described him as a "first-class division commander: intelligent,
resourceful, and with much initiative. Deserves promotion to the rank of corps
commander." In 1924 he became commander of the Fifth Rifle Corps, and
from 1926 to 1933 was deputy commander of the Belorussian, Central Asian,
and Moscow military districts. Unsparing of his strength and time, he devoted
all his knowledge and experience to the military and political training of troops.
A. I. Egorov, the commander of the Belorussian Military District, recommended
him as follows:

> A first-class and expert commander, a tried Party man who takes an active
> part in the life around him. Fully capable of handling a wide range of problems
> on the district level. A true and valuable assistant to the district commander
> and one who in due course well deserves promotion to an independent command.
> Fit to command an army in wartime.

In 1932, during the reorganization of the armed forces, five new military
academies were created, including the Red Army Academy for Mechanization
and Motorization, of which Germanovich became head in 1933 while it was
still in a formative stage. The necessary material and technical basis was lacking,
and there were not enough skilled instructors and hardly any manuals. During
his three years in charge, with the help of the Party organization and the teaching
staff, Germanovich made a substantial contribution to the training of skilled
engineers and commanders of armored units. Under his direct guidance, the

necessary equipment and techniques were acquired. Apart from well-equipped lecture rooms and laboratories in Moscow, the academy acquired a tankodrome for the training of command staff, and a tank for firing practice. Scientific and research work went on at a good pace. From 1934 to 1936, sixty-five manuals and aids to learning were written and published, and teaching standards were improved. In the 1937 competition among military academies, the Mechanization and Motorization Academy achieved first place, owing primarily to Germanovich's leadership.

In March 1937 Germanovich became deputy commander of the Leningrad military district. In the same year he was a victim of arbitrary rule. His good name has now been restored.[56]

VLADIMIR MIKHAILOVICH GITTIS

Biographical data

Born 1881, died 1938. A colonel in the Tsarist Army; joined the CP in 1925. In the Civil War he commanded the sixth and eighth armies and the southern, western, and Caucasian fronts. After the war he commanded the Petrograd military district, was Red Army deputy chief of supplies and held other important command posts.[57]

VLADIMIR DAVIDOVICH GRENDAL'

Biographical data

Born 1883, died 1940. A lieutenant general of artillery. An officer in the Tsarist Army, he joined the Red Army at its inception and took an active part in the Civil War. Later he was an artillery commander of military districts and head of the artillery committee of the chief artillery administration of the Red Army, deputy head of artillery administration, and professor at the Frunze Military Academy.[58]

NIKOLAI EVGEN'EVICH KAKURIN

Biographical data

Born 1883, died 1936. A colonel in the Tsarist Army; joined the Red Army in 1919. Commanded a division and was deputy commander of a front. After the Civil War he became senior instructor at the Frunze Academy.[59]

VALENTIN ALEKSANDROVICH KANGELARI

Biographical data

Born 1883, died 19—. Studied at Kharkov University and became a physician. Arrested several times for revolutionary activity. Joined the Red Guard in 1917, fought on the eastern and western fronts and took part in the suppression of the Kronstadt mutiny. After the Civil War he held command and staff appointments in the Soviet Army and was an adviser to the Mongolian People's Army. From 1930 he worked as director and commissar of the Military Medical Academy and was first deputy PC for health of the RSFSR and later of the U.S.S.R. He was a victim of the cult of Stalin's personality.[60]

A humane and courageous life

This man of true courage and energy would today be eighty years old. He combined the firmness of a revolutionary fighter with a sensitive and tactful disposition. That is how we thought of our old war comrade, the true fighter for the Leninist Party Valentin Aleksandrovich Kangelari.

The son of a mechanic at Kerch, his talent and application secured him a medical degree at Kharkov University. From student days his life was inextricably bound up with the revolutionary movement. He took part in political demonstrations, was arrested and imprisoned, and fought in the trenches during the imperialist war. When the October Revolution came, he returned from the front to Omsk, where he joined the Red Guard and commanded a detachment of local Communists.

On the eastern front during the Civil War, he was deputy commander of a detachment led by the celebrated Baltic Fleet sailor and Bolshevik, Pavel Khokhriakov. For courage and devotion to duty he received the Order of the Red Banner for the first time. One of his fellow soldiers recalls: "At every battle we discover fresh heroes. Just now, our regiment is talking with pride of the deputy commander of the Kamyshlov Regiment, Comrade Kangelari, who although badly wounded did not desert comrades and bravely led them into the attack."

On the western front he became commander of the Tenth Rifle Division and received the Order of the Red Banner for the second time for exceptional bravery and distinction at the defeat of the White Guard troops of Bulan-Balakhovich.

At the time of the Kronstadt mutiny he was attached to Army Commander Tukhachevsky and took part in storming the fortress in the glorious ranks of the cadets from the military-training schools. For his services the RMC of the Republic presented him with an inscribed gold watch.

During the period of peaceful construction he occupied command and staff posts in the Red Army, and was assigned the responsible task of advising the Mongolian People's Army. In 1930 he became director and commissar of the Military Medical Academy. His successful work in this important sector and his organizing ability were fully appreciated by the Party, and he became first deputy PC for health of the RSFSR and later of the U.S.S.R., in which capacity he served for three years. Together with PC G.N. Kaminsky this intrepid Communist raised his voice against the repressions which set in during the cult of Stalin's personality. Kaminsky was arrested and died shortly afterward, as did Kangelari.[61]

NIKOLAI DIMITRIEVICH KASHIRIN

Biographical data

Born February 4, 1888; died June 14, 1938. Hero of the Civil War; Army Commander, Second Class in 1935. Joined the CP in 1918. Born in the Cossack village of Verkhneural'sk, Orenburg gubernia; his father, a teacher, became ataman of the village. Worked as a teacher from 1902 to 1906 and completed studies at Orenburg cadet school in 1909. In 1912 he was expelled from the Fifth Orenburg Cossack Regiment for anti-government agitation among the lower ranks. Decorated six times in the First World War and rose to be first lieutenant. Invalided home in 1916. In March 1917 he became a leader of the Cossack rank and file against their counterrevolutionary leaders. In 1918 he organized a volunteer Cossack detachment in Verkhneural'sk to fight the Dutov forces. On June 16, 1918, he was elected commander in chief of the southern Ural composite partisan force operating behind the White lines; he was wounded and became assistant to Bliukher, the new commander in chief. In September 1918, after the force had joined with the Red Army, he became deputy commander and then commander of the Fourth Ural Division, later the Thirtieth Rifle Division. In 1919 he was named commander of the Ural Fortified Zone and of the Forty-ninth Division on the Turkestan front. In 1920, chairman of the Orenburg-Turgai gubernia executive committee, and commander of the Third Cavalry Corps on the southern front and of the Aleksandrov group of forces operating against the Makhno bands. In 1923-25, commander of the Fourteenth Rifle Corps; then was attached to the Red Army staff for duties of special importance, then commander of the First Red Cossack Cavalry Corps. In 1925-31, deputy commander of a number of military districts; 1931-37, commander of the North Caucasus military district; from 1934, member of the Military Council of the U.S.S.R. In July-August 1937, head of the main administration of military training. Subjected to illegal repressions during the cult of personality, rehabilitated posthumously. A monument has been erected to his memory at Verkhneural'sk.[62]

GRIGORII DAVIDOVICH KHAKHAN'IAN

Biographical data

[Corps commander.] Born December 28, 1895; died February 22, 1939. Born in Runsi village, Gori uezd, the son of a village teacher. Graduated from high school in Tiflis in 1915 and entered the historical and literary faculty of Moscow University. Mobilized in summer 1916 and sent to Moscow Ensigns' College. On February 1, 1917, he became an officer and was appointed to the 157th Reserve Regiment at Kamyshlov, Perm gubernia. Joined the Bolshevik Party in March 1917 and was soon elected chairman of the Kamyshlov soviet of workers', peasants' and soldiers' deputies (*See Great Soviet Encyclopedia*, 1st edition, vol. 59, p. 474). Courtmartialed for revolutionary activity, and sent to the western front in a draft battalion which was directed from Petrograd to join a reserve regiment at Gorodok in Vitebsk gubernia. During the October Revolution he was in Petrograd and, as a member of a composite detachment of the RMC, took part in the capture of the Baltic railroad station and the night assault on the Winter Palace. Was a delegate to the second congress of soviets. During the Krensky-Krasnov rebellion he had the important task of stopping counterrevolutionary forces that were advancing toward Petrograd to aid Kerensky, and in fact not a single enemy train got through Gorodok. He was a member of the Gorodok uezd executive committee, vice chairman of the army committee of the old Fifth Army, member of the Pskov gubernia executive committee and secretary of its Cheka, head of the operational section of the military revolutionary commissariat of the Velikie Luki raion, and military commissar of the group of forces in the Novorzhevsk raion.[63]

The career of a corps commander

The Bolshevik warrior and hero of the Civil War Grigorii Davidovich Khakhan'ian had a splendid war career, for which he received the Order of the Red Banner three times and a Revolutionary Sword of Honor. Having served in the ranks of the October Revolution, from the very first days of the Soviet state he devoted his strength and knowledge to the task of building up the Red Army.

In July 1918 he was military commissar of the Pskov Division and was sent to the eastern front. At the beginning of August he became deputy head of the operational section of the staff of the Fifth Army. At that time the enemy was attempting to strike at the Fifth Army in the Sviiazhsk area by encircling and destroying the Soviet troops around Kazan. On August 29 a brigade of White Guards under Colonel Kappel' with 2,000 bayonets, 340 sabres, 14 heavy guns, and many machine guns broke through toward Sviiazhsk station together with the SR detachments of Savinkov and Fortunatov. The appearance of the Whites in the rear of the Fifth Army brought about an extremely serious situation, and the RMC of the Fifth Army entrusted the defense of Sviiazhsk to Khakhan'ian. V. K. Putna, who was an eye-witness of these events, described the defense of the town as follows:

> Every single available man was in the ranks of those who stood shoulder to shoulder, rifle in hand, defending Sviiazhsk—from the members of the RMC to the humblest clerk in the Administration.... The Red soldiers fought as only those do who have no retreat, knowing that more than Sviiazhsk was at stake.... The enemy charged fiercely with bayonets more than once.

The defenders were reinforced by sailors from the Volga flotilla, and Kappel''s troops, though clearly superior in numbers, were repulsed. On behalf of the RMC the commander of the Fifth Army, P.A. Slaven, rewarded Khakhan'ian's bold organization of the town's defense with a gold watch inscribed "To a brave warrior of the Red Army."

Khakhan'ian was unable to take part in the liberation of Kazan, having been wounded in the leg. After recovery he returned to the staff of the Fifth Army, and in February 1919 became head of the operational section of its staff. But he longed to get back to the front line, and after several requests on his part the RMC appointed him commander of the Simbirsk Brigade, later the Third Brigade of the Twenty-seventh Rifle division.

Having defeated the enemy forces, the regiments of the Third Brigade broke across the Belaia and Ufimka rivers in the direction of Zlatoust, which they liberated after an eighty-mile march. Then, on November 13, 1919, the Twenty-seventh Division approached Omsk. Having crossed the Irtysh River at Nikolaevka, units of the First Brigade, (which were now under Khakhan'ian's command) began to encircle Omsk from the north and thus ensured the victory of the Second Brigade, which attacked the town directly. After the encirclement the brigade commander led his troops to the eastern outskirts of the town, and Kolchak's forces, finding the enemy in their rear, were obliged to evacuate Omsk.

For his bold and decisive command on this occasion Khakhan'ian received the Order of the Red Banner, the highest distinction awarded at that time. But the Twenty-seventh Omsk Division was not to remain in Siberia for long: it was soon ordered to take the field against White Poland. Khakhan'ian's Seventy-ninth Brigade, formerly the First, entered the fight forthwith and experienced both the joys of victory and the bitterness of defeat.

The order issued by the Republican RMC, conferring on Khakan'ian the Order of the Red Banner for the second time, stated that "by his soldierlike qualities and constant presence in the thick of the fighting during the retreat of our troops from the Bug River during August 20-23, this officer was able to sustain his brigade's morale to the end of the operation and to win the action at Belostok.... His skillful command of this action, the firmness and personal courage of the heroic Comrade Khakhan'ian, enabled our surrounded troops and transports to extricate themselves safely."

The commander of the sixteenth Army, N. V. Sologub, stated in an Order of the Day that of the fifteen brigades which composed the army, only four, including Khakhan'ian's Seventy-ninth, had preserved their organization and battle efficiency and, having broken through the enemy front, had returned to their formations headed by their commanders. He recommended that these four commanders be rewarded with the Order of the Red Banner. Accordingly, on December 31, 1920, Khakhan'ian received this order for the third time.

At the beginning of March 1921, a week before the Tenth Party Congress opened, the counterrevolutionary revolt broke out at Kronstadt. The capital needed help urgently, and the Twenty-seventh Omsk Division set out in haste. The first brigade to arrive was Khakhan'ian's Seventy-ninth, which was ordered by A. I. Sediakin, the Commander of the southern group, to capture the southern Kronstadt forts and occupy the western part of the fortress-town, thus threatening the rebels' line of retreat toward Finland. On the evening of March 16 Khakhan'ian issued an order ending with the words, "Let no one think of returning to the mainland without capturing Kronstadt." At 4:00 a.m. on the 17th, his troops set out across the ice. In the forefront were Division Commander Vitovt Putna; Brigade Commander Khakhan'ian; the military commissar of the brigade, M. L. Belotsky; its chief of staff Berezovsky; the regimental commanders I. V. Tiulenev, I. I. Assarit, and P. S. Terent'ev; and delegates from the Tenth Party Congress. Before dawn on the 18th, after twenty-four hours of fierce fighting, the banner of the Soviet Republic again flew over Kronstadt. The country duly appreciated the military feats of the Seventy-ninth Brigade and its commander, who received the Revolutionary Sword of Honor for having "contributed to victory by his calm and skillful leadership, under fierce enemy fire, of the assault columns which took the fortress of Kronstadt on March 18, 1921."

After the Civil War Khakhan'ian remained in uniform, and at the head of his brigade defeated many irregular bands on the Volga. At the beginning of January 1923 he was appointed commander of the Twenty-seventh Omsk Division. In October of that year he commenced attendance at senior academic courses, [and at the academy] he was elected secretary of the Party organization. Having completed his studies, on the recommendation of the chief of the air force he was appointed head of the tactical faculty of Zhukovsky Air Force Academy. But his talent as an organizer and instructor was most fully displayed in the Higher Infantry Tactical School of the Red Army (the "Third International" or "Vystrel"), whose director and commissar he became on January 7, 1925. During this appointment he began work on his book *Osnovy voennoi psikhologii* (Elements of Military Psychology), which he finished at the end of 1929 and which contains a wealth of illustration of the problems of individual and collective psychology.

In March 1927 Khakhan'ian became commander and military commissar of the Nineteenth Maritime Province Rifle Corps at Khabarovsk. On October 10, 1928, the commander of the Siberian military district, N. N. Petin, reported on him as follows:

> An officer of very high quality. His lively, penetrating mind, exceptionally serious and politically responsible approach to all problems, objectivity, endurance, moral fiber, breadth of mind in both military and other respects, and wide Party and military experience—all this gives promise of rich further development and advancement to high positions in the Red Army, both on the military side and on that of the central political administration.

In August 1929 he became head of political administration and a member of the RMC of the Ukraine military district, where he remained until 1934. At the Seventeenth Party Congress he was elected a member of the Commission of Soviet Control as head of the military group. Though this was interesting work, he preferred to be in the front line and was glad when, in December 1936, the Party appointed him head of political administration and a member of the RMC of the Special Red Banner Army of the Far East. He reached Khabarovsk at the beginning of January 1937. However in autumn he was recalled to Moscow, where troubled times were approaching. He wrote to Mekhlis, the Head of the Red Army political administration:

> I am not in the least discouraged and burn with anxiety to return to my work in the Far East, which I know and love and where I can be useful. I beg you to hasten the examination of my case.... to imagine the stress and bitterness which I have undergone for so long, conscious as I am of being an honest and devoted son of the Party and of our country.

Khakhan'ian was arrested on February 1, 1938, and perished, a victim of slander, on February 22, 1939. The life of this able Soviet commander and political worker was cut short at the height of his creative powers.[64]

DIMITRII IOSIFOVICH KOSICH

Biographical data

Born 1886, died 1937. Joined the Bolshevik Party in 1918. In the Civil War he commanded a regiment and was military commissar on the staff of the Fifth Army. After the war he was commander and commissar of the Ninth

Rifle Division, chief of supply of the North Caucasus Military District, inspector of formations of the Red Army, and chief of transport and equipment administration of the Red Army.[65]

EPIFAN IOVICH KOVTIUKH

Biographical data

[Corps commander.] Born May 9, 1890; died July 28, 1938. Corps commander, 1935. Joined the CP in 1918. Born in Baturino village, Kherson gubernia, the son of a poor peasant who afterward settled in the Kuban. Called up in 1911; in the First World War he fought on the Caucasian front. Passed cadet school in 1916 and rose to be junior captain. Elected to the committee of his regiment, 1917. In 1918, company commander and deputy commander of a Red Guard detachment in the Kuban area; fought against White Guardists in the northern Caucasus. During the heroic campaign of the Taman Army (August-September 1918), he commanded the First Column which formed the vanguard: cf. A. S. Serafimovich's novel *Zheleznyi potok* (The Iron Deluge), in which the hero Kozhukh represents Kovtiukh. From October to December 1918 (with intervals of absence owing to illness) he commanded the Taman Army; in 1919-20 he headed the Third (Taman) Rifle Division and the Fiftieth Division, which fought at Tsaritsyn, Tikhoretskaia, Tuapse, and Sochi. In 1920 he commanded the composite corps of the Second Army, and in the fall of that year led a force which landed in the rear of General Ulagai's force in the Kuban area. Graduated from military academy in 1922 and commanded a division, then a corps. Completed advanced course for command staff, 1928. From 1936, army inspector and deputy commander of the Belorussian military district. Subjected to repressions during the cult of Stalin's personality; rehabilitated posthumously.[66]

A commander and man of the people

Epifan Iovich Kovtiukh (1890-1938) was born in Baturino village, Kherson gubernia. His father, Iov Prokop'evich, an impoverished peasant, moved with his family—eleven persons in all—to the Kuban and settled in Poltava village, Taman sector, where he worked as a herdsman for rich Cossacks. Epifan also worked for the kulaks as a boy, but when he grew up he became a factory hand.

In 1911 he was called up, and soon became a noncommissioned officer. He was almost court-martialed for defending soldiers against ill treatment by their officers, but was saved by the outbreak of war. For exceptional bravery on the Caucasian front he received the George Cross more than once and was sent to a cadet school. Later he commanded a machine-gun company and a battalion, and rose to be junior captain.

After the October Revolution, in January 1918, the first Taman revolutionary congress proclaimed the Soviet power as sole legitimate authority in its area. But the kulaks, monarchist officers, Cossack sergeants, and reactionaries who had flocked to the Kuban from the center of the country began a frenzied agitation against the soviets. In many places armed uprisings of counterrevolutionary Cossacks broke out, led by former Tsarist officers. To combat these the Bolsheviks set up revolutionary committees and organized detachments of workers, farm laborers and poor Cossacks. Kovtiukh, who was demobilized and returned from the front at this time, became commander of a revolutionary company, forming part of a detachment under the Bolshevik sailor Rogachev, which fought with distinction against the Whites in the Taman peninsula. Kovtiukh's military experience stood him in good stead and he became deputy commander of the detachment, which was later reformed into the First North Kuban Regiment.

In summer 1918, when Denikin's "volunteer army" began its advance, a serious situation developed in the Kuban. In July the Denikin forces captured Tikhoretskaia village and marched on Ekaterinodar, the center of the Kuban. The First North Kuban Regiment was sent to help the Soviet troops in this area. The army committee under N. I. Podvoisky called a meeting of command staff and troop representatives which decided to defend the town and to unite all the defense forces under the command of E. I. Kovtiukh. The new commander set to work energetically. Despite stubborn resistance, the enemy was defeated at the villages of Dinskaia and Platnirovskaia and was repulsed from Ekaterinodar. Meanwhile the counterrevolutionaries had taken a number of other villages in the Taman sector, and the First North Kuban Regiment was one of the units detailed to suppress the rebellion. In August the Poltava battalion under Kovtiukh was moved to Novonikolaevskaia village.... At a general meeting of the command staff and representatives of companies it was decided to unite the troops in the Griven sector into a column under Kovtiukh's command.

Kovtiukh prepared his men to attack, but instead they had to retreat. On August 16 Denikin took Ekaterinodar, and the Soviet forces, commanded by Sorokin, were obliged to withdraw toward Belorechenskaia and Armavir. The counterrevolutionary Cossack leaders of the Taman sector chose this moment to intensify their activity: they drove out the soviets, hanged soviet workers, and carried out reprisals against the poorer Cossacks. The revolutionary forces in the area were thus cut off from the main body of the Red Army in the northern Caucasus. Kovtiukh's column had to retreat, fighting as it went, toward Slavianskaia and then via Krymskaia to Novorossiisk. It took with it the families of Red Army men and impoverished Cossacks. All who were capable of bearing arms joined the battalion, which transformed itself into a regiment ....

Kovtiukh's column passed through Novorossiisk, followed by the rest of the Soviet forces. The situation called for the uniting of all the retreating forces under a single command. At a council of commanders and commissars, held at Gelendzhik in the presence of local Party and political workers, it was decided to form the retreating detachments into an army, to be called the Taman Army, under the command of a sailor named I. I. Matveev, with the Bolshevik G. N. Baturin as his chief of staff. Kovtiukh's column was to constitute the First Column of the new army, the Second and Third being composed of the forces immediately following it.

The line of troops, accompanied by thousands of refugees, stretched out for many miles along the narrow mountain road. The hot southern sun blazed mercilessly by day, while the nights were cold. Provisions ran out, and the only food was raw maize, acorns, and wild berries. Children starved to death; clothing and shoes were full of holes. Only five to ten cartridges were left to each soldier. The enemy carried out sudden attacks from time to time and bombarded the retreating force from the sea. The Whites kept on the heels of the Red detachments and terrorized the civil population. In Novorossiisk alone, on August 27 they killed about 10,000 men and women, burying dozens of them alive....

On September 1, 1918, Tuapse was liberated and the remnants of the enemy fled to Sochi. Ordzhonikidze telegraphed to Lenin: "At Tuapse the Georgian troops of General Mazniev were routed together with Alekseev's forces and withdrew to Sochi, leaving their artillery in our hands."

After leaving Tuapse the First Column, led by the resolute and energetic Kovtiukh and supported by the Second and Third columns of the Taman Army, defeated the White troops under Generals Pokrovsky and Geiman at the village of Belorechenskaia. The army's legendary 300-mile march ended on September 18, 1918, with the capture of Dondukovskaia village. Its escape from encirclement and reunion with the main revolutionary forces in the Kuban strengthened the fighting spirit of the whole Red Army. A former member of the RMC of the Second Army, S. Petrenko, wrote afterward:

> This march by the Taman Army, which at times had nothing but bayonets to fight with, should be inscribed in the annals of our struggle as one of the most glorious exploits of the revolutionary forces. Thanks to the bravery, battle experience, and personal example of Comrade Kovtiukh, commanding the First Column, and the able, self-assured leadership of the army, the soul of which was its chief of staff Comrade Baturin, this force was able to extricate itself from what seemed hopeless difficulties. The news of their reunion with the main forces filled us with hope for a new and victorious period of our struggle.

On October 11, 1918, the RMC of the northern Caucasus appointed Kovtiukh commander of the Taman Army with orders to advance toward Stavropol. Denikin had sent three divisions into the Armavir area and was attacking the town with officer regiments and a large force of cavalry, artillery, armored cars, and trains. Kovtiukh was in the forefront of the defense and in moments of crisis himself handled a machine gun. Thanks to his ability and the heroism of his troops, the enemy was driven back to his initial positions. In this battle two enemy officer regiments were destroyed and a White composite regiment suffered severe losses; many prisoners were taken.

At the end of 1918 Kovtiukh joined the CP, with which his fate was linked ever afterward. In 1919, after a severe attack of typhus, he went to Moscow, where the RMC granted his request to form a special Taman division, the nucleus of which would consist of commanders and men of the former Taman Army. At the head of this, the Fiftieth Division, Kovtiukh took part in the battle for Tsaritsyn and the final defeat of Denikin's soldiery in the northern Caucasus. On March 8, 1920, the division took Tikhoretskaia by a sudden attack; it then marched triumphantly through the Kuban fields to the shores of the Black Sea, while soviets were set up in the liberated areas.

But the counterrevolutionaries would not accept defeat. In August 1920 Baron Wrangel landed troops in the Kuban, and his forces threatened Ekaterinodar. The commander of the Ninth Kuban Army, M. K. Levandovsky, appointed Kovtiukh commander of the Krasnodar Fortified Zone. The Soviet command made a bold decision: to send troops by the way of the Protok River into the enemy's rear area near Grivenskaia. The force was composed of men from the Taman area who knew the terrain well; its commander was Kovtiukh and its commissar D. A. Furmanov. As a precaution, Kovtiukh sent cavalrymen along both banks of the river; during the night these men destroyed several enemy patrols. At dawn the force was a mile and a quarter from Grivenskaia while the enemy staff was still sound asleep. As Furmanov put it later, a blow was struck "at the enemy's very heart." The main Red forces supervened at this moment, and the Whites were thrown into the Sea of Azov. So ended Wrangel's design of raising the Kuban Cossacks in revolt against Soviet power.

After the Civil War, Kovtiukh was sent to study at a military academy. Later he commanded a division and a corps and became inspector and deputy commander of the White Russian military district. In 1936 he was elected a member of the All-Union CEC for the Western oblast. For his war services he received the Order of the Red Banner three times.

In 1937 he became a victim of unjustified repression owing to the cult of Stalin's personality, and perished tragically. A great commander was lost to the Soviet Army.

The name of E. I. Kovtiukh, Communist, corps commander and hero of the Civil War, will live forever in the people's memory.[67]

DIMITRII ALEKSANDROVICH KUCHINSKY

Biographical data

Born 1898, died 1938. An officer in the Tsarist Army; joined the Bolshevik Party in 1918 and fought in the Civil War. Subsequently held senior command posts: chief of staff of the Ukrainian Military District and head of the General Staff Academy. Subjected to repression and perished in 1938.[68]

Corps Commander
Nikolai Vladimirovich Kuibishev (left)

NIKOLAI VLADIMIROVICH KUIBISHEV

Biographical data

[Corps commander.] Born 1893, died 1938. Joined the CP in 1918. Brother of V. V. Kuibishev. Born in the town of Kokchetak; graduated in 1914 from Aleksandrovsky Military School. In the First World War he commanded a company and then a battalion. In 1917 he was a member of a regimental committee, and after the October Revolution was elected commander of his regiment. From June 1918 he was a member of the senior military inspectorate; from January 1919 a military commissar, and from October 1919 commander of the Third Brigade of the Ninth Rifle Division. From January 1920 he commanded this division on the southern front. In 1921 he became a corps commander, and in 1922-23 he was commander and commissar at Kronshtadt. In 1923-25 he directed the advanced rifle school known as Vystrel. In 1925-26 he was deputy commander of the Turkestan front and then commanded a corps. In 1927-28, chief of command administration of the Red Army and deputy commander of the Moscow military district. From 1928 to 1936, commander of the Siberian military district, and in 1937 of the Trans-Caucasian military district. Received the Order of the Red Banner three times. Deputy to the Supreme Soviet of the U.S.S.R., first convocation. Subjected to illegal repression during the cult of Stalin's personality; rehabilitated posthumously.[69]

Put to death for opposing Stalin

Many Party, Soviet, and military leaders spoke out against the unjustified repression of honest Communists and pointed out its grave consequences for the Soviet state and the country's defense. At the November 1937 session of the Military Council, N. V. Kuibishev, commander of the Trans-Caucasian military district, declared that the repressions had depleted the military cadres of his district and were the main cause of a drop in its fighting efficiency. Soon afterwards, he himself was subjected to repression.[70]

ALEKSANDR IVANOVICH KUK

Biographical data

Born 1886, died 1937. Joined the Bolshevik Party in 1927. Junior captain in the Tsarist Army; joined the Red Army in 1918. In the Civil War he commanded the operations divisions of the Estonian and Fifteenth armies, then commanded the Sixteenth Army and was chief of staff of the southern group of the Seventh Army. After the war he held senior posts on the Red Army staff, was chief of staff of the Western military district, deputy commander of the Leningrad military district, commander of the Karelian Fortified Zone and military attaché in Japan.[71]

IVAN SEMENOVICH KUTIAKOV

Biographical data

[Corps commander.] Born 1897, died 1942. Joined the CP in 1917. Corps commander, 1935. Born in Krasnaia Rechka village, Nikolaevsky uezd, Samara gubernia, the son of a peasant. Called up in 1916, became a junior NCO and chairman of a regimental committee. Delegate to the second all-Russian congress of peasants' deputies. Elected commander and commissar of the Twentieth Turkestan Rifle Regiment. After demobilization he became chairman of the volost revolutionary committee and formed a Red Guard detachment which became part of the Second (Stenka Razin) Rifle Regiment commanded by V. I. Chapaev. From October 1918 he commanded the Seventy-third Brigade of the Twenty-fifth Chapaev Division. After Chapaev's death, from September 6, 1919, to October 1920, he commanded the Twenty-fifth Division and took part in fighting the Ural White Cossacks and the White Poles. Graduated from military academy in 1923 and completed advanced course for senior officers in 1931; commanded a division and a corps. Received the Order of the Red Banner three times. 1936-37, deputy commander of the Volga military district. Subjected to illegal repression and posthumously rehabilitated.[72]

NIKOLAI NIKOLAEVICH KUZ'MIN

Biographical data

Joined the Party in 1903, and in 1918 was military commissar of the Sixth Army. After the close of operations on the northern front in April 1920 he was appointed commissar of the Baltic Fleet, and was soon transferred to the Soviet-Polish front as a member of the RMC of the Fifteenth Army and then commander of the Twelfth Army. After the Civil War he was again commissar of the Baltic Fleet and took part in the suppression of the Kronstadt mutiny. In later years he served as procurator of the military collegium of the Supreme Court of the U.S.S.R., chief of political administration of the Turkestan front and of the Siberian military district, chief of administration of military educational establishments and chief of territorial administration at Arkhangelsk. He was a victim of the cult of Stalin's personality.[73]

Commissar, tribune, and warrior

A Red Army Commissar. The phrase calls to mind the heroic figure of a strong-willed, courageous man whom others were willing to follow to the death and in whom they believed at moments of crisis more firmly than in themselves. Lenin's Party conferred this exalted and difficult role on the best of its sons, tried revolutionaries who were inflexibly devoted to the October cause. They were the true leaders of the Red Army masses: it was their ardor which inspired its warriors with revolutionary enthusiasm, their iron will and faith in victory which enhanced the army's fighting ability. Under their Bolshevik influence, a whole galaxy of Red commanders came into being and received their training. One such commander and gifted political worker was our wartime comrade and friend Nikolai Nikolaevich Kuz'min.

We may ask ourselves today—what was the main characteristic which enabled this man to conquer everyone's heart? Perhaps his most striking quality was inflexibility in the battle for one great idea— the inflexibility which he learned from V. I. Lenin.

Describing a conversation with Lenin, Kuz'min wrote:

> I remember how in November 1917, when the Left SRs were oscillating like a pendulum, he sent me to a meeting with this admonition: "The great thing is to present problems sharply—harass them without mercy and strip them of pretenses, so that they will either have to declare themselves for us or join the enemy's camp."

All his life long, the commissar stoutly defended the cause of communism. Wherever the Party sent him, he was a passionate advocate of Bolshevik ideas and exponent of Leninist policy.

In summer 1918 the interventionists were occupying Arkhangelsk and revolutionary Petersburg was threatened. On Lenin's instructions, the Sixth Army was formed in the north, and Kuz'min became its military commissar and member of the RMC. From the outset, the Red Army units had to fight in exceptionally difficult conditions. They were short of food, arms, and uniforms. But despite all difficulties, the Sixth Army not only barred the enemy's path but destroyed the combined forces of external and internal counterrevolution.

The victory in the north was largely a result of the selfless work of the Red commissars. Thanks to the Bolshevik cells created even in the smallest units, the political apparatus of the Sixth Army united its soldiers into a single force with full awareness of its goals: soldiers' meetings, the reading and explanation of the most important Leninist documents, information about developments on the front, even amateur theatricals—there is no end to the list of activities organized by the political officers.

The political department members scattered pamphlets among the enemy's troops and in his rear area, denouncing the predatory aims of the interventionists. Educational work was promoted on a large scale among prisoners of war. The enemy troops refused to carry out their officers' orders and came over to our side singly or in groups. Kuz'min as military commissar was not only the soul of these activities but set an example to Red Army men in the thick of the fighting....

In 1920 he had the gratifying duty of reporting to Lenin that the interventionists had been expelled from the north thanks to the brotherly cooperation of the Red Army, the partisans, and the local working population. The northern front having thus been cleared, in April 1920 he was appointed commissar of the Baltic Fleet. However, he did not stay there long, for in July he was sent to the Polish front. As a member of the RMC of the Twelfth Army [sic] he devoted his exceptional abilities and experience to the fight with the White Poles. A month later he became commander of the Twelfth Army.

After the Civil War the Party once more appointed him to the Baltic Fleet, where a serious situation was developing. Taking advantage of the weakening of Bolshevik organization, bourgeois agents prepared a counterrevolutionary outbreak at Kronshtadt. From the first day of his arrival the commissar was constantly at meetings among the sailors, but it was too late to prevent the mutiny, and in the course of one of his speeches Kuz'min himself was seized by the mutineers. After escaping he took part, rifle in hand, in the assault on Kronshtadt. For his courage and valor on this occasion the Soviet Government conferred on its faithful son the Order of the Red Banner.

In the title of this article we called Kuz'min a "tribune." He earned this description by his brilliance as a speaker and journalist. He addressed the men of the Red Army and the Red Fleet literally every day and often twice a day, attending numerous meetings and writing even more frequently in the press. He had an amazing capacity for work. In the eight months from May to the end of 1920 he published more than three-hundred articles, chiefly in the military press. These daily articles provide a vivid picture of the life of the army and fleet at that unforgettable time....

Kuz'min's life was cut short as a result of the repression during the cult of personality. At that time he was serving in the main administration of the Northern Sea Route, as chief of territorial administration at Arkhangelsk—the town in which, in February 1920, he had served in the front ranks of the glorious Eighteenth Rifle Division which expelled the interventionists from the Soviet Union.[74]

AL'BERT IANOVICH LAPIN

Biographical data

[Corps commander.] Born 1899, died 1937. Corps commander; joined the Bolshevik Party in 1917. In the Civil War he was commissar on the staff of the Fifth Army, commanded a regiment, a brigade, a division, and finally the Amur and Trans-Baikal military districts. After the war he was chief of staff of the Special Red Banner Army of the Far East, commanded a corps, and was subsequently chief of administration of Red Army Staff and air force commander of the Belorussian Military District and the Special Far Eastern Army.[75]

IAN IANOVICH LATSIS

Biographical data

[Corps commander.] Born 1897, died 1937. Corps commander; joined the Bolshevik Party in 1917 and the Red Army in 1918. In the Civil War he commanded the Fourth Latvian Rifle Regiment and the Fifteenth Division, was deputy commander of the rear of the Twelfth and Ninteenth armies and commander of the rear of the Sixth Army. After the war he commanded a division and a corps.[76]

MIKHAIL KARLOVICH LEVANDOVSKY

Biographical data

[Army commander, second class.] Born 1890, died 1938. Joined the Russian CP in 1920. In the Civil War he commanded the Eleventh, Twelfth, and Ninth armies. After the war he commanded the Turkestan front, the Caucasian Red Banner Army, and the Siberian military district and occupied other senior command posts in the Red Army.[77]

A gifted commander

The life and military career of Mikhail Karlovich Levandovsky, who together with G. K. Ordzhonikidze, S. M. Kirov, and A. I. Mikoyan led the Eleventh Army into Trans-Caucasia, is inseparably bound up with Georgia. Levandovsky was born in Tiflis, where he began his military service. This was the headquarters for staff and administration of the Caucasian Red Banner Army and the Trans-Caucasian military district, in which he spent seven years in charge of training the troops defending the southern borders of our country.

Today is the seventy-fifth anniversary of the birth of Army Commander, Second Class Mikhail Karlovich Levandovsky, an eminent Soviet commander and hero of the Civil War.

Levandovsky was one of those officers of the Tsarist Army who devotedly served the people from the first days of the October Revolution and took an active part in forming and building up the armed forces of the young Soviet state. Trained by the Communist Party, which he joined in 1920, he was a man of unshakable courage, strong will, transparent moral purity, and great military experience. His whole life was an inspiring example of service to the motherland in the name of great ideals and of the victory of communism. He was, too, a man of great personal courage and self-control. Sergo Ordzhonikidze referred to him as "the intrepid Levandovsky."

Once, returning from a reconnaissance with a small escort, he drove into a village occupied by the Whites and found his way blocked by a cavalry screen of Wrangel's troops. Unperturbed, he took control of a machine gun and told the driver to go full speed ahead. Thanks to his accurate fire, the Whites were dispersed and his party was able to traverse the village.

The Party and government appointed him to the most crucial sectors of the Civil War, to posts requiring the utmost strength and energy in combating the enemies of Soviet power. He was military commissar of the Terek People's Republic and a leader of the heroic defense of Groznyi in 1918. Under his command, the Thirty-third Kuban Rifle division and, in 1920 the Ninth Kuban Army fought fiercely against the White Guardists in the Don and Kuban areas and took an active part in destroying Denikin's soldiery. The troops under his command liberated Azerbaidzhan, drove Wrangel's Kuban and Ukraine forces into the sea, put down anti-Soviet revolts in Dagestan and the Tambov gubernia, and destroyed Basmachi gangs in Central Asia.

Levandovsky rendered particular service in developing and improving methods of military training for both officers and men during the years of peaceful construction. His first and basic duty was to train fighting men in conditions as close as possible to those of actual warfare. He devoted special attention to methods of mountain warfare, to developing the independence and initiative of each commander, to cooperation between different arms, to enveloping and outflanking movements and the art of striking at the enemy's rear in offensive actions. A combative army commander and a great Soviet military specialist, a convinced Bolshevik and a veteran of the First World War and the Civil War, Levandovsky did much to train the nation's military cadres and to cement friendship among the peoples of Transcaucasia. The fighting men of Georgia, Azerbaidzhan, and Armenia well knew and loved their commander. He often visited national units and took a personal interest in their successes and the development of their officer cadres....

He was in constant touch with local Party and Soviet organs and took an active part in their work. He was a member of the Transcaucasian CEC and the CEC of the Georgian SSR, of the Transcaucasian regional committee of the CPSU and the CC of the Georgian CP. In 1927 he was elected a member of the CEC of the U.S.S.R.

He was a close friend of F. I. Makaradze, the chairman of the CPC of the Georgian SSR and later of its CEC. The two men fought together against Denikin in the northern Caucasus in 1918, when they were both members of the government of the Terek People's Republic....

Levandovsky was a delegate to the Fourteenth, Fifteenth, and Sixteenth congresses of the Party. In celebration of the Fifteenth anniversary of Soviet Georgia he received the Order of Lenin—his fourth Red Army decoration—for his service to the southern defenses of our motherland. In June 1937 he became commander of the First Red Banner Far Eastern Army. In 1938, he became a victim of unjustified repression.

The memory of this great commander and Party worker, a fearless fighter for Soviet power, lives in the hearts of the Soviet people and army.[78]

MIKHAIL EVGEN'EVICH MEDVEDEV

Biographical data

Born 1898, died 1937. In the Civil War he was chief of staff of a brigade, commanded the Gomel Fortress Brigade and the First Kazan Rifle Division. After the war he was chief of air staff of the Red Army, chief of staff of a corps, and chief of staff of the Red Army.[79]

KONSTANTIN ALEKSANDROVICH MEKHONOSHIN

Biographical data

Born 1889, died 1938. A military leader; took an active part in the October Revolution. Born at Zavod Aleksandrovsky (now Aleksandrovsk), Perm gubernia, the son of a teacher. Joined the revolutionary movement in 1906 and the CP in 1913. While a student at Petersburg University (1909-14) he was twice arrested and expelled from the city. In 1914-15 he was a scientific adviser to the Caspian Sea expedition of the Academy of Sciences. From 1915, served in Petersburg as a guardsman in the Grenadier Regiment. After the February revolution of 1917 he became a member of his regimental committee and of the Petrograd soviet of workers' and soldiers' deputies, also of the Petrograd Bolshevik committee. From April he was a member of the Bolshevik military organization, and from June of the all-Russian bureau of front and rear military organizations under the CC of the RSDWP(B). In July 1917 he was arrested by the Provisional Government and imprisoned at Kresty until October. Before and during the October Revolution he was a member of the Petrograd military revolutionary committee. Member of the All-Union CEC, second convocation. From November 20 to December 3, 1917, he served as deputy PC for military affairs, and from December 1917 to September 1918 he was a member of the collegium of the PC for Military Affairs. From January 21 to February

3, 1918, he was a member of the collegium for the formation and organization of the Red Army, and from March 1918 of the Supreme Military Council. In 1918-20, during the Civil War, Mekhonoshin was a member of the RMC of the eastern, southern and Caspian-Caucasian fronts, of the Eleventh Special Army and the Eleventh Army of the southwestern front and the Third Army of the western front, also of the RMC of the Republic (September 1918 to July 1919). In 1921-26, deputy director and then director of universal military training, chairman of the supreme council for physical culture and sport, and later worked in the Red Sporting International. In 1926-27, he was a military attaché in Poland; in 1927-31, worked in U.S.S.R. Gosplan and Osoaviakhim; in 1931-34, member of the collegium of the PC for Communications, then director of the All-Union Scientific Research Institute of Oceanography and Maritime Economy. Subjected to unjustified repression in 1937; rehabilitated posthumously.[80]

SERGEI ALEKSANDROVICH MEZHENINOV

Biographical data

Born 1890, died 1937. An officer in the Tsarist Army. Studied at Kiev Air Observation School and the General Staff Academy. Joined the Red Army in 1918. Commanded armies in the Civil War. Subsequently chief of staff of military districts and of the air force; from 1933, deputy chief of staff of the Red Army.[81]

MIKRAMID MIRSHARAPOV

Biographical data

Date of birth unknown; died before 1940. Joined the CP in 1918. Was a farm laborer before the Revolution. Fought for Soviet power in October 1917. In 1919 he attended the Lenin School for Military Instructors in Turkestan, and after graduation commanded a cavalry troop which was to be the nucleus of the Red Army in Khoresm (Khiva). On April 26, 1920, when the Khurultai (Assembly) proclaimed the Khoresmian People's Soviet Republic (KPSR), he was elected deputy chairman of the Council of Nazirs (Ministers). Shortly thereafter the RMC of the Turkestan front recalled him to Tashkent to form national units of the Red Army. In spring 1924 he returned to Khoresm, where the Central Asia bureau of the CC of the RCP(B) appointed him deputy nazir of war for the KPSR and he again saw military service. For his skill and bravery the CEC of the KPSR awarded him the Labor Order of the Red Banner and a complimentary address [sic]. When the KPSR had been cleared of Basmachi he was transferred to the Republic of Bukhara where they were still causing trouble, and for personal bravery there he received the Order of the Golden Star, First Class. In 1925 he was transferred to Moscow to attend the Frunze Military Academy of the Red Army. After graduation he became commander and then commissar of the Uzbek Cavalry Brigade. In 1932 he commanded a separate Uzbek composite brigade, and later the Sixth Uzbek Order of Lenin Mountain Cavalry Division. In 1935 he was Soviet millitary attaché in the Mongolian People's Republic, and a year later commanded a multinational division in the North Caucasian military district. While in this post he met an untimely death at the height of his creative powers.[82]

NIKOLAI NIKOLAEVICH MOVCHIN

Biographical data

Born 1896, died 1938. Served in the Civil War and was a senior member of Red Army staff and a graduate of the Frunze Military Academy.[83]

ROMUAL'D ADAMOVICH MUKLEVICH

Biographical data

Born 1890, died 1938. Born at Suprasl', Grodno gubernia, the son of a Polish textile worker. After leaving parish school he worked with his father at the textile factory. In 1906 he joined the Social Democratic Party of Poland and Lithuania; he was secretary of its Belostok committee in 1907-9 and of its Lodz committee in 1911. Imprisoned in 1907 for organizing a strike at Belostok. Called up for naval service in 1912. Served in the Black Sea coastal cruiser flotilla and carried on revolutionary work among soldiers and sailors at Izmail and Ochakov. Transferred from the cruiser *Korshun* to Kronshtadt to attend a school for motor mechanics; completed the course in 1915 and remained at the school as a noncommissioned officer. Took part in the February revolution and was a member of the Petrograd soviet of workers' and soldiers' deputies. Served in the military organization under the CC of the RSDWP.[84]

A sailor of the revolution

The sailors of the revolution were Lenin's support in the October uprising, the days of the establishment of Soviet power, and the years of the Civil War. They were such men as A. Zhelezniakov, I. Kozhanov, K. Dushenov, N.

Markin, E. Berg, P. Dybenko, T. Ul'iantsev and many others. The ablest of them commanded fleets and flotillas in times of peace and became military and political leaders in the army or the fleet. [Among] this distinguished company was Romual'd Adamovich Muklevich. One of those who stormed the Winter Palace, he also led the group which suppressed the counterrevolution at the Vladimir Cadet School. In February 1918 he joined, as a volunteer, the partisan unit under Fabritsius which was fighting advancing German troops. From August 1918 he did valuable service as a commissar on the German border, directing a recruiting bureau for the Reserve Rifle Division. He was then chief of staff of the Sventsian group of forces, military commissar for Minsk gubernia, commissar on the staff of the Sixteenth Army, staff commissar for the western front and, from April 1921, member of the RMC of the western front. During this period he carried out several other duties: member of the military council of the Bobruisk Fortified Center, chairman of the field commission for preventing desertions, and chairman of the Revolutionary Committee of the Vilna gubernia.

From 1922 to 1925 he was commissar at the Red Army Military Academy. At this time he wrote a book, *Politrabota v boevoi obstanovke* (Political Work in Combat Conditions), which was the first general work on the subject. In it he developed the view that political work is not an end in itself but must be subordinated to the commander's strategic and tactical intentions. The work went through four editions between 1924 and 1929.

In 1925 he was appointed deputy chief of the Red Air Force and also chairman of the editorial collegium of the air force journal *Vestnik vozdushnogo flota*. In 1925 he was one of the organizers of the flight of a Soviet aircraft from Moscow to Peking. From August 1926 he was chief of Soviet naval forces and a member of the RMC of the U.S.S.R.

These were the years in which problems of the development of the Soviet Navy were being decided. In reply to the question "What sort of fleet do we need and how fast should it be built?" Muklevich took the line that the development of our fleet should be proportionate to our resources and to the tasks it was required to perform. He felt that our shipbuilding program should be based on three principles: (1) to build only as much as we could afford at any given time; (2) to begin with such ships as we need for defense purposes; (3) to limit ourselves to the capacity of Soviet industry. He repeatedly emphasized that a fleet could not be built in one year or even in several years. For it to be strong and up to date we must be prepared for constant hard work and moral effort.

With his help, the first combat regulations and ship's regulations of the Red Navy were drawn up and introduced. He also helped to edit the journals *Morskoi sbornik* (Naval Miscellany) and *Krasnyi flot* (Red Fleet).

In 1931 V. M. Orlov became chief of the Soviet Navy, and Muklevich, while remaining a member of the RMC of the U.S.S.R., was appointed inspector of naval forces. At the same time he carried out a number of important tasks for the government. For example, he headed a commission which was sent to the Far East to investigate the possibilities of creating a Pacific fleet.

From 1934 he was chief of the main administration of the shipbuilding industry, and at the end of 1936 he became deputy PC for the defense industry. He was a delegate to the Third Congress of the Comintern, the Fifteenth and Seventeenth Party congresses, and several convocations of the CEC of the U.S.S.R. and the All-Russian CEC. In 1928 he received the Order of the Red Banner for his Civil War services.

In all the positions he occupied, he distinguished himself by a broad statesman-like approach to problems, by the search for new, rational methods, and by adherence to Bolshevik principles.

He was unjustly arrested in 1937 and perished on February 9, 1938. The men of the Red Navy remember him with affection as one of the creators of the Soviet Fleet.[85]

SHAMIR ARAKELOVICH OSENIAN

Biographical data

Born at Sanain in the Alaverdi raion; joined the underground Party organization there in 1918. In 1920 he became a teacher in Karindzh village, and in February 1921 took part in the fighting for Khodzhori. After the establishment of Soviet power in Georgia he became instructor and organizer in the Dsekh student committee of the Party and later in the Uzunlarsky raion. Called up in 1923 and became political instructor in the Second Armenian Rifle Regiment; later held other important posts. In 1937 he became principal secretary of the regional Party commission under the political administration of the Trans-caucasian Military District. In the same year he was arrested and became a victim of the cult of personality.[86]

A life devoted to the Party

In the fall of 1932, at exercises held in mountainous conditions, the Armenian Rifle Division showed itself to be one of the best units of the Special Red Banner Caucasian Army. But this did not satisfy its commander and commissar, who was not a man to rest on his laurels. Soon afterward, a number of changes took place in the political and military command. The president of the military tribunal at this time was Shamir Arakelovich Osenian.

Throughout the units and subunits of the division, systematic political and military training was being carried out. The new president of the tribunal visited units, talked to officers and men, and gave valuable advice. I was among those whom he saw two or three times, and I noticed his considerate and thoughtful attitude toward all whom he met. It was not surprising that in March 1933 the divisional Party conference elected him secretary of the [regional] Party Commission, a post in which he gave brilliant proof of his abilities as a Communist organizer. He took part in company tactical exercises and helped the Party bureau secretaries in their tasks of placing personnel and preparing and conducting meetings. He was often to be seen in friendly conversation amid a group of fighting men. He organized close contact with the men's parents and with the factories and farms from which they had been called up. In his letters he spoke warmly of those who had distinguished themselves in training, fighting, and political instruction.

In May 1936, on the Fifteenth anniversary of its foundation, the Armenian Rifle Division received the Order of the Red Banner in recognition of its high state of military and political training. Besides its commander, Akon Atoian, and the head of the political department, Khoren Abramits, Osenian was one of those sent to receive this high award from the Presidium of the CEC of the U.S.S.R.

In May 1937, the Communists of the Transcaucasian military district showed their confidence in Osenian by electing him principal secretary of the regional Party Commission under the political administration of the military district. He had earned this confidence by hard work, ability, and true Communist modesty.

Osenian was born in a poor peasant family at Sanain in the Alaverdi raion. His childhood was spent in cheerless toil. Besides heavy manual labor he worked as an errandboy for the village teacher and at the local medical center. In 1918 he came into contact with the Bolsheviks, who introduced him to underground Party work in Sanain. In 1920 he went as a teacher to Karidzh village, where he organized an underground Bolshevik cell. During the rule of the Georgian Mensheviks and Dashnaks in the "neutral zone" he took an active part in organizing the peasant movement. During the Lori armed uprising in February 1921* he led a small detachment of partisans in the fight for Khodzhori. When Soviet power was established in Georgia he returned to Karindzhi and worked as an instructor and organizer of the Dsekh student committee of the Party and later in the Uzunlarsky raion.

Toward the end of 1923 he was called up for service in the Red Army and was appointed to the medical company of the Armenian Division. In October 1923 he joined the Second Armenian Rifle Regiment, and later held other important posts.

This worthy son of the Leninist Party perished while holding the post of principal secretary of the regional Party commission under the political adminis-

---

* This rebellion was started in the district of Lori, south of Tiflis, by Georgian Mensheviks and Dashnaks. Subsequently it spread through all of Georgia and parts of Armenia. Native participants were helped by the British. The rebellion was suppressed by the Red Army in May 1921, at which time the council of people's commissars of Armenia was created.—ED.

tration of the Transcaucasian Military District. His memory is recalled with affection not only by the comrades who served with him but by all who came in contact with this transparently honest and unswerving Communist.[87]

GAIK ALEKSANDROVICH OSEPIAN

Biographical data

[Army commissar, second class.] A physician; joined the Bolshevik Party in 1913. During 1913-17 he carried on revolutionary work among the troops on the Caucasian front. In 1917-18, member of the organization committee for the establishment of the CP of Armenia, and secretary of its CC. In 1921, secretary of the uezd committee of Aleksandropol' (Leninakan). In 1927, first secretary of the CC of the Armenian CP. In 1929-31, head of the agitation and propaganda department of the political administration of the Red Army, head of the organization department, and then deputy head of the Red Army political administration. From 1931-37, editor of the Armenian Party journal and secretary of the Party organization of the PC for Defense. Arrested during the night of June 30-July 1, 1937; perished shortly thereafter, a victim of the cult of personality.[88]

A commissar's life

On May 30, 1937—a quiet, sunny morning on the last day but one of spring—Gaik Aleksandrovich Osepian sat at his desk and frowned as he idly turned over some sheets of paper. He was to speak next day at the military council of the PC for Defense. Ian Borisovich Gamarnik, head of the Red Army political administration, was seriously ill, and it fell to Osepian as his deputy to deliver a report on the political and moral state of Red Army personnel. The report was ready, but now Osepian was thinking of something else. It was about a month since Tukhachevsky had been arrested and the case against him entrusted to the security authorities. An eminent commander, highly valued by Lenin, a staunch Communist, and now suddenly "a traitor to the motherland."

Every day there were new arrests. It was as though someone had determined to deprive the army of its heads, to remove all its most experienced and devoted commanders and political officers.

The telephone interrupted his thoughts. It was Marshal Bliukher, an old friend.

"Good morning, Vasilii Konstantinovich," said Osepian. "Yes, my report's all ready. A trip to the country? Yes, why not? It's a marvelous day."

Half an hour later, Bliukher arrived. He seemed in a cheerful, even a joking mood. Osepian tried to behave in the same way, but neither could conceal his inner anxiety from the other.

Back from the country, they went to see Gamarnik, who was still in bed, but said he felt better and expected to be able to attend the council next day. Then they returned to Osepian's apartment. It was late in the evening, and they fell into a long and frank conversation on the all-absorbing topic. They could not bring themselves to believe that the best Communists, the pride of the Red Army, had become "enemies of the people."

At one o'clock Bliukher departed, and an hour later a group of strangers opened the apartment door with their own key. "You are arrested," said one of them. He showed a warrant and ordered Osepian to put on civilian dress. The latter replied, "I am a commissar of the Red Army, and I have no clothes except my uniform." Then he called to his wife: "Don't worry, Lisa. It's a mistake—I'll be back soon."

He did not come back.

We members of the agitprop department of the Red Army political administration first met Gaik Aleksandrovich Osepian when he became head of the department in the fall of 1929, having previously served in the Volga military district. I remember our conversation before his arrival:

"Comrades, guess what kind of a specialist Osepian is?"

"A historian? A literary expert? A lawyer?"

"No, he's a doctor!"

Osepian had in fact begun his revolutionary career while still a medical student at Moscow University. He joined the CP in Moscow in 1913 and later carried on underground work among the troops on the Caucasian front. In 1917-18 he was a member of the organization committee set up to found the Communist Party of Armenia, and was secretary of its CC. In 1921, when Armenia was a Soviet state, he was secretary of the uezd committee of Aleksandropol' (now Leninakan). He was in charge of the formation of the First Armenian Division and became its commissar. In 1927 he was elected first secretary of the CC of the Armenian CP, and later the Party again assigned him to war work....

The year, 1930, was the year of collectivization. By a decision of the RMC, the political organs of the army were to furnish, from among the rank and file and junior officers of the Red Army, 100,000 men for work in the countryside. Osepian became the animator and direct organizer of this operation. Soon afterward he was appointed head of the organization department of the Red Army and then deputy head of its political administration. He took on this immense burden without apparent strain, feeling himself in his element. In line with the technical reconstruction of the Red Army, changes were taking place in the nature of the troops called up, increased demands were being made of political officers serving with the forces, and in the political administration itself new departments were being created to deal with the air force and motorized units....

Osepian's tasks were not confined to political administration. When in 1931 it was proposed to start a political journal for the armed forces, he was chosen as its editor. For six years he was secretary of the Party organization in the PC for Defense, which was one of the most important Party units in Moscow.

In 1935 there was a checkup of Party members in the PC for Defense, under a commission headed by Elena Dimitrievna Stasova. Osepian, along with others, was examined in the usual way at a public meeting. Stasova mentioned his good qualities and valuable work as a Party secretary, and then, turning to him, said: "I see from your file that you were awarded the Order of the Red Banner. Why do you not wear it?"

Osepian was indeed a man of extraordinary modesty. Even those of us who had worked with him for years had no idea that he possessed this order.

From whatever angle one surveys his life, it is a shining example of humanity and the beauty of Leninism. How right the Red Army soldier was whom I once heard say this of him: "He's a fine man and no mistake. A commissar through and through!"[89]

PETR MATVEEVICH OSHLEI

Biographical data

Born 1886, died 1937. Joined the Bolshevik Party in 1917 and the Red Army in 1919. In the Civil War he was commissar of a rifle brigade and later of a division, member of the RMC of the Sixth Army, military commissar on the staff in the Ukraine and Crimea. After the war he was secretary of the RMC of the U.S.S.R., administrator of the PC for the Army and Navy, and head of the Red Army military-economic administration.[90]

ALEKSANDR VASIL'EVICH PAVLOV

Biographical data

Born 1880, died 1937. Joined the Red Army in 1918. Political instructor in screen detachments. Commanded a division and the Tenth Army. After the war he commanded a corps and was deputy commander of the Western and Volga Military Districts, assistant inspector of infantry of the Red Army, and head of the Special Faculty of the Frunze Academy.[91]

LEV FILIPPOVICH PECHERSKY

Biographical data

Born 1885, died 1937. A professional revolutionary; joined the Bolshevik Party in 1903. Took an active part in the barricade fighting in 1905. In the

Civil War he was a member of the RMC of the Tenth Army, and after it
of the RMC of the Turkestan front; also commanded special purpose units
on that front. Performed important government work after 1924.[92]

ALEKSEI MAKAROVICH PEREMYTOV

Biographical data

Born 1888, died 1938. A captain in the Tsarist Army; joined the Red Army
in 1918. In the Civil War he was chief of staff of a division, head of the
operational department of the staff on the southern front, deputy chief of staff
on the western front, and chief of staff of the North Caucasian Military District.
After the war he was chief of staff of the Fifth Red Banner Army and several
Military Districts, and an instructor at the Red Army Military Academy.[93]

EVGENII LEONIDOVICH PERFIL'EV

Biographical data

Born before 1900; date of death unknown. In 1917 he was a member of
the RMC and assistant to the chairman of the executive committee of the Tashkent
soviet. He was arrested, but set free on the night of October 31 by the victorious
workers and soldiers. After the October Revolution, at the third regional congress
of soviets of Turkestan, he was elected PC of military affairs of the Turkestan
region and military commissar of the Turkestan Republic. With I. O. Tobolin,
A. Ia. Pershin, A. A. Kazakov, D. I. Mandzhara, and others, he took an
active part in forming the first Red Guard and Red Army units. In December
1917, on the orders of the Turkestan CPC, he led a detachment to Ashkhabad,
where he helped to restore the situation and consolidate Soviet power. At the
end of December he led the First Tashkent revolutionary fighting detachment
of soldiers and railroad workers to defeat the troops of ataman Dutov. Afterward
he led the detachment to Samarkand, where it took an active part in defeating
and disarming the White Cossacks who were trying to overthrow Soviet power
in Turkestan. As military commissar of the Turkestan Republic he was responsible for the disarming of soldiers of the old army, after which the more
revolutionary-minded were enlisted in the Red Guard and the Red Army. In
February 1918 he commanded a group of detachments which defeated the counterrevolutionary "Kokand autonomy" movement. In summer 1918 he fell gravely
ill and was recalled to the Urals, where he later took an active part in routing
the White Guardists. After the Civil War he held several high posts in the
Red Army. In 1930-38 he was military procurator of the Ukraine military
district. Arrested in 1938, he became a victim to the cult of Stalin's personality.[94]

IAKOV KHRISTOFOROVICH PETERS

Biographical data

Born 1886, died 1942. Soviet Party and state leader. Joined the CP in 1904. Born in Latvia, the son of a farm laborer. While working at Libava (Libau) he joined the local branch of the SDPLR. During the revolution of 1905-7 he carried on propaganda among peasants and farm laborers; was arrested in 1907. From 1909 to 1917 he lived in exile and was a member of the London group of the SDPLR. After the February revolution he returned to Russia and did propaganda work for the Riga branch of the SDPLR, was elected a member of the CC of the SDPLR and represented it on the CC of the RSDWP(B), and edited the newspaper *Tsinia*. During the October Revolution he was a member of the Petrograd RMC, a delegate to the Second All-Russian Congress of Soviets, and a member of the All-Russian CEC. After the revolution he was a member of the collegium and deputy chairman of the All-Russian NKVD and chairman of the Revolutionary Tribunal. In 1919-20 he was commander of the Petrograd and Tula fortified zones and a member of the Tula military council. In 1920-22 he was a member of the Turkestan bureau of the CC of the RCP(B) and plenipotentiary representative of the All-Union NKVD in Turkestan. From 1923 he was a member of the OGPU collegium. During the Twelfth to Sixteenth Party congresses he was elected a member of the Central Control Commission of the CPSU and was chairman of its Moscow control committee and a member of the commission of Party control under the CC of the CPSU. Subjected to illegal repression; posthumously rehabilitated.[95]

RUDOL'F AVGUSTOVICH PETERSON

The Kremlin commandant

It was early spring, 1920. A Red Army detachment marched along the street singing. The houses were covered with posters advertising public debates, lectures, meetings. The Russian Telegraph Agency's daily sheet gave the latest news from the fronts.

A man in uniform left the office of the Party CC. He had just had a conversation there which determined the whole future course of his life. The CC had decided that he, Rudol'f Avgustovich Peterson, was to be commandant of the Moscow Kremlin.

This was an immense responsibility. From now on he would answer for Lenin's personal safety, for the maintenance of order at the seat of the Soviet government, and for the protection of congresses of soviets, CC plenums, and the various conferences held in Moscow. And he was not yet twenty-three years old. Would he be equal to the difficult task? When he expressed his doubts to the CC, they answered: "We did not choose you at random. You have done well in several responsible jobs and we are sure you can manage this one. Lenin himself took a personal concern in your appointment."

It was true that since the beginning of the Civil War the Party had directed him to one crucial sector after another. When the Left SRs had rebelled in the Tambov gubernia, he had been put in command of the detachment which suppressed the rebellion. Later he had fought the White Cossacks on the Don and had been a division commissar on the front against Iudenich.

Once in the fall of 1918, in the Voronezh raion, when Peterson was commandant of a train of the PC for the Army and Navy, Iakir, then a member of the RMC of the Eighth Army, had come to him with alarming news. A mutiny had broken out in one of the regiments: a unit incited by counterrevolutionaries had refused to carry out the orders of the Red command. Together, without any escort, Iakir and Peterson [detached the train's] engine and set off on it for Ostrogozhsk. A patrol of mutineers stopped them and brought them to the staff headquarters, where drunken revelry was going on. The prisoners were in a highly dangerous position, but boldness saved the day.

Iakir said sternly to the regimental commander Sakharov: "The High Command has been informed that you intend to betray Soviet power and open the way to the enemy. If this is true, I have orders to shoot you."

Sakharov, taken aback, submitted. His regiment, stiffened by Communists, later fought bravely on various fronts of the Civil War.

Peterson could remember many such episodes. How often death had stared him in the face from the black barrel of a revolver!

So here he was in the Kremlin. He met the deputy commandant, Kruklis, who was, like him, a Latvian rifleman. A vast number of urgent matters had to be decided. Despite the efforts of the previous commandant, Mal'kov, many were still living in the Kremlin who had no business there and for whom it was necessary to find other quarters. Part of the area was encumbered with debris and building materials. A general clearing-out of the governmental quarters was overdue. Important Party workers and their families were constantly visiting the Kremlin and had to be housed properly.

On May 1 the CC organized an all-Russian day of overtime labor, which also applied to the Kremlin. Before 8:00 a.m. Peterson called at Lenin's apartment —the latter was already dressed—and they walked to the CPC building, before which were students attending the Kremlin machine-gun courses. Peterson went up to Borisov, the commissar in charge of the courses, and said that Lenin wished to take part in the working day. Lenin stood alongside Borisov and said to him: "Show me what I must do."...

Some days later there was a graduation parade of Red commanders, and those who had attended the course asked that Lenin be photographed with them before they went to the front. Peterson passed on their request and the photograph was taken, with Peterson standing beside Lenin.

The young commandant had much to do on Lenin's orders. Sometimes Lenin would make observations. Once, having heard that those attending the course were poorly fed, he went to the kitchen himself and tasted one or two dishes and ordered portions to be sent to the commandant, as a reminder to take an interest in the men's welfare. Later Peterson reported to Lenin that he had done everything possible to improve the quality of the food in the Kremlin military school.

Gradually conditions of peace returned, and the Soviet seat of government developed the traditions and atmosphere of imperturbable order which have become an example for all Soviet institutions. In recognition of the commandant's services, the RMC of the Republic in 1922 conferred on him the Order of the Red Banner....

In January 1924 a fearful, tragic event afflicted the country: Lenin's death. The committee which organized the great leader's funeral consisted of Dzerzhinsky, Voroshilov, Bonch-Bruevich, Avanesov, and Peterson. The last-named was entrusted with the duty of supervising the construction of a mausoleum. The work went on in bitter cold around the clock. The teams which hacked at the earth on the site were relieved every two hours, and beams and planks were brought by hundreds of carts. At the end of four days a simple, modest mausoleum of dark gray wood was completed; it somewhat resembled the present one in appearance, and stood for several years. At that time the solemn ritual of changing the guard at the mausoleum was instituted, in the form in which it has since been carried out by generations of Kremlin soldiers.

In 1928 reports were made on the command staff of the Red Army, and Peterson was described as follows by B. M. Shaposhnikov, chief of staff of the Red Army and future Marshal of the Soviet Union:

A strong-willed, energetic, and resolute officer with much initiative. Is himself disciplined and knows how to enforce discipline in others. Has great organizing ability and knows how to lead and teach. Studies thoroughly the tasks entrusted to him and works them out in detail. An excellent worker.

In 1932 Peterson received the Order of Lenin, and two years later he was elected a member of the CEC of the U.S.S.R. He remained commandant of the Kremlin for fifteen years and perished tragically in 1937, a victim of slander and arbitrary rule.[96]

SERGEI ANDREEVICH PIONTKOVSKY

Biographical data

Born October 8, 1891; died March 8, 1937. Party names Ivanovsky, Espe. A Soviet scholar, one of the first professional Marxist historians; corresponding member of the Communist Academy and the Academy of Sciences of the Belorussian SSR. Joined the CC in 1919.

Born at Odessa, the son of a professor of law. In 1914 he graduated at the history and language faculty of Kazan University and continued his studies in order to become a professor of Russian history. Took part in the students' revolutionary movement from 1910. After the October Revolution he was PC of labor of the Kazan gubernia. In 1919-20 he worked in the Higher Institute of Popular Education at Kazan. In 1920 he moved to Moscow, where he was an original member of the commission for the study of the history of the CP and helped to found the archives of the October Revolution. From May 1921 he was a professor at Sverdlov Communist University and at the same time deputy editor of the journal *Prolatarskaia revolutsiia*. From 1922 he was a lecturer and then professor at Moscow State University, and in the 1930s a professor at Moscow Institute of Philosophy, Literature and History, and at the Institute of Red Professors. From 1929 he was a member of the section for the study of the history of the proletariat, a part of the historical institute of the Communist Academy. In 1934, in accordance with a decree of the CC of the CPSU and the CPC of the U.S.S.R., he was co-author of a textbook history of the U.S.S.R. and a member of the editorial board of the fourth volume of the History of the Party, under the chairmanship of Emelian Iaroslavsky. Author and editor of many works of documentation and monographs on the history of the working class and the revolutionary movement in Russia, the February and October revolutions and the civil war, and works on historiography. Subjected to illegal repression; posthumously rehabilitated.[97]

SEMEN ANDREEVICH PUGACHEV

Biographical data

Born 1889, died 1938. An officer in the Tsarist Army; joined the Red Army in 1918. In the Civil War he was head of the administrative department of the staff of the Ural military district, head of the operational department of the staff of the Second Army, and chief of staff of the Caucasian front. After the war he became chief of staff of the Special Red Banner Army, commander of the Turkestan front, deputy chief of staff of the Red Army, and chief of staff of the Ural and Central Asian military districts.[98]

IURII VLADIMIROVICH SABLIN

Biographical data

[Division commander.] Born at Iur'ev (Tartu) on November 24, 1897. Studied at Moscow Commercial Institute (now the Plekhanov Institute of Political

Economy) and was a nonresident student at Moscow University. Joined a student SR group at the institute, end of 1915. In summer 1916, having completed the first part of his course, he volunteered for active service and fought on the southwestern and Rumanian fronts as a junior ordnance technician in an artillery battery. He was gassed and, after recovery, attended the Second Moscow School for Ensigns, which he left in May 1917. He then served as a junior company officer in the Fifty-sixth Reserve Infantry Regiment.[99]

The career of a division commander

On October 31, 1917, Sablin actually commanded the revolutionary detachment which advanced from Strastnoi Boulevard to the Nikitskie Gates, capturing the headquarters of the municipal authorities and 300 cadets who were defending it. The fight went on until late evening, and Sablin was wounded by a bullet. Aleksei Tolstoy has recorded the episode in his *Khozhdenie po Mukam* (The Road to Calvary). At this time Sablin was a Left SR, but the Moscow Bolshevik paper nevertheless wrote: *"Our comrade,* the Left SR Sablin, was wounded." In March 1917 the soldiers had elected him to the executive committee of the Moscow soviet of soldiers' deputies, and at the second congress of soviets he became a member of the CEC. Next day, on October 27, he was appointed to the staff of the Moscow revolutionary committee, and soon after the victorious October uprising in Moscow he became a member of the presidium of the Moscow soviet of workers' and soldiers' deputies.

In the central state archives of the October Revolution, among the documents relating to the stormy times of the revolution and Civil War there is a certificate, No. 2104 issued on December 14, 1917, by the staff of the Moscow military district, which reads:

> The present document is issued to Comrade Georgii Sablin, member of the CEC of the Soviet of Peasants', Workers' and Soldiers' Deputies and the presidium of the Moscow Soviet of Workers' and Soldiers' Deputies, to certify that he has been appointed commander of the First Moscow Revolutionary Composite Force, in token of which our signature and seal are appended.

With this mandate and at the head of a force of 1,500 Red Guards, Sablin proceeded to Kharkov, where he placed himself at the disposal of Antonov-Ovseenko. Having routed the Whites who were occupying Kupiansk, his force advanced on Debal'tsevo. On December 25 he telegraphed to the Moscow soviet: "First Moscow Revolutionary Detachment, having received orders and proceeded to its destination, fully conscious of urgent need to suppress Kaledin's adventurers, greets Moscow workers and soldiers and all revolutionary organizations." Later came a second telegram:

> Moscow revolutionary troops together with Red Guardists and workers have taken Debal'tsevo. Advance guard has taken Rodakovo. Hour of decisive blow at counter-revolutionaries is at hand. Sablin, Commander of Moscow Detachment.

From then until the final defeat of General Kaledin, the papers printed victorious communiqués from the front on the Don, where Sablin was pursuing the counter-revolutionaries.

At this time, the western screen was created to defend the Soviet Republic against German invasion. Sablin and Tukhachevsky were appointed commissars for the Moscow raion. At the fourth all-Russian congress of soviets, Sablin was again elected to the All-Russian CEC, though he still remained a Left SR. On July 6, 1918, the Left SR leaders organized a revolt against Soviet power. Sablin played a part of some importance in the revolt: it was he, with Prosh'ian, who arrested F. E. Dzerzhinsky, the president of the All-Russian Cheka, when the latter came to the rebel headquarters.*

In December Sablin went to the Ukraine, where power had been usurped by a counterrevolutionary directorate under Vinnichenko and Petliura. Sablin took command of the insurgent forces in the Kharkov area, and commanded first a regiment and then a brigade against Petliura and later Denikin. He showed his devotion to the Soviet power by valiant fighting, and in May 1919 he joined the Bolshevik Party.

In October-November 1919, when Denikin's troops were fighting at Orel, Sablin commanded a group of Fourteenth Army troops, after which he succeeded R. P. Eideman as commander of the Forty-first Rifle Division. This unit, which formed part of the Fourteenth Army, decisively defeated Denikin's forces. Eideman, then commanding the neighboring Forty-sixth Division, recalled subsequently: "The Forty-first Division on our right flank advanced with remarkable speed, rolling back the disorganized cavalry forces of General Iuzefovich, which ceased to offer resistance. Thus Kharkov's fate was decided." At 10:00 p.m. on December 9 Sablin issued the order to "consolidate on the right flank and conduct on the left flank a vigorous attack with the object of taking Kharkov by the evening of December 10, advancing from the west by way of the Kholod-naia hill." On the night of the 11th-12th, units of the Forty-first and Eighth Cavalry divisions entered Kharkov. The next day victory was crowned by an order posted in the streets of the town: "All state property within the limits of the city of Kharkov is hereby declared to be the property of the working people." The order was signed "Iu. V. Sablin, Division Commander and Chief of the Garrison."

The troops of the southern front rapidly pursued Denikin's retreating forces. Two White corps (those of Kutepov and Iuzefovich) retreated southwestward

---

*The German ambassador to Moscow, Count Wilhelm Mirbach, was assassinated on July 6, 1918, by Iakov Blumkin, a Left SR who served in the Cheka. Feliks Dzerzhinsky, head of the Cheka, went to the headquarters of the SRs with the intention of arresting the leaders. He was disarmed by Iurii Sablin and was placed under arrest. Other Cheka officials were also arrested. A detachment of 940 SRs then succeeded in capturing the central post and telegraph office and held Dzerzhinsky as hostage. While under arrest, Dzerzhinsky talked to the SR soldiers and persuaded them to free him; subsequently, twelve of the SRs were shot. Blumkin fled, but surrendered in April 1919 and censured the SRs. In May he was granted amnesty. See Feodor Gladkov, "The 'Rooster Conspiracy,'" *Molodoi kommunist,* no. 12 (December 1967), 48-53. -ED.

from Kharkov toward Rostov and those of Shilling and Dragomirov retreated toward Odessa, while Slashchev's corps, losing hope of maintaining itself in the northern Tauris, withdrew across the Crimean isthmuses. At the beginning of March 1920 the Estonian Division, whose command Sablin took over on February 20, together with the Eighth Cavalry Division, forced its way across the Perekop Isthmus and dislodged Slashchev's troops from their positions at Iushun'. However, there were not sufficient forces to exploit the victory, and the command of the southwestern front did not send reinforcements. This mistake was noted by Lenin on March 15 ("They did not move up sufficient force"). The Whites counterattacked in strength and drove the Soviet troops out of the Crimea. This was the beginning of the confrontation between the battle-weakened Thirteenth Army and Wrangel's forces, which strove to emerge from the Crimea into the side spaces of the southern Ukraine and the Don basin—a situation which continued, with fluctuations of fortune, until the final liquidation of Wrangel's forces in November 1920.

The Forty-sixth Rifle Division covered the Isthmus of Perekop, the shores of the Sivash and the Sea of Azov, opposing again and again the attempts of Wrangel's troops to force the Perekop Isthmus and effect landings south of Melitopol and at Genichesk. Sablin took over command of this division on April 3. Ten days later, Wrangel's forces made a landing at the village of Kirilovka south of Melitopol and at the port of Khorly, and attempted to advance northward. Sablin at once went to Melitopol and personally took charge of operations. But while the fight was proceeding, the enemy landed more forces at Genichesk, from which town they dislodged the division's 409th and 410th regiments. Sablin himself led these regiments into the counterattack and was in the thick of the street fighting. When the RMC of the army learned of the defeat of both landings, it recommended Sablin for the Order of the Red Banner. He did not, however, receive the decoration for this exploit until later, after another one had already been conferred on him. Order No. 226 of the Republican RMC, dated July 31, 1921 stated:

> The Order of the Red Banner is conferred for the second time on Comrade Iurii Vladimirovich Sablin for valor displayed in the course of stubborn fighting against the enemies of the workers' and peasants' power in the Ukraine in 1920, when his outstanding military exploits contributed to the defeat of counterrevolution in the south. In action against landing forces of the Wrangel army southeast of Melitopol from April 15 to 17, 1920, comrade Sablin directed the operations of his division ably and energetically, broke the enemy's resistance and drove him into the sea, so that the enemy troops were drowned or taken prisoner.
>
> Kamenev,
> Commander-in-Chief of
> Armed Forces of the Republic
> Danilov,
> Member of the Republican RMC.

... In 1921-23 Sablin was enrolled in advanced courses, at a military academy. The heat of fighting had given place to peaceful studies. For Sablin's active nature, this was an abrupt change. Having a wider military background than his fellow students, he found the courses easy. The impetuous energy of the twenty-five-year-old commander required a fuller outlet.

This was a time of vigorous activity for the Military-Scientific Society, formed at the end of 1920 on the initiative of the Party organization of the academy. Sablin was elected to the governing presidium of the society and became chief secretary of the presidium and afterward head of the publishing department and member of the society's editorial collegium. In July 1921 the society began to publish its journal *Krasnaia armiia* (Red Army), to which Sablin was the most active contributor. Apart from numerous articles, he reviewed books on the history of the Civil War, White Guardist memoirs, and the journals published by branches of the society, such as *Voennaia mysl'* (Military Thought—Tashkent), *Armiia i revoliutsiia* (Army and Revolution—Kharkov), and *Voenno-politicheskaia mysl'* (Military and Political Thought—Chita). The society devoted much attention to studying the experience of the Civil War, and in addition to *Krasnaia armiia* it began to publish collections of works by its members. Its staff lectured on the history of the war, both on its own premises and in civilian colleges. Sablin lectured at the Sverdlov Communist University on the inception and termination of the campaigns against Wrangel, which he knew from his own experience....

While still studying at the academy and playing an active part in the work of the Military-Scientific Society, Sablin worked as military editor of *Izvestiia*. At this time he became interested in aviation. The Soviet Air Force was being created, and many Party, state, and military authorities were studying how to arouse public interest in this subject. One of the first steps taken was to set up the Society of Friends of the Air Force, the precursor of Osoaviakhim and the present DOSAAF. Sablin was among the initiators of this development.

His rich all-around experience as a military commander was once again brought into play when in November 1926 he became commander and military commissar of the Ninety-ninth Rifle Division (Ukrainian military district). His seniors no longer made mention in their reports of "lack of balance and staying power." The report on him for 1927-28, signed by K. A. Rakh'ia, describes [Sablin] as "a well-developed all-around commander ... interested and active in social life; looked up to by his subordinates ... well disciplined; thinks out his assignments carefully and executes them quickly, taking due account of circumstances; shows much initiative and firmness of character....

On November 22, 1933, Sablin reported to the commission charged with purging the Party. He described his career and how he had broken with the SRs on perceiving the "errors" of their policy, and had joined the Bolsheviks. Lebedev, who spoke after him, declared: "Sablin is one of those who have earned their Party membership by shedding blood for the sake of Soviet power." Another Party member who had known Sablin since the Civil War summarized his career as follows: "From terrorist romanticism to that of armed combat

... I served under Sablin in the Forty-first Division. We Red Army men went into battle inspired by the example of this intrepid commander and Bolshevik.'' Nazarov, who was not a Party member and had not known Sablin in Civil War days but only later in the field of military organization, added: "He is a strong, staunch Bolshevik, to whose leadership we owe our present achievements. He managed to instill the spirit of shock workers into us all.''

On November 26, 1935, the PC for Defense, in Order No. 2484, conferred on Sablin the rank of Division Commander. He was only thirty-eight years old and at the height of his powers, having had not only rich war experience and theoretical training but also fifteen years of varied service in the Red Army during its formative period and reconstruction, as well as thorough political education in the service of the Communist Party. In him, the Red Army possessed a commander of wide vision. But he too was engulfed by the wave of unjustified repression which swept away part of the Red Army command in the fall of 1936. He was arrested on a slanderous charge on September 25 and shot on June 19, 1937. He has now been posthumously rehabilitated as a true-hearted warrior, citizen and Communist.[100]

ALEKSANDR IGNAT'EVICH SEDIAKIN

Biographical data

[Army commander, second class.] Born 1893, died 1937. Joined the Bolshevik Party in 1917. In the Civil War he was a commissar and commanded a regiment, a brigade, and a division, also the Kronshtadt fortress and the Petrograd Fortified Zone. After the war he commanded the Fifth Red Banner Army and the Volga military district and occupied other senior command posts.[101]

EVGENII NIKOLAEVICH SERGEEV

Biographical data

Born 1887, died 1938. A lieutenant colonel in the Tsarist Army; joined the Red Army in 1918. In the Civil War he was chief of staff of a division and then of an army. After the war, chief of staff of several military districts and lecturer at the Red Army Military Academy.[102]

ERNEST GENRIKHOVICH SHAKHT

Biographical data

[Major-general of the air force.] Born 1904, died 1941. Born at Basle, Switzerland. Joined the Bolshevik Party in 1926. Worked from the age of fourteen as assistant to a painter, then to an electrician. Joined the Komsomol in 1918. In 1922 the bureau of the Communist Youth International appointed him to Berlin, then to Moscow, where he worked on the international workers' committee for aid to starving peoples. Attended the Borisoglebsk Aviation School and afterward became commander of a detachment. Received the Order of Lenin May 25, 1936. Fought in the Spanish Civil War, and in 1937 was made a Hero of the Soviet Union. Executed in 1941, a month before the outbreak of war with Germany, on Beria's personal instructions.[103]

We shall not die

"I had no doubts about him, and I believe that he did his duty honestly as a member of the CPSU and a Soviet citizen." Those words were written by Shakht about a colleague who was in disfavor during the cult of personality. Every syllable of this brief report reflects its writer's nobility and faith in human nature. The sheet bears the date November 10, 1940, and on the right, at the top, the clearly written signature: E. Shakht.

The Communist General Shakht was not mistaken—the man for whom he spoke was not guilty. Justice triumphed and the man was rehabilitated at the Twentieth Congress, which restored the good name of so many who had suffered unjustly, including Shakht himself, general of the air force and a true soldier of the Party.

His fate was a strange and surprising one. I shall relate what I have heard from his war comrades and discovered in archives. I first saw him in a photograph. When I turned the first page of his dossier, I saw the face of a man with lively eyes and an open face lit by a scarcely perceptible smile. In the buttonhole of his tunic was a badge of rank, and on his left breast the Order of the Red Banner. The photograph dated from 1936, when he wrote his autobiography.

He was born in 1904 at Basle, Switzerland. By origin and circumstances he belonged to the working class. He knew German and French. At the age of fourteen he went to work, first as an assistant to a painter and then in a power plant. He joined the Komsomol in 1918, and worked in Switzerland smuggling Communists across the frontier. He was twice arrested, and was tried for incitement of youth at the time of the general strike. In 1922 the Communist Youth International assigned him to Berlin and then to Moscow, where he worked in the international workers' committee for aid to starving peoples. He joined the CPSU in 1926....

The U.S.S.R. became his second fatherland. Having come to the Soviet Republic born in the fires of October, how could he remain indifferent to the rapid growth of national construction that was in progress and to the need for thousands of brave men to defend the Soviet state? He joined their ranks.

"Are you determined to do this, Ernst?" they asked him. "Yes," he replied laconically, and added, with a gleam of enthusiasm: "My dream is to be an aviator."

So he was directed to the Borisoglebsk school for pilots. But this, it turned out, was in its infancy, and it would be a long time before he could fly. Lecture halls were being built alongside the barracks which had once housed dashing cavalrymen, and hangars were being erected on the airfield. The would-be fliers took a hand in the work, and there was nothing to distinguish the blue-eyed twenty-year-old youth who worked as hard as the rest. Only the Russian language gave him trouble at first. Going to fetch bricks on one occasion, he explained "I go to bricks." When his new friends burst out laughing, he replied with a cheerful smile.

In the evenings a man of short stature used to visit the pupils' quarters. As soon as he crossed the threshold a shout would go up from end to end of the large barracks, which had been buzzing like a beehive "Boys, here's the Commissar!" It was Zhan Robertovich Akkerman, member of the Party, who at once became the center of a lively group. He seemed about thirty, but was a pupil on the same footing as the others. Nevertheless, they listened to him with unconcealed excitement. He had tales to tell, for he had been one of the legendary Latvian sharpshooters in the Civil War, had seen Lenin and met Karl Liebknecht. This was the war commissar for whom Shakht spoke years later, on the eve of the war, during the period of the cult of personality.

It came about naturally that Akkerman took Shakht in hand and became his instructor, helping him with his Russian and with political self-education.

In the spring, flying at last began. Shakht's instructor was named Kish—an experienced pilot, a real old hand....

Shakht fearlessly took on any and every assignment, risking his own life in the fight for human happiness, led on by a sense of duty and the promptings of his Communist heart....

His war service ended with the defeat of the Basmachi bands; but the pilot Shakht still had much work to do. He taught his juniors to fly, and the unit which he commanded stood in high repute. He was one of those chosen by reason of their ability to attend a course in "blind" flying. Later he attended another course, this time for the advanced training of officers, and was then appointed to command a squadron. The documents do not show in detail how successfully he performed his task, but we know that on May 25, 1936, he received the supreme award—the Order of Lenin.

In that year storm clouds formed over Spain, and the fight for freedom called. "A man dangerous as a whirlwind flew to Madrid, to the destruction of fascism"—thus the poet wrote of the Communist Shakht. True to his international duty, he was one of the first Soviet flying men who volunteered to fight for the Spanish people's sake. As regards the quality of his service, the documents say briefly: "A brave commander, organizing and taking part in all his squadron's flights over the battle field and deep into the enemy lines. By bold attacks on enemy airfields and accurate fire he has put out of action dozens of enemy planes including heavy bombers."

What do his war comrades relate of their former commander? We have been able to trace some of them, and have talked to the squadron's former navigator, Hero of the Soviet Union G. M. Prokof'ev, now a major general in the reserve air force. "Ernst?" he said thoughtfully, and after a short pause went on with conviction:

> Yes, he was a strong man and a true Communist. I was navigator to lots of pilots, but Nikolai Ostriakov and Shakht were in a class by themselves. I met Shakht in Spain and we soon got used to flying together. He was a first-class pilot....
>
> At the New Year they told some of us we had been decorated—I got the Red Banner. Just then, Shakht and some others were called away on an urgent mission. When they returned I told him about my award. He congratulated me warmly and invited me to his quarters. In my excitement I had forgotten to say that for some reason his name was not on the list of those decorated. When we got to his room I remembered this and asked him the reason. With evident emotion, he replied quietly: "I have been named a Hero of the Soviet Union." We embraced, and suddenly, perhaps for the first time in his life, this brave man burst crying.
>
> "What is it, Ernst?" I exclaimed. Recovering himself, he stammered out: "You and I flew together—you've even flown more than I have. It's embarrassing—do you understand?"
>
> We talked for a long time that evening. When we parted, he said: "They've forbidden me to fly again here. But you and I will fly together—next time." And we did—the whole squadron, under my old commander, Hero of the Soviet Union Ernst Shakht.

Such was General Prokof'ev's story; and I remembered a short newspaper item and certain other words—those spoken by Major General Ernst Shakht on February 27, 1937, when he received at the Kremlin the country's supreme award of a Golden Star, No. 15. Speaking also on behalf of the others decorated, he ended with words that rang like an oath: "It is easy to give one's life for the Soviet socialist motherland. But we shall not die—we shall conquer."

But as things turned out, he did not ride the fiery skies in the turmoil of war; a month before the struggle broke out he was shot by Beria's own order. None the less, he remains in our ranks, since he believed implicitly in victory. He believed, then and always—when he was a Komsomol member, when he flew into battle as a Communist, and when, as a general and the director of an advanced school of flying tactics, he and other commanders forged our country's air power.

This is what the Communist Party had done for him. He was its soldier. The words that he wrote about one of his comrades in arms were true of himself: "He did his duty honestly as a member of the CPSU and a Soviet citizen."[104]

IOSIF EREMEEVICH SLAVIN

Biographical data

Born 1893, died 1938. Army commissar, second class. Joined the Bolshevik

Party in 1918. In the Civil War he was head of the political department of a brigade, a division, and a district. After the war, member of the RMC and head of political administration of several military districts and of military educational establishments of the Red Army. Member of the military council of the PC for Defense.[105]

ANDREI EVGEN'EVICH SNESAREV

Biographical data

Born 1865, died 1937. A lieutenant general in the Tsarist Army. Joined the Red Army in May 1918 and took an active part in the Civil War. For two years from August 1919 he was director of the General Staff Academy, later professor and chief instructor in military geography and statistics. Directed the oriental faculty of the academy and was member of the Senior Military Editorial Council. Hero of Labor. Subjected to repression. Released from concentration camp because of illness and died at home in 1937.[106]

IVAN IAKOVLEVICH STROD

Biographical data

Born 1894 at Ludz (Latvia); died 1937. Joined the Red Army in 1918. Commanded a special purpose detachment in Iakutia. In 1920, commanded a shock cavalry regiment and took part in fighting the Japanese and Semenov forces. In 1921, fought for the establishment of Soviet power in Iakutia. During the Civil War he received the Order of the Red Banner three times. After the war he became a writer. In 1937 he fell victim to the cult of Stalin's personality.[107]

"The Chapaev of Iakutia"

Such was the nickname of Ivan Iakovlevich Strod, a Latvian born in the small town of Ludz who became a national hero of the Iakut people. A monument is to be raised to him at Amga, the scene of his successful battles with the White Guardists. His name has been given to a street in Iakutsk, a motor ship which plies on the Lena River, an important collective farm, and a secondary school.

Strod, a young worker, was called up as a private in the First World War and returned from the front as an ensign, decorated with all four grades of the St. George's Cross. In April 1918 he began his career as a Red Army fighter, serving in the First Irkutsk Cavalry Division against the White Czechs and Semenov's bands. Finding himself in territory occupied by Kolchak, he succeeded, together with the Communist I. A. Zakharov, in organizing the armed uprising which led to the overthrow of Kolchak's forces in the Olekminsk district.

The military revolutionary staff of Iakutia appointed Strod commander of a special purpose detachment which, in fierce December weather near the coldest point on the earth's surface, effected the arduous march to Suntar, where it established Soviet power.

In 1920 Strod commanded a shock cavalry regiment which routed the Japanese interventionists and Semenov forces. In the fall of that year he carried out a raid which penetrated deep into the enemy's rear area, and scored a crushing victory at Verkhne-Ul'khunskaia, the headquarters of the White units led by Colonel Tokmakov and the Cossack captain Tapkhai. For this he received his first Order of the Red Banner.

At the end of 1921 the position in Iakutia was again critical. The remoteness of the area and the bad state of the roads enabled the counterrevolutionaries to set up a new anti-Soviet group. The White kulaks occupied nearly all of the Iakut territory, under a "government" headed by nationalists, White Guard officers, kulaks, and merchants. The defenders of Soviet power retained only a small area around Iakutsk and Viliuisk. At this desperate hour regular Soviet forces from Irkutsk came to the aid of the Yakut people. Their commander was Nestor Kalandarashvili, and the first detachment was led by I. Ia. Strod. The march was one of extraordinary difficulty—some 2,000 miles of dense wintry taiga and mountain passes lay between Irkutsk and beleaguered Iakutsk. Strod's detachment covered the distance in forty days, beating off White raids as they went, establishing Soviet power and organizing volunteer detachments. Exceptionally severe fighting took place at Amga, where Strod's men took an active part in defeating the enemy's "northern group," while his "southern group" was soon liquidated at Tekhriur, thus sealing the fate of the kulaks and White Guards.

Many in the White Guard army had been enrolled by force or deceit, and on the Party's orders Strod now became an agitator and diplomat. He performed these tasks in masterly fashion, and after the negotiations he conducted, the main White forces in the Viliuisk district surrendered peacefully. Strod thus became immensely popular with the local inhabitants.

The civil war in Iakutia came to an end, but a new danger soon appeared. Forces under General Pepeliaev landed at the port of Aiai and advanced inland. Strod rapidly assembled his troops and marched to meet the enemy. The latter surrounded Strod's forces at Sasyl-Sysy in the so-called "ice siege"—one of the most heroic pages in the fight against the Whites in Iakutia. During eighteen days of incessant enemy attack, Strod, who was twice wounded, displayed exceptionally brilliant qualities as a commander. His troops, by their stubborn resistance, diverted the main force of Pepeliaev's attack and prevented him from advancing on Iakutsk. It was at this time that the Iakut people gave

Strod the name of "Our Chapaev," and the Iakut government bestowed on him a gold medal.

During the Civil War, Strod received the Order of the Red Banner three times. He was a gifted commander, a humane, sensitive person, and a talented writer. His works *V taige* (In the Taiga) and *V iakutskoi taige* (In the Iakutian Taiga) describe the fight to establish Soviet power in the Far East.

In 1937 this true Communist became a victim of slander and arbitrary rule. After the Twentieth Party Congress the hero's name and the memory of his military deeds were once more restored to the people. This news was received with particular joy in Iakutia, where the memory of the Red commander had never ceased to live in story and word-of-mouth tradition.[108]

NIKOLAI ALEKSANDROVICH SULEIMAN

Biographical data

Born 1878, died 1938. A general in the Tsarist army; joined the Red Army in 1918. Taught and did research work in military academies.[109]

ALEKSANDR ANDREEVICH SVECHIN

Biographical data

Born 1878, died 1938. Major general in the Tsarist Army; joined the Red Army in March 1918. In the Civil War he was chief of staff of the western sector of the screen, military instructor for the Smolensk raion of the screen, and chief of the All-Russian General Staff. Later he was lecturer at the Red Army Military Academy, chief instructor on strategy to all military academies, and a professor.[110]

VLADIMIR KHRISTOFOROVICH TAIROV (TER-GRIGOR'IAN)

Biographical data

Born 1894, died 1937. Born on September 4, 1894, in the village of Ispagandzhuk in the Karabakh Mountain area (Azerbaidzhan). Joined the Bolshevik Party in 1918, and the Red Guard during the October Revolution. Was subsequently state commissar for the four Moscow banks. Served in the Red Army from 1918; commissar of the First (Kamyshin) Division, member of the RMC of the Special Group on the southern front, commissar on the staff of the Ninth and later the Tenth Army. In 1922, political commissar on the staff of the First Cavalry Army. Attended senior courses at the [Moscow] Military Academy. In 1926, military adviser to the Soviet mission in China, then in France. Subsequently member of the military council of the Special Red Banner Army of the Far East. In February 1935, ambassador of the U.S.S.R. to the Mongolian People's Republic. Received Order of Lenin, January 1937. He was a victim of the cult of personality, June 1937.[111]

A bold warrior and a gifted diplomat

Vladimir Tairov is among the most eminent military and political leaders our Party has produced. Tempered in the fire of revolution, he devoted his whole life to fighting for the victory of the people's cause. A modest, tactful comrade, a cool fighter in emergency—that is how he was known to all who came into contact with him.

Tairov joined the CP in 1915 and fought the enemies of the revolution on the shores of the Volga, around Tsaritsyn, in the Northern Caucasus and the Ukraine. He was commissar of the First Kamyshin Division and commissar on the staffs of the Ninth and Tenth armies.

He did not like to talk about his revolutionary services and exploits during the Civil War, and left no memoirs. Whenever questioned, he would reply: "I did and do nothing but what every Communist does and should do for the victory of his ideals."

Vladimir Khristoforovich Tairov (Ter-Grigor'ian) was born on September 4, 1894, in the village of Ispagandzhun [sic] in the Karabakh Mountain area. He spent his childhood there, but the family later moved in search of work to Baku. His uncle sent him to commercial school, where he gave an excellent account of himself; he then entered the Kiev Commercial Institute. Owing to the war, the institute was evacuated to Saratov, where Tairov was imprisoned for two months for taking part in social-democratic student demonstrations. After his release he went to Moscow and entered the commercial institute there (now the Plekhanov Institute of Political Economy), where his Marxist outlook was enriched and deepened, and where he met another Marxist student from Azerbaidzhan, Artashes Khalatov. The two friends were active in Marxist student circles and took part in proletarian and student demonstrations. Thus in Moscow they perfected their training as revolutionaries.

During the October Revolution Tairov fought on the barricades and was among the Red Guards who stormed the Kremlin. After October he became state commissar for the four Moscow banks, and was a member of the financial council of the Moscow soviet.

When, on the night of February 21–22, 1918, the radio and telegraph announced the terms of Lenin's decree "The Socialist Fatherland in Danger,"

Tairov at once joined the Red Army. In August 1918 he became commissar of the First Kamyshin Division. He was an exceptional orator, and his fiery appeals inspired Red Army men, commanders, and political officers to perform heroic deeds in defense of the conquests of the revolution. He displayed great energy and initiative in the fighting against the White Guardists, and in October 1918 was appointed a member of the RMC of the Special Group on the southern front, where he spared neither strength nor energy.

Later he was made commissar on the staff of the Ninth and then the Tenth Army. It was his good fortune to work and fight shoulder to shoulder with the commander of these armies, Aleksandr Il'ich Egorov, later a Marshal of the Soviet Union, who defeated and destroyed the White Guardists on the banks of the Volga at Tsaritsyn, in the northern Caucasus, and on the Donbass steppes. Many times at the height of the battle and under a rain of bullets, Tairov would take over from a machine-gunner and set a personal example of heroism and devotion. As staff commissar and deputy chairman of the RMC, his valor in these stubborn battles was twice rewarded with the Order of the Red Banner.

An ardent revolutionary and intrepid political worker, in 1922 he became political commissar on the staff of the legendary First Cavalry Army. In October of that year he left the Cavalry Army and came to Moscow to study at the Military Academy. In 1926 he became military adviser to the Soviet mission to China, and later he performed similar duties in France. Besides his native Armenian, he spoke fluent Russian, Georgian, Azerbaidzhani, Turkish, French, and English. As an army commissar second class, he rendered valuable service for many years as deputy head of a department in the PC for Defense.

Years later he was in Khabarovsk, working with Marshal of the Soviet Union V. K. Bliukher, the legendary commander of the Special Red Banner Army of the Far East, as a member of that army's military council. The two men worked together for two years and became friends. Bliukher admired Tairov for his patriotism, honesty, sincerity and devotion to the motherland. He was sorry when, in February 1935, Tairov was transferred from Khabarovsk to be ambassador to the Mongolian People's Republic, a post which he occupied for about two years.

Tairov's ability as a diplomat was greatly appreciated by the CC of the Party and the Soviet government. By a decree of January 20, 1937, the CEC of the U.S.S.R. conferred on him the Order of Lenin. In June 1937 he became a victim of the cult of personality.

The Communist Vladimir Tairov is no longer among our ranks; but the country will not forget his services to our Party and people. Many veterans of the armed forces remember him with affection as a gifted military and political officer, a subtle diplomat, a bold warrior, a modest and sensitive comrade and friend who devoted all his strength to his people and worked without stint to strengthen the defenses of the motherland.[112]

BENEDIKT USTINOVICH TROIANKER

Biographical data

Born 1901; joined the CP in 1917 and in that year took part in the overthrow of the Provisional Government at Uman'. Worked in the underground during the German occupation of the Ukraine. In 1918 he was director of the agitation and propaganda department of the Party committee at Petrograd, secretary of the Vasilievsky, Ostrov soviet of workers' deputies, then served at the front in the Civil War. In 1922, military commissar of the Thirteenth Dagestan Rifle Division. In 1923, chief of organization of the political department of the North Caucasian military district; later, deputy head of the political department of the Belorussian military district. Member of CC of the Belorussian CP. In 1932, head of the cultural propaganda department of the Red Army political administration, political assistant to the chief of the Red Air Force, head of the department of chief political organs of the Red Army, head of political administration of the Civil Air Fleet, member of the military council of the Moscow military district. Received Order of the Red Star, May 25, 1936. A victim of the cult of personality.[113]

Our Commissar

In January 1922 a new head of the political department joined our Special Dagestan Brigade. He was of middle height, black-haired, and seemed to us very young. In actuality Benedikt Ustinovich Troianker was only twenty-one years old. But from the expert and energetic way in which he tackled the Party-political work and familiarized himself with every aspect of military life, we realized that he must be rich in practical experience. We were not mistaken.

As a mere youth, in September 1917, he had joined the Bolshevik Party. He took part in the overthrow of the Provisional Government at Uman', and when the Ukraine was occupied by German interventionists he fought against them as a member of the underground. Then, clandestinely crossing the frontier laid down by the Brest Litovsk treaty, he made his way to Petrograd, where he directed the propaganda work of the Vasilievsky Ostrov party committee and was secretary of the Vasilievsky Ostrov soviet of workers' deputies. As a regimental Party organizer he fought against Iudenich and then the White Finns. Later he was transferred to the Caucasus, where he took part in operations against illegal bands in the Elbruz area. From the Caucasian Red Banner Army he came to us in Dagestan, where the Thirteenth Rifle Division had been formed in summer 1922. As its military commissar, the duty assigned to him by the Party oblast committee and the Dagestan government was to direct the struggle against the armed bands of iman Gotsinsky, which were preventing a return to normal life in the towns and villages. The success of the operation was in large measure a result of the thorough educational work carried on by the division's political staff among the soldiers and population. Banditism in the hills was suppressed almost without bloodshed: the mountaineers themselves caught and disarmed the bandits and brought them into captivity.

In the spring of 1923 we said goodbye to Troianker, who had been appointed chief of organization of the political department of the North Caucasian military district. Six years later, I was transferred to the Belorussian MD as chief of the political section of a rifle division, and was glad to find my old commissar serving as deputy head of the political department of the military district. During the interval he had forged even farther ahead as a political officer. As a member of the CC of the Belorussian CP, he often addressed workers' meetings on current themes; he also maintained close contact, as before, with the officers and men of various units and formations, being well acquainted with their lives and needs.

In March 1932 he was appointed head of the cultural propaganda department of the Red Army political administration. Thereafter he served in Moscow in the responsible posts of political assistant to the chief of the Red Air Force, head of the department of chief political organs in the political administration of the Red Army, head of political adminstration of the Civil Air Fleet, and member of the military council of the Moscow military district.

I would probably be correct to say that during this time his talents as an organizer and military man developed to an exceptional extent. He was an ardent propagandist and political officer, combining the Marxist education of a Bolshevik commissar with the ability to understand all aspects of military life and ways, influencing his subordinates by word and deed. On May 25, 1936, the CEC of the U.S.S.R. conferred on him (he was by now a corps commander) the Order of the Red Star for "outstanding personal achievements in mastering aviation techniques and bold direction of the military and political training of the Red Air Force." Together with Alksnis, the head of the Red Air Force (both men were to perish during the period of the cult of personality), he encouraged all aspects of progress in the air force and in particular the achievement of record flights, as well as creating conditions for the successful work of aircraft designers.

Troianker was elected a delegate to the Fifteenth and Sixteenth Party congresses. To his last breath, he devoted his life to the cause of our Leninist Party and the workers of our country.[114]

Iosif Stanislavovich Unshlikht

IOSIF STANISLAVOVICH UNSHLIKHT

Biographical data

Born 1879, died 1938. An eminent member of the Party and state administration. Joined the revolutionary movement in 1900. Member of the CEC of the U.S.S.R. and a candidate member of the CC of the CPSU. In the Civil War he was a member of the RMC of the Sixteenth Army on the western front. From 1921, vice-president of the All-Union Cheka; from 1925, member of the RMC of the U.S.S.R. and chief of supplies for the Red Army; from 1925, vice-chairman of the RMC of the U.S.S.R. From 1930, vice chairman of the Supreme Council of the National Economy of the U.S.S.R.; and from 1935, secretary of the CEC of the U.S.S.R.[115]

A man of iron will

Iosif Stanislavovich Unshlikht was a professional revolutionary. The workers of Warsaw, Lodz, Belostok, and the Dombrova coal mines well knew this energetic young man in pince-nez, sparing of words but impetuous in action. Comrade, Iuzef Iurovsky (Jóef Jurowski), as he was called in the Party, spoke at meetings where he urged the workers to rise against Tsarism; along with them, he took part in political demonstrations and the revolutionary clashes of 1905. Between 1902 and 1916 he was arrested seven times by the Tsarist gendarmerie; the February revolution of 1917 liberated him from exile in Siberia. During the October Revolution he was a member of the Petrograd RMC and the Petrograd soviet; in February-March 1918 he organized resistance to the German interventionists as chief of defense of the Pskov sector.

In 1919-20 he fought on the western front. A member of the CC of the Lithuanian and Belorussian CP, he took an active part in the creation of the Soviet Lithuanian and Lithuanian-Belorussian republics.

At Vilna, in the winter of 1919, a meeting was held at 5 Vron'ia Street (now Paris Commune Street) to set up the Lithuanian division of the Red Army. Among others, Komsomols and Red Guardists of the Karl Liebknecht detachment were present. With their commissar, the Ural Bolshevik Nikolai Volovyi, they sat in the center of the hall directly in front of the chairman's table and cheerfully struck up the *Warszawianka*. The rest of the meeting took up the song and the words rang out: "Fiercely the storm howls around us ...." Then V. Mitskiavichius-Kapsukas, one of the leading members of the Soviet Lithuanian government, reported on the formation of the first Lithuanian unit of the Red Army, ending with the words: "We must bring our division up to full strength. Our Party's slogan is: 'Volunteer for the Red Army!' " There was a storm of applause, and the chairman went on: "We shall now hear one of the oldest revolutionaries, a member of the Party since 1900 and a political exile, our dear comrade Józef Jurowski."

Unshlikht was wearing a black leather coat with a belt and a revolver at his side. His pince-nez glittered as he raised his hand and spoke. "I have remembered his words ever since," declares A. I. Kronik, then a Komsomol and now a major general in the reserve. "He said: 'We must arm the broad masses of the people and follow the example of the Russian workers and peasants. Young men and women, your place is in the front ranks of those defending the revolution!' " Again applause filled the hall; everybody rose and sang the *Internationale*, and volunteers enrolled then and there for service in the Red Army.

In April 1919 Unshlikht became a member of the RMC of the Lithuanian-Belorussian Army, and from December of that year to the end of the Civil War he was a member of the RMC of the western front. At this period he was seriously wounded and received the Order of the Red Banner.

In the fall of 1921 the Party appointed him to the All-Union Cheka as deputy to F. E. Dzerzhinsky; in 1923 he returned to the Red Army. As deputy PC of the army and navy and vice chairman of the RMC of the U.S.S.R. he worked hard at the reorganization of the armed forces. His former secretary, N. N. Krizhanovsky, relates:

> The quality about him which astonished us all was his immense capacity for work. As Deputy PC for the army and navy he was in charge of army supplies and intelligence. His other great quality was his iron will. He worked hard and made others do so too. On the day when his only son, a student, was tragically drowned in the Moskva River, he came to work as usual and only his closest friends knew of his grief.

In June 1930 Unshlikht became vice chairman of the Supreme Council of the National Economy of the U.S.S.R. On the occasion of his leaving the army, the chairman of the RMC issued an order which stated:

> ... In Comrade Unshlikht the Red Army possessed an old Bolshevik and revolutionary, a genial comrade and a skilled leader. We part from him with regret, and in the name of the Red Army, I express to him our deep gratitude for his work in building up our national defenses.

In all the posts to which he was later appointed by the Party, Unshlikht worked in the same energetic and conscientious manner. He was a member of the CEC of the U.S.S.R. at all convocations and was elected a candidate member of the CC of the CPSU at the Fourteenth, Fifteenth and Seventeenth Congresses. In 1935 the seventh congress of soviets elected him secretary of the Union Council of the CEC of the U.S.S.R., and on July 7, 1937, he attended a session of the council for the last time. He became a victim of slander and illegality during the period of the Stalin cult.[116]

Semen Petrovich Uritsky

SEMEN PETROVICH URITSKY

Biographical data

Born 1895, died 1937. Served in the Tsarist Army from 1915 and carried on propaganda among the soldiers. In 1917 he became a Red Guard instructor. After the establishment of Soviet power in Odessa he was assistant inspector of cavalry for the Odessa military district, then fought on civil war fronts. In 1919, head of the operational section of the intelligence administration of Red Army Staff and brigade commander in the Special Purpose Second Cavalry Army. In 1921, commander and commissar of the Odessa Fortified Area. At the end of that year he was called to Moscow to complete a course at the Red Army Military Academy and was then sent abroad on special duties. After returning to Moscow he was director of the International Infantry School. From 1927 he held command appointments in the field, and in 1935 he became head of intelligence administration of the Red Army. In 1937, on government orders, he carried out extensive duties in connection with aid to the Spanish Republic. He was arrested on the night of November 30, and perished soon afterward.[117]

Chief of military intelligence

In the middle of August 1919 the Fifty-eighth Soviet Rifle Division commanded by I. F. Fed'ko was defending the Kherson-Nikolaev-Voznesensk area against Denikin's forces, while the Makhno bands were causing disorder in its rear. When the Whites took Kherson, Makhno declared that the Bolsheviks were retreating because they did not want to defend the Ukraine. Incited by Makhno's agitators, men of the rear units of the Fifty-eighth Division arrested Fed'ko and Commissar Mikhelovich and threatened them with death. At this point the deputy chief of staff of the division, S. P. Uritsky, conducted himself brilliantly. He alerted a liaison battalion, led it to the armored train which the Makhno bands had captured, and rescued the commander and commissar from the enraged crowd. The mutineers took to their heels; order was restored in the division and Fed'ko led it back to Voznesensk. Here it joined the southern group of forces, with which it took part in a 250-mile march through the enemy's rear area. Uritsky's skill in rescuing the commander and commissar was recognized in an order of the RMC of the Republic devoted solely to the exploit of this young officer, who received the Order of the Red Banner. Uritsky, the order stated, ''more than once proved his loyalty in the fight against enemies of the Workers' and Peasants' Republic.''

Uritsky's fight for the revolution started in 1912, when he received his Party card at the age of seventeen. He was led to the Party first and foremost by the environment in which he grew up. In the family circle, meetings of revolutionary youth, under the guise of social gatherings, were frequently organized by his uncle, M. S. Uritsky, who later became a prominent Party member and chairman of the Petrograd Cheka.*

Semen Uritsky was called up in 1915 and served in a dragoon regiment, where he carried on propaganda on the Party's instructions. After the February revolution in 1917, detachments of young people formed by him in Odessa joined the local Red Guard. In December of that year he became a Red Guard instructor, and after Soviet power was established in the city he became assistant inspector of cavalry for the Odessa military district.

Then came front-line service in the Civil War—at Tsaritsyn, in the Crimea, and with the southern group of forces in the Ukraine. From then until the end of his life he was united in close friendship with the Civil War hero and commander of the Fifty-eighth Division Ivan Fedorovich Fed'ko.

In October 1919, Uritsky was wounded and shell-shocked during the assault on Kiev. After recovery, he became head of the operations section of the intelligence administration of the Red Army Staff. While appreciating the importance of this position, he expressed a wish to return to the front, where, as a brigade commander in the Special Purpose Second Cavalry Army, he inflicted a defeat on Wrangel.

In March 1921, before dawn on a cold, misty day, Uritsky was advancing across the ice-covered Gulf of Finland, in the front line of the 561st Rifle Regiment, which was attacking the Kronshtadt mutineers. Brigade Commander Fed'ko was at his side. They had both been studying at the [Red Army] Military Academy a few days earlier when the news of the mutiny came through, and both had asked to be sent immediately to the front. Now they were leading their men toward a rebel fortress bristling with cannon and machine guns. Despite its strength, the fortress surrendered to its steel-hearted assailants. Uritsky was among those who received the Order of the Red Banner, and the Petrograd soviet presented him with an inscribed gold watch.

At the end of 1921, when commander and commissar of the Odessa Fortified Area, he was summoned to Moscow to complete a course at the Red Army Military Academy which he had been pursuing at intervals during the Civil War. He was then sent abroad on a special mission. Back in Moscow, he became director of the International Infantry School.

From 1927 he again served in the field, commanding a division and various rifle corps and also acting as chief of important staffs. At the beginning of 1935 the CC of the CPSU and the higher authorities of the PC for Defense promoted him to be head of the intelligence administration of the Red Army. His work there was not, and probably for a long time will not be, a subject for publicity. The intense struggle which still continues on an invisible front

---

*Mikhail Solomonovich Uritsky (1873-1918) was chairman of the Petrograd Cheka and a member of the Petrograd RMC. He was assassinated August 30, 1918, by a young officer, one Kenigiesser, who is said to have belonged to a group called the "Union of Regeneration."—ED.

for the defense of the Soviet state demands the observance of secrecy. Nevertheless, of late our people have come to know and pay due honor to the exploits of its heroes Richard Sorge and Lev Manevich. Uritsky not only directed these intrepid agents but himself engaged in similar work. He took over the direction of the intelligence administration from I. K. Berzin, that eminent organizer of Soviet strategic intelligence whose methods and lines of activity Uritsky adopted as the foundation for his own. His great organizing talent, knowledge, and inexhaustible energy, and the close contact he established with his fellow-workers, who understood and supported him, had an excellent effect on the work of Soviet strategic military intelligence, which is appreciated even by its enemies.

Although absorbed in his work, Uritsky had other interests as well. He studied higher mathematics, physics, and astronomy, spoke French and Polish and knew some German. His leisure time was devoted to literature. He wrote a good deal, and had many stories published in the magazine *30 dnei* (30 Days) and elsewhere. When in Germany in 1931-32 he planned and wrote a long novel about the German military which was edited by one of his close friends, the writer Pavlenko. Other intimates of his were Mikhail Kol'tsov, the Komsomol leaders Kosarev and Luk'ianov, and the well-known writer Boris Lavrenev. All these men took a lively interest in a satirical journal which [Uritsky] produced and to which Fed'ko contributed from the Far East.

In 1937 the Soviet government entrusted him with the important task of aid to the Spanish Republic. He selected cadres of military advisers, organized supplies for the Republican troops, evacuated the children of Spanish antifascists from ruined and burning towns and arranged for their settlement in the Soviet Union. This work went on in difficult conditions. The trials of so-called "enemies of the people" had already begun. The hysterical campaign of slander and spy mania, instigated and blessed by Stalin, robbed our armed forces of their most experienced cadres on the very eve of the showdown with fascism.

Uritsky was arrested on the night of November 30 and perished soon after. Today his name has been restored to the people, and he is numbered once more among the heroes and builders of the Red Army.[118]

PAVEL IVANOVICH VAKULICH

Biographical data

Born 1890, died 1937. An officer in the Tsarist Army; joined the Red Army in 1918 and the Bolshevik Party in 1919. During the Civil War he was in charge of the First Saratov Course; after the war he was head of the first section and deputy head of the first department of the Red Army Staff, head of the operational faculty of the Red Army Military Academy and holder of a chair at the General Staff Academy.[119]

MATVEI IVANOVICH VASILENKO

Biographical data

Born 1888, died 1937. An officer in the Tsarist Army. Joined the Red Army in 1918. During the Civil War he commanded the Second, Ninth, and Fourteenth armies. After the war he commanded the Forty-fifth Rifle Division and the Ninth and Seventeenth rifle corps, was an inspector of infantry for the Red Army and deputy commander of the Ural military district.[120]

IOAKIM IOAKIMOVICH VATSETIS

Biographical data

[Army commander, second class.] Born 1873, died 1938. A colonel in the Tsarist Army at the time of the October Revolution, he transferred his allegiance to the Soviet power with a body of Latvian riflemen. In 1918, on Lenin's orders, he commanded the troops which put down the uprising of left-wing SRs in Moscow. From July 10, 1918, he commanded the eastern front, and from September 1918 to July 1919 he was commander in chief of the armed forces of the RSFSR. From August 1919 to 1921 he carried out assignments of special importance for the RMC of that republic. From 1922 he was senior instructor on war history at the Red Army Military Academy. Wrote several works on military science.[121]

MIKHAIL DIMITRIEVICH VELIKANOV

Biographical data

[Army commander, second class.] Born December 27, 1895; died July 27, 1938. Took an active part in the Civil War and joined the Communist Party in 1924. Born in the village of Nikolskoe, Sapozhkov raion, Riazan oblast: son of an official. Graduated from cadet school in 1915 and joined the Red Army in 1918. Brigade commander of the Twenty-fourth "Iron" Division; took part in the liberation of Simbirsk; commanded the special group of forces defending Orenburg against Kolchak's troops, and later the shock group of Tenth Army troops which defeated the White cavalry at Egorlykskaia and the Cossack village of Ataman. After the Civil War he occupied senior posts in the Red Army. In 1930-33 he was deputy commander of the North Caucasus military district, from 1933 commander of the Central Asian military district, and from June 1937 commander of the Trans-Baikal military district. He was a victim of slander and repression during the cult of Stalin's personality. Rehabilitated posthumously.[122]

A gifted commander

Although I did not serve very long under Mikhail Dimitrievich Velikanov, his image will always remain in my memory. A Communist and Leninist utterly devoted to the Party, a gifted commander with a wide range of special knowledge and a wealth of war experience, a man of great personal charm, his influence on his junior commanders was both deep and beneficial. I should like to describe him to readers of *Krasnaia zvezda*. It is all the more necessary to do so since his name has been unjustifiably blackened: he was one of the victims of arbitrary rule during the period of the cult of Stalin's personality. In 1937 Army Commander of the Second Class M. D. Velikanov, then commanding the Trans-Baikal Military District, was arrested on the basis of slanderous accusations and died in jail. Moreover, some authors have adopted an uncritical attitude toward the false charges brought against this highly honorable man and have given a distorted picture of his career.

M. D. Velikanov's military career began during the First World War. A teacher in a local school, he was enrolled in a cadet college and soon after graduation in 1915 was sent to the front, where he distinguished himself in the dark days of the retreat of the Russian forces. He succeeded in withdrawing his company without loss from the region of the Masurian Lakes, for which he received a decoration.

In 1917 he unhesitatingly joined the revolution and was elected by the troops as a member of the regimental revolutionary committee. In February 1918 he volunteered for the Red Army, and for the rest of his life he faithfully served the socialist motherland.

While still a company commander, he fought to consolidate Soviet power at Kozlov (now Michurinsk). He became deputy commander of the Kozlov Revolutionary Regiment, and in this capacity took part in crushing the White Czech revolt.

Later the First Army was formed on the eastern front, comprising among others the Second Simbirsk Regiment with Velikanov as its commander and Nikolai Mikhailovich Shvernik as its military commissar. Velikanov's military talents were fully revealed under the beneficial influence of the conscientious and tactful Shvernik and the leadership of such eminent commanders as M. N. Tukhachevsky, then commanding the First Army, and G. Gai, commanding the Iron Division. This period of Velikanov's career was well characterized in the recently published memoirs of the former chief of staff of the First Army, now Major General N. I. Koritsky (retired), who wrote:

Young Misha Velikanov was everybody's favorite.... In the most complicated
tactical situations he found original solutions and ways of checkmating the adversary. His decisions were marked by flexibility, versatility, and the element of
surprise. In his hands, even defensive operations turned into attacks, thanks to
his command of fire-power and maneuver.

The rout of the Whites by the Second Regiment near the village of
Bukhteevka, during the fighting for Simbirsk, was due to Velikanov's action
in leaving a single company to cover the enemy's front while he with his main
forces executed a detour, struck suddenly at the enemy's flank and rear, and
entered the village. He carried out a similar bold maneuver at the village of
Griaznukha. An active participant in these events subsequently wrote: "The
success of the Second Simbirsk Regiment was of decisive importance for the
eventual capture of the town."

The heroic defense of Orenburg stands out among Velikanov's later exploits
on the eastern front. This town was of key importance to the Red Army's
advance on this front, since its loss would have laid bare the army's southern
flank and rear. It was held by one brigade and one regiment of regulars and
two regiments of Orenburg workers, while the attacking forces consisted of
two corps of White Cossacks. Lenin, aware of the serious position, telegraphed
to M. V. Frunze on May 12, 1919: "Do you realize danger at Orenburg?
... Report at once plans and measures taken...." Frunze gave orders that the
town was to be held at all costs, and laid personal responsibility on M. D.
Velikanov, commander of the special group of defending forces.

In the defense of the town Velikanov again displayed outstanding skill in
maneuver. Concentrating his battalions first at one point and then at another,
he kept the White Cossacks at bay and inflicted considerable losses on them.
Finally the Whites gave up the attempt to capture the city and went on the
defensive.

Velikanov was later appointed commander of the Twentieth Rifle Division,
which fought on the southwestern front and scored several important victories
over Denikin's forces. He subsequently rendered important services in Transcaucasia, where he helped the workers of Azerbaidzhan, Georgia, and Armenia
to expel the White Guardists and foriegn interventionists and the Musavat and
Dashnak adventurers. For his meritorious services during the Civil War the
All-Union CEC awarded him the Order of the Red Banner and a gold watch;
he also received the Azerbaidzhan and Armenian Orders of the Red Banner.

When peace returned, Velikanov was assigned to courses of study at senior
military academies, after which he became commander of a rifle corps. I saw
a lot of him during the time when he was deputy commander of the North
Caucasian military district. He spent a great deal of time with the troops, and
I accompanied him on several journeys. I was struck by the range of his military
knowledge and ability. If he was displeased with the standard of shooting in
any unit, he would seize a rifle or operate a machine gun and obtain the desired
results. He was a master of all forms of rifle and gunfire, and drove a car
in days when it was not as simple a matter as it is now. When preparing

to inspect the physical training of troops (sports and gymnastics were just then being introduced into the army), he also went through a rigorous course of gymnastic training.

His main attention, however, was given to tactical training. At that time the opinion was sometimes expressed that the next war, unlike the Civil War, would be one of positions. Velikanov did not agree, and I remember how firmly he opposed this view in a lecture on the French military manuals of that time. Thanks to his efforts, commanders were fully trained in the art of maneuvering on the field of battle.

Many eminent Soviet commanders knew Velikanov well and had a high opinion of him. Marshal of the Soviet Union S. M. Budennyi thus described him in his book *Proidennyi put'* [My Life's Journey]:

> Velikanov belonged to the glorious band of able Soviet commanders who were brought forward and trained by the Communist Party and tempered in battle against the enemies of the young Soviet Republic.... He showed himself a bold, wise and resolute commander.

The name of M. D. Velikanov is one with which the younger generation of Soviet fighting men ought to be acquainted.[123]

ALEKSANDR IVANOVICH VERKHOVSKY

Biographical data

Born 1886, died 1937. A major general in the Tsarist Army, and minister of war in the Provisional Government. Joined the Red Army in 1919. During the Civil War he was an inspector of colleges of the Reserve Army, a chief inspector of the Main Administration of Military Schools, a lecturer on military history, and member of the academic council of the Red Army Military Academy. Attended the Genoa conference (1922) as an expert. Subsequently director of military-academic courses for the senior command personnel of the Red Army, senior lecturer at the Red Army Military Academy, director of tactical studies at all military academies, and chief of staff of the North Caucasian military district.[124]

IAKOV IL'ICH VESNIK

Biographical data

Born 1894, died 19—. Served in the Tsarist Army from 1914 and joined the Communist Party in 1917, when he became a member of the Vyborg raion soviet, commissar in the central supply department of the Red Army, and member of the RMC of the Eighth Army on the southern front. From 1924 he was head of the Red Army department of military engineering, and later served in economic posts in the Altai. From 1931 he was in charge of buildings at the Krivoi Rog steel works. Perished tragically during the cult of personality.[125]

A warrior and builder

Iakov Il'ich Vesnik belonged to the generation which carried out the October Revolution. In 1905, when a mere boy of eleven, he aided the Bolshevik underground fighters of Minsk by performing liaison duty and hiding arms and the red flag. Called up in 1914, he fought in East Prussia and was wounded. After his recovery he worked as a mechanic at Petrograd, where he met Mikhail Ivanovich Kalinin. The young workman learned many things from the future "grand old man" of the Soviet Union.

During the period of preparation for the October uprising, Vesnik was elected a member of the soviet of the Vyborg raion, and became a member of the Communist Party. During the uprising he fought the counterrevolutionaries at Tsarskoe Selo and on the heights of Pulkovo. He joined the Red Army as soon as it was formed; in July 1918 he became commissar in the central supply department of the Red Army and, in October, a member of the RMC of the Eighth Army on the southern front. He personally took part in the battles of Kupiansk and Valuiki on the Millerovo sector. Later he served in the northern Caucasus and Transcaucasia, where he was seriously wounded. For his Civil War services he twice received military decorations.

In April 1924 he was named head of the Red Army department of military engineering. Soon afterward the Party assigned him to a responsible economic task in the Altai. He restored to activity the Ridlerovo mines which had been flooded by the White forces, built the Magnitogorsk and Kuznetsk groups of mines, and from 1931 was in charge of buildings at the Krivoi Rog steel works. The Soviet government conferred on him the Order of Lenin. At the time of the cult of personality he was slandered and perished tragically.[126]

IAN MATISOVICH ZHIGUR

Biographical data

Born 1895, died 1937. A senior member of the Red Army staff and instructor at the Frunze Academy and later the General Staff Academy. Deputy head of military-chemical administration.[127]

DIMITRII PETROVICH ZHLOBA

Biographical data

Born 1887, died 1938. Born at Kiev; joined the CP in 1917. In 1894 his parents settled at Krivchik in Podolsk gubernia. Educated at parish school and at a two-class teachers school in the village of Velikii Zhvanchik. Left school to work as a mechanic at the Zeifel'd factory in Dunaevtsy. Wanted by the police for revolutionary activity, he avoided arrest by traveling to the south, where he worked successively as a farm laborer, metalworker, and miner in Bessarabia, the Ukraine, and the Kuban area. Was at Moscow at the time of the February revolution, and joined the CPSU immediately before the October Revolution. After the establishment of Soviet power in Moscow, on November 5, 1917, the Moscow RMC sent him to the Donbass, where he took an active part in organizing the Red Guard. At the head of the first Donets detachment of the Red Guard he fought against Kaledin's troops and the National Central Rada of the Ukraine. During the Civil War in the Ukraine he fought on the Don and in the Kuban area, at Tsaritsyn, and later in the Astrakhan steppes and Georgia. At the beginning of 1919, on Lenin's orders, he formed in the Astrakhan steppes a special partisan detachment, many of whose officers and men had belonged to the former Iron Division. This unit later became the First Partisan Brigade and, as part of the Second (Composite) Cavalry Corps, helped to liberate Novocherkassk and Krasnodar. In summer 1920 the corps was transferred to the Ukraine and fought against Wrangel's troops. In March 1921 Zhloba commanded the Eighteenth Cavalry Division, which played an important part in the liberation of Batumi and all of Georgia. After the Civil War, in 1922, he was appointed commissioner of the All-Union CEC to deal with the problem of homeless children in southern Russia. He also presided over a commission to study the establishment of labor colonies. On his initiative a number of popular orchestras were created, one of which was associated with a children's home. He was a pioneer of collectivization in the northern Caucasus. Having secured the allotment of a small piece of land in the village of Pavlovsk, he transformed it into a model nursery for fruit and vegetables with the help of partisans and the inmates of the children's home. Here, in 1924, the former partisans and orphans organized an agricultural collective which led the way for the collectivization of neighboring villages. Over a period of fifteen years Zhloba was elected member of a regional committee and a regional executive committee, and a delegate to most of the congresses of soviets of the U.S.S.R. and RSFSR. His life was tragically cut short in 1938.[128]

Rehabilitated Writers of Military Theory

ALKSNIS, IAN IANOVICH (1895-1938). [See p. 84 for biographical data.] Chief works: *Militsionnoe stroitel'stvo* (The Creation of a Militia), [n. p.], 1925; *O kharaktere budushchei mobilizatsii burzhuaznykh armii* (The Nature of the Future Mobilization of Bourgeois Armies), Moscow, 1927; "Nachal'nyi period voiny" (The Initial Period of a War), *Voina i revolutsiia* (War and Revolution), nos. 9 and 10, 1929; a series of articles on the mobilization of troops in *Voiskovaia mobilizatsiia* (Military Mobilization), Moscow, Red Army Staff, 1928-34.

BUBNOV, ANDREI SERGEEVICH (1883-1940). [See p. 199 for biographical data.] Chief works: *1924 god v voennom stroitel'stve* (The Year 1924 in Military Construction), Moscow, 1925; *Boevaia podgotovka i politicheskaia rabota* (Military Training and Political Work), Moscow, 1927; preface to the first volume of *Istoriia grazhdanskoi voiny* (History of the Civil War), Moscow, 1928; *Grazhdanskaia voina, partiia i voennoe delo* (The Civil War, the Party, and Military Matters), Moscow, 1928.

GRENDAL', VLADIMIR DAVIDOVICH (1883-1940). [See p. 133 for biographical data.] Chief works: *Ogon' artillerii* (Artillery Fire), Moscow, 1926; *Polevaia sluzhba artilleriiskogo komandovania i shtabov* (Field Service of Artillery Command and Staffs), Moscow, 1927; *Rol' artillerii v obshchevoiskovom boiu* (The Role of Artillery in Combined Operations), Moscow, 1937; *Artilleriia v pozitsionnoi voine* (Artillery in a War of Positions), Moscow, 1938; *Razvitie artilleriiskoi tekhniki* (The Development of Artillery Technique), Moscow, 1938; *Artilleriia vo vstrechnom: Nastupatelnom i oboronitel'nom boiu strelkovogo korpusa i divizii* (Artillery in Battles of Encounter: Offensive and Defensive Engagements by Rifle Corps and Divisions), Moscow, 1938; *Artilleriia v osnovnykh vidakh boia* (Artillery in the Main Forms of Combat), Moscow, 1940.

ZHIGUR, IAN MATISOVICH (1895-1937). [See p. 192 for biographical data.] Chief works: *Vlianie sovremennoi voennoi tekhniki na kharakter budushchikh voin* (The Influence of Present-day Military Technique on the Character of Future Wars), Moscow, 1927; *Budushchaia voina i zadachi oborony SSSR* (The Coming War and Problems of Defense of the U.S.S.R.), Moscow–Leningrad, 1928; *Razmakh budushchei imperialisticheskoi voiny* (The Scale of a Future Imperialist War), Moscow, 1930; *Khimicheskoie oruzhie v sovremennoi voine* (The Chemical Weapon in Modern War), Moscow, 1933; "Proryv oboronitel'noi sistemy po opytu mirovoi voiny" (The Breach of Defensive Systems in the Light of World War Experience), *Voina i revolutsiia*, January-February 1935; "Proryv i ego razvitie" (The Breakthrough and Its Development), *Voennaia mysl'*, no. 5-6, 1937.

KAKURIN, NIKOLAI EVGEN'EVICH (1883-1936). [See p. 133 for biographical data.] Chief works: *Strategiia proletarskogo gosudarstva* (The Strategy of a Proletarian State), Moscow, 1921; *Strategicheskii ocherk grazhdanskoi voiny* (Outline of Civil War Strategy), Moscow-Leningrad, 1926; *Kak srazhalas' revolutsiia* (How the Revolution Was Fought), Moscow, 1925, vol. 2, 1926; *Obshchaia taktika* (General Tactics), Moscow, 1931; *Operatsii na otdalennykh i na svoeobraznykh teatrakh pustyni* (Operations in Distant and Unusual Desert Theaters of War), Moscow-Leningrad, 1930.

MEZHENINOV, SERGEI ALEKSANDROVICH (1890-1937). [See p. 152 for biographical data.] Chief works: *Voprosy primeneniia i organizatsii aviatsii* (Problems of the Use and Organization of Air Forces), Moscow, 1924; *Osnovnye voprosy primeneniia VVS* (Basic Problems of the Use of Air Power), Moscow, 1926; *Vozdushnye sily v voine i operatsii* (Air Forces in War and Operations), Moscow-Leningrad, 1927.

MOVCHIN, NIKOLAI NIKOLAEVICH (1896-1938). [See p. 153 for biographical data.] Chief works: *Komplektovanie v Krasnoi Armii* (Red Army Recruitment), Moscow, 1926; *Posledovatel'nye operatsii po opytu Marny i Visly* (Successive Operations in the Light of the Marne and Vistula Battles), Moscow-Leningrad, 1928.

SLAVIN, IOSIF EREMEEVICH (1893-1938). [See p. 172 for biographical data.] Chief work: *Voprosy voennogo dela v svete materialisticheske oi dialektiki* (Military Problems in the Light of Dialectical Materialism), Moscow, 1935.

SNESAREV, ANDREI EVGEN'EVICH (1865-1937). [See p. 173 for biographical data.] Chief works: *Severo-Indiisky teatr (Voenno-biograficheskoe opisanie)* (The North Indian Theater [a Military and Biographical Description]), [n.p.], 1903; *Indiia, kak glavnyi faktor v Sredneaziatskom voprose* (India as a Main Factor in the Central Asian Question), [n.p.], 1906; *Voennaia geografiia Rossii: chast' obshchaia* (Russian Military Geography: General Section), [n.p.], 1909; *Afganistan* (Afghanistan), 1921; *Vvedenie v voennuiu geografiiu* (Introduction to Military Geography), [n.p.], 1924.

SULEIMAN, NIKOLAI ALEKSANDROVICH (1878-1938). [See p. 175 for biographical data.] Chief work: *Tyl i snabzhenie deistvuiushchei armii* (The Rear and Supply Problems of an Operational Army), Moscow-Leningrad, 1927.

FEL'DMAN, BORIS MIRONOVICH (1890-1937). [See p. 65 for biographical data.] Chief works: *K kharakteristike novykh tendentsii v voennom dele* (A Comment on New Tendencies in Military Theory), Moscow, 1931; "O budushchei voine" (On a Future War), *Mirovoe khoziaistvo i mirovaia politika* (World Economics and World Politics), no. 11-12, 1933 (preface to book by Ettore Bastico, *Budushchaia voina* [A Future War], translated from Italian, Moscow, 1934).

EIDEMAN, ROBERT PETROVICH (1895-1937). [See p. 61 for biographical data.] Chief works: "Povstanchestvo i ego rol' v sovremennoi voine" (Insurgence and Its Role in Modern War), *Armiia i revolutsiia* (Army and

Revolution), no. 3-4, 1922; "M. V. Frunze i oborona SSSR" (M. V. Frunze and the Defense of the U.S.S.R.), *Voina i revolutsiia*, no. 10, 1926; "Voprosy voenno-nauchnoi raboty" (Problems of Military-Scientific Work), *Krasnaia zvezda* (Red Star, February 23, 1929; "Kharakter operatsii sovremennykh armii" (The Character of the Operations of Modern Armies), *Krasnaia zvezda*, January 1, 1930; "K izucheniiu istorii grazhdanskoi voiny" (On Studying the History of the Civil War), *Voina i revolutsiia*, no. 2, 1932; *"K voprosu o kharaktere nachal'nogo perioda voiny"* (On the Nature of the Initial Period of War), *Voina i revolutsiia*, no. 8, 1931.[129]

III. PROMINENT LEADERS OF THE CPSU

IAKOV ANDREEVICH ANDREEV

Biographical data

Born 1888, died 1937. A Party and stafe official in Chuvashia; joined the CPSU in 1919. Born in Ananasovo-Temiashi village, Tetiushi uezd, Kazan gubernia. Began his revolutionary career in February 1917 as a member of the 125th Infantry Regiment at Iamburg (Kingisepp) near Petrograd. In 1918-19 he directed the Chuvash and extramural sections of the Tetiushi uezd department of popular education. In April 1919 he was mobilized and directed to the eastern front as commander of a Communist detachment fighting against Kolchak.

In 1920-25 he carried out various important Party and governmental tasks in the Tatar Republic. In 1926 he was transferred to Chuvashia, where he worked until 1937 in the Chuvash oblast committee of the Party as a lecturer and propagandist, committee instructor, secretary of the Cheboksary city committee of the Party, secretary of the Party collegium, director of the organization and training section of the oblast committee, and second secretary of the Chuvash oblast committee of the CPSU (1932-37). In 1937 he was subjected to illegal repression; fully rehabilitated in 1956.[1]

NIKOLAI KIRILLOVICH ANTIPOV

Biographical data

Born in 1894, died 1941. Joined the Bolshevik Party in 1912. In 1917 he was a member of the Petrograd committee of the RSDWP(B) and of the central soviet of factory and works committees; after October 1917 he held important Party and government, military, and economic posts. In 1928-31 he was PC for posts of the U.S.S.R.; from April 1935, deputy chairman of the CPC and the Council of Labor and Defense of the U.S.S.R. and chairman of the Commission of Soviet Control.[2]

EREMIIA SAIADOVICH BAKUNTS

Biographical data

Born in 1892, died 1937. Joined the second class of the Echmiadzin seminary in 1905. In 1908 he was representative of a social-democratic group and worked among students. In 1914 he entered the Petersburg Psychoneurological Institute and was at once in the thick of the student movement. During the February revolution he took part in armed street fighting in Petrograd and later worked in the Party's Petrograd committee as an organizer and propagandist; was secretary of the propaganda collegium, spoke at Sestroretsk, fought in a machine-gun regiment in the Vyborg district and at the main post office, and attended the Party's April conference. As a result of starvation and lack of sleep he became sick and went south to Baku; from there the Bolshevik committee sent him to Zangezur to organize a Party cell. There commanded Communist units, was secretary and chairman of the revolutionary committee, worked in the Cheka, was chairman of a revolutionary court and secretary of the Leninakan uezd committee; he then became secretary and head of the organization department of the CC of the Armenian CP. Was a member of the CECs of Armenia, Transcaucasia, and the U.S.S.R. Perished in 1937. The year 1967 marked the seventy-fifth anniversary of his birth.[3]

KARL IANOVICH BAUMAN

Biographical data

Born 1892, died 1937. The son of a peasant, he was born on the Lachi estate in the Vil'ka volost, Lifliand gubernia. As a child he helped his parents with agricultural work....

In the fall of 1906 he entered the Pskov agricultural school, where he joined a social-democratic group including both Bolsheviks and Mensheviks: Karl adhered to the former. In 1907, as a youth of fifteen, he joined the Pskov social-democratic organization, and became the leader of a teachers' group distributing clandestine literature to railroad workers and performed other Party tasks....

During the February revolution he was one of the founders of the Latvian section of the social-democratic organization in Kiev, formed as a subsection of the Kiev Bolshevik organization. At the same time he was active in the professional union of bank workers, where he was one of the leaders and within which he organized a Bolshevik wing. During the October Revolution this union, in which Bolshevik influence was strong, rejected the call of the All-Russian Council of Unions for a strike and declared itself in support of Soviet rule. Bauman deserves much of the credit for this stance. After the revolution he was appointed to the finance division of the Revolutionary committee as commissar for the nationalization of private banks, and on Party instructions evacuated gold reserves from Kiev. When the Germans occupied Kiev he was evacuated with the Latvian detachment to Poltava. There he contracted pneumonia and went to convalesce with his family in the Putivl' uezd, Kursk gubernia.

At the beginning of 1919, after the restoration of Soviet rule in Kiev, he became manager of a branch of the National Bank and also worked in the PC of finance of the Ukraine. He was active in the Party organization in the National Bank and the Latvian Party organization, and was elected to the Kiev soviet of workers' deputies.

At the end of August 1919, on the eve of the Denikin invasion, Bauman and other members of the Ukraine PC of finance were evacuated to Moscow by way of the Dnieper. In October-November, having contracted spotted typhus, he was granted leave and once more went to Putivl'. After recovery he served as chairman of the uezd executive committee and on the bureau of the Party committee for the Putivl' uezd. Later he was sent by the Kursk gubernia committee of the RCP(B) to Gaivoronsk, where as chairman of the executive committee he organized the fight against kulak bands ....

At the end of 1928 he was elected second secretary of the Moscow committee of the CPSU, and in 1929 first secretary of the Moscow oblast committee and a secretary of the CC of the CPSU. In the fall of 1930 the Party CC directed him to work in Central Asia, where in February 1931 he was elected first secretary of the Central Asian bureau of the CC of the CPSU. On his initiative, new irrigation works were begun in the Fergana and Vakhsh valleys and the Golodnaia Steppe; old irrigation systems were rebuilt and the Chirchik nitrogen-fertilizer combine was set up. In 1934 he returned to work in the Party CC, where he headed the department of science, technical discoveries, and inventions. He encouraged scientists to concentrate in fields that gave most promise of benefit in the spheres of economy and national defense.

In 1929-30 he was secretary of the Party CC and a candidate member of the Politburo; after the Sixteenth Congress he was secretary of the CC and a member of its Organization Bureau, also a member of the CEC of the U.S.S.R. and the All-Union CEC at several convocations. He was a delegate to all Party congresses from the Tenth to the Seventeenth, and was elected a member of the CC from the Fourteenth Congress onward.[4]

ANDREI SERGEEVICH BUBNOV

Biographical data

Born March 23, 1883; died January 12, 1940. Party names "Khimik", Iakov; literary pseudonyms A. Glotov, S. Iaslov, A. B., etc. Government and Party worker, historian and publicist. Joined the CP in 1903. Born at Ivanovo-Voznesensk, the son of a petty bourgeois. Studied at Moscow Agricultural Institute; expelled for revolutionary activity. In 1905 he became a member of the Ivanovo-Voznesensk committee of the RSDWP(B), and in 1906 of the Ivanovo-Voznesensk Union bureau of the RSDWP(B). Took part in the Fourth and Fifth congresses (1906 and 1907) of the RSDWP, and became a member of the Party's committee in the latter year; in 1908, member of the oblast bureau of the RSDWP(B) for the central industrial area. In 1909-17 he carried on Party work in Nizhnii Novgorod, Sormovo, Petersburg, Samara, and other cities, and was several times imprisoned and exiled. In 1910 he was co–opted onto the Bolshevik Center for Russia. At the sixth all-Russian conference of the RSDWP (Prague 1912) he was elected a candidate member of the CC of the RSDWP. After the February revolution in 1917 he was a member of the Moscow oblast bureau of the RSDWP(B). Represented the CC in the Petrograd committee of the RSDWP(B). At the session of the CC which was held October 10 to 23, 1917, he was elected to the Politburo, and at the session of October 16 to 29 to the Revolutionary Military Party Center for the direction of the October uprising; member of the Petersburg revolutionary military committee and commissar for all railroad stations. After the second Congress of soviets he was a member of the All-Union CEC and of the collegium of the PC of Communications. In November 1917, as republican commissar for railroads, he was ordered to the south and took part in operations against Kaledin's troops. In 1918 he joined the "left-wing Communists." In March 1918 he became a member of the Ukraine soviet government and the CC of the Ukraine CP; in October he was assigned to underground work in Kiev and joined the Kiev oblast bureau of the Ukraine CP. In 1919 he became a member of the RMC of the Ukrainian front and the RMC of the Fourteenth Army. After 1919 he worked in Moscow in the main adminis-tration of textile enterprises, and was a member of the Moscow committee in the bureau of the Moscow committee of the CPSU. Took part in the suppression of the Kronshtadt mutiny in 1921. In 1921-22 he was a member of the RMC of the North Caucasian Military District, and in 1923 director of agitprop in the CC of the CPSU. In 1920-21 he joined the anti-Party group of "democratic cen-tralism," and in 1923 the Trotskyist opposition, which he later abandoned. From the beginning of 1924 to September 1929 he was head of political administration of the Red Army and a member of the RMC of the U.S.S.R. and of the orga-nization bureau of the CC of the CPSU. In 1925, secretary of the CC of the CPSU, and from 1929 to 1937 PC of education of the RSFSR. At the Thirteenth, Fourteenth, Fifteenth, Sixteenth, and Seventeenth congresses of the CPSU he was elected a member of the Party CC. Slandered and subjected to repression during the cult of Stalin's personality; rehabilitated posthumously.

Bubnov wrote a number of valuable works on the history of the CP, and was one of the first authors of articles on the subject: see, e.g., "Turning Points in the Development of the Russian CP" (1921); "Basic Problems of the History of the RCP (four editions, 1924-26); and monograph on the CPSU for the first edition of the *Great Soviet Encyclopedia* (vol. 2, pp. 8-544), also published separately. These works contain a great deal of factual historical material.[5]

An eminent Party and government worker

Andrei Sergeevich Bubnov belongs to the glorious pleiad of proletarian revolutionaries. His vivid and combative career taught the young generation of builders of Communist society to devote all their strength to the cause of the Party and people.

Young Bubnov's revolutionary views were formed under the influence of Lenin's *Iskra* and in contact with the workers of Ivanovo-Voznesensk. He joined the RSDWP in 1903 and became a Bolshevik after the Party's Second Congress. From the very beginning, he underwent all the experiences that could befall a professional revolutionary: thirteen arrests, nearly five years of imprisonment, exile to the Turukhan region, and all the anxieties of underground existence. But none of this could shake his faith in the victory of the proletariat; each time he was released, he devoted himself with fresh energy to serving the Party that had nurtured and hardened him.

In 1905 he helped to organize revolutionary outbreaks in the Ivanovo-Voznesensk industrial area....

During the years of reaction, 1907-10, though arrested several times, he continued to work vigorously as a Party organizer in the Sokolniky and then the Rogozhsky quarters of Moscow, and was elected a member of the oblast bureau of the RSDWP for the central industrial area. As an agent of the Party CC in this area he restored Bolshevik organizations and took part in the preparation of the oblast Party conference.

The revolutionary workers' movement once more forged ahead, and in 1911, having been released from captivity, Bubnov worked at Nizhnii Novgorod and Sormovo. At the sixth (Prague) conference he was elected a candidate member of the CC. In 1912-13 he worked in Petersburg on the staff of *Pravda* as a member of the Duma. Later he carried on revolutionary work in Kharkov, Poltava, and Samara. At the time of the February revolution he was en route to the Enisei, where he and other Bolsheviks, including V. V. Kuibyshev, were being sent under strong guard to be deported to the Turukhan region. Returning, he made his way to Ivanovo-Voznesensk and then to Moscow. The Sixth Congress, at which armed rebellion was discussed, elected him a member of the Party CC.

In the crucial days when the assault on the old regime of exploitation was being planned, Bubnov was one of the main organizers of the victory of the working class. At the session of the CC on October 10 he was elected to the Politburo headed by V. I. Lenin.

On October 15 he delivered a report at the secret session of the Petrograd committee of the RSDWP(B) which discussed practical problems of the armed rebellion. "The present state of things may be defined as follows," he declared; "we are approaching a decision, the crisis has come to a head and events are starting to develop. "Having pointed out the necessity of improving liaison between the center and the outlying districts, and between these and the factory committees, he emphasized the importance of bringing the Red Guard to a state of preparedness.

At the enlarged session of the CC on October 16 he was elected to the Military Revolutionary Party Center which was to direct the uprising. Bubnov's own task was to organize the seizure of stations and of control over the railroad system.

On the morning of October 25 the CC decided to set up a field staff for the direct supervision of operations against the counterrevolutionary forces of Kerensky and Krasnov. The members of this staff, besides Bubnov, were N. I. Podvoisky, V. A. Antonov-Ovseenko, G. I. Chudnovsky, and K. S. Eremeev.

After the second congress of soviets, Bubnov was appointed a member of the collegium of the PC of Communications and people's commissar for the southern roads....

Reaching Rostov shortly thereafter, he set about vigorously organizing armed resistance to the generals and cadets of the old order. As a result of the successful advance of the revolutionary forces on November 28, the remains of the cadets and Cossacks headed by General Pototsky and his staff surrendered. As Bubnov recalled in his memoirs, "I sent a wireless telegram about this from the yacht *Kolkhida* to Comrade Lenin, the chairman of the CPC in Petrograd."

Bubnov played a most active part in the Civil War. At the beginning of 1918 he became a member of the Soviet government of the Ukraine, and from April 1918 he was a member of the bureau which directed the fight of the insurgents in the enemy's rear. As a member of the CC of the Ukraine CP and of the Ukraine RMC, he directed the fight of the insurgents in the enemy's rear. As a member of the CC of the Ukraine DP and of the Ukraine RMC, he directed the formation of partisan units. Later he was a member of the RMC of the Ukraine front and of the defense council of the Ukraine SSR, carrying out important instructions of the workers' and peasants' defense council of the RSFSR. In 1933 his services in the Civil War in the Ukraine were recognized in a message of congratulation on the occasion of his fiftieth birthday and the thirtieth anniversary of his revolutionary career, in which K. E. Voroshilov, G. K. Ordzhonikidze, S. V. Kosior, P. P. Postyshev, Ia. B. Gamarnik, S. I. Gopner, E. I. Kviring and others wrote: "We remember your devoted work as an organizer of the partisan struggle with the Petliura and White Cossack underground; how you helped to found the Ukraine CP and how, after the establishment of Soviet rule, you were one of the foremost fighters for socialism in the Ukraine."

In June 1919 Bubnov became a member of the RMC of the Fourteenth Army, and in October, of the revolutionary committee of the Kozlov shock group. In 1921 the government awarded him the Order of the Red Banner for his heroism in the suppression of the Kronshtadt mutiny. As G. M. Krzhizhanovsky wrote, Bubnov "did not shrink from risking man's most precious possession—his life—in combat under the Ukrainian sun and on the Kronshtadt ice."

During the years of the New Economic Policy, when it became one of the Party's foremost tasks to eradicate bourgeois ideology, Bubnov was assigned to the most important ideological sectors. From May 1922 to January 1924 he directed the agitprop department of the CC of the RCP(B), while also serving on the collegium of the PC of Education and the main committee of political education. In these posts of key importance for mass education, he devoted special attention to the guidance of youth. "The question of youth, its Party training and political education in the spirit of Bolshevism," he wrote in January 1924, "must be tackled in a far more serious manner and on a broader basis than hitherto. For this we need strength, means and people. It is the Party's job to find them."

He himself devoted great energy to Party propaganda and the ideological strengthening of the Party and government press, that sharpest of weapons in the fight for socialism. He demanded that scientific works bear a militant Party character. His attitude was well expressed in his replies to a series of questions posed by the journal *Proletarskaia revolutsiia* in 1923, in one of which he said: "The journal in its present form suffers, as it were, from eclecticism: it is not sufficiently scientific, and not enough of a propaganda instrument; its material is too desultory, too fragmentary." In reply to the question whether and what changes should be made in the composition of the journal, he said, "It should be made less lightweight and contain more reference material. The section devoted to memoirs should be more concise, solid, and systematic, and the whole journal more historical in character." Since he wrote these words much time has gone by and our press has made great strides, yet his views are still topical.

Bubnov himself made important contributions to the work of Marxist-Leninist propaganda, lecturing frequently to workers and in establishments of higher learning on the history of the Revolution and the Party.

At the height of the struggle against the Trotskyists on questions of military development, the CC appointed him head of political administration of the Red Army, a post he occupied from the beginning of 1924 to September 1929. At the same time he belonged to the RMC of the U.S.S.R. and was chief editor of the main military newspaper, *Krasnaia zvezda*. A vivid account of his work during this period was given in 1933 in the message addressed to him by the PC of Army and Navy Affairs and the RMC of the U.S.S.R., which stated: "You deserve a place of honor as regards the achievement of unitary command, the instilling of iron military discipline, the strengthening of the political apparatus and the Party and Komsomol organization of the Red Army, the Bolshevik education of Red Army officers and men and, finally, the study of basic problems of military development in the light of Marxist-Leninist theory.'' The message also spoke of Bubnov's role in carrying out the military reforms of 1924-25, which formed the basis for the subsequent steady development of the Soviet armed forces.

Bubnov wrote such works on military history and theory as *Krasnaia armiia i edinonachalie* (The Red Army and Unitary Command), 1925, and *Boevaia podgotovka i politrabota* (Battle Training and Political Work), 1927. In 1928 he published a collection of articles entitled *Grazhdanskaia voina, partiia i voennoe delo* (The Civil War, the Party, and Military Affairs). He was a member of the board of the Military-Scientific Society for the Study of the Experience of the Class War, attached to the Red Army Military Academy. In 1928-31 he edited, together with S. S. Kamenev and R. P. Eideman, the three-volume work *Grazhdanskaia voina 1918-1921* (The Civil War, 1918-1921). He also edited for the press Lenin's correspondence on military subjects and a collection of the writings of M. V. Frunze.

Bubnov was one of the most important workers in the field of Soviet education. In September 1929 he became PC of education of the RSFSR, and held this post until the end of 1937. Then he successfully tackled various tasks of the cultural revolution, such as the introduction of universal compulsory primary education, the polytechnization of schools, the improvement of teacher training, and the Communist instruction of youth. He wrote several pedagogical works, some of which are still valuable.

He was also one of the chief authorities on the history of our Party, about which he wrote many major works. For many years he was a member of the council of the Marxist-Leninist Institute and the presidium of the Socialist Academy. In November 1920 he published in *Pravda* a series of articles entitled ''Turning Points in the Development of the Russian CP,'' which were reissued as a separate work in 1921 by the state publishing house, and also by the local Party committees in Petrograd, Kiev, Odessa, Tiflis, Tashkent, Vladimir, Ivanovo-Voznesensk, Samara, Mogilev, and Kaluga. His next book, *Osnovnye voprosy istorii RKP* (Basic Problems of the History of the RCP), ran through five editions in three years (1924-28). In 1930 he contributed a monograph on the CPSU to the second volume of the *Great Soviet Encyclopedia*.

The value of his work on Party history consists not only in its wealth of factual material but also in his endeavor to display and illuminate the inner logic of the Party's development and its many-sided activity, its program, tactics, and organization throughout the changes of economic and political conditions, both at home and abroad.

Bubnov was a fighter against objectivism in the study of Party history. The weighty words in his article on the CPSU are truer than ever today:

> In the course of expounding the ideas and facts of the history of the CPSU, we have been constantly guided by the principles of Party ''contemporaneity.'' Our basic

position is that a proletarian revolutionary and member of the Leninist Party who takes up his pen as a historian cannot be an "objective" chronicler of Party history but must be an active fighter for Leninism against any and every distortion of the revolutionary theory of Marx, Engels, and Lenin.

At the same time it must be noted that Bubnov's works on Party history contain a number of incorrect theoretical positions and inaccuracies of detail. For instance, he is wrong as regards the time at which Russia entered the monopolistic phase of capitalistic development, which he assigns to the eve of the First World War, and in describing the work of the Second International he deviates from Lenin's assessment of the role of Trotskyism during the period of trade union discussions.

After the October Revolution he was a delegate to the Seventh and all succeeding Party congresses through the Seventeenth. At the Eighth Congress he was a member of the commission set up to draft the CPSU program. At the Twelfth Congress he was elected a candidate member of the Party CC and at the subsequent congresses, a full member. In 1925 he was secretary of the CC. He was also a member of the All-Union CEC and the CEC of the U.S.S.R. at several convocations.

Such was the career of A. S. Bubnov, an eminent servant of the CP and the Soviet state. In the course of a long and difficult road he made occasional mistakes for which the Party and Lenin himself criticized him sharply. This just and honest criticism helped him to correct his mistakes and fight on valiantly for the victory of the Party line.

During the cult of Stalin's personality he was slandered and subjected to repression, and his name and leading role in the fight for a better life for the workers fell into oblivion. The Party has restored the historical truth, and the memory of this devoted member of Lenin's Old Guard will henceforth be cherished by the Soviet people.[6]

VLADIMIR ALEKSANDROVICH DEGOT'

Biographical data

Born 1889, died 1944. Joined the Bolshevik Party in 1904. Born at Golubovka-Brikvanovo, Podol'sk gubernia, the son of an unskilled worker. During the period 1904-17, worked in illegal printing presses and workers' circles, organized many strikes and armed uprisings. After the collapse of an underground press in Odessa, emigrated to France and was active in the Paris section of the Bolshevik Party. After finishing Party school, worked to set up the Party organization in Odessa, organized an illegal press there, and was at the same time correspondent for the newspaper *Sotsial-Demokrat*. Was arrested and exiled to the

Enisei gubernia. Escaped, emigrated, and again worked in the Paris section of the Bolshevik Party. In July 1917 returned to Odessa and worked in a factory; was a member of the Odessa soviet of workers' deputies and of its presidential collegium, chairman of the printers' trade union, organizer of the "Foreign Collegium"; later carried out important Comintern work in France and Italy, was chairman of the gubernia trade union council, and member of the bureau of the Party gubernia committee at Ivanovo-Voznesensk (1924). In 1924-38 was head of agitprop and deputy chairman of the All-Union Central Council of Trade Unions; member of the collegium and later deputy PC of labor of the U.S.S.R.; deputy PC of justice of the RSFSR, and chief public prosecutor of the RSFSR. Arrested on July 31, 1938; died in prison, April 3, 1944.[7]

The career of V. A. Degot'

The older generation of the Soviet people well remember the name of Vladimir Aleksandrovich Degot', one of the Leninist old guard who devoted his life to the liberation of the workers.

He was born on February 20, 1889, in the village of Golubovka-Brikvanovo in the Podol'sk gubernia, the son of an unskilled laborer. He lost his parents in childhood and from the age of eight lived and worked in Odessa, first in a box factory and various binderies and later at the Vysotsky factory. From the age of fourteen he took an active part in the revolutionary movement, in strikes, political demonstrations, and spreading illegal literature. He had very little education—only two years of evening classes—but in evenings after work he used to read Marx and Lenin, Chernyshevsky, and Gor'ky. In 1904 he joined the RSDWP and worked in illegal printing presses and workers' circles. At the time of the mutiny on the battleship *Potemkin,* and also in October 1905, he organized strikes, armed uprisings, and street fighting by the Odessa proletariat. During the period of reaction in 1906-7 he led several strikes in Odessa enterprises.

In 1908, after the appearance of the newspaper *Odesskii rabochii* (The Odessa Worker) and the detection of the underground press, Degot' had to emigrate to France. There he was active in the Paris section of the Bolshevik Party and first met Lenin and Krupskaia. Soon the section assigned him to printing work, with the task of hastening the appearance of the minutes of the London Congress of the RSDWP. At the same time he studied in the Party school organized by Lenin to instruct in Communist theory those who were to carry out illegal work in Russia. In his book *Pod znamenem bolshevizma* (Under the Bolshevik Banner), written at Lenin's suggestion, he relates:

> We studied in the evenings, two or three times a week. Lenin instructed us
> on the land question, which he expounded from his own manuscript, criticizing

the Menshevik policy of municipalization and the SR policy of socialization.*...
We worked ... in a large, almost empty apartment, the home of a comrade
who had escaped from Siberia.... Lenin explained a number of difficult points,
[and] we asked him questions and he would question us in turn. Besides explaining
the theoretical side of the problem, he told us how we would have to work
in Russia and how our opponents would do their best to exploit our weak points
at bigger and smaller meetings and in private contacts. He gave as an example
an incident that had happened in Switzerland. He had been lecturing on the land
question and, as he told us, "although I had not asked Chernov to come with
me and speak at my lectures, he always did so and, instead of talking about
the matter in hand, tried to divert attention by raising questions about terrorism,
the role of personality in history, and so forth." Lenin added humorously that
when he came to the end of his talk he had invited Chernov to give a lecture
of his own on land problems, "so that we can get to grips." Then he drew
the moral by telling us we should have to deal with many Chernovs of our
own—"petty intellectuals who will do their best not to answer your points but
to distract you by talking of other matters. You must not let them divert you
from the subject on which you have prepared yourselves. They may try to put you
off by quoting false statistics: be sure you always get your figures right, and
never speak at meetings on subjects you have not prepared."

In 1909, having finished Party school, Degot' was sent by Lenin to Odessa
to restore the disrupted Party organization. Before he left Lenin talked with
him at length, giving him full instructions and explanations and several messages
for V. V. Vorovsky. He was also to deliver to Odessa, Ekaterinoslav, and
Nikolaev the newspapers *Proletarii, Sotsial-Demokrat,* and other illegal literature.

After reaching Odessa, Degot' organized with Vorovsky's help an underground press on which two numbers of *Rabochii* were printed. He also acted
as a correspondent for *Sotsial-Demokrat.* As a leading member of the Odessa
Party committee, under the instructions of the CC of the RSDWP, he actively
combated the "liquidators" and "recallists." At the beginning of January 1910
he was arrested and, after two years in jail, sentenced at the trial of the "22"
to exile in the Enisei gubernia.

In 1912 he escaped from Siberia to Odessa, again emigrated, and at once

---

*Agrarian programs were adopted by all the major political parties in about 1905. The SRs advocated
"socialization," i.e., confiscation of landlords' estates and their equal distribution among the peasants. All land was to be controlled by "central and local organs of popular self-government."
Its use was to be "equalized on the basis of labor."

The program propounded by the Social Democrats, known as "municipalization," was formulated
by Peter P. Maslov (1867-1946), a Marxist agrarian theoretician who proposed the transfer of
confiscated landlords' estates to regional bodies of local self-government which were to be organized
on democratic principles. This program was accepted by the fourth congress of the SD Party
in 1906.

Lenin objected to both of these programs for reasons of tactical expediency. He proposed
that all privately or communally owned lands be "nationalized" and turned over to the peasants.—ED.

rejoined the Paris section of the Party. Together with Grigorii Belenkii he organized and directed all of the section's secret liaison with Lenin. In 1915, with Inessa Armand, he translated into French and organized the publication of Lenin's book *Socialism and War: The Attitude of the RSDWP toward the War*. In July 1917 the Party once more directed him to Odessa, where he became a factory worker and was soon elected to the Odessa soviet of workers' deputies and later became a member of its collegium. He also headed a section concerned with the work of the soviet's executive committee and was a member of the board of the Printers' Union and later its chairman.

Until the Bolshevik takeover of power the Odessa Party committee was not unified, as many experienced Bolsheviks were still abroad. Consequently, when Lenin's pamphlet *K lozungam* (On Slogans) was received at Odessa, the committee refused to publish it. But Degot', by selling all his possessions, managed to publish it from the press of *Odesskiia novosti* (The Odessa News).

He took an active part in the fight to establish Soviet rule, was elected to the Odessa Party committee and was a delegate to the third all-Ukraine congress of soviets. During the foreign occupation of Odessa he was active in the Bolshevik underground. Documentary evidence and the recollections of others concerned show that at the end of 1918, on the instructions of Comrade Lastochkin, the secretary of the Odessa oblast committee of the Ukraine CP, he organized the "Foreign Collegium" and directed its work until the end of February 1919. As will be recalled, the propagandist activity of this body achieved the result that the mass of the French occupation troops refused to act as destroyers of the Russian revolution. The heroic revolt of the French sailors at Odessa and Sevastopol will always stand out as an example of proletarian internationalism.

In February 1919, when enemy intelligence was on Degot''s trail, the collegium advised him to hide. This alone saved him from sharing the sad fate of other members of the Foreign Collegium. At Petroverevka he organized an underground revolutionary committee and maintained liaison with the Party oblast committee. When Odessa was liberated, the members of the Foreign Collegium who had survived—Elena Sokolovskaia, Zalik, Buzhor, and others—presented a full report to the Party's Odessa committee describing the part played by each of their members during the underground period. In this report Degot' was named as the organizer and chairman of the collegium.

At the beginning of April 1919 a legal foreign collegium was set up under the Party's Odessa committee, and Degot' was elected its chairman. The French newspaper *La Victoire* stated with justification on July 9, 1920, that Degot' had been at the head of a department which "controlled Communist propaganda for all of Europe."

In August 1919 the Party assigned Degot' to important Comintern work in France and Italy. At that time Odessa was already occupied by Denikin's troops, and the Whites were seeking him everywhere.

I heard by chance [Degot' later recalled] that a former foreign officer whose life I had saved when he was a prisoner of ours was serving in one of the embassies.... I sent a comrade to tell him that a rich Russian merchant wanted to see him on important business. We arranged to meet next day at an agreed hour at the Writers' and Artists' Club on Grecheskaia Street. I duly appeared, and in my heavy disguise passed unrecognized among the smartly dressed crowd.

"Don't you know me?" I asked.

He paled. "Is it really you?"

"Yes, it is. You can arrest me if you like, and get a big reward, but it'll be the end of you if anything happens to me. Instead, you'd better do something for me—you'll be well rewarded for that too."

"Well, I won't give you away and I'll do whatever it is you want, but let's talk about that later. The man with me is an intelligence agent." And he introduced me to his companion under my alias as a rich merchant....

Their second meeting at the club almost resulted in capture, but the officer kept his word and helped Degot' to obtain a foreign passport.

En route to France he stopped in Italy, where as a result of the October Revolution there was a great popular upsurge in 1919-20. Here he met the chief members of the Italian Socialist Party and Gramsci, the leader of the Turin group publishing the newspaper *L'Ordine Nuovo*, who served the revolutionary wing of the Party well in its fight against reformism. In France Degot' saw Vaillant-Couturier, Lefebvre, and other leaders and discussed with them the prospects of developing the workers' movement, stepping up propaganda, and publishing newspapers.

Before long he returned to Russia, and on October 1, 1920, saw Lenin in Moscow. The latter took a close interest in the French workers' movement and the Turin group. He remembered "Vladimir the bookbinder" from his Paris school, and saw that his pupil had now become a full-fledged Marxist.

Degot' was once again assigned to Comintern work, but this time the French police tracked him down and arrested him. After a few months in jail he escaped with the help of the French Communist, Céline Catella (who later became his wife) and returned to Soviet Russia via Germany.

In 1921 the CC of the RCP(B) sent him to Ivanovo-Voznesensk, where he was elected chairman of the gubernia trade union council and a member of the bureau of the Party's gubernia committee. At the same time he was head of the Committee's propaganda collegium and edited the journal *Trud* (Labor) and the newspaper *Rabochii krai* (Workers' Country). He also wrote many articles and books about trade unions....

The gubernia trade union council devoted much attention to fighting illiteracy, setting up schools and workers' colleges, furthering higher education, etc. "Our students must ... come closer still to the working masses, especially when they work shoulder to shoulder with them in the works and factories during summer vacations. Another task for the students is to come into close touch with the brain of the working class—the Russian Communist Party. Every revolutionary student must keep in mind Lenin's precepts, not shut himself up within his subject but take an active part in the political and economic development of our country,'' Degot' wrote. He obtained a special decree of the Supreme Council of the National Economy whereby 40 percent of the sum allocated for national education was devoted to the needs of gubernia schools and colleges. Under his direction, much work was done in the gubernia to assist the International Aid Society for Revolutionary Fighters. On October 9, 1923, the Party faction of the gubernia trade union council resolved as follows: ''Having heard the report by Comrade Degot' on developments in Germany and the difficulties of the German worker comrades in the fight against the German and French bourgeoisie, we consider it essential not to weaken the campaign at present being carried on among the workers of our country for material aid to the German workers.''

Degot' was at Ivanovo when he heard of Lenin's death. Recalling this, he wrote:

> Ivanovo-Voznesensk, the Red Manchester and old capital of the revolution, the citadel of Bolshevism before and after 1905, the birthplace of the first soviet of workers' deputies in that year—the city which after the October Revolution sent its best proletarian sons to the front under the leadership of Comrade Frunze, the veteran convict-Bolshevik—Ivanovo was shaken to the core at the tragic news of Lenin's death. Despite a minus thirty-degree frost, workers and peasants came by the thousands from many miles around to pay their respects to the memory of Vladimir Il'ich. I had to stay at Ivanovo, but I longed to be in Moscow for a last look at my dear teacher. I made a speech. It was difficult ... but I had to. Tens of thousands of working people listened to me ... workers, peasants, old men, women, weeping and fainting. I talked first at one factory, then at another—my throat choked with tears, as if my heart were breaking to pieces. In the factories where the exploiters once reigned and foremen dismissed and humiliated the workers at their bidding—that is where the proletariat knows and feels what Lenin meant to them. And everybody realized, in that hour of heavy loss, that we must close our ranks more firmly than ever before.

On Degot''s initiative, one of the first monuments to Lenin was erected at Ivanovo-Voznesensk in a square opposite the Palace of Soviets, and the square itself was named for him.

In 1924 the Party assigned Degot' to work in the All-Union Central Council of Trade Unions, where he was in charge of agitprop and also deputy chairman of the council. At this time he carried out a number of important assignments for the CC of the RCP(B). He was a delegate to the Third, Fourth, Fifth and Sixth Comintern congresses. From 1931 he was a member of the collegium of the U.S.S.R. PC of Labor, and later deputy PC. Afterward he became deputy PC of justice of the RSFSR and procurator general of the RSFSR. His work in the field of Soviet justice was characterized by keenness in the defense of Leninist principles of socialist legality and by an acute sense of justice toward individuals.

He was arrested on July 31, 1938, and accused of heinous crimes which he denied having committed. After his young son came to see him in camp, he wrote: "Remember, my son, that an old Bolshevik and pupil of Lenin cannot be a traitor. I swear to you before Lenin's tomb that my conscience toward the Party is as clear as crystal." He died on April 3, 1944.

The Party, having liquidated the consequences of the personality cult, has restored the good name of V. A. Degot'. His letters from camp and the testimony of those who met him in those sad days show that he maintained to the last his courage and faith in the Party of the great Lenin, to whose cause he devoted all his strength.[8]

NAUM IGNAT'OVICH DUBOVOI

Biographical data

Born 1875, died 1941. Joined the CP in 1903. Born in Novoselitsa village, Chigirin uezd, Kiev gubernia, the son of a poor peasant. From the age of nine he worked as a shepherd and farm laborer in the Kiev and Kherson gubernias. Called up for military service in 1897, and learned to read and write in the army. After demobilization, worked in the Donbass mines. From 1901, took an active part in workers' circles and in the revolutions of 1905-07. On the instructions of the local Party organization he and a group of fellow workers created self-defense groups in the Donbass which protected the Jewish population from pogroms. In 1912-13 he maintained liaison with the Bolshevik faction in the Fourth State Duma and the editorship of *Pravda:* one-hundred copies of this paper were sent to him at the Nelepov mine for distribution among the miners. In 1916 he took an active part in the strike in the Gorlovka-Scherbinovka coalfields. After the February revolution of 1917 he was elected first chairman of the combined soviet of workers' deputies of the Nelepov, Shcherbinov, and Mititov mines. After the October Revolution he was one of the organizers and leaders of the Donbass Red Guard and for a time commanded a special military unit which collected food and supplies for the Donbass workers' units. During the German occupation of the Ukraine he was on the southern front at Kozlov; after the liberation of the Ukraine he was a member of the gubernia executive committee at Slaviansk and then a political officer with the Forty-fourth Division. After the Civil War he worked for a few years in the Zhitomir gubernia control commission and was in charge of workers' and peasants' inspection for the gubernia. In 1921 he also became a member of the Ukraine central commission for aid to the starving. In 1924 he was transferred to Kharkov, where, as a member of the central control commission of the Ukraine CP and the Ukraine PC of workers' and peasants' inspection, he devoted all his powers to socialist construction. Dubovoi was deputy chairman of the central complaints bureau of the PC of workers' and peasants' inspection of the Ukraine, and at the same time chairman of the All-Ukraine Council of Militant Atheists. In 1934-37 he served on the Commission of Soviet Control. Arrested in 1937 and perished in 1941.[9]

EVGENIIA NIKOLAEVNA EGOROVA (ELLA-MARTA LEPIN')

Biographical data

Born at Ruen, Latvia. Carried on revolutionary work at Riga, then in Moscow; arrested and exiled to the Irkutsk gubernia. On return to Petersburg worked as a propagandist and secretary of the Vyborg raion committee, then served at the front; was chairman of the Party committee at the "Red Triangle" factory, chairman of the CC of the garment industry trade union, and secretary of the All-Union Council of Trade Unions. Perished during the cult of Stalin's personality.[10]

Party card No. 600

I rang the bell of apartment No. 14 at 45 Nevsky Prospekt. The door was opened by Erna Iakovlevna Lepin', a brisk gray-haired woman with a long, narrow face.

"Yes," she said, "I am Zhenia Egorova's sister. Please come in and take off your things." Indeed I could see she was Egorova's sister: she had the same look, the same profile, although the photograph of Egorova which I had seen somewhere in a book had been taken in the thirties. Yet their surnames were different—because of marriage perhaps? But again, Erna had a foreign accent and an un-Russian name, and the patronymics were different—how could they be full sisters?

"I know you must be puzzled," said Erna with a friendly smile. "Zhenia was a Latvian, and so am I. Her name was Ella-Marta—Latvian girls sometimes have two Christian names—but we used to call her Marta. She took the name Egorova after her exile. It's a long story—but if you want to hear it ..."

Erna sighed deeply and began to tell me about their childhood. They had grown up in Ruien [sic], in a house on narrow Lumbezhu Street. It was a big, friendly family: Marta, Mil'da, Erna, Sil'va, El'mar, and Victor. Their father was a wood worker and their mother a washwoman. Their neighbors used to wonder why the police were constantly breaking in on them. Then they realized that it was to look for forbidden literature, and that it was Marta, the eldest, who was responsible. She would go off in the evenings to some mysterious place and come back excited, her gray eyes shining and her blond hair falling across her broad forehead.

Marta belonged to a Marxist group, and her Party name was "Mulap." Afterward she went to Riga, where she distributed Party literature, and then worked at an illicit printing press in Moscow. She was caught red-handed and received a cruel sentence from the Tsarist court: deprivation of all civil rights and permanent exile. She was sent to the Irkutsk gubernia, to Bol'shegody village. Far from losing heart, she made friends with all her Bolshevik fellow prisoners, read, and prepared herself for the coming struggle. But she longed to return to central Russia, where her comrades were working and where the revolution was being brought daily nearer.

One day the prisoner Kozitsky was joined by his wife, a doctor named Evgeniia Nikolaevna Egorova. The news she brought—that the workers were striking and the soldiers refusing to fight—both delighted and saddened Marta. She began pacing about the room. "What can I do—what can I do?" she exclaimed to the other woman, with whom she had quickly become friendly. "My head is in a whirl!"

"I know what, Marta. Let's change!"

"Change—what do you mean?"

"Change our names. You can be Zhenia Egorova, and I'll be Marta Lepin'. You take my passport—it's a clean one—and you can have my fur coat as well."

"Zhenia, darling, how can I thank you?" And thus Marta Lepin' became Evgeniia Egorova.

She got to Petersburg safely and worked as a propagandist, then became secretary of the Vyborg raion committee. Krupskaia knew her well, and so did Lenin, for whom she found safe places to live and organized protection. In September-October 1917, immediately before the revolution, she spent weeks without sleeping in her own home. Krupskaia wrote about this period: "The Vyborg raion was arming itself and preparing for the uprising: one workers' group after another came to the committee for arms and instructions. Egorova and I attached ourselves to a truck that our people were sending to Smolnyi for some purpose or other. I wanted to know whether Lenin had reached Smolnyi...."

Zhenia Egorova was also at the front. At Luga the Whites saw in their trenches a frantic fair-haired girl in a leather jacket with a revolver at her belt. After the revolution she remained the same combative, fascinating, tireless person: "our dear Zhenia," they called her. She headed the Party Committee at the "Red Triangle" factory, and in Moscow, where she was transferred soon afterward, she was chairman of the CC of the garment industry trade union and then secretary of the All-Union Council of Trade Unions. In 1933 she was one of the first women to receive the Order of Lenin. Her name is on the list of delegates to many Party congresses.

She died young, during the period of the cult of personality. By then she was already a widow: her husband, Mikhail Seliverstovich Ivanov-Mikhailov, an eminent organizer of Soviet industry, is buried in Red Square. Her two small children, Boris and Lena, were brought up after her death by her sister Erna. "They're grown up now," the latter told me, "but they often come to see me. They'll be here today—you must wait and see them. I'll get tea ready.

Not long ago, Boris made a trip to the little town of Ruien, which had grown and improved beyond recognition. Limbazhu Street was now named Egorova-Lepin' Street, and many remembered the Lepin' "family of revolutionaries."[11]

ROBERT INDRIKOVICH EIKHE

Biographical data

Born 1890, died 1940. Joined the CP in 1905. Born in Kurland (Latvia). Joined the Social Democratic Party of the Lettish Region (SDPLR) in 1905. In 1907, member of the raion committee of the first raion of the Elgava organization, and of the propaganda collegium which was set up by that committee. He was arrested several times. In 1908, he became a member of the Elgava committee of the SDPLR. Emigrated to London at the end of the year and worked in the Party's émigré group there. In 1911, returned illegally to Riga and worked at the Fel'zer factory. In 1912, elected a member of the Bolshevik center of the SDPLR. In 1914, member of the CC of the SDPLR and member of the editorial board of its chief publication, *Tsinia* (The Fight). In 1915, exiled to the Kansk uezd of the Enisei gubernia. In 1917, after the February revolution, he moved to Krasnoiarsk and then to Latvia. Arrested in 1918; escaped, and returned to Soviet Russia. Was agent of the PC of Food of the RSFSR in the Tula gubernia. Recalled for work in Latvia in December 1918. In 1919 he was PC of food of the Latvian Soviet Republic, and chief agent of the Food Commissariat and Latvian Supply Council in the RSFSR. After the overthrow of Soviet power in Latvia he returned to Russia, where he was deputy gubernia food commissar at Cheliabinsk, then deputy PC of food of the Kirgiz Republic. Later worked in the CC of the Latvian CP until June 1921. In 1921-22 he was agent of the PC of Food for the southeast [sector]. In 1922-23, food commissar for Siberia; in 1924-25, deputy chairman of the Siberian revolutionary committee. In 1925-29, chairman of the Siberian regional executive committee. In 1929-37, secretary of the West Siberian regional commission of the CPSU. In 1937-38, PC of agriculture of the U.S.S.R. At the February plenum of 1935 he was elected a candidate member of the Politburo of the CC of the CPSU. Arrested in 1938 and perished on February 2, 1940.[12]

The life work of R. I. Eikhe

In 1905 all Russia was astir with revolution, and the flames spread to Latvia, an outlying national area of Tsarist Russia. The workers' and peasants' fight was directed by the Lettish social-democratic workers' party. Later, in 1910, Lenin wrote in an article on the anniversary of the newspaper *Tsinia* as follows: "In the revolution, the Latvian proletariat and Social Democratic Party [of the Lettish Region] were in the forefront of the struggle against autocracy and all the forces of the old order." Lenin emphasized also that the SDPLR was the "most proletarian" of parties in its composition and that its leaders were mainly workers. One such proletarian leader of the SDPLR was Robert Indrikovich Eikhe.

Eikhe was born on July 31, 1890, on the Avotin' estate in the Doblen uezd of the Kurland gubernia, the son of a farm laborer. In 1904 he left the two-class school at Doblen, where he received primary education. He worked from an early age, first as a shepherd and then as a blacksmith's apprentice at Bikstengof (Kurland). In December 1905, at the age of fifteen, he joined the SDPLR. From then on his life was inseparable from the revolutionary movement and the CP.... At the end of 1908, when in danger of arrest, he emigrated to England and at once joined the émigré group of the SDPLR in London. It was difficult to live and find work in a foreign land, but he became a stoker on a steamship going to Africa, and after his return worked as a coal miner near Glasgow where on one occasion he was nearly killed when part of a shaft caved in. He continued his revolutionary activity [in Scotland], studied Marxism diligently, and became head of a social-democratic group in Glasgow. However, he longed to be back at work in his own country, and in 1911 he returned illegally to Riga. Here he took a job at the Fel'zer works and at once joined the Party organization of the Fourth District (the Alexander Gates).

During the years of reaction the Party was weakened by numerous arrests of Bolsheviks.... The Latvian Bolsheviks carried on a stubborn fight with the Mensheviks, who aimed at liquidating the proletarian Marxist Party. One of the [Menshevik] strongholds was the Fourth District, the strongest and most combative in the city, which provided the nucleus of the Bolshevik center set up at Riga in June 1912 at a conference of local organizations of the SDPLR. Among the members of the center were the eminent Latvian Bolsheviks R. Eikhe, Ia. Shilf-Iaunzem, E. Evirbulis, and K. Ozolin-Pagana. The center did much to influence the working masses and educate them in the spirit of the revolutionary struggle.

At the end of 1912 Eikhe was elected to the Party committee of the Fourth District and joined first the district, then the central propaganda collegium of the Riga Party organization. The Fourth District collegium served the entire Riga organization and was of great help in the fight against Menshevik influence not only in the other Riga districts but in the village organizations of the SDPLR. Soon Eikhe was elected to the Riga Party committee.

In the preparations for its fourth congress the SDPLR received much help from Lenin, who composed a work on its draft program which was widely distributed among Latvian Social Democrats and was a powerful weapon against the "liquidators." He carried on a lively correspondence with the Latvian

Bolsheviks, followed the preparations for the congress in detail and, on behalf of the CC of the RSDWP, took part in the congress itself, which was held at Brussels January 13-26, 1914. Eikhe, as a delegate for the Fourth district, took an active part in the congress and, with other Bolsheviks, defended Lenin's views on the need for close union between the SDPLR and the RSDWP, on defending Party unity against the dissenting "liquidators," and on upholding true Marxist principles. His services were much appreciated by the Party, and he was elected to the CC of the SDPLR and the editorial board of the newspaper *Tsinia*. On returning to Latvia he at once began working for the establishment of a liaison with the CC of the RSDWP. However, on the evidence of a provocateur, he was soon arrested (for the fifth time). In October 1914 the Petersburg court found him guilty of belonging to the Social Democratic Party and sentenced him to lifelong exile to Siberia and deprivation of civil rights. In 1915 he was sent to the Kansk uezd of the Enisei gubernia. This was his first acquaintance with the Siberian region which he was to do so much to transform in the future. The village of Cherviansk, which had been assigned as his place of settlement, was some 440 miles from the uezd center of Kansk and seventy-five miles from the nearest inhabited place. By thus relegating Eikhe to the back-of-beyond, the Tsarist government thought itself rid of him forever. But he was not a man to reconcile himself to exile and give up revolutionary work. At the first opportunity he made his way from Chervinsk [sic] to the village of Ialanskoe, thence to Irkutsk and Achinsk, where he lived under a false name. Later he worked at a creamery in the village of Krutoiarka, and after the February revolution moved to Krasnoiarsk, whence the CC of the SDPLR summoned him to Latvia. He reached Riga in May 1917.

In the difficult conditions of the front-line area he carried on much propaganda and educational work among the town workers and landless peasants of the Riga uezd and also among the soldiers, whose revolutionary outbreaks he organized. In May he was elected to the executive committee of the Riga soviet and, with his colleagues, vigorously opposed the counterrevolutionary forces which became active at Riga during the spring of 1917. At the beginning of July he took part in his first conference on behalf of the CC of the SDPLR, and pointed out that the Party organization had taken deep root among the Lettish regiments, which were a source of faithful support for the revolution. The conference expressed itself in favor of close union with the RSDWP.

The revolutionary movement throughout the country was gaining in strength, as was the influence of the Bolshevik Party. Demonstrations in Latvia coincided with those in Petrograd on June 18. Over 60,000 took part in demonstrations at Riga with the slogans "All power to the soviets of workers, the soldiers and the landless!" "Peace without annexations or tribute!" "Down with the ten capitalist ministers!" and "Self-determination for all peoples!" Eikhe was in the thick of revolutionary events. During the demonstrations he spoke at meetings together with other Bolsheviks—Iu. Danishevsky, Ia. Peters, Ia. Khermanis, Ia. Berzin-Anderson, and others—to the effect that only the transfer of all power to the soviets could preserve the revolutionary conquests of the proletariat and satisfy the workers' demands.

At the beginning of July 1917, when counterrevolution was in the ascendant at Riga, the SDPLR held its fifth congress, which summed up the results of the first stage of the revolution and discussed means of further uniting the workers in the fight for socialist revolution. Eikhe attended as a delegate, and was once more elected to the CC of the Latvian Social Democratic Party (LSDP)—as the SDPLR renamed itself at the congress. The Party organizations and revolutionary Latvian soviets fought vigorously for the fulfillment of the decisions of the sixth congress of the RSDWP and the fifth congress of the LSDP. At the end of July a meeting was held at Riga of the soviet of deputies of Latvian workers, soldiers, and landless peasants, a majority in which was held by the LSDP. The soviet decided upon its future tasks in the revolution and elected an executive committee of twenty-seven members, including the eminent Latvian Bolsheviks R. Eikhe, O. Karklin', Ia. Berzin-Anderson, Iu. Danishevsky, R. Endrup, and others. This body became the central organ of the revolutionary soviets of Latvia.

In August 1917 General Kornilov surrendered Riga to the German forces in order to open the way for them to revolutionary Petrograd. By a decision of the CC of the LSDP, Eikhe and six other members of the CC stayed in Riga to direct underground Party work in German-occupied Latvia. In January 1918 Eikhe was arrested by the German authorities and confined first to a military jail and then to a concentration camp. In July he escaped from the camp and crossed the front line into Soviet Russia. By August he was in Moscow, where the Party assigned him to a key sector of socialist construction, that of food supplies. He worked as agent of the PC of Food of the RSFSR in the Tula gubernia, but not long afterward, in December, was recalled by the CC of the LSDP to Latvia, which had by then been liberated from the Germans. One of the Party's main tasks now was to create and strengthen the Soviet regime in Latvia. An important role was played by the First Latvian congress of soviets, held at Riga in January 1919. Eikhe was a delegate to this congress, at which he was elected a member of the CEC and PC of food for the Latvian Republic. The Soviet government of Latvia, headed by P. Stuchka, also appointed him chief agent of the Food Commissariat and Latvian Supply Council in the RSFSR. In this post he did much to organize help from the RSFSR to Soviet Latvia, which was in serious difficulty over food supplies.

After the overthrow of Soviet rule in Latvia he returned to Russia and continued to work in the PC of Food of the RSFSR, where he held the important posts of deputy gubernia food commissar at Cheliabinsk and, later, deputy PC of food of the Kirgiz Republic. Then, at the request of the Latvian section of the Comintern, he was transferred to Latvia and placed at the disposal of the Party CC, where he worked until June 1921. He was a delegate to the

Third Comintern Congress, representing the Latvian CP which had gone into hiding. After the congress, on the CC's orders, he returned to the food sector, working at Rostov as agent of the PC of Food for the southeastern area.

In May 1922 he was directed to Siberia, where he was to spend more than fifteen years helping to build socialism in that rich area. In 1922-23 he was food commissar for Siberia: he did much to ensure the execution of food policy there, and organized aid to the starving at the time of the bad harvests in European Russia. In 1924-25 he was deputy chairman of the Siberian revolutionary committee. The first Siberian regional congress of soviets, held in December 1925, declared in a resolution that this committee, formed at the height of the Civil War, had honorably fulfilled its tasks. The congress also welcomed the CP proposal for the industrialization of Siberia, and elected a Regional executive committee under Eikhe's chairmanship. He remained at this post until 1929, and from then until September 1937 was secretary of the West Siberian regional committee of the CPSU.

Eikhe made no small contribution to solving the basic problems of the industrialization of Siberia and of the whole country. A man of exceptional breadth of view who well understood the meaning of industrialization, he saw a close connection between the problems of socialist construction in Siberia and the transformation of the country as a whole. "For us Bolsheviks," he used to say, "there is no such thing as Siberian, Caucasian, or Ukrainian interests. For us, the interests of the revolution as a whole are paramount." He also held that the industrialization of Siberia must rest on five basic things. "The first is coal—the immense reserves of Siberian coal; second, chemistry and the chemical industry; third, metals and the Kuznetsk metallurgical plant; fourth, electric power; and fifth, the immense possibilities of the timber industry." In his report to the fifth Siberian Party conference in 1930 he mentioned the chief centers of Siberian industrialization:

> The first is the Kuzbass [the Kuznetsk coal basin] with its huge coal reserves and metal ores ...; second, the Baikal area, Irkutsk and its surroundings, the Angara hydroelectric stations. Third, the Minusinsk and Abakansk areas, where the metal ore deposits are far from having been fully explored.... And fourth, the Novosibirsk area, which will be devoted mostly to processing industries—textiles and leather goods, and the very important combine-harvester plant.

He emphasized that two of these centers—Irkutsk and Minusinsk—were still only in the planning stage, and that Kuzbass and Novosibirsk were at that time in the forefront of attention.

He brought all the fervor of a Bolshevik-Leninist to the execution of the Party's plans, emphasizing the need for industrial cadres to make possible the development of the Kuzbass, and urging its high priority from the point of view of the allocation of resources. Speaking at a West Siberian congress of teachers and shock workers on May 13, 1936, he said: "Our region is striving to turn the Kuzbass into a second Donbass, and to create a second Ukraine in respect to wheat production." His speeches at the Fifteenth, Sixteenth, and Seventeenth Party congresses were devoted chiefly to problems of the economic development of Siberia. At the Seventeenth Congress, he spoke with pride of the prodigious changes that had taken place in the region during the years of Soviet power and the successful creation of a second coal and steel base in the eastern part of the country in accordance with the Five Year Plans. "The creation of the Ural-Kuzbass combine," he emphasized in this speech, "deserves to rank as one of the Party's greatest victories. Where there was once a desert we now have blast furnaces, open-hearth furnaces, and rolling mills. The degree of mechanization at Kuzbass is already higher than that of the British coal industry.... Nor is Kuzbass merely a coal base: it is fast becoming a major center of the chemical industry."

At the same congress he proposed the organization of an all-Union agricultural exhibition to display the achievements of the state and collective farms.

By virtue of his exceptional organizing talents and adherence to principle he won the respect and love of the Siberian working masses. More than once he drew attention to the harm done by self-praise and complacency. As he said at the plenum of the Oirot oblast committee of the CPSU in November 1935:

> Complacency is a form of blight or decay, the ruin of strong men and organizations. It turns us away from the true Leninist path into a bourgeois morass.... We have spoken of our successes only that we may better understand our tasks and shortcomings, concentrating our attention and powers of Bolshevik self-criticism on the latter....

In so arguing, he emphasized that objective criticism was a motivating force in the development of socialist society. He resolutely opposed the distortion of the Party's general line in matters of socialist construction by the Trotskyist-Zinovievite bloc and right-wing deviationists.

The Party and government greatly appreciated his services. For his successful direction of the socialist economy of western Siberia he received the Order of Lenin in 1935. At the Fourteenth and Fifteenth Party congresses he was elected a candidate member of the CC of the CPSU, and at the Sixteenth and Seventeenth congresses a full member. At the plenum of the CC in February 1935 he was elected a candidate member of the CC Politburo. In October 1937 he was assigned by the Party to another important post—that of PC of agriculture of the U.S.S.R. He had occupied this post for barely six months when in April 1938 he was arrested on a contrived charge. It was a cruel blow for one who had a glorious career behind him as a Bolshevik and Leninist, who had fought for Soviet rule and several times looked death in the face, and had labored selflessly for his socialist mother country. But his faith in the CP, its strength, and the great ideals of communism remained unshakable. His life was tragically cut short on February 2, 1940.

The Latvian people have given birth to many great revolutionaries, true

Leninists and patriots devoted to the Party and the Communist cause; and one such fighter, to the very last day of his life, was the Party's true son Robert Indrikovich Eikhe.[13]

AVEL' SAFRONOVICH ENUKIDZE

Biographical data

Born 1877, died 1937. Born in Tskadisi village, Racha uezd, Kutaisi gubernia. Attended village school and studied from 1889 to 1892 at the uezd school in Mingrelia, then in Tiflis. By that time revolutionary ideas were gaining much ground among students; a political strike broke out in the Tiflis theological seminary and various revolutionary circles were formed, one of which Enukidze joined in 1894.

His political education advanced rapidly. In 1896 he joined a Marxist circle for young workers and students, and in 1897 he became an organizer of social-democratic groups and a propagandist in the Tiflis railroad works, where he was employed in an assembly shop. From September 1898 he was assistant engineer at the Baku depot, and in the same year he joined the Bolshevik Party. The next year, with V. Ketskhoveli, he organized the first workers' Marxist circles, first in the railroad area, then in nearby factories and in the oil industry.

The year 1900 saw the creation of the Baku committee of the RSDWP, a directing center for local social-democratic groups. Enukidze was a member of the committee, and in the spring of 1901, together with Ketskhoveli and V. Sturua, he set up the first underground press, known as "Nina." Through the aid of exiled social-democrats in Astrakhan and also L. M. Knipovich, Enukidze and his companions established contact with the editorship of *Iskra* and thus Lenin, to whom they submitted plans for illegal printing work and the distribution of *Iskra*. Lenin approved the plans, and Enukidze, Ketskhoveli, and L. B. Krasin worked hard to put them into practice. Soon the Baku press began to print *Iskra* from matrices sent from abroad. "Nina" continued to function for nearly a year, but at the beginning of 1902 the police discovered the press and it had to be closed down. About five hundredweight of type was packed into small bundles and hidden away in a railroad depot near Baku, while the press itself was stored near the wharves.

On *Iskra's* instructions Enukidze engaged in the transportation of illegal literature; ... [also] at this time he took an active part in all the work of the Baku committee. In 1902 he helped to organize the First of May demonstration: he was arrested immediately afterward, but soon set free.... Meanwhile, the Party's draft program together with Lenin's pamphlet *What Is to Be Done?* had found their way to the Metekh castle in Tiflis (where Enukidze was imprisoned), and had been read by many of his fellow inmates.

Avel' Safronovich Enukidze

Enukhidze was again arrested about the end of 1903 and exiled to eastern Siberia, whence he escaped. He returned secretly to Baku where the illegal press was being set up again. New equipment was bought and a rented house furnished with a stereotype press and stitching and cutting machines. The work was directed by Krasin, a member of the CC of the RSDWP representing *Iskra,* and Trifon Enukidze. The operation was well camouflaged, and the seven men employed were not allowed to leave the house or even show themselves at the windows. All but one of them were specialists in printing. The exception, Avel' Enukidze, performed various duties: correcting proofs, operating and cleaning the machines, folding and stitching the printed sheets, tying up and weighing packages, and helping to cast stereotypes.

The press printed *Iskra,* separate articles from *Iskra,* leaflets and pamphlets (including the *Communist Manifesto),* and many other illegal publications. Baku was a long way from Petersburg, and several times the question was raised of bringing the press closer to the industrial centers. This question became critical in 1905 with the growth of the revolutionary movement and the increasing need for Party literature. At the end of that year Enukidze was summoned to Petersburg, where he met Lenin for the first time in person at a conference of members of the CC of the RSDWP. He had corresponded with the Party leader since 1901, but was abashed when Lenin greeted him with the words "So this is Comrade Avel'!" Lenin immediately began to inquire about the situation in the south, particularly the Caucasus.

The conference decided to move the press to Petersburg, and Enukidze returned to Baku to make the arrangements. In 1906 he was back in Petersburg; there he set up the press, which had arrived from Baku, and began to work in the Party's legal printing establishment. He also carried out various Party tasks and remained in touch with Lenin. He returned to Baku in the fall of 1906, took part in the congress of Caucasian social-democratic organizations, and became a member of the Union Committee of the RSDWP and the Baku Committee of Bolsheviks....

In 1910 he again returned to Baku after a period of exile. A new revolutionary wave was in progress and he threw himself into Party work, but in September 1911, when busily preparing for the all-Russian Party conference, he was again arrested together with S. Shaumian, V. Kasparov, and others....

In summer 1912 he was expelled from the Caucasus and, after living for a time at Rostov-on-Don and Moscow, he moved to Petersburg, where he did extensive Party work. He was closely connected with the Bolshevik faction in the Fourth State Duma, worked in Party organizations beyond the Neva Gate, contributed to *Pravda,* and corresponded with Lenin, Krupskaia, and Shaumian. Once more the police tracked him down, and on July 4, 1914, he was arrested and exiled to the Enisei gubernia. At the end of 1916, when still in exile, he was called up and served at Krasnoiarsk as a private in the Thirteenth Company of the Fourteenth Siberian Rifle Regiment. He had long talks with his fellow soldiers and when, on February 27, 1917, his regiment passed through Petersburg on its way to the front, they poured out into the city streets and greeted with delight the first day of revolution. Enukidze played a prominent part that day in the street demonstrations of his own comrades and soldiers from other regiments.

After the February revolution he worked as a Party organizer and propagandist among units of the Petersburg garrison. In October he was a member of the RMC set up by the CC of the Bolshevik Party, which took practical steps to organize the armed uprising. He was a member of the second congress of soviets, which entrusted the government of the country to the genuinely national organs of power which it elected—the All-Russian CEC and the CPC. Along with Lenin, Sverdlov, Volodarsky, Dzerzhinsкy, and other front-rank Bolsheviks, Enukidze was elected a member of the CEC and appointed head of its military department. From the fall of 1918 he was a member of the Presidium and secretary of the All-Russian CEC, and when the U.S.S.R. was formed on December 30, 1922, he became a member of the Presidium and secretary of the CEC of the U.S.S.R.

He was a delegate at the Sixth, Eighth, Ninth, and Eleventh to Seventeenth Party congresses. At the Thirteenth, Fourteenth, Fifteenth, and Sixteenth congresses he was elected a member of the Central Control Commission of the CPSU, and at the Seventeenth Congress he became a member of the CC of the CPSU.

A creator of the Transcaucasian Party organization who joined the RSDWP from its very inception, A. S. Enukidze was a true and unswerving Leninist. For many years he was a counselor of the great Lenin, working under his direct guidance and carrying out his instructions. Many communications between Lenin and local Party organizations passed through his hands. Letters and notes which have come down to us show how Lenin consulted him on political questions. All who had dealings with him remember him as a kindly, warm-hearted man.[14]

ARTEMII GRIGOR'EVICH GEURKOV

Biographical data

Born 1902, died 1937. Joined the Bolshevik Party in 1919 and in the same year was one of the founders and active members of the Spartak organization. In 1921-23, secretary of the Telavi uezd Komsomol committee and of the Adzhar oblast committee. In 1925-26, head of the organization department of the CC of the Leninist Komsomol of Georgia. Performed Party duties in 1926-28. In 1928-30, studied at the Communist Academy at Moscow, then became head of the organization department of the Tbilisi oblast committee of the Georgian CP and of the organization and instruction department of the Transcaucasian regional committee of the CPSU. In 1931-32, head of the Transcaucasian department of Traktorotsentr (Tractor Center) and deputy chairman of the Transcaucasian Kolkhoztsentr (Collective Farms Center). In 1932-37, secretary of the Adzhar oblast committee of the Georgian CP and at the same time head of Kolkhidstroi (Kolkhida Construction Administration). In 1937 he was a victim of the cult of Stalin's personality.[15]

A veteran

It is sixty-five years since the birth of Artemii Grigor'evich Geurkov, one of the old guard of the Georgian Komsomol and a staunch fighter for communism.

In 1910-20 Geurkov studied at the Telavi high school, where he took an active part in revolutionary work among the young. In 1917 the "Spartak" youth organization of international socialism was set up at Tiflis (Tbilisi) and developed great activity. Cells belonging to this organization were soon created in many other Georgian towns and areas, and at the beginning of 1919 one was set up in the Telavi uezd. Guerkov was one of its founders and leaders. In the same year he joined the Bolshevik Party and performed important Party duties in the struggle to establish Soviet power in Georgia. As a result he was persecuted and subjected to repression by the Menshevik government of Georgia. After the victory of Bolshevism he occupied key Party and Komsomol posts, devoting all his strength, knowledge, and experience to building up his new fatherland.

From March 1921 to November 1923 he worked first as secretary of the Telavi uezd Komsomol committee and then, when the Adzhar oblast Komsomol committee was created, as secretary of that body. In 1925-26 he was in charge of the organization department of the CC of the Lenin Komsomol of Georgia. He performed Party duties from March 1926 to August 1928 and was at different times head of the organization department of the Party's raion committee at Tbilisi and secretary of the Telavi uezd committee of the Georgian CP.

In 1928-30 he studied at the Communist Academy in Moscow. After completing his course he was first head of the organization department of the Tbilisi oblast committee of the Georgian CP, and then of the organization and instruction department of the Transcaucasian regional committee of the CPSU. In 1931-32 he was head of the Transcaucasian department of Traktorotsentr and deputy chairman of the Transcaucasian Kolkhoztsentr. He fought energetically for the observance of the Party's general line as regards kolkhoz construction.

From 1932 until his death in 1937 he was secretary of the Adzhar oblast committee of the Georgian CP, and was at the same time head of Kolkhidstroi. He took part as a delegate in the work of Party and Komsomol congresses in Georgia and Transcaucasia. He was a member of the control commission of the Transcaucasian regional committee of the CPSU, of the CC of the Komsomol of Georgia, of the commission which drafted the constitution of the Georgian SSR, and of the budget commission of the CPC of the Georgian SSR.

In all his work he displayed profound knowledge and fidelity to principle, fighting zealously for the fulfillment of Party and government directives. His whole life was devoted to the cause of Soviet power in Georgia and the triumph of Lenin's great ideals.[16]

NIKOLAI FEDOROVICH GIKALO

Biographical data

Born 1897 at Odessa; died 1939. Took an active part in the fight to establish Soviet power in the northern Caucasus. Joined the CP in 1917. Graduated from the Tiflis school for medical orderlies in 1915. From March 1917 he was chairman of the Groznyi city soviet, and from May commanded local units of the Red Army. Commanded a partisan detachment and later a group of Red insurrectionary forces in the Terek oblast during the campaign against Denikin. From 1919 he was a member of the Caucasian regional committee of the RCP(B). After the Civil War he served as commander and commissar of the Terek oblast and was at the same time deputy chairman of its executive committee. Later he was successively secretary of the Gori oblast committee of the RCP(B), head of agitprop and secretary of the Party's North Caucasian regional committee, and secretary of the CC of the CPs of Uzbekistan, Azerbaidzhan, and Belorussia. At the Seventeenth Party Congress in 1934 he was elected a candidate member of the CC of the CPSU. Slandered and subjected to illegal repression during the cult of Stalin's personality; posthumously rehabilitated.[17]

LEVAN DAVIDOVICH GOGOBERIDZE

Biographical data

Born 1896, died 1937. Took an active part in the fight for Soviet power in Transcaucasia. Joined the CP in 1916. After the February revolution in 1917 he became deputy chairman of the Dzhivizlik (Trapezund district) soviet of workers' and soldiers' deputies and worked on the Bolshevik newspaper *Kavkazsky Rabochii* (The Caucasian Worker). From February 1918 he performed Party and government work in Baku. After the temporary defeat of Soviet power in Baku he did responsible underground work. In November he took part in a conference of Transcaucasian Bolshevik organizations at Tiflis, was arrested by Menshevik authorities and expelled to Baku. From December 1918 he was a member of the bureau of the Baku committee and then of the Caucasian regional committee of the Party. In May 1919 he was one of the leaders of the Baku workers' strike against the Musavat faction, and in summer of that year was seriously wounded by a Musavat terrorist. At the end of 1920 he became a member of the presidium of the Nizhnii Novgorod gubernia committee of the RCP. From 1921 to 1930 he occupied important posts in Georgia: chairman of the Tiflis revolutionary committee, secretary of the Tiflis committee of the RCP, in 1923 deputy chairman of the Georgian CPC, and in 1926-30 secretary of the CC of the Georgian CP. In 1930-34 he worked and studied in Moscow. From May 1934 he was secretary of the Eisk Revolutionary Committee of the Party, and from January 1935 of the Party committee of Rostsel'mash (Rostov-on-Don Agricultural Machinery Plant) and a delegate to the Fifteenth and Sixteenth congresses of the CPSU. He was subjected to illegal repression during the cult of Stalin's personality; rehabilitated posthumously.[18]

A fighter for the people's happiness

"Comrade Gogoberidze was Dzhaparidze's right-hand man and worked in the Baku underground as a true and tried Communist." Such were the words used by Sergo Ordzhonikidze, at the first congress of the Georgian CP, to describe the well-known professional revolutionary Levan Davidovich Gogoberidze, whose name is inseparably associated with the fight of the working people of Transcaucasia for the victory and consolidation of Soviet power.

Gogoberidze was born in 1896 in the village of Gocha-Dzhikhanshi. After finishing his studies at the Kutaisi Technical High School he went on to the Petrograd Polytechnic School. He was called up in 1915 and carried on active propaganda work among the soldiers, for which he was soon arrested and sent to a penal battalion. He then worked in an infirmary at Dzhivizlik, not far from Trapezund (Trabzon, or Trebizond, in Turkey), where he met the Bolshevik underground worker A. Dzhaparidze. Afterward recalling this period of his life, he wrote: "I received my Party education and 'literacy' from Alesha Dzhaparidze during our work together ... and in February 1916 I was admitted to the Party on his recommendation."

After the bourgeois-democratic revolution of February 1917 Gogoberidze was elected a member of the presidium and head of the department of education of the Dzhivizlik soviet of workers' and soldiers' deputies, and then a member of the presidium of the Platan soviet. In February 1918 he was elected to the presidium of the Baku soviet of workers' and soldiers' deputies. In March, during the Musavat uprising against Soviet power,* he was in the front rank of the defenders, and fought rifle in hand against the enemies of the Baku proletariat. After the victory of Soviet power in Baku he was sent by the Baku

---

*Although after the October Revolution the Bolsheviks dominated the Baku soviet, they were in fact a minority in it. Their subsequent attempts to strengthen their control in Baku provoked a revolt against Soviet power by the Musavat, an Islamic nationalist party, on March 18, 1918. After only a few days of fighting, the struggle ended in a Bolshevik victory. A massacre of the rebels ensued, for which the Bolsheviks blamed the Armenians.—ED.

CPC on a special mission to Tiflis. On the way back, at Adzhikabul, he was arrested by counterrevolutionaries, and escaped execution thanks only to the unexpected arrival of a Bolshevik armored train.

In August 1918 he was appointed captain of one of the ships which were to take the Baku commissars to Astrakhan. The ships, however, were turned back by the counterrevolutionary "Central Caspian dictatorship," and the leaders of the Baku commune were imprisoned at Bailov. The situation in Baku was tense: the working masses were indignant at the treacherous act of the SRs, Mensheviks, and Dashnaks and demanded the immediate release of the arrested men. In this state of affairs the Mensheviks and SRs decided to hold fresh elections to the Baku soviet. In spite of all obstruction the workers reelected all the imprisoned members of the CPC. At this time Gogoberidze also became a member of the soviet. In September 1918, when the Turkish forces took Baku, he remained in the town and together with other Bolsheviks carried on underground work, re-establishing liaison and Party organizations. The Turks condemned him to death together with his comrades G. Sturua and S. Agamirov, and it became dangerous to stay in Baku. Gogoberidze managed to escape to Tiflis, but was arrested there. After his release from prison he continued revolutionary work, taking part in the conference of representatives of Transcaucasian Bolshevik organizations at Tiflis in November 1918.

Before long he returned to Baku, where the Bolsheviks had built up their strength for a showdown with the Musavat government. Gogoberidze, together with L. Mirzoian, F. Gubanov, and others, inspired the activity of the factory, works, and industrial committees which were later united in the "Baku workers' conference"—a political organ with full authority to represent the Baku proletariat. Gogoberidze was elected its chairman and a member of its presidium. This body, a sort of workers' parliament, offers a striking example of the Communists' exploitation of legal possibilities.

Alarmed at the growing pressure of the working masses, the Musavat government resorted to terror and repressions against the workers' and peasants' leaders, especially the Communists. Gogoberidze was arrested several times, and in summer 1919 was gravely wounded by a Musavat terrorist. After his recovery he again took up active underground work and went to Central Asia to organize the supply of arms to the Baku proletariat. However, at the end of 1920 he was transferred by the Party CC to Nizhnii Novgorod to take charge of the political education department. Here he became a member of the presidium of the Party's gubernia committee.

Gogoberidze took an active part in the fight to establish and consolidate Soviet power in Georgia. After the victory of the socialist revolution he was chairman of the Tiflis Revolutionary Committee, deputy chairman of the Georgian CPC, and first secretary of the Tiflis Party committee. In 1926-29 he was second secretary of the CC of the Georgian CP, and in 1930 its first secretary. In his last years he worked in the Azov-Black Sea region as secretary of the Eisk raion committee of the Party, and then as secretary of the Party committee of Rostsel'mash.

Gogoberidze devoted all of his adult life to the struggle for the great cause of the Party, the workers, and the victory of communism. His selfless devotion to the people and to the revolutionary cause won him the love and gratitude of all Soviet people engaged in building communism under the leadership of the Leninist Party.[19]

FILIPP ISAEVICH GOLOSHCHEKIN

Biographical data

Born 1876, died 1941. State and Party worker and veteran of the October Revolution. Born at Nevel'; joined the CP in 1903 and carried on Party work in Petersburg, Kronshtadt, Sestroretsk, Moscow, and other cities. Elected member of the Petersburg committee of the RSDWP, 1906. After the dissolution of the First State Duma he was arrested and sentenced to two years' confinement in a fortress; he was set free a year later but again arrested on May 1, 1907. After release he worked as an organizer and member of the Petersburg executive committee of the RSDWP. In 1909 he took part in the conference of editors of the journal *Proletarii*, then published in Paris; returned to Russia and worked in the Moscow committee of the RSDWP. He was arrested in 1909 and exiled to the Narym region; escaped in 1910, and carried on Party work in Moscow; later elected to the CC of the RSDWP at the Sixth (Prague) Congress in 1912. He worked again in Moscow, but was soon arrested once more and exiled to the Tobolsk gubernia. Escaped and worked in Petrograd (1913), then in the Urals, where he was arrested and exiled to the Turukhan region. Remained there until the February revolution. Was a delegate to the Seventh (April) conference and the Sixth Congress of the RSDWP(B). After the October Revolution he was Secretary of the Perm and Ekaterinburg gubernia committees and the Ural oblast committee of the Party, then a member of the Siberian bureau of the CC. During the Civil War he was military commissar of the Ural oblast, head of the political department of the Third Army, and member of the RMC of the Turkestan Army. In 1922-25, chairman of the Samara gubernia executive committee and the Samara gubernia committee of the RCP(B). From October 1924, secretary of the regional committee of the Kazakhstan CP. Elected a candidate member of the CC of the CPSU at the Twelfth to Fourteenth Party congresses, and a full member at the Fifteenth and Sixteenth congresses. From 1933 he worked as chief arbitrator for the CPC of the U.S.S.R. Subjected to illegal repression during the cult of Stalin's personality; posthumously rehabilitated.[20]

GRIGORII FEDOROVICH GRIN'KO

Biographical data

Born 1890, died 1938. Born at Shteshivka village, now Sumsk oblast. Political and social worker of the Ukrainian SSR. Belonged first to petty bourgeois parties—the SRs and the Borot'ba faction. During the Civil War he took part in the fight to establish Soviet power in the Ukraine. In 1919 he represented the CC of the Ukrainian CP (Borot'bists) on the CEC of Soviets and the CPC of the Ukraine; he was also a member of the CEC of the RSFSR and of the All-Ukrainian RMC. Joined the CP in March 1920. In 1920-26 he was PC of education and chairman of Gosplan of the Ukrainian SSR; in 1926-29 deputy chairman of Gosplan of the U.S.S.R., and from 1930 PC of finance of the U.S.S.R. At the eighth conference of the Ukraine CP he was elected a candidate member of its CC, and at its ninth congress he became a full member.[21]

MIRZA DAVUD BAGIR-OGLY GUSEINOV

Biographical data

Born 1894, died 1938. Azerbaidzhan Party worker. Joined the CP in November 1918. Born at Baku; studied at Moscow Commercial Institute. Joined the Gummet organization at the beginning of 1919 and became a member of its committee; then was elected to the Caucasian regional committee of the RCP(B). In February 1920, became a member of the CC of the Azerbaidzhan CP. Took part, as a member of the military revolutionary staff, in preparing the armed uprising in Azerbaidzhan against the Musavat government. After the victory of Soviet power he became PC of finance and subsequently of foreign affairs for the Azerbaidzhan SSR, then PC of finance of the Transcaucasian SFSR, then deputy chairman of the CPC of the Transcaucasian SFSR. In 1930-33, first secretary of the CC of the Tadzhikistan CP. Delegate to the Fourteenth (1925) and Sixteenth (1930) congresses of the CPSU. Served for the last few years of his life in Moscow as PC of education of the RSFSR. Subjected to illegal repression during the cult of Stalin's personality; posthumously rehabilitated.[22]

A fighter for the Party

In the fight against the exploiters and oppressors, the workers of Azerbaidzhan produced from their ranks a galaxy of fighters devoted heart and soul to the proletarian cause. One such was Mirza Davud Bagir-ogly Guseinov. Born at

Baku in 1894, he studied at the technical high school and then in the economics department of the Moscow Commercial Institute, returning to Baku in May 1917. At that time events in Transcaucasia were developing with dramatic speed. The propertied classes, alarmed by the progress of the socialist revolution, were joined by foreign imperialists in opposing the people's conquests. Under the pressure of superior enemy forces, Soviet power in Azerbaidzhan gave way in July 1918, and there followed a dismal period of rule by foreign interventionists and Musavat counterrevolutionaries. The latter ... permitted foreign invaders to plunder the wealth of Azerbaidzhan.

Despite cruel persecutions, the workers of Azerbaidzhan under Bolshevik leadership carried on a determined fight for social and national independence. This fight was the chief influence in forming the views of M. D. Guseinov. He saw through the false slogans of the bourgeois nationalists and firmly took his stand on the side of Soviet power.

In November 1918 he entered the CP, having already [sic] gained a leading position in the Communist organization known as "Gummet," which operated under the direction of the Baku Party committee. Together with A. I. Mikoyan, V. I. Paneishvili, D. Buniadzade, G. Sultanov, A. G. Karaev, and others, he carried on intensive political and organizational activity among the workers, summoning them to overthrow the bourgeois and landlords' regime. In one of his speeches in May 1919 he said: "The people will come into their own by means of revolution and national power, and in no other way." In August of that year he became a member of the Baku Party committee, and then of the Caucasus regional committee of the RCP(B). He took an active part in the creation of the Azerbaidzhan Communist Party, and was one of those who reported at the illegal first congress of Azerbaidzhan Communist organizations, held in February 1920, the result of which was to unite all the organizations concerned into a single Azerbaidzhan Bolshevik CP as an integral part of the RCP(B). At the first plenum of the CC of the new party he was elected chairman of the CC presidium. Together with other Bolsheviks he took an active part in organizing the workers' fight to overthrow the antinational Musavat government. He was also Chairman of the military revolutionary staff set up by the Party's regional committee of the Caucasus to prepare for an armed uprising.

On April 28, 1920, Soviet power prevailed in Azerbaidzhan. As deputy chairman of the Azerbaidzhan revolutionary committee and also acting PC of finance of the Azerbaidzhan SSR, Guseinov displayed inexhaustible energy in restoring the republic's economy. He was a warm advocate of friendship and brotherly cooperation between all the Soviet republics, and always emphasized the immense aid which Soviet Russia gave to the Azerbaidzhan people. "Every socialist country," he said in 1921, "feels at its back the strength of all other socialist countries, and if, for example, anyone today should attack us, we can call on the help of socialist Russia, Georgia, Armenia, and so on."

As a representative of the Azerbaidzhan CP, Guseinov, together with Kirov, Narimanov, and R. Akhundov, took part in June 1923 in a conference of chief editors of the national republics, called by the CC of the RCP(B) to discuss the subject of implementing the decisions of the Twelfth Party Congress on the nationalities question.

In connection with the formation of the Transcaucasian Federation, the Party assigned M.D. Guseinov to important work in Transcaucasia. In 1923-29 he was deputy chairman of the CPC, PC of finance, and PC of foreign affairs of the Transcaucasian SFSR. All his strength, knowledge, and organizing ability were devoted to developing the productive forces of the Transcaucasian republics and to securing the triumph of Lenin's nationalities policy....

During his work in Transcaucasia Guseinov met and worked with such eminent Party leaders as S. M. Kirov, A. I. Mikoyan, G. K. Ordzhonikidze, N. N. Narimanov, E. D. Stasova, F. N. Makharadze, and many others.

In February 1930 he was assigned to important Party work in Tadzhikistan, where he was elected first secretary of the CC of the republican CP, a post which he held for many years. Afterward he worked in the PC of Education at Moscow. He was elected several times to the CC of the Azerbaidzhan CP, and served on the Transcaucasian and Central Asian bureau of the CC of the CPSU and on the presidium of the CEC of the Azerbaidzhan SSR and of the Tadzhik and Transcaucasian SSRs; he also became a member of the CEC of the U.S.S.R. and was a delegate to the Fourteenth and Sixteenth congresses of the CPSU.

At the height of his creative powers he was a victim of arbitrary rule, during the cult of Stalin's personality.

The glorious image of M. D. Guseinov, a true son of the Party and people, like that of other revolutionary champions, inspires the working people of Azerbaidzhan to fight selflessly for the realization of the historic decisions of the Twenty-second Congress of the CPSU and the glorious program for the construction of a Communist society in the U.S.S.R.[23]

AKMAL' IKRAMOV

Biographical data

Born 1898, died 1938. A Party and government worker, one of the organizers of the Uzbekistan CP. Born at Tashkent, the son of an Uzbek peasant. Joined the CP in February 1918 and carried on Party work in Fergana, Tashkent, and Namingan. Was deputy chairman of the Namingan revolutionary committee and later secretary of the Fergana and Syr'dar'ia oblast committees of the RCP(B). In 1921-22, head of the organization department and secretary of the CC of the Turkmenistan CP. From 1922 he studied in Moscow at Sverdlov

Communist University, and was later secretary of the Tashkent oblast Party committee. From March 1923, secretary of the CC of the Uzbekistan CP, secretary of the Central Asia bureau of the CC of the CPSU, and delegate at the Twelfth to Seventeenth congresses of the CPSU. Member of the CEC of the U.S.S.R. and candidate member of its Presidium. He was a victim of slander and repression during the cult of Stalin's personality; posthumously rehabilitated.[24]

A true fighter for the Party

This spring [1964] Akmal' Ikramov, an organizer of the Uzbekistan CP, would be sixty-five years old.

In 1925 M. I. Kalinin, speaking on proletarian internationalism and solidarity at the first constituent congress of the Uzbekistan CP, declared: "The speech of the worker Ikramov from Central Asia had the same effect on me as though he were a worker from Leningrad." This was high praise from the lips of a veteran Petersburg working man, but it was not unfounded.

Ikramov joined the Party at the very beginning of 1918. He was admitted without a specific personal recommendation. As he wrote later in his autobiography, "the organization was a small one, consisting of a few comrades almost all of whom knew me." Yes, he was well known in Tashkent. As a child he worked for the local notables, and later he became a plasterer in the mountain villages. At sixteen he decided to leave home, his father being a fanatical Moslem. From the moment of the February revolution of 1917 he made contact with Russian Bolsheviks living in Tashkent, and on their instructions he organized his fellow workers into groups, read them newspapers, and talked to them about life and the proletarian revolution. At that time the only formal education he had had was in the *mekteb* (religious primary school), where the only instruction was from the Koran. But he had read extensively on his own account and taught himself Russian.

Ikramov had a long career as a Communist and Leninist. Immediately after the October Revolution he organized evening classes for adults where he expounded revolutionary ideas, and after joining the Party he threw himself into organization and propaganda work.

In 1919, as the class conflict became more acute, the Party sent him to the town of Namangan, where he did much to create Party cells among building workers and also headed a commission for the mobilization of Red Army detachments. In addition to these important tasks he devoted special attention to the creation of the first Soviet schools for Uzbek children. Soon the Communists of the Fergana valley promoted him to the bureau of the Fergana oblast committee. Later he was secretary of the Syr-Dar'ia oblast committee, the largest in Central Asia, and in 1921-22 he became secretary of the CC of the Turkestan CP.

After a course at Sverdlov University in Moscow he returned to Tashkent, and at the first congress of the Uzbekistan CP he was elected secretary, and in 1929 first secretary, of the CC of the Uzbekistan CP. During 1931-34 he was also secretary of the Central Asia bureau of the CC of the CPSU.

His name is linked not only with the creation of the Uzbekistan CP but with its great achievements in the first ten years of its existence. Following the course mapped out by the great Lenin, this backward country with its semifeudal agricultural population became a land of socialism and the main supplier of cotton to Soviet industry, so that the problem of Soviet independence with respect to cotton was solved.

As a true disciple of Lenin, Ikramov fought ceaselessly for the triumph of Lenin's nationalities policy. He resolutely opposed all manifestations of nationalism, pan-Turkism, and pan-Islamism, as well as the Trotskyists and other opportunists. He devoted many interesting articles and speeches to problems of agrarian reform and irrigation and to the collectivization and industrialization of Uzbekistan, as well as to popular education and youth problems. One who studied all his life, he became a full-fledged Marxist and was learned in the history and culture of the peoples of Central Asia. He took an active part in the preparation of a new edition of the works of Alisher Navoi and their translation into Russian.

Ikramov's life is a shining example of how Lenin's nationalities policy, by kindling the political initiative of the masses, called forth true Party leaders from their midst. As befits a true Communist, he was modest and considerate, attentive to the workers' needs, implacable toward enemies of Soviet power and all who sought to undermine friendship among the Soviet peoples.

He was a member of the CEC of the U.S.S.R. and a candidate member of its Presidium. The Communists of Uzbekistan sent him five times to Party congresses in Moscow. At the Fourteenth, Fifteenth, and Sixteenth congresses he was elected a candidate member of the CC of the CPSU, and at the Seventeenth a full member. In his speech at the Seventeenth Congress he emphasized that we must not give way to conceit over our achievements or to adulation. Stalin interrupted him sharply and, as events were to show, did not forget the incident. When the phase of illegal repressions reached its height in 1937, Ikramov protested and was arrested on Stalin's personal order. He perished tragically before the age of forty. The memory of this true fighter of Lenin's Party and outstanding son of the Uzbek people lives in the hearts of all citizens of the U.S.S.R.[25]

ALEKSANDR FEDOROVICH IL'IN-ZHENEVSKY

Biographical data

Born 1894, died 1941. A Party and state worker and publicist. Joined the CP in 1912. Born at Petersburg. In 1914 he worked for *Pravda* and the journal

Voprosy strakhovaniia (Insurance Questions). In 1917 he carried on active Party work among the sailors of the Baltic Fleet, editing the Bolshevik papers *Golos pravdy* (Voice of Truth), *Volna* (The Wave) and *Soldatskaia Pravda* (Soldiers' Pravda). He was a member of the Petrograd soviet. In October 1917 the Petrograd RMC appointed him commissar of the Reserve Regiment of Grenadier Guards; later he was sent at the head of a detachment of sailors to aid the insurgents in Moscow. After his return to Petrograd he was a secretary in the PC of Military Affairs, then commissar of the armed forces judicial department. During the Civil War he was head of political administration of the Petrograd Military District and commissar of the department of universal primary education. After 1923 he edited a number of newspapers and journals and was head of the Leningrad oblast commission for the study of the history of the CP. From August 1930 he was counselor of the Soviet embassy in France and later [held the same position] in Czechoslovakia. In 1932 he became deputy director of the Institute of Party History. Subjected to illegal repression during the cult of Stalin's personality; posthumously rehabilitated.[26]

U. D. ISAEV

Biographical data

Born 1899, died 1938. A Party and state leader of Kazakhstan. Joined the CP in 1921. In 1919-24 he worked in local soviets of the Ural gubernia, later in the gubernia Cheka and the Ural gubernia committee of the RCP(B). In 1924-25 he was deputy chairman of the regional control commission and deputy PC of workers' and peasants' inspection. In 1925-29 he was a member of the bureau and later second secretary of the Kazakh regional committee of the CPSU. In 1929-38, chairman of the CPC of the Kazakh SSR. Was elected a delegate from the Fifteenth to the Seventeenth CPSU congresses and attended many congresses of soviets of the RSFSR, U.S.S.R., and Kazakh SSR; was a candidate and full member of the CC of the CPSU, a member of the All-Union CEC and its Presidium. Committed certain errors in practical and theoretical work.[27]

V. I. IVANOV

Biographical data

Born 1893, died 1938. Delegate for the Party's Moscow organization to the Eleventh Congress of the RCP(B). Joined the CP in 1915 and carried on Party work in Moscow. During the October Revolution he was a member of the RMC of the Basmannyi district of Moscow. In later years he held important Party posts as secretary of the Yaroslavl gubernia committee of the RCP(B), and head of the organization department of the Moscow committee and chairman of that committee. From 1924, he was secretary of the CC of the Uzbekistan CP, later secretary of the North Caucasus and the Northern regional committee of the CPSU. From 1937, PC of forest industry of the U.S.S.R.[28]

ASATUR KAKHOIAN

Biographical data

Born 1874, died 19——. In 1898 organized Marxist groups among Armenian workers in Tiflis. In 1907 he was a delegate to the Seventh Congress of the RSDWP. Took an active part in the establishment of Soviet rule in Transcaucasia; member of the Transcaucasian regional committee of the CPSU and the Transcaucasian CEC. He became a victim of the cult of personality.[29]

His memory lives

When Lenin learned of the tragic fate of his beloved pupil and counselor I. V. Babushkin, he said: "All that has been conquered from Tsarist autocracy was won thanks to the struggle of the masses led by such men as Babushkin." We may well apply these inspiring words to the eminent workers and Bolsheviks Asatur Kakhoian, Melik Melikian ("grandfather"), and their close friends—the "Babushkins" of the Armenian proletariat, veteran revolutionaries of Transcaucasia and unswerving champions of the Leninist Party. As early as 1898 they organized the first Marxist group of Armenian workers in Tiflis, and in 1900 they founded the first illegal newspaper in the Armenian language, *Banvor*.

Kakhoian was born in 1874 in the village of Akhpat, where he spent his childhood and youth. He maintained contact throughout his life with the workers of Lori, mindful of the needs and cares of his native village. As an experienced Party organizer and propagandist, he has a special place among the Bolshevik old guard. His activity during the underground years may be described as truly heroic.... He was skilled in the arts of conspiracy, organized underground printing presses, and was a close and loyal comrade of the legendary Kamo—who before taking some decisive step would often say: "I shall not be happy about this until I have consulted my friend Kakhoteli" (as he used to call Kakhoian). The latter played a major part in organizing the strikes of 1904-5 at Batumi and Alaverdi, when the bosses and factory managers were forced to make concessions to the workers' demands.... The Party cell which he and Melikian created at Akhpat was one of the first Leninist *Iskra* cells in Armenia.

In 1923, on the twentieth anniversary of the heroic outbreak of "Red Akhpat" and the creation of a Bolshevik cell there, the Armenian CP and press gave prominence to this glorious date and to the name of Asatur Kakhoian. The old Bolshevik publicist Amot Khumarian wrote of him in the newspaper *Martakoch:* "A modest, hard-working revolutionary veteran, prepared for every self-sacrifice and deprivation, the worker Khecho [sic] was an example of a true fighter of the working class."

Kakhoian took an active part in establishing Soviet rule and fighting for the victory of socialism in Transcaucasia. He occupied important posts and was several times elected to the Transcaucasian regional committee of the CPSU and the Transcaucasian CEC [sic] of the CC of the Armenian CP.... He also left us a literary testimony in his interesting memoirs, extracts from which were published by the Armenian branch of the Marxist-Leninist Institute of the CC of the CPSU. It is to be wished that others of his works might be published.

He was an ardent advocate of friendship among peoples, and belongs equally to those of Armenia, Georgia and Azerbaidzhan. This Bolshevik of pure soul and steadfast will traversed the thorny but honorable path of an ardent warrior. He was a victim of repression during the cult of personality, but he lives among us, in our hearts. Today on the ninetieth anniversary of his birth, we honor the memory of this brave fighter.[30]

BETAL EDYGOVICH KALMYKOV

Biographical data

Born 1893, died 1940. Joined the CP in March 1918. Born of poor parents in the mountain village of Kuba, now in the Baksan raion of the Kabardino-Balkarian ASSR. Worked as a laborer from the age of fourteen, and in 1913 was a leader of the peasant revolt against the local nobility whose first interest was the breeding of race horses. In 1915-16 he organized the illegal revolutionary-democratic movement known as "Krakhalk" (The Poor). In 1917 he played an important part in organizing and carrying out the October Revolution in the northern Caucasus. In 1918 he was a delegate to all five congresses of the peoples of the Terek oblast, directed the work of the first congress of the Nal'chik district which proclaimed Soviet rule in Kabardia and Balkaria (March 1918), and was commissar extraordinary and commissar for nationalities of the Terek oblast. During the Civil War he was an organizer and leader of partisans in the northern Caucasus and commanded a regiment and a division of the Red Army. In 1921-24 he directed military operations for the suppression of banditry in Kabardia and Balkaria. In 1920-29 he was chairman of the Kabardino-Balkarian oblast executive committee, and in 1929-38 first secretary of the Kabardino-Balkarian oblast committee of the CPSU. He was a member of the CEC of the RSFSR and the CEC of the U.S.S.R. at all convocations; deputy to the Supreme Soviet of the U.S.S.R. at the first convocation and a delegate at the Eleventh to the Seventeenth Party congresses. Subjected to repression during the cult of Stalin's personality; posthumously rehabilitated.[31]

Our Betal

It was January 1919. The Red Army, overwhelming Denikin's troops, was advancing toward Rostov. Denikin decided to make a thrust for the northern Caucasus. He collected some shock troops and attacked the Eleventh Army which was barring his way. The North Caucasian Bolsheviks, led by Ordzhonikidze and Kirov as emissaries of the Party CC, stirred up the working population of Kabardia and Balkaria to defend the Soviet regime. In those strenuous days Betal Kalmykov, commissar extraordinary for the Terek oblast, never unsaddled his horse or let the weapon drop from his hand. But the forces were unequally matched. Denikin's men took Vladikavkaz and shot Kalmykov's father and brother. He himself hid with his companions in the forests of Kabardia, Balkaria, Ossetia, and Ingushetia. Not until March 1920 did he return to his own territory, at the head of the Kabardino-Balkarian revolutionary committee.

This was only one military episode in Kalmykov's life—the life of an eminent leader of the Bolsheviks of Kabardino-Balkaria. His name is permanently associated with the heroic deeds and victories of his compatriots during the fight for Soviet rule and the subsequent building of socialism.

He was born on October 24, 1893, the son of a poor peasant. In youth he worked as a loader, herdsman, and unskilled laborer. In 1913 he was one of the organizers of the major uprising of Kabardinian and Balkarian peasants in the Zol' pastures and the Cherek gorge. At that time he met S. M. Kirov, who was to play a most important part in his life.

In 1917-18 Kalmykov carried on intensive organizing work among the masses, mobilizing and forging them into a fighting force for the victory of socialism in the Terek area. In March 1918 he joined the Piatigorsk Bolshevik organization, and he remained a faithful son of the Party to the end of his life. He was an organizer and leader of the first Bolshevik organization formed in Kabardia at the beginning of 1918, and he was in the chair at the session of soviets which proclaimed Soviet power in Kabardia and Balkaria.

When the Civil War broke out, the Party directed him to the most dangerous and responsible sectors. The government showed its high appreciation of his services in liquidating counterrevolutionary bands and directing the partisan movement in the northern caucasus by awarding him the Order of the Red Banner. "You and your comrades," Ordzhonikidze wrote to him, "have, in the years of the Civil War and under the guidance of Lenin's Party, led the workers in the forefront of the struggle for Soviet power in the northern Caucasus."

From 1920 to 1930 he was chairman of the Kabardino-Balkarian oblast executive committee, and in 1930-38 first secretary of the Kabardino-Balkarian oblast committee of the CPSU. In those years he displayed his ability to organize most clearly, showing himself to be an outstanding leader, recognizing no interests but those of the Party and people. He was an eminent Party and government worker, a member of the All-Russian CEC and the CEC of the U.S.S.R. at all convocations, a deputy to the Supreme Soviet of the U.S.S.R. at the first convocation, and a delegate at the Eleventh to Seventeenth Party congresses.

He became a victim of arbitrary rule during the cult of personality and perished at the height of his powers in 1940. A monument to his memory was erected in 1961 at Nal'chik, the capital of the Kabardino-Balkarian ASSR, by a decision of the Soviet government.[32]

Kalmykov's career

The name of B. E. Kalmykov is dear to all the workers of Kabardino-Balkaria. He earned this love and universal gratitude by his faithfulness to the Communist Party, his selfless service of the people and the cause of socialism and communism.

From his youth he carried on revolutionary work among the poor folk of Kabardia and Balkaria. More than once he was subjected to repression by both the Tsarist and the bourgeois Provisional Government. In 1919 the Whites shot his father and younger brother.

A friend and counselor of the eminent revolutionaries Ordzhonikidze, Kirov, and S. T. Buachidze, during the fight for the preparation and execution of the socialist revolution Kalmykov emerged as a leader and powerful organizer of the workers, a skillful propagator of the ideas of the Bolshevik Party among the mountain dwellers of the northern Caucasus. He was in close touch with the leading Bolsheviks and rank-and-file Communists of Chechen-Ingushetia, northern Ossetia, Dagestan, Karachai-Cherkessia, and other regions of the northern Caucasus, where the masses rose in arms to defend Soviet power.

In 1918, when a bitter struggle was raging for the victory of Soviet power in the northern Caucasus, he was elected a delegate to all five congresses of the peoples of the Terek oblast, where he and other Bolsheviks mercilessly denounced the anti-national activity of the local princes, landowners, and kulaks and forged the workers into a revolutionary force.

At the beginning of 1918 he joined the CP, and in that year the CPC of the Terek oblast appointed him its commissar extraordinary and commissar for nationalities. In March 1918 he presided over the first national congress of the Nal'chik district, which proclaimed Soviet power in Kabardia and Balkaria. During the Civil War and foreign military intervention, he was one of the first organizers of partisans and Red Guard detachments in the northern Caucasus.

In summer 1918 he commanded a regiment, and later a division of the Red Army.

From 1920 to 1929 he was chairman of the Kabardino-Balkarian oblast executive committee, and from the end of 1929 to 1938 he was first secretary of the Kabardino-Balkarian oblast committee of the CPSU. In these years he showed himself to be an outstanding leader of the Leninist type, having no interests but those of the Party and people. His whole career was a model of service to the people, close contact with the masses, and ability to listen to the workers, profit by their experience, and encourage their initiative. As *Pravda* declared on October 26, 1936,

> Kalmykov, the oblast first secretary, understands ploughing and stockbreeding as well as he does folk art and the building of schools. His daily concern is the life and interests of the masses.... As a good Bolshevik, he does not lie down under difficulties but remains faithful to the people in good and bad times.

The Party and government highly valued his revolutionary and organizing ability, and he received the Order of the Red Banner for his work in liquidating counterrevolutionary bands and his leadership of the partisans in the northern Caucasus. He was a Party and government worker of the first rank: a member of the CEC of the RSFSR and of the U.S.S.R. at all convocations, a deputy to the Supreme Soviet of the U.S.S.R. at its first convocation, a permanent member of the North Caucasus regional committee of the Party and of the regional executive committee, and a delegate at all Party congresses from the Tenth to the Seventeenth.[33]

ALIGEIDAR AGAKERIM-OGLY KARAEV

Biographical data

Born in 1896, died 1938. Joined the CP in 1919. Born at Shemakha (Azerbaidzhan). In 1916, entered the Don Polytechnic Institute at Novocherkassk. In May 1917, returned to Azerbaidzhan. In 1918, took part in the Baku Workers' Conference and in the December strike of the Baku proletariat. In 1919, member of the presidium of the Baku conference and subsequently its chairman; member of the Baku committee of the RCP(B). In 1920, member of the CC of the Azerbaidzhan CP, and subsequently of its presidium. In 1923-25, secretary of the CC of the Azerbaidzhan CP. In 1925-29, first secretary of the Azerbaidzhan CC. In 1929-30, secretary of the Transcaucasian regional committee of the CPSU. In 1930-31, secretary of the Gandzha district committee of the Azerbaidzhan CP; elected several times to the CC of the Azerbaidzhan CP and the Transcaucasian regional committee of the CPSU; member of the Azerbaidzhan CEC and the Transcaucasian CEC. At the end of his life he was working in the Institute of Extramural Education of Party Cadres under the CC of the CPSU. Liquidated in 1938.[34]

A fighter for the people's freedom and happiness

Aligeidir Agakerim-ogly Karaev was born at Shemakha on June 7, 1896. At the age of six he entered the local religious school, and in 1906-15 he attended the Shemakha technical high school. As a youth he was much influenced by the poems of the revolutionary satirist M. A. Sabir and the poet A. Sikhkhet, which taught him to understand the life of town paupers as well as the peasantry he had known since childhood. He worked for the journal *Molla Nasreddin*, opposing the arbitrary rule of the rich and the ignorance and obscurantism of the clergy, and took an active part in the cultural and educational society known as Nidzhat. In 1916 he entered the Don Polytechnic Institute at Novocherkassk, where he was an active member of the student social-democratic movement.

In May 1917 he returned to Shemakha, where he met the local social-democrats and became chairman of the soviet of workers' and soldiers' deputies. In June he was sent by the peasants of the Shemakha uezd as a delegate to the Transcaucasian congress of peasants' deputies. At this time he had not sufficiently grasped the development of the revolution, and he joined the Menshevik Gummet in Tiflis.

The Socialist revolution did not triumph at once in Transcaucasia. The bourgeois-nationalist Mensheviks and SRs, with the help for foreign intervention-ists, attacked the conquests of the workers and peasants, and Soviet power in Baku was eclipsed by the dark days of intervention and counterrevolution. But the workers of Azerbaidzhan and Transcaucasia did not lay down their arms, but fought stubbornly to restore Soviet power. These events opened Karaev's eyes to reality, to the true nature of counterrevolution and the treacher-ous role of petty bourgeois and nationalistic parties. His move to proletarian Baku in December 1918 was a decisive step in his life and put the seal on his Bolshevik outlook. In February 1919 he joined the CP and united his fate once and for all with the struggle of the Azerbaidzhan workers for the victory of the socialist revolution. Soon he became one of the chief leaders of the Communist Gummet under the direction of the Baku Committee of the RCP(B). Together with A. I. Mikoyan, G. Sultanov, D. Buniatzade, I. I. Anashkin, M. D. Guseinov, V. I. Naneishvili, and other Bolsheviks, he carried out inten-sive political and organizational work among the Baku workers and the Azer-baidzhan peasants, mobilizing them to overthrow the power of the bourgeois and landlords.

The Bolsheviks, at this time an underground movement, exploited all possi-ble legal means, one of which was the Baku Workers' Conference. This perma-

nent political organ directed the fight of the Baku workers and the toiling population of Azerbaidzhan against the British interventionists, the Whites, and the
Musavat government. In December 1918 Karaev became a member of the conference, and in that year took an active part in the strike of the Baku propetariat.
In March 1919 he was elected a member of its presidium, and in May became
its chairman. Occupying this post until the victory of Soviet power, he often
appeared at works, factories, and other concerns, carrying on propaganda and
speaking at meetings. The voice of Bolshevism was also heard in the Musavat
parliament, where he relentlessly denounced the treasonable policy of the government of bourgeoisie and landowners.

Karaev did excellent work in organizing, publishing, and editing Bolshevik
newspapers and journals, especially in the Azerbaidzhani language.... These
newspapers published the Bolshevik Party program adopted at the Eighth Congress of the RCP(B), propaganda articles explaining this program, Lenin's ideas
on the nationalities question, his statements on problems of the revolution,
the nature of Soviet power, Soviet Russia, the foundations of socialism, etc.
They also familiarized the workers with the life history of the revolutionary
leader [Lenin]. All this had a great effect on the political education of the
whole working people of Azerbaidzhan. Most of the articles were written by
Karaev himself. In articles and other short pieces he relentlessly denounced
the colonial policy of the imperialists in Azerbaidzhan and Transcaucasia and
the counterrevolutionary aims of the Musavatists, Dashnaks, Mensheviks, and
SRs, calling upon the people to combat foreign interventionism and internal
counterrevolution....

In October 1919 Karaev was elected a member of the Baku committee
of the RCP(B). In February 1920 the first congress of the Azerbaidzhan CP
was held illegally and called on the Party organization and the workers of
Azerbaidzhan for an armed uprising. At this congress Karaev was elected to
the CC of the Azerbaidzhan CP, and later became a member of its presidium.
As a leader of the Azerbaidzhan CP and a member of the Azerbaidzhan
revolutionary committee and the revolutionary committee for Baku and the surrounding area, he took part in the organization of the uprising.

On April 28, 1920, Soviet rule was established once and for all in the
ancient land of Azerbaidzhan. Occupying at various times the posts of PC
of justice, of labor, and of the army and navy, and also being chairman of
the Baku soviet, Karaev devoted himself heart and soul to consolidating the
conquests of the young Soviet republic. Under his direction the armed forces
of Soviet Azerbaidzhan were built up and strengthened. In 1921 S. M. Kirov
wrote of him: "Comrade Karaev is a devoted servant of the Party who has
displayed energy in both Party and state affairs and in organizing the Azerbaidzhani Red Army."

Karaev saw the freedom and happiness of the Azerbaidzhan people in
friendly alliance with Soviet Russia and the Russian people. He spoke with

deep gratitude of the October Socialist Revolution which had brought freedom to all the peoples of our country....

In 1923 he was elected secretary of the CC of the Azerbaidzhan CP. From January 1925, after Kirov was transferred to Leningrad, he became first secretary of the Azerbaidzhan CC. As head of the republic's Party organization he worked hard to mobilize the energies of the Communists and the entire working people for the development of industry and agriculture and for the cultural revolution. He devoted great attention to the electrification of enterprises, the adoption of new techniques, the creation of new industrial centers, the development of transport, and the improvement of the material welfare of the workers and peasants. During these years his organizing talent showed to the greatest advantage. His whole life and work were an example of steadfastness, hard work, and true Communist modesty, as well as close contact with the people. He adhered strictly to the Party's general line, taking a firm stand on Leninist principles, decisively and relentlessly opposing the foes of Leninism, defending the unity of the Party and the ideological purity of its ranks....

In October 1929 he was elected secretary of the Transcaucasian regional committee of the CPSU, and in 1930-31 he was secretary of the Gandzha (Kirovabad) district committee of the Azerbaidzhan CP. He was elected several times to the CC of the Azerbaidzhan CP and the Transcaucasian regional committee of the CPSU, and was a member of the Azerbaidzhan CEC and the Transcaucasian CEC; he was also a delegate at the Eleventh and Fifteenth congresses of the CPSU. At the latter congress, in 1927, he was elected a member of the Central Control Commission of the CPSU. After attending a course at the Moscow Institute of Red Professors he worked during the last years of his life at the Institute of Extramural Education of Party Cadres under the CC of the CPSU. In 1938 his career was tragically cut short.

The workers of our republic revere the memory of the great Bolshevik A. Karaev, who gave his life for the triumph of the ideas of Lenin's Party.[35]

LAVRENTII IOSIPOVICH KARTVELISHVILI

Biographical data

Born 1891, died 1938. Joined the Bolshevik Party in 1910. Born in Georgia. Arrested for revolutionary activity in 1916. After the February revolution of 1917 he returned from exile to Kiev, was a member of the city committee of the RSDWP and chairman of its raion committee. During the period of hetman rule* he worked in the Party underground in Kiev and took part in

---

*The "period of hetman rule" refers to the period between April 29 and December, 1918, when under the Austro-German occupation the head of the Ukrainian government, Pavel Petrovich Skoropadsky, was proclaimed hetman of the Ukraine.—ED.

the All-Ukraine Congress of Trade Unions. In 1918 he was a member of the CC of the Ukrainian CP. After leaving the underground he edited the newspaper *Kommunist* at Odessa. In June 1919 he was elected to the gubernia Party committee and later became its secretary. In August he became a member of the RMC of the southern group of forces. After Denikin's defeat and the liberation of Odessa in February 1920 he was appointed head of the agitprop department, and later editor of the oblast newspaper *Izvestiia*. Later he was elected to the presidium of the gubernia committee and was head of the agricultural department, then chairman of the Odessa gubernia committee of the Party. From the end of 1921 to 1925, with short interruptions, he directed the Kiev oblast Party organization. In 1925-29 he was secretary of the CC of the Georgian CP, then chairman of the Georgian CPC. In 1929 he returned to the Ukraine as head of the political administration of the Ukraine MD. In November 1929 he became secretary and a member of the politburo and organization bureau of the CC of the Ukrainian CP. In 1931 he was made secretary of the Transcaucasian regional committee of the Party; in November, second secretary of the West Siberian regional committee of the CPSU, and later first secretary of the Far Eastern committee of the CPSU. In 1936-37 he served as secretary of the Crimean oblast committee of the Party. At the Sixteenth Congress of the CPSU he was elected a candidate member of the CC of the CPSU. He was a victim of the cult of Stalin's personality.[36]

MENDEL' MARKOVICH KHATAEVICH

Biographical data

Born 1893, died 1939. Soviet Party and government worker. Joined the CP in 1913. From 1914 to the February revolution of 1917 he was in jail or in exile. Took part in the October Revolution, in Belorussia, and the Civil War. He was secretary of the Gomel and Odessa gubernia committees, the Tatar oblast committee and the Central Volga regional committee of the Party, also secretary of the CC of the Ukraine CP. At the Sixteenth and Seventeenth Party congresses he was elected a member of the CC of the CPSU.[37]

An unswerving Communist

The name Mendel' Markovich Khataevich conjures up in my mind the picture of a man of resolute features and few but decisive gestures. I saw him once delivering a report to a crowded hall in Kharkov. As he spoke he kept waving his left hand and striking his other hand with it as though hammering in nails. His right hand was paralyzed—a momento of the dark days of the White Guard revolt at Samara.

On July 28, 1918, when the counterrevolutionary Czechoslovak forces attacked Samara, Khataevich and other local Bolsheviks fought bravely in the streets of the town. Their forces were too few, and they had to retreat. During the street battle Khataevich was badly wounded in the chest and right hand. By some miracle his comrades got him away from the scene of the fighting and hid him in a hospital for two months, but in the end he was arrested by the Whites and brutally tortured. As he himself later related:

> Not wishing to betray those who had helped me to hide, I refused to tell my questioners where I had been. In revenge I was cruelly beaten: my torturers hit me about the head and face with a pistol butt, thrust the muzzle into my mouth and threatened to shoot at once, and drove their heels into my chest where the wound had not yet healed under the bandages. But they got nothing further out of me. That evening I was sent to jail and straight to the prison hospital. I looked such a sight that the warden who took me in said: "Well, here's one that won't last three days."

But the Whites underrated their prisoner's toughness. Half dead from torture, he still had the strength to defy the jail authorities and to stir up his fellow prisoners to resist evacuation from the city. The Whites, retreating in panic before the advancing Red Army, were obliged to leave Khataevich and his comrades.

This episode is characteristic of the career of this staunch, brave Communist. While still a youth he took part in the fight against autocracy by distributing illegal literature. In 1913, at the age of twenty, he was already the leader of an underground group of Bolsheviks at Gomel. A year later he was arrested for printing and distributing leaflets calling for support for the Baku strikers. He remained in jail or Siberian exile until the February revolution. Returning to Gomel in March 1917, he soon managed to strengthen the city's Bolshevik organization: a group of eleven or twelve men had grown by September 1917 to a monolithic organization of over 800. He was elected deputy chairman of the Gomel Party committee and a member of the presidium of the city soviet. On all basic questions—those of the war, political power, and land ownership—the Gomel organization of the RSDWP and the Gomel city soviet adopted resolutions put forward by the Bolsheviks.

On August 28, the occasion of Kornilov's counterrevolutionary revolt, Khataevich organized a meeting of workers and soldiers in the town park. Directly after the meeting, dozens of workers enlisted in the Red Guard. A "committee of revolutionary defense" was set up at Gomel to fight Kornilov: this committee, of which Khataevich was a member, sent its representatives to telegraph and railroad stations and organized patrols on the main roads and highways linking the staff of the supreme command with the southwestern front.

The importance which the CC of the RCP(B) attached to Khataevich's activity during the preparation and carrying out of the October Revolution may be judged from the fact that his private address (No. 3 Hospital Street, Gomel) was noted in the CC address book drawn up by Ia. M. Sverdlov and E. D. Stasov. When Gomel was occupied by the Germans Khataevich was sent to Samara, where he was elected chairman of the Party's city committee, a member of the gubernia committee, and a member of the Defense Staff commission. Together with V. V. Kuibyshev, E. S. Kogan and other Samara Communists he took part in the suppression of the Anarchist-Maximalist revolt and the armed struggle with the White Czechs. In the last year of the Civil War the Party sent him to the Polish front as head of the political department of the Fourth Army and later of the Twenty-first Division, with units of which he advanced as far as Warsaw.

Returning to Samara, he found the gubernia committee in the hands of the ''workers' opposition'' and at once embarked on a sharp struggle in defense of the Leninist Party line. At the next gubernia congress of soviets, the Bolshevik group refuted the theses of the oppositionist speaker and put forward Khataevich as their spokesman.... At the city assembly of the Party which was held before the gubernia conference, anti-Party views were put forward by representatives of all the opposition groups, including Trotsky, who had come to Samara for the occasion. At this meeting Khataevich cast into Trotsky's face the angry words ''Until such time as you conform to the true Party line, I will oppose you.''

Kuibyshev, who was sent to Samara to explain the decisions of the Tenth Party Congress, said to the Party's city *aktiv:* ''The Party organization in Samara is lucky that Khataevich came back from the front in time to organize the defense of Lenin's line in true Party fashion.'' Indeed, throughout his career Khataevich displayed implacable hostility toward enemies of the Party, devotion to its interests, and firmness in defending Lenin's ideas against Trotskyists, Zinovievites, and right-wing opportunists. These qualities brought him to the front rank of Party leaders and organizers of the masses and of socialist construction.

In 1924-25 he worked as a senior instructor and deputy head of the organization and distribution department of the CC of the CPSU, studying the course of the Leninist enrollment of Party members.... Later he was secretary of the Tatar gubernia committee of the Party (1925-28) and of the Central Volga regional committee (1928-32). A champion of the concrete approach and an enemy of empty phrases, he studied the special features of Volga agriculture and saw to it that account was taken of them in the Party's work of fostering agriculture and collectivization. In a comparatively short time the regional committee achieved notable successes in collectivization and the replanning of agriculture.

When the growth of the kolkhoz movement called for a revision of the five-year plan of kolkhoz construction and collectivization deadlines, the Party CC in December 1929 set up a commission to study various questions ''of major practical and theoretical importance.'' Khataevich became a member of this body together with other Party and agriculture experts such as Ia. A. Iakovlev, A. A. Andreev, S. V. Kosior, and N. M. Vareikis.

In March 1933 he was elected first secretary of the Dnepropetrovsk oblast committee of the Ukraine CP. At that time agriculture in the oblast was in a bad way, and the Party organization was called upon to retrieve the position. In this task Khataevich's abilities found plenty of scope. He studied questions of agricultural techniques, the material and economic interests of collective farms, the problem of fodder, the organization of machine tractor stations, and the role of village soviets as organs of power and mass organizations in the villages. He mobilized all organizations and the whole population to improve agriculture. He expounded to the Komsomol *aktiv* a specific program for the acquisition of agricultural techniques and the training of machine operators, called special conferences on questions of profitability and rural trading, and discussed with the editors of raion newspapers how to improve the standard of the village press. All the crucial questions of kolkhoz life were discussed at oblast meetings of kolkhoz shock workers, stockbreeders, and women workers on state and collective farms. By 1933 the oblast had overcome its backwardness and was successfully fulfilling its quotas for output and delivery of agricultural products to the state. For this achievement, Khataevich in 1935 received the Order of Lenin. He was constantly among the people, learning from them, listening to their advice and benefiting from their experience. In 1934 he invited thirty-seven "grandfathers" or veterans of the kolkhoz movement to attend a meeting of the oblast committee and advise on how and when it was best to sow winter crops and prepare seeds, and how to improve the quality of cultivation. He also laid stress on the participation of women in public activities and in running the kolkhozes....

His wide interest and varied activities are attested by the list of his writings. The Library contains more than sixty books and pamphlets by him, including works entitled: *Bol'sheviki Dnepropetrovshchiny v bor'be za stakhanovskie pokazateli 1936 g.* (The Dnepropetrovsk Bolsheviks and the Fight to Achieve the Stakhanovite Indices of 1936); *Za polnokrovnuiu, b'iushchuiu kliuchem partiinuiu zhizn'* (For a Full-blooded, Vigorous Party Life); *Bol'she vnimaniia shkolam i detiam* (More Attention to Schools and Children), a speech delivered at a city conference of parents; *Za peredovoe mesto v riadakh literaturnogo dvizheniia* (For a Place in the Forefront of the Literary Movement); *Za bol'shevistskie vysokodokhodnye, ustoichivye i krepkie kolkhozy* (For Strong, Durable, High-yielding Bolshevik Collective Farms); *Za ovladenie agrotekhnikov* (How to Obtain Agrotechnicians); *O sliianii politotdelov s raikomami* (On the Merging of Political Departments with Raion Committees); and *Za vypolnenie finansovogo plana* (For the Fulfillment of the Financial Plan). In these short works we feel the tremendous energy of a tireless Party leader who devoted his life to the triumph of the ideas of socialism.

During the cult of Stalin's personality, when democratic principles for the direction of agriculture were being distorted, Khataevich declared war on gross violations of the kolkhoz system, bureaucratism, "administrationism," and arbitrary rule. At the beginning of 1931, in a conversation with the Komsomol *aktiv* of the Central Volga region, he sharply criticized leaders who on occasion used coercive measures instead of explanation and persuasion, and appealed to Party workers not to substitute command for guidance. He always insisted that Party workers should listen to the opinions of the masses, and condemned those who tried to stifle the criticisms of rank-and-file Communists. As early as 1928, in a report delivered at Samara, he observed that some leaders regarded any worker who spoke out plainly as a trouble-maker and oppositionist... Many of his utterances at the time of the personality cult reveal deep anxiety and concern over the position in the Party. In his speech in 1937 at the thirteenth congress of the Ukraine CP, of which he was then second secretary, he urged that a stop should be put to arbitrary rule and the defamation of honest Bolsheviks for the slightest criticism, and also to the atmosphere of empty pomp and show and self-congratulation. He described to the delegates how a certain old Donbass worker had been expelled from the Party and declared an "enemy of the people"—a man who had fought in the Civil War and lost two brothers in it—merely for daring to make critical remarks about the central organs of the Ukraine.

Khataevich was a delegate to many Party congresses, from the Eighth to the Seventeenth. At the Fourteenth, he was elected a member of the central commission of inspection, at the Fifteenth a candidate member of the CC, and at the Sixteenth and Seventeenth a full member of the CC of the CPSU. From 1932 to 1937 he was a member of the politburo of the CC of the Ukraine CP. In 1937 he was slandered and subjected to repression.

After the Twentieth Congress the Party restored the good name of this inflexible Communist, true Leninist, and selfless fighter for the people's happiness.[38]

VIL'GEL'M GEORGIEVICH KNORIN

Biographical data

Born 1890, died 1939. Party and government worker, historian and publicist. Joined the CP in 1910. Born in Latvia; herded sheep from the age of eleven, then worked at a wadding factory. Attended a teachers' college; worked on social-democratic newspapers in Petersburg, Riga, and Libava (Libau). After the February revolution of 1917 he helped to organize the Minsk soviet of workers' and soldiers' deputies and Bolshevik organizations on the Western front. From May 1917 he was secretary of the Minsk soviet, then editor of the Bolshevik newspaper *Zvezda*. In October 1917 he became a member of the Minsk RMC. In 1918-22, he carried out key Party and government work in Smolensk, Minsk, and Vilna (Wilno). In 1922-25 he served on the CC of the CPSU as deputy head of the department of accounting and distribution and head of the information department, then head of agitprop of the Moscow committee of the CPSU. In 1926-27, head of the agitprop department of the CC of the CPSU. In 1927-28, secretary of the CC of the Belorussian CP. At the Sixth Comintern Congress he was elected a candidate member of the Comintern Executive Committee; served on this committee from 1928 to 1935. From 1932 he was director on this committee from 1928 to 1935. From 1932 he was director of the Party history section of the Institute of Red Professors, and in 1932-34 a member of the editorial board of *Pravda*. From 1935, he was deputy head of the agitprop department of the CC of the CPSU. Became a Doctor of Historical Sciences in 1935; wrote several, works on Party history. Subjected to illegal repression during the cult of Stalin's personality; posthumously rehabilitated.[39]

A true son of the Leninist Party

August 30, 1965, will be the seventy-fifth anniversary of the birth of Vil'gel'm Georgievich Knorin.

The son of a poor Latvian peasant, he worked for a kulak from childhood and at the age of fifteen became a factory worker in the town of Ligatne. The 1905 revolution occurred while he was there and determined the future course of his life. The defeat of the revolution and the brutal repressions which followed only strengthened his revolutionary fervor. In 1906 he entered a teachers' college and studied philosophy, including the Marxist classics.

At the outbreak of the First World War he was called up and served as a private soldier on the western front, in Belorussia. He created an underground Party organization at the thirty-second evacuation station. Long before the revolution he was a member of the Latvian social-democratic group and was in contact with numerous comrades, including such tried Bolsheviks as M. V. Frunze, K. I. Lander, A. F. Miasnikov, and others. At Minsk, after the February revolution, he resolutely opposed the "conciliating" policy of the petty bourgeois parties and supported the creation of a consistent Leninist Bolshevik Party organization. A large part was played in this by the Minsk soviet of workers' deputies, led by the Bolsheviks. Knorin was elected secretary of this body in May 1917. The Minsk Bolsheviks, having split up the notorious *ob"edinenka,* ("writer group"), created an independent Bolshevik organization of which Knorin was the moving spirit.

Later, he was a member of the RMC of the western region which took over power in Minsk, the whole of Belorussia, and on the western front. The break-off of negotiations at Brest Litovsk put a stop to the intense activities of Soviet power in Belorussia, which the German troops began to occupy.

Knorin, as chairman of the Party's Minsk city committee, organized cadres for underground Party work, and at the end of 1918 and the beginning of 1919 contributed largely to the creation, under Lenin's direction, of the Belorussian CP.

In the difficult conditions of civil war and the fight against the interventionists, he was intensely active in the fields of Party organization and propaganda. After Minsk and Belorussia were liberated from White Polish occupation, he headed the Party organizational triumvirate and then the revolutionary committee set up by the RMC of the western front. In the course of the establishment of the Belorussian SSR he fought on two fronts: against great-power chauvinism and local bourgeois nationalism.

A Party leader of the Leninist type—organizer, agitator, propagandist—he was at the same time a simple, modest, wholehearted comrade, much loved and admired by the Belorussian workers.

He was a delegate at the Fifth to Seventh congresses of the Comintern, and at the Sixth Congress was elected a member of the Comintern Executive Committee. In 1928-31 he served abroad as a Comintern representative, and in 1931-35 in Moscow as a member of the Comintern Executive Committee and head of its Central European secretariat. He took part in the Comintern's elaboration of the tactics of a single proletarian front and a broad popular front against fascism and the approaching world war. He did much to overcome sectarianism and dogmatism in the international Communist movement.

From 1932 until 1935 he was a member of the editorial board of *Pravda,* and in 1934-37 of the journal *Bol'shevik.* He left many writings, and in 1935 received the degree of Doctor of Historical Sciences. He was director of the Institute of Red Professors and published several works on Party history. His life was tragically cut short in 1937, when he was busily working on a popular textbook of the history of the CPSU. The great Leninist Party, to which he devoted his life, will never forget its faithful son.[40]

ALEKSANDR VASIL'EVICH KOSAREV

Biographical data

Born 1903, died 1939. Active in the Communist youth movement. Joined the Young Communist League of Russia in 1918 and the CP in 1919. Born in Moscow, the son of a worker. During the Civil War he volunteered for the front at the age of fifteen, and in 1919 took part in the defense of Petrograd against Iudenich's forces. After the war he was secretary of the Bauman raion committee of the All-Union Komsomol in Moscow, the Moscow-Narva raion committee in Leningrad, and the Penza gubernia committee of the Komsomol. In 1926 he was elected secretary of the Moscow committee of the Komsomol, and in 1927 secretary of the organization's CC. From March 1929 to 1939 he was secretary general of the CC of the Komsomol and enjoyed great prestige as a youth leader. At the Fifteenth Congress of the CPSU in 1927 he was elected a member of the Central Control Commission of the CPSU; at the Sixteenth Congress in 1930 he became a candidate member of the CC of the CPSU, and a full member of the CC at the Seventeenth Congress in 1934. He was a member of the organization bureau of the CC of the CPSU and a member of the CEC of the U.S.S.R. During the cult of Stalin's personality he was slandered and subjected to illegal repression. Posthumously rehabilitated.[41]

An eminent youth organizer

A dashing youth with a mop of hair presented himself at the raion committee and demanded to be sent to the front. When he was refused he made no special protest, but pulled his battered cap over his eyes and smiled mysteriously. A few days later he was discovered under the seat of a railroad coach which was carrying Moscow volunteers to Petersburg to fight Iudenich's White Guard bands. At that time he was not yet sixteen. This was Aleksandr Kosarev, in later years an eminent leader of the Communist youth movement.

Born on November 14, 1903, he was one of those young revolutionaries who from the first days of Soviet rule devoted their whole lives to fighting for the great ideals of the Communist Party. Bold and decisive, yet at the same time full of human sympathy, he soon became a leader of the young Moscow factory workers. In 1918 he was one of the first to join the "Third International" socialist league of working youth, and afterward the Komsomol. In 1919, when aged sixteen, he became a member of the CP. Later he was wounded at the front, attended Communist courses, and thereafter was an active leader of the Komsomol for some twenty years.

An episode which has recently come to light is connected with his activity at the beginning of the twenties, when he was secretary of the Bauman raion committee of the Komsomol. A meeting of the committee bureau was discussing a proposal to send greetings to Lenin. It was resolved to send to the leader the newspaper *Put' molodezhi* (The Way of Youth) and "greetings from the youth of the Bauman raion to the leader of world revolution." Not long afterward the excited Kosarev read Lenin's reply to his comrades: "Dear friends: I thank you warmly for your greeting, and send you in return my greetings and best wishes. Yours, V. Ul'ianov (Lenin)." Their beloved leader's cordial greetings and friendly wishes went to the heart of the young fighters for the revolution and remained a lasting memory throughout their lives.

Kosarev devoted all his strength and ability to the Komsomol and the Party, to which he was selflessly attached. As he declared at the plenum of the Komsomol CC in June 1935, "We must cherish the Party's confidence [as we cherish] life itself, for the strongest, finest, and most wonderful thing in the life of a young revolutionary is that confidence which the great Party displays towards every one of us.''

Kosarev had a splendid career from rank-and-file member of the Komsomol to secretary general of the Komsomol CC. It was a career of fighting and study, the conquest of difficulties without thought of self, from everyday labors to heroic achievements. His invariable message to youth was to learn from the Party to work, fight, and conquer in Leninist fashion. As he used to say, ''to arm young people with Party knowledge and the experience of the past, to foster their loyalty to Bolshevik ideals—this means instilling in them a profound confidence in the rightness of our Party's cause.''

Kosarev soon became an organizer of the Bolshevik type. He was no bureaucrat but longed to be among the masses. He frequently appeared at factories, works, and building sites, in schools, colleges and collective farms, at youth meetings, [and he often could be found] engaged in simple, friendly conversation with some young engineer or raw factory hand. His name is associated with many fine achievements initiated by the Lenin Komsomol, such as the first youth shock brigades and ''light cavalry,'' the construction of Young Pioneer palaces and aero clubs, rationalization and factory training schools, large-scale sport exercises, and the campaign for universal literacy and culture. One and all were inspired by his fervent, inexhaustible energy.

He was a convinced, passionate fighter for peace. How topical today are the words he uttered at Geneva on September 3, 1936, at the international youth congress for the defense of peace: ''When the aggressor's bombers appear over peaceful towns and cities, the same sufferings and torments will be in store for young Catholics, socialists, republicans, Christians, Communists, and all others. Young men and women of all countries, let us unite our forces in the struggle to defeat all that threatens peace.''

Kosarev's simplicity, friendliness, common sense, and wide range of interest made him irresistibly attractive to youth. The Communist Party highly valued its faithful son. He was a delegate at all Party congresses from the Thirteenth to the Seventeenth. At the Fifteenth he was elected to the Central Control Commission of the CPSU, at the Sixteenth a candidate member of the CC, and at the Seventeenth a full member of the CC. From the Fifth all-Union congress of soviets he was a member of the CEC of the U.S.S.R. In 1933 he received the Order of Lenin. The decree of the CEC of the U.S.S.R. ran: ''The Order of Lenin is conferred on A. V. Kosarev—an experienced leader of the Lenin Komsomol, an outstanding organizer of the Komsomol masses in the fight, under Party leadership, for the victory of the Five Year Plan.''

The late 1930s was a period of unjust mass repression of Komsomol workers. Kosarev was distressed by the arrests of comrades, many of whom he knew and trusted, and he took every opportunity to stand up for them. In June 1937 he was summoned to appear before Stalin together with P. S. Gorshenin, the secretary of the Komsomol CC, and V. F. Pikina. Ezhov was present, and Stalin began to upbraid Kosarev on the ground that the Komsomol was not helping the PC of Internal Affairs to "unmask enemies." He went on in this manner for an hour and a half, heedless of Kosarev's explanations and of the lives and interests of young people, insisting that the CC must help to unmask "enemies of the people" within the Komsomol. Later Stalin took under his protection one Mishakova, an instructress under the Komsomol CC, who slandered many Party and government workers and treacherously accused the whole Komsomol organization of the Chuvash oblast of failing to "destroy the people's enemies," at whose hands she herself claimed to have suffered.

From November 19 to 22, 1938, a plenum of the Komsomol CC was held on Stalin's orders and in his presence together with Molotov and Malenkov. This became in effect an arraignment of the honest cadres of Komsomol workers. At the plenum Kosarev declared: "I personally feel absolutely at ease, because my conscience is clear. I never have and never shall betray the Party or the Soviet people." A few days later, he and most of the other members of the Komsomol CC were arrested: Kosarev was taken in charge by Beria himself. In this way many true sons of our Party were cut off in their prime, victims of arbitrary rule during the period of the Stalin cult.

Liquidating the consequences of the cult of personality, the Party has restored Kosarev's good name, which will never be forgotten by the people.[42]

STANISLAV VIKENT'EVICH KOSIOR

Biographical data

Born 1889, died 1939. Party and government leader. Joined the CP in 1907. Born at Vengerovo, Sedlets (Siedlce) gubernia, the son of a Polish worker. In 1907, member of RSDWP Party committee at the Donetsk-Iur'evsk metal works. Arrested several times for revolutionary activity in 1907-11. In 1912-14, carried on illegal Party work in Kharkov, Poltava and Kiev. In 1915 carried on Party work in Moscow; was arrested and exiled for three years to Irkutsk gubernia. After the February revolution in 1917 he was in Petrograd as a member of the Narva-Petergof committee of the RSDWP(B), and of the Petrograd committee and the executive commission of the Petrograd committee of the RSDWP(B). Delegate to the seventh (April) conference and the Sixth Congress of the RSDWP(B). Took part in the October uprising in Petrograd and was commissar of the Petrograd RMC. In 1918 he was in charge of illegal Party work in the German-occupied Ukraine. In October 1918 he was elected secretary of the underground Right-Bank Committee of the CP; he was also a member of the Party's oblast committee for the preparation of an armed uprising. Joined the "left-wing Communists" at the time of the Brest Litovsk treaty. In 1919

Stanislav Vikent'evich Kosior

he headed the Western Front bureau of the CC of the Ukraine CP and was in charge of underground work in the rear of Denikin's forces. In 1920, secretary of the CC of the Ukraine CP. In 1921-22, in charge of food supplies. From November 1922, secretary of the Siberian bureau of the CC of the RCP(B). From December 1925, secretary of the CC of the CPSU. From July 1928 to January 1938, at the first session of the Supreme Soviet of the U.S.S.R., he was elected deputy chairman of the CPC of the U.S.S.R. and chairman of the Commission of Soviet Control. Delegate at the Twelfth through the Seventeenth Party congresses, and elected to the CC from the Thirteenth to the Seventeenth Congress. From 1927, candidate member of the Politburo of the CC of the CPSU; full member from 1930. Delegate to the Sixth and Seventh Comintern congresses. Member of the Presidium of the CEC of the U.S.S.R. Slandered and subjected to illegal repression during the cult of Stalin's personality. Posthumously rehabilitated.[43]

A true son of the Party

Today [November 18, 1964] is the 75th anniversary of the birth of the eminent Party and government worker Stanislav Vikent'evich Kosior. The son of a Polish peasant, he worked at the Sula and later the Donetsk-Iurevsk metal works. He joined the Bolshevik Party as a youth in 1907 and devoted his whole life to serving this great cause.

His name is associated forever with the history of the CPSU. The Petersburg workers remember him: in 1917 he was Party organizer for the Narva-Petergof raion, and in the October Revolution led the Putilov workers, the flower of the Petersburg working class, in the assault on the old regime. In the stormy years of Civil War he helped to create the CP of the Ukraine, and in 1922-25, as secretary of the Siberian bureau of the CC of the RCP(B), he was one of the authors of the great transformation of Siberia. As secretary of the CC of the CPSU he did much to strengthen the Party's ranks. In 1926-27 he directed the all-Union Party census and revision of Party cards. In 1928 he was elected secretary of the CC of the Ukraine CP, a post which he occupied until 1938. Not long before his arrest he was appointed deputy chairman of the CPC of the U.S.S.R., and was at the same time in charge of the PC of State Control of the U.S.S.R. At the Twelfth Party Congress he was elected a candidate member of the CC of the CPSU, and at the Thirteenth Congress a full member. From 1930 he was a member of the Politburo of the CC of the CPSU.

The whole of his short but brilliant career was devoted to the fight for communism. He published more than eighty works—lectures, speeches, and articles containing much valuable material on themes of socialist construction, Communist education, the training of cadres, Party organization, and international affairs.... His whole life and work were a model of steadfastness and self-criticism, hard work, modesty, and close attachment to the people. R.

Ia. Terekhov, a former second secretary of the CC of the Ukraine CP and a close colleague, recalls that "Kosior's great quality was his interest in the masses, in the Party rank and file. He was accessible to everyone." ... He was particularly fond of talking to young people, who found in him a close friend and mentor as well as a senior Party colleague....

He used to emphasize that the task of rebuilding society requires helpers who work not from fear or from love of money but who believe in the strength of the proletariat and are themselves ready to devote all their strength to the building of socialism.

Many of his speeches had a great effect abroad and were widely discussed in the foreign press. In 1933 his report to the November plenum of the CC of the CPSU on "Achievements and Tasks of National Policy in the Ukraine" was acclaimed as an important summing up of the achievements of Leninist national policy in the Ukraine. Jean Sedoil, the French writer and friend of the Soviet Union, wrote on this occasion: "It is important to realize that the inclusion of the Ukraine in the U.S.S.R. is an accomplished fact and that separatist plans, from whatever quarter they may originate, are the merest illusion." A patriot for his great motherland and an ardent internationalist, Kosior was a passionate adherent and agent of Leninist national policy and friendship among all peoples of the earth.

Along with many other disciples of Lenin, he became a victim of arbitrary rule during the cult of Stalin's personality. The Soviet people cherish his memory as that of a staunch fighter for Leninism. His name and his deeds will not be forgotten.[44]

AIKAZ ARKAD'EVICH KOSTANIAN

Biographical data

Born 1897, died 19—. Joined the CP in 1916. Born at Tiflis; educated at Nersinsian seminary, then for three years at Saratov University, which he left during the following year to become a professional revolutionary. In 1916 he carried on underground work for the Tiflis Bolshevik organization. After the October Revolution he was PC of education for the city of Saratov and at the same time chairman of the Armenian Committee of the Commissariat of Nationalities Affairs of the RSFSR. During the Civil War he was political commissar of a Red Army regiment. At the end of 1919 he carried on underground work in Armenia. At the January Conference of 1920 he was elected to the Armenian committee of the RCP(B) and later secretary of [the committee's] foreign bureau. After the establishment of Soviet power in Armenia he became PC of social welfare and later of internal affairs. In 1923-25 he was head of the organization department of the CC of the Georgian CP. In 1925-28 he did important work in the Red International of Trade Unions (Profintern), and in 1928-30 was first secretary of the CC of the Armenian CP. In 1930-34 he was first secretary of the Party's Crimea oblast committee, after which he again worked in the Profintern. In 1934 he was appointed head of the political department of the Moscow-Kursk railroad. During this assignment he became a victim of slander.[45]

A professional Party worker

As the fiftieth anniversary of the October Revolution draws near, we recall with pride the names of its faithful soldiers who, with sword and gun, carried its banner into every corner of our huge country, motherland of many nations.

The present generation of Soviet people has rightly adopted the slogan: "Nothing and no one shall be forgotten." The names of our country's glorious sons and their services to the revolution live in the hearts of all builders of communism. Among the shining band of prerevolutionary fighters for Lenin's Party we recall that great Party and state leader Aikaz Arkad'evich Kostanian.

He was born, a tanner's son, at Tiflis in July 1897. He received his secondary education at the Nersisian seminary and then spent three years in the medical faculty of Saratov University. Having devoted himself to fervent political activity, he left in his fourth year and became a professional revolutionary. While still at the seminary, he had belonged to political groups and underground organizations and had taken part in illegal rallies and meetings. In those years he began to study Marxist literature and take an interest in the history of the workers' revolutionary movement in Europe and Russia. In September 1916 he joined the RSDWP(B) and carried on underground work for the Tiflis Bolshevik organization. At the Echmiadzin seminary he belonged to the same Marxist group as Anastas Mikoyan and Artak Stambol'tsian, and when he came to Saratov he was already an experienced underground worker. After the October Revolution he became PC of education for that city, and was at the same time head of the Armenian committee of the PC of Nationalities of the RSFSR. During the dark days of the Civil War he served in the Red Army as a regimental political commissar, and at the end of 1919 he was assigned to underground work in Armenia. At the conference of January 1920 he was elected to the Armenian committee of the RCP(B), and later became Secretary of the committee's foreign bureau. After the suppression of the May uprising in Armenia he moved to Tiflis to avoid persecution by the Dashnaks, but was arrested there by the Mensheviks. His friend and companion G. Voskanian, also a Party member since 1916, writes: "After the First of May demonstration in 1920 a large number of Bolsheviks were arrested, including Aikaz Kostanian. He told me in jail about the May uprising at Aleksandropol, which he compared with the Paris Commune. The heroic rebels, as he put it, were truly storming the heavens."

After the establishment of Soviet power in Armenia, Kostanian became first PC of social welfare and then PC of internal affairs. In 1923 he was transferred to the post of head of the organization department of the CC of the Georgian CP. In 1925-28 he did important work in the Profintern. In 1928, at the request of the Transcaucasian regional committee, he was recalled to Armenia, where he was elected first secretary of the CC of the CP. Although he remained in this post for only a short time, his experience enabled him to accomplish a great deal of useful work. He paid particular attention to developing the republic's industry and agriculture, and to furthering the Party's growth and the ideological training of cadres while intensifying the fight against the false ideologies of Trotskyism and nationalism. The ranks of the new intelligentsia swelled, and proletarian culture advanced by leaps and bounds. Vagram Alazan, the well-known prose writer who was at this time secretary of the Association of Armenian Proletarian Writers, said of him: "Thanks to his energy and fine character, Kostanian became universally popular in a short time. He attached particular importance to creating favorable working conditions for writers and artists."

In 1930 Kostanian became first secretary of the Crimea oblast committee of the Party, after which he returned to the Profintern as its chief secretary. He proved himself an outstanding leader of the international workers' movement, cooperating closely with such eminent Comintern leaders as Dimitrov, Togliatti, Thälmann, Thorez, and others.

In 1934 the CC of the CPSU appointed him head of the political department of the Moscow-Kursk railroad. In this post he became a victim of slander which cut short a busy life that was inspired to the last by devotion to the people and Party. This true son of the Party belonged to the band of those who stood firmly by Lenin's principles and standards of Party life. He was a man of the utmost integrity and nobility of character, a brilliant speaker and organizer and a profound student of Marxism. He was fluent in Armenian, Georgian, Russian, and German. In private life he was extremely modest, demanding as much of himself as he did of others.[46]

ALEKSANDR IVANOVICH KRINITSKY

Biographical data

Born 1894, died 19—. Joined the Bolshevik Party in 1915. In 1917 he was chairman of the Tver' committee, and food commissar of the Tver' gubernia. Later he worked in the political department of the southern front and was secretary successively of the Party's Moscow raion committee, of the gubernia committees of Saratov, Omsk, and the Donbass, the CC of the Belorussian CP and the Transcaucasian regional committee. From 1927 to 1929 he was head of the agitprop department of the CC of the CPSU. In 1924-25 and 1927-34 he was a candidate member of the CC of the CPSU, in 1934-37 a full member of the CC and a candidate member of its organization bureau; in 1933-34 he was deputy head of the agricultural department of the CC and chief of political administration of the PC of Agriculture. In 1934-37 he was secretary of the Saratov regional committee of the Party. He was arrested in 1937, and perished together with his wife, Iu. F. Alekseeva.[47]

A true soldier of the Party

The First of May holiday of 1917 is still remembered by the older generation of inhabitants of the town of Kalinin, then still called Tver'. For the first time, workers, soldiers, and students were able to march in the streets by the thousands. The most impressive column was from the Berg factory, marching with Bolsheviks at its head to the strains of the *Internationale*, which the other bands had not yet learned to play.

A man approached the column and was warmly greeted by the workers. "Well," he said, "I can say what I think to you at least. Your band plays well, but we must see to it that all the other factory bands can play the same tune." It was Aleksandr Ivanovich Krinitsky, the chairman of the Tver' committee of the Bolshevik Party. It was not long since he had returned from exile in Siberia, but he already had great prestige among the masses. The more politically conscious workers also knew him from underground work. He had begun to study Marxism under the influence of Lenin's *Pravda*, had joined the Party in 1915 and was an active, skilled propagandist who knew how to explain to the workers Lenin's program and Party tactics.

In April 1917 he attended the Party conference as a delegate from the Tver' organization. He was deeply affected by Lenin's speeches at the conference and by the decision to engage the Party in the fight for socialist revolution. He and his comrades on the committee unswervingly led the Party organization and the proletarian masses on the Leninist course, and their work was crowned by a swift and decisive victory in the October days, when power was seized by the Tver' Revolutionary Committee which numbered Krinitsky among its members. As well as directing the Party organization he became food commissar for the Tver' gubernia.

Later he was transferred to one crucial sector after another, wherever an experienced organizer with a firm theoretical background was needed. He served in the political department of the southern front, and was secretary of the Party's Moscow raion committee and the gubernia committees of Saratov, Omsk, and the Donbass, then of the CC of the Belorussian CP and the Transcaucasian regional committee. In 1927-29 he headed the agitprop department of the Party CC. Year by year his knowledge and political experience widened. Wherever he worked he found a way to the people's hearts, uniting them in the task of building a new society.

In 1924 he was elected a candidate member of the CC of the CPSU, and in 1934 a full member. He fought fiercely and remorselessly against anti-Leninist groups in the Party.

A large part of his career was devoted to agricultural problems and the socialist transformation of the countryside. His Party comrades recognized in him a man who understood the special problems of rural development. At the Thirteenth and Fifteenth congresses he was elected to commissions for the purpose of studying problems of Party work in the countryside and the strengthening of bonds between the working class and the peasants. At the Fifteenth Congress he made a speech of particular interest on the cultural revolution in the countryside. In this he linked the raising of cultural levels in rural areas with the progress of collectivization, and urged that agricultural schools should turn out agronomists who were capable of making collectivization a reality and organizing large-scale agricultural production.

In 1933 the Party appointed him to one of the most important posts in the field of collectivization. While deputy head of the agricultural department of the CC of the CPSU, he also headed the political administration of the PC of Agriculture, which was in charge of the day-to-day practical direction of the political departments of the machine and tractor stations.

In 1934 he was elected secretary of the Saratov regional committee of the Party, and he devoted all his strength and ability to the economic and cultural development of that large region. But in 1937 his closest collaborators one after another, were arrested and slandered. He tried to stand up against arbitrary rule and defend his comrades, but he too became a victim of the illegal repressions of the period of the cult of Stalin's personality. Today the good name of this outstanding leader and true son of Lenin's Party has been restored to the Soviet people.[48]

MIKHAIL MAKSIMOVICH KUL'KOV

Biographical data

Born 1891, died 1939. Joined the CP in 1915. Born at Konstantinovo village, Bronnitsky uezd, Moscow gubernia. Began his working life at the age of twelve. In 1907 he became a representative of the Tanners' Union, and in 1908 a member of its governing body. In 1908-12 he worked in Petersburg, first as a saddler at the Osipov factory, then at the Ostrem works; was a member of the administrative body of the city tanners' union, later its treasurer and deputy chairman, also labor correspondent of the Bolshevik newspapers *Pravda* and *Zvezda*. Was arrested in 1912; after release from jail returned to the Tanners' Union, and in 1914 switched to underground work in the Petersburg port organization (Bolshevik). During the February revolution of 1917 he was a member of the Committee of Social Security, and later of the Soviet of Workers'

Deputies. In April he was an RSDWP organizer at Briansk, and after the Bolshevik constituent assembly at the end of May he was chairman of the Bolshevik organization in that city. In September, at the first Orel gubernia Party conference, he was elected a candidate member of the gubernia bureau. Before the October Revolution he was deputy chairman, and a member of the presidium, of the uezd soviet of workers' deputies. In December 1917 he was elected to the CPC of the Briansk uezd committee of the RSDWP and deputy chairman of the gubernia Cheka, while at the same time head of the department of internal administration of the gubernia executive committee. In 1919 he was elected chairman of the Briansk gubernia Party organization, and in 1920 chairman of the Bezhitska Soviet. From the end of 1920 he was in Moscow, working at the Shorkozh and Krasnyi Postavshchik works; was elected cell secretary and member of the Party's Zamoskvorech'e district committee. In 1924-25 he served in the administration of the central control commission and the [department of] workers' and peasants' inspection of the RSFSR. In 1922-26 he was a member of the Moscow soviet of the Party's Moscow committee, and of the administration of the Tanners' Union; [during the same period] he was also chairman of the Moscow organization of the International Aid Society for Revolutionary Fighters. In 1926 he was assigned to a course of Marxism at the Sverdlov Communist Academy; after he completed the course the Party sent him to Central Asia as a deputy representative of the Central Control Commission of the CPSU on the Central Asia bureau of the CC of the CPSU, and as a member of the Turkmen central control commission. In 1929-30 he was first secretary of the Kirgiz oblast committee of the CPSU and a member of the Central Asia bureau of the CC. From 1931 to 1935 he was secretary of the CPSU's Zamoskvorech'e district committee in Moscow, and later of the Proletarsk district committee; from 1935 to 1937 he was secretary of the Moscow city committee of the CPSU. At the Seventeenth Congress of the CPSU in 1934 he was elected a candidate member of the CC. In February 1937 he was appointed to the Azov-Black Sea region as agent of the Commission of Party Control. He was arrested in October 1938 and perished in 1939.[49]

A Bolshevik's career

As Lenin wrote in *What Is to Be Done?* "the broader and deeper the elemental upsurge of the working masses becomes, the more they produce from their midst not only skilled agitators but gifted organizers, propagandists, and 'practical workers' in the best sense of the term." Mikhail Maksimovich Kul'kov was a good example of this type of Bolshevik organizer. He was born on May 9, 1891, in Konstantinovo village, Bronnitsky uezd, Moscow gubernia, the son of a textile worker. The family was a large one, life was hard, and his childhood was of short duration. In 1903, after finishing primary school, the twelve-year-old boy was sent to Moscow to the Karl Thiel tanning and saddlery works. Despite his youth he took part in the revolutionary movement of 1905, speaking at meetings and rallies and executing Party commissions. After the suppression of the revolution he was dismissed from the factory and took employment at the Dement works, where he joined the Tanners' Union and a Marxist circle. In 1907 the workers elected him a representative of the union, and in 1908 he was already a member of its governing body. In the same year he was obliged to move to Petersburg, where he first worked as a saddler at the Osipov factory and then at the Ostrem. At this time he was elected a member of the administrative body of the Petersburg Tanners' Union, and later its treasurer and deputy chairman. In addition, he was labor correspondent of the Bolshevik newspapers *Pravda* and *Zvezda* and helped to organize political strikes at factories for such occasions as the Lena Goldfield events, the January 9 and May 1 anniversaries, etc. In 1912, although he was not yet a Party member, the Bolshevik fraction of the Tanners' Union made him their representative with *Pravda,* where he worked directly with Konkordiia Samoilova. In April 1912 he was arrested for his part in a strike at the Ostrem works. After release from jail he again worked with the Tanners' Union until it was closed down in 1914, when he took up underground work in the Petersburg port Bolshevik organization. In January 1915 he became a Party member through the Vasilii Ostrov Party organization, and thenceforth his whole life was connected with the Bolshevik Party.

During the imperialist war the "conciliationist" Mensheviks and SRs endeavored to imbue the working masses with defensist-chauvinistic ideas, but from the outset of the war Kul'kov held fast to the Leninist line. After being again arrested and serving a term in the Kresty prison at Petersburg, he moved to Briansk to avoid exile. The years of reaction, arrests, and exile dealt heavy blows to all Bolshevik organizations, including that at Briansk, which had gone underground. Kul'kov, who worked as a saddler at the "Arsenal" works, wrote later that it was some time before he could get the organization on its feet again. In 1916 he was a member of the Arsenal strike committee, which was later reorganized for the purpose of aiding exiles and others who had suffered as a result of the strike. During the February revolution the Arsenal workers elected him to the social security committee, and, after this was dissolved in March, to the soviet of workers' deputies. The Mensheviks and SRs at first secured a majority in this body, but the Bolsheviks worked hard for their expulsion.

In April 1917 Kul'kov was one of those who organized the RSDWP at Briansk. In his autobiography, written after his admission to the All-Union Society of Old Bolsheviks, he wrote: "I took immediate steps to organize the united RSDWP, and served as chairman of the city organization until the arrival of Ignat Fokin of the district committee of the Moscow Bolshevik organization.

After the split in the Party, I remained chairman.'' The united RSDWP ceased to exist in Briansk on May 28, when the Bolsheviks formed a separate organization at their constituent assembly. That Kul'kov remained its chairman for some time is shown by a letter of August 11 from the Briansk committee of the RSDWP(B) to the Bolshevik Party's oblast bureau, informing it of the committee's change of address and signed by Kul'kov as chairman. He was also more than once in contact with the Party CC: for example, the latter's secretary, E. D. Stasova, wrote on October 27 to the publishing house Priboi requesting that 380 rubles' worth of Party literature be sent to Comrade Kul'kov for the Briansk organization.

After Ignat Fokin arrived in Briansk in April, Kul'kov became one of his closest collaborators in strengthening the city's Party organization, soviets, and trade unions. Together with other Bolsheviks he made numerous appearances at large meetings and workers' gatherings, describing what was going on in the country, explaining Bolshevik policy and the Party's attitude toward the Provisional Government, and giving practical instances of Menshevik and SR objectives. During the Kornilov revolt he and other Bolsheviks formed a Red Guard with the help of the Arsenal workers and those of the Bezhitsa engineering works. Everywhere the soviets were becoming Bolshevized, and the Briansk area was no exception: the Bolsheviks held a majority in the Briansk soviet by the end of September. When the first Orel gubernia Party conference was held at this time, Kul'kov was elected a candidate member of the gubernia bureau. The conference took note that the town and country Bolshevik organizations had expanded considerably and had done much to prepare the workers and the peasant masses for the decisive struggle with the bourgeoisie for control of the soviets.

At the second all-Russian congress of soviets the Briansk representatives were all Bolsheviks, and Kul'kov was of their number. When news of the October Revolution reached Briansk on the evening of October 25/November 7, the Briansk soviet at once ordered the Red Guard, consisting for the most part of Arsenal workers, to seize the post and telegraph office, the city treasury, and the railroad stations and arms depots. There was no armed resistance by counterrevolutionaries, and Soviet rule was proclaimed in Briansk on October 26. At this time Kul'kov, Fokin, and other Bolshevik delegates were attending the congress of soviets at Petersburg. The uezd congress, which took place in December, approved the overthrow of landowners' and bourgeois rule and called on the workers of the area to strengthen local soviets and ensure the execution of Soviet decrees. It also elected a council of people's commissars of the Briansk industrial area, and Kul'kov became a member of this body and of its presidium. In 1917-18, while continuing to work at the Arsenal, he was elected first a member and then chairman of the works trade union committee, and took an active part in setting up trade unions in the city and uezd. At the Orel gubernia Party congress held on March 1, 1918, he delivered the report on factory and works committees and trade unions.

During the Civil War he carried out various forms of Party and government work and was elected chairman of the Briansk uezd committee of the RSDWP. From the spring of 1918 he served for about a year as deputy chairman of the gubernia Cheka and was at the same time head of the department of internal administration of the gubernia executive committee.

In February 1918 Briansk went through dark days; the Germans were only a short distance away, at Klintsy, Starodub, and Mikhailovsky farmstead. The Party and government organs of Briansk, Bezhitsa, and other towns in the uezd called on the workers and peasants to organize Red Guard units to defend the Soviet Republic, and Kul'kov was a leader in this activity. The counter-revolutionary parties, defeated in open battle, had gone underground and were biding their time. In August 1918 there was an armed uprising in Briansk of left SRs and anarchists who demanded the dissolution of the soviets and the Food Requisition Detachment. The Briansk workers, with Communists in the forefront, stood by the Soviet regime. On the instructions of the Briansk uezd committee, Kul'kov addressed the Arsenal workers in a passionate speech denouncing the treason of the left SRs. The workers took good heed of his words. "He was full of energy and the Arsenal workers loved and respected him"—such was the later comment of A. I. Ivaniuta, a Party member since May 1917. The meeting was a stormy one, as the Mensheviks and SRs tried to break it up, but they did not succeed. The workers resolved to ask the uezd committee to liquidate all counterrevolutionary organizations and to strengthen the worker element in the Food Requisition Detachment and the Red Guard: volunteers for the purpose came forward at the meeting itself. On September 2, 1918, the executive committee of the Briansk uezd soviet of workers', peasants', and Red Army deputies, after hearing a report on anarchist activities, adopted the following resolution: "The swift suppression of the terrorist threat and open armed rebellion of local anarchists against the Soviet regime and its representatives has still further united the ranks of the revolutionary proletariat of the city of Briansk, who have spared no effort to nip counterrevolution in the bud." The same meeting saw the provisional establishment of a RMC of seven members, including Fokin and Kul'kov.

During the Civil War Briansk was of great importance as a rail and industrial center. In March 1919 the Thirty-fourth and Thirty-fifth regiments, which were at the railroad station on their way to the front, were incited to mutiny by SR and anarchist propaganda and attempted to march on the city and overthrow the soviets. In this emergency a five-man military command was set up on Fokin's initiative, of which he, Kul'kov, and Liudvigovsky were members. They decided to attack the garrison troops at night before the latter, who were much superior in numbers, could organize themselves. On Fokin's orders two Communist groups were sent out to intercept the mutineers, and one of these, led by Kul'kov, made its way toward the Black Bridge. A guard battalion went with it, but on arriving at the bridge refused to intervene further. The situation was critical, but with much difficulty Kul'kov persuaded the soldiers to return to the city, leaving a guard of Communists at the bridge. After two days of fierce struggle the counterrevolutionary mutiny was put down.

In the fall of 1919 the country was again in difficulty with Denikin's advancing troops only a few dozen miles from Briansk. The Mensheviks and SRs used every possible chance to slander the young Republic and recover a majority in the soviets. At this juncture the uezd committee received news that an artillery battalion in barracks on Trubchev Street had mutinied, refused to go to the front, and was about to shell the town. "All members of the Party organization, with Kul'kov at their head," Ivaniuta writes, "were sent out to deal with this battalion," and they succeeded in foiling the counterrevolutionary attempt to help the interventionists. No small part of the credit for this success was due to Kul'kov.

In 1919 Kul'kov was elected chairman of the Briansk gubernia Party organization, and in 1920 chairman of the Bezhitsa soviet. From 1917 to 1920 he took part in all uezd and gubernia committees. The workers and Bolsheviks of the Briansk area knew and loved him well, and in March 1920 sent him as their voting delegate to the Ninth Party Congress. All together he spent six years at Briansk. Under Fokin's guidance and along with such Bolsheviks as A. Antsyshkin, A. Bogomolov, G. Krapivnitsky, G. Pankov, G. Kireev, and many others, he took an active part in establishing and strengthening the young Soviet regime in those difficult years.

From the end of 1920 he was in Moscow, where the Party committee and the Tanners' Union assigned him to the Shorkozh and later the Krasnyi Postavshchik works; he was elected cell secretary and member of the Party's Zamoskvorech'e district committee. One of his colleagues at the Krasnyi Postavshchik works was A. P. Seregina, a Party member since 1919. She recalls how attentive he was to the workers' interests and how as cell secretary he frequently visited their quarters and got to know how they lived doing all he could to improve their housing conditions. He did much for young people and helped to organize antireligious evenings.

At the Thirteenth Party Congress he was elected a member of the Central Control Commission by the Moscow organization, and worked in this body in 1924-25. He devoted his organizing experience to strengthening the unity of the Party and state apparatus, fighting bureaucratism, stagnation, red tape, and abuses. In 1922-26 he was elected a member of the Moscow soviet and the Moscow Party committee and also of the administration of the Tanners' Union, and was chairman of the Moscow organization of the International Aid Society for Revolutionary Fighters. In 1926 he was assigned to take a course of Marxism at the Sverdlov Communist Academy, where he studied hard to perfect his knowledge. The Moscow Communists sent him as their delegate to the Fourteenth and Fifteenth Party congresses. After his course was completed the Party CC sent him to Central Asia as deputy representative of the Central Control Commission of the CPSU with the Central Asia Bureau of the CC of the CPSU, and as a member of the Turkmen central control commission. In this new sector he again displayed the utmost zeal in carrying out Party and government orders. In 1929-30 he was elected first secretary of the Kirgiz oblast committee of the CPSU and a member of the Central Asia bureau of the CC. The Communists of Central Asia sent him as a delegate to the Sixteenth Party Congress, where he was again elected to the central control commission. In 1931-35 he was secretary of the Party's Zamoskvorech'e and Proletarsky district committees, and in 1935-37 secretary of the Moscow city committee of the CPSU. At the Seventeenth Party Congress he was elected a candidate member of the CC. In February 1937 the CC appointed him to the Azov-Black Sea region as agent of the Commission of Party Control. The workers and officials showed their confidence in him by electing him a deputy to the first convocation of the Supreme Soviet, representing the Salsk constituency.

He was arrested on a false charge in October 1938, and perished in 1939.

Whatever post he occupied, he always remained sincere and straightforward in his relations with people. While in Moscow he kept in touch with Briansk and its people and did all he could to help them. He used to say: "I cannot be impartial about Briansk—I spent my best years there, and have so many memories." The workers of Briansk for their part revere his memory, and in 1965 one of the city streets was named for him.[50]

U. D. KULUMBETOV

Biographical data

Born 1891, died 1938. Joined the CP in 1920. Was a teacher before the October Revolution. In 1919-23 he was chairman of the criminal investigation commission of the Irgiz uezd executive committee, head of the uezd department of public education, head of the Aktiubinsk gubernia social security and public education departments, and head of the agitprop department of the Party's gubernia committee. During 1923-25, he was chairman of the Akmolinsk gubernia executive committee. From April 1925 to September 1926 he was chairman of the central council of national economy of the Kazakh ASSR; from September 1926, deputy chairman of the CPC and chairman of the republic's Gosplan, and in 1935-37 chairman of the CEC of the Kazakh ASSR. Was a member of the plenum and bureau of the Kazakh regional committee of the CPSU and a member of the CEC of the Kazakh SSR, and was several times elected a delegate to regional Party conferences and congresses of soviets. Committed practical errors in carrying out the policy on nationalities.[51]

BELA KUN

Biographical data

Born 1886, died 1939. Joined the Hungarian Social Democratic Party in

1902. Member of the Hungarian and international revolutionary movement. Born at Lele, the son of a village clerk. Joined the workers' movement at sixteen. Carried on propaganda among Budapest students, taking part in the creation of Marxist groups. In 1905 he directed strikes which led to clashes with the police, and was arrested several times. In 1909 he took a firm line against the action of Social Democrat leaders in deserting their principles by compromising with the bourgeois parties on the subject of the electoral law. Called up in 1914, he was taken prisoner by the Russian Army in 1916 and sent to a camp at Tomsk. There he made contact with the local organization of the RSDWP(B), became a Bolshevik, and carried on active social-democratic propaganda among his fellow prisoners. After the February revolution he worked in the Tomsk gubernia committee and on the staff of the Bolshevik journal *Sibirsky rabochii* and the daily *Znamia revolutsii*. He rallied to the October Revolution from the outset, came to Petrograd and met Lenin. Together with Tibor Szamuely he edited the Hungarian newspaper *Nemzetközi Szocialista* (The International Socialist) and later *Szocialis Forradalom* (Socialist Revolution), which were distributed to prisoners of war together with pamphlets by Kun expounding Marxist ideas. In March 1918 Kun organized a Hungarian group of the RCP(B), and in May he became chairman of the newly founded Central Federation of Foreign Groups of the RCP(B). He was a leader of the international units of the Red Army, and took part in the defense of Petrograd, the fighting at Narva, and the suppression of the SR revolt in Moscow. Organized propaganda among German and Austro-Hungarian troops in the Ukraine. In November 1918 he returned secretly to Hungary, where he and other Hungarian Communists shortly afterward founded the Hungarian Communist Party (HCP). He was one of a group of Communists arrested by the bourgeois government in February 1919; he remained in jail until March 21, when the Hungarian Soviet Republic was proclaimed and he became its PC of foreign affairs, later PC of war. He played an important part in organizing Soviet power and laying the basis of the internal and external policy of the young proletarian state.

After Soviet rule in Hungary was overthrown he withdrew to Austria and was interned. In 1920 he came to Soviet Russia and took part in fighting the Whites in the Crimea. He was a member of the RMC of the southern front and chairman of the Crimea revolutionary committee. In 1921 he was in Germany and was one of the leaders of the March demonstrations of the German proletariat. In 1921-23 he was engaged in important Party work in the Urals. He was a member of the Presidium of the All-Russian CEC, and in September 1923 was appointed representative of the CC of the RCP(B) on the CC of the Russian Komsomol. He was active in the Comintern, and was a member of its Executive Committee from 1921, while also directing the work of the illegal Hungarian CP. In 1927 the RMC of the U.S.S.R. awarded him the Order of the Red Banner. In April 1928 he was arrested in Vienna, but was soon released thanks to the pressure of public opinion. He returned to the U.S.S.R. and continued political work. Wrote works on the history of the international workers' movement. He was subjected to illegal repression in 1937, posthumously rehabilitated.[52]

PETR MIKHAILOVICH KUZNETSOV (DARBINIAN)

Biographical data

Born 1896, died 1938. Joined the CP in 1918. Born at Nakhichevan'. Served in the Tsarist Army until 1918. In 1918-20, mechanic and Party cell secretary at the Aleksandropol' depot. In 1921-38, representative of the railroads committee at Karaklis (Kirovakan); later worked in Leningrad, Erevan, and Tbilisi; chairman of Armenian trade union council, secretary of the CC of the Armenian CP, and chairman of the Transcaucasian trade union council. After the dissolution of the Transcaucasian Federation he was chairman of the commission of party control of the CC of the Armenian CP. In 1938 he was a victim of the cult of Stalin's personality.[53]

The adventurous life of a fighter

In the life of every individual there is one main theme that determines his career. For Communists this theme is the struggle for the liberation of the masses and for a bright future—communism. One who devoted his whole life to this struggle was the steadfast Bolshevik Petr Mikhailovich Kuznetsov (Darbinian), whose name is associated with the heroic May rebellion at Aleksandropol' (Leninakan), the establishment and consolidation of Soviet rule in Armenia.

Born at Nakhichevan' in the former Erevan gubernia, Kuznetsov attended the Tiflis vocational school and, after being demobilized from the Tsarist Army, found himself at Aleksandropol', where he worked for three years as a depot mechanic. While still a private in the army he had grasped the full injustice of the existing order, embraced the idea of the liberation of the working class, and joined the revolutionary movement. He became a Party member in 1918. At Aleksandropol' he soon made contact with the underground organization and became one of its active members. His revolutionary activity as secretary of the Party cell of the depot did not go unnoticed, and in 1919 he was arrested by the Dashnaks and imprisoned for a short time. On his release, under the direction of the experienced Bolsheviks B. Garibdzhanian, E. Sevian, and S. Musaelian he learned how to carry on the revolutionary struggle and took an active part in the heroic uprising of the Aleksandropol' workers. The Red Guard detachment under his command had the task of seizing the post office, bank, jail, and other important objectives....

After the suppression of the May rebellion he went into hiding and escaped to Baku. The CC of the Armenian CP prepared the masses to strike a decisive blow for Soviet rule, and Kuznetsov was appointed commander of a company of the special Communist detachment which entered Armenia together with Red Army troops.

In the dark days of February 1921 he was once more among the active defenders of the conquests of the revolution. The Party appointed him representative of the railroads committee at Karaklis (now Kirovakan), where he soon organized the force of railroad workers known as the "Iron detachment." Having expelled the Dashnaks from the Baiazet raion, this unit was incorporated in the group of forces under Velikanov and Atarbekov and took part in the liberation of Erevan.

Subsequently Kuznetsov worked until 1936 at Leninakan, Erevan, and Tbilisi. He was chairman of the Armenian trade union council, secretary of the CC of the Armenian CP (after finishing a course at the Transport Academy in Moscow), and chairman of the Transcaucasian trade union council. He was elected several times to central Party and state organs, being a member of the Transcaucasian regional committee and CEC, the Armenian CEC, the Erevan city soviet, and the bureau of the CC of the Armenian CP; he was also elected as delegate to CPSU congresses. After the dissolution of the Transcaucasian Federation he was elected chairman of the commission of Party control of the CC of the Armenian CP. In 1938 he became a victim of repression during the cult of personality.[54]

EMMANUIL IONOVICH KVIRING

Biographical data

Born 1888, died 1939. Party and government worker. Joined the CP in 1912. In 1913 he was secretary of the Bolshevik fraction in the Fourth State Duma. Arrested and exiled for revolutionary activity. In October 1917, secretary of the Ekaterinoslav committee of the RSDWP(B) and chairman of the local soviet. From 1918 to June 1919, chairman of the supreme council of the national economy of the Ukraine. In 1920-22, secretary of the Donetsk gubernia committee of the Party. In 1918-25, member of the CC of the Ukraine CP. In 1925-27, deputy chairman of the Supreme Council of the National Economy of the U.S.S.R., and in 1927-30 deputy chairman of the U.S.S.R. Gosplan. In 1931, deputy PC of communications; 1932-34, deputy chairman of the supplies committee of the Council for Labor and Defense; 1932-36, director of the economic institute of the Communist Academy. From 1934, deputy chairman of the U.S.S.R. Gosplan. At the Twelfth to Sixteenth congresses of the CPSU he was elected to the CC of the CPSU. Member of the CEC of the U.S.S.R.

at several convocations. Wrote several books on problems of socialist construction. Subjected to unjustified repression during the cult of Stalin's personality; posthumously rehabilitated.[55]

A tireless fighter for communism

A founder of the Ukrainian CP and an eminent organizer of socialist construction in our country, Emmanuil Ionovich Kviring belonged to the Party generation of "Pravda workers." He joined the Party in 1912 and was soon given the important post of secretary of the Bolshevik group of deputies to the Fourth State Duma for the purpose of illegal liaison with Party organizations. This work, and his active participation in Lenin's *Pravda*, threw him into the thick of Party life, rapidly widened his political horizons, and sharpened his journalistic abilities. In the atmosphere of revolutionary upsurge, the Bolshevik fraction of the Duma and *Pravda* were the most important strongholds of the Leninist Party. The fight of Lenin and the Party against all opposition and enemy groups, the discussion of major problems of home and international politics armed the new generation of the Party with tremendous political experience. Kviring, who had found his way to Marxism by means of self-education during the years of black reaction, later described *Pravda* as the best imaginable Party school. "It was *Pravda*," he wrote in his autobiography, "which directed my Marxist inclinations onto the road of Bolshevism."

The news of the second Russian revolution reached Kviring in Siberian exile. By now he was a full-fledged Marxist-Leninist with considerable experience as a Party worker. His high sense of responsibility, gift of organization, personal courage, delicacy of feeling, and implicit devotion to the Communist cause aroused the deepest admiration of his comrades.

At the beginning of April 1917 he reached Ekaterinoslav, where he had worked in the underground in 1914-15, and was received joyfully by his old Party comrades. The Bolsheviks of the metal works (now named after Petrovsky) at once elected him secretary of their works committee, and before long he was chairman of the Ekaterinoslav committee of the Party and an editor of the newspaper *Zvezda* (Star). Under his leadership and that of V. Averin, the committee was victorious in the armed struggle against the Ukrainian nationalists at the end of 1917. This victory not only gave power to the local soviet, of which Kviring was chairman, but prevented the forces of the Central Rada from joining with the Don Cossacks.

During the Civil War Kviring, as a member of the CC of the Ukraine CP, directed the work of underground Party organizations in the Ukraine, and during the campaign against Denikin he fought in the Red Army. When the Ukraine CP was set up he followed the Leninist line in resolutely opposing all separatist tendencies and defending the principle of the unity of aims of the Ukrainian and Russian peoples, as well as the organization of the Ukrainian

CP as an inseparable part of the CPSU.... On many occasions he met Lenin and received directions from him.

In May 1921 the CC of the RCP(B) sent him to the key sector of the Donbass. The grave situation there was of concern to the whole Party, and Kviring devoted much effort to restoring the country's main coal field and strengthening the Donetsk Party organization despite Trotskyist opposition. In him the Party found a true adherent of the Leninist general line, and it was no surprise that the Bolsheviks of the Ukraine later elected him secretary of the CC of the Ukrainian CP.

He was especially active in 1921-25 against various opposition groups and families, and in defending the purity of Marxism-Leninism, above all against Trotskyism. He wrote a number of articles and pamphlets which are still of value as a sharp weapon in defense of Party unity. His reputation among Ukrainian Bolsheviks stood high. When the Trotskyist at the height of their onslaught against the Leninist line, made him the object of sharp attacks and vile slanders, the members of the CC of the Ukraine CP spoke out firmly in his defense at all the important discussion meetings at Kharkov.

In 1925 he was transferred to Moscow, where for twelve years he worked in various sectors of socialist economic construction as deputy chairman of the Supreme Council of the National Economy of the U.S.S.R., deputy chairman of the U.S.S.R. Gosplan, and deputy PC of communications. He was the representative of the CC of the Party at Dneprostroi, and his likeness is preserved in the memorial plaque set into the first slab of concrete of the historic Dnepr Hydroelectric Station (Dneproges). He was also well known as an eminent economist. In 1931-36 he was head of the economic institute of the Communist Academy. He wrote a number of important works on problems of the Soviet economy, especially those concerning planning. In 1934 Kviring was made a Doctor of Economic Science.

A tireless Party worker and skilled organizer of economic construction as well as a true Leninist, at the Twelfth to Sixteenth congresses of the CPSU he was elected a member of the CC; he was also several times a member of the All-Ukrainian CEC, the All-Russian CEC, and the CEC of the U.S.S.R. The name of this stalwart fighter for October, for the victory of socialism and the U.S.S.R., will live forever in our people's memory.[56]

VASILII DIMITRIEVICH LAKOBA

Biographical data

Born 1897, died 1938. Born at Lykhny village, Gudaut district, the son of a poor peasant. In 1914 he was a trooper in an Abkhaz squadron of a

Circassian regiment of the Caucasian Native Cavalry Division, also known as the "Wild Division." At the outbreak of the February revolution he was at Kiev, where he had been sent with a mounted unit of the Circassian Regiment to make up the local cavalry force. On the orders of the Kiev Bolshevik committee he carried on Party work in the Wild Division stirring up the troops and peasantry and distributing appeals and leaflets. Before long the revolutionary unit which he had formed at Bendery mutinied (the unit consisted of cavalry and some infantrymen who had left the front); however, the mutiny was suppressed and Lakoba was jailed at Kishinev. The officers there wanted him to be shot at once, but the peasant troopers stood up for him and a tense situation arose within the division. In accordance with a telegram from General Brusilov, then commanding the southwestern front, Lakoba was moved to Kiev, stripped of his rank as a trooper, and given the chance of leaving the front area at once.

At the end of 1917 he returned to Abkhazia and settled in the Gudaut district, where the Bolsheviks headed by Nestor Apollonovich Lakoba had great influence among the workers. At the beginning of 1918 Vasilii Lakoba joined the CP. During the armed uprising in Abkhazia in the spring of that year he helped to organize the flow of arms from Batumi. After the proclamation of Soviet power at Sukhum he became a member of the RMC and took part in its work, directing operations during the fight against foreign interventionists at the beginning of May. In 1919-20 he was a member of the Party's Gudaut uezd committee; arrested in 1920, he was released in March 1921. He then returned to his home territory and worked actively to strengthen the workers' and peasants' rule. For outstanding military services to the motherland he later received the Order of the Red Banner. He took part in strengthening Soviet rule and socialist legality in the young Abkhaz Republic, occupying such important posts as military commissar of the Abkhaz Cavalry Regiment, chief of militia of the Gagra and Gudaut uezds and at Sukhum, chairman of the Gudaut executive committee and chief of the republican militia; was also head of various social organizations. He was elected to the Abkhaz oblast committee of the Georgian CP and to the Abkhazian CEC. His life was tragically cut short in 1938.[57]

DIMITRII ZAKHAROVICH LEBED'

Biographical data

Born 1893, died 19—. Joined the Bolshevik Party in 1909. Born at Nikolaevka village, Novocherkassk uezd, Ekaterinoslav gubernia, the son of a poor peasant. In 1905, at the age of twelve, he entered a two-class railroad school at Nizhnedneprovsk, but had to leave owing to his father's death. In 1908 he worked as a mechanic, and later in the railroad workshops at Nizhnedneprovsk. In 1910-11 he took an active part in a social-democratic group for which he carried out several assignments. In 1912 he was an organizer and active member of a Bolshevik organization in the workshops, and at the end of that year he was arrested. In 1913-14 he took an active part in the work of the Ekaterinoslav Party organization. Called up in 1915, but was invalided out and returned to Ekaterinoslav, where he was active in restoring the Bolshevik organization in the railroad workshops. In 1916 he organized strikes in the Nizhnedneprovsk workshops. He was arrested in 1917 and released after the February revolution, when he was again active in the Ekaterinoslav Party organization. Was a member of the soviet of workers' deputies and later of the gubernia executive committee at Ekaterinoslav, then gubernia commissar for the militia, deputy chairman of the executive committee, and chairman of the committee of the Bolshevik organization of the Ekaterinoslav railroad. After the October Revolutionary Lebed' continued to work on the executive committee and the military revolutionary staff of the railroad, and edited the newspaper of the railroad executive committee and later the Bolshevik newspaper called *Revolutsionnyi signal zheleznodorozhnika* (The Railroad Worker's Revolutionary Signal).

During the German occupation of the Ukraine he worked at Debal'tsevo, Saratov, and Moscow on the newspaper *Vestnik Narodnogo Komissariata Vnutrennikh del RSFSR* (News of the PC of Internal Affairs of the RSFSR). In January 1919 he returned to Ekaterinoslav, where he was elected deputy chairman of the gubernia executive committee and member of the Party's gubernia committee. In May 1919 he took part in the suppression of the Grigor'ev revolt, and was later commissioner of the Fourteenth Army in the campaign against Denikin. In July-December 1919 he did Party and government work at Vladimir. In December he returned to Ekaterinoslav and edited the newspaper *Zvezda* and was head of the railroad political department and chairman of the trade union committee of the Ekaterinoslav railroad. At the third congress of the Ukraine CP in March 1919 he was elected a member of the revision commission, and on November 23, 1920, he became a member of the organization bureau and second secretary of the CC of the Ukraine CP. In 1921 he became a candidate member, and in 1922 a full member, of the politburo of the CC of the Ukraine CP. From May 1924 to December 1925 he was chairman of the central control commission of the Ukraine CP and PC of workers' and peasants' inspection of the Ukraine. During 1926-29 he was deputy PC of workers' and peasants' inspection and a member of the presidium of the Central Control Commission of the CPSU. In 1930 he was appointed deputy chairman of the CPC of the RSFSR. At the Eleventh and Twelfth Party congresses he was elected a candidate member of the CC of the RCP(B), at the Thirteenth and Fourteenth congresses a member of the Central Control Commission, at the sixteenth and seventeenth congresses a member of the CC of the CPSU. He became a victim of the cult of Stalin's personality.[58]

NIKOLAI MIKHAILOVICH LUKIN

Biographical data

Born 1885, died 1940. Pseudonym P. Antonov. Historian and Academician (1929). Joined the CP in 1904, graduated from Moscow University in the same year. Became a lecturer at the university in 1915. Took an active part in organizing the Moscow Bolshevik newspaper *Nash put'* (Our Way). After the February revolution he became a member of the editorial collegium of the Bolshevik newspaper *Sotsialdemokrat*. In October 1918 he resumed lecturing at Moscow University; in 1921 he was elected dean of the faculty of social sciences. From 1920 to the early 1930s he taught at the General Staff Academy and gave courses in Marxism at the Socialist Academy and at the Institute of Red Professors. In 1925 he was one of the founders of the Association of Marxist Historians. In 1932-36, director of the institute of history of the Communist Academy, and in 1936-38, director of the institute of history of the Academy of Sciences of the U.S.S.R. From 1935, chief editor of the journal *Istorik Marksist* (The Marxist Historian). Took part in international historical congresses (Oslo 1928, Warsaw 1933) and sessions of the International Committee on Historical Sciences (Cambridge) in 1930, the Hague in 1932 and Paris in 1934.

Lukin's special field was the modern history of Western Europe, especially France and Germany. In 1919 he published *Maksimilian Robespierre* (Moscow 2d ed. Moscow-Leningrad, 1924), which was the first attempt at a consistent Marxist analysis of the history of the great French Revolution. He paid particular attention to the class struggle in the French countryside during the Jacobin dictatorship (see his *Bor'ba klassov vo frantsuzskoi derevne i prodovol' stvennaia politika konventa* [The Class Struggle, in the French Countryside and the Convention's Food Policy], 1930; and *Revolutsionnoe pravitel'stvo i sel'skokhoziaistvennye rabochie* [The Revolutionary Government and the Agricultural Workers], 1930). He also made an important contribution to the historiography of the French Revolution. In 1922 he published *Parizhskaia Kommuna 1871 goda* (The Paris Commune of 1871), on the elaboration of which he worked almost to the end of his days. The first volume of his revised and enlarged version of this study was published in 1932; the second was finished in the middle 1930s but never published.

Lukin made a valuable contribution to the study of Germany in the age of imperialism, especially the German social-democratic movement (see *Ocherki po noveishei istorii Germanii, 1890-1914* [Notes on Modern German History, 1890-1914], Moscow-Leningrad, 1925). He also paid much attention to the study of French socialism under the Third Republic, and wrote works assessing Marx and Lenin as historians *(Marks kak istorik* and *Istorik-Marksist,* vol. 1, 1934). In 1923 he published the first Marxist textbook of modern history for senior schools: *Noveishaia istoriia Zapadnoi Evropy* (Modern History of

Western Europe) (2d ed. Moscow, 1925). He was subjected to illegal repression in 1938, posthumously rehabilitated.[59]

ALEKSEI VASIL'EVICH MEDVEDEV

Biographical data

Born 1884, died 1936. Joined the CP in 1904. Born at Sereno-Zavodsk, Bunashev volost, Kozel' uezd, Kaluga gubernia, the son of a worker. Worked from 1897 at the local factory. In 1902 he was an apprentice smelter at the engineering works at Bezhitsa. In 1903 he moved to Moscow and worked at the cast-iron foundry of Dobrovykh and Nabgol'ts. Carried on revolutionary activity among the Zamoskvorech'e workers. Dismissed in 1905 for participation in strikes and demonstrations, he then worked at Briansk and Lugansk and was a member of the Lugansk organization of the RSDWP. In 1907, was assistant mechanic at the depot of the Kursk railroad station in Moscow. To escape arrest, he moved in 1909 to Koz'ma-Demian near Iaroslavl, then to Nizhni Novgorod, Tsaritsyn, Debal'tsevo, and Torets. In 1911, worked as a mechanic at the Makeevka metal works, and in 1912-13 at the Novyi Aivaz works in Petersburg, where he was arrested. After his release, moved to Revel (Tallin), then to Riga, where he worked as a mechanic at the Fel'zer works. In 1915 he was arrested and expelled from the Baltic area. Worked at the Alekseev works at Kharkov and was a member of the Party's Kharkov committee; contacted Bolshevik organizations at Ekaterinoslav and in the Donbass. After a short period of detention at the end of 1915 he returned illegally to Petersburg, where he carried on revolutionary activity at the Renault, Puzyrev, and Novyi Lesner works; was a member of the Vyborg raion committee and the Petersburg committee of the RSDWP. After the February revolution he was a member of the Petrograd soviet of workers' and soldiers' deputies and of the city duma. After the October Revolution he was a member of the press tribunal of the Petrograd soviet, volunteered for the front, carried on Party work at Syzran', was bank commissar and a member of the soviet's executive committee. In June 1918 he was chairman of the volost committee of the RCP(B) at Kozel'sk, chairman of the local revolutionary committee, and member of the Kaluga gubernia committee of the Party. In 1919-21, chairman of the volost committee of the Ukraine CP and of the revolutionary committee at Belaia Tserkov'; fought as a volunteer on the Polish and southern fronts. After the liquidation of the Wrangel front he was commissar for railroad construction, chairman of the Crimea Metallurgical Works, and member of the Bakhchisarai volost committee of the Party. In 1921-22 he served on the CC of the metallurgists' trade union at Kharkov and in the main administration of the metalworking industry; also as secretary of the Party organization of the Ukraine council of the national economy, member of the Petinsk (Plekhanovsk) regional committee of the Ukraine CP, and chairman of the Kharkov gubernia trade union council. In April 1923 he was elected chairman of the central control commission of the Ukraine CP, and in November PC of workers' and peasants' inspection of the Ukraine. In May 1924 he was elected secretary and member of the politburo and organization bureau of the CC of the Ukraine CP. In February 1925 he became secretary of the Ekaterinoslav gubernia committee of the Ukraine CP. In November 1927 he was elected Second Secretary for Organization and a member of the organization bureau and politburo of the CC of the Ukraine CP. In 1930 he was elected a candidate member of the Presidium and secretary of the CEC of the U.S.S.R. In 1935 he was confirmed as a member of the Supreme Court of the U.S.S.R. At the Thirteenth to Fifteenth Party congresses he was elected a member of the CC of the CPSU, and at the Sixteenth Congress a member of the Central Control Commission of the CPSU. While serving in the Ukraine he was elected at the sixth Party conference a candidate member, and at the seventh conference a full member, of the central control commission of the Ukraine CP. At the eighth conference and the ninth and tenth congresses he was elected a member of the CC of the Ukraine CP. In 1924-25 and 1927-29 he was a member of the politburo and orgburo of the CC of the Ukraine CP. He became a victim of the cult of Stalin's personality.[60]

ARAM MIKHAILOVICH MIRZABEKIAN

Biographical data

Born 1895, died 19—. Born at Baku. Took part in the February and October revolutions. From 1918 to 1932 he served in the Red Guard, then in the Cheka at Astrakhan and Moscow. Assistant to the Commissar Extraordinary for Southern Russia; then held an important post in the control commission of workers' and peasants' inspection in the Transcaucasian Federation. In 1932-37 he was secretary of the CC of the Armenian CP and later deputy PC of workers' and peasants' inspection for Georgia.[61]

A member of Lenin's old guard

It is seventy years since the birth of the eminent Bolshevik Aram Mikhailovich Mirzabekian. He was born [in 1895] at Baku, studied at the commercial school there and entered the Kiev Institute. Here, as a youth of twenty, he joined the Bolshevik underground and, on the Party's orders, directed student Marxist circles.

He took an active part in the February and October revolutions. From the beginning of 1918 he was assistant to the Red Guard commander in Baku, and later worked in the Cheka until the fall of the Baku Commune. He also worked for the Cheka in Astrakhan and Moscow. From 1920 he was assistant to Sergo Ordzhonikidze, the Commissar Extraordinary for Southern Russia, and took part in all operations for the establishment of Soviet power in Transcaucasia.

After the Transcaucasian Federation was set up, the Party assigned him to important work in the control commission of the workers' and peasants' inspection of the Transcaucasian Federation. In 1932-33 he was secretary of the CC of the Armenian CP, and in 1934-37 deputy PC of workers' and peasants' inspection for Georgia.

A stalwart Bolshevik, Mirzabekian worked hard to effect Lenin's nationalities policy and to develop the economy of the federation. His strong principles won him respect and love. He was liquidated together with Sergo Ordzhonikidze's brother and others, a victim of the arbitrary rule of that enemy of the people Beria. But his glorious image will live forever in the nation's memory.[62]

LEVON ISAEVICH MIRZOIAN

Biographical data

Born 1878, died 1938. Joined the Bolshevik Party in 1917. Born in Ashan village, Shushin uezd, Gandzha gubernia. In 1918, after the temporary overthrow of Soviet rule in Baku, he carried on underground work in that city. In 1919 he was a member of the Baku Workers' Conference and the Baku trade union council, as well as the Baku committee of the Azerbaidzhan CP. Sent by the Party to Dagestan, he was arrested and expelled to Georgia, where he was again arrested and expelled to Armenia. In 1920 he was chairman of the Azerbaidzhan trade union council, and in 1921 chairman of the Baku committee of the Azerbaidzhan CP. In 1925-29 he was secretary of the CC of the Azerbaidzhan CP; in 1929-33, secretary of the Perm' district committee, then second secretary of the Ural oblast committee of the CPSU; in 1933-38, first secretary of the Kazakhstan regional committee of the CPSU, and (from June 1937) first secretary of the CC of the Kazakhstan CP. In 1938 he became a victim of the cult of personality.[63]

Mirzoian's career

Levon Isaevich Mirzoian occupies a worthy place in the ranks of fighters of the Bolshevik old guard. The name of this outstanding revolutionary, gifted organizer of the masses, and true Leninist is closely linked with the class struggle of the proletariat against Tsarism and the bourgeoisie, the achievement and consolidation of Soviet rule, the struggle to create heavy industry, and the victory of socialism. Wherever he served he was tireless and self-effacing, with the power to inspire achievement in others.

He was born, the son of a peasant, in November 1897 in Ashan village, Shushin uezd, Gandzha gubernia. In 1912, having come to live in Baku, he joined the revolutionary movement and became a member of an illegal social-democratic teachers' group. Later a subgroup evolved from this, working under the direction of the Baku committee of the RSDWP, and in this body the young Mirzoian played an active part. In March 1917 he joined the Bolshevik Party.

During 1917-20, under the guidance of S. G. Shaumian, P. A. Dzhaparidze, S. M. Kirov, and G. K. Ordzhonikidze, he carried on intensive propaganda and organizational work in the trade unions and performed difficult assignments for the Party. He was secretary of the Binagadin department of the trade union of boilermakers and riveters and later of the trade union of metalworkers; he was also a member of the Bolshevik armed workers' detachment and a deputy to the Baku soviet of workers' and soldiers deputies. After the temporary over-throw of Soviet rule in Baku in July 1918, he remained in the city and carried on underground work under Party instructions. Together with his Communist colleagues he organized Party work, stirred up the sailors and workers of the military port to overthrow the bloody regime of Musavatists and foreign invaders, and helped to organize the transport of fuel from Baku to Soviet Astrakhan. At the end of November 1918 an illegal meeting of Bolsheviks elected him to the provisional bureau which was in charge of all underground work.

The Communists' widespread activity in mobilizing the working masses of Baku for revolution led to the formation of workers' organizations. In November 1918 the Baku Workers' Conference—a political organ of the Baku proletariat—was already in existence. At the re-election of its presidium in March 1919, Mirzoian, A. G. Karaev, and other Bolsheviks became members of it and also of the Baku trade union council. Later Mirzoian was elected to the Baku committee of the Azerbaidzhan CP.

Soon the Party sent him to Dagestan to organize liaison with local Bolshevik groups there. After his return he took an active part in preparations for a general political strike of Baku workers. In May 1919 he was arrested by the Musavatist authorities and expelled to Georgia, where he joined in the work of the Party's Transcaucasian regional committee. Soon he was again arrested and expelled to Armenia, whence he escaped to Baku.

When Soviet rule was established in Azerbaidzhan he devoted himself to trade union work. At the first congress of Azerbaidzhan trade unions at the end of August 1920 he was elected chairman of the Azerbaidzhan trade union council. In 1921 he became chairman of the Baku committee of the Azerbaidzhan CP, and devoted all his energy to overcoming the economic and cultural back-wardness inherited by the republic from the former regime. He encouraged the development of the oil industry by advocating an accelerated drilling program, opposing the monthly revision of norms and lowering of rates. He expressed to the CC of the RCP(B) his views on the need to do away with excessive centralization of control over the Azerbaidzhan petroleum industry by the Supreme Council of the National Economy, which he said fettered the initiative of local Party and economic groups; he also argued in favor of raising the workers' pay satisfying their cultural needs, and improving their living standards. At the same time, he gave great attention to the training of Party and economic cadres, believing that a good Bolshevik requires both theoretical and practical experience. He devoted much energy to the work of the special commission of the CC of the Azerbaidzhan CP that was set up in January 1925 to consider questions of Party work in the countryside. He also took an active part in working out a plan to intensify the activity of the soviets.

At the end of 1925 the CC of the CPSU appointed S. M. Kirov, the chairman of the CC of the Azerbaidzhan CP, to serve on the Party's Leningrad oblast committee. On Kirov's recommendation Mirzoian was at this time elected secretary of the CC of the Azerbaidzhan CP. In this post he continued to concentrate on developing the economy of the republic, reconstructing the oil industry, and strengthening Party organization. He led the fight against Trotskyists and other anti-Leninist groups, demanding unity in the Party's ranks. In vivid speeches at meetings of Party organizations, conferences, and congresses he denounced the Trotskyists' anti-Party, factionalist activity and their unfounded attacks on the Party. At the eighth congress of the Azerbaidzhan CP on November 18, 1927, he appealed to Communists to defeat the Trotskyists' attempts to create a separate opposition party of their own.

In October 1929 the CC of the CPSU appointed him to the Ural area, first as secretary of the Perm' district committee and then as second secretary of the Ural oblast committee of the CPSU. In those years the chief concern of the Ural Bolsheviks was to speed up industrial construction. The best Communists of the area were assigned to the Ural heavy machinery plant, the Magnitogorsk metallurgical combine then under construction, the Bereznikov chemical combine, the Cheliabinsk tractor plant, the Nizhnii Tagil metallurgical combine, the Solikamsk chemical combine, and other enterprises. The Ural area was being transformed into a center of metallurgy, engineering, and chemical works.

In 1933 the Party sent Mirzoian to Kazakhstan, where he was elected first secretary of the Party's regional committee. When the Kazakhstan CP was formed in June 1937 he became first secretary of its CC. His organizing talent, sense of purpose, and devotion to the Party and people were not the only outstanding qualities of this leader of the Kazakhstan Party organization. He constantly strove for progress, never resting on his laurels or becoming complacent with success.... He realized that the fulfillment of tasks assigned by the Party depended on the ruthless elimination of shortcomings and mistakes in the work of local Party, state, and social organizations.

His outstanding services in the development of Kazakhstan agriculture and industry were recognized in 1935, when the Soviet government conferred on him the Order of Lenin. He was a delegate to the Fifteenth, Sixteenth, and Seventeenth CP congresses. At the Fifteenth and Sixteenth congresses he was elected a candidate member, and at the Seventeenth a full member, of the CC of the CPSU. He was also a member of the CEC of the U.S.S.R. at several convocations.

In May 1938 the life of this eminent Bolshevik, Leninist, and gifted organizer of socialist construction was tragically cut short, when he became a victim of unjustified repression during the cult of personality. With Stalin's approval he was dismissed, arrested, and accused of serious crimes. His last declaration contained these words: "I have faithfully served the Party and people for twenty-two years. I have never betrayed the Party's interests. I swear with my last breath, on the life of my children, that I was never an enemy to the Party and people." His fate was shared by his wife and true companion, Teodorovna Tevosian, who joined the Party in 1918 and was director of the Marxist-Leninist Institute of the CC of the Kazakhstan CP.

In January 1956 Mirzoian and his wife were rehabilitated on the ground that the accusations against them were not substantiated. The Party thus restored the good name of its faithful son, an outstanding Party and administrative leader of the Leninist type.[64]

MUZAFFAR AKPER-OGLY NARIMANOV

Biographical data

Born 1897, died 1937. Joined the Bolshevik Party in 1918. Born at Tiflis. In 1918 he joined the Gummet party, then worked for Musavat intelligence. After the victory of Soviet power in Azerbaidzhan he was in charge of the Azerbaidzhan revolutionary committee, commissar extraordinary for the committee, and special plenipotentiary of the Party CC for the Zakataly district and the Nukha uezd. In 1921-27, having completed a course at the Plekhanov Institute of Political Economy, he was head of a department of the CC of the Azerbaidzhan CP. In 1928-32 he was an instructor for the Sverdlovsk oblast committee of the Party, then first secretary of the Sverdlovsk district committee of the Party. In 1932-33 he studied in Moscow. In 1933-37 he was successively head of the Agitation and Mass Campaigns department of the CC of the Azerbaidzhan CP, first secretary of the Ordzhonikidze raion committee of the Party, third secretary of the Baku oil committee of the Azerbaidzhan CP, and second secretary of the Party's city committee. He was arrested in 1937.[65]

A life devoted to the fight for socialism

A sturdy man of middle height with a handsome, virile face and a gentle expression—such was Muzaffar Narimanov, a prominent leader of the Azerbaidzhan CP. Profoundly devoted to Lenin's Party, a gifted organizer and educator of the masses, a man of great culture and personal qualities, he devoted his entire adult life to the fight for the victory of socialism in our country.

He was born on July 28, 1897, at Tiflis, the son of a poor handicraftsman. His parents soon died, and he and his brothers and sisters had a difficult childhood. From 1898 he was at Baku, where he attended the Russo-Tatar school and then the Baku technical high school. The hardships of his life, the revolutionary outbreaks of the Baku proletariat, the First World War, the influence of N. Narimanov, G. Sultanov, and other Bolsheviks—all this was bound to have a lasting effect on his outlook. After the February revolution he took up active revolutionary work. Two events which particularly impressed him were the defeat of the anti-Soviet revolt at Baku at the end of March 1918 and the creation and activity of the Baku CPC. As he wrote later, "the events of March were decisive in shaping my political views, and at the end of March or beginning of April I joined the Gummet party (the Turkic section of the Baku organization of the RSDWP[B]).

After the temporary overthrow of Soviet power in Baku, on the instructions of the Bolshevik Party he worked in Musavat counterespionage. Keeping in close touch with G. Sultanov and V. Naneishvili and receiving instructions from them, he carried out Party assignments and underground work and kept the Party thoroughly informed of the state of the Musavat armed forces, the activity and plans of Musavat intelligence, etc.

After the victory of Soviet rule in Azerbaidzhan he took an active part in the fight to consolidate Soviet power in the various districts, to put an end to economic dislocation and revive the oil industry. He was in charge of the Azerbaidzhan revolutionary committee, was commissar extraordinary for the committee and special plenipotentiary of the Party CC for the Zakataly district and the Nukha uezd. In these posts he did much to create centers of Soviet power, suppress counterrevolution, and ensure food supplies.

In November 1921 he went to Moscow to study at the G. V. Plekhanov Institute of Political Economy. On his return he was appointed head of a department of the Azerbaidzhan CP, which post he held until November 1927. In October 1928 the CC of the CPSU directed him to work in the Urals, where he was an instructor for the Sverdlovsk oblast committee and later first secretary of the Sverdlovsk district committee of the Party. The Ural Communists elected him their delegate to the Sixteenth Congress of the CPSU.

At the end of 1932 he once again went to Moscow to study, but did not complete his course [because he was] transferred in May 1933 to the important Party post of head of the Agitation and Mass Campaigns department of the CC of the Azerbaidzhan CP.

In 1933 the Soviet people, who under the guidance of Lenin's Party had laid the firm economic foundations of socialism, embarked on the fulfillment of the Second Five Year Plan and the completion of the construction of a socialist society in our country. In this plan, the Party and government made great and important demands on the Baku oil workers: the Azerbaidzhan oil industry was called on to provide, without interruption and in sufficient quantity, oil and petroleum products for the purpose of socialist construction throughout the country. Narimanov at this time devoted all his energy, knowledge, organizing talent, and experience as a Party worker to organizing ideological and political work and improving its quality so that it should become an integral part of the day-to-day practical struggle of the Baku Party organizations for the production of oil. He was active in explaining to the working masses the aims and problems of the Second Five Year Plan in general and in particular the Republic's economic plan for 1933—the significance of the fight for oil to the whole country and to the fate of socialism in the Soviet Union.

The CC and the Baku committee of the Azerbaidzhan CP took various measures to ensure the realization of the plan for increased oil deliveries. Every enterprise was assigned specific tasks: to increase the number of drills and bore-holes, to step up the rate of daily output and the target for the second half-year, and so on. All secretaries and senior members of the staff of the CC and Baku committee were attached to one enterprise or another, and the Party raion committees were stiffened by the addition to their staff of experienced and energetic Party workers.

In August 1933, on the recommendation of the CC and Baku committee of the Azerbaidzhan CP, Narimanov was elected first secretary of the Ordzhonikidze raion committee of the Party. As head of the Party organization of one of the key oil areas he devoted himself heart and soul to the cause of oil production. In the first two years of the Second Five Year Plan the oil wells of the Ordzhonikidze raion gave the country almost 9.3 million tons of oil. For his successful work in exceeding the 1933-34 oil output plans, he received the Order of the Red Banner of Labor. In July 1935 he was elected third secretary of the Baku oil committee of the Azerbaidzhan CP, and six months later second secretary of the Party's city committee—a post which gave full play to his talent and skill as a Party leader, organizer, and mass educator. His unswerving fidelity to Leninist ideas and the general line of the CP, his knowledge and experience, especially of oil production and the cadres of the oil industry, and finally his outstanding personal qualities—strong will, self-control, and powers of organization, level-headedness, endurance, conscientiousness, interest in and understanding of the smallest details of the work at hand, ability to heed the voice of the masses and keep in close contact with Party organizations—all these traits enabled him to acquit himself with honor in carrying out the tasks laid upon him by the Party.

But it was not given him to see with his own eyes the fruits of our people's heroic struggle for the building of socialism. A victim of the cult of personality, he was falsely accused of the gravest crimes and arrested on September 3, 1937.

He belonged to the generation that was brought up by the October Revolution and the Communist Party. All his life he was unshakably faithful to the great ideas of Lenin's Party, devoted to the struggle for socialism and communism. The glorious memory of this great man and true son of the Party will live forever in the people's memory.[66]

AMAIAK MARKAROVICH NAZARETIAN

Biographical data

Born 1889, died 1938. Joined the Bolshevik Party in 1905. Born at Akhal-kalaki (Georgia). Entered the law faculty of Petersburg University in 1909. In 1911 he was expelled for revolutionary activity and sent to prison in Tiflis; he escaped and lived until 1913 in Switzerland. From 1913 to 1916 he carried on revolutionary work in Petersburg. In 1916-18 he was chairman of the commit-tee of the soldiers' union at Tiflis and a member of the Tiflis Party committee, the Caucasian regional committee, and the presidium of the Caucasian bureau of the CC of the RCP(B); also worked on the Bolshevik newspaper *Kavkazsky rabochii* (Caucasian Worker). In 1918-19 he was commissar of labor and deputy chairman of the CPC of the Terek Soviet Republic. In 1919-20 he was in Georgia, where he was arrested in 1920 and expelled into Soviet Russia. In 1921-22 he was a member of the Georgian revolutionary committee. In 1922-27, chief of the bureau of the Secretariat of the CC of the RCP(B) and later secretary of the Transcaucasian regional committee of the CPSU. In 1927-28, chairman of the Transcaucasian control commission of the CPSU, PC of workers' and peasants' Inspection of the Transcaucasian Federal Republic, and a member of the editorial board of the newspapers and journals *Izvestiia* (organ of the Transcaucasian control commission of the CPSU), *Zaria vostoka,* and *Kavkazskii bol'shevik*. In 1928-36 he did important Party, government, and economic work in Transcaucasia. In 1936-37 he was a member of the collegium of the PC of Workers' and Peasants' Inspection of the U.S.S.R. In 1937 he was arrested when en route to Moscow; liquidated in 1938.[67]

A fighter for the people's cause

In the glorious cohort of fighters for the victory of the proletarian revolution in Transcaucasia, an important place belongs to Amaiak Markarovich Nazaretian—one of the illustrious band of revolutionaries of Lenin's Party who, as the great leader himself wrote, "did not waste their energies on useless, isolated acts of terrorism but worked steadily and vigorously among the proletarian masses, developing their political awareness, organization, and self-reliance. These were the people who led the mass armed struggle against Tsarist autocracy when the critical moment came, when the revolution broke out and men and women joined our movement by the millions."

Nazaretian was born on November 17, 1889, at Akhalkalaki (Dzhavakheti), the son of a small tradesman. He received his first education at home and then entered the Third Tiflis High School for boys, where he joined other pupils in an illegal revolutionary organization. In 1905 he became a member of the RSDWP. From then on he performed important tasks for the Bolshevik Party, carried on revolutionary propaganda among workers and high school pupils, and took an active part in illegal rallies and mass meetings held in the country around Tiflis. He also helped to organize the escape of prisoners from the Tiflis gubernia jail.

In 1909 he entered the law faculty of Petersburg University. As a student he was an active member of the university Bolshevik group and directed Marxist circles of workers at the Putilov factory. For his revolutionary work he was expelled from the university in 1911 and confined in the gubernia jail at Tiflis. He escaped with the aid of the Party underground organization and later emigrated to Switzerland, where he stayed until 1913. On return to Petersburg he took up revolutionary work with renewed energy, conducting courses at works and factories, carrying on propaganda among soldiers against the imperialist war, and expounding Bolshevik tactics on questions of war, peace, and revolution.

In 1916 he moved to Tiflis, where for a time he was chairman of the committee of the Union of Soldiers, Workers, and Officials and was in charge of the Bolshevik group of the third Tiflis raion. From the time of the February revolution of 1917 till the establishment of Soviet power in Georgia, he carried on organizing and propaganda work—as a leader of Caucasian Bolshevik organizations fighting for the victory of the socialist revolution and the establishment of Soviet rule in the Caucasus, and denouncing the Georgian Mensheviks, the Armenian Dashnaks, and the Azerbaidzhani Musavatists. At this time he was also a member of the Party's Tiflis committee, the Caucasian regional committee, and the presidium of the Caucasian bureau of the CC of the RCP(B). He did valuable work for the Bolshevik press in 1917-18 as a member of the editorial staff of *Kavkazskii rabochii*.

In 1918, pursued by the Menshevik authorities, he went from Tiflis by way of the Georgian Military Highway to Vladikavkaz, where he fought actively for the victory of Soviet power in the northern Caucasus. He was PC of labor, and subsequently deputy chairman of the CPC, of the Terek Soviet Republic. At the beginning of 1919 he returned to Georgia, and in the fall of that year he was one of the leaders of the working people's uprising against the Mensheviks for the establishment of Soviet power. In 1920 he was arrested by the Mensheviks and expelled to Soviet Russia. At the beginning of 1921 he was busy with organizational work for the establishment of Soviet power in Georgia. When the Georgian revolutionary committee was set up on February 16, 1921, he became one of its members. The great services he rendered in the fight for Soviet rule in Georgia are attested by a remark of Ordzhonikidze's during the first days of Soviet rule: when asked his opinion of a proposal to transfer Nazaretian to the capital, Ordzhonikidze replied, "He has done excellent service here; I think he had better stay."

In 1922 Nazaretian was recalled for service under the CC of the RCP(B), where he became head of the bureau of the Secretariat. He remained in close touch with the Transcaucasian Bolsheviks and took a lively interest in the first steps toward the building of a new life in the fraternal republics of Transcaucasia.

In 1924-26 he was secretary of the Transcaucasian regional committee of the CPSU, and in 1927-28 chairman of the Transcaucasian control commission of the CPSU and PC of workers' and peasants' inspection of the Transcaucasian Federal Republic. He was also a member of the editorial board of *Izvestiia* (the organ of the Transcaucasian control commission of the CPSU), *Zaria vostoka*, and *Kavkazskii bol'shevik*. In the execution of his important Party, government, and economic duties in Transcaucasia he devoted all his powers, energy, and knowledge to the economic and cultural development of the Transcaucasian republics and the realization of Lenin's plan for the building of socialism in our country. He did much to strengthen the bonds of friendship between the peoples of Azerbaidzhan, Armenia, and Georgia and to educate the working people of Transcaucasia in the spirit of the great ideals of proletarian internationalism.

In October 1936 he was appointed a member of the collegium of the PC of Workers' and Peasants' Inspection of the U.S.S.R. He was a delegate to several congresses of the CPSU and of Communist organizations in Transcaucasia, and was several times elected to the bureau of the Transcaucasian regional committee of the CPSU and to the CEC of the U.S.S.R.

In 1938 he became a victim of slander and injustice. Our own day has seen the restoration of the good name and illustrious memory of this devoted fighter for the peoples's welfare and the cause of Lenin's Party.[68]

N. N. NURMAKOV

Biographical data

Born 1895, died 1938. Joined the CP in 1920. An eminent political leader of Soviet Kazakhstan. Took part in the fight for Soviet power in the Karkaralinsk uezd and was a member of its revolutionary committee and that of the Semipalatinsk gubernia, 1919-20. In 1920-22 he was deputy head of the organization department of the Kirgiz oblast committee of the RCP(B) and president of the supreme court of the Kirgiz ASSR; in 1922-24, PC of justice, procurator of the republic, and head of the Agitprop department of the Kazakh regional committee of the CPSU. From October 1924 to 1937 he occupied several important posts: chairman of the CPC of the Kazakh ASSR, deputy secretary of the All-Union CEC and head of the nationalities department of the Presidium of the All-Union CEC and the Supreme Soviet of the U.S.S.R. He was a member of the Kirgiz oblast committee and the Kazakh regional committee of the CPSU, of the CEC of the Kazakh ASSR, and of the Presidium of the All-Russian CEC, and a delegate to the Eleventh and Fourteenth CPSU congresses.[69]

MAMIIA DIMITRIEVICH ORAKHELASHVILI

Biographical data

Born 1883, died 1937. Joined the Bolshevik Party in 1903. Born in Sakara village, Shoropain uezd, Kutaisi gubernia, Georgia. Served at the front in 1917; then was chairman of the Vladikavkaz committee of the Bolshevik Party and chairman of the Vladikavkaz soviet of workers' and soldiers' deputies. Arrested, released in 1920, then became chairman of the CC of the Georgian CP and member of the Caucasian bureau of the CPSU. In 1921-27 he was chairman of the Georgian revolutionary committee, chairman of the CPC of the Georgian SSR, and chairman of the CPC of the Transcaucasian Federation. In 1921-22 he was also secretary of the CC of the Georgian CP and later secretary of the Caucasian regional committee of the CPSU. After the First and Second all-Union congresses of soviets he was chairman of the CPC of the U.S.S.R. In 1930-31 he was a member of the editorial board of *Pravda;* in 1931-32, chairman of the CPC of Transcaucasia, then first secretary of the Transcaucasian regional committee of the CPSU. In 1932-37, deputy director of the Marx-Engels-Lenin Institute of the CC of the CPSU. Liquidated in 1937.[70]

A true fighter of the Leninist Party

Among the fighters of the Bolshevik old guard, a worthy place is occupied by Mamiia (Ivzi) Dimitrievich Orakhelashvili. It is impossible to imagine the history of Bolshevik organizations in Transcaucasia without his distinguished name. He was born on June 10, 1883, in a poor peasant family in the village of Sakara, Shoropan uezd [sic], Kutaisi gubernia, Georgia. Having attended high school at Kutaisi he entered the medical faculty of Kharkov University and later the Petersburg Military-Medical Academy. While still a schoolboy he joined a social-democratic group, and at Kharkov University headed a group of students whom he coached in historical materialism. In the summer of 1903 he was tried by a military court for "taking part in disturbances" in student camps near Iaroslavl'. From that time on he was a steadfast member of the Social Democratic Party, and immediately after the Party's Second Congress he threw in his lot with the Bolshevik Leninists, taking an active part in the revolutionary events of 1905 in Petersburg.

In the summer of 1906 he went to Paris and Geneva, and on his return was arrested and kept in captivity for eight months, then sent to Tiflis for trial in connection with the Aklabar underground printing press. In 1908 he was sent to Transcaucasia, where he worked as a medical officer and at the same time contributed to progressive and Bolshevik newspapers. At the end of 1913 he was back in Kutaisi, where he continued his Party activity. When the February revolution of 1917 broke out he was at the front. Soon afterward he was in the northern Caucasus as chairman of the Vladikavkaz committee of the Bolshevik Party and chairman of the Vladikavkaz soviet of workers' and soldiers' deputies.

In the fall of 1917, after the temporary victory of counterrevolutionary forces in the northern Caucasus, he and other Bolshevik leaders were sentenced to death, but his comrades succeeded in rescuing him. He then worked at Tiflis, Batumi, and Kutaisi in the illegal Caucasian regional committee of the Bolshevik Party. Arrested several times by the Menshevik intelligence service, he was confined in Metekh jail and released in 1920, after the conclusion of peace between Soviet Russia and the Menshevik government of Georgia. He then again went underground as chairman of the CC of the Georgian CP and member of the Caucasian bureau of the CC of the RCP(B).

In December 1926 he was elected first secretary of the Transcaucasian regional committee of the CPSU, and for some years was at the same time chief editor of *Zaria vostoka*. In 1930 he came to Moscow as a member of the editorial board of *Pravda*. In January 1931 he returned to Transcaucasia as chairman of the CPC and later first secretary of the Transcaucasian regional committee of the CPSU. From November 1932 to 1937 he was again in Moscow as deputy director of the Marx-Engels-Lenin Institute of the CC of the CPSU. He was several times elected a candidate and then a full member of the CC of the CPSU.

His whole career was that of a fighter for Lenin's great cause. He was a close friend and wartime counselor of Mikha Tskhakaia, Sergo Ordzhonikidze, S. M. Kirov, N. Narimanov, and A. I. Mikoyan, and enjoyed great popularity and prestige among Communists and non-Communists alike. He earned the reputation of a man of principle, exacting of himself and others, and internationalist of modest life, a good comrade, and an excellent publicist. Stepan Shaumian described him in a speech on June 15, 1918 as "one of the best Marxists in the Caucasus." He actively opposed Stalin's promotion of the scoundrel and adventurer Beria. When the latter published a book falsifying the history of Bolshevik organizations in Transcaucasia, Orakhelashvili openly expressed indignation at Beria and his work. He paid the price for his honesty and attachment to principle: he was arrested and died a victim of arbitrary rule during the cult of Stalin's personality. His fate was shared by his wife and faithful companion Mariia, a prominent member of the women's movement who had been a Party member since 1906 and PC of education in Georgia.

The glorious name of the Leninist Bolshevik Orakhelashvili will live forever in the memory of the working peoples of Georgia, Armenia, Azerbaidzhan, and the northern Caucasus, and in the memory of all Soviet people.[71]

MARIIA PLATONOVNA ORAKHELASHVILI-MIKELADZE

Biographical data

Born 1887, died 1937. Born at Kulashi village, Kutais uezd, Georgia. Studied at Platon Teachers College in Petersburg, but was expelled for taking part in student disorders and finished her education at the law faculty of the Bestuzhev Institute. Her acquaintance with Marxism began in 1903-4, when she met Sasha Tsulukidze while on vacation at home in Kutais. She joined the Bolshevik Party in 1906. After the defeat of the first Russian revolution she was active in the military organization of the Petersburg Bolshevik committee and in illegal student social-democratic organizations: one of the leaders of these was the well known state and political leader Mamiia (Ivan) Dimitrievich Orakhelashvili, whom she later married.

At the outbreak of the October Revolution she was living at Vladikavkaz, where from 1914 she was a teacher in addition to taking a leading part in Social Democratic work among the toilers of the Terek oblast. At the end of 1917, when counterrevolution for a while triumphed at Vladikavkaz and reaction was in full swing, she remained on the Party's orders to do underground work and aid Bolsheviks to escape. She worked at Vladikavkaz with such prominent members of the CP as S. M. Kirov and Samuil (Noi) Buachidze. Here too she was elected to the city soviet and the presidium of its executive committee; she took an active part in organizing trade unions, and was chairman of the Vladikavkaz city central bureau and the city committee of the Bolshevik organization. At the beginning of 1918, again on Party orders, she made her way by the Georgian Military Highway from Vladikavkaz to Tiflis. As a skilled Party organizer she was also sent to Kutais, where she was elected to the gubernia committee of the Georgian Bolshevik organization and was active in preparations for an armed uprising. From summer 1920 she worked in the CC of the Georgian Bolshevik Party and in the clandestine publishing concern *Krasnaia zvezda*. In September she attended the Congress of Eastern Peoples at Baku. Arrested in January 1921, she was jailed first at Kutais and then at Batumi. After her release she was active in the fight to establish Soviet power in Adzharia. After the soviets triumphed in Georgia the CC appointed her to several important posts, chiefly in the field of popular education. At different times she was head of the women's department of the CC of the Georgian CP and deputy PC and later PC of the Georgian Republic. She was a member of the collegium of the PC of education of the RSFSR, was several times elected to the CC of the Georgian CP and the presidium of the CECs of Georgia and the RSFSR, and was chairman of the editorial board of the State Publishing House and editor of various journals *Mshromeli kali, Kul'tstroitel'stvo, and Tsiteli skhivi).* In 1924 she attended the third international conference of Communist women. In March 1933 she was awarded the Order of the Red Banner of Labor. Arrested in 1937 together with her husband Orakhelashvili, she became a victim of the cult of Stalin's personality.[72]

SERGEI PORFIR'EVICH PETROV

Biographical data

Born 1889, died 1942. Joined the CP in August 1917; an eminent Party worker of Chuvashia. Born in Attikovo village, Cheboksary uezd, Kazan gubernia, the son of a peasant of middle status. Attended primary school and then worked from 1903 to 1907 as an unskilled laborer at Kazan. Became an active revolutionary in 1917 while in the army. In 1918 he took part in the expulsion of the White Czechs from Samara, then served on a committee for aid to the poor and on the Samara city soviet. In April 1919 he was called up to fight Kolchak and became military commissar in the Seventh Samara Regiment, which was later transformed into a separate rifle brigade. In 1921-23 he was deputy head of military-political courses of the district political administration. After 1923 he was engaged exclusively in Party work. From 1923 to 1926 he was secretary of the first raion committee of the city of Samara, chief instructor of the Samara gubernia committee of the RCP(B), and secretary of the Buguruslan uezd committee of the Party. In September 1926 the CC of the Party assigned him to Chuvashia, where he served without a break until November 1937 as chief secretary and first secretary of the Chuvash oblast committee of the CPSU. In June 1935 he received the Order of Lenin on the occasion of the fifteenth anniversary of Chuvash autonomy. At the end of 1937, at the height of the cult of Stalin's personality, he was unjustly expelled from the Party and subjected to repression. Posthumously rehabilitated in 1956.[73]

IOSIF (OSIP) ARONOVICH PIATNITSKY

Biographical data

Born 1882, died 1939. Party names Piatnitsa, Freitag. One of the earliest participants in the revolutionary movement; an eminent member of the Communist Party and the international workers' movement. Born at Vil'komir, Kovno gubernia; joined the RSDWP in 1898. In March 1902 he was arrested for belonging to the *Iskra* organization, and imprisoned at Kiev. Escaped in August 1902, hid for a time at Zhitomir and then went abroad. On the instructions of *Iskra* he settled in Berlin and organized the movement of persons and literature into Russia. Took part in the convocation of the Second and Third congresses of the RSDWP. In July 1905 he was assigned to Party work in Odessa, where he was arrested in January 1906, but soon released under police surveillance. In September 1906 he moved to Moscow, where he was in charge of passports and transport for the Moscow committee. Arrested in 1908 while trying to cross the border, but soon released on bail. In 1909 he was sent to Germany

Iosif (Osip) Aronovich Piatnitsky

by the Foreign Bureau of the CC of the RSDWP(B) for the purpose of restoring border-crossing arrangements. In 1912 he took part in the Prague conference of the RSDWP(B). In 1913 he came to Russia and worked in the Saratov gubernia. Arrested in June 1914 and exiled to the Enisei gubernia, where he stayed until March 1917. Returned to Moscow, was elected to the Moscow committee and the executive committee of the Moscow Soviet of workers' and soldiers' deputies. After the October Revolution he served in important Party posts. In 1920 he was secretary of the Moscow committee; from 1921 he worked in the Comintern, and from 1923 was secretary of its Executive Committee. Took part in the Sixth, Eighth, and Twelfth to Seventeenth Party congresses. From the Thirteenth Congress onward he was a member of the CC of the CPSU. Author of several works publicizing the international revolutionary and trade union movement, and also memoirs (*Zapiski bol'shevika*). His works were translated into foreign languages. He was liquidated in 1939.[74]

OL'GA VLADIMIROVNA PILATSKAIA

Biographical data

Born 1883, died 1937. Joined the CP in 1904. Born in Moscow, the daughter of a mechanic. In 1901 she started training as a doctor's assistant and joined the revolutionary movement. During the 1905 revolution she organized a hospital unit for armed workers' detachments; later worked in the underground movement in Moscow. In 1909 she emigrated to England to join her husband, V. Zagorsky. On her return to Moscow she was arrested and exiled to Saratov. In 1911 she again went abroad to join her husband at Leipzig, and worked in a Bolshevik group there with Piatnitsky and Savel'ev. On the eve of the First World War she returned to Russia, and after her son was born lived at Nizhnii Novgorod. In 1915 she returned to Moscow and worked as an English translator in the Russo-American Chamber of Commerce. After the February revolution she directed Party work in the Gorodskoi raion of Moscow and was a member of its military revolutionary committee. After the October Revolution she served as a people's judge for the Moscow Cheka and was agitprop secretary of the CC of the RCP(B) and later of the chief committee of political education. From 1922 she worked in the Ukraine, and during 1922-26 was head of the agitprop department of the Party's gubernia committee at Ekaterinoslav. In 1926-30 she was head of the central department of the CC of the Ukraine CP for work among female workers and peasant women and a member of the organization bureau of the CC of the Ukraine CP; at the same time she contributed to the journals *Kommunarka Ukrainy* and *Selianka Ukrainy*. From 1930 to 1937 she worked in the state planning commission (Gosplan) of the Ukrainian SSR. In 1932-34 she was also director of the Institute of Red Professors, and in 1934-36 director of the institute of the CC of the Ukraine CP, [which dealt with] the history of the Party and the October Revolution in the Ukraine. She served on the CC of the Ukraine CP, the presidium of the Ukraine CEC, and the CEC of the U.S.S.R. She was arrested in 1937 and became a victim of the cult of Stalin's personality.[75]

MIKHAIL GEORGIEVICH PLESHAKOV

Biographical data

Born 1886, died 1938. Joined the Bolshevik Party in 1904. Born at Saratov. In 1904, joined the Balakhana raion committee of the RSDWP. After the February revolution of 1917 he was a member of the food committee of the Balakhana raion and chairman of the raion soviet of workers' and soldiers' deputies. In 1919, member of the provisional bureau of the Party's Baku committee. In 1920, member of the CC of the Azerbaidzhan CP. In 1921, member of the Baku revolutionary committee and of the Caucasus bureau of the CC of the RCP(B). In 1922, member of the Party's Transcaucasian regional committee, and in 1925 of the Central Control Commission of the CPSU. Liquidated in 1938.[76]

A glorious fighter for the Party

The Bolshevik organization of Baku was the breeding-ground for a whole band of distinguished revolutionary leaders sprung from the proletariat. Many and strenuous were the paths that led into revolutionary life such men as M. Mamed'iarov and P. Montin, I. Fioletov and B. Sardarov, Kh. Safaraliev and M. Melikian, M. B. Kasumov, I. Anashkin, and many others. But all of them were one hundred percent sons of the Baku proletariat. And so too was Mikhail Georgievich Pleshakov, an eminent revolutionary, a worker and the son of workers.

He was born at Saratov but his family came to Baku in search of work, and he began to earn his living as a mechanic's assistant at the age of eleven. In 1903 he came into contact with the social-democrats and carried out assignments for them, distributing proclamations and taking part in the work of Marxist study groups. He was often to be seen in the ranks of strikers from the local oil industry. In 1904 he joined the Bolshevik Party.... Kirov later said of him: "From 1904 onward [Pleshakov] was an active member of the Bolshevik fraction of the Party and took a prominent part in political strikes and demonstrations, May Day rallies, and so on. He grew up with the Baku workers' movement and became a part of it."

When reaction swept the country after the defeat of the 1905 revolution, Pleshakov engaged in underground activity which he combined with various forms of legal work. The Baku Bolshevik organization made good use of his experience as a leader in connection with the union of oil industry workers. Pleshakov was a regular and active participant in all the activities of the Balakhana workers' club.

In February 1917 the Tsarist autocracy was overthrown. The Bolshevik Party came out of hiding, and its organizations in Azerbaidzhan began to work legally. Together with other Bolsheviks, Pleshakov spoke at workers' meetings and rallies, explaining the course of events and appealing for the destruction of the institutions of the old regime and the creation and strengthening of soviets. He became a member of the food committee of the Balakhana raion. The oil workers showed their confidence in him by electing him chairman of the raion soviet of workers' and soldiers' deputies. He devoted much strength, energy, and labor to improving the defenses of the Baku Commune.... When the Musavatists and foreign invaders seized control in Azerbaidzhan, he was one of the leaders of the Baku Bolshevik organization. At the beginning of 1919 he, M. B. Kasumov, and M. Mamed'iarov became members of the provisional bureau of the Party's Baku committee. At the same time he served as Party organizer of the Balakhana-Sabunchi raion. He took part in the first congress of Azerbaidzhan Communist organizations held on February 11-12, 1920, which set up the CP of Azerbaidzhan and prepared Party organizations for an armed uprising against the anti-national regime. Pleshakov was elected to the CC together with other noted Communists, including D. Buniatzade, M. D. Guseinov, I. Dovlatov, V. Egorov, A. G. Karaev, V. Naneishvili and G. Sultanov.

After Soviet power triumphed in Azerbaidzhan in April 1920, Pleshakov worked tirelessly in various sectors of socialist construction, in responsible Party and government posts. In 1921 he was a member of the Baku revolutionary committee, and in the same year he was elected to the Caucasus bureau of the CC of the RCP(B). At the first congress of Communist organizations in Transcaucasia in February 1922 he became a member of the Party's Transcaucasian regional committee. At the Fourteenth Congress of the CPSU he was elected to the Central Control Commission of the CPSU.

All told, he rendered great services to the mother country as a gifted organizer of socialist construction in Azerbaidzhan. Among Azerbaidzhan Bolsheviks he was universally respected. As Kirov said of him, "his gentle character, long experience, and devotion to the Party's cause made him beloved by all its members." The workers of Azerbaidzhan honor his memory as that of a true Leninist and staunch champion of the Communist Party.[77]

VLADIMIR IVANOVICH POLONSKY

Biographical data

Born 1893, died 1939. Joined the CP in 1912. In 1913-14 he was a member of the presidium of the central board of the Petersburg union of metalworkers. In 1914-17 he was in exile in Siberia. In 1917 he was a leading member of the Moscow RMC and commissar of the Vitebsk Division at Petrograd. Toward the end of the Civil War he was chairman of the southern bureau of the All-Union Central Council of Trade Unions in the Donbass; later he became a member of the presidium of the CPC of the Ukraine, and engaged in trade union work until 1925. During 1925-30 he served as secretary of the Moscow city committee of the Party. In 1930-33 he was first secretary of the CC of the Azerbaidzhan CP and secretary of the Transcaucasian regional committee of the Party. From 1933 to 1935 he was head of the organization department of the CC of the CPSU; in 1935-37, second secretary of the All-Union Central Council of Trade Unions; from 1937, PC of communications of the U.S.S.R. Perished in 1939.[78]

A true Leninist

The older generation of the Baku proletariat—the generation of storm detachments which fought on the fronts of the First Five Year Plan—remembers with pride its eminent commander Vladimir Ivanovich Polonsky. He was one of those leaders of the Party organization of the Azerbaidzhan of the Republic whose names are permanently linked with the republic's successes during the First Five Year Plan. Born in 1893, he joined the Bolshevik Party in 1912, and from then rode the crest of the revolutionary wave. In 1913 on the recommendation of *Pravda* the Party's central organ, he was elected to the presidium of the central board of the Petersburg union of metalworkers. He did much at that time to unite the industrial proletariat of Petersburg around the Marxist-Leninist banner. In the late spring of 1914 he was arrested during an anti-militarist demonstration of the Petersburg workers and exiled to Siberia. In February 1917 he was once more in the thick of revolutionary events, as one of the chief leaders of the Moscow RMC. In October 1917 he led revolutionary detachments which defeated cadet and White Guard bands on the Moscow barricades. As commissar of the Vitebsk Division he was among the leaders of the revolutionary defense of Petersburg.

Toward the end of the Civil War the Party assigned him to the Donbass as head of the southern bureau of the All-Union Central Council of Trade Unions. At the same time he was a member of the presidium of the Ukraine CPC in charge of various sectors of the economy. In the course of the tense struggle to save the revolution on the military and economic fronts he stood out as a Party leader who, wherever he was and whatever his duties, always performed honorably, successfully, and in Leninist style. At the first all-Russian miners' congress he was elected secretary of the CC of the miners' union. After the Tenth Party Congress he was assigned once more to the trade-union front, the strengthening of which was judged especially important during the implementation of the New Economic Policy. He devoted all his energies to this task until 1925, when he headed the Party organization of the ''Proletariat'' raion of the capital; later he was elected secretary of the Moscow city committee of the Party. The Party organization under his direction was a true proletarian mainstay of the Party in the fierce ideological battle for Leninism.

In August 1930 he was elected first secretary of the CC of the Azerbaidzhan CP. In the first days of his tour of duty there he became a popular figure at all the factories, works, new constructions, etc., and was accepted by the Baku workers as one of the proletarian family. In November 1930 he was elected secretary of the Transcaucasian regional committee of the Party, while remaining first secretary of the CC of the Azerbaidzhan CP. At the beginning of February 1933 he became head of the organization department of the CC of the CPSU. During the years of intense struggle for the strengthening of Party control over rail transport he was deputy PC of communications. He was a victim of unbridled arbitrary rule during the cult of Stalin's personality, and perished in 1939.[79]

IAN VASIL'EVICH POLUIAN

Biographical data

Born October 9, 1891; died October 8, 1937. Of Kuban Cossack origin. Took an active part in the October Revolution and the Civil War. Joined the CP in 1912, having been active in the revolutionary movement since 1907. Sentenced to five years hard labor in 1915; liberated by the February revolution of 1917. In that year he was chairman of the executive committee of the Ekaterinodar (Krasnodar) soviet and a member of the Ekaterinodar committee of the RSDWP(B). In 1918-20 he was chairman of the Kuban oblast revolutionary committee and executive committee, chairman of the CPC of the Kuban-Black Sea Soviet Republic, chairman of the RMC of the North Caucasus Second Army, member of the RMC of the Ninth (Kuban) Army, and chief of the political department of the southwestern front. In 1920-22 he was chairman of the Kuban revolutionary committee and oblast executive committee and a member of the Kuban-Black Sea oblast committee of the RCP(B); he was also a member of the Caucasian and southwestern bureaus of the CC of the RCP(B). From 1922 he was chairman of the Tver (Kalinin) gubernia executive committee. He was a delegate to the Tenth Party Congress in 1920; a member of the All-Russian CEC from 1918 to 1931, and of the All-Union CEC from 1922 to 1931. In 1925-29 he worked in the apparatus of the All-Russian CEC and was a member of its Presidium. In 1929-30 he was chairman of the Far Eastern regional executive committee, and in 1931-37 head of power administration of the PC of communal economy of the RSFSR. He was a victim of unjustified repression; posthumously rehabilitated.[80]

IAKOV ABRAMOVICH POPOK

Biographical data

Born 1894, died 1938. Joined the CP in 1909. Born in the small town of Khislavichi, Mogilev gubernia and called up in 1915. In 1918 he was in charge of the fuel department of the Moscow soviet, then served in the Ukraine. During the Civil War he was deputy head of the political department of the Reserve Army on the Southeastern front. Head of the political department of the Eleventh Cavalry Army and member of the RMC of the North Caucasian Military District. After demobilization he carried out important Party work. During 1930-37 he was first secretary of the CC of the Turkestan CP. In 1937-38, first secretary of the Party's oblast committee for the Volga area. He became a victim of the cult of Stalin's personality in 1938.[81]

A worthy son of the Party

Seventy years have elapsed since the birth of a great Party worker, Iakov Abramovich Popok, the former first secretary of the CC of the Turkmenistan CP and member of the Central Inspection Committee of the CPSU.

Born on September 20, 1894, at Khislavichi in the Mogilev gubernia, he moved when fifteen years old to Ekaterinoslav (now Dnepropetrovsk), where in 1909 he joined the CP. He was called up in 1915 but soon deserted from the army, having become liable to courtmartial for distributing revolutionary propaganda among the ranks. At the end of 1916 he returned to his home territory, and when the February revolution of 1917 broke out he set up the local Bolshevik organization. At the beginning of 1918, after the victory of the October Revolution, he went to Moscow, where for a time he was in charge of the fuel department of the Moscow soviet, and was then sent as a representative of the All-Russian CEC to organize labor departments in the Ukraine. He was a delegate to the sixth all-Russian congress of soviets, and was there elected a member of the All-Russian CEC. During the Civil War he performed military duties as deputy head of the political department of the Reserve Army on the southeastern front, head of the political department of the Second Cavalry Army, and member of the RMC of the North Caucasian Military District. After demobilization, nearly all of his career was spent in Party work....

In August 1930 he was sent by the CC of the CPSU to Turkestan as first secretary of the Party CC. He held this post until April 1937, and from July 1937 to April 1938 was first secretary of the Party's oblast committee for the Volga area. He was a delegate to the Seventeenth Congress of the CPSU, where he was elected a member of the Central Inspection Committee of the CPSU. At the height of his powers, in 1938, he became a victim of arbitrary rule owing to the cult of Stalin's personality.

In the important posts he held he showed himself to be a man of principle, an exacting and at the same time considerate Party leader. He devoted much energy to raising the economic and cultural level of Turkmenistan. For this he was rewarded with the Order of Lenin in 1935. As a true Leninist, he laid stress on the deepening of fraternal friendship between the Turkmenian, Russian, and other peoples of the U.S.S.R. He will always be remembered by those who worked with him as a worthy son of the Party who placed its interests and those of the people above all else.[82]

PAVEL PETROVICH POSTYSHEV

Biographical data

Born 1887, died 1940. Born at Ivanovo-Voznesensk, Vladimir gubernia, the son of a textile worker. Went to work for a brushmaker in 1896, and in 1899 became an apprentice in A. Garelin's cotton print factory. Joined the RSDWP in 1904, and in 1905 carried on propaganda in support of the struggle of the Ivanovo textile workers against their bosses. On June 12, 1906, at the constituent meeting of the Union of Print Workers, he was elected a member of the union's governing body. In November of that year he was dismissed from the factory for protesting against its regulations, and became a professional Party worker. In 1908, after the arrest of O. Varentsova, he became one of the leaders of the Ivanovo Party organization, and on April 24 was arrested with some of his comrades. He served a prison sentence at hard labor at Vladimir from April 1908 to February 1910. He was again jailed at Vladimir from February 1910 until December 1912, when he was exiled for life to Siberia. In 1913-14 he lived in a settlement at Ust'-Ude on the Angara, and from March 1914 to March 1917 he worked at Irkutsk. There, in March 1917, he became a member of the soviet of workers' deputies and was one of the founders of the central bureau of the Trade Union Council; organized strikes and took an active part in denouncing Mensheviks and SRs. In August he was elected deputy chairman of the soviet of workers' deputies of the city of Irkutsk, and on December 5 a member of the newly created Irkutsk district RMC. On August 26, 1918, he represented the Siberian central committee at the fifth Far Eastern congress of workers. In September, on the instructions of the Party's central organs, he transferred to underground work. In 1919 he was commissar of the partisan detachment formed by I. Shevchuk and chairman of the agricultural soviet of the Tungus volost. In 1920 he took part in the formation of regular units from partisan detachments. Appointed representative of the CC of the RCP(B) for the Khabarovsk raion, he organized the social and administrative department of the Amur region. When the Far Eastern Bureau of the CC of the RCP(B) was set up he became a candidate member of it. In August 1921 he was appointed representative of the government of the Far Eastern Republic for the Baikal oblast and took part in fighting against Baron Ungern's White Guard bands. In October he became a member of the provisional revolutionary committee and the military council of the re-formed eastern front. In February 1922 he and Bliukher directed the assault on the White fortified positions at Volochaevka. After the success of this operation he was elected a delegate to the Eleventh Congress of the RCP(B). In April he took up his duties as oblast representative of the government of the Far Eastern Republic. In August 1923, when the Baikal gubernia ceased to exist, he was recalled by the CC of the RCP(B) and attached to the Kiev Party organization as acting head of the organization and training section of the Party's gubernia committee. In 1924 he was assigned to the gubernia control commission. In May, at the ninth Kiev gubernia Party conference, he was elected chairman of the gubernia control commission and delegate to the eighth all-Ukraine conference and the thirteenth Congress of the RCP(B). At the eighth conference of the Ukraine CP he was elected to the central control commission, and in autumn he became secretary of the Kiev gubernia committee of the Party. In December 1925, at the ninth congress of the Ukraine CP he was elected to the politburo and organization bureau of the CC and also became secretary of the CC. In 1926-30 he was secretary of the Kharkov district and city committees of the Party. At this time he took part in Party congresses and was elected to the CC of the CPSU and to the CC of the Ukraine CP. On July 13, 1930, the plenum of the CC of the CPSU elected him a member of its organization bureau and secretary of the CC. From July 1930 to January 1933 he was secretary of the CPSU CC in charge of agitprop and organization. On January 29, 1933, the joint plenum of the Kharkov city and oblast committees of the Ukraine CP elected him secretary of the city and oblast Party organizations. From 1933 to June 1934 he was in charge of the Kharkov Party organization and also second secretary and member of the politburo and organization bureau of the CC of the Ukraine CP, as well as a secretary of the CC of the CPSU. From July 1934 to January 1937 he was in charge of the Kiev oblast Party organization; in 1935 the Order of Lenin was conferred on the Kiev oblast and on him personally. In January 1937 he was relieved of his duties as secretary of the Kiev oblast Party committee, and in March, allegedly on account of shortcomings, he was relieved of the duties of secretary of the CC of the Ukraine CP. At the beginning of 1938 his name was removed from the list of candidate members of the Politburo of the CC of the CPSU and he was arrested. In December 1940 his life was cut short.[83]

The last months of his life

January 1937. Every day brings news of some fresh victory in the field of production. The new enterprises in List 518 are already in full swing. In an amazing upsurge, the First Five Year Plan has transformed the country into an industrial one. And yet people are alarmed: in Moscow trials are being held for leaders of opposition groups and tendencies. In the factories, people are denouncing Trotskyists, Zinovievites, Bukharinites, and various other right- and left-wing deviators. No one indeed, can forgive these schismatics for their opposition during the period when the Party was leading the nation toward the building of socialism. But people can not understand why other workers who were true Communists and served with the Red Guard are being dismissed and expelled from the Party.

At various works I have been asked by acquaintances and correspondents why Postyshev has not been seen there recently. "He could tell us what's going on—we know where we are with him." I too have not seen him for some time at meetings and discussions, even on subjects about which he always had something to say. At the newspaper office it is said that he is being groomed for some other work; there are rumors that he is leaving Moscow. There has been a vague announcement that he is being released from the duties of first secretary of the Kiev oblast committee of the Ukraine CP because it is impossible to combine this post with that of second secretary of the CC. At the same time, the plenum has removed Il'in from the post of second secretary of the Party oblast committee because of some technical blunders or even political mistakes; and Il'in was working under Postyshev's direction. It is impossible to discover what has happened from anyone in the oblast or city committee. It appears, however, that L. M. Kaganovich attended the plenum which relieved Postyshev of his duties as oblast committee secretary. On that occasion the woman Nikolaenko was described as a "heroine" and "unmasker of enemies," while the Kiev Party organization was blamed for relaxing its vigilance and sheltering enemies of the Party. Surely Stalin will step in and correct this mistake?

On January 25 my brother came from Kharkov and told me what was going on at the tractor and locomotive works, where people were being arrested who had fought in the Civil War. Bludov, the rector of the university, had also been arrested, as had some writers.

February 5. I am glad I am being sent on a rural assignment, away from these incessant meetings and denunciations.

February 7. This country spot near Radomyshl', far away from the railroad, is no more peaceful than Kiev. The chairman of the raion executive committee has been dismissed and the head of the agitprop department has been expelled from the Party. They were both arrested while on the way to Kiev. People in the raion organizations have stopped working and are simply wondering when they will be discharged. The collective farms are working virtually without guidance from the Party people. But the peasants are working together well and preparations for sowing are far better than in former years.

March 10. An urgent telegram asking me to prepare an article on how the Party oblast committee gave wrong directions in agricultural matters. But in every village people have had nothing but praise for the oblast committee workers, who have not been interfering in farming matters or imposing their own plans but helping with the large-scale aspects and the liaison between the kolkhozes and urban enterprises.

March 12. I have sent off an article on some shortcomings in agricultural planning and the improvement of crops and livestock. This subject has often been raised by Postyshev, Kosior, and Liubchenko at congresses, conferences, and rallies of agricultural Stakhanovites. I mentioned in my article an example given by Postyshev at the oblast congress not long ago, when he said that if a thousand grains weigh an ounce and a half, with close sowing you can get a yield of 27-30 bushels per acre, whereas if they weigh a half to three-quarters of an ounce the yield will be only 15-18 bushels.

March 14. Received a telegram telling me to report immediately to Kiev. In our office there I found Negreba looking haggard and depressed: he has been declared politically unreliable and dismissed from the Bureau of the Party organization. He told me: "You'd better forget about your article. You've been summoned to the Party meeting. There's a plenum of the oblast Party committee. I wasn't there, but they said openly that Killerog and Sodin, the editor of *Proletarskaia pravda*, are Trotskyists and that Postyshev and Il'in have been shielding them. The orders are that the resolution of the oblast Party authorities is to be followed up at all meetings. I expect it'll be published in the newspapers."

March 16. The resolution of the oblast Party *aktiv* was read at today's Party meeting. I do not know how the *aktiv* could have adopted it, knowing Postyshev and Il'in as they do. These two and all the other members of the oblast committee of the Party are accused of having transferred the basis of their work from the city to the oblast and thus in some strange way "downgraded" the city. It was also strange that they were accused of having concentrated too much on economic work and neglected politics and the Party's role, and strangest of all to hear that Postyshev had protected enemies of the people. There were also unconvincing charges of laxity, complacency, and self-serving.

March 18. The newspapers publish a communiqué on the plenum of the CC of the Ukrainian CP. Postyshev is relieved of his duties as second secretary of the CC "in connection with his transfer to other work."

* * *

People in the Ukraine who knew Postyshev—and they were to be found in every kolkhoz, workers' settlement and small town—were astonished and upset at his dismissal. Few indeed of those who knew his strength of principle and the high standards he set for himself and others could believe that he had protected enemies of the people, practiced self-advertisement, or tried to drive a wedge between the countryside and the town. These were the sort of accusations which the advocates of the "cult" used to justify repressions during that period of arbitrary rule. A true Leninist was thus in grave danger.

The announcement that Postyshev had been elected secretary of the Kuibyshev regional committee of the Party did not reassure his friends and well wishers. The wiles of Beria and his minions were by this time well known. Party and government workers were given fresh jobs and transferred to other oblasts or republics and, soon afterward, were subjected to repressions. None the less, Postyshev did remain for a few months at the head of the Party organization of the large Volga area, and his name appeared from time to time in Tass communiqués. But from the beginning of 1938 nothing more was heard of the new secretary of the Kuibyshev regional committee of the Party, and few knew what had happened to Postyshev. Suddenly his name was removed from the list of candidate members of the Politburo of the CC of the CPSU and he was arrested.

The masters of slander and illegality did not dare to accuse Postyshev openly, as they had other Party and state leaders, of diversionary activity, conspiracy, espionage, or anti-Leninism. They knew too well with what respect millions of workers spoke his name. For this reason his fate was shrouded in silence. But he remained a favorite of the Party and the people. A report went around the country of the last conversation he was believed to have had with Stalin. In this, the people put into his mouth words expressing the unspoken indignation which was in everyone's mind in those tragic days of 1937-38: "Why are they arresting Communists, honest Soviet citizens who risked their lives in the underground, in the October Revolution, and on the fronts of the Civil War, who gave their strength and their abilities in the great days of the First Five Year Plan?"

Years later it became known that this was not mere imagination—Postyshev did put this very question to Stalin, knowing what the consequence would be. He was faithful to his inviolable oath, not spoken but sealed in his heart and mind—the oath he had sworn to the Party as a youth of sixteen, when he first took his stand in the Leninist ranks. His question showed that he did not intend to kowtow to Stalin even after he had been dismissed from his work in the Ukraine on a false charge of "protecting enemies of the people." He knew too that Beria and his men would settle accounts not only with him but with his family. But like a true Leninist he spoke out fearlessly against the arbitrary actions of the servants of the cult of personality. He could not suppress the question which was burning the minds and hearts of millions of Soviet people.

Postyshev was arrested and he met the fate which was to be expected.[84]

SHARIF RADZHABOV

Biographical data

Born 1900, died 1937. Born at Khodzhent (now Leninabad), the son of an impoverished craftsman. As a worker in a shoe factory, a forge, and on a railroad, he experienced the full force of cruel exploitation. Meeting Russian workers, he soon learned their language and became familiar by degrees with the revolutionary and liberating ideas of the proletariat. He entered the Khodzhent

Russo-native school, but did not complete the course owing to the onset of revolutionary events.

After the establishment of Soviet rule in Azerbaidzhan on November 11, 1917, Radzhabov devoted himself wholly to revolutionary activity: attending rallies and meetings, serving on the city soviet, breaking up counterrevolutionary conspiracies, and strengthening the organs of Soviet power in the Khodzhent uezd. In 1919 he was admitted to the Leninist Party. During the Civil War the Party made him chairman of the politburo of the uezd of the OGPU. He dispatched units to fight the Basmachi bands, saw action himself, and displayed great heroism, intrepidity, firmness, and ingenuity. His organizing ability and devotion to the Party were fully recognized, and he became chief secretary of the Party's Fergana oblast committee.

In 1923 he was sent to study at the Sverdlov Communist Academy. After graduating in 1926 he occupied an important post under the CC of the Uzbekistan CP, after which he became chief secretary of the Party's Khodzhent district committee.

When the CP took measures to thwart counterrevolutionary machinations and to hasten the military and political training of national army units, it assigned a number of its best men to army work. Radzhabov was attached to the special Composite Cavalry Brigade, which was engaged in active fighting against the Basmachi bands. As chief of the brigade's political department, he was the first Tadzhik to reach the rank of general (i.e., brigade commander). For his success in carrying out Party orders by supressing the Basmachi he received the Order of the Red Banner for the second time. After this he was recalled to work in the Central Asia bureau of the CC of the CPSU, where he was head of the department of native villages, culture, and propaganda. When the bureau was dissolved in 1934 he was sent to Moscow to study at the [Institute of] Red Professors of the CEC of the U.S.S.R., but before finishing his course he was recalled to work under the CC of the CPSU.

During his career Radzhabov was several times elected to major Party and state organs of Uzbekistan and Tadzhikistan. In 1927-34 he was a member of the CEC of the Uzbek SSR; in 1929 he was elected to the CEC of the Tadzhik SSR, and in 1934 to the Central Asia bureau of the CC of the CPSU. In 1937 he was slandered and subjected to unjust repression, and his life was tragically cut short.[85]

DZHAINAK SADEEVICH SADAEV

Biographical data

Born before 1900; date of death unknown. Of poor peasant origin, born at Buran village, Pishpek (Frunze) uezd. His father died when he was young, and he and his brothers had to work as farm laborers for Russian kulaks and the local beys. At the end of 1916 he was enlisted in the transport unit of the second Rifle Division and saw service on the Austrian front. After the February revolution of 1917 he joined a Red Guard detachment which fought in the October Revolution. In December 1917 he moved to Semirech'e, joined a Red Guard unit at Tokmak, and fought for Soviet power in Kirgizia. During the Civil War he fought on the northern and Semirech'e fronts against the forces of Annenkov and Dutov.

After successfully completing academic studies he became local representative of the [All-Union] Cheka; [in this post he] combated counterrevolution and introduced agrarian and irrigation reform, organizing and directing the *koshchi* (peasants' unions) at Tokmak. In 1922 he was elected secretary of the Tokmak raion committee of the Turkestan CP, and in 1923 chairman of the Pishpek city executive committee; at the same time he acted as chairman of the uezd committee of the *koshchi,* and of the committee for the resettlement of refugees returning from China. In 1925-28 he was chief secretary of the Kirgiz oblast committee of the RCP(B), and from 1925 to 1930 a member of the CEC of the U.S.S.R. During the period when socialism was advancing on all fronts the Party assigned him to the key posts of chairman of the oblast control commission of the CPSU and PC of workers' and peasants' inspection. As a member of the Central Asia bureau of the CC of the CPSU and the Central Asian Economic Council, he took a large part in developing the political, economic, and cultural life of the republics of the region. He became a victim of the cult of Stalin's personality.[86]

SAKHIBGAREI SAID-GALIEV

Biographical data

Born 1894, died 1939. Joined the CP in 1917. Born at Ufa, the son of an unskilled laborer. Attended a Tatar primary school, 1901-4; sold newspapers from the age of ten. In June 1906 he was beaten by gendarmes and obliged to abandon his work as a punishment for concealing forbidden proclamations and selling revolutionary pamphlets. In 1906 he worked as an unskilled laborer on the Siberian railroad, a stoker on a steamboat, and a packer at the Ufa sawmills; also collected subscriptions for Brockhaus and Efron publications at Saratov, Samara, and Orenburg. Began revolutionary work in 1916 when serving in the 126th Reserve Infantry Regiment at Ekaterinburg. After the February revolution the soldiers elected him to the regimental soviet; later he became a member of the presidium of the regimental committee, a member of the Ekaterinburg Soviet of workers' and chairman of the oblast committee of Moslem soldiers. On the instructions of the Ekaterinburg Party organization he carried out propaganda among Tatar and Bashkir soldiers at Ekaterinburg and other

Ural towns. After the October Revolution he was commissar for Moslem affairs of the Forty-seventh Brigade at Ekaterinburg, and the First Ural Moslem Battalion was formed on his initiative. In 1918 he was a delegate to the second all-Russian Moslem military congress, which set up a Bolshevik section headed by Said-Galiev and K. Iakubov. On February 28, 1918, the General assembly of the Kazan soviet elected him commissar for nationalities. During the Civil War and foreign intervention he mobilized Tatar and Bashkir workers to fight the interventionists and White Guards. From November 1918 to April 1919 he was a member of the Tatar-Bashkir bureau of the Ufa gubernia committee of the RCP(B). In spring 1919 the central bureau of Moslem organizations of the RCP(B) sent him to Kazan, where he carried on political work among Red Army soldiers of the Reserve Moslem Battalion and instruction of Moslem military-political courses. At the second all-Russian congress of Communist organizations of Eastern peoples, held November 22-December 3, of the CC of the RCP(B) for Communist organizations of Eastern peoples. In January 1920, by a decision of the politburo of the CC of the RCP(B), he became a member of the interdepartmental commission which drafted the decree on the organization of the Tatar ASSR. In June 1920 he was recommended for the post of chairman of the RMC and co-opted onto the Bureau of the Kazan gubernia committee of the RCP(B). At the first plenary session of the CEC of soviets of the Tatar ASSR he was elected first chairman of the CPC of the republic. On October 9, 1920, an attempt was made on his life. At the second congress of soviets of the Tatar ASSR in June 1921 he was removed from the post of chairman of the CPC, called to Moscow, and on Lenin's recommendation elected chairman of the CPC of the Crimean Republic. After Lenin's death he held Party and government posts in Moscow and Saratov. In 1939 he became a victim of the cult of Stalin's personality.[87]

SHIRINSHO SHOTEMORE

Biographical data

Born 1889, died 1937. Born in the village of Porshnev in the Pamirs. In 1914 he worked as an unskilled laborer at a brewery and as a streetcar driver at Tashkent. During the Civil War he was an agent of the food committee in the Khodzhent uezd. In 1921-23, chairman of the Pamir revolutionary committee. In 1923-24, instructor of the national minorities section of the CC of the Turkestan CP and at the same time head of the Tadzhik Communist section; took an active part in the formation of the Tadzhik ASSR. Helped to produce the first Tadzhik-language newspaper, *Ovozi Tadzhik* (The Tadzhik Voice), and to organize the Tadzhik Educational Institute. In 1924-26 he was PC of workers' and peasants' inspection and representative for the Tadzhik ASSR on the central control commission of the CP of Uzbekistan. In 1926-27, permanent representative of the Tadzhik ASSR in the Uzbek SSR. In 1927 he entered the Moscow Communist University for Eastern Workers, but did not complete his course, as he was elected chief secretary of the Tadzhik oblast committee of the Uzbekistan CP. In 1929-32 he was secretary of the CC of the Tadzhikistan CP. In 1932-33 he studied at the Institute of Red Professors at Moscow. Recalled to Tadzhikistan in 1933 and appointed chairman of the presidium of the CEC of the Tadzhik SSR, (until 1937). He was a member of the CEC of the U.S.S.R. from 1925 to 1937; arrested in October 1937, and became a victim of the cult of Stalin's personality.[88]

A fine son of the Tadzhik people

The Tadzhik people reverently preserve the memory of a great Party and state worker of our republic, one who had a large share in creating and developing the Tadzhik SSR—Shirinsho Shotemore, an innocent victim of slander and arbitrary power during the period of the cult of Stalin's personality.

Shotemore was born in 1889 in a poor peasant family in the Pamirs, in the settlement of Porshnev. He was orphaned at an early age, and at thirteen began to earn his living as a farm laborer in the service of the commander of a Pamir detachment. In 1914 a Tsarist officer brought him to Tashkent, and until the revolution he worked at a brewery and as a streetcar driver. The victory of the October Revolution opened up a new life to the young man from the Pamirs and he was sent to a teachers' training school, but did not finish his course. At that time our country had only just emerged from the Civil War and was going through difficult days. Many parts of Soviet Russia were stricken by famine. The Communists of Turkestan were organizing help for the central parts of the country, and Shotemore, as agent for the food committee, was dispatched to the Khodzhent uezd to supervise the collection of grain. The team under his authority beat off the attacks of Basmachi bands and successfully fulfilled its mission by the due date.

In 1921, by a decision of the CC of the Turkestan CP, he was made head of the military-political triumvirate and sent to the Pamirs, where he was chairman of the revolutionary committee until August 1923. In 1923-24 he served the CC of the Turkestan CP as an instructor in the section of national minorities, and was at the same time head of the Tadzhik Communist section. During the national-territorial demarcation of Central Asia he took an active part in the creation of the Tadzhik ASSR. At the end of 1924 he helped to launch the first Tadzhik-language newspaper in Turkestan, *Ovozi Tadzhik* and to organize the Tadzhik Educational Institute. When the first revolutionary Tadzhik government was set up in Tashkent in December 1924 he was appointed PC of workers' and peasants' inspection and agent of the central control commission of the Uzbekistan CP in the Tadzhik ASSR. He did much work in connection with the transfer of the Tadzhik ASSR government [to its new seat] at Dushanbe, and in the establishment there of the central institutions of the republic, including both state and Party organs. He was also active in suppressing Basmachi counterrevolution in Tadzhikistan. In 1925, together with A. Iarmukhamedov, the PC of internal affairs of the republic, he headed a government commission which carried out a campaign to liquidate the Basmachi in the Kuliab area. At various meetings he explained the policy of the CP and Soviet government to the masses, organized volunteer detachments of local inhabitants, and personally took part in the pursuit and destruction of many of the bands.

In December 1926, after the suppression of Basmachi counterrevolution in the Republic, he was appointed permanent representative of the Tadzhik ASSR in the Uzbek SSR. In August 1927 he was sent to take a course at the Moscow Communist University for Eastern workers, but did not finish it as he was elected chief secretary of the Tadzhik oblast committee of the Uzbekistan CP. Back in Tadzhikistan, he devoted himself with still greater energy to Party work and the solution of the republic's economic, political and cultural problems. The social and economic processes which took place in Tadzhikistan during 1924-29 showed that in order to achieve socialist construction in the republic it was necessary to pursue a firmer policy with regards to the development of industry and agriculture, especially in the more intensive aspects of development—land and irrigation reform, the organization of the poorest peasants and those of medium status and increasing their political activity, the education of the workers, and the cultural development of the Tadzhik nation. All these aims could most easily be achieved if the Tadzhik people were reunited and formed into an independent Tadzhik SSR, and accordingly Shotemore boldly proposed this course. "At the present time," he wrote to the Politburo of the CC of the CPSU, "we attach particular importance to uniting with Tadzhikistan the Khodzhent district of Uzbekistan: this would fully correspond to the political and economic interests both of the district itself and of Tadzhikistan."

A convinced internationalist and Leninist, Shotemore vigorously combated manifestations of narrow local patriotism and national deviationism, which occurred among some of the leading Party and state workers of the republic. At the same time he resolutely opposed great-power chauvinism.

In 1929 an Extraordinary Congress of soviets of the Tadzhik ASSR, expressing the will of the people, declared itself in favor of the formation of an independent Tadzhik SSR as a separate member of the U.S.S.R. The CEC of the U.S.S.R. granted this request and the Khodzhent (Leninabad) district was united with the new Union Republic of Tadzhikistan. Thus the Tadzhik nation was reunited thanks to the consistent application of the Leninist nationalities policy of the CP. The Khodzhent district Party organization was merged into the Tadzhik oblast Party organization, which not only increased the latter's numbers but gave it more of a working-class composition. On November 25, 1929, the Politburo of the CC of the CPSU resolved "to transform the Tadzhik oblast organization of the CP of Uzbekistan into a national CP directly subordinate to the CC of the CPSU on the same footing as the national CPs of the other republics of Central Asia, and to transform the Tadzhik oblast committee into the CC of the Tadzhikistan CP."

Shotemore remained secretary of the CC of the Tadzhikistan CP until 1932, when on his urgent request he was transferred to Moscow to study at the Institute of Red Professors.... In December 1933, after the national deviationists at the head of the state organs of the republic were unmasked, he was once more recalled to Tadzhikistan and appointed chairman of the presidium of the CEC of the Tadzhik SSR, which post he held until 1937. Slandered in 1937, he died an innocent man.

During his service in Tadzhikistan he was several times elected to leading Party and state organs. From 1925 to 1937 he was a member of the CEC of the U.S.S.R. In 1930 his services to the mother country were rewarded with the Order of the Red Banner of Labor.

The Tadzhik people, commemorating the fortieth anniversary of the formation of their republic, recall with profound gratitude the name of Shirinsho Shotemore, who gave his life for Party and people and for the triumph of communism.[89]

ELENA KIRILLOVNA SOKOLOVSKAIA

Biographical data

Born 1894, died 19—. Born at Odessa, a lawyer's daughter. While studying at Bestuzhev in Petrograd she took an active part in the work of the Bolshevik group; later worked in the Bolshevik underground in Petrograd, and during vacations at Chernigov. After the February revolution she was a member of the Chernigov committee, and deputy and member of the presidium of the soviet of workers' and peasants' deputies. After the establishment of Soviet rule she was first chairman of the executive committee of the Chernigov soviet. During the Austro-German occupation of the Ukraine she was active in organizing insurgent detachments in the Chernigov area. Later the Party CC sent her to the Kiev gubernia as a member of the underground gubernia committee and secretary of the revolutionary committee. During the Anglo-French intervention the CC of the RCP(B) assigned her to work in Odessa, where, under the name of Elena Svetlova, she carried on underground work with Nikolai Lastochkin and others, taking part in the creation of the foreign collegium under the Party's oblast committee. After the establishment of Soviet rule in Odessa she was a member of the presidium of the oblast executive committee, commissar for justice, and member of the bureau of the Party's gubernia committee. In December, on the Party's orders, she went to France and Italy, and on returning to Moscow attended courses in Marxism and Leninism. At the Sixteenth Party Congress she was elected a member of the Central Control Commission of the CPSU, for which body she worked until 1934. In her last years she was deputy director, then director, of the Gorky film studio. She perished during the cult of Stalin's personality.[90]

KARL PETROVICH SOMS (KAUFMAN)

Biographical data

Born 1894, died 1937. Born the son of a peasant in the Zel'burg volost, Kurland gubernia. In 1911-13 he was a member of the executive committee of the social-democratic organization of the Madlenas-Gaisma raion. Arrested in 1913 and expelled from the Baltic area for three years. On return, carried out propaganda and organization work for the CC of the Latvian Social Democratic Party. Again arrested in 1915 and exiled to Vyshnii Volochek. In 1917-20 he organized the Red Guard at Kharkov, was secretary of the Samara city committee of the Party, chairman of the revolutionary committee of the Shtokmansgof raion, and deputy chairman of the Riga soviet and the Party's Riga committee. In 1920-33 he worked in the foreign bureau of the CC of the Latvian CP, was secretary of the Pskov uezd committee of the Party and secretary of the Pskov gubernia committee, later of the Novgorod committee. In 1933-37, head of political administration of the PC of State Farms (solkhozes). In 1934, member of the Commission of Soviet Control. In 1937 he became a victim of the cult of Stalin's personality.[91]

A Bolshevik and Leninist

Karl Petrovich Soms (Kaufman) was born on September 17, 1894, the son of a peasant, in the Zel'burg volost, Kurland gubernia. His working life began early: he helped his father as a ferryman on the Western Dvina River, and later earned a living by timber-rafting. This enabled him to pay for schooling in the town of Iakobshtat; he finished in the spring of 1913.

The revolutionary events of 1905-7 made a deep impression on him. As he wrote later: "The suppression of the revolutionary movement by the Tsarist Army, and especially the burning and destruction of whole settlements and the shooting of groups of local revolutionaries, were something I shall never forget." In 1910 he joined an underground study circle for young people which was part of the Latvian social-democratic workers' organization. Soon he was carrying on revolutionary propaganda among the workers, taking part in demonstrations and writing, printing, and distributing proclamations.... In April 1917 the CC of the RSDWP sent him to Kharkov to step up activity among Latvians in that area. There he took part in the formation of the Red Guard.

Wherever the Party sent him, he made a highly favorable impression by his organizing talents and was elected to lead Party organizations. He was secretary of the city committee of the Party at Samara, chairman of the revolutionary committee of the Shtokmansgof raion, and deputy chairman of the Riga soviet and the Party's Riga committee. From 1920 he belonged to the foreign bureau of the CC of the Latvian CP and was at the same time secretary of the Pskov uezd committee of the Party. Later he was secretary of the gubernia committee, first at Pskov and then at Novgorod.

In 1933 he was promoted to be head of political administration of the PC of State Farms. In this capacity he frequently wrote articles in the press on current agricultural problems, of which he had a wide knowledge. He attached great importance to the mechanization of field-crop cultivation and stockbreeding, which required the introduction of technical improvements and cadres of tractor and combine operators. His articles displayed great attention to practical matters and powers of analysis. For example, in an article entitled "Socialist Grain Factories" he raised one of the most crucial questions of socialist agriculture, that of planning production on state farms which, being the largest agricultural undertakings in the world, must, as he pointed out, be constructed in accordance with a well-thought-out-plan. In general, Soms worked with great energy and determination on all problems of state-farm production. He was a delegate to many Party congresses, and at the Seventeenth Congress was elected to the Commission of Soviet Control.

His life was tragically cut short in 1937. Today his good name is restored to the Party and people.[92]

VLADIMIR GORDEEVICH SORIN

Biographical data

Born 1893, died 1944. Joined the Bolshevik Party in 1917. Born in the Ukraine. Graduated from high school in Odessa in 1912 and entered the historical and philological faculty of Moscow University. In 1917-18 he was editorial secretary of the newspapers *Sotsial-Demokrat* and *Pravda*. In 1918-19, secretary of the Serpukhov city committee of the Party and chairman of the eastern front military tribunal; then member of the bureau and head of agitprop of the Moscow committee of the Party, and member of the Moscow gubernia executive committee and RMC. In 1920-24, member of the Moscow city committee of the Party, also member of the committee's bureau in charge of agitprop. In 1924, deputy head of the press department of the CC of the RCP(B) and assistant director of the Lenin Institute. In 1936-39, director of the Marx-Engels-Lenin Institute.

Arrested in 1939 as an "enemy of the people" and perished at the end of 1944.[93]

V. G. Sorin's carrer

V. G. Sorin, a fighter on the ideological front of the CP and an active propagandist of Marxism-Leninism, belonged to the generation of revolutionaries who in the stormy year of 1917 joined the Bolshevik ranks without hesitation and thereafter devoted their lives to the Party's service in its fight for the victory of socialism and the building of Communist society.

He was born in the Ukraine in 1893, the son of an official. Leaving high school in Odessa in 1912, he entered the historical and philological faculty of Moscow University. When the revolution broke out in February 1917 he joined the revolutionary movement though he had not yet completed his studies. Moscow in those days was like a seething cauldron: the revolution had awakened to political life even the most inert sections of the community. Meetings were being held in profusion and the voices of speakers were heard on every hand. The Bolsheviks appealed to the workers to make the revolution a full reality and continue the struggle against the imperialist war. But their voice was often drowned by those of the Mensheviks, SRs, Kadets, and Anarchists who urged that the war be fought to final victory. The bulk of the intelligentsia was attracted toward the petty bourgeois parties.

Sorin, at twenty-four years of age, determined to fight for the Bolshevik program. He joined the Party in April 1917 and was at once assigned to one of the most crucial sectors of the work of the Moscow Party organization—that of ideology. In 1917 and at the beginning of 1918 he was editorial secretary of *Sotsial-Demokrat*, the organ of the Party's Moscow committee, and subsequently of *Pravda*.

The situation in the country during the first few months after the victory of the October Revolution was extremely complicated. The main question was whether to conclude peace with the German imperialists in order to preserve Soviet power. Lenin and the Party had a hard struggle with the "left-wing Communists" and Trotsky, who were pressing for an immediate "revolutionary war" with imperialist Germany so as to touch off revolution in the West. Sorin himself at this time succumbed to the pseudo-revolutionary arguments of the left wing. But he soon understood, after the discussion at the Seventh Congress of the RCP(B), that if the left wing gained the upper hand its adventurist policy would bring disaster on the revolution. In June 1918 he broke with the Bukharin group and rallied to the Leninist position.

Before long he went to Serpukhov and was elected secretary of the Party's city committee, which post he held until September 1918. The Civil War, unleashed by the White Guardists and foreign interventionists, threatened the very existence of Soviet Russia, while the Red Army was still in process of formation and had yet to gain military experience. The need of the moment was to strengthen the army, to introduce military order and discipline into its ranks. At this crucial time the Party sent Sorin to the eastern front as representative of the front-line military tribunal. He served in the army from September 1918 to February 1919 and, together with the front command, did much work in educating the personnel of the Red Army units in question. Returning from the eastern front, he served on the Moscow city committee of the party, as being a member of its bureau in charge of agitprop. At the same time he was a member of the Moscow gubernia executive committee and RMC. At this juncture the Denikin bands, as will be remembered, were presenting a serious threat to the capital, and Sorin, like the other members of the RMC, devoted all his strength and energy to mobilizing material and human resources in the defense of Moscow city and gubernia.

From the beginning of 1920 the CP was confronted with the problem of economic construction and the restoration of the production system, which lay in ruins. The immense difficulties of this task were aggravated by the petty bourgeois element in the country and the revival of its ideology in the Party. The question of how to organize economic construction and what role the Party should play was the subject of argument with the "democratic centralism" group, to whose views Sorin inclined on the eve of the Ninth Congress of the RCP(B). Failing to understand the correct combination of the principles of collegiality and unity of command in the administration, he advocated the collective management of enterprises as a "democratic" measure. However, he soon recognized his mistake and disavowed it at the congress itself, after Lenin had spoken. In 1939 he wrote in his autobiography: "At the Ninth Congress, after Lenin's speech I voted for the CC line, and since then I have always been on the Party's side." This was true. After the Ninth Congress he was consistent in defending and putting into effect the Leninist Party line.

In May 1920 he was elected a member of the Moscow city committee of the Party, and for several years was a member of the bureau of the committee in charge of agitprop.

In January 1924 a great misfortune befell our Party and people and the international proletariat—the death of V. I. Lenin, founder and leader of the Bolshevik Party, creator and guide of the Soviet state and the Communist International. The Soviet working class responded to the death of its beloved leader by offering to the Party more than 200,000 of its best sons. It thus became the Party's task to educate its new members and confirm them in the spirit of Marxism-Leninism. They had to be familiarized with Party history, the fight against Tsarism and the bourgeoisie, the Party's hostility toward opportunism and all deviations from the Leninist line, the problems of ensuring the victory of socialism in the U.S.S.R., and the fact that the Lenin enrollment constituted a priceless treasure, the means of preserving Leninism and ensuring its progress.

At this time, the task of preparing a popular work on the history and theory of Bolshevism was entrusted to Sorin. In March 1924 he finished work on his book *Uchenie Lenina o partii* (Lenin's Teaching Concerning the Party), which was published soon afterward by the Party's Moscow committee. To compose this important and useful work within two months of Lenin's death clearly required immense application and creative fervor..... Describing the vast importance of Lenin's teaching ..., Sorin called upon his readers to "spread as widely as possible Lenin's teaching about the Party, proclaim it as fully and in as many ways as possible to the working masses of all countries."...

Later in 1924, he was appointed head of the press department of the CC of the RCP(B). But he did not occupy this post for long, for at the end of the year the CC appointed him to the important post of assistant director of the Lenin Institute, with responsibility for the publication of Lenin's works, a task of which he acquitted himself with great ability and devotion. After the Lenin Institute and the Marx-Engels Institute were merged, he was appointed deputy director of the combined institute in 1936 and remained in this post until 1939, while continuing to supervise the publication of Lenin's works. He did excellent work in preparing the first three editions of the complete Works and of a number of selections. Thanks to his experience, knowledge, and active participation, the form of the editions for which he was responsible has, in all essentials, been adhered to up to the present.... He was also an active propagandist of Marxism-Leninism and an eminent Party historian, publishing such books and pamphlets as *Rabochaia gruppa* (The Working Group), 1924; *Partiia i oppozitsiia* (Party and Opposition), 1925; *V. I. Lenin: Kratkaia biografiia* (V. I. Lenin: A Short Biography), 1932; *Pervye shagi Lenina po sozdaniiu partii* (Lenin's First Steps in Founding the Party), 1934; *Lenin v dni Bresta* (Lenin and Brest-Litovsk), 1936, etc. "The "Short Biography" reflects with particular clarity the author's endeavor to paint a clear and accurate picture of the greatest man of our age in simple, heartfelt language that could be understood even by the unlearned. It gives a true and inspiring picture of Lenin's life and activity, his amazing capacity for work and the vital energy which persisted until the end of his life.... Sorin vividly describes Lenin as a man of irresistible charm, simplicity, and tact, a true comrade to all Party members and to workers and peasants alike. All who read this book (until it was banned during the cult of Stalin's personality) must have been filled with love for Lenin and his Party, the struggle for Lenin's cause and the realization of his precepts. In the conclusion to the book Sorin wrote: "History tells of no other man who enjoyed such authority, confidence, love and respect on the part of the broad popular masses, as Vladimir Il'ich Lenin."

"Lenin's First Steps" was another scholarly work which, using a wealth of factual material, described Lenin's fight for true Marxism against the populists and "legal Marxists," his struggle to create a Party of a new type, to free the working class from exploiters and exploitation and bring about the triumph of socialism. Sorin rightly emphasized that the Bolshevik tradition of combating all forms of deviation within the Party and the working class goes back to 1894-95, when Lenin founded the Petersburg "alliance for the liberation of the working class." The book contains many interesting facts and accounts of the views of a number of important public figures.

In the pamphlet on Lenin and Brest-Litovsk (1936), Sorin gives an analysis from the Party point of view of the hard struggle waged by Lenin and the Party to conclude peace with the German imperialists and to refute the adventurist views of the "left-wing Communists" and Trotsky which threatened the ruin of Soviet power....

Sorin was not only an able historian and popularizer of Leninism, but an outstanding Party worker. He was elected a delegate to the Eighth, Ninth, and Eleventh to Thirteenth Party congresses. At the Twelfth Congress he spoke on the Party's external policy. In connection with the proposed admission to the Party of the well-known former Menshevik Martynov, he pointed out that in recent years some 30,000 former members of petty bourgeois groups had joined the Party, and expressed the view that the CC should exercise more care over such admissions in future.... He also took issue with Stalin's view that the CC was first and foremost a school of administration—a view which displayed a tendency on Stalin's part whose dangers Lenin himself had pointed out. "Yes," Sorin replied, "the CC is a school of administration among other things, but that is far from being its principal role. What we chiefly demand of it is that it should be a guiding and governing organ." In other words, it should teach, educate, direct, correct when necessary—but mere administration was the least of its duties.

While working in the Marx-Engels-Lenin Institute Sorin performed many public duties, delivering reports and lectures and advising on points of theory and Party history. He was closely connected with the Party history faculty of the Institute of Red Professors, where he conducted examinations and enlisted his hearers to help in the republication of Lenin's works. He was several times elected to the Party committee of the institute and carried on much political organizational work, being deservedly looked up to by the institute's staff.

In 1939 he was unexpectedly subjected to repression as an "enemy of the people." Many who knew him well could not believe this grave accusation could be true. But in the atmosphere of the personality cult it was impossible to fathom the reasons that lay behind Stalin's mass repressions. By the end of 1944 Sorin had ceased to live.

The denunciation and condemnation by the Twentieth CPSU Congress of the anti-Leninist ideology of the personality cult have cleansed the atmosphere and put an end to violations of socialist legality. The Party has restored the honor and good name, from a state and Party point of view, of all those, including Sorin, who suffered unjustly during the period of the cult. Our people will always remember this brave, modest man, devoted to the CP, whose whole life was dedicated to hard work for the good of his country and the triumph of communism.[94]

ALESHA SVANIDZE

The death of Stalin's brother-in-law

A tragic fate also befell Alesha Svanidze, who is less widely known within our Party [than others mentioned earlier], but who was the brother of Stalin's first wife. He was an old Bolshevik, but Beria contrived by all sorts of machinations to suggest that he had been "planted" by German intelligence, though in fact he was Stalin's close friend. So Svanidze was shot. Beforehand they gave him a message from Stalin stating that if he asked for pardon he would be granted it. When he heard this he said: "What am I supposed to ask pardon for? I have done nothing wrong." So he was shot, and after his death Stalin said: "What a proud man he was—you see, he would sooner die than ask forgiveness." It did not occur to him that Svanidze was above all an honest man.[95]

Nikolai Samsonovich Svanidze

NIKOLAI SAMSONOVICH SVANIDZE

Biographical data

Born 1895, died 1937. Joined the CP in 1917. Finished technical high school in 1916 and entered the Moscow Commercial Institute. In 1917-20 he carried on underground activity in Abkhazia, was secretary of the Sukhumi soviet and a member of the revolutionary committee in the Samurzakan uezd. In 1920-27 he was arrested, freed by the Red Army, then was successively secretary of the Abkhazian and Adzharian oblast committees of the Party. In 1931-37 he was PC of supplies and deputy chairman of the CPC of Transcaucasia. Arrested in 1937 and was a victim of the cult of Stalin's personality.[96]

A true son of the Party

March 21, 1965 was the seventieth anniversary of the birth of Nikolai Samsonovich Svanidze, an ardent Bolshevik and Leninist and a true son of the CP. The life of this remarkable man is a shining example of selfless devotion to the great cause of the socialist revolution.

He was twenty-one years old when he left the Sukhumi technical high school for the Moscow Commercial Institute, where he met revolutionary-minded students and began to frequent a Marxist study group and to read seriously the works of Marx, Engels, and Stalin. A year later he returned to Abkhazia, and in June 1917 he joined the Leninist Bolshevik Party. From then on he lived the life of a professional revolutionary with all its alarms and dangers. During the tense period that preceded the October Revolution, together with his comrades Eshba, Kukhaleishvili, and Akirtava he created an underground Bolshevik organization at Sukhumi. When the Sukhumi oblast soviet of workers' and peasants' deputies was set up, Svanidze became its secretary, and set about improving his knowledge by dint of practical work as an underground revolutionary.

The working masses of Abkhazia received the news of the October Revolution with joy. At the beginning of 1918 the local Bolshevik organizations prepared for an armed uprising. The plan of attack was carefully worked out. In April, after fierce fighting with the counterrevolutionaries at Novyi Afon, the insurgents took Sukhumi and proclaimed Soviet rule. But external and internal counterrevolutionaries bent all their efforts to overthrow the new regime, and Soviet rule in Abkhazia at this time lasted only forty-two days.

The Mensheviks, who seized power from the Soviets, were agents of foreign imperialists, and their rule was marked by arbitrariness and violence. But the revolutionary forces were preparing for fresh decisive battles. Svanidze became a member of the revolutionary committee and took an active part in the fight with the White Guardists in the Samurzakan uezd. In June 1920, when the

Bolsheviks were still preparing for a second uprising, Svanidze was arrested by the special department of the Menshevik government of Georgia and was courtmartialed. There followed agonizing months of confinement in the jails of Sukhumi, Poti, Kutaisi, and Batumi. Endless interrogations, beatings, and humiliation could not break the stern Bolshevik's iron will. In March 1921 units of the heroic Red Army took Batumi. The flag of victory waved over the town, and Svanidze along with other political prisoners was set at liberty.

After the establishment of Soviet power in Georgia the Party assigned him to the most responsible posts. He was elected secretary of the Abkhaz oblast committee of the Party. In 1927 he became secretary of the Tiflis committee of the RCP(B). At this time a sharp struggle was going on with the national-deviationists and the Trotskyist right-wing opposition. Svanidze resolutely and consistently defended Leninist principles in the control of Party organizations, showing great organizing ability. Four years later, he became PC of supply and deputy chairman of the CPC of Transcaucasia.

A firm Leninist, an upright and irreconcilable enemy of attempts to undermine Party authority, he sharply and directly opposed the dictatorial methods of the traitor Beria. But the atmosphere became intolerable and he had to leave Georgia. The CC of the CPSU made him its representative for the improvement of crop yields, first in the northern Caucasus and then in the Ukraine. In 1937, on Beria's personal orders, he was arrested in Kiev and brought back to Georgia. Soon afterward, his noble life was tragically cut short.

A thoroughgoing Leninist, an honorable and passionate fighter for the revolutionary cause, Svanidze was one of the glorious band of those who served the revolution without thought of self, for whom loyalty to the Party was the guiding principle of their entire lives.[97]

IOSIF MIKHAILOVICH VAREIKIS

Biographical data

Born 1894, died 1939. Joined the Bolshevik Party in 1915. After the February revolution in 1917 he was deputy chairman of the Podol'sk soviet of workers' and soldiers' deputies, member of the Ekaterinoslav city committee of the Party and secretary of the Donetsk-Krivoi Rog oblast committee of the RCP(B). During and after the Civil War he was chairman of gubernia Party organizations in Simbirsk and Kiev, deputy chairman of the Baku soviet, secretary of the CC of the Turkestan CP, head of the press department of the CC of the RCP(B), secretary of oblast and krai committees of the Party in the Central Chernozem oblast, the Volga, and the Far East. At the Thirteenth, Fourteenth, and Fifteenth Party congresses he was elected a candidate member of the CC of the CPSU, and at the Sixteenth Congress a full member. Arrested on October 9, 1937; his life came to a tragic end in autumn 1939.[98]

A staunch Leninist

A political rally was in full swing at the sewing machine factory at Podol'sk owned by the American Singer company. Thousands of workers crowded the yard, many wearing red ribbons on their chests. A revolution had broken out in Petrograd! The Tsar was overthrown, the autocracy had collapsed! At last the workers could breathe freely! One speaker succeeded another at the rostrum hastily improvised from a few planks. Then a youth with a dark, energetic face sprang up. "Comrades!" he cried, "Do not let yourselves be fooled! It has happened often enough in history that the bourgeoisie have snatched the people's victory out of their hands. Remember, the revolution has only just begun!"

The speaker seemed scarcely more than twenty, but he clearly knew something about politics and had been schooled in revolutionary doctrine. Some workers from the neighboring arms factory who were also at the meeting asked who he was and received the reply: "He's one of our men, a turner called Iosif Vareikis. His father Mikhail is a stoker. We've known him since he was a baby."

Iosif Mikhailovich Vareikis was born on September 18, 1894, in Pavinkshnia village, Vilkomir uezd, Kovno gubernia, the son of a poor Lithuanian peasant. When he was ten years old the family moved to Podol'sk. After attending a handicrafts school the boy went to work at the same factory as his father. Meeting the Bolshevik Leonov, one of the leading members of the revolutionary circle at the factory, listening to the tales of his older comrades about the fighting at Presnia, taking part in May Day meetings, reading Marxist literature in a clandestine group—all this brought the young workman into the front ranks of those fighting against oppression. In 1913 Vareikis became a member of the Bolshevik Party. His ardent devotion to the revolutionary cause and his exceptional organizing ability endowed him with well-earned authority among the workers.

After the February revolution he became deputy chairman of the Podol'sk soviet of workers' and soldiers' deputies. He helped to form Red Guard detachments, denounced the anti-national policy of the Provisional Government, carried on tireless propaganda in favor of Lenin's ideas for the development of the revolution and spoke out sharply against Mensheviks and SRs.

At the beginning of August 1917 the Party sent him to the Ukraine, where he was first elected a member of the Ekaterinoslav city committee and later secretary of the Donets-Krivoi Rog oblast committee of the RCP(B). Still later the Party and working class entrusted many other important tasks to him. During the Civil War he was in charge of the Simbirsk Party organization, then Chairman of the Vitebsk gubernia executive committee, deputy chairman of the Baku soviet, chairman of the Kiev gubernia committee of the Party, secretary of the CC of the Turkestan CP, head of the press department of the CC of the RCP(B), secretary of oblast and krai Party committees in the Volga area, the

Central Chernozem oblast, and the Far East. At the Thirteenth, Fourteenth and Fifteenth Party congresses he was elected a candidate member of the CC and after the Sixteenth Congress he was a full member. He was a delegate to many congresses of soviets and took an active part in the preparation and drafting of the Soviet Constitution of 1936.

In all his various assignments, Vareikis fully justified the high confidence shown in him by the Party and the people. He was a selfless revolutionary, an honest, conscientious Bolshevik, a true Leninist, a man of exceptional steadfastness and courage. An episode from the Civil War will illustrate his self-command, ingenuity, and implicit devotion to the Soviet regime.

At the beginning of June 1918, when the Left SRs stirred up a counterrevolutionary revolt in Moscow and peasant rebellion raised its head in many parts of the country, a grave situation arose in the Volga area, where the Left SR Murav'ev, commanding the eastern front, attempted to strike a treacherous blow at the regime. Appearing unexpectedly at Simbirsk, he declared that he did not recognize the Treaty of Brest Litovsk and advocated continued war with Germany. By dint of demagogic speeches he won over part of the local garrison, and intended to advance from Simbirsk to Moscow to overthrow the Soviet regime. The rebels occupied a number of important buildings in Simbirsk and arrested many Soviet officials and officers, including M. N. Tukhachevsky, the commander of the First Army. Vareikis, then secretary of the gubernia committee of the Party, at once organized local Communists and sent them out among the troops to spread correct information and organize the fight against the rebels. Soon loyal detachments were formed, and on the night of July 11-12 Murav'ev was summoned to a meeting of the Simbirsk executive committee, where Vareikis denounced him as a traitor and demanded his arrest. Murav'ev resisted and was killed; his accomplices were arrested and the revolt was subdued.

Describing Vareikis's services in strengthening Soviet power on the eastern front, Tukhachevsky wrote in February 1919:

> The creation of the First Army and suppression of counterrevolution would have been impossible if the Simbirsk Party committee and executive committee had not come to our aid.... Comrade Vareikis, I regard your action and that of the Party in the defense of Simbirsk as a brilliant service to the state. Once more, a hearty greeting to our dear Communist comrades, with whom we have worked and fought hand in hand for communism and against counterrevolution.

In the days of peaceful socialist construction, Vareikis worked to improve his knowledge and, with the passion of a true revolutionary, fought to implement the Party's general line for the achievement of socialism in our country. At the head of the Party organization of the Central-Chernozem oblast, one of the most important in the country, he worked hard to build up major industrial undertakings, to develop electrification, among other things by creating raion power stations, and to carry out Lenin's directives for the exploitation of the mineral resources of the Kursk Magnetic Anomaly (KMA). In 1930, on the proposal of the Party Committee for the Chernozem oblast, the government allocated six and one-half million rubles for prospecting in the area; but the industrial exploitation of its rich resources was impeded by conservative elements in the planning organization. Vareikis raised the question at the Seventeenth all-Union Party conference, and on February 13, 1932, addressed a letter to Stalin covering a report on the results of prospecting and specimens of ore. "The attached material," he wrote, "shows that the reserves of ore in the KMA in the area which has recently been prospected are at least no less than those in the areas where metallurgical works are now being constructed. In my opinion, there is good reason to propose here and now the high-speed development of work on the industrial exploitation of the ore in question."

Without waiting for a decision from Moscow, the oblast Communists under Vareikis made immense efforts to put their recommendation into action. Shortly before the First of May holiday in 1933, the country learned that the first ore had been extracted from the KMA. On April 21 the mine named after academician I. M. Gubkin was visited by Vareikis, Gubkin himself, the chairman of the [local] executive committee E. I. Riabinin, the engineer in charge of KMA construction I. G. Aleksandrov, the writers V. P. Il'enkov, and F. I. Panferov, and other representatives of society. At a meeting on this occasion Vareikis said: "For centuries peasants ... have been walking over the area on which this mine has been built. Nobody knew what riches lay under his feet, and even today many regard the works here as something strange and obscure. But the extraction of the first high-quality ore will finally dispel all doubts."

Vareikis is also remembered as one of the main organizers of kolkhoz (collective farm) movement and the radical transformation of the rural economy on the basis of the latest achievements of science and technology. Collectivization in the Central Chernozem oblast took place under his auspices, and he took a firm line against left-wing deviation in this field. On February 14, 1930, on his initiative, the Party oblast committee instructed workers not to collectivize pigs, sheep, poultry, and private buildings. But as in other oblasts, there was some undue haste in the first stage of the kolkhoz movement. Vareikis responded with Bolshevik honesty and self-criticism to the CC's decree of March 14, 1930, indicating mistakes committed, and firmly carried out the remedial measures enjoined by the Party.

In spring 1930 Kaganovich, who was then secretary of the CC, visited the oblast and pressed for administrative measures to bring the peasants into the kolkhozes; but the local Communists under Vareikis did not consider it possible to comply with his demands. On March 27, at a meeting of the bureau of the committee, Vareikis sharply criticized Kaganovich's proposals to abolish work-days and pay the collective farmers a wage. "As regards the instructions of which Kaganovich spoke at our last session," he said, "I regard them as quite unsuitable to our purpose. The wage system should not be introduced into the kolkhozes. Cash payment today is a fiction. No one pays in cash and no one has any: the result would be an absurdity.''

Vareikis was a gifted organizer of socialist construction and a brilliant example of a leader of the Leninist school. Bureaucratic methods of leadership were foreign to him. He was always to be found where the basis of a new life was being created by means of purposeful labor. He knew intimately the life of peasants and workers and strove to improve their conditions of work and daily existence, their cultural level and technical training.... Under the guidance of the Communist organization with him at its head, the oblast was transformed from an agriculturally impoverished area, as it had been before the revolution, to one of the foremost kolkhoz and industrial areas of the Soviet Union. In recognition of the progress made in socialist construction the Voronezh oblast, which was formed in 1934 after the reorganization of the Central-Chernozem oblast, was rewarded with the Order of Lenin, as was Vareikis himself, the first secretary of the oblast Party organization.

* * *

Vareikis was an active propagandist of Marxist-Leninist ideas and relentlessly fought all kinds of falsifiers of Party history, the history of the October Revolution, and the building of socialism in the U.S.S.R. Between 1917 and 1937 he published about seventy books and pamphlets and more than 100 articles in central and local periodicals. His works showed deep thinking and unusual literary talent.

In his articles entitled "The Meaning of Personality," "V. I. Lenin," "The Aniversary of Lenin's Death," "The Third Anniversary," etc., he vividly described Lenin's activity and his contribution to the development of Marxism, giving a lively and fascinating portrait of the great leader. Analyzing Lenin's work "What Are 'Friends of the People' and How Do They Fight Against the Social-Democrats?'' Vareikis wrote:

> By virtue of these writings, Lenin became a leader of Russian Marxism.... It is noteworthy that already in this period Lenin stood out as a fully formed personality with all the brilliant qualities which distinguished him throughout the revolutionary struggle as a theoretician, politician, and Party tactician.

Together with the Party as a whole, Vareikis defended Leninism against the attacks of Trotsky and his followers. In articles and pamphlets such as those entitled "Intra-Party Disagreements," "The Party's Relation to Trotskyism," "The Historical Meaning of Trotskyism," "The Historical Meaning of Trotsky's Latest Statement," and "Moving Forces of the Russian Revolution and the Theory of 'Permanent Revolution,' " he refuted the false positions of the Trotskyists in regard to the "rearmament" of the Party and demonstrated that the October Revolution was the culmination of Bolshevik strategy and tactics and a victory for the organization with which Lenin had armed the Party over the years and decades. In studying the history of the Party, as Vareikis observed, we must be guided by the only correct method, that of Marxism-Leninism: "No one who wishes to adopt a Marxist-Leninist approach to the lessons of the October Revolution, the study of the preconditions and historical preparation for that event of the Russian workers and peasant masses, can do so by following Trotsky's methods."

Many of Vareikis's works were devoted to the defense of the Leninist plan for building socialism in the U.S.S.R., and to defining the problems of industrialization and collectivization. Such, for instance, were his works "Is the Victory of Socialism in One Country Possible?" "The Achievements and Difficulties of Socialism," "Problems of the Village Communist in Kolkhoz Construction," "Complete Collectivization and the Liquidation of the Kulak Class," "Marx Was Right," etc.

Describing Lenin's role in deciding the fate of socialism in our country, he wrote with inspiration: "Lenin's great merit lies in the fact that he studied questions of the building of socialism ... in relation to the economic level of the U.S.S.R.—not on the basis of some 'ideal' condition of higher technical achievement but of the state of affairs which we inherited from the bourgeoisie and landowners."

From his first days as a Party member Vareikis fought relentlessly for unity in the Party's ranks and the strengthening of its organizations. In an article on "Unity and Factionalism," in which he attacked Trotskyist demands for the liberty of factions and groups, he urged that a merciless struggle be fought against the slightest tendency to factionalism. "To permit factional struggles within the Party," he wrote, "would mean putting an end to its existence."

* * *

With his profound knowledge of artistic and literary questions, Vareikis did much to develop literature and art. He met many workers in this field, often visited exhibitions and theatres, and took part in literary debates. Keenly concerned that literature and art serve the interests of socialist construction, he urged experienced Soviet writers and editors to pay more attention to budding talent in workers' and peasants' study groups and to train and help the younger writers. He was an ardent supporter of everything new and progressive which served the interests of the people and enhanced the role of the printed word.

Much interest attaches to his article, published in February 1925, on "Literature and Proletarian Writers." "At the present time," he wrote, "the Party must set before itself a clearly defined task, that of fostering the development of a literature that will promote the education of the broad masses in the spirit of socialism and assist the fulfillment of the historical and revolutionary tasks which confront the working people of the Soviet Union. Only writers who

are ideologically linked with the worker and peasant masses can create the literature which the Party and people require." While concerned for the formation of
a new Soviet intelligentsia in accordance with the Party's teaching, Vareikis
had a considerate attitude toward the old intelligentsia and creative writers of
the kind then called "fellow travelers." In his view, "the Party and working
class should not repulse these people but do everything possible to get them
on its side, while ensuring that their activity is subject to ideological and political
leadership." Defending the Leninist principle of Party leadership in the cultural
field, Vareikis opposed those who thought the Party should "farm out" its
responsibility by entrusting control over literature to the All-Union Association
of Proletarian Writers. "The Party," he wrote, "cannot and must not entrust
its leadership in the field of creative writing to any organization of literary
men and women, however excellent and revolutionary they may be."

In August 1935 a group of Moscow and Leningrad painters arrived at Volgo-
grad [sic] in connection with the preparations for an all-Union exhibition on
the theme of socialist industry. Vareikis, then secretary of the Party's regional
committee, had a lively discussion with I. E. Grabar', A. A. Rylov, and others
of the group on questions of artistic production. He emphasized that the exhibition
should not be turned into a "catalogue of machines" or a collection of photographs
of enterprises, but should truly reflect the country's industrial growth, its renova-
tion, the transformation of the countryside and of those who work the land
At the same time, it must comprise a collection of genuinely artistic productions.
"Above all," he urged the artists, "show plenty of gaiety and the joy of life!
Let us see what Soviet youth looks like—not only in the factory but in its
everyday life, its games and sports."

In January 1937 Vareikis was elected secretary of the Far Eastern regional
committee of the CPSU. With his usual energy he threw himself into the task
of transforming that vast, rich area, which, like the rest of the country, was
then in a state of upsurge. Vareikis was especially delighted by the enthusiasm
of the young patriots who, responding to the Party's call, came to the Far
East to help in the work of construction. But his joy was mixed with bitterness,
for at this time there were ever stronger signs of the arbitrary rule and abuse
of power associated with the cult of Stalin's personality. In summer 1937 charges
of treason were made against Tukhachevsky, Iakir, Uborevich, and other famous
Civil War leaders. Vareikis was linked by ties of war comradeship with many
of these, especially with Tukhachevsky, whom he admired and knew to be
an able commander and a devoted soldier of the socialist army.

On September 30, 1937, Vareikis received a telegram summoning him
urgently to Moscow. That very day he left Khabarovsk by train, and on October
9 he was arrested at a tiny station near Moscow. Later in the fall of the same
year his life was tragically cut short.

Vareikis was a true disciple of Lenin and a steadfast fighter for communism.

When the Party had put a stop to the cult of personality it restored the good name of its faithful son, one of the foremost Party and governmental workers of the Leninist type.[99]

EVGENII IL'ICH VEGER

Biographical data

Born 1899, died 19—. Born in Listrosovo village, Kostroma gubernia. Started revolutionary work at an early age, first distributing illegal literature and pamphlets, then, while in the senior classes of the Astrakhan technical high school, carrying on propaganda in workers' circles in the city. Joined the CP in 1917. Before the October Revolution he worked as an instructor in the Moscow uezd soviet of workers' deputies. After the revolution he occupied a number of responsible posts. In January 1918 he was chairman of the Kursk gubernia CPC, and later chairman of the Kazan gubernia Party committee. In 1919 he was a political officer on the southwestern and Caucasus front and member of the Fourth Army RMC. After the Civil War, commissar of the group of forces that took part in the assault on the Kronshtadt fortress: received Order of the Red Banner. In May 1921, member of the RMC of the Kharkov Military District; then studied at the Higher Moscow Technical School. Transferred a year later to head the trade and industry department of the RSFSR PC of Finance; then served at Sverdlovsk and Bezhitsa, and from July 1928 in the apparatus of the CC of the CPSU. In 1930-33, appointed first secretary of the Odessa oblast Party committee. At the Seventeenth CPSU Congress, elected candidate member of the CC of the CPSU. From February 1933, member of CC and candidate member of the politburo of the CC of the Ukrainian CP. From 1935, member of the Ukrainian CEC. He perished during the cult of Stalin's personality.[100]

I. A. ZELENSKY

Biographical data

Born 1890, died 1938. Joined the CP in 1906. Carried on revolutionary work in Saratov, Samara, and other towns of the Volga region. Subjected to repression by the Tsarist government. After the February revolution of 1917 he became a Party organizer in the Basmannyi district of Moscow and a member of the presidium of the Moscow soviet. After the October Revolution he did Party and government work as head of the Moscow food department, member of the collegium of the People's Food Commissariat, secretary of the Moscow committee of the RCP(B), secretary of the Central Asia bureau of the CC of the RCP(B); from 1931, chairman of the Central Union of Consumers' Cooperatives.[101]

TENGIZ GIGOEVICH ZHGENTI

Biographical data

Born 1887, died 1937. An eminent fighter for Soviet rule in Georgia. Joined the CP in 1903. Took an active part in the peasants' revolutionary movement in Georgia; carried on Party work in Batumi, Chiaturi, and Kutaisi. In 1918-20 carried on illegal Party work in Tbilisi and Baku and helped to prepare the armed uprising against the Menshevik government and the Musavatists. From 1921 he was engaged in important Party and governmental work; was chairman of the Batumi soviet of workers' deputies, first secretary of the Adzhar oblast committee head of the commission for the study of the history of the Communist Party under the CC of the Georgian CP, and secretary of the CEC of the Georgian SSR. Elected to the CC of the Georgian CP. Subjected to illegal repression during the cult of Stalin's personality. Posthumously rehabilitated.[102]

A soldier for the Party

From his early youth, T. G. Zhgenti took part in the fight against Tsarist autocracy and the revolutionary movement of the Georgian peasants. In 1903 he joined the RSDWP, and on the Party's orders formed fighting groups in Chokhatauri. His activity was intense and many-sided. He organized meetings, carried on revolutionary propaganda among the population, and distributed anti-government leaflets. His work soon attracted the attention of Tsarist authorities, and in June 1903 he was arrested together with other revolutionaries. After his release he continued to carry on illegal activity in Chokhatauri and Batumi. He took an active part in the revolution of 1905-7, carried out Party assignments in Guriia and Cheatura, helped to organize fighting bands, and took part in armed clashes with the Cossacks.

To unite the broad masses in support of Bolshevism, the Georgian Party organizations in 1905 instituted theoretical discussions which were highly effective. Some of these were organized by Zhgenti and took place in Guriia. As he recalled:

> I took part in debates in Guriia, at Chokhatauri and Partskhmakh. Comrade I. V. Stalin, who came especially for the occasion, spoke for the Bolsheviks, and for the Mensheviks there were M. Arsenidze, G. Lordkipanidze and many others. I well remember how in the village of Ianeuli the Mensheviks opposed holding

the meeting on the ground that it was illegal, but on the peasants' demand we held it nevertheless next day. Among those who came was the academician Nikolai Marr, who supported the Bolsheviks on scientific questions.

At the beginning of 1907 Zhgenti was arrested and imprisoned, first at Shorapan and then at Kutaisi. He was not released for two years, and was again arrested in 1911. After coming out of prison for the second time he continued illegal Party work in Kutaisi, and was once more arrested, on December 10, 1913. When next released he reverted to revolutionary work, and with other comrades organized strikes at Poti, Batumi, and Chiatura, distributing proclamations and working to strengthen the Party ranks.

When the February revolution broke out in 1917 he was serving on the Caucasus front, ai Sherifkhan in Iran. There he was elected chairman of the soviet of soldiers' and workers' deputies, and in December 1917, as a delegate of the Sherifkhan garrison, took part in the work of the second congress of the Army of the Caucasus. Here he was elected a member of the army's regional council.

In April 1918 he proceeded to Tiflis and, under the direct instructions of M. Tskhakaia, organized the publication of illegal bulletins. Soon thereafter he went with L. Kartvelishvili to Kiev, where they made contact with the eminent Ukrainian Party worker D. Z. Manuil'sky and on the instructions of the local Party organization, took an active part in the fight of the Ukrainian working people against the Petliura bands. In November 1918 Zhgenti was instructed to organize an uprising in Odessa, and executed his task with great ability. Under his leadership, in November and December 1918, the Volosts of Maiaki, Beliaevka, Iaska, Dal'nik, and others were liberated from the Petliura bands. In January 1919 the Odessa military committee was reorganized and took into its ranks, besides local Party workers, Zhgenti, Kale Sadzhaia (known in the Ukraine as Kalenichenko), and others. Important tasks were also carried out for the committee by D. Makharadze, S. Lekishvili, and others.

Zhgenti had several encounters with Petliura's bands. During one skirmish he was captured and sentenced to death. Fortunately an armed detachment came on the scene in time and forced the bandits to retreat.

In February 1919 Zhgenti was appointed military commissar and commander of the Elizavetgrad (now Kirovograd) garrison. Here he did much to defeat Grigor'ev's bands.* Soon afterward he was transferred to Odessa as deputy military commissar for the gubernia, and took part in the fighting against Denikin.

*In the spring of 1919 there were numerous anti-Soviet bands, largely recruited from among the peasantry, roaming about the Ukraine attacking Red patrols and wrecking trains. The ataman Grigor'ev became the leader of many of these bands—of about 16,000 troops in all—and appealed to his forces to march on Kiev and Kharkov to overthrow the Soviet government. By the end of May 1919, however, these forces had been driven from the large towns and from strategic positions along the railway lines. Grigor'ev thereupon made overtures to the rival leader Makhno, only to be rebuffed and shot by one of Makhno's lieutenants on July 27, 1919, in the village of Sentovo. Some of Grigor'ev's followers then joined the Makhno bands.—ED

In September 1919 he entered Georgia in secret and, together with F. Makharadze and A. Nazaretian, began to prepare Bolshevik organizations for an uprising. Before his plans were ripe he was captured by a special unit under the Menshevik government, but escaped and on Sturua's advice went to Baku. Here he carried on illegal Party work with Egorov, Sarkisov, Pleshakov, Buniatzade, Navenshvili, Karaev, and others. In January 1920 he published articles in the Baku Bolshevik newspaper *Novyi mir* denouncing the counterrevolutionary policy of the Menshevik government of Georgia, which had started a bloody persecution of Communists. He was arrested by the Musavatists, and after his release made his way secretly to Kutaisi. Here he was tracked down by the Mensheviks and arrested in April 1920. Released in May, he worked as secretary in the editorial office of *Komunisti*.

In June 1920 he and other Bolsheviks were once more arrested. They were released after the fall of the Menshevik government and the establishment of Soviet rule in Adzharia, and thereafter carried on a bitter struggle with the Turkish forces which had occupied almost half the city of Batumi. On the orders of the Adzhar Revolutionary Committee under the chairmanship of S. Kavtaradze, Zhgenti led several operations against the Turkish troops.

After the victory of the socialist revolution in Georgia, the CP and the Soviet government assigned Zhgenti to important posts. At different times he was military commissar of the Batumi oblast, first secretary of the Adzhar oblast committee of the Party, an instructor for the CC of the All-Russian CP, head of the press and Party history department of the CC of the Georgian CP, and secretary of the Society of Old Bolsheviks. In his later years he was secretary of the CEC of the Georgian SSR. He was several times elected a member of the CC of the Georgian CP and the CEC of the Georgian SSR.

He devoted his whole life to the cause of liberating the workers from the capitalist yoke and achieving the victory of communism. The working people of Georgia, who have made such strides toward the construction of a Communist society, remember Zhgenti and other active leaders of the revolutionary movement with warm gratitude.[103]

IV. LEADERS OF THE NATIONAL COMMUNIST PARTIES

THE DESTRUCTION OF CADRES IN THE REPUBLICS: OVERVIEW

Armenian SSR

As is clear from the documents of the Twenty-second Party Congress and the report by Comrade Ia. N. Zarobian, first secretary of the CC of the Armenian CP, the black hand of the factionalists and adherents of the personality cult did not spare the Armenian Republic. In September 1937, Malenkov, one of the leaders of the anti-Party group, came to Armenia on a mission to deal with the republic's *aktiv*. The ground had been suitably prepared: in July 1936 that contemptible enemy of the people, Beria, had disposed of Comrade A. Khandzhian, the first secretary of the CC of the Armenian CP; in August 1937 Comrade S. Tergibrielian, the chairman of the CPC of the Armenian SSR, had been arrested in Moscow, and later he too was subjected to reprisals. What had he done, what were the grounds for his arrest? No documents can be found, and it is safe to say that there was no ground whatever. No doubt it was necessary to discredit the chief leaders of the republic so that charges could then be concocted concerning an alleged highly organized counterrevolutionary nationalistic group under their direction. In this way, by Malenkov's orders, cruel punishment was meted out to innocent people. Within a month of his team's entering into action over 1,000 persons were arrested, including 100 senior workers in Erevan alone. According to former members of the NKVD, Malenkov in several cases himself took part in the interrogations, which grossly violated the rules of socialist legality.[1]

Azerbaidzhan SSR

The greatest abuse of power and illegality during the cult of personality was perpetrated in Azerbaidzhan by the political adventurer Bagirov and his accomplices. Bagirov was a close companion of the master criminal and adventurer Beria; he and his men treated with cynical cruelty all who stood in their way and subjected innocent people to repression. Their despicable actions inflicted severe loss on the Azerbaidzhan Party organization. Among these who were shot and posthumously rehabilitated were Rukhulla Akhundov, Ali Geidar Karaev, Dadash Buniatzade, Gazanfar Musabekov, Sultan Medzhid Efendiev, Levon Mirzoian, Mirza Davud Guseinov, Gamid Sultanov, and many other true sons of the Leninist Party who had fought for the revolution in the glorious ranks of the Baku proletariat. Those who, with Bagirov's knowledge and on his direct orders, were persecuted, arrested, and executed included many outstanding writers, artists, scholars, industrial and agricultural specialists, workers, collective farmers, and others. By his threats and persecution Bagirov drove to suicide the eminent Azerbaidzhan scholar Geidar Guseinov, whose only crime was that, having written a book about the history of social and philosophical thought in Azerbaidzhan in the nineteenth century, did not ascribe its authorship to Bagirov!

Things got to the point where repressions were no longer conducted against individuals but by lists. In October 1937 Bagirov sent to his accomplices Sumbatov and Borshchev lists of "suspicious persons" living in the Lenin and Kirov raions who were to be dealt with: the number for the Lenin raion alone was 104. In a letter of December 29, 1937, Borshchev duly reported to his master that "those whose numbers are ringed with a circle on the attached list (covering two sheets) are either in custody or have already been sentenced".

The documentary evidence and statements by witnesses present a revolting picture of the cruelty, bestiality, humiliation, and abuse to which innocent Soviet citizens were subjected. Many of them, none the less, maintained their courage and firmly rejected the slanderous charges. Thus Ali Geidar Karaev, accused among other things of having ignored, in his book "The Recent Past," the historic role of Stalin as the founder and leader of the Transcaucasian Bolshevik organizations, declared in court that he had always fought honorably to strengthen socialism in Azerbaidzhan and had never belonged to any counterrevolutionary nationalist groups. In an appeal to Stalin, Karaev declared that he had "worked under the direction of Comrades Mikoyan, Ordzhonikidze, and Kirov and ... never deviated from the Party's general line." None the less, he was accused on the basis of forged documents and shot.

Rizaev, the former chairman of the Azerbaidzhan GPU, was fearfully tortured and beaten while under arrest, but did not admit himself to be guilty. In a letter to Stalin he declared that most of the so-called discoveries of counterrevolutionary organizations in Azerbaidzhan were bogus, and added boldly: "As for the adventurers Bagirov and Sumbatov, I assure you once again that sooner or later they will be unmasked by the CC of our Party." But this courageous statement, imbued with faith and devotion to the CP, fell on deaf ears, and Rizaev was shot.

Many other documents could be quoted to show the atmosphere of arbitrary rule and gross violation of socialist legality which Bagirov and his associates created in Azerbaidzhan during the cult of Stalin's personality.[2]

*   *   *

Certain limitations of intra-Party and Soviet democracy were inevitable by reason of the intensive struggle against class enemies. Stalin, however, erected these into a law and began to completely ignore the collective views of the Party and its CC. As the cult of his personality grew, he increasingly violated the principles of collective leadership in Party and state. His acts showed an ever-widening gap between theory and practice. In 1937, after the victory of socialism at home, he advanced a thesis, contrary to Marxism-Leninism, to the effect that the intensity of the class struggle increased in proportion to the conquests of socialism. This thesis was used as a pretext for mass repressions not only against the Party's theoretical opponents who had been defeated on the political plane, but against honest Soviet citizens who were devoted to the cause of socialism.

The scoundrel and adventurer Beria, who at this time rose to high office in the Party and state, with the help of his henchmen slandered and destroyed many honest men and women who were devoted to the Party and the people. The emergence and development of the cult of Stalin's personality and the abuses connected with it were abetted by Molotov, Kaganovich, Malenkov, and others then holding high places in the Party and state. In this atmosphere the adventurer Bagirov, then first secretary of the Azerbaidzhan CP, grossly violated revolutionary legality and the Leninist norms of Party life. The bureau of the CC and the [CC itself] of the Azerbaidzhan CP virtually ceased to act as collective Party organs. Grossly violating the CPSU rules, Bagirov and his accomplices encouraged wholesale expulsions from the Party and fostered an atmosphere of careerism, denunciation, and contempt for the views of the Party rank and file. These criminals sowed mistrust and undue suspicion throughout the republican Party organization. As a result, the CC and the bureau of the Azerbaidzhan CP [and the Party's] city, raion and local organizations were inundated with thousands of slanderous denunciations of Party members. In the Bailovo-Bibi Eibat district of Baku there was scarcely a single Communist or economic or Party worker who had not been informed against, and the number of such denunciations was as many as 600!

* * *

Bagirov and his gang used these false accusations to get rid of people who stood in their way and to carry out mass repressions. The Bureau of the CC of the Azerbaidzhan CP rubber-stamped hundreds of lists of expulsions from the Party, each containing the names of many honest and devoted Communists. Thus, at a single session of the bureau on November 5, 1937, 279 people were expelled from the Party without consideration or debate.

* * *

Bagirov, the enemy of the Party and the people, was especially ferocious in pursuing the old Bolsheviks who had fought in their time for Soviet rule and socialism. He organized repressions against the heads of Party, state, and social organizations, leading cultural and industrial figures. He was actively abetted by other enemies who were later condemned along with him, such as Sumbatov-Topuridze, Markarian, Emel'ianov Grigorian, Borshchev, and Atakishnev. In order to expel Old Bolsheviks from the Party and subject them to repression, he falsified the revolutionary history of the Azerbaidzhan Party organizations and slandered many of their chief leaders. He declared young Azerbaidzhanis "politically suspect" and persecuted Party members and others who had come from southern (Persian) Azerbaidzhan. Among his chief victims in Party and state were: A. P. Akopov, R. Akhundov, M. F. Barinov, D. Buniatzade, M. Gadzhiev, M. D. Guseinov, Ch. Il'drym, M. Israfil'bekov (Kadirli), A. G. Karaev, M. Kuliev, L. I. Mirzoian, G. Musabekov, M. Narimanov, U. Rakhmanov, G. Sultanov, Aina Sultanova, and S. M. Efendiev. Old-guard Bolsheviks who were expelled from the Party and declared enemies of the people at his demand were: B. Agaev, K. Agaev, B. Aliev, I. I. Anashkin, L. A. Arustamov, I. I. Dovlatov, M. G. Pleshakov, I. V. Ul'ianov, and A. B. Iosifzade. Unjust repressions were visited on several able commanders of the Azerbaidzhan Division, such as G. Vezirov, D. Aliev, M. Talyb-zade, and many others, thus inflicting damage on the military cadres of the Red Army. Cultural leaders subjected to repression in the same period included T. Shakhbazi, V. Khuluflu, B. A. Talybly, Gusein-Dzhavid, Seid Gusein, Mikhail Mushaig, and Iosif Vezir (Chemenzeminli). All this was not the end of the harm done by the personality cult, which damaged the republic's political, economic, and cultural life.

January 19, 1938, saw the publication of a decree of the January plenum of the CC of the CPSU "On the Mistakes of Party Organizations in the Expulsion of Party Members, the Bureaucratic Attitude Adopted toward Appeals against Such Expulsions, and Measures to Remedy These Abuses." By this measure Stalin and those close to him attempted to divest themselves of blame for the mass repressions and place it on the shoulders of local organizations. On February 4, 1938, the bureau of the CC of the Azerbaidzhan CP discussed the above decree and resolved to correct the mistakes committed in regard to the expulsion of Party members; but in practice its resolutions did not put an end to the mass repressions of innocent men and women expelled from the Party. Because of Bagirov's underhanded work the vile slanderers and instigators of mass repression were not punished and appeals were not dealt with within the prescribed time limits. In fact, a fresh trial was organized, at which several members of the republic's PC of agriculture were in the dock.[5]

Belorussian SSR

The results of this man's [Malenkov's] activity were especially tragic as regards the Belorussian Party organization. As will be recalled, an inspection and renewal of Party documents took place in 1935-36. Malenkov, who was then a member of the CC apparatus, took advantage of this campaign to eliminate many honest Communists, and together with Ezhov concocted a story of the existence in Belorussia of a widespread anti-Soviet underground headed by Party and government leaders. On the strength of this fable, about half the members of the Belorussian Party organization were deprived of their Party cards. When Comrade Goloded, the chairman of the republican CPC, called these findings into question at a plenum of the CC of the Belorussian CP, Malenkov himself came to Belorussia and carried out a purge of the republic's leading cadres. This led to the expulsion from the Party, and in many cases the arrest, of nearly all the republican leaders, including the secretary of the CC, the chairman of the CPC, the people's commissars, many leaders of local Party and state organs, and representatives of the creative intelligentsia. All these innocent people have now been rehabilitated, many of them posthumously.[6]

Destruction of the CP of Western Belorussia.   The revolutionary and national liberation movement in Western Belorussia was affected by unjust repressions in 1933. The victims at that time were former leaders of the BKRG* and of [the publication] *Zmagannie* who were then in the Belorussian SSR. Former members of the Polish Sejm, P. P. Voloshin, F. I. Volynits, I. E. Gavrilik, I. Gretsky, I. S. Dvorchanin, P. S. Krinchik, P. V. Metla, S. A. Rak-Mikhailovsky, and B. A. Tarashkevich [were all men who] had been sentenced to many years' imprisonment in bourgeois Poland but later, thanks to an exchange, given refuge in the U.S.S.R. from the persecutions of Polish fascism. All of these men were arrested on false charges of counterrevolutionary conspiracy and anti-Soviet activity. At the same time several leaders of the CC of the Belorussian CP were arrested: R. Bobrovich, A. G. Kaputsky, P. A. Klintsevich (Gorbatsevich), L. I. Rodzevich, and others. Under the influence of these false charges, the Party CC in 1934 adopted two resolutions, one entitled "Fight Nationalist Opportunism," the other "The Basic Causes of Nationalist Opportunism in the CP of Western Belorussia." These resolutions reflected a false appreciation of some aspects of the Party's past activity, especially in the leadership of the movement for national liberation. The BRO* was wrongly assessed as an agency of White Russian nationalism, and the admission of its members to the CP was condemned. Many who belonged to the revolutionary and national liberation movement in Western Belorussia were unjustly accused of bourgeois nationalism.

Thus in 1938, on the eve of the Second World War, after undoubted successes had been attained in creating a united workers' popular front against fascism and in stepping up the revolutionary and national liberation movement in Poland,

---

*Belorussian Peasant-Workers Gromada, created in 1925.—ED.

*Belorussian Revolutionary Organization, created in 1923, a group that split off from the Belorussian Left SRs to become an independent party.—ED.

the Western Ukraine, and Western Belorussia, the CPs of these areas were dissolved and ceased to exist. The dissolution was preceded by the repression in 1937 of leading members of all three parties who were then in Moscow, Kiev, Minsk, and certain other towns.

Among the leaders of the CP of Western Belorussia who were arrested were R. D. Vol'f, E. A. Idel', I. K. Loginovich (P. Korchik), M. S. Maisky, N. P. Maslovsky, S. A. Mertens (Skulsky), A. A. Ol'shevsky, A. M. Rozenshain, I. F. Semenikov, A. S. Slavinsky, M. D. Slovik, V. Z. Khoruzhaia, E. I. Sholomov, L. M. Iankovskaia, and many others. The dissolution of the Party and repression of its chief members dealt a severe blow to the revolutionary and national liberation movement in Western Belorussia.[7]

Estonian SSR

The successful fight of the Estonian CP against fascism, and the consolidation of the Party's ranks, were gravely hampered by the adverse phenomena associated with the cult of Stalin's personality. In the 1930s many Estonian Communists, including leading members of the Party, were living in the U.S.S.R., as well as many non-Party activists of the working-class movement who had taken refuge from bourgeois terror and repression. The majority of these comrades actively helped the Estonian CP in its struggle, whether by direct participation in the work of its main organs, by helping to produce Party literature, or by material contributions [to such organizations as] the International Society for Aid to Revolutionary Fighters. But the atmosphere of distrust and suspicion brought about by the cult of personality had a dire effect on the activity and fate of these comrades. Many honest fighters for the working class who had escaped from bourgeois Estonia were absurdly accused of liaison with the bourgeois police, removed from political work, and even arrested. The unjustified repressions due to abuse of power in 1937-38 were an especially heavy blow. Among the leaders and veterans of the Estonian CP who became victims at that time were Ia. Anvel't, Kh. Pegel'man, N. Ianson, R. Mering, O. Riastas, I. Kiaspert, R. Vakman, Ia. Saks, E. Alas, and A. Sakkart. In addition, the repressions affected many ordinary Communists and activists of the workers' movement living in the U.S.S.R. In consequence, by the beginning of 1938 the CC of the Estonian CP and its organization and foreign bureaus had ceased to function and the Party had lost its link with the Comintern, while it became impossible to publish *Kommunist* in Scandinavia (the last number came out in Stockholm in March 1938). Thus the Estonian Communists had to continue their fight in extremely difficult and distressing circumstances. Bourgeois propaganda skillfully exploited the illegal repressions due to the personality cult, launching a campaign of slander against communism and deforming the whole of socialist construction. This slander awakened some response, especially in petty bourgeois circles, which made the task of the Estonian CP still more difficult.[8]

Georgian SSR

The facts show that as part of the cult of Stalin's personality, state and Party life were characterized by the curtailment of democracy and by arbitrary rule which led to the destruction of thousands of innocent people including many Party, state, and military leaders. It has been proven that the repressions of 1935-37, like those of 1949-50, were carried out either on Stalin's direct orders or with his knowledge and approval.

For instance, it sufficed for German espionage to plant a forged document to the effect that the eminent commanders Tukhachevsky, Iakir, and others were agents of the German General Staff, for Stalin to have them arrested and executed.

Comrade Shelepin, the chairman of the Committee of State Security of the Council of Ministers of the U.S.S.R., gave appalling facts in his speech at the [Twenty-second] Congress concerning illegal mass punishments and executions of outstanding leaders of our state whose existence was for some reason inconvenient to Stalin or to his close companions Molotov and Kaganovich. Among the innocent persons who were executed and have since been rehabilitated are such Party and state leaders as Postyshev, Kosior, Eikhe, Rudzutak, Chubar', Voznesensky, Krylenko, Unshlikht, Bubnov, and many others. In Georgia too, the Party organization suffered severely from this illegal and arbitrary rule. Among the innocent leaders who perished we may mention Mamiia Orakhelashvili, Mikha Kakhiani, Shalva Eliava, Levan Gogoberidze, Nestor Lakoba, Soso Buachidze, Lavrentii Kartvelishvili, and many others, all of whom have since been rehabilitated. Besides these, how many of our best writers, poets, artists, scholars, and engineers were repressed without a shadow of justification, tortured, exiled, or shot as a result of the false accusations of Beria and his minions! Among those arrested and shot were Sergo Ordzhonikidze's brother and the old Bolshevik Alesha Svanidze, brother of Stalin's first wife, whom Beria made out to be an agent of German intelligence. As for Sergo Ordzhonikidze, a true disciple of Lenin, he committed suicide so as not to share responsibility for Stalin's misuse of power.[9]

*   *   *

Together with his accomplices, Beria, the accursed foe of the Party and people, organized and carried out the mass extermination of cadres and thus inflicted enormous loss on the Party, on socialist construction and on the country's defense capabilities. This scoundrel and upstart worked his way into Stalin's confidence and, while still secretary of the CC of the Georgian CP, destroyed by treacherous means many Party and state workers and leaders of our intelligentsia, while hosts of innocent people were obliged to leave the Republic.... Stalin knew of Beria's intrigues against Sergo Ordzhonikidze, but did not stop them in time: that true disciple of Lenin, rather than share responsibility for

Stalin's misuse of power, committed suicide. Beria stopped at no villainy to gain his criminal ends. As later became clear, he was a thoroughgoing adventurer and provocateur. Those who had been subjected to unjust repressions were fully rehabilitated in 1954-55.[10]

Iakut ASSR

The cases of many citizens who were subjected to unjust repression in 1937-39 have been reviewed and the honest victims rehabilitated. Among those who perished were the leaders of the [Iakut Autonomous] Republic, organizers of Soviet power, and old Bolsheviks M. K. Ammosov, S. M. Arzhakov, I. N. Barakhov, P. A. Ouinsky-Sleptsov, S. V. Vasil'ev, S. F. Gogolev, and A. F. Popov.[11]

Kazakh SSR

The personality cult also had dire results for Kazakhstan. The divorce between word and deed in Stalin's behavior did considerable harm to the execution of Lenin's nationalities policy. During the cult of Stalin's personality there was an ever-growing tendency to restrict the rights of the Union Republics, to over-centralize their economies and to exercise petty control over their administrative organs. Questions of capital construction, material and technical equipment, the marketing of products, and other matters which now fall within the competence of the Union Republics were then decided at the center. The Constitution of 1936 deprived the republics of the right to their own criminal and civil codes and reserved to the U.S.S.R. the right to make laws concerning the judicial system and judicial proceedings.

Stalin in his writings many times reiterated Lenin's precepts concerning the need for a sympathetic and helpful attitude toward national cadres, but in practice these cadres suffered to the fall from his arbitrary rule and abuse of power. The young Kazakh Republic thus lost its best Party, state, and economic cadres and many eminent scientists and cultural workers. Those slandered and subjected to repression included all the members and candidate members of the bureau of the CC of the Kazakhstan CP elected at the Party's first congress, including L. I. Mirzoian and S. Nurpensov, the CC secretaries; U. D. Isaev, the representative of the CPC; many other members of the CC; secretaries of oblast committees and representatives of oblast executive committees and nearly all the secretaries of city and raion committees. The charges leveled at members and candidate members of the CC and other bodies were never properly investigated. Many Party workers were expelled from the Party after being subjected to repression. Some of those who suffered—U. K. Dzhandosov, Iu. Babaev, M. Ma San-chi, A. Rozybakiev, A. M. Asylbekov, and others—had taken an active part in the establishment of Soviet power in Kazakhstan and in setting up the first Party organs. The Kazakh intelligentsia suffered severely. Among the eminent public figures and writers who underwent repression were I. Dzhangusurov, B. Mailin, and S. Seifullin. Later, in 1954-55, those who had thus suffered unjustly were rehabilitated.[12]

Latvian SSR

The Party was carrying on its work in difficult conditions. As a result of intensified repressions against Communists and all democratic forces, links were being broken between the Party leadership and a number of lower organizations, and the arrests of Communists multiplied. The Party organizations needed help and support, but instead their difficulties increased. The consequences of the cult of Stalin's personality affected the whole international Communists movement and were especially serious for the Latvian CP. The fact that some hundreds of Latvian Communists had been arrested by the Ulmanis' fascist clique was represented to be a consequence of the alleged contamination of Party organizations by provocateurs and was used as a pretext for manifesting distrust toward the leaders of the Latvian CP. Thus many of the latter, working in the foreign bureau and senior posts in the CPSU, were slandered, falsely declared to be nationalists and enemies of the people, and subjected to repression. This was a heavy blow to the Latvian CP and the revolutionary movement led by it, at a time when the Party was contending selflessly with extremely difficult conditions.

The effect of the cult of Stalin's personality in 1936-38 was to cast aspersions of treachery on tried Party cadres who had been through the hard school of the revolutionary struggle. Isolated mistakes committed in the past by Party leaders were now inflated and exaggerated. The legend was spread that the Latvian CP was going through a profound political and organizational crisis which was paralyzing its activity. The Party was blamed even for the fact that, working as it was in a strictly clandestine manner, it had never carried out a mass purge of its members. On the strength of these baseless fabrications, the CC of the Latvian CP was virtually disbanded and replaced by a new governing organ, the Provisional Secretariat. The foreign bureau of the Party's CC was dissolved, a body which had existed for sixteen years and had done the Party great service; the same fate befell the Riga committee, one of the Party's most important organs.

In the second half of 1936, a check of all personnel of the Latvian CP was carried out. In underground conditions this measure could not ensure that the Party's ranks were cleansed of individual provocateurs and unreliable elements. In some places the result was an artificial reduction in numbers, so that many devoted Communists found themselves expelled from the Party.

Incorrect appreciations of the situation within the Party were reflected in the resolution of the plenum of its CC "On the Position and Tasks of the

Latvian CP" (the minutes of this plenum, incidentally, have never been found), which stated that the Party was going through a critical phase from the political and organizational points of view, and inferred from this the necessity of a mass purge of the Party and the dissolution of its principal organs. The Party was in fact virtually decapitated during the cult of Stalin's personality, a great many of its chief members being subjected to repression. These included the members of the foreign bureau of the CC, Ia. Berzin-Ziemelis and Ia. Lentsmanis, and members of the Provisional Secretariat Ia. Krumin-Pilat and E. Apins. The same fate overtook many active members of the Leninist Party who had at various times assisted the Foreign Bureau of the CC of the Latvian CP: Ia. Rudzutak, R. Eikhe, Iu. Danishevsky, V. Knorin, K. Pechak, R. Endrup, R. Bauze, and others. Repression also befell many comrades who had for a longer or shorter time been in charge of Party underground work in Latvia: E. Sandretier, F. Pauzer, O. Dzenis, and others. All these were slandered, and their names, like that of the eminent Leninist P. Stuchka and many others, were erased from Party history. As a result of mass repressions the Latvian CP was for a long time cut off from the Executive Committee of the Comintern, which placed it in a very difficult position.[13]

Lithuanian SSR

The arbitrary rule which developed widely in 1937-38 inflicted a heavy blow on the Lithuanian CP. Many of its chief leaders who were then living in the U.S.S.R. became victims and have now been rehabilitated. How many valuable cadres Soviet Lithuania would now have if it were not for the machinations of criminals who had their will during the cult of Stalin's personality! Concocting false charges, these enemies laid their vile hands even on cadres of the Lithuanian CP who were laboring underground or confined in fascist jails. They tried, by sowing suspicion, to create an atmosphere of mistrust among the chief members of the Lithuanian CP. But the underground workers stood firm and refused to be taken in by provocation.

The liquidation of the consequences of the cult of personality was a vital necessity for our Party, which could not otherwise have moved forward toward the building of communism.[14]

Moldavian SSR

During the cult of personality, many important Party, state, and economic workers in the Moldavian Party organization were subjected to illegal repression, and some were shot. They included Golub, Bikhman, and Dochul, the secretaries of the Moldavian oblast committee of the Ukraine CP; Voronovich, the chairman of the CEC of the Moldavian Autonomous Republic; [G. I.] Stary (Borisov), the chairman of the CPC of the republic; the Bessarabian political émigrés

Milev and Krivorukov; and others. These were staunch Bolsheviks, tried in the battles of the Revolution, many of them members of the old guard of Bolsheviks.[15]

South Ossetian Autonomous Oblast

The workers of our South Ossetian oblast also suffered heavily. According to incomplete data, hundreds of people were subjected to repression and shot in 1937-38, including the secretaries of the Party oblast and raion committees, the chairmen of the oblast and raion executive committees, and such active members of the revolutionary movement and the fight for Soviet power in Georgia and South Ossetia as Lado Sanakoev, formerly chairman of the South Ossetian district committee of the RCP(B), and the district committee members Aleksandr Abaev, Sergei Gagloev, Aron Pliev, and others. All these were accused of counterrevolution and so-called anti-Soviet terrorist nationalist activity. Later, when Beria and his crew were unmasked, it became clear that there had never been an anti-Soviet nationalist center in South Ossetia. Nearly all the victims of illegal repression have been rehabilitated, most of them posthumously.[16]

Tadzhik SSR

At the February-March, 1937, plenum of the CC of the CPSU, at which the Party made important decisions aimed at developing inner-Party democracy, Stalin put forward the anti-Leninist thesis that the class struggle would become intensified as socialism grew stronger. This was intended to justify his exercise of arbitrary rule and violation of socialist legality. After the plenum, still more mass repressions took place against thousands of honest Soviet people who were deeply devoted to the CP. In these mass repressions and the extermination of Party and government cadres, a criminal role was played by the adventurers Ezhov and Beria at the head of the state security system. Responsibility for the downfall of many Party and government leaders falls also on Molotov, Kaganovich, and Malenkov, who actively abetted these crimes.

The violation of socialist legality and the democratic norms of Party and political life dealt a serious blow to the CP and the Soviet state. The cult of Stalin's personality was detrimental to the work of republican Party organizations, of the soviets, and of all public bodies. In conditions of mass repression it was impossible to prevent frequent changes in the composition of leading cadres, which meant that they could not be systematically trained or educated. The atmosphere of suspicion and mistrust affected work at all levels in the Party and state apparatus and prevented the objective discussion of economic problems. Many shortcomings in Party, state, and economic work were attributed to the activities of "enemies of the people," which made it impossible to discover the real causes and eradicate them.

Grave harm was done in this way to the Party organization of Tadzhikistan. At the third congress of the Tadzhikistan CP sweeping and unjust accusations were leveled against many of the republic's leaders, especially S. Shalund, the former secretary of the CC. In the summer of 1937 many other Party and state leaders of the Tadzhik SSR were arrested on false charges, including S. Shotemore, the chairman of the CEC, and A. Rakhimbaev, the chairman of the CPC. In autumn U. Ashurov and A. Frolov, the secretaries of the CC of the Tadzhikistan CP, were dismissed; later they were arrested and perished. And this took place at a time when the workers of Tadzhikistan, led by the CP of the republic, had built the foundations of socialism. The atmosphere of suspicion and mistrust favored the criminal activities of careerists, slanderers, and informers. As a result, many Communists were expelled without cause from the Tadzhikistan Party organization. In some raions the organization was virtually liquidated. Thus, in the Komsomolobad raion only one Party member and three candidate members were left. The figures for other raions were: Shul'mak, one and five; Vanch, three and ten; Nurek and Rokhatin, four members only.[17]

Turkmen SSR

In the Turkmen SSR socialist legality and the Leninist norms of Party life were violated [during the 1930s], and the principle of collective leadership was disregarded in the CC of the CP. For some months, from October 1937 to February 1938, there was no bureau of the CC. The first secretary of the CC, Ia. Chubin, and a number of senior members of the CC and the oblast committees permitted the stifling of criticism, encouraged toadyism, and introduced nepotism in the selection of cadres. In this atmosphere, mass repressions and expulsions from the Party took place in our republic on an exceptionally large scale. Those who suffered included Anna Mukhamedova, the secretary of the CC of the Turkmen CP; K. Atabaev, chairman of the CPC; N. Aitakov, chairman of the CEC, and such important Party, state, and social workers as Ch. Velekov, Kh. Sakhatmuradov, O. Tashnazarov, D. Mamedov, B. Ataev, and Kurban Sakhatov. Many Communists were expelled from the Party on unfounded and slanderous grounds. In the Mary (Merv) raion alone, 107 persons were expelled from the Party in 1937; of these, forty-eight were later reinstated. Wholesale expulsions took place in gross violation of established rules, in the absence of the person affected and without public discussion. In this way, the Party organization of the Ashkhabad railroad lost 22.5 percent of its staff.[18]

Ukrainian SSR

Among the victims of unjust repression in the Ukraine and its CP were nearly all of the leading cadres of the central and oblast committees of the

CP, leading members of state and economic organizations and of research institutions. The mass repressions created an atmosphere of mistrust and suspicion, an atmosphere fostered by provocative and slanderous letters and statements. At Kiev a woman named Nikolaenko perpetrated especially malicious slanders against many leading members of the CC of the Ukraine CP, the Kiev oblast and city committees, and for so doing was expelled from the Party. But Stalin at the February-March plenum of the CC of the CPSU in 1937, and Kaganovich at the meeting of the Kiev oblast Party aktiv praised this woman as a "heroic unmasker" and accused the CC of the Ukraine CP and the Kiev oblast organization of relaxing their political vigilance and sheltering enemies of the Party. Among the victims of arbitrary rule and abuse of power were such old, experienced Party leaders and Leninist cadres as N. N. Demchenko, V. P. Zatonsky, L. I. Kartvelishvili, E. I. Kviring, I. E. Klimenko, S. V. Kosior, P. P. Postyshev, K. V. Sukhomlin, M. M. Khataevich, V. I. Cherniavsky, V. Ia. Chubar', I. E. Iakir, and others.[19]

Destruction of the CP of the Western Ukraine. It is legitimate to ask why a Marxist-Leninist Party with a highly militant history and great revolutionary traditions suddenly ceased to exist in 1938 and was erased from the history of the international Communist movement until the Twentieth Congress of the CPSU. The reason lies in the distortions and violations of the Leninist norms of Party life which were permitted during the period of the cult of Stalin's personality and which had an adverse effect not only on the CPSU but on the whole international Communist movement.

The CP of the Western Ukraine was gravely affected by the provocative acts of Kaganovich in 1927-28. At that time the Party had committed errors in regard to the national question which required criticism and correction. But instead of helping it to overcome these errors in a quiet, comradely spirit and with consideration for the difficulties of clandestine work, Kaganovich took the course of accusing the whole CC of the Party, then headed by Vasil'kov and Turiansky, of nationalism and treason. The result was to bring about a schism in the Party. In addition, Kaganovich went so far as to discredit the Party as a whole. In November 1927, at a session of the politburo of the CC of the Ukraine CP, he cynically stated that he did not know which side the CP of the Western Ukraine would be on, in the event of a war against the U.S.S.R. (see Archives of the Institute of Party History of the CC of the Ukraine CP, f. 1, op. 69, item 11, pp. 59-60). This accusation was based on the state of affairs which Kaganovich himself had created by his intrigues in the CC of the Ukraine CP, and which was thus described by V. Ia. Chubar' in June 1928 in a speech at the joint session of the politburo of the CC and the central control commission of the Ukraine CP: "Mutual confidence and contact between us have been broken, so that no one trusts anyone else. Questions have been decided without the knowledge of the politburo.... I find this state of affairs oppressive." (Archives of the Institute of Party History of the CC of the Ukraine CP, f. 1, op. 145a, item 99, pp. 101-3.) On the strength of false information, the majority of the leaders of the CP of the Western Ukraine in 1928 were declared to be clandestine agents of fascism. Later events not only did not confirm these allegation but on the contrary proved their malicious character, as was stated in the declaration of the Five Communist Parties in 1956.

The unfounded accusations against the CC of the CP of the Western Ukraine in 1927-28 had tragic consequences. In the atmosphere of the cult of Stalin's personality they served as a pretext for fresh blows against the Party. In 1933 its leaders, then M. T. Zaiachkovsky (Kosar) and G. V. Ivanenko (Baraba), were once more accused of nationalism and treason, and were declared to be secret agents of a Ukrainian nationalist organization. Shortly afterward a whole group of the Party's leaders were similarly falsely accused and subjected to illegal repressions.

In 1938 the Executive Committee of the Comintern, believing the lying accusations made against the Polish CP in connection with the cult of Stalin's personality, made its unjustified decision to dissolve the Polish CP and its component parts, and the CP's of the Western Ukraine and Western Belorussia. A heavy blow was thus dealt to the revolutionary movement in Poland, the Western Ukraine, and Western Belorussia.[20]

ZIGMAS IONOVICH ANGARETIS

Biographical data

Born 1882, died 1940. Real name Aleksa. A leader of the Lithuanian CP. Born at Obeliutsiai village, Volkovyshki (Vilkavishkis) uezd, Lithuania, the son of a peasant. Studied at Warsaw Veterinary Institute; expelled in 1904 for taking part in an anti-war demonstration. Joined the Lithuanian Social Democratic Party (LSDP) in 1906 at Vilna (Vilnius). In 1907, at the seventh congress of the LSDP at Cracow (Kraków) he was elected a member of the party CC. In 1908-9 he edited the newspaper *Darbininku žodis* (The Workers' Voice). In 1909 he was arrested and sentenced to four years hard labor in Pskov jail, after which he was exiled to Angara region of Siberia. There he carried on Bolshevik propaganda and wrote articles which appeared over the signature "Angaretis" in émigré Lithuanian social-democratic newspapers. From 1917 he was in Petrograd editing *Tiesa* (Truth), was elected secretary of the Lithuanian raion committee (Lithuanian Section) of the Petrograd organization of the RSDWP(B) and became a member of the Petrograd Bolshevik committee. Was a delegate to the seventh (April) all-Russian conference and the sixth Congress of the RSDWP(B). Member of the central bureau of the Lithuanian section of the CC, RSDWP(B). Took part in the October uprising in Petrograd. On

December 8, 1917, he was appointed deputy commissar for Lithuanian affairs in the PC of Nationalities. During the Brest Litovsk negotiations he adhered to the "left-wing Communists". In November 1918 he was directed to underground work at Vilnius, where he was co-opted onto the CC of the Lithuanian CP. At the end of 1918 and beginning of 1919 he was a member of the first Soviet government of Lithuania as PC of internal affairs. Was a delegate to the eighth Congress of the RCP(B). From 1920, secretary of the foreign bureau and member of the CC of the Lithuanian CP; from 1924, member of the politburo of the Party's CC and representative of the Lithuanian CP on the Executive Committee of the Comintern. At the Fifth, Sixth, and Seventh Comintern congresses he was elected to the International Control Commission, of which he was secretary from 1926 to 1935. Wrote *Istoriia revolutsionnogo dvizheniia i bor'by rabochikh Litvy* (History of the Revolutionary Movement and Struggle of the Workers of Lithuania), vols. 1 and 2, 1921; also published pamphlets and articles on the history of the working-class and Communist movement.[21]

IAN IANOVICH ANVEL'T

Biographical data

Born 1884, died 1938. Literary pseudonym Elssaare Aadu. Professional revolutionary and leader of the Estonian CP. Son of a peasant; born in Orgu village, Fellin uezd, Livland gubernia. Joined the CP in 1907. Studied at the Iur'ev (Tartu) teachers college and passed examination at Petersburg as a primary schoolteacher. Taught in 1906-7, then entered the law faculty of Petersburg University. Helped to organize the newspaper *Kiir* (The Ray). During the February revolution of 1917 he headed the provisional PC at Narva, then the Narva soviet; was a member of the Revel' (Tallin) and North Baltic committees of the RSDWP(B) and of the executive committee of the Estonian soviet. Arrested by the Provisional Government in July 1917. From October 1917, member of the RMC and later chairman of the Estonian regional executive committee of soviets. From February 1918, military commissar of the Northwestern oblast in Petrograd. From November 1918, chairman of the government of the Estonian Workers' Commune and PC of military affairs. In 1919-20 he held senior Red Army posts, and in 1920 he was elected to the CC of the Estonian CP. In 1921-25 he carried on underground Party work in bourgeois Estonia and was a leader of the uprising of December 1, 1924. In 1925 the Party assigned him to Moscow, and in 1926-29 he was commissar at the Zhukovsky Air Force Academy. During 1929-35 he served as deputy head of main administration of the Civil Air Fleet. Delegate to the Fourteenth, Fifteenth, Sixteenth, congresses of the CPSU and the Sixth and Seventh congresses of the Comintern. In 1935-37, member and chief secretary of the International Control Commission of the Comintern. Wrote several literary works, including a novel, *Vne zakona* (Outlawed).[22]

A glorious son of the Estonian people

> An Estonian worker cannot be a slave. After centuries of slavery in our land, the sun of freedom shines once again. Let us do all in our power so that this sun may shine from a cloudless sky over all Estonia, dissipating darkness and slavery, and a new world may begin for us and our descendants. We are ready, if need be, to give our lives for the freedom of the Estonian workers—it is better to die for their future than to be slaves.

These passionate words belong to that glorious son of the Estonian people and eminent revolutionary Ian Anvel't, who devoted his whole life to selfless service of the workers....

At the beginning of the century, Lenin's *Iskra* touched off the bright flame of revolution, and the movement gathered strength in Estonia under the influence of the Petersburg proletariat. The first social-democratic revolutionary organizations in Tallin were formed in 1903. At this time the nineteen-year-old Ian Anvel't left the Tartu teachers college and settled in Petersburg, where he lived on a clerk's modest salary and by dint of self-tuition passed the examination qualifying him as a primary schoolteacher.

Revolutionary Petersburg had a strong influence on him. From the end of 1905, working as a teacher in Estonia, he carried on propaganda among the poor peasants and fishermen. Returning to Petersburg as a student in 1907, he soon entered the circle of revolutionary students and in the same year joined the RSDWP. In 1911 he was arrested and expelled from the capital. Settling in Estonia, he continued his revolutionary work and, because he was wanted by the police for publishing the Marxist journal *Meie Syna* (Our Word), he went into hiding.

In 1912 he was at Narva, where the Social Democrats formed the plan of creating a newspaper on the model of Lenin's Pravda to unite the Estonian revolutionary workers and educate Party cadres.... The idea was quickly put into practice by Anvel't together with I. Kiaspert, V. Buk, and other local revolutionaries, and the first number of *Kiir* came out on June 15, 1912, Anvel't being the principal editor. The newspaper was much interfered with by the police, who imposed fines and confiscated and banned it from time to time, but like its parent *Pravda* it continued to appear under new names. It maintained close links with *Pravda,* reprinting the latter's articles and sending it material from Estonia. Recognizing its services, Lenin wrote in a reply to the "liquidators" in 1914 that *"Pravda* is not alone ... first of all, there are Estonian and Lithuanian papers of the *Pravda* type."

During the February revolution in 1917 a soviet of workers and soldiers' deputies was set up at Narva under Anvel't's chairmanship. In April he presided over the conference of North Baltic Bolshevik organizations and became a member of the North Baltic bureau of the RSDWP(B) and the Party's Tallin committee. Soon thereafter he was elected chairman of the Tallin city duma, and then of the executive committee of the Estonian regional soviet. Then came the October Revolution. Anvel't was a delegate to the historic Second Congress which declared the assumption of all power by the soviets, and he became chairman of the first Soviet government of Estonia. But in February 1918 the country was occupied by the Kaiser's forces and the government was evacuated to Petrograd, where Anvel't took an active part in directing underground activity behind the enemy lines while at the same time taking a course for Red Army commanders.

When the peace treaty of Brest Litovsk was annulled as a result of the November revolution in Germany, the Red Army, including its Estonian regiments, liberated a large part of Estonian territory. The Estonian SSR was proclaimed at Narva under the name of the Estonian Workers' Commune, and Anvel't became its president [sic]. But it was not possible to consolidate the victory of the Estonian proletariat, and from 1921 to 1926 he was engaged in underground work in bourgeois Estonia. In the trying conditions of White terror he and V. Kingisepp directed the struggle against the anti-national bourgeois government.

From 1925 onwards Anvel't worked in the U.S.S.R., where he held a number of important posts, including that of deputy head of the chief administration of the Civil Air Fleet. His services in the development of Soviet civil aviation were rewarded with the Order of Lenin. He was also secretary of the International Control Commission of the Comintern and took an active part in the direction of the Estonian CP. In 1937 he became a victim of arbitrary rule and the violation of socialist legality during the cult of Stalin's personality.

The name of this steadfast Bolshevik, who played an important part in the growth and organization of the Estonian CP from the moment of its creation, will never grow dim in our people's memory. A monument has been erected to him at Tallin, and Estonian streets, schools, and enterprises have been named for him. His literary works have been published. The people honor the memory of this staunch fighter for the cause of the working masses.[23]

SEMEN BANTKE (RUBAN)

Biographical data

Born 1898, died 19—. Joined the Bolshevik Party in 1917. Born at Kishinev, the son of an artisan. During the occupation of Bessarabia by Rumanian troops he was evacuated to Russia, where he began college studies but later volunteered for the Red Army and became military political commissar of the First Special

Bessarabian Brigade. In 1919 he served in the underground in Bessarabia, was arrested and tried by a Rumanian court-martial in 1920. Freed in 1922, he resumed underground revolutionary activity; [this time he] escaped arrest and returned to the U.S.S.R., where he studied at the Sverdlov Communist University and the Institute of Red Professors and then enrolled in post graduate studies. On concluding these he became a professor of general history at the Institute of Red Professors and later director of the historical section of the Leningrad department of the Communist Academy. He was on the editorial staff of *Bor'ba klassov* (The Class Struggle), *Voprosy grazhdanskoi istorii* (Problems of Civil History) and *Krasnaia Bessarabiia* (Red Bessarabia). He became a victim of the cult of Stalin's personality.[24]

The legacy of the revolutionary scholar S. Bantke

The reader will of course have encountered the name of Semen Bantke (Ruban) in Party-historical and popular scientific literature. But few are aware that this eminent Soviet Party historian was a native of Kishinev. An active fighter for Soviet power in Moldavia and underground worker in Bessarabia, he wrote a history of our republic and threw a wealth of light from the Marxist-Leninist point of view on the history of the Communist and workers' movement.

He was born on December 17, 1898, the son of an artisan. In high school he impressed his comrades and teachers by the extent of his knowledge and the logical consistency of his judgments. Soon his passion for social sciences also became clear, and on his nineteenth birthday he joined the Communist Party. The future scholar's outlook was much influenced by conversations with the Bolsheviks of the Rumanian front who had been swept into Bessarabia by the tide of the First World War, they also supplied him with Communist books, newspapers, and journals.

When the troops of royalist Rumania occupied Bessarabia with the aid of Entente forces, many fighters for Soviet power temporarily withdrew across the Dniester. Bantke was of their number. He went to college in Soviet Russia, but the young Communist could not ignore the call of the "Socialist motherland in danger." He joined the Red Army, was elected a political commissar, and then became military political commissar of the First Special Bessarabian Brigade.

The news of the revolutionary fight of the working people of Bessarabia, the uprisings at Khotin and Bendery, brought many Bessarabian Communists back to their homeland to defend the conquests of the October Revolution and Soviet Russia. The CP, supporting the working people's struggle for social and national liberation, sent the Bessarabian Communists into the thick of the battle on their native soil. On the night of July 16-17, 1919, the elderly peasant Terentii Bogus secretly ferried across the Dniester a group of Communists which included Bantke, I. Cherkashin, and A. Zakharopulos. They delivered to the Communist underground fighters the works of Marx, Engels, and Lenin and the program of the RCP(B).

As an underground worker, Bantke threw himself into Party political work and the production of Bolshevik newspapers, leaflets, and appeals. His articles and other writings were imbued with Bolshevik passion and hatred for enemies of the people. Addressing Communists and Komsomols in underground workers' and youth groups he described to them the social-economic, political, and cultural transformations in Soviet Russia. All this had an immense effect on the growth of the Bessarabian revolutionary movement.

On the night of July 29-30, 1919, the police, who had been tipped off by a spy, broke into the house at No. 35 Kiev Street, searched it and arrested all of Bantke's family. Under interrogation he, his mother, and two sisters were subjected to gross indignities. The period of interrogation and torture lasted 176 days. On January 28, 1920, Bantke was tried by a Rumanian court-martial on a charge under which he could have been sentenced to death. Despite a complete absence of evidence, the court imposed a long term of imprisonment. He managed to regain his freedom in 1922, however, and, life outside the Party being unthinkable, resumed his underground revolutionary activity. But the treachery of provocateurs and risk to his life obliged him to leave Kishinev and return, with immense difficulty, to the U.S.S.R. Here he continued his studies, first at the Sverdlov Communist University, then at the Institute of Red Professors, and finally in a postgraduate course.... The completion of this course opened the way into the fascinating research world of Soviet historians. From this time on he taught general history at the Institute of Red Professors and was then director of the history institute of the Leningrad department of the Communist Academy. [At the same time] he worked on the editorial board of the journals *Bor'ba klassov, Voprosy grazhdanskoi istorii,* and *Krasnaia Bessarabiia....* The young scholar's interests were extremely wide, but he concentrated especially on two subjects: the international Communist and workers' movement and the history of Soviet Moldavia.

As a writer, Bantke was tireless in popularizing Lenin's immortal teachings. Among his works explaining the greatness of the founder of the Bolshevik Party, the creator of the first proletarian state in the world and leader of the international workers' movement are *Lenin i bol'shevizm na mezhdunarodnoi arene v dovoennyi period* (Lenin and Bolshevism in the Prewar International Arena) and *Lenin i Tsimmerval'dskoe dvizhenie vo Frantsii* (Lenin and the Zimmerwald Movement in France). These appeared in the large collection of documents and material entitled *Bor'ba bolshevikov za sozdanie Kommunisticheskogo Internatsionala* (The Bolsheviks' Fight to Create the Comintern). These works, written about 1930, helped our Party defend the purity of Marxism-Leninism against the inroads of Trotskyism, opportunism, and social-reformism. Another work of enduring merit is the Marxist study (the first of its kind) *Bor'ba za sozdanie Kommunisticheskoi partii Frantsii* (The Fight for the Creation of the French CP), written in 1934 on the basis of original documents in the archives of Paris, Lyons, Tours, and other French cities. This monograph is highly valued today by French Communists and all Marxist historians. Bantke also published about a dozen works on the history of the class struggle and the Communist movement in Germany and Italy. In addition, he was one of the first Soviet historians to undertake and publish research on the history of Moldavia....

When, at Gorky's suggestion, preparations were being made for a history of the Civil War, Bantke was put in charge of the group whose task was to collect materials and write the eleventh chapter of the second volume on the "Fight with Rumanian Counterrevolution for Bessarabia." In this connection he wrote several articles describing the method of collecting and sifting historical material and writing the "History of the Civil War in Bessarabia and Moldavia—the History of Battles in Which the Moldavian People took part."

Among his major contributions to the development of culture and scholarship in Soviet Moldavia were the following works: *Otnoshenie Marksa i Engelsa k krest'ianskomu i natsional'nomu voprosam na Balkanakh* (The Attitude of Marx and Engels toward the Peasant and National Questions in the Balkans); *Protiv meshchansko-obyvatel'skogo izobrazhenia revolutsionnogo dvizheniia v Bessarabii* (Against the Petty-Bourgeois Interpretation of the Bessarabian Revolutionary Movement); *Rabota po podgotovke Istorii grazhdanskoi voiny dolzhna stat' udarnoi* (The preparation of the History of the Civil War Should Be Speeded Up); *10 let bor'by protiv rumynskikh boiar* (Ten Years of Fighting against Rumanian Boyars); *Bessarabskaia molodezh' pod sapogom rumynskogo zhandarma* (Bessarabian Youth under the Jackboot of the Rumanian Gendarme); *Khotin v ogne vosstaniia* (Khotin in the Fire of Revolt); and *V grobu Doftany* (In Doftana's Grave). These were the first Soviet historical works to throw light from the Marxist-Leninst standpoint on the revolutionary movement of the Moldavian people. They contain vivid pages on the fight for Soviet power in Moldavia, the widespread participation in that struggle by the popular masses and especially the youth, and the acute class struggle in the Bessarabian countryside during the royalist Rumanian occupation. Bantke's works depict the strategy and tactics of the Communists of the Bessarabian underground—leaders of the working people's fight to overthrow the occupation regime, restore Soviet power, and reunite Bessarabia with the U.S.S.R.

In the archives of the Institute of Party History of the CC of the Moldavian CP there is a document showing that [when he died] Bantke was working on a book to be entitled"Outline of the History of the Communist Organizations of Bessarabia." The Moldavian oblast committee of the Party was giving him every help in this enterprise.

Bantke was obliged to leave much historical research unfinished. He perished tragically in the period of the cult of Stalin's personality. Today he has been posthumously rehabilitated. He has left us a great legacy in the field of historical science. The time is more than ripe for a thorough study of his works, which have become a bibliographical rarity and deserve a high place among Soviet historical studies.[25]

ALEKSANDR GRIGOR'EVICH CHERVIAKOV

Biographical data

Born 1892, died 1937. Joined the CP in 1917. Born at Dukorka village near Minsk. From 1909 he was a primary school teacher in the Trakai uezd, Vilna gubernia. Took part in the February revolution and organized Belorussian patriotic groups which carried on revolutionary work alongside the Bolsheviks. In 1918-19 he was commissar of Belorussian affairs attached to the CPC of the RSFSR, then on the southern front. In 1919-20 he was PC of education for Belorussia, and member of the CEC of Lithuania and Belorussia and of the Minsk gubernia revolutionary committee. In 1920-37, chairman of the CEC of the Belorussian SSR; in 1924-37, member of the bureau of the CC of the Belorussian CP. His life was tragically cut short on June 16, 1937.[26]

The "headman" of Belorussia

Aleksandr Grigor'evich Cherviakov was born not far from Minsk, in the village of Dukorka, Pukhovichi raion, on March 8, 1892. He attended the parish and town schools and qualified as a primary school teacher. From the age of seventeen he taught in the Trakai uezd, Vilna gubernia, where he discovered the works of Marx and Lenin and explained the ideas of scientific socialism to the impoverished peasantry. After leaving the Vilna Teachers Institute he was called up for service in the army, where he joined a social-democratic organization. He took an active part in the February revolution at Petrograd, and in May 1917 joined the Bolshevik Party. At Petrograd he also organized the Belorussian patriotic groups which carried on revolutionary work alongside the Bolsheviks. In February 1918 he was attached as commissar of Belorussian affairs to the CPC of the RSFSR. Afterward the Party sent him to the southern front, where he held the important posts of divisional commissar and head of the culture and education department of the All-Russian Bureau of Military Commissars. He thus took part in framing the first regulations on political education in the Red Army.

He was also one of the founders of the Belorussian SSR. In 1919 he was PC of education for Belorussia, and a member of the CEC of Lithuania and Belorussia and of the Minsk gubernia revolutionary committee. At the second all-Belorussian congress of soviets in December 1920 he was elected chairman of the CEC of the Belorussian SSR. At the end of 1922, in a speech at the tenth all-Russian congress of soviets which was discussing the creation of the U.S.S.R., he said: "The working people of Belorussia will be proud if you accept our proposal and allow the Belorussian workers and peasants to be among the first toilers to enter the ranks of the newly created U.S.S.R."

From 1920 onward he took part in all CPSU congresses, and from 1924 he was a member of the Bureau of the CC of the CPSU. A devoted Bolshevik and Leninist, he fought without respite for the application of the Party's general line, the industrialization of the republic, the collectivization of agriculture, and the cultural revolution in Belorussia. He often emphasized the special responsibility of the Belorussian SSR for the defense of the U.S.S.R.'s western borders, and exhorted the working people of the republic to be ready at all times to defend their socialist motherland.

The Belorussian toilers admired him for his modesty, simplicity, and understanding of others. He often visited farms, factories, and building sites, giving political talks, answering workers' and peasants' questions and paying careful heed to their requests and complaints. His life was tragically cut short on June 16, 1937.[27]

VLAS IAKOVLEVICH CHUBAR'

Biographical data

Born 1891, died 1939. Born at Fedorovka village, Ekaterinoslav gubernia (now Chubarevka village, Zaporog oblast), the son of a poor peasant. In 1904, having attended a two-class village school, he entered the technical high school at Aleksandrovsk (now Zaporozhe). During the revolution of 1905-7 he took an active part in revolutionary activity at Aleksandrovsk. In 1907 he joined the Bolshevik Party, and on the orders of the underground Party organization he carried on propaganda work among the city's railroad workers, distributing illegal literature and performing other tasks. He was arrested several times. In 1911-15 he worked at various plants in the Ukraine and later in Moscow. Here he was called up for army service, and as a skilled metalworker was employed as a lathe operator in a Petrograd arms factory. When the February revolution broke out he was elected at the first conference of factory and plant workers' committees to be a member of the Petrograd soviet of those committees. During the October Revolution the Party appointed him commissar of the chief artillery administration at Petrograd. Soon he was elected to the Council of Workers' Control, and after its reorganization to the presidium of the Supreme Council of National Economy. In June 1918 he was appointed chairman of Sormovo-Kolomna, the first big amalgamation of state engineering works. In 1919 the Party sent him to the Urals as head of a commission of the Supreme Council of the National Economy to restore Ural industry, and at the beginning of 1920 he went on a similar mission to the Ukraine SSR, where he worked until 1934. In 1920-21 he was chairman of the supreme soviet of national economy of the Ukraine SSR, and in December 1921 head of the central administration of the coal industry of the Donets basin. From 1920 he was a member of the CC of the Ukraine CP and of its politburo. At the Tenth Congress of the CPSU he was elected a candidate member of the Party CC, and at the Eleventh Congress a full member. He was also a member of the all-Ukraine CEC. In July 1923 he became chairman of the CPC of the Ukrainian SSR, and held this post without a break until 1934. From 1934 he was deputy chairman of the CPC and PC of finance of the U.S.S.R. In December 1937 he was elected a deputy to the Supreme Soviet of the U.S.S.R. by the Kharkov agricultural electoral district. In 1926-35 he was a candidate member of the Politburo of the CC of the CPSU, and from 1935 a full member. Arrested in 1937, he fell victim to the cult of Stain's personality.[28]

PETR IUR'EVICH DIATLOV

Biographical data

Born 1883, died 1933. Born at Starodub in the Chernigov area, the son of a craftsman. Left high school (where he earned a silver medal) in 1901, and entered the law faculty of Moscow University. Joined the students' revolutionary movement, was arrested and expelled from the university. Served a prison sentence and then lived in administrative exile at Kursk, Vorozhba, Nezhin, Glukhov, and other towns. Despite the Tsarist authorities' ban he succeeded in 1903 in enrolling in the financial and economic faculty of the Petersburg Polytechnical Institute. Expelled in the fall of 1904 for revolutionary activity, he returned to the Ukraine and worked in the petty-bourgeois nationalistic Ukrainian Revolutionary Party [Ukrainian Social Democratic Workers' Party] as an active member of its left wing. Emigrated in December 1908 and lived in Zurich, 1909-10, Prague, 1911-14; and Vienna, 1915-21. During this period he carried on literary and translation work, gave private lessons, took part in the social-political life, and improved his education and training. He graduated from the engineering faculty of the Prague Polytechnic [Institute] and the philosophical faculty of Vienna University. For anti-war revolutionary activity he was arrested by the Austrian government and sent to the concentration camp at Eter-Chab, Drosendorf. In 1918 he joined the Ukrainian section of the Austrian CP, and from 1921 to 1924 was chairman of the foreign committee of the CP of Eastern Galicia. At the end of 1921 he went to Berlin, where he worked in the Soviet embassy, joined the German CP and the Ukrainain Communist group, and worked on the editorial staff of *Nasha Pravda,* the chief organ of the CP of the Western Ukraine. In summer 1924 he moved to Prague, worked in the Soviet legation and the Ukrainian section of the Czechoslovak CP, and helped to edit the miscellany *Chuiesh surmy zagraly* (Sound of the Trumpet) for Ukrainian workers and students. Returned to the Ukraine in January 1925 and joined the Ukraine CP in January 1926. In 1926-33 he was academic secretary of the PC of education of the Ukrainian SSR and an editor of *Narodnyi uchytel'* (The People's Teacher). He also taught the history of the revolutionary movement, political economy, historical and dialectical materialism, and history of the Soviet economy at Kharkov colleges, was an editor and translator for the Ukraine State Publishing House, and held the chair of political economy at the Kharkov Institute of Communal Economy. In 1933 he became a victim of the cult of Stalin's personality.[29]

BUTABAI DODOBAEV

Biographical data

Born 1888, died 19—. Born at Chust (Uzbek SSR). Joined the Bolshevik Party in 1918. Until that year he was servant to a cotton agent, worked at a tannery and as watchman and messenger for a Tashkent doctor, was a clerk in the Namangan uezd, and worked in the Chust office of the Singer Company and as a police station clerk in the town of Skobelev (now Fergana). From the first days of the October Revolution he threw himself into revolutionary work, took an active part in setting up the Union of Moslem Workers and Artisans, served in militia organs, and was a member of the Fergana oblast committee of the Moslem artisans' union. Later he was first deputy chairman of the Skobelev soviet of workers', peasants' and Red Army deputies, editor of the newspaper *Akhbori,* chairman of the uezd and city executive committee, head of a department of the Fergana oblast executive committee, chairman of the Andizhan uezd and city revolutionary committee, member of the military council of the Fourth Rifle Brigade, deputy chairman of the Fergana oblast revolutionary committee and later of the oblast executive committee, and PC of justice and state procurator of the Turkestan Republic. When the Tadzhik ASSR was formed he became a member of the organization bureau of the CP of Uzbekistan and the Tadzhik ASSR, first deputy chairman of the presidium of the Provisional Government of Soviet Tadzhikistan (the Revolutionary committee of the Tadzhik ASSR, manager of the Tadzhik agricultural bank, and permanent representative of the Tadzhik ASSR on the Central Asian Economic Council. He was a victim of the cult of Stalin's personality.[30]

A soldier of the revolution

It was the fall of 1916; the pupils of the Russo-native school at Skobelev were on their way home. My classmate Iuldash Dodobaev invited me to go home with him so we could prepare our lessons together. There we were welcomed by his brother Butabai, a young man of twenty-seven or twenty-eight. This was my first meeting with that stout-hearted Bolshevik, later an eminent member of the Turkestan CP.

Butabi had a hard life as a child, as did most workers' and peasants' children in Turkestan. His father died when he was twelve, and as the eldest child he had to leave school and hire himself out as a worker. First he was servant to a cotton agent named Niiaskhodzha; then he worked at a tannery and a cotton-cleaning plant. But his miserable wages did not help the family's position, and poverty drove him to Namangan and then Tashkent. Here the work was equally strenuous and badly paid, but as watchman and messenger at a Tashkent doctor's clinic he learned to speak Russian and, with the help of the doctor's children, to write it, which greatly widened the Tadzhik youth's horizons. In 1907, when he was nineteen, his mother died and he returned to Fergana and his home town of Chust in order to look after his younger brothers....

In 1918 he joined the CP at Fergana. With other Bolsheviks, including Shomansur Alikhodzhaev (later a member of the presidium of the CEC of the Turkestan ASSR) and Mullo Umar Gulimov, he took an active part in founding the Union of Moslem Workers and Artisans. He also served in the militia, and was a member of the Fergana oblast committee of the Moslem artisans' union and first deputy chairman of the Skobelev soviet of workers', peasants, and Red Army deputies. The Party also assigned him to a great variety of other posts.... He took an active part in combating the Basmachi for which he received an inscribed sword and the Order of the Red Banner of the Turkestan Republic. When the Tadzhik ASSR was set up, he was sent to Tadzhikistan as a member of the organization bureau of the CP of Uzbekistan as a member of the organization bureau of the CP of Uzbekistan and the Tadzhik ASSR. At the same time he was first deputy chairman of the presidium of the Provisional Government of Soviet Tadzhikistan—the revolutionary committee of the Tadzhik ASSR. Selflessly devoted to the CP and to Soviet power, he worked ceaselessly for the good of his people, fought its enemies relentlessly and took an active part in the socialist reconstruction of the national economy of Tadzhikistan. He did much good work as manager of the Tadzhik agricultural bank and permanent representative of the Tadzhik ASSR on the Central Asian Economic Council.

His life and activity were unexpectedly cut short during the cult of Stalin's personality, to which he fell a victim. But the Tadzhik and Uzbek peoples, led by the CP onto the broad highway of prosperous life, will not forget the part played in their prosperity by Butabai Dodobaev. The shining figure of this true soldier of the revolution will live forever in the national memory.[31]

MIKHEI NIKOLAEVICH ERBANOV

Biographical data

Born 1889, died 1937. Joined the Bolshevik Party in 1917. Born in the Bakhtai *ulus* (settlement) of the Irkutsk oblast. Came into contact with a social-democratic group at Barnaul in 1913, and in 1917 was a member of the Buriat group of Bolsheviks at Irkutsk. In 1919 he was a leading member of the revived Buriat section of the Bolshevik Party, which had disintegrated during the Czechoslovak counterrevolutionary coup in June 1918. In 1920 he served on the gubernia committee of the RCP(B) and later on the gubernia revolutionary committee at Irkutsk. In 1921 he was chairman of the Buriat revolutionary committee, and in 1922 of the executive committee of the Buriat autonomous oblast. In 1923, chairman of the CPC of the Buriat ASSR; in 1925-27, simultaneously chairman of the CEC and of the CPC of the republic. In 1928-37, first secretary of the Buriat oblast committee of the Party. In 1937 he became a victim of the cult of Stalin's personality.[32]

A true son of the people

It is seventy-five years since the birth of Mikhei Nikolaevich Erbanov, a true son of the people whose name is closely linked with the struggle of the Buriat workers to establish Soviet power and build socialism.

He was born in 1889, the son of a peasant of middle status in the Bakhtai settlement of the Irkutsk oblast. The cheerless and arduous life of the Buriat workers, groaning under the double yoke of Tsarist colonialism and exploitation by local kulaks, aroused the young man's hatred of the existing order. In 1913 he came into contact with the social-democratic group at Barnaul. At the end of 1917 the first Buriat Bolshevik group came into existence at Irkutsk, to be transformed later into a section of the gubernia Party organization. Erbanov was an active member of this group, and in December 1917, he joined the RSDWP(B). On the orders of the Party's gubernia committee he visited towns and villages, setting up local organs of Soviet power, lecturing workers' meetings on the nationalities policy of the Party and the Soviet State, and denouncing bourgeois nationalists. At the end of 1919 the Irkutsk underground gubernia committee of the RCP(B) decided to revive the Buriat Bolshevik section which had disintegrated as a result of the Czechoslovak counterrevolutionary coup of June 1918. Erbanov was one of the Buriat Communists who took control of the section and, despite difficult conditions, worked to create underground Party cells in the settlements and organized fighting groups and partisan detachments at Alari, Bokhana, Nelkhai, and other places. In December 1919 and at the beginning of 1920 Erbanov took part in the armed uprising against the Kolchak regime. After the latter's defeat he served on the Irkutsk gubernia committee of the RCP(B) and on the gubernia revolutionary committee, taking an active part in organizing the Soviet state apparatus in the gubernia. In 1920 he was a delegate to the Moscow all-Russian congress of representatives of republics, oblasts, and national minorities. He also took part in the all-Russian congress of soviets, at which he heard a report delivered by Lenin. The latter's energetic, vivid words made an indelible impression on Erbanov and played a great part in his life and work.

In 1921 he was elected chairman of the Buriat revolutionary committee, to which full powers were entrusted by a decision of the All-Russian CEC pending the convocation of the first congress of soviets of the Buriat autonomous oblast.... At the sixth oblast Party conference in December 1928 he was elected first secretary of the Buriat oblast committee of the Party, which post he held until September 1937. During these years his organizing talent displayed itself to the full, and he showed himself a leader of the Leninist type. All who worked with him or even met him at this time were struck by his infectious optimism, warm-heartedness, and simplicity. His life was devoted to the interest of the Party and the people, and to Lenin's great ideals.

Thanks to the endeavors of the CP and the Soviet State, the Buriat nation freed itself in a short time from the backwardness of centuries. In those years many industrial enterprises were created, cadres came into existence in every branch of national economy, agriculture was collectivized, and a cultural revolution took place. Speaking at a reception for delegates of workers of the Buriat ASSR at the Kremlin in 1936, Erbanov gave a vivid account of the radical changes in the life of the Buriat people under the Soviet regime, adding proudly: "Let our enemies realize this, and not compare the 'native' Buriats of former times with the Soviet Socialist Buriat Republic of today."

Erbanov was a delegate to a number of CPSU congresses, and at the Seventeenth Congress was elected a member of the Central Inspection Commission. From the time of the second congress of soviets of the U.S.S.R. in 1924 he was a member of the CEC of the U.S.S.R., and was a candidate and then a full member of its Presidium at the fourth, fifth, and seventh convocations. For his services to the Party and state he received the Order of Lenin and that of the Red Banner. At the end of 1937, at the height of his powers, he became a victim of arbitrary rule and the cult of Stalin's personality. Today the Party, condemning the cult, has restored his good name among others. The Buriat working people will never forget their faithful son.[33]

NIKOLAI MATVEEVICH GOLODED

Biographical data

Born 1894, died 1937. Joined the CP in 1918. In 1917 he carried on revolutionary work in the army, and in 1918 did important work for the Party and government. In 1925-27 he was secretary of the CC of the Belorussian CP and member of the presidium of the CEC of the Belorussian SSR. At the Sixteenth and Seventeenth CPSU congresses (1930 and 1934) he was elected a candidate member of the CC.[34]

A true son of the Party

It was 1919—a time of trial for the young Soviet Republic. The Red Army was fending off enemy pressure on all fronts, and special groups headed by men of outstanding courage were formed to deal with internal counterrevolution.

One of the detachments that put down rebels in Gomel' was commanded by the twenty-five-year-old Communist Nikolai Goloded. In a fierce struggle his detachment inflicted a decisive defeat on superior enemy forces and put the rebels to flight. Not long afterward, he took an active part in breaking up a terrorist organization in the local agricultural institute, organizing and placing his activists in such a way that the band was completely shattered. In the battle with the terrorists the young Communist showed courage, boldness, and ingenuity.

Nikolai Matveevich Goloded was born on May 22, 1894, the son of a poor peasant in the Gomel' area. He had a hard childhood, working as a laborer on a kulak's farm, herding cattle, cleaning out stables and cowsheds. At sixteen, driven by poverty, he became a miner in the Krivoi Rog area. The peasant boy learned much from his fellowworkers and became a skilled machinist and electrician. He began to attend Marxist groups, to take part in May Day rallies and Bolshevik meetings. From 1917 he carried on active revolutionary work in the army: as a member of the committee of several units on the southwestern front he firmly defended Bolshevik ideas. Weapon in hand, he took part in the October Revolution, and in 1918 he joined the CP. He performed with success many Party tasks as secretary of the agricultural soviet, member of the volost revolutionary committee, and agent of the uezd executive committee. His thorough studies, his ability to grasp a complicated situation, and his great powers of organization all made him an excellent Party worker.

In January 1924 he was elected a member of the Provisional Belorussian Bureau of the CC of the RCP(B). He soon became a member of the CC of the Belorussian CP, and in December 1925 second secretary of the CC. In 1927 he became chairman of the CPC of the Belorussian SSR, a post which made good use of his organizing ability. His great services to the Soviet state were rewarded with the Order of Lenin. He was a delegate to the Fourteenth through Seventeenth congresses, and at the Seventeenth Congress was elected a candidate member of the Party's CC. All his knowledge and energy were devoted to the cause of the Belorussian workers in their fight to establish Soviet power and build socialism. He often said that "all our work in all fields of construction must be permeated by Bolshevik intransigence and moral tenacity." He was a staunch internationalist and regarded friendship among the peoples of the U.S.S.R. as a cornerstone of policy.

In 1937, at the height of his creative powers, he was subjected to unjust repression and became a victim of arbitrary rule and the cult of personality. Today, the honorable name of this remarkable man and true Leninist has been restored, and the Belorussian people faithfully preserve his memory.[35]

GRIGORII VASIL'EVICH IVANENKO (BARABA)

Biographical data

Born 1893, died 19—. Party names Svii, Neznaiko, Gritsenko, Zadorozhnyi, Kariienko, Dovhenko, Vasil', Mikhail's'kyi. Born at Dovgii village, Drohobycz district, Austria-Hungary, the son of a peasant. Attended village school and Drohobycz high school, but left because of its poor quality. Called up for service in the Austrian army in 1914; captured at the battle of Stryi, 1916. He became acquainted with the social-democratic movement in Siberian prisoner-of-war camps at Omsk and Mariinsk. With other Galician prisoners he took an active part in the revolutionary movement in Siberia, the establishment of Soviet power, and the fight against Kolchak. When, on the proposal of the Slav group of the CC of the RCP(B), Communist organizations were set up at Omsk among former prisoners of war of the Austrian army, Ivanenko joined the Ukrainian Communist group. At the beginning of 1920 he and others arrived at Kiev and were placed at the disposal of the Committee of Communists of Eastern Galicia and the Bukovina under the CC of the Ukraine CP, which before long sent him to carry out underground work in Galicia. In 1921 he organized a strike of oil workers at Borislav, and was an active contributor to the legal paper *Sprava robitnycha* (The Workers' Cause). He was arrested in September 1921, his case being linked with that of the so-called "Świętojurcy," (St. George Cathedral group)* but was acquitted for lack of evidence. At the end of 1923 the CC of the Eastern Galicia CP dispatched him to Volhynia, where he made close contact with the Communists of Lutsk, Rożyszcze, Holoby, Łokacze and Vladimir Volynsk, preparing the way for them to unite into a single Volhynian Party organization. In 1923 he was elected to the Party's Volhynian district committee. On February 16, 1924, he and Olga German were arrested at Kovel, but he was released a year later for lack of evidence. In 1926 the CC of the CP of the Western Ukraine sent him to its Party school, then located in the Artem Communist University at Kharkov. After completing a course there he became head of the revolutionary movement of western Ukrainian workers. In 1928 he was co-opted onto the CC, and later the politburo, of the CP of the Western Ukraine. He remained a member of the politburo until the end of 1933 and was also secretary of the CC. At the fifth and sixth congresses of the Polish CP (1930 and 1932) he was elected a candidate member of its CC. During the cult of Stalin's personality, unfounded charges of nationalism that had been leveled against the old leadership of the CP of the Western Ukraine (the leadership headed in 1927-28 by Vasil'kov and Turiansky) were used to buttress the pernicious theory of the "permanent nationalism" of the Party's ruling group. As a result, in 1933 Ivanenko and other comrades were accused of nationalism, removed from the leadership, and later subjected to repression. The Twentieth and Twenty-second congresses of the CPSU restored to the people the good name of Grigorii Vasil'evich Ivanenko (Baraba).[36]

FAIZULLA KHODZHAEV

Biographical data

Born 1896, died 1938. Joined the Bolshevik Party in 1920. Born at Bukhara,

*The Świętojurcy were a strongly nationalistic, anti-Communist Ukrainian group led by Archbishop Shyptycky, who was the spiritual leader of the Greco-Catholic community in Eastern Galicia.—ED.

the son of a rich merchant. In 1917 he joined the underground CC formed by the Young Bukhara Party and took an active part in organizing a major demonstration against the emirate. When the widely based movement of revolt was defeated by the Emir, Khodzhaev, in danger of the death sentence, fled to Turkestan, where he soon became a leader of the left-wing Young Bukhara Party. In 1919 he served in Moscow in the office of the Turkestan ASSR and as representative of the Young Bukhara bureau. Returned to Tashkent in September 1919. In August-September 1920 he was active in organizing the armed uprising against the Emir. After the latter's overthrow he became chairman of the Council of People's Nazirs (commissars) and nazir of foreign affairs of the Bukhara People's Soviet Republic. In the ensuing years he took a direct part in fighting the Basmachi. By a decision of the CC of the RCP(B) he was appointed chairman of the RMC of eastern Bukhara. In 1922 he was a member of the Central Asian bureau of the CC of the RCP(B), and in 1924 chairman of the CPC of the Uzbek SSR. In 1927 he was elected a chairman of the Presidium of the CEC of the U.S.S.R. In 1938 he became a victim of the cult of Stalin's personality.[37]

He grew up in the thick of the fight

Pictures of him used to hang in Uzbek villages and in the tents of the Chukchi, in Moscow offices and public buildings, and even in a commercial gallery in the capital of Weimar Germany, as part of an exhibition of world-famous men and women. In some of these he appeared as he had in Bukhara, wearing a striped robe and a high white turban; in others he wore a commander's jacket with rank insignia, and more often still he was dressed in an elegant suit and tie. But all the portraits bore the same brief inscription: "Faizulla Khodzhaev, Chairman of the CEC of the U.S.S.R." At that time there were seven such chairmen, of whom he was one. He was elected to this high post at the fourth congress of soviets of the U.S.S.R. before the May festivities of May 1927, and was unanimously re-elected at the Fifth, Sixth, and Seventh congresses. For ten years in all, together with M. I. Kalinin, G. I. Petrovsky, and others, he carried out the exalted duties of President of the great Soviet power....

At the beginning of September 1920, when the people of Bukhara overthrew their Emir with the help of the Red Army, the twenty-four-year-old revolutionary Faizulla Khodzhaev became chairman of the Bukhara people's government and nazir [commissar] for foreign affairs. A month earlier, during the Second Comintern Congress, Lenin, reflecting on the nature of power in a newly liberated Eastern country where "the greater part of the population consists of peasants who have been exploited in medieval fashion," noted on a report by the Iranian Communist A. Sultan-zade: "We must think about this and try to find concrete answers." (First printed in the complete edition of Lenin's works in Russian, vol. 41, p. 457). The "answers" were given first, and were soon enlarged upon, by the Soviet People's Republics of Khoresm and Bukhara.

In the calendar of revolutionary battles, Bukhara's September followed Russia's October. Bukhara leaned heavily on the right arm of its neighbor and friend, the RSFSR, and especially its component Republic of Turkestan. Thanks to this help and to the political initiative of the Bukhara Communists and their government, as well as the natural desire of the Uzbeks, Tadzhiks, and Turkmens of Bukhara to reunite with those of their countrymen who had come under the Soviet flag in 1917, only four years elapsed before the Soviet People's Republics of Bukhara and Khoresm were prepared to merge themselves in the main tide of socialist construction. Faizulla Khodzhaev played a great part in achieving this....

I remember a conversation about this man, who was for a time almost forgotten and who [still] is practically unknown to our young people, at the World Youth Festival in Moscow in the summer of 1957. I was a member of the Uzbekistan group, and during a break in a philosophical discussion a young French Communist with a degree in politics, a Senegalese by race, came up to us and said: "I am very much interested in Bukhara and its leader Faizul Khodzha" (as he called him). He explained why: "Ninety percent of the leaders of the emergent countries of Afro-Asia are very like him, and the transformation of a bourgeois into a Communist, and of Bukhara's national democracy into a socialist democracy, is most interesting and instructive. How did I hear of him? Oh, plenty has been written about him—but by Western enemies of the U.S.S.R."

I myself was already much interested in Khodzhaev's personality. His full name was a long one—Ubaidulla-Khodzhaev—and his revolutionary career was also long and intricate. There is, incidentally, one document in which his name is given in full—his foreign-travel passport. In the early twenties it was suggested to him that he should go to Germany for a cure and to start up trade relations. The RSFSR government approved, and his full name was written in his passport. This was no accident. Ten years before, in 1912, his father, a man of slight build with a thin beard but a "big shot" and a millionaire, had died in Moscow on the way to Mecca, bequeathing to his sixteen-year-old son Faizulla the ownership of the biggest astrakhan fur trading concern in the east of Russia. At this time the son added to his own name that of his venerated grandfather, so as to emphasize that he would carry on the family business. Thus the young merchant with eight million gold rubles of capital became known abroad under his full name—but he was now not the head of a Bukhara trading firm, but of the Bukhara Soviet Government.

Young Faizulla had gone to school in Moscow, and had lived for nearly three years in the home of a rich merchant of the Kadet (Constitutional Democratic) Party, where he was taught by cultivated and democratic tutors. It is not surprising that the young Bukhara merchant "in Moscow clothes," carried away by the ideal of a bourgeois transformation of Russia, became a follower of the Dzhadid movement.* Later, in his book *K istorii revolutsii v Bukhare* (On the History of the Revolution in Bukhara), Khodzhaev vividly described the evolution of the Bukhara Dzhadids, who "as class differentiation became more acute, retreated more and more from their positions, and after the October Revolution ... came to play a counterrevolutionary role as class opponents of the workers and *dekhkany* (peasants)" (p. 100). But for the time being the Bukhara Dzhadids were progressive, aiming as they did at liquidating the feudal despotism of the emirate. A "secret society" came into being within the Bukhara bourgeois-liberal movement; the energetic Faizulla became a member of it, and soon also of the CC of the Young Bukhara Party. Many of his colleagues never rose above bourgeois nationalism, but Faizulla, as he wrote of himself, "though slowly and with difficulty, in ceaseless fight," went the whole way as a revolutionary and devoted himself entirely to the socialist cause.

For him, the new road began in April 1917, when a demonstration took place in Bukhara and was dispersed by the Emir. Faizulla, who in absentia was sentenced to death for his part in organizing the popular movement, escaped at dawn by narrow side streets to the nearby Russian town of Kagan, where he joined the circle of "glorious sons of Russia"—P. G. Poltoratsky and other working men—who helped him to "clear his mind and come over to the Bolshevik side." But this did not happen at once. In the spring of 1918, conscious of his share in responsibility for the failure of the "Kolesov campaign" against Bukhara, Khodzhaev set out for Moscow, to find out [from a source] near to Lenin what should be done next. He was arrested at Orenburg, and the doctors at Samara barely succeeded in saving his life. His journey took months, but it was itself an education. When he returned from Moscow to Tashkent, he was in many respects a changed man. His companions "did not know him." His former bourgeois ideals seemed to him untenable, suggestions of a pro-British orientation were suspect, and the ideas and methods of the Young Bukhara revolutionaries seemed ineffectual.... By the beginning of August 1920 he had declared that he considered his program identical with that of the Communists. On the seventh day of the Bukhara revolution in which he had had so great a share, the Young Bukhara Party, although more numerous than the Bukhara Communist Party at that time, dissolved itself on Khodzhaev's suggestion, and he, together with other active revolutionaries, declared himself a Communist and became a member of the CC of the Bukhara CP....

In 1922 Khodzhaev was in Moscow on his way to the Genoa conference. As a trade expert and the head of Soviet Bukhara, commanding export possibilities

*The Dzhadid (Jadid) party of Bukhara was a moderate reform party originally organized to bring about some democratic reforms in the government of the emir. After the February revolution the emir promised certain reforms but reneged, whereupon members of this party arrested him and appealed to the Red Guards for support. In the ensuing struggle the emir prevailed; on March 1, 1918, the Reds were suppressed. Later the emir gave support to the Basmachi, the native insurgents, in their struggle against the Bolsheviks.—ED.

and with experience of direct trading relations with foreign countries, he was much needed at the conference. But events in Bukhara were threatening. The traitor and foreign agent Enver Pasha had united the Basmachi under the green banner of Islam. Khodzhaev changed his route: "I was told to go to Bukhara"—and he did so, as chairman of the eastern Bukhara RMC. For directing the operations in which the Basmachi were defeated, he received the Order of the Red Banner, being the first representative of the Soviet East to receive what was then the highest award of the RSFSR. The Soviet People's Republic of Bukhara likewise conferred its highest military honor upon him: he and the principal Soviet commanders each received a golden sword....

"At first I thought one way was right, and then I saw it must be another." Such was Khodzhaev's experience. The way he trod was a clear one, but it became visible step by step, and everything in it was new. But he was an honest seeker after truth, and above all he knew, like a true Bolshevik how to draw conclusions from criticism of his mistakes.... His straightforwardness and honesty helped him to acquire Bolshevik methods of working. Firm and resolute, he also possessed the cultural background without which, as Dzerzhinsky has said, one cannot imagine a Party and Soviet leader. The testimony of former colleagues and the CPC show that he was a practical man of few words who would study a problem carefully, consulting specialists and gathering background information, and would then penetrate swiftly and accurately to the essence of the problem. His training in Party principles helped him to grow in stature as a thinker and comprehend the dialectics of our nation's development. His theoretical, economic, and practical knowledge were shown in his approach to problems of irrigation and cotton-growing, for the improvement of which he received the Order of Lenin.

He spared no effort to improve his education and became a highly cultivated man, combining the duties of chairman of the CPC with academic and journalistic activity. He wrote more than twenty books, pamphlets, and monographs, including his large work, which was reprinted, on the history of the revolution in Bukhara. This and his other works contain not only useful facts and records but were original and profound (although not always indisputable), theoretical statements [concerning], for example, bourgeois liberal tendencies and the primary accumulation of capital in the old emirate, the evolution of races and tribes, the politico-geographical division of Central Asia, etc. His book which bears the deliberately simple title *Narodnoe khoziaistvo Uzbekistana* (The Political Economy of Uzbekistan) is a splendid example of impassioned polemics based on vivid facts and figures, written in reply to slanderous critics from the imperialist camp. The edge of his journalistic acumen was frequently directed against manifestations of nationalism and chauvinism. He wrote with emotion of the beauty, nobility, and depth of feeling of the true internationalist, holding that "the Party's general policy on the nationalities question constitutes the moral strength of every individual and of society as a whole."

His last public utterance was his speech at the first congress of scientists and scholars of Uzbekistan, held at Samarkand in May 1937. Among other things he then described the future irrigation system of Uzbekistan—the big canals in the Fergana valley, the linking of the Amu Darya with the Zarafshan, etc. He had this speech recorded verbatim and, on his way home to Bukhara through the Zarafshan valley, telegraphed to Tashkent expressing the hope that it would be published "in order to throw light on future problems."

In March 1938 his life was tragically cut short when he was less than forty-two years of age. He had come to the revolution at dawn through the dark, narrow lanes of Bukhara, and it had led him to the highway of progress for both Party and people. He strove to keep to the sunny side, and it is from that side too, that he is best seen and that our people will remember him.[38]

IURII MIKHAILOVICH KOTSIUBINSKY

Biographical data

Born 1895, died 1937. Son of the classic Ukrainian writer Kotsiubinsky. Born at Vinnitsa. Joined the Bolshevik Party in 1913. In 1911, while still at high school, he took an active part in organizing revolutionary youth. At the time of the February revolution in 1917 he was at Petrograd, doing his military service and carrying on revolutionary work among the troops. Arrested in July. After his release he was appointed commander of Red Guard detachments in the Moscow-Zaslavsky raion of Petrograd. During the October Revolution he was a member of the Petrograd RMC and took part in the assault on the Winter Palace. After the revolution he returned to the Ukraine. At the first congress of soviets of the Ukraine in December 1917 he was appointed deputy people's secretary for military affairs. In 1918 he was commander in chief of the troops of the Ukraine Workers' and Peasants' Republic. Under his command the Soviet troops destroyed the forces of the Central Rada and liberated Kiev. He was chairman of the Special Defense Committee of the Ukraine, and during the German occupation organized underground work in occupied territory. He took an active part in setting up the Ukraine CP, and at its first congress was elected to its CC. In 1919 he was chairman of the gubernia executive committee at Chernigov; in June he became a member, and in August secretary, of the gubernia committee of the Ukraine CP at Chernigov. During the invasion of the Ukraine by Denikin's forces, as chairman of the defense committee, he organized the formation of units for the Twelfth Army and the northward evacuation gubernia institutions and property. In 1920 the Party directed him to work at Poltava, where he performed important duties in the gubernia committee and the gubernia executive committee. In December 1921 he was appointed representative of the Ukrainian SSR at Vienna. In September 1922 the CC of the Ukraine CP sent him to study at the Socialist

Academy of Political and Academic Sciences. In 1925-30 he was again employed in diplomatic work at Vienna and then at Warsaw. In 1930-34 he was deputy chairman, then chairman, of the Ukrainian Gosplan. In 1937 he was a victim of the cult of Stalin's personality.[39]

IVAN IULIANOVICH KULIK

Biographical data

Born 1897, died 1941. Literary pseudonyms R. Rolinato, Vasil' Rolenko. Joined the CP in 1914. Born at Shpole (now in the Cherkassy oblast), the son of a teacher. In 1900 his parents moved to Uman', where he spent his childhood. Entered Odessa Arts School in 1911. Went to America in 1914 and took part in the work of the Social Democratic Party. Returned to the Ukraine in May 1917. Took part in the October Revolution and the Civil War. During the October armed uprising in Kiev he was a member of the local RMC. In December 1917, at the oblast congress in Kiev of the RSDWP(B) for the southwestern region, he was elected to the Main Committee of the Social Democratic Party of the Ukraine, and at the first all-Ukrainian congress of soviets he became a member of the CEC of Soviet Ukraine. After taking part in the restoration of Soviet power at Kremenchug and Uman', he worked in the Ukrainian section of the PC of Nationalities affairs at Moscow, and in 1919 was a member of the collegium of the PC of Foreign Affairs. From July 1919 he took an active part in the Communist underground in the Western Ukraine and Poland, and was arrested by the White Poles. In 1920 he was a member of the Galician revolutionary committee and took part in the fighting against the White Poles. In 1923 he joined the organization of proletarian writers known as "Gart." In 1924-26 he was a Soviet consul in Canada. After returning home he performed Party and government work. From 1924 he was chairman of the Union of Soviet Writers of the Ukraine. At the thirteenth congress of the Ukraine CP in 1937 he was elected to the CC of the Ukraine CP. In 1936-37 he was chairman of the radio committee of the Ukrainian SSR and director of its Party publishing house. In 1937 he was arrested and became a victim of the personality cult.[40]

IAN DAVIDOVICH LENTSMAN

Biographical data

Born 1881, died 1939. Party names Kentsis, Misinbart, Krums, Tseris Grike, Grikis, Boris. Joined the CP in 1899. Born in the Kurland gubernia, the son of a farm laborer. Became a worker and joined the revolutionary movement in 1897. Exiled to the Arkhangelsk gubernia in 1903. Escaped in 1904 to Libava (Libau) and became a member of the committee of the Latvian social-democratic workers' party. From 1905 he was a member of the CC of the Social Democratic Party of the Lettish Region (SDPLR); in 1907 a delegate to the Fifth Congress of the RSDWP. At the beginning of 1908 he became a member of the CC of the RSDWP as representative of the CC of the SDPLR. From the end of 1908 to 1911 he was a member of the Baku committee of the RSDWP, and from 1911 a member of the Riga committee and CC of the SDPLR. In 1917 he also became a member of the Riga soviet of workers' deputies. He was a member of the All-Russian CEC at its first convocation and deputy to the seventh (April) conference and Sixth Congress of the RSDWP(B). During the German occupation of Latvia he did illegal work in Riga; from December 1918 he was deputy chairman of the government and PC of internal affairs of Soviet Latvia. In 1919-21 he was a member of the RMC of the Fifteenth Army and served on the RMC of the RSFSR. In 1921-24, controller of the commercial port of Petrograd and member of the Petrograd gubernia committee of the RCP(B). In 1925-31, chairman of the board of the Soviet merchant marine. In 1931-37, worked in the Latvian section of the Comintern. He was slandered and liquidated during the cult of Stalin's personality. Posthumously rehabilitated.[41]

AVIS SOGOMONOVICH NURIDZHANIAN

Biographical data

Born 1896, died 1937. Joined the Bolshevik Party in 1917. In 1913 he left the Shusha technical high school for the economics faculty of the Kiev Commercial Institute. Called up in 1914 and sent to the Caucasian front. In 1917 he joined the bourgeois nationalist party Dashnaktsutiun, but soon altered his views and joined the Bolsheviks. In 1918 he did underground work at Baku and was secretary of the Baku committee of the RCP(B). Arrested in 1919; after his release went to Armenia and was a member of the [RCP(B)] Armenian committee, taking an active part in the formation of the Armenian CP. In 1920 he represented the Armenian CP at the Second Comintern Congress with the right of casting a vote, and was a member and then secretary of the CC of the Armenian CP. In 1920-21 he was PC of war of the Armenian Republic; in May-September 1921 commander of Special Purpose Forces, then PC of internal affairs and member of the presidium of the Armenian CPC. In 1921 he studied in Petrograd. In 1923-26 he was head of the organization department of the Volodarsky raion committee of the city of Leningrad. In 1926-30, head of the Press department of the Riazan' gubernia Party organization. In 1930-37 he was in Transcaucasia as chairman of the Council of Collective Farms. In 1937 he became a victim of the cult of Stalin's personality.[42]

"Our Avis"

Avis Nuridzhanian was one of the chief members of the glorious generation of Armenian Leninist Bolsheviks. He took an active part in the defense of the Baku Commune, helped to direct the May uprising, and fought selflessly to establish Soviet power in Armenia. While still young, he embarked on the struggle for the liberation of the working class, and he remained faithful throughout his life to the Leninist banner.

Avis Sogomonovich Nuridzhanian had a hard life. He lost his parents at an early age and had to study and work simultaneously in his native village of Vagachan (Kafan raion, Armenian SSR). Despite their scanty means, his relatives did everything possible to procure him an education. In 1913, having passed through the Shusha technical high school, he entered the economic faculty of Kiev Commercial Institute. He did not stay there long, however, as the imperialist war broke out. Called up in 1914, he was sent to the Caucasian front. In 1917 he joined the bourgeois nationalist party Dashnaktsutiun. However, he came to Baku in that year and, under the impact of the revolutionary struggle of the multi-national Baku proletariat, soon revised his political views, left the Dashnak party, and joined forces with the Bolsheviks together with a large number of "left-wing Dashnak" workers. During the period of the Baku Commune the Bolsheviks, with the help of Avis and his companions, extended their influence over the masses who had been led astray by Dashnak propaganda. On August 25, 1918, he, together with S. Shaumian, A. Dzhaparidze, G. Petrov, and V. Polukhin, signed a telegram to Lenin and Sverdlov denouncing the treacherous behavior of the commune's enemies and expressing the conviction that Soviet power would triumph at Baku and that its proletariat of many nations would once more be united with the workers of Soviet Russia.

After the fall of the Baku Commune the "left-wing Dashnak" group ceased to exist, and Nuridzhanian and his friends joined the Bolshevik Party, accepting its ideas without reserve. The Baku Bolshevik organization directed him to the most crucial sectors of underground work. His great gifts as a speaker, propagandist, and organizer, his power to convince and inspire, made him a key member of the organization. By a decision of the Baku committee of the RCP(B) he attended the "Adaliat" Party conference as a delegate, and was later elected secretary of the Baku committee of the RCP(B). His revolutionary activity did not go unnoticed by agents of the Musavatist government, and he was arrested in the fall of 1919. After holding him in jail for six weeks the government expelled him from Azerbaidzhan, and with the approval of the Transcaucasian committee of the RCP(B) he went to Armenia, where he soon became a leader of the Aleksandropol Bolshevik organization. He spared no effort to strengthen Armenian Bolshevik organizations and develop the revolutionary movement. At the September conference of 1919 and the January conference of Bolsheviks he was elected a member of the Party's Armenian committee. He took a major part in setting up the Armenian CP and in the struggle to establish Soviet rule. His name is associated with the resolution adopted by the Aleksandropol Bolsheviks on the subject of the "present situation," which was submitted to the January conference and published as one of its major documents in the Baku newspaper *Novyi mir* (New World): it played an important part in the establishment of Soviet rule in Armenia by means of an armed uprising. Nuridzhanian was in fact the author of this resolution....

In July-August 1920, together with A. M. Nazaretian, he represented the Armenian CP at the Second Comintern Congress, with the right of casting a vote. He presented to that congress a report on "Communism in Armenia," which was published some months later in Petrograd in a collection of reports delivered to the congress. [Nuridzhanian's report] summarized the course of the revolutionary movement in Armenia, described the Party's organizational work there, and expressed the hope that the Executive Committee of the Comintern would take measures to put a stop to the arbitrary treatment of the working masses by the Dashnak regime. In September of the same year he took part in the conference of Armenian Communist organizations, and in the congress of Eastern peoples at which he was elected to the propaganda council together with S. M. Kirov, G. K. Ordzhonikidze, E. D. Stasova, and others. He took an active part in the council's work and in publishing its organ *Krasnyi Vostok* (The Red East), while remaining a member of the CC of the Armenian CP, of which he became secretary in November [1920]. His prestige among the workers was great, as were his services to the people. He was also a member of the Armenian revolutionary committee, along with Sarkis Kas'ian, Aleksandr Vekzadin, Isaak Dovlatian, Askanaz Mravian, and Saak Ter Gabrielian....

In 1921, at the time of the Dashnaks' February adventure, he took part in directing the operations of the Red Army. After the defeat of the Dashnaks he devoted himself entirely to peaceful economic work. In September 1921 he went to Petrograd to study. In 1923-26 he was head of the organization department of the Volodarsky raion committee of the city of Leningrad, and in 1926-30 of the press department of the Party organization of the Riazan' gubernia. In 1930 he returned to Transcaucasia and devoted himself to the socialist reconstruction of the countryside, as chairman of the Council of Collective Farms.

Nuridzhanian was an energetic and honest worker, a man of principle and a firm devotee of the unshakable international friendship between the peoples of Transcaucasia and the whole Soviet Union. Both his practical activities and his literary output, modest as it was, bear witness to this. He also did much to develop the Armenian Bolshevik press, helping to found the newspapers *Golos krest'ianina* (The Peasants' Voice), and the *Kommunist* and *Izvestiia* of the CC of the Armenian CP. He wrote several articles for newspapers and journals, pointing out and illuminating the main problems of organizational and political work confronting the Armenian CP. He attended the Eleventh, Twelfth, and Thirteenth CPSU congresses and was many times elected to leading Party and government posts. His life, cut short in 1937, was a shining example of devoted service to the Communist cause.[43]

SADYK NURPEISOV

Biographical data

Born 1904, died 1938. In 1925 he was head of the organization department of the Kazakh regional committee of the Komsomol, first secretary of the same committee, a member of the Kazakh regional committee of the CPSU, and a member of the Kazakh CEC. After completing a course in Marxism-Leninism under the CC of the CPSU he became first secretary of the Merke raion committee, then secretary of the Karaganda oblast committee of the Party. In 1934-38 he was second secretary of the CC of the Kazakhstan CP. In 1937-38 he was deputy to the Supreme Soviet of the U.S.S.R., and in 1938 chairman of the credentials committee of the Council of Nationalities of the Supreme Soviet of the U.S.S.R. In 1938 he became a victim of the cult of Stalin's personality.[44]

The Party's pupil

Sadyk Nurpeisov was born in a Kirgiz village, the son of a poor peasant. His early childhood was a cheerless one, sunk in ignorance and poverty. But his family set a high value on learning, and when his elder brothers began to earn their living as farm hands they were able to send little Sadyk to school, first in the village and then to a Russo-Kirgiz establishment. When the Revolution came, literate people were needed, and he began to work as secretary of the village soviet. But brave fighters were needed too: the Whites and imperialists thirsted to put out the torch of October and stifle Soviet power. Sadyk could not bear to remain a secretary: he exchanged his pen for a rifle and enlisted in a Red Army detachment. His resolve to become a Komsomol was strengthened in battle, and on returning home he organized the first Komsomol cells. Two years later he became a candidate member of the CP, while remaining in close touch with the Komsomol. He worked at Kustanai as deputy secretary of the uezd committee, and was head of the organization department of the Komsomol gubernia committee. Later he became chief secretary of the organization bureau of the Kirgiz oblast committee of the Komsomol, with responsibility for the youth organizations of the Syr-Daria, Dzhetisui, and Kara-Kalpak oblasts. This was the period of the delimitation of Central Asia into national political units, and Sadyk did much work explaining the necessity of this to the population and at the same time ruthlessly denounced the national-deviationists and chauvinists who endeavored to distort the problems and goals of the measure.

In 1925 he became responsible for the organization department of the Kazakh regional committee of the Komsomol, which dealt with the selection, training, and placement of Komsomol leaders and in which his organizing talent became especially evident. Soon he was elected first secretary of the Kazakh regional committee of the Komsomol, which post he held for two years. He was also a member of the Kazakh regional committee the Fifteenth Congress of the CPSU. Under his direction the local Komsomol organization fought fiercely against the Trotsky Zinovievite opposition, right-wing opportunists, and national deviationists. All his tireless energy was devoted to educating the youth of many nationalities in the spirit of proletarian internationalism.

His name is associated with the Komsomol campaign on the cultural front, especially in eradicating illiteracy. He spent many years among young people in villages and settlements. The creation of soviets, the division of ploughing and pasture land, the confiscation of livestock from the semi-feudal beys—all this called for wise leadership and great energy on the part of the Komsomol chief. Then came the toil involved in fresh constructions: the Turkestan-Siberia railroad, nonferrous metallurgical plants and the oil industry. The creators of this new world had no source of experience to turn to; they acquired it as they went along, in the hurly-burly of everyday work. But the road into the future was lit by the brightness of Marxist-Leninist teachings.

To complete his theoretical knowledge, Nurpeisov attended Marxist-Leninist courses under the CC of the CPSU, after which the Party again assigned him to important posts. He was first secretary of the Merke raion committee, then secretary of the Karaganda oblast committee of the Party. For the last four years of his life he was second secretary of the CC of the Kazakh CP. During this time he was elected a delegate to the Seventeenth CPSU Congress and the eighth all-Union congress of soviets, also a member of the CEC of the U.S.S.R. and a deputy to the Supreme Soviet of the U.S.S.R. at its first convocation. At the first session of this body, in January 1938, he was elected chairman of the credentials committee of the Council of Nationalities. In his report to that committee he said: "By sending its deputies to the supreme organ of state power, the Soviet people has shown high confidence in us, its elected representatives. But we must never forget that the deputy's duty is one of selfless devotion to his people and to Lenin's great cause."

In the CC of the Kazakhstan CP he dealt with questions of Party and state construction and the selection and promotion of cadres. He was in charge of the checking and renewal of Party credentials at a time that brought to light the presence in the Party of various unworthy elements which had entered it by stealth: former White Guardists, beys, kulaks, and members of the Alash-orda.... When his candidacy as a deputy to the Supreme Soviet of the U.S.S.R. was put forward in November 1937, *Kazakhstanskaia pravda* wrote: "Comrade Nurpeisov has spent his entire adult life in the ranks of the Komsomol and the Party. One of the finest sons of the Kazakh people, he has devoted and continues to devote all his strength and energy to his motherland. Risen from the common people, hardened in the class struggle with the counterrevolutionary Alash-orda and nationalists of all shades.... Comrade Nurpeisov has become the foremost leader of the Bolsheviks of Kazakhstan."

Only a year later he became a victim of arbitrary rule and unjust repression, and perished at the height of his strength and talents. But his good name has been restored. All who knew him well feel a special gratitude to the CC of the Party, which has restored Leninist norms of Party and state life.[45]

AGA GUSEIN RASULZADE

Biographical data

Born 1884, died 19—. Joined the CP in 1903. Member of the Baku soviet in 1917. In 1918, assigned by the Party to organize soviets in Dagestan; after the temporary overthrow of Soviet power at Baku he worked in the underground. In 1919 he was chairman of the workers' conference of the Balakhany-Sabuchin raion. In 1918-19 he took an active part in publishing *Izvestiia*, the organ of the soviet of workers', soldiers' and sailors' deputies of the Baku raion; was a member of the editorial board of the newspaper *Khurriiat* (Freedom); worked on the staff of the legal satirical journal *Mashal* (Torch) and of *Azerbaidzhan fugarasi* (The Azerbaidzhan Poor); also organized underground Party organizations at Giandzha. In 1920 he carried on propaganda and organizational work at Balakhany. After the establishment of Soviet rule in Azerbaidzhan he was a member of the revolutionary committee of the Balakhany-Sabuchin raion and edited the newspaper *Kyzyl Giandzha* (Red Giandzha). In 1921 he was commander of the militia of the Baku uezd, and member of the central control commission of the CC of the Azerbaidzhan CP. He was a victim of the cult of Stalin's personality.[46]

A true son of the Party

Aga Gusein Ali-ogly Rasulzade lived a life devoted to the revolutionary struggle and to serving the Party and the working people. He was born in November 1884 in the Balakhana settlement, Baku uezd. At ten years of age he attended the village religious school, and at sixteen he became assistant to a maker of boring implements. Such was the way in which workers' children began their careers. In 1903 he joined the RSDWP, and to the last day of his life he remained steadfastly faithful to Lenin's Bolshevik banner. He took part in the first political demonstration at Baku, on May 1, 1902.... Together with G. Sultanov, M. Mamed'iarov, and S. Iakubov he founded the "Balakhany circle" whose members studied and distributed the newspaper *Tekamiul*

(Development) and worked among Moslem youth. He was a revolutionary publicist and an active propagandist of the important works of M. A. Sabir, D. Mamedguluzade, A. Akhverdiev, A. Gamgusar, and others. These helped him to carry on the fight against Tsarism, religious fanaticism, ignorance, and social injustice. Many of his articles appeared in 1907-12 in the newspaper *Baky khaiaty* (Baku Life), on which he worked with D. Buniatzade and G. Sultanov. In addition, in 1911 he wrote and had published his first book, *Nogsanlarmyz* (Our Defects), which cannot be read without emotion. It is amazing how this simple, self-taught worker describes profoundly and in an admirable literary style the situation of the workers and toilers, how he calls on peasants and women to fight against the old world with steadfast determination.

Rasulzade occupies a worthy place among those who fought actively for the victory of Soviet power in Azerbaidzhan. He was absolutely devoted to the cause of proletarian revolution and was a straightforward, upright, sensitive and sympathetic person. The workers loved and admired him. After the February revolution of 1917 he was for the first time elected a member of the Baku soviet, and in a short time showed himself to be a gifted organizer. In February 1918 the Party sent him, together with Kazi Magomed Agasiev and Gaidar Ali Tagizade, to Dagestan to organize soviets there. After the temporary overthrow of Soviet power at Baku in 1918 he went underground and did much Party work among Baku workers in the difficult conditions of the counterrevolutionary Musavat regime. In April 1919 he was elected chairman of the Workers' Conference of the Balakhany-Sabuchin raion. In 1918-19, together with R. Akhundov, Kh. Zeinally, and A. I. Mikoyan, he took an active part in producing *Izvestiia*, the organ of the Baku raion soviet of workers', soldiers', and sailors' deputies. He was also a member of the editorial board of the legal newspaper *Khurriiat* and worked on the legal satirical journal *Mashal* and on *Azerbaidzhan fugarasy*. In June 1919 he was often to be seen at workers' and youth meetings in Balakhany. A fiery speaker, he denounced the anti-national policy of the Musavatist government, the Dashnaks and Mensheviks, calling upon the toilers to unite under the international banner of Lenin's Party.

In 1918-19 the Baku Party organization gave much assistance to the uezd Party organizations of Azerbaidzhan. In the same year the Baku committee [sic] ordered Rasulzade and other Bolsheviks to Giandzha, where he coordinated the work of underground Party organizations and saw to it that the poor peasants were represented on them. When he became a member of the Union of Old Bolsheviks, S. M. Efendiev had this to say of him: "I know Rasulzade as a fighter against the Musavat party and as an active Party member who has worked hard to set up Soviet power."

He was a delegate to the first congress of the Azerbaidzhan CP in February 1920, and before and after that time he carried on propaganda and organizing work at Balakhany. After the establishment of Soviet rule in Azerbaidzhan he was a member of the revolutionary committee of the Balakhany-Sabuchin raion and took part in suppressing the counterrevolutionary revolt at Giandzha in May 1920. After this he remained at Giandzha doing Party work and editing the newspaper *Kyzyl Giandzha*. In 1921, by a decision of the CC of the Azerbaidzhan CP, he moved to Baku and occupied several important posts there: he was commander of the militia of the Baku uezd, was elected chairman of the Shusha uezd executive committee and a member of the central control commission of the CC of the Azerbaidzhan CP. In all these posts he justified the Party's confidence.

He was an active fighter for the international education of the Transcaucasian peoples. At the fifth congress of soviets of the Transcaucasian SFSR he was elected to the Transcaucasian CEC. He edited numerous papers: *Akinchi* (The Raider), *Put' rabfakovtsev* (The Road Ahead for Worker-Students, *Eni iol* (The New Way), *Kyzyl asker* (The Red Soldier), etc. Describing his literary and journalistic activity, he wrote: "At the same time I continued the literary work I had begun in 1907, writing for many papers in the Azerbaidzhani language." He was a worker of the Leninist type, a true Leninist, ruthless toward enemies of the Party and people. But like many others, he became a victim of arbitrary rule during the cult of personality. The Azerbaidzhan people honor the memory of this true son of the CP.[47]

TURAR RYSKULOV

Biographical data

Born 1894, died 1937. Joined the CP in 1917. In 1918 he was chairman of the soviet of the Aulie-Ata (Dzhambul) uezd, a member of the Turkestan CEC, and PC of health of the Turkestan ASSR. In 1919-20, deputy chairman of the Turkestan CEC, chairman of the Extraordinary Anti-Famine Commission, and member of the extraordinary commission for the suppression of the Basmachi movement. In 1920, chairman of the Turkestan CEC. In 1921-22, member of the collegium and later second deputy PC of nationalities affairs of the RSFSR. In 1923-24, chairman of the CPC of the Turkestan ASSR, member of the Central Asian Bureau of the CC of the RCP(B), and member of the bureau of the CC of the Turkestan CP. In 1925, Comintern representative in Mongolia. From 1926 to 1937, head of the press department of the Caucasian Regional Commission of the RCP(B) and at the same time chief editor of the Kazakh regional newspaper *Enbekshi-Kazakh* and deputy chairman of the CPC of the RSFSR. In 1937 he became a victim of arbitrary rule and the cult of personality.[48]

Ryskulov's career

It is now seventy years since the birth of Turar Ryskulov, one of the generation of young revolutionaries who took up the struggle in the historic days of the October Revolution. His life and manifold activities during the fight to establish and consolidate Soviet rule, the years of civil war and socialist construction, are closely bound up with the history of the CPs of Turkestan and Kazakhstan, two militant detachments of the CPSU.

Ryskulov began his revolutionary career by taking part in the national liberation movement of the peoples of Central Asia and Kazakhstan in 1916, for which he was arrested and thrown into jail by Tsarist authorities. He welcomed with joy the overthrow of Tsarism in February 1917, but soon realized that this had not yet brought the people freedom and a better life. The bourgeois Provisional Government which had replaced the Tsar continued the old policy of national oppression. Ryskulov supported the Bolsheviks' fight against the Provisional Government and was again arrested. In the spring of 1917, together with the Russian revolutionary N. Chernishev, he organized at Merke the "Revolutionary Union of Kirgiz Youth," which took an active part in the work of the local soviet. Ryskulov belonged to that part of the Kazakh national-democratic intelligentsia which, during the period of preparation for socialist revolution, took the side of the working class and its vanguard, the CP. He joined the Party in September 1917 and fought actively to establish Soviet rule in the Aulie-Ata uezd, being elected to Party and soviet organs. In 1918 he was chairman of the Aulie-Ata uezd soviet. At the first congress of soviets of the Turkestan Republic he was elected a member of the CEC and PC of health of the Turkestan ASSR. In 1919-20 he was deputy chairman of the Turkestan CEC, chairman of the Extraordinary Anti-Famine Commission, and a member of the extraordinary commission for the suppression of the Basmachi. He was also active in Party organizations as a member of the Presidium of the RCP(B). At the beginning of 1920 he was elected chairman of the Turk-estan CEC. Thus in a short time he had risen from the ranks of the Party to one of the top posts of the republic. He showed himself an outstanding organizer in various sectors of Party and state activity.

It must be noted that in his practical and theoretical activity in the 1920s he committed serious mistakes of a nationalistic character, which did much harm to the international education of the workers. He pressed for the transformation of the Turkestan CP into a "Turkic CP" and for the creation of a Turkic republic uniting all peoples of Turkic speech in Central Asia and Kazakhstan. This was in contradiction to Lenin's principles of international Party structure. Today, the rabble of pan-Turkism and pan-Islamism seek to exploit these mistakes of his for their own sordid ends, falsifying the history of the peoples of Central Asia and Kazakhstan. But these foreign counterfeiters suppress the fact that the Party highly valued Ryskulov's services to the revolution—his intelligence, willpower, energy, and experience—and helped him to correct his errors. These were subjected to sharp criticism and condemned by the Party organizations of Turkestan and Kazakhstan. His plan for the Party and state organization in Turkestan was rejected by the CC of the RCP(B) and by Lenin himself. Recognizing his mistakes, he later wrote an article entitled "Against the Distortion of the History of the Kazakh People," in which he said:

> A group of Party members, headed by myself, which had pursued the Bolshevik line and helped at the beginning of the revolution to weld the indigenous working population in support of Soviet power, committed several grave errors in 1920-21. Having overcome the so-called "colonial deviation" and being in control of the Turkestan Republic (I was then the chairman of the CEC), we were led astray by nationalist slogans, wished to be "national leaders," underrated international problems, strove to introduce our own national officials into the apparatus of public life, and so on. During the past fifteen years the Party has sufficiently tested me and I have not once diverged from the Party line. My mistakes of 1920-21 have taught me to be a staunch Bolshevik in day-to-day work, and I hope I shall never deviate from this course.

The Party CC and Lenin himself did everything possible to help the creation and development of the Party organization of Turkestan and Dazakhstan, to see that the Party's nationalities program was implemented and to strengthen friendship and brotherly solidarity between the peoples of the Soviet East and the great Russian people. This is shown by Lenin's directions and letters to the Communists of Turkestan and Kazakhstan and the creation of the Turkestan commission of the All-Russian CEC and the CPC of the RSFSR. Lenin and the CC took all possible steps to raise the economic and cultural level and to redress the unequal treatment of the formerly oppressed peoples of the Soviet East. In subjecting to honest Party criticism the serious errors of Ryshkulov and others concerning the nationalities question, Lenin and the CC showed patience and the utmost concern in training national Marxist cadres, and helping them to correct mistakes, to perfect their Marxist training and achieve political maturity. Ryskulov was highly thought of by M. Frunze and V. Kuibyshev, who knew their colleague's merits as well as his shortcomings. Kuibyshev, for example, in a letter of August 9, 1920, to E. D. Stasova, the secretary of the CC of the RCP(B), mentioned [Ryskulov's] mistakes but described him as a "person out of the ordinary, who may develop in Moscow into an outstanding Communist."

By a decision of 1921 of the CC of the RCP(B), Ryskulov was recalled to Moscow and became a member of the collegium of the PC of nationalities affairs of the RSFSR; shortly afterward, he became second deputy PC. This was a striking example of Lenin's policy of educating leading national Party cadres. In 1923-24 he was chairman of the CPC of the Turkestan ASSR and was elected a member of the Central Asian bureau of the CC of the RCP(B) and of the bureau of the CC of the Turkestan CP. In April 1923 he was a delegate to the Twelfth Congress of the RCP(B). In his speech at that congress he stated that in connection with the introduction of the New Economic Policy certain feudal elements of the beys' regime had raised their heads and would have to be firmly combated. At that congress also he was elected a candidate member of the CC of the RCP(B).

Lenin's death was a great blow to Ryskulov. A few days after Lenin died, *Pravda* published on its front page an article by Ryskulov entitled "Lenin—The Banner Uniting Two Worlds." This article, which is still topical today, condemned the theoreticians who preached nationalism and racism and who, to the detriment of proletarian unity, placed two worlds in opposition to each other: the East and the West, Asia [against] Europe, Asians [against] Europeans. He wrote: "I remember a conversation I had with the great man in 1920. I felt like a schoolboy being examined, and of course I could not get all the answers right from the Marxist point of view. But Lenin, though he did not know all about Turkestan, drew the proper conclusions from his knowledge."

After the national demarcation of Central Asia and Kazakhstan, Ryskulov worked as deputy head of the Eastern department of the Comintern. In 1925 he was sent as Comintern representative to Mongolia, where he stayed for about a year, helping our Mongolian friends to advance along non-capitalist lines of development. Chicherin, then PC of foreign affairs, wrote of him at that time that "his political line is in general profoundly right and we should support it." (Letter to Peters dated August 21, 1925.) From March 1926 Ryskulov was head of the Press department of the Caucasian regional commission of the RCP(B), and at the same time chief editor of the Kazakhstan regional newspaper *Enbekshi-Kazakh* (now *Sotsialisticheskii Kazakhstan*). In the same year, by a decision of the CC of the RCP(B), he became deputy chairman of the CPC of the RSFSR, a post which he held for eleven years.

While occupying important posts in the Turkmen Republic, the Kazakh SSR, and the RSFSR, he took an active part in deciding questions of socialist construction of the republics of Central Asia and Kazakhstan. As deputy chairman of the CPC of the RSFSR and head of a special government commission, as described in *Ocherki istorii Kommunisticheskoi partii Kazakhstana* (Outline History of the Kazakhstan CP), he did much in 1926-30 to further the construction of the Turkestan-Siberia railroad and the socialist industrialization of the Kazakh SSR. The Party displayed great confidence in him. He was a delegate to the Twelfth (1923), Fifteenth (1927), Sixteenth (1930), and Seventeenth (1934) congresses of the CPSU and was several times elected a member of the All-Union CEC and the Supreme Soviet of the U.S.S.R. Besides practical work he took an interest in theoretical problems. He lectured at the Communist University of the Eastern Peoples at Moscow and published several books on the national liberation movement in Kazakhstan, the history of the Kazakh press, and the construction of the Turkestan-Siberia railroad.

In 1937, during the cult of personality, he was a victim of arbitrary rule. He was posthumously rehabilitated after the Twentieth Party Congress.[49]

BORIS PETROVICH SHEBOLDAEV

Biographical data

Born 1895, died 1937. Joined the Bolshevik Party in 1914, in which year he was arrested for revolutionary activity. Served on the Turkish front in 1915. In 1917 he was a member of the regional army soviet; in 1918 chairman of the RMC at Staryi Kamyshev, member of the Baku soviet of Bolsheviks, and deputy commander of armed forces of the Baku RMC. In 1920, chairman of the RMC of the Dagestan region and secretary of its Party committee; later, first secretary of the CC of the Tadzhikistan CP, head of the organization section of the CC of the CPSU, and secretary of the Party's Middle Volga committee. In 1930-32, secretary of the Party's North Caucasian regional committee. Was a member of the CC of the CPSU. In 1937 he became a victim of the cult of Stalin's personality.[50]

A bold fighter for the revolution

The name of Boris Petrovich Sheboldaev is written in golden letters in the chronicle of the fight for socialist revolution, for the victory of Soviet power and the building of socialism.

He was born in Paris, the son of a doctor, on May 28, 1895. At the age of sixteen he went with his parents to Stavropol, where he made contact with the Bolshevik organization of social-democrats, and joined the Bolshevik Party in 1914. When the first imperialist war broke out, he carried on active anti-war propaganda among the students and proletariat of Petersburg and was thrown into jail. In March 1915 he was at Sarykamysh on the Turkish front, where he met the well-known revolutionaries P. Dzhaparidze, S. Alaverdin, O. Sarukhanian, A. Ovsenian, and F. Solntsev, and became one of the principal Bolsheviks active on the Caucasian front.

The news of the victory of the October Revolution in Petersburg was received with joy and enthusiam by the 30,000-strong garrison of Sarykamysh. The soldiers, led by Sheboldaev and his comrades, showed their willingness to defend the proletariat's conquests with their lives. In 1917 Sheboldaev took part in the second congress of the Caucasian regional soviet of the army and was elected a member of that soviet. Here he met Lenin's wartime counselor Shaumian, who headed the Bolshevik group at the congress.

In January 1918 an RMC was set up at Sarykamysh under the guidance of the revolutionary soviet elected by the second congress. Sheboldaev was the chairman of this body, which included among its members the stalwart Bolsheviks Alaverdin, Solntsev, I. Kiasev, and S. Petrenko. The RMC took power into its hands and proclaimed Soviet rule. For the next six weeks

Sarykamysh flew the Red flag in imitation of the Petrograd garrison. But it was cut off from the proletarian centers of Russia and Transcaucasia and could not withstand the superior counterrevolutionary and German-Turkish forces. In 1918 Sheboldaev, G. Korganov, and other Bolsheviks joined the troops at Baku, where with the help of the fearless Baku proletariat leaders Shaumian, Dzhaparidze, V. Fioletov, and M. Azizbekov they carried on an active struggle for the victory of Soviet power in Baku and the whole of Transcaucasia. On Shaumian's proposal, Sheboldaev was elected a member of the Baku Bolshevik committee, and in March 1918 he was appointed deputy to Korganov, commander of armed forces of the Baku RMC. He showed heroism in the fight against counterrevolution: Shaumian speaks of him as a brave Party and war leader.

In 1920, after the defeat of counterrevolution and the consolidation of Soviet power, he was appointed chairman of the RMC of the Dagestan region and secretary of its Party committee. Later, after attending senior courses of Marxism-Leninism, he was first secretary of the CC of the Tadzhikistan CP, head of the Organization section of the CC of the CPSU, and secretary of the Party's Middle Volga oblast committee. In 1930-32 he was secretary of the Party's North Caucasian regional committee. He was elected a delegate to the Fourteenth through the Seventeenth congresses of the CPSU and a member of its CC. An honest and devoted Bolshevik, he was cut off at the height of his creative powers in 1937, a victim of arbitrary rule during the cult of personality.[51]

NIKOLAI ALEKSEEVICH SKRIPNIK

Biographical data

Born 1872, died 1933. Joined the Bolshevik Party in 1897. Born at Sloboda Iasinovataia, Ekaterinoslav gubernia (now Iasinovata, Donetsk oblast), the son of a minor railroad official. Educated at two-class village school at Barvenkovo and then at the Iz'ium technical high school, Kharkov gubernia, where he began revolutionary activity. Joined the RSDWP in 1897. In 1900 he entered the Petersburg Technological Institute and took part in the work of the Petersburg committee of the social-democratic organization Rabochee Znamia (The Workers' Banner). Arrested in 1901 for taking part in a demonstration in March on Kazan Square, and exiled to Ekaterinoslav, where he took part in the work of the local committee of the RSDWP. Shortly thereafter he returned to Petersburg, where he joined the *Iskra* organization and carried on propaganda among Marxist groups beyond the Neva Gate and in the Petrograd quarter. Arrested early in 1902 for planning demonstrations, he was sentenced to five years' exile in Yakutia, but escaped on the way there. He did much work at Tsaritsyn and later Saratov to rally Social Democrats around Lenin's paper *Iskra*. Pursued by the authorities, he moved to Samara and made contact with *Iskra* adherents there. In the first half of 1903 he carried on revolutionary work at Ekaterinoslav; in the fall, again pursued by the police, he moved to Odessa where he organized Party groups in the Moldavanka-Kamennolomnia and Peresyp districts and the port area. In January 1904 he returned to Ekaterinoslav, where he took an active part in the work of the local committee of the RSDWP and bitterly fought the Mensheviks. He was arrested again and sentenced to be deported to the Arkhangelsk gubernia, but escaped on the way and returned to Odessa. He was Odessa delegate to the Third Party Congress (1905), after which he worked as secretary to the Petersburg committee. In October 1905 the CC of the RSDWP sent him to Riga to assess the readiness of local Bolsheviks for an armed uprising. He addressed a meeting of armed workers at Riga on the tactics of street fighting. Pursued by the police he moved to Yaroslavl, where he was again arrested and sentenced to five years in the Turukhan region. Escaped from his place of exile and in October 1907 carried on propaganda work in Petersburg, organizing the second city raion. Was member of the governing body of the "Trudovik" cooperative; edited a trade union journal and was a delegate to legal all-Russian cooperative congresses. Soon he was again arrested and deported without trial to the Viliuisk uezd of Yakutia, whence he escaped to Petersburg in 1913. From the end of 1913 he edited a legal Bolshevik organ, the journal *Voprosy strakhovaniia* (Insurance Questions). Was a member of the editorial board of *Pravda*. Arrested and sentenced to five years at Morshansk (Tambov gubernia). Returned to Petrograd in June 1917. On the orders of the CC of the RSDWP(B) he worked in the Central Union of Factory and Works Committees, which he represented at the first and second convocations of the All-Russian CEC. The Petrograd organization appointed him a delegate to the Sixth Party Congress, at which he was elected a candidate member of the CC of the RSDWP(B).

During the fighting against Kornilov he was a member of the Petersburg defense committee and organized the distribution of arms to workers. Took an active part in the October Revolution. Was a member of the Petrograd RMC. After the victory of the revolution in Petrograd, in December 1917 Skripnik was sent to the Ukraine on Lenin's proposal as representative of the Party CC, and there became people's secretary of labor. On March 4, 1918, the CEC of the Ukraine SSR appointed him chairman of the Soviet government of the Ukraine. Took an active part in the formation of the Ukraine CP. After the Taganrog Party conference he headed the organization bureau for the convocation of the first congress of the Ukraine CP; at the congress he was elected a candidate member of the CC of the Ukraine CP, and from December 1918 he was a full member.

He took an active part in the Civil War. In 1918 he was a member of the collegium of the All-Russian Cheka, in charge of the department for combating counterrevolution. At the beginning of 1919 he was appointed PC of state control of the Ukraine SSR. In summer 1919 he organized the defeat of the

Zelenyi band and carried on political work in the Red Army, being commander of the political department of the Gomel fortified zone and later commander of the Special Section of the Caucasian front. In April 1920 he returned to the Ukraine, where he became people's secretary of workers' and peasants' inspection.

In 1921 Skripnik was PC of internal affairs of the Ukrainian SSR, in 1922-27 PC of justice and procurator-general, and in 1927-33 PC of education. From February 1933 he was deputy chairman of the CPC and chairman of Gosplan, of the Ukraine SSR. He was a delegate to the Eleventh through the Sixteenth congresses. At the Twelfth and Fourteenth congresses he was elected a candidate member, and at the Fifteenth and Sixteenth a full member of the CC of the CPSU. He was a delegate from the fifth to eighth conferences and the ninth to eleventh congresses of the Ukraine CP. From 1920 to 1933 he was a member of the CC of the Ukraine CP; during 1923-25 he was a candidate member, and in 1925-33 a full member, of the politburo of the CC of the Ukraine CP. He took an active part in the work of the Comintern, and was a delegate from its First through its Sixth congresses. At the Sixth Congress in 1928 he was elected a member of the Executive Committee of the Third International. He was active in the fight against "left-wing Communists," Trotskyists, right-wing opportunists, nationalists, and other anti-Leninist groups. In his work as PC of education of the Ukraine he committed errors in the field of national cultural development.

He received the Order of the Red Banner in 1922 for bravery in the Civil War, and in 1928 the Order of the Red Banner of Labor of the Ukraine for his services to socialist construction. He published about 270 papers on scientific and cultural subjects, especially Party history, the national question, art, and literature. For his outstanding services to the development of Soviet learning he was elected a member of the Communist Academy of the U.S.S.R., and to the Academy of Sciences of the Ukraine SSR and that of the Belorussian SSR. He was an inspiring orator and publicist.

In 1933, during the influence of the cult of Stalin's personality, Skripnik was falsely accused of nationalism. Deeply grieved by this injustice, he committed suicide in a moment of despair on July 7, 1933. He was buried at Kharkov. After the Twentieth and Twenty-second congresses of the CPSU, which condemned the cult of Stalin's personality, the grave and unfounded charges against Skripnik were annulled and the good name of this true son of the Party was restored.[52]

GRIGORII IVANOVICH STARYI (BORISOV)

Born 1880, died 1937. Joined the Bolshevik Party in 1900. A Moldavian, born at Bozieni village, Kishenev uezd. Carried on revolutionary activity and in 1910 was deported to Bendery and there called up for army service. During the February and October revolutions of 1917 he was a member of military committees, and at the end of 1917 he joined the Army committee as a representative of the Communists. In 1918 he helped to organize resistance to the interventionists in Bessarabia, where he directed a partisan movement. In 1918, at the trial of the "108," he received a death sentence in absentia from a court-martial of the Third Rumanian Army Corps. On the left bank of the Dniester he took part in the formation of the Forty-fifth Division and commanded its Special Section; then was recalled from the army to work behind Denikin's lines and to organize the Communist underground in Bessarabia. Was a member of the Provisional Soviet Government of Bessarabia. In 1920-21, chairman of the Tiraspol uezd Party committee; in 1924, chairman of the CEC of the Moldavian ASSR. In 1926-37, except for a short period, he was chairman of the CPC of the Moldavian ASSR. In 1937 he became a victim of the cult of Stalin's personality.[53]

A fighter for the triumph of Lenin's ideals

It is eighty-five years today since the birth of that professional revolutionary and true Leninist, the former chairman of the Moldavian ASSR Grigorii Ivanovich Staryi (Borisov).

Just sixty years ago, on December 9, 1905, the young Grigorii lay in the prisoners' car of a Tsarist train, where he had been thrown by gendarmes who had beaten him half-dead for his part in leading a twenty-three-day strike of Golubov miners in the Donbass. His head ached and his wounds burned savagely.... Yet on December 17, 1905, he [joined] other progressive Donbass workers to clash with Cossacks on the barricades at Gorlovka. Once more he was arrested, beaten, and thrown into jail. When released he went on with the revolutionary struggle, and again he was imprisoned. In 1908 he was sentenced to three years' detention in a fortress. Cut off from the world, he devoted himself to studies in preparation for the fights to come.

* * *

Staryi was a Moldavian, born at Bozieni village, Kishenev uezd, the son of a railroad worker. He began his revolutionary career while working as a carpenter at the main Kiev railroad workshops. Here, in 1900, he joined the RSDWP. He carried out many assignments for the Party's Southern bureau at Rostov, Nikolaev, Kremenchug, Mariupol, and in the Donbass, and was often harried by the Tsarist police for his part in organizing political strikes in the Ukraine. In 1910 he was transported to Bendery under special police supervision, but there too he continued his revolutionary activity. When called up for army service he carried on anti-war propaganda among the troops on the southwestern front.... At the time of the February and October revolutions he was elected to military committees, and at the end of 1917 he joined the Army committee as a representative of the Communists. At the beginning of January 1918 he arrived at Bendery, where there were important railroad workshops and depots.

The victory of the socialist revolution in Russia provoked fierce resistance on the part of [the forces of] internal counterrevolution and of international imperialism, which unleashed a Civil War in the hope of overthrowing Soviet power. One of the first moves of the rapacious imperialist states was the military invasion of Bessarabia in January 1918. The working masses rose up to fight the invader. The railroad workers played a big part, and one of those who organized their resistance was G. I. Staryi. The Party's orders were to organize a Communist underground and a widespread partisan movement in the occupied areas. In the summer of 1918 Staryi and I. D'iachishin came to Moscow and received directives from the CC of the RCP(B) for the intensification of this work.... The CC attached great importance to revolutionary propaganda among the interventionist troops. The Communist underground workers of the Dniester area, in liaison with the Odessa oblast committee of the Ukrainian CP, did highly successful work in undermining the invader's forces. Most of the agitators they selected knew foreign languages, and they printed and distributed leaflets. At Staryi's suggestion a phrasebook was prepared in several languages which helped the agitators in their work. He spent a year and a half in the underground, but had to leave Bendery after the uprising there in May 1919. At the trial of the "108" a court-martial of the Third Rumanian Army Corps condemned him, in absentia, to death. On the left bank of the Dniester he took part in the formation of the Forty-fifth Division and commanded its Special Section. Soon by a decision of the CC of the Ukraine CP, he was recalled from the army to work behind Denikin's lines and organize the Communist underground in Bessarabia. He was a member of the Provisional Soviet Government of Bessarabia and a delegate to the second oblast conference of Bessarabian Bolsheviks, at which he was elected to the oblast committee.

In 1920-21 he was elected chairman of the Tiraspol uezd Party committee and devoted much strength and energy to peaceful socialist construction and the training of Party and government cadres. By 1924 definite progress had been made in the left-bank Dniester area with the restoration of industry and agriculture and the improvement of cultural standards. Guided by Party directives and expressing the general wish of the Moldavian population, the third session of the All-Ukrainian CEC at its eighth convocation on October 12, 1924, passed a decree establishing the Moldavian ASSR within the Ukrainian SSR. The organizational work necessary to put this decision into practice was carried out by the revolutionary committee of the Moldavian ASSR under G. I. Staryi, who had the honor of opening the first all-Moldavian congress of soviets which adopted the Constitution of the Moldavian Republic. He was also elected the first chairman of the republic's CEC, and from 1926 to 1937, with a short interruption, acted as chairman of its CPC. He was a delegate to the Fifth Comintern Congress, the Seventeenth CPSU Congress, the tenth through the twelfth congresses of the Ukraine CP, and the third all-Ukrainian conference of the Ukraine CP. He was a member of the CEC of the U.S.S.R. and of the Ukrainian SSR, and a member of the presidium of the Council of Nationalities. At the eighth extraordinary congress of soviets he was elected to the commission which drafted the Constitution of the U.S.S.R.

As chairman of the CPC of the Moldavian ASSR, he took an active part in the fight for socialist construction of the republic's Party organization. He was noted for his friendly contacts with the workers. He was to be seen at the sites of new enterprises, on collective farms, in schools and hospitals, skillfully organizing the masses to fulfill the complicated tasks of socialist reconstruction of industry and agriculture. During the First and Second Five Year Plans, thanks to the enthusiasm of the workers and the unselfish help of the fraternal Russian, Ukrainian, and other peoples of the U.S.S.R., the Moldavian ASSR developed a food and building industry and created cadres of workers and a technical intelligentsia. The socialist system became universal in agriculture and new methods were introduced into the villages. The Party and soviet organs of the republic devoted much attention to land improvement and reclamation. Staryi was active in organizing the work of strengthenting the Dniester's banks and creating the Karagash and Malovat irrigation systems.

In his care for the republic's development and in accordance with the Party's wishes, he did much to raise the cultural level of the working masses. In 1935 he received the Order of Lenin. Grigorii Ivanovich Petrovsky once wrote of him: "Staryi was beloved by the people"—high praise that was well deserved.

A high-principled Communist, an outstanding propagandist and organizer taught in the hard school of the Bolshevik underground, Staryi devoted twenty years of his life to the prosperity of Soviet Moldavia. These were years of strenuous work for the triumph of Lenin's ideals, the reunion of the whole Moldavian people with the Soviet motherland, and the victory of socialism.[54]

GAMID SULTANOV

Biographical data

Born 1889, died 1938. Joined the Bolshevik Party in 1907. Born in the settlement of Shinykh, Kazakh uezd, the son of a peasant. In 1907 he did Party work in Baku. Arrested in 1908; after his release emigrated to Germany and graduated from the Leipzig Polytechnical Institute. Returned to Baku in 1913 and resumed revolutionary work. In 1917, on the Party's orders, he organized the peasants to fight counterrevolution and was a leader of the Baku

Gummet organization. In 1918, after the temporary overthrow of Soviet rule in Azerbaidzhan, he worked at Astrakhan; was chairman of the Moslem section of the RCP(B) in the Astrakhan gubernia, member of the presidium of the Astrakhan gubernia committee of the RCP(B) and of the presidium of the gubernia executive committee, and head of the land department of the executive committee. In 1919 he did underground Party work in Azerbaidzhan and was a member of the Caucasian regional committee of the RCP(B). In 1920, member of the CC of the Azerbaidzhan CP. During 1920-38 he served as PC of industry and trade of the Azerbaidzhan SSR, chairman of the republic's supreme council of national economy, chairman of the CPC of the Nakhichevan ASSR, deputy PC of trade of the Transcaucasian Federation, and secretary of the CEC of the Transcaucasian SFSR. In 1938 he became a victim to the cult of Stalin's personality.[55]

A glorious son of Lenin's Party

In the spring of the unforgettable year 1920 ... on April 26, a special joint session of the CC of the Azerbaidzhan CP and the Baku bureau of the [Caucasian] regional committee of the RCP(B) resolved on a plan for the overthrow of the counterrevolutionary Musavatist government. At this time the troops of the glorious Eleventh Red Army, having defeated the remnants of Denikin's bands, stood on the northern border of Azerbaidzhan. Conditions were at last favorable for an armed uprising. The Musavatist government appraised the situation in an atmosphere of confusion, panic, and fear of the people's wrath. The war minister, asked whether he could cope with the Bolsheviks, could only answer helplessly, "No." Parliament, hastily summoned, met early one morning but found nothing to debate: the terrified "statesmen" had lost their heads.... Shortly after the session opened, a Communist delegation headed by Gamid Sultanov and representing the CC of the Azerbaidzhan CP, the Baku bureau of the Caucasian regional committee of the RCP(B), and the Central Workers' Conference presented to the Musavatist government and parliament an ultimatum demanding that the parliament be dissolved and power entrusted to the Bolsheviks. This was at ten o'clock in the morning on April 27, 1920. The ultimatum had a shattering effect on the assembled politicians. Sultanov later wrote that "the members of parliament were so dumbfounded that for some minutes they could not get a word out. Then, when the chairman read the ultimatum, Agamali-ogly shouted from his seat: "That's enough! The bazaar's closed!"

At the moment when Sultanov presented the ultimatum, on the Party's orders a war flotilla, flying the Red flag and commanded by that true son of the Bolshevik Party Chingiz Il'drym, had moved into the roadstead and trained its guns on the parliament building. Thus, during the night of April 27-28 power passed into the hands of the Provisional Revolutionary Committee headed by N. Narimanov. This body, one of whose members was Gamid Sultanov, appealed by radio for help to Lenin and the Soviet Russian government. The Red Army men, sons of the Russian people, performed their historic mission and helped the workers of Azerbaidzhan to liberate themselves. On the day when Soviet rule was established, Sultanov became PC of internal affairs of the republic....

Gamid Gasan-ogly Sultanov was born on May 26, 1889, in the settlement of Shinykh, Kazakh uezd, the son of a peasant. After attending village school he entered the school in Tiflis in 1902. Here he took part in anti-regime activities with his fellow pupils and was arrested for the first time. In September 1906 he was at Baku, working as a mechanic in the Ramany oilfield. In the early years of the century, Baku, as Lenin noted, had become "a Russian industrial center of the first rank," providing almost all of the country's oil. At the same time it had become a powerful center of the workers' movement. Here, in this crucible of revolution, Sultanov received his training and became a seasoned Bolshevik. He was a leading spirit in strikes and demonstrations and an active member of the Oil Industry Workers' Union. He joined the Party in January 1907, and worked at Baku with such noted Communists as S. Shaumian, N. Narimanov, P. Dzhaparidze, S. Spandarian, M. Azizbekov, I. Fiole, V. Knuniants, V. Efimov (Saratovets), Kazi Magomed, and S. M. Efendiev. Soon he was recognized as a skilled organizer and propagandist for the proletarian cause, loved and respected by the workers and hated by the minions of Tsarism. He was arrested in 1908, and as the police continued to harry him after his release he emigrated to Germany, where he graduated from the Leipzig Polytechnical Institute.

When the new revolutionary storm blew up in Russia, Gamid hastened home. In 1913 he was again at Baku and wholly engaged in revolutionary work. After the February revolution of 1917 he displayed even more fervent energy, and on the Party's orders toured the Baku gubernia, organizing the peasants, and summoning them to fight against counterrevolution, and strengthening Bolshevik organizations. He was well known by the Bolsheviks Sal'ian and Lenkorani, Astary and Kuby, and was prominent in the Baku organization Gummet.

After the temporary overthrow of Soviet power in Azerbaidzhan in August 1918 he moved to Soviet Astrakhan together with many other Bolsheviks, including G. Musabekov, D. Buniatzade, B. Sardarov, V. Naneishvili, A. Korinian, Aina Sultanova, I. Eminbeili, S. Kvantaliani, and I. Vatsek. Under his guidance, Bolshevik cells were created in many villages of the Astrakhan gubernia. He was elected chairman of the Moslem section of the RCP(B) in the gubernia, a member of the presidium of the Astrakhan gubernia committee of the RCP(B), and a member of the presidium of the gubernia executive committee with responsibility for its land department. At the same time he commanded a Communist detachment operating against White Guard bands.

In June 1919 the CC of the RCP(B) assigned Sultanov to underground Party work in Azerbaidzhan together with Buniatzade, Naneishvili, Kvantaliani, and others. They reached Baku with some difficulty—in fishing boats—and Sultanov at once threw himself with enthusiasm into the work of the local organization. As A. I. Mikoyan later wrote: "Toward the end of the summer we were helped by the arrival from Astrakhan, for illegal Party work, of Buniatzade and Sultanov." In September 1919 Sultanov was co-opted onto the Caucasian Red Committee of the RCP(B). At the end of 1919, on the Party's orders, he went to Tiflis, posing as an engineer named Omarov, for the purpose of secretly acquiring supplies and dispatching them to units of the Red Army fighting Denikin's forces in the northern Caucasus, as well as to the Baku Bolsheviks and the Gikalo partisan detachments. He performed this important task with success.

He took an active part in the formation of the Azerbaidzhan CP. At its first congress in February 1920 he became a member of its CC and of the RMC set up on the proposal of the Caucasian regional committee of the RCP(B) to direct the armed uprising.

After the overthrow of the bourgeois landowners' regime and the establishment of Soviet power, the Azerbaidzhan people turned to constructive labor in fraternal comradeship with the other nations of the Soviet Union. In these years, Sultanov's exceptional powers and organizing ability came especially to the fore.... He was several times elected to the CC of the Azerbaidzhan CP and the Transcaucasian Regional Committee of the CPSU, and was also a member of the Azerbaidzhan CEC, the Transcaucasian CEC, and the CEC of the U.S.S.R. Wherever the Party sent him he devoted all his powers to building communism.

His life was cut short at the height of his creative powers. In 1938 he was slandered and became a victim of arbitrary rule during the cult of Stalin's personality. But the Party has restored the good name of this ardent Bolshevik. Today, on the eve of the 150th anniversary of the great day on which Azerbaidzhan became a part of Russia, the workers of our republic do reverent honor to the memory of this true son of Lenin's Party who gave all his strength to affirming the unbreakable friendship between the peoples of our motherland.[56]

SAAK MIRZOEVICH TER-GABRIELIAN

Biographical data

Born 1886, died 19—. Joined the Bolshevik Party in 1902. Born at Shusha, Karabakh Mountain Asia region of the Azerbaidzhan SSR, the son of a tailor. Arrested for revolutionary activity in 1902. Returned to Baku in 1903, and became a leading organizer of the revolutionary movement and the big strike of 1904. For many years, beginning in 1905, he was a member of the Baku

Union of Oil Industry Workers. In 1917 he was a member of the Baku soviet of workers' deputies and commissar of the Baku municipality. In 1918 he was commissar for the Baku telephone system and for the distribution and sale of oil and oil products, also chairman of the Extraordinary Commission (Cheka) for Combating Counterrevolution and Espionage. Was arrested, and after his release went to Astrakhan. In August 1918 he was called to Moscow by the CPC of the RSFSR, and in November became commissar with responsibility for the transport of all forms of fuel. In March 1919 he went to the Donbass to organize the supply of coal, was assistant to the Extraordinary Agent for Red Army Supplies, then head of the Special department of the All-Russian Cheka. In 1920 he was an agent on the Caucasian front, counselor to the RSFSR mission in Armenia, representative of the Caucasian bureau of the CC of the RCP(B) in Armenia, and member of the Armenian revolutionary committee. In 1921-23, plenipotentiary representative of Soviet Armenia in Moscow. In 1923-28, plenipotentiary representative of Soviet Armenia in Moscow. In 1923-28, plenipotentiary representative of the Transcaucasian Federation accredited to the government of the U.S.S.R. In 1928-35, chairman of the Armenian CPC and deputy chairman of the Transcaucasian CPC. He was a victim of the cult of Stalin's personality.[57]

Selfless devotion to the Party

It is eighty years since the birth of Saak Mirzoevich Ter-Gabrielian, a professional revolutionary and an eminent Party worker and Soviet statesman.

He was born, the son of a tailor, at Shusha in what is now the Nagorno-Karabakh region of the Azerbaidzhan SSR. In 1900, when he was fourteen, he was obliged, owing to his father's death, to leave high school and go to work at Baku to support his large and destitute family.... After the Second RSDWP Congress he joined the Bolshevik Party, and remained a true Leninist to the end of his days. Lively, energetic and possessed of a winning manner, he soon enjoyed the love and confidence of the Baku workers. During the years of underground work he was several times elected to the principal Baku Party organs.... In 1907, when mass repressions followed the defeat of the first Russian revolution, he was arrested together with a group of Party workers including V. Kasparov, A. Bekzadian, M. Kasumov, and S. Zhgenti. After eight months in jail he was deported from Transcaucasia. He soon returned to the Baku industrial area, and continued to take an active part in underground revolutionary work.

When the February revolution broke out, Ter-Gabrielian represented the Bolshevik group of the presidium at the first all-Russian conference of soviets of workers' and soldiers' deputies, held at Petrograd. At the same time he took part in the all-Russian conference of Party workers called by the Bureau of the CC of the RSDWP.

His organizing ability was displayed particularly during the period of the

Baku Commune and the later years of civil war in Russia and Transcaucasia. In June 1917 he was elected a delegate to the Transcaucasian congress of soviets of workers' and soldiers' deputies, and was deputy chairman of the congress.... On the instructions of the Party's Baku committee he left with a number of oil tankers for Astrakhan, whence he traveled to Moscow to report to Lenin on the position at Baku and the organization of military aid. Although Soviet Russia was itself in a difficult economic situation, it managed to help the Baku Commune. On Lenin's proposal the government decided to provide money, arms, uniforms, and bread. With the help of military and government authorities, Ter-Gabrielian returned safely with an armored and air detachment and military equipment, as well as a letter from Lenin to S. Shaumian, the chairman of the Baku soviet. In his reply, Shaumian wrote: "Dear Vladimir Il'ich: Today Ter-Gabrielian returned at last and brought us four armored cars, thirteen airplanes, and many other useful things. Many, many thanks to you for all this. We have got what we needed and it will be of tremendous help to us." Ter-Gabrielian himself, reporting on his visit to Lenin, said: "Comrade Lenin ... many times expressed delight with the policy of the Baku soviet and his dear comrade Shaumian. He declared himself ready at all times to support the Baku proletariat both morally and materially."

During his stay in Moscow Ter-Gabrielian was appointed a member of the collegium of the chief oil committee of the Supreme Council of the National Economy, and was instructed by the CC of the RCP(B) and the CPC of the RSFSR to organize the supply of oil from Baku and Astrakhan. Lenin's orders in this matter were successfully carried out. Soviet Russia received over a million and a quarter tons of oil from Baku, which greatly eased its transport and fuel problems in 1918-19.

On his return to Baku, Ter-Gabrielian was appointed chairman of the [local] Cheka. On July 31, 1918, after the fall of the Soviet regime, the counter-revolutionary "Central Caspian" government ordered the warship *Astrabad* to stop all ships under Bolshevik control and to arrest Shaumian, Dzhaparidze, B. Shoboldaev and Ter-Gabrielian. The Bolshevik leaders escaped being shot thanks only to the workers' pressure and to the fact that the Soviet artillery was still active and had trained its guns on the "Central Caspian" government building. When [the prisoners] were released, the Baku committee directed Ter-Gabrielian to proceed secretly to Astrakhan to seek emergency help, which however was not forthcoming. In Baku the Musavatists held sway, and before the Turks occupied the town twenty-six commissars there were taken to Transcaspia and shot by British invaders with the help of SRs and Mensheviks.

In August 1918 the CPC of the RSFSR recalled Ter-Gabrielian to Moscow. At this time Lenin signed the following order:

> To all soviets of workers', peasants' and Red Army deputies in the Volga area:
> The CPC directs you to conform unreservedly to all orders of the office headed by comrades Ter-Gabrielian and Kviatkovsky as regards the movement

of oil, gasoline, and petroleum products into and out of your area. Any obstruction in this matter by members of your soviet will be regarded as an act of hostility toward the Soviet power and will be punished with the full rigor of revolutionary law.

Lenin valued highly Ter-Gabrielian's organizing ability, his efficiency and devotion to the Party's cause, and on November 18, 1918, made him commissar responsible for the movement of all kinds of fuel. On the instructions of the CC of the RCP(B), Ter-Gabrielian left for Astrakhan with S. M. Kirov and a staff consisting of engineers, technicians, clerks, and a military escort with the hope of getting through to Groznyi, but this proved impossible.

During these war years and for many years afterward, Ter-Gabrielian was linked by a close friendship with S. M. Kirov. On March 1, 1919, he left for the Donbass to organize the supply of coal from that area. After Denikin's occupation of the Ukraine Ter-Gabrielian returned to Moscow and was appointed assistant to the Extraordinary Agent for Red Army Supplies, then head of the Special Department of the All-Russian Cheka. In February 1920 he became an agent on the Caucasian front. At the end of April 1920 Soviet power was established in Azerbaidzhan, and he was recalled to Moscow. This time the Party sent him to Armenia, then in Dashnak hands, as counselor to the RSFSR diplomatic mission.... November 1920 saw the victory of the workers and peasants of Armenia, aided by the Eleventh Army, in their armed uprising against the hated Dashnak regime. The Armenian revolutionary committee, of which Ter-Gabrielian was a member, announced the birth of the new socialist republic. With his fellow member of the committee, A. Mravian, he was received by Lenin on December 13. They described the difficult situation in which Soviet Armenia had been placed: Turkish troops were occupying Aleksandropol; there was a food crisis and the country was full of refugees and orphans. Lenin listened attentively to what the Armenian representatives had to say, and replied: "It goes without saying that we shall do all we can to help our Armenian comrades." Despite the vast difficulties caused by the Civil War, Soviet Russia did in fact render unselfish fraternal help to Soviet Armenia. The CPC of the RSFSR allocated for this purpose 600,000 gold rubles, many manufactured goods, medical supplies, and bread and other foodstuffs. In a speech of December 1920 to the eighth all-Russian congress of soviets, Ter-Gabrielian greeted the workers of Soviet Russia on behalf of Soviet Armenia and expressed his conviction that with the help of the Russian people the Armenian people would build a new socialist life.

From 1921 to 1923 he served in Moscow as the representative of Soviet Armenia, and from 1923 to 1928 as the representative of the Transcaucasian Federation accredited to the government of the U.S.S.R. From 1928 to 1935 he was chairman of the Armenian CPC and deputy chairman of the Transcaucasian CPC. He rendered immense service in the development of the industry, agriculture, and cultural institutions of the peoples of Armenia, Georgia, and Azerbaidzhan. A tireless organizer of socialist construction, he energetically put into practice Lenin's policy for the industrialization of the country.... He was a delegate to the Tenth and the Thirteenth through the Seventeenth congresses of the CPSU. Together with S. Kas'ian he represented the Armenian CP at the Third Comintern Congress and took part in several congresses of soviets. He was a member of the All-Russian CEC and a candidate member of its presidium; a member of the CEC of the U.S.S.R. and a candidate member of its presidium; a member of the bureau of the Armenian CC and of the Transcaucasian regional committee.

Saak Mirzoevich Ter-Gabrielian was a true son of the Bolshevik Party—a man of transparent purity, modesty, and charm. His career is an example of selfless service to the Party, the Soviet people, and the cause of building a communist society.[58]

DANIIL IVANOVICH VOLKOVICH

Biographical

Born 1900, died 1937. Born at Zanemansk village in the former Mostovskaia volost, Grodno uezd. Volunteered for the Red Army in 1918, member of uezd collegium of the Cheka, deputy chairman of the uezd Cheka. In 1920 secretary of the Malmyzh uezd committee of the RCP(B), Viatka gubernia. In 1922 attended a workers' college, and in 1924 became secretary of the Party's raion committee at Koidanovo. In 1926, secretary of the Liachovich raion committee of the city of Minsk, head of the organization department of the Mogilev district committee, secretary of the Klimovich and Bobruisk raion committees of the Party, and deputy PC of agriculture of the Belorussian SSR. In 1934-37, second secretary of the CC of the Belorussian CP. In June-September 1937, chairman of the CPC of the Belorussian SSR. He was arrested in 1937 and became a victim of the cult of personality.[59]

A soldier, worker, and fighter

In August 1918, during heavy fighting on the eastern front, a White Guard -SR mutiny broke out at the Izhevsk war factory. Taking advantage of the fact that the greater part of the Izhevsk proletariat, including every single Communist, had gone to the front, the SR–Mensheviks managed to seize the town on the night of August 7-8. The Bolshevik Party sent some of its best sons to suppress the mutiny. This they soon succeeded in doing, thanks largely to a group of Komsomols under the eighteen-year old Communist Daniil Volkovich, who proved himself a strong-willed and brave commander.

This was only one episode in the wartime career of Daniil Ivanovich Volkovich, an ardent fighter for the cause of the CP and a true son of his people. He was the son of a poor peasant, born in the village of Zanemansk in the former Mostovskaia volost of the Grodno gubernia. As a child he knew poverty and privation, the hard struggle for a morsel of bread. But he was a capable and gifted youth and in spite of all difficulties finished the course at the village school. At the end of 1915, as the front drew closer, the family was evacuated to the Viatka gubernia. To keep starvation at bay, the young Daniil hired himself out for various kinds of heavy work. In April 1918 he volunteered for the Red Army. Starting as a private, he became a member of the uezd collegium of the Cheka and later deputy chairman of the uezd Cheka, taking an active part in the suppression of counterrevolutionary revolts and in combating Kolchak's forces. In 1920 he was elected secretary of the Malmyzh uezd committee of the RCP(B) in the Viatka gubernia, and in August was sent by the CC of the RCP(B) to the Polish front. In Belorussia, as commander of a Komsomol platoon he fought banditism in the Mozyr' area. Soon he was directed to the CC of the Komsomol of the republic as head of the department for village work, and then became an instructor for the Party CC.

Early in 1922, while still holding his CC job, he entered a workers' college, where his fellow students were young people from the front, Party and Komsomol members all tempered by the fire of battle.... He enjoyed great prestige among them, knowing how to talk to his fellows and help them in case of need. He was a modest man, fair-minded and full of human sympathy, and his comrades elected him secretary of their Party cell. In June 1924, having finished his studies, he was sent to Koidanovo (now Dzerzhinsk), in the most unsettled frontier region of Belorussia, as secretary of the Party's raion committee. His war experience stood him in good stead in the fight against diversionists and terrorists. In 1926 he was elected secretary of the Liakhovich raion committee of the city of Minsk. Later he was head of the organization department of the Mogilev district committee, secretary of the Klimovich and Bobruisk raion committees of the Party, and deputy PC of agriculture of the Belorussian SSR. In August 1934 he was elected second secretary of the CC of the Belorussian CP, and threw himself with his usual fervent energy into the tasks confronting the republic. He often visited construction sites, factories and works, raions and villages. He was constantly among the workers, urging them to greater efforts in all sectors of socialist construction.... On June 1, 1937, the CEC of the Belorussian SSR elected him chairman of the CPC of the republic. Arrested on September 9 of that year, he fell victim to arbitrary rule and the cult of personality. Today our Party, condemning the cult, has restored his good name. The Belorussian people reverently honor the memory of this staunch fighter for the workers' cause.[60]

VLADIMIR PETROVICH ZATONSKY

Biographical data

Born 1888, died 1940. Soviet Party leader and statesman. Joined the CP. in 1917. Born at Lysets village, Ushchits uezd, Podolsk gubernia, son of a

volost clerk. Graduated from Kiev University in 1912 and taught physics at
Kiev Polytechnical Institute. Joined the RSDWP (Mensheviks) in 1905.
Arrested several times for revolutionary activity. After the February revolution
of 1917 he broke with the Mensheviks, and in March 1917 joined the
RSDWP(B). From May 1917 he was a member of the Party's Kiev committee;
in October he was one of the leaders of the armed uprising at Kiev and became
a member of the [local] revolutionary committee. In November 1917 he was
chairman of the Kiev committee of the RSDWP(B). At the first all-Ukraine
congress of soviets (December 1917) he was elected to the National Secretariat
(government of the Ukraine SSR) as head of the secretariat (PC) of education.
At the second all-Ukrainian congress of soviets (March 1918) he was elected
chairman of the Ukraine CEC. Headed the delegation of the Ukraine CEC
to the fourth extraordinary all-Russian congress of soviets, and supported
Lenin's line concerning the necessity of concluding the treaty of Brest Litovsk.
In 1918 he was a member of the organization bureau for the convocation of
the first congress of the Ukraine CP, at which he was elected to the CC.
Directed Ukrainian underground Party organizations. PC of education of the
Ukrainian SSR from March 1919. In 1919-20 he was a member of the RMC
of the Twelfth, Thirteenth, Fourteenth armies and the RMC of the southern
front, also of the All-Ukraine revolutionary committee. Was delegate to the
Tenth Congress of the RCP(B) and a member of the commission on the
nationalities question for that congress. Took part in the suppression of the
Kronshtadt mutiny. In 1923 he was PC of education of the Ukraine SSR.
Performed military work from 1924 to 1926. In 1927-33 he was chairman
of the central control commission of the Ukraine CP and PC of workers' and
peasants' inspection of the Ukraine SSR, and in 1933-38 he again served as
PC of education of the Ukraine SSR. Was elected to the CC and the central
control commission of the Ukraine CP and was a member of the CC politburo,
also a delegate to the Tenth through the Seventeenth congresses of the CPSU.
At the Seventeenth Congress he was elected a candidate member of the CC
of the CPSU. He was a member of the Presidium of the CEC of the U.S.S.R.
and the presidium of the all-Ukrainian CEC, also of the Ukrainian Academy
of Sciences (from 1929). He became a victim of slander and repression during
the cult of Stalin's personality. Posthumously rehabilitated.[61]

V. STATESMEN

KAIGYSYZ SERDAROVICH ATABAEV

Biographical data

Born 1887, died 1937. Born at Miana village, Tedzhen uezd. Graduated in 1907 from teachers college in Tashkent, but was prevented from exercising his profession for a time because of his membership in revolutionary groups. In 1909 he was employed as a teacher at the Russo-native school at Merv (Mary), after which he became headmaster of the Bakharden Russo-native school. In 1912-17 he was a clerk at the Discount and Loan Bank at Merv. Here he came into contact with progressive workers and soldiers and engaged in active revolutionary work. After the February revolution he took an active part in organizing the soviet of workers' and soldiers' deputies at Merv and was elected chairman of the uezd food committee. After the triumph of the October Revolution in Turkestan he remained head of the food committee and dealt with famine problems on a large scale. After the Transcaspian oblast was occupied by the interventionists he moved to Tashkent and became a member of its Party workers' militia.

Atabaev played an important part during the Civil War and the restoration and consolidation of Soviet power in Turkestan. He was an instructor in the political department of the RMC of the Transcaspian front, deputy chairman of the Merv uezd executive committee and of the Transcaspian oblast revolutionary committee; performed major organizational work in mobilizing the toilers of Transcaspia, especially in regard to supplying the front. In July 1920 he became PC of agriculture of the Turkestan Republic, and in September, at the ninth Turkestan congress of soviets he was elected chairman of the republic's CPC. He was one of the internationally-minded local political workers who, grouped around the Turkestan Commission, combated national deviationism and fought for the Party's general line on the nationalities question.

In July 1920 the regional committee of the Turkestan CP, which had become swamped by nationalist elements, was dissolved, and a temporary CC of the Turkestan CP was formed consisting of Atabaev, N. T. Tiurakulov, Iu. I. Ibragimov, and others. In September the fifth congress of the Turkestan CP was held and the immediate tasks in the field of Party, government, and economic development were defined. The congress fully approved the work of

389

the temporary CC, and elected a CC with an executive Bureau whose members included Atabaev, Tiurakulov, and A. R. Rakhimbaev. During the fight with the Basmachi, Atabaev, while remaining chairman of the CPC, was assigned to the Fergana oblast as chairman of the RMC of the Fergana force. In 1922 he became a member of the collegium of the PC of Nationalities Affairs of the U.S.S.R. After a year's work in Moscow the Party assigned him to the Bukhara People's Republic as deputy chairman of the council of nazirs (commissars).

His outstanding qualities as a Party member and statesman became increasingly noteworthy during his tenure as chairman of the CPC of the Turkmen SSR. He was elected to this position at the first all-Turkmen congress of soviets, held in February 1925, which proclaimed the formation of the SSR. At the first session of the republic's CEC he was elected head of the government, and at the first congress of the Turkmenistan CP he became a member of the CC. At the plenum he was elected a member of the bureau of the CC. He held this high office without a break until his death in 1937. For his services in developing the industry, rural economy, and culture of the Turkmen SSR he received the highest government award, the Order of Lenin.[1]

MAZHID MUKHAMEDZHANOVICH CHUMBALOV

Biographical data

Born 1874, died 1940. Born in Tal volost, Bukeev gubernia (now the Ural oblast). After attending high school he studied at the medical faculty of Kazan University and graduated as a physician and plague specialist. From 1903 to 1917 he was in charge of a hospital in the city of Urda. After the October Revolution he took an active part in establishing Soviet power in Kazakhstan and was a member of the RMC. Joined the Bolshevik Party in 1918. In 1919-23 he was chairman of the Bukeev gubernia executive committee and a member of the Bureau of the gubernia committee of the RCP(B); in 1923-30, deputy PC of health of the Kirgiz (Kazakh) ASSR. In 1929 he was transferred to the post of director of the pharmaceutical center at Alma-Ata. He was a victim of the cult of Stalin's personality in 1940.[2]

A true son of the people

This spring marks the ninetieth anniversary of the birth of Mazhid Mukhamedzhanovich Chumbalov, one of the organizers of the Kazakhstan health services. During the period of unjustified repression he fell victim to arbitrary rule and the cult of Stalin's personality, and died tragically in 1940.

Born in the Tal volost of the Bukeev gubernia (now the Ural oblast), he was sent by his father at the age of ten to a Russian elementary school at the local township of Novouzensk. At that time, a Tatar who was a pupil at the Kazan High School was working as a teacher in Chumbalov's home village. When Mazhid left school he went with this youth to Kazan and entered high school there. A few years later he became a student at the medical faculty of Kazan University. He was one of the first Kazakh doctors to return to his own territory, where he was active in combating epidemics. This period determined his future career as a plague specialist. From 1903 to 1917 he was director of a hospital at Urda, while continuing to work on the liquidation of plague concentrations in the Caspian depression and the Kalmyk steppes. For his selfless work in this field he was twice rewarded with medals by the Astrakhan health authorities.

After the October Revolution he took an active part in establishing Soviet power in Kazakhstan; he was a member of the RMC and in 1918 joined the Bolshevik Party. In 1919 he was elected chairman of the Bukeev gubernia executive committee and a member of the bureau of the gubernia committee of the RCP(B), while also directing the gubernia health department. During these years he organized a number of medical institutions and a wide range of village clinics. In 1923 he moved to Orenburg, the then capital of the Kirgiz (Kazakh) ASSR, where he was deputy PC of health of the republic and was elected a member of its Party CC of the second convocation. After the capital was transferred to Kzyl-Orda he remained deputy PC for health until 1930.

He did much teaching, lecturing, and health propaganda work in various medical and training institutions and in the Kazan Institute of Popular Education. In 1929 he was transferred to Alma-Ata in order to strengthen what was at that time a backward sector, as director of the pharmaceutical organization of the Kazakh Republic, which he almost completely reorganized. He also did much to organize the first Kazakhstan medical institute at Alma-Ata. A tireless worker, he spared no effort to protect the workers' health and train medical cadres. He organized the first Kazakh regional pharmaceutical technical school at Semipalatinsk, and enabled many of his countrymen to receive higher medical education and in their turn to become defenders of the workers' health. He also wrote a number of popular works on medical subjects.

His whole life was a shining example of devoted service to the Soviet people. The memory of this true son of Lenin's Party and the Kazakh people lives on in the hearts of Soviet men and women.[3]

ARAMAIS ARTEMOVICH ERZNKIAN

Biographical data

Born 1879, died 1937. Born at Akhpat village; attended Nersisian Seminary at Tiflis, then Geneva University. Joined the Bolshevik Party in 1899. In 1899-1907 he was a member of the Party's Tiflis committee and an organizer of the Marxist "Union of Armenian Social-Democrats." In 1907 he took part in the Fifth RSDWP Congress in London. Arrested in 1912; after his release, helped to edit the newspaper *Paikar*. In 1917-21, member of the Center of the Transcaucasian workers' and peasants' soviet and of the Tiflis soviet of workers' deputies. Arrested in 1921. Joined the CP after the establishment of Soviet rule in Georgia. In 1921-30, PC of agriculture of Armenia; in 1930-31, PC of agriculture of the Transcaucasian Federation. In 1931-37, first deputy chairman of the Armenian CPC. In 1937 he became a victim of the cult of Stalin's personality.[4]

A soldier of the Party

Aramais Erznkian belonged to the generation of those first Armenian Marxists who came on the political scene at the end of the nineteenth century and the beginning of the twentieth century and raised the standard of class struggle on their native soil, bringing the workers and peasants into the mainstream of the Russian revolutionary movement. Erznkian's own political journey, it is true, was not a straightforward one: joining the CP meant a complete reversal of his ideas. Nevertheless, we should not pass over or forget the services he rendered in founding the Union of Armenian Social Democrats in 1903, in publishing the newspapers *Proletariat, Kaits,* and *Nor khosk* in 1906; and above all his strenuous and fruitful activity in the field of socialist construction in Soviet Armenia, when he showed himself a major political and administrative leader.

Aramais Artemovich Erznkian was born in 1879 in the Lori village of Akhpat. He attended the Nersisian Seminary at Tiflis and the University of Geneva, Switzerland. In 1899 he joined the RSDWP, and later became a member of the Party's Tiflis committee. In summer 1902, under sponsorship of the RSDWP, the first Armenian Marxist organization was set up under the name of the "Union of Armenian Social Democrats." Erznkian took an active part in founding it, together with S. Shaumian, B. Knuniants, A. Zurabian, S. Khanoian, M. Melikian, R. Dashtoian, and D. Shaverdian. In October of that year it began to bring out a newspaper entitled *Proletariat:* Shaumian and Zurabian were its editors and Erznkian was responsible for its publication. The formation of the union was a major event in the revolutionary struggle of the Armenian people and was warmly welcomed by Lenin.

After the Second RSDWP Congress [1903] Erznkian joined the Mensheviks. In 1907 he took part in the Fifth RSDWP Congress in London. In 1912 he was thrown into the Metekh jail in Tiflis, where he spent several months in the same cell as Suren Spandarian. After his release he engaged in legal work, and in 1916 he helped to produce the newspaper *Paikar*. In 1917, after the February revolution, he was elected a member of the Center of the Transcaucasian workers' and peasants' soviet, and also a member of the Tiflis soviet of workers' deputies.

The October Revolution had a decisive effect on Ernzkian. The experience of the counterrevolution and the nationalistic activity of the Caucasian Mensheviks, especially their leaders, led him to take a fresh look at the road he had traveled. As a member of the Transcaucasian Assembly which, in 1918, considered the question of Transcaucasia seceding from Soviet Russia and declaring its independence, he voted against this proposal and later, as he wrote subsequently, "went into opposition against the Menshevik regime." In October 1921 he was arrested by the Georgian Menshevik government. Released after Soviet power was established in Georgia, he joined the CP. This marked a turning point in his life and the beginning of his fruitful activity. In 1921 he became a member of the Armenian CPC headed by Aleksandr Fedorovich Miasnikian, and remained PC of agriculture until 1930. This was the period of land reform, of the organization of land tenure and the first collective farms in Lori, Kotaika, and the Echmiadzin and Dilizhan raions. With characteristic energy Erznkian applied himself to the socialist transformation of the countryside. In 1930-31 he was PC of agriculture of the Transcaucasian Federation. From the end of 1931 he was first deputy chairman of the Armenian CPC, and in 1932-33 was in addition chairman of the executive committee of the Erevan city soviet. He devoted much energy to the reconstruction of the Armenian capital, and with the help of the academician Tamanian brought into being part of the Lenin Square ensemble (Government House) and laid the foundations of the Spendiarov opera and ballet theater. His contempories well remember how this tall, handsome, eagle-nosed son of the Lori mountains would visit the site each morning, inspect the work, give directions on the spot, and encourage the workers. He also rendered important services in regard to the construction of the republic's first hydroelectric power stations and the repatriation of Armenian workers from abroad.

Erznkian was a man of great charm: direct, straightforward, incorruptible, with a delicate sense of humor, full of life and optimism.... With good reason, he was deeply respected by the Party and Soviet cadres and wide circles of the intelligentsia of Georgia, Azerbaidzhan, and Armenia. In 1937 he became a victim of arbitrary rule during the cult of personality....[5]

IAKOV ARKAD'EVICH IAKOVLEV (EPSHTEIN)

Biographical data

Born 1896, died 1939. Joined the CP in 1913. Took part in the October Revolution and the Civil War in the Ukraine. Was chairman of the Kharkov revolutionary committee and the Kiev and Ekaterinoslav gubernia committees, then head of the political department of the Fourteenth Army. From 1919 he was a member of the politburo of the CC of the Ukraine CP; from 1926, deputy PC of workers' and peasants' inspection and of the central control commission; from 1929, PC of agriculture of the U.S.S.R.; and from 1934, head of the agricultural department of the CC of the CPSU. Author of works on the history of the October Revolution and Soviet construction.[6]

GRIGORII NAUMOVICH KAMINSKY

Biographical data

Born 1895, died 1938. Joined the Bolshevik Party in 1913. Born at Ekaterinoslav, the son of a tube-rolling mill worker. In 1912-17 he carried on propaganda in underground workers' circles, organized a tailors' trade union, and while studying medicine at Moscow University carried on underground revolutionary work at the Schmidt furniture works and the "Trekhgorka" [sic]. In 1917-20 he was a member of the Moscow oblast bureau of the RSDWP, worked actively for the formation of a unified RSDWP organization at Tula, was chairman of the Tula gubernia executive committee and at the same time chairman of the Party's gubernia committee. In September 1920 he was sent with other Party members to work in Azerbaidzhan: there he was a member of the politburo and organization bureau of the CC of the Azerbaidzhan CP and chairman of the Baku soviet of workers' and Red Army deputies. In 1921-29 he held senior posts in the All-Russian Union of Agricultural Cooperatives at Moscow. In 1929-31 he was head of the Agitation and Mass Campaigns section of the CC of the CPSU and third secretary of the Party's Moscow city committee; he was second secretary of this committee in 1931-32. In 1932-36 he was chairman of the Moscow oblast executive committee, PC of health of the RSFSR, and chief state sanitary inspector of the U.S.S.R. In 1936-37, first PC of health of the U.S.S.R. At the Fourteenth through the Seventeenth CPSU congresses he was elected a candidate member of the CC; he was also a member of the All-Russian CEC and the All-Union CEC. Arrested in 1937; died in jail 1938.[7]

Kaminsky's career

The Sixth Congress of our Party was hard at work in the anxious July days of 1917. Among the relatively few participants in this historic congress which set the Party's course for armed rebellion was the twenty-two-year-old Grigorii Kaminsky, leader of the Tula Bolsheviks, who had joined the RSDWP in 1913 and was in later years to become an eminent figure in the CP and the Soviet State....

He was born on November 1, 1895, at Ekaterinoslav, the son of a tube-rolling mill worker. After his father's death the family moved to Minsk, where Grigorii lived with an uncle and his schooling was paid for by another relative who worked as a railroad engineer in Poland. While still at school, Grigorii joined the revolutionary movement. In 1912 he began distributing *Pravda,* and after becoming a member of the RSDWP carried on propaganda among underground workers' groups and, on the Party's orders, organized a tailors' trade union. From 1915, while studying medicine at Moscow University, he carried on underground revolutionary work at the Schmidt furniture factory and the "Trekhgorka." He was also well known in progressive student circles. In 1916 he was arrested.

After the February bourgeois-democratic revolution Kaminsky was elected to the Moscow oblast bureau of the RSDWP. In the second half of March 1917 the Party sent him to Tula—a major industrial center whose importance for the revolution was more than once emphasized by Lenin. Kaminsky had already been there in 1916, on the instructions of the Moscow oblast bureau, to renew contacts with the Bolshevik organization of the arms factory. Even then it was clear that the Mensheviks and SRs were increasing their influence on the working masses, while the Bolsheviks were weakened by arrests and the departure of Bolshevik workers for the front. As workers at the Tula arms factories were exempt from military service, a good many of them were sons of bourgeois and kulaks.

As soon as he arrived at Tula, Kaminsky got busily to work.... At the end of March 1917 a united RSDWP organization had been created there as a result of the weakness of the Bolsheviks and the dominance of the "conciliator" parties. A decisive role in strengthening the Tula Bolshevik organization was played by Lenin's April theses and the decisions of the seventh all-Russian (April) conference of the RSDWP(B). Kaminsky was one of the initiators of the Bolshevik withdrawal from the united social-democratic organization. At the end of May 1917 he was elected secretary of the Tula committee of the RSDWP(B)....

Returning from the Party's Sixth Congress [1917], Kaminsky and other Tula Communists set about strengthening the Bolshevik organization and preparing the proletariat to seize power. Whereas at the moment of the break with the Mensheviks there were only150 Bolsheviks among the 2,000 Tula Social Democrats, the number rose to over 500 at the end of June, about 1,000 in July, and over 1,500 by October. When the October Revolution broke out, the Tula Bolsheviks set up their RMC which, with Kaminsky at its head, organized the dispatch of large quantities of arms to the Red Guards in Petrograd, Moscow, Kharkov, the Donbass, and other workers' centers. To Moscow, in particular, substantial truckloads of arms and ammunition were sent on November 12, 1917. V. A. Kul'nev, a Party member since 1913, remembers that in acknowledging the great value of this help ... for the Moscow workers and revolutionary soldiers, Sverdlov said: "We know that the Tula Bolsheviks gave much help to Moscow by sending supplies at the moment of the armed uprising."...

In difficult conditions of the first years of the revolution, when oppositionists involved the Party in all kinds of discussions, the Tula Party organization under Kaminsky stuck to the Leninist line, notably during the debate over the peace of Brest-Litovsk....

In the fall of 1919 the Soviet Republic went through dark times, when the Whites took Orel and advanced to the borders of the Tula gubernia. Lenin said that the enemy was never so near Moscow as in October 1919.... The organizing work of the Tula Party machine under Kaminsky, and the heroic labor of the workers at the arms and cartridge factories, ensured a steadily increasing rate of production for the front. The CP and Soviet government highly valued this exploit of the Tula armament workers, who in April 1921 were rewarded with the Order of the Red Banner of Labor for having—as stated in the citation of the All-Russian CEC—successfully fulfilled the 1918-20 program for the production of supplies for the Red Army.

In September 1920 the Party CC sent Kaminsky and other comrades to Azerbaidzhan. The Bolsheviks already working at Baku included Ordzhonikidze, Kirov, Mikoyan, E. D. Stasova, and others. In October the plenum of the CC of the Azerbaidzhan CP elected Kaminsky a member of the politburo and organization bureau and secretary of the CC. Under the direction of the Caucasian bureau of the CC of the All-Russian CP, headed by Ordzhonikidze, Kaminsky worked actively to consolidate Soviet power in Azerbaidzhan and restore the oil industry.

Carrying out the decisions of the second congress of the Azerbaidzhan CP, the Azerbaidzhan Communists at the end of 1920 set about organizing committees of the village poor to accelerate class equalization in the countryside and the transition from revolutionary committees to soviets.... Kaminsky, who was at the same time chairman of the Baku soviet of workers' and Red Army deputies, did much to strengthen the links between the Baku working class, which then consisted chiefly of Russian and Armenian workers, and the Azerbaidzhan peasantry. Speaking at a session of the Baku soviet in June 1921, he said: "We shall not get far unless we bring about an exchange of goods between our own industry and the Azerbaidzhan countryside, and transfer to the latter large cadres of the Baku proletariat."...

Kaminsky resolutely fought the Trotskyists. In the discussion on trade unions, the plenum of the CC of the Azerbaidzhan CP pronounced itself by a huge majority in favor of Lenin's program, appointing Ordzhonikidze to report on this subject at the third congress of the Azerbaidzhan CP.

At the Tenth Congress of the RCP(B) Kaminsky, together with the other Azerbaidzhan delegates Kirov and R. Akhundov, was elected to the commission which prepared the congress's resolution on the nationalities question. Kaminsky supported without reserve the resolution concerning Party unity and the syndicalist and anarchist deviation within the RCP(B).

In the fall of 1921 he was transferred to Moscow for important work in the All-Russian Union of Agricultural Cooperatives. Fulfilling the Party's decisions, he devoted himself with his usual energy and initiative to developing agricultural cooperatives, improving their methods and increasing the efficiency of their organs. At the fourteenth conference of the RCP(B) he sharply criticized the "administrative" methods which had prevailed in the cooperative setup.... In speeches at congresses of the All-Union Council of Collective Farms and at all-Russian and all-Union collective farm congresses during 1926-28, he defended the Leninist policy and reverted time and again to Lenin's ideas on cooperatives. "Lenin laid down the general line of progress to socialism in the countryside through cooperatives. Our task is to interpret it correctly. It would be wrong to hasten the swallowing up of the peasants' economy by that of the state: we must seek ways of persuading them to join voluntarily in the general system of socialist construction." So said Kaminsky in a report of 1926, adding: "Not only are we moving in the direction pointed out by Lenin, but we are already beginning to discern, in its concrete aspects, what he spoke of only in general terms." Speaking at the third all-Russian collective farms congress, he observed that the kolkhozes could not develop without the general guidance and control of the state organ whose task it was to plan for the whole country's agriculture, namely the PC of Agriculture. "The kolkhoz movement," he said, "grows and develops under the joint influence of Party and state organs and cooperative organizations. It involves a close union between the poor peasants and rural proletariat on the one hand and the peasants of middle status on the other.... Only in this way can the kulak be overcome and socialist construction be achieved in the countryside."

He considered that peasant women had a special part to play in the collective farm construction. As if seeing into the future, he declared that in war conditions women would be the mainstay of the kolkhozes, with the duty of supplying food to the front and the civilian sector. It was therefore necessary to train women to manage kolkhozes well before the outbreak of war.

In November 1929 the CC of the CPSU held a plenum at which Kaminsky, on the instructions of the Politburo, reported on "the achievements and further tasks of kolkhoz construction." The plenum noted that the conversion of the broad masses of the peasantry to socialism meant the beginning of a new historical stage of the socialist transformation of agriculture....

At the beginning of 1932 Kaminsky became chairman of the Moscow oblast executive committee. In this and other senior posts he took an active part in solving problems of the socialist reconstruction of industry and agriculture in the Moscow area. He solved in a creative fashion problems of the reorganization of the Party's work, and frequently addressed toilers in Moscow and its surrounding district. Thanks to the selfless work of the Moscow Party organization and the whole labor force, the oblast in 1930-33 fulfilled the basic tasks laid upon it by the First Five Year Plan for the development of the national economy. On January 3, 1934, the oblast was rewarded with the Order of Lenin for its success in developing agriculture, strengthening the collective and state farms, and discharging its obligations toward the state. Much of the credit for this is due to Kaminsky, who devoted unremitting attention to agriculture. He was well acquainted with agricultural production, and believed strongly in creating large kolkhozes and in increasing material incentives for every state and collective farm worker. He often emphasized that problems of socialist construction must be solved "on the ground," and criticized those who settled things only in accordance with instructions from above....

In February 1934 he became PC of health of the RSFSR and chief state sanitary inspector of the U.S.S.R. When, in July 1936, the All-Union PC of Health was formed, he was the first to occupy [the commissariat's leading] post, which he held for over three years, leaving a mark on the history of Soviet health services. In February 1936, in his regular report to the sixteenth all-Russian congress of soviets, he declared that public health is one of the major concerns of the socialist revolution and that the health services are inseparable from socialist construction in general, with all its vast possibilities for improvement in this sphere. He laid particular stress on improving the efficiency of the health services and their links with other social organizations.... Under his guidance, and with his active participation, much work was done to extend the system of clinical and prophylactic services, higher and intermediate medical schools, and research institutes. He took a direct part in preparing several Party and government decisions in the public health field, concerning, e. g., the training of doctors, better pay for medical workers, higher allocations for health purposes, anti-malaria work, and the All-Union Institute of Experimental Medicine.

A prominent Party member and politician, he was a delegate to the Eighth through the Seventeenth Party congresses, and at the Fourteenth through the Seventeenth of these was elected a candidate member of the CC. He was also a member of the All-Russian and the All-Union CEC at several convocations. He was distressed by the cult of personality, and in 1937 spoke out against unjustified repressions at the June plenum of the CC. He was arrested on the same day, and his life was tragically cut short in 1938.

The CPSU, liquidating the consequences of the personality cult, has restored the good name of its son, an able and devoted fighter for communism whose deeds earned him the gratitude of the Party and all the Soviet people.[8]

SARKIS OGANESOVICH KAS'IAN (TER-KASPARIAN)

Biographical data

Born 1876, died 1937. Joined the CP in 1905. Born at Shuma. Studied from 1900 to 1904 at the Leipzig Commercial Institute, then at Berlin University. In 1904-10 he was a member of the Baku committee of the RSDWP and edited the newspaper *Banvori Dzain* (Voice of the Workers). In 1910-12 he was active in setting up Bolshevik organizations in Georgia and edited the newspapers *Listok-kopeika* and later *Trudovaia kopeika*. In 1912-15, after the illegal printing press was closed down, he and those of his comrades who were not arrested revived the Party's Tiflis committee and helped to launch Bolshevik papers along the lines of *Pravda* in Transcaucasia. In 1915-17 he was in exile at Astrakhan, then at Vologda. In 1917-18 he was back at Tiflis, was a member of the Caucasian Committee of the RSDWP, and edited the papers *Banvori Kriv* (The Workers' Fight) and *Banvor* (The Worker). In 1918-19 he headed local Bolshevik organizations at Tiflis, and in 1919-20 carried on underground work in Armenia. In 1920-21 he was a member of the Armenian committee of the RCP(B), and at the end of January was sent from Armenia to Tiflis as secretary of the regional committee. He was arrested there, and after his release in the summer of 1920 moved to Baku, where he worked in the foreign bureau of the CC of the Armenian CP, and was a member of the CC and chairman of the Armenian revolutionary committee. In 1921-22 he edited the Armenian newspaper *Karmir Atskh* (Red Star), published at Tiflis, and later the journal *Nor Ashkar* (New World). In 1923-24 he was a member of the CEC of the Transcaucasian Federation and of the auditing committee of the Transcaucasian regional committee of the CPSU; in 1924-27 rector of the Transcaucasian Communist university named for the Twenty-six Commissars, and chairman of the federation's council of national minorities; in 1927-28 he served as chairman of the Transcaucasian CEC, and in 1928-29 as chairman of the CEC of the Armenian SSR. In 1929-33 he was a member of the CEC of the U.S.S.R. and chairman of the Transcaucasian supreme court. In 1937 he became a victim of the cult of Stalin's personality.[9]

A staunch fighter in Lenin's old guard

In November 1920, Dashnak terror and despotism, famine and epidemics, disputes between nationalities and persecutions had brought our country to an unprecedented state of collapse. The Turkish slaughterers were planning to repeat in eastern Armenia the massacre of 1915. At this time of crisis in the nation's destiny, the Armenian revolutionary committee at Idzhevan, headed by Sarkis Kas'ian, raised aloft the liberating banner of the October Revolution, and in a decree signed by Kas'ian proclaimed the Armenian SSR.

Sarkis Oganesovich Kas'ian (Ter-Kaspar'ian) was born at Shuma January 28, 1878 [sic]. Shortly afterward his family moved to Baku, the proletarian center of Transcaucasia. While attending technical high school there he took an active part in anti-government demonstrations, and in consequence was expelled. He finished his schooling by correspondence in 1893, and in 1900 went to the Leipzig Commercial Institute. Having graduated there from the faculty of economics, he took a degree at the philosophical faculty of Berlin University. In Germany he studied the works of Marx and Engels in depth, and was in close touch with German social-democratic leaders. At this time he read Lenin's *What Is to Be Done?* which, as he later testified, made a "tremendous impression" on him. In September 1903 he attended the congress of German Social Democrats at Dresden. He was much impressed by August Bebel's speech; of Bernstein he said that he "was trying to sit on two stools at once."

In 1904 he returned to Baku, and in 1905 he joined the Leninist Party. As a member of the Baku committee of the RSDWP he carried on extensive revolutionary work among employees of the oil industry. He displayed journalistic talent, and in 1906 he brought out the newspaper *Banvori Dzain,* the organ of the Baku committee of the RSDWP, the first number of which contained an article by Lenin on boycotting the State Duma. He also helped to publish the Armenian Bolshevik newspapers *Kaits* (The Spark), *Nor Khosk* (The New Word) and *Orer* (Days). A professional revolutionary and staunch member of Lenin's old guard, he denounced, in his Marxist articles, not only the Tsarist autocracy but also the bourgeois nationalists who did all they could to stand in the way of the class education of the workers. At Tiflis in 1910 he took part in reviving the local Bolshevik organizations, and with Suren Spandarian edited *Listok-kopeika* and later *Trudovaia kopeika.* He was among the leaders of the Tiflis organization of the RSDWP, along with Spandarian, Elena Stasova, Petr Arveladze, Akop Akopian, and others.

In 1912 the Tsarist police discovered the illegal Bolshevik printing press and arrested S. Ordzhonikidze, Spandarian, Stasova, and others. Kas'ian and other comrades who were still at liberty revived the Party's Tiflis committee and maintained contact with Lenin and the CC of the RSDWP. On November 25, 1913, Kas'ian wrote to inform the CC that the Tiflis Bolsheviks were in liaison with Party organizations at Kutaisi, Elisavetpol, Erivan, Aleksandropol, and elsewhere, and requested help in the form of literature and instructions, as well as aid with the local Bolshevik press. He wrote: "We ask Comrade Lenin, for whom we have great respect and deference, to help us with his articles and thus strengthen our influence and fighting power." He added that Lenin's name would "at one stroke increase the importance of our paper not only among workers of various nationalities in the Caucasus, but throughout the local community."...

The police administration of the Tiflis gubernia having decided that Kas'ian's further presence in the Caucasus was undesirable, he was exiled in 1915, first to Astrakhan and then to Vologda. The inhuman conditions of exile did not break the spirit of this staunch revolutionary or his unquenchable faith in future victory. His faith was justified: the Romanov dynasty fell and the February revolution was victorious. Kas'ian returned to Tiflis and the front line of the battle. In October 1917, at the first regional congress of Caucasian Bolsheviks, he was elected a member of the Caucasian committee of the RSDWP. He also edited the newspapers *Banvori Kriv* in 1917, and *Banvor* in 1918. In the latter year, owing to persecution by the Menshevik government, the Party's regional committee moved to the northern Caucasus, but Kas'ian remained at Tiflis with M. Tskhakaia and F. Makharadze and, in difficult conditions, directed the work of local Bolshevik organizations. In May 1919 he attended the celebrated conference at Baku where the proposal was put forward by himself and others to create national Soviet republics and Communist parties. Later, on the orders of the regional committee, he took up illegal work in Armenia. He was active in organizing the September conference of Armenian Bolshevik organizations, at which he reported on the urgent tasks of the revolutionary movement, and at which the Armenian Committee of the RCP(B) was elected....

The Dashnak "Mauzerists" were ferocious in their persecution of the revolutionaries, and at the end of 1920 Kas'ian was arrested and expelled from Armenia to Tiflis, where he took an active part in the work of the regional committee of the RCP(B), of which he was secretary in 1919-20. He was arrested by the Menshevik government but set free at the request of S. Kirov, at that time the RSFSR representative, and in summer of the same year he moved to Baku. Here he at once joined the foreign bureau of the CC of the Armenian CP, and on November 11, 1920, became a member of the CC itself.

When the Caucasian bureau of the CC of the RCP(B) and the CC of the Armenian CP jointly set up an Armenian revolutionary committee, Kas'ian became its chairman. In November 1920 the committee declared over his signature that "henceforth the red banner of Soviet Armenia will protect its working people from the age-old yoke of the oppressor." The committee called on Soviet Russia for aid, and in his telegram to Lenin, Kas'ian used these words: "We make known to the leader of world revolution that the peasants of the Dilizhan and Karavansarai raions, indignant at the criminal policy of the Dashnak government and the growing anarchy in the country, have raised the standard of revolt." The heroic Red Army gave brotherly help to the Armenian people, the great October banner was raised over their ancient land, and freedom dawned for the nation that had suffered so cruelly.

In summer 1921 Kas'ian represented the Armenian CP at the Third Comintern Congress, and in a passionate speech denounced the anti-national policy of the Dashnak lackeys of imperialism.... From 1928 he was chairman of the CEC of the Armenian SSR; in 1929 he was elected to the CEC of the U.S.S.R. and later was a delegate to the Sixteenth Congress of the CPSU. In 1931-33 he was president of the supreme court of Transcaucasia. Everywhere and at all times he displayed limitless faith in the Leninist Party and a firm belief in the victory of its great ideals. He was not only a political worker and statesman but also a major theoretician and fervent propagandist of Marxist-Leninist teaching. He organized many translations of the works of the founders of Marxism into Armenian, and his own translation of the Communist *Manifesto* appeared in 1927. A dauntless Communist and a man of principle, he left many theoretical works. He perished in 1937, but he is one of the great men whose memory will live forever in the hearts of Soviet people.[10]

ALEKSEI SEMENOVICH KISELEV

Biographical data

Born 1879, died 1938. Party and political leader. Born at Avdotino village near Ivanovo-Voznesensk, the son of a worker. Worked as a mechanic at a factory from the age of fourteen. Joined the CP in 1898 and carried on Party work at Ivanovo-Voznesensk, Moscow, Kharkov, Baku, and Odessa. Arrested and exiled several times. In 1914 he went on Party business to Austria, where he met Lenin; was co-opted onto the CC of the RSDWP(B). In summer 1914 he was arrested and exiled to Eniseisk, but soon escaped and lived clandestinely at Eniseisk, Krasnoiarsk and Verkhne-Ukinsk. Returned to Ivanovo-Voznesensk after the February revolution and was elected chairman of the city soviet and a member of the local committee of the RSDWP(B). At the Sixth Congress of the RSDWP(B) he was elected a candidate member of the CC. At the first all-Russian congress of soviets he was elected to the All-Russian CEC. After the October Revolution he was chairman of the CC of the textile industry and a member of the presidium of the Supreme Council of the National Economy, later a member of the CPC commission for Turkestan affairs. In 1918 he headed the Orenburg Defense Group against the Kolchak and Dutov forces. In 1920 he was chairman of the Miners' Union; in 1921-23 chairman of the Smaller CPC, and, from the second all-Union congress of soviets, member of the CEC of the U.S.S.R. At the Twelfth Congress of the RCP(B) in 1923 he was elected to the Central Control Commission of the RCP(B); he was later a member of the commission's presidium, PC of workers' and peasants' inspection of the RSFSR, and deputy PC of the U.S.S.R. At the Tenth, Eleventh, and Fourteenth through the Sixteenth CPSU congresses he was elected a candidate member of the CC, and at the Seventeenth a member of the auditing commission. From 1924 until his tragic death he was secretary of the All-Union CEC and a member of its Presidium. Subjected to illegal repression as a result of the cult of Stalin's personality; posthumously rehabilitated.[11]

IVAN EVDOKIMOVICH KLIMENKO

Biographical data

Born 1891, died 1938. Joined the CP in 1912. Born at Rivchaki village, Nezhin uezd, Chernigov gubernia, the son of a peasant. Herded sheep as a child. In 1905 he was apprentice printer at the staff of the Kiev military district; was dismissed for joining a revolutionary group there and worked at various private presses in Kiev. Carried on active revolutionary work from 1911; was arrested several times; worked clandestinely at Poltava and Kharkov. Arrested in 1914 and exiled for three years to the Narym krai. Escaped to Irkutsk and led an unsuccessful strike at a local press in spring 1916; then moved to Verkhne-Udinsk and in the winter of 1917 to Novo-Nikolaevsk. During the February revolution he was deputy chairman of the local soviet of workers' and peasants' deputies, secretary of the printers' union and a member of the Kiev central soviet of factory and plant workers' committees. Took an active part in the uprising of January 1918 against the Central Rada; was chairman of the strike committee and served in the Red Guard at the Kiev arsenal and in Podolia. In March 1918 he was elected a member of the Ukraine CEC and PC of labor. After the first congress of the Ukraine CP in July 1918 he did underground work at Kharkov, and after the second congress at Odessa; was member of the Party's Odessa oblast committee and chairman of the illegal Odessa revolutionary committee. He was later a member of the Party's gubernia committee, and from April 10 to August 23, 1919, was chairman of the gubernia executive committee. From August 1919 he was military commissar of the Forty-fifth Division, chairman of the Zhitomir RMC and, from October, again military commissar of the Forty-fifth Division. From December 1919 to 1921 he was deputy chairman of the Kiev gubernia revolutionary committee, a member and later chairman of the Party's gubernia committee, chairman of the Odessa gubernia revolutionary committee, and chairman of the Ekaterinoslav revolutionary committee. In 1922-24 he was PC of agriculture of the Ukraine; in 1925-27, secretary of the CC of the Ukraine CP; in 1927-29, deputy PC of agriculture of the RSFSR; in 1929-30, chairman of the Tractor Center and of the Union of Agricultural Co-operatives and deputy PC of agriculture of the U.S.S.R. In 1930-31 he was chairman of the Siberian regional executive committee. After the Sixteenth CPSU Congress he was appointed director of the Central Asian railroad, and from the beginning of 1931 a member of the collegium of the PC of Communications. In 1933-34 he was director of the Riazan-Ural railroad and in 1934 head of grain administration of the PC of Agriculture of the U.S.S.R. He was a member of the organization bureau and politburo of the CC of the Ukraine CP and a member of the Ukraine CEC. In 1938 he became a victim of the cult of Stalin's personality.[12]

Nikolai Vasil'evich Krylenko

NIKOLAI VASIL'EVICH KRYLENKO

Biographical data

Born 1885, died 1938. Party name "Comrade Abram." Political and Party leader; joined the CP in 1904. Born at Bekhteevka village, Sychevka uezd, Smolensk gubernia, the son of an exiled official. Graduated from the historico-literary and law faculties of Petrograd University. In 1904-5 he was a leader of the students' revolutionary movement; in 1906 he carried on Party propaganda work in and around Petersburg and in Moscow, on the instructions of the local committees of the RSDWP. He went abroad in June 1906, and on his return became a member of the military organization of the Petersburg committee of the RSDWP, where he carried on propaganda among the garrison troops. Arrested again [sic] in 1907 and sent to Lublin. From 1911 he worked on *Zvezda* and later *Pravda,* and on Lenin's orders organized the movement of Party literature and underground workers across the frontier. In summer 1912 Lenin sent him to Petersburg to take part in preparations for the elections to the Fourth State Duma.

In August 1913, after he had done his military service, he was again sent to Petersburg by the CC of the RSDWP(B) to work on *Pravda* and in the Bolshevik fraction of the Duma. Betrayed by the *agent provocateur* Malinovsky, he was arrested and in March 1914 sent to Kharkov, where he took part in preparations for the south Russian Party conference. To avoid another arrest he emigrated to Austria and then Switzerland, where he took part in the Bern conference of foreign sections of the RSDWP.

In summer 1915 the Party CC assigned him to illegal work in Moscow; he was arrested in November, and sent to the front in April 1916. In the February revolution of 1917 he was elected chairman of a regiment committee and a division committee of the Fourteenth Army. Represented the CC of the RSDWP(B) at the congress of the southwestern front at Kremenets. In April 1917 he was elected chairman of the Army committee of the Eleventh Army, and in May he was a delegate to the all-army congress of front-line soldiers at Petrograd. Was a delegate to the first all-Russian congress of soviets and, representing the Bolshevik group, became a member of the presidium of the congress and of the first all-Russian CEC. Carried on active work among workers and soldiers and was on the staff of *Soldatskaia pravda.* Lenin (*Works,* vol. 27, chap. 25) spoke of him as "one of the keenest Bolsheviks and among those closest to the army." In June 1917 he took part in preparing the all-Russian conference of front and rear organizations of the RSDWP(B), at which he delivered a report on "War, Peace and Our Advance" and was elected to the central bureau of the all-Russian military organization of the CC of the RSDWP(B). In the summer of 1917 he was arrested by the Provisional government [and was in detention] from June till August.

From March 1918 he worked in the administration of Soviet justice and the establishment of the courts and the procurator's office. From 1918 he worked in the administration of Soviet justice and the establishment of the courts and the procurator's office. From 1918 to 1931 he was public prosecutor in major political trials. In 1922-31 he was assistant procurator and then procurator of the RSFSR; from 1931 he was PC of justice of the RSFSR, and from 1936, of the U.S.S.R. At the Fifteenth and Sixteenth Party congresses he was elected a member of the Central Control Commission; he was several times elected to the All-Union CEC, and became a member of its Presidium in 1935.

He wrote many works on the theory and practice of political and legal work in the U.S.S.R.: *Sud i pravo v SSSR* (Law and Justice in the U.S.S.R.), 3 vols., 1927-30; *Chto takoe revolutsionnaia zakonnost'* (The Nature of Revolutionary Legality), 1927; *Lenin o sude i ugolovnoi politike* (Lenin on the Courts and Criminal Law Policy), 1934; *Sovetskoe pravosudie: Sud i prokuratura v SSSR* (Soviet Justice: The Courts and Procurator's Office in the U.S.S.R.), 1936, etc. He was a member of the commissions that drafted the constitutions of the RSFSR and the U.S.S.R. and various codes of laws. He took part in the compilation of the History of the Civil War and the Great Soviet Encyclopedia; taught at colleges and the Institute of Red Professors and was professor of criminal law at the Moscow Institute of Soviet Law. Was an organizer and participant in the sixth scientific expedition of the U.S.S.R. Academy of Sciences to the Pamirs in 1928-34, and for several years was director of the All-Union Society for Proletarian Tourism. Was prominent in U.S.S.R. chess circles, and organized international chess tournaments from 1925 to 1936.

In 1938 Krylenko was slandered and became a victim of unjustified repression. Posthumously rehabilitated.[13]

Krylenko's career

On October 18, 1904, some 2,000 pro-revolutionary students of Petersburg University held an illegal meeting which filled one of the biggest of the university lecture halls. A quite young student, Nikolai Krylenko, addressed the meeting and spoke with passion of the day when the people would overthrow the autocracy and men and women would be able to live, work, and think in freedom. He called on his audience to support the students of the polytechnical institute, who had demanded that the government at once put a stop to the shameful war in the Far East and call a constituent assembly on the basis of universal suffrage.

Such was the first public appearance of a future hero of the October Revolution, the first Supreme Commander of the Soviet Republic, later PC of justice—the eminent Soviet politician and statesman, Nikolai Vasil'evich Krylenko.

*   *   *

[N. V. Krylenko] was born on May 14, 1885—the son of Vasilii Abramovich Krylenko, who had taken an active part in the revolutionary outbreaks of Petersburg students in the 1880s and had been banished under police supervision to the remote village of Bakhteevka [sic] in the Smolensk gubernia. Not until five years later was the family allowed to move to Smolensk and subsequently to Lublin, where they lived for many years.

In 1903 Nikolai left high school for the historico-literary faculty of Petersburg University, where he at once joined the students' revolutionary movement. In December 1904, when he was nineteen he became a member of the RSDWP, and from then on he was well known among the progressive youth of Petersburg as a revolutionary leader and organizer of illegal meetings, rallies, strikes, and demonstrations. In the tense days of autumn 1905 Nikolai (whose Party name was "Abram") spoke daily at works and factory meetings in the Vyborg quarter and beyond the Neva Gate. As V. D. Bonch-Bruevich recalls, "Krylenko ... with his exceptional oratorical gifts ... spoke everywhere in those days in his thundering style. Young though he was, his speeches, full of moral fervor, made a profound impression on workers' meetings in the industrial districts."

It was at this time that Krylenko first met Lenin at a meeting of the Petersburg committee of the RSDWP, of which he was a member. In 1906 the Party assigned him to work among the troops, but before long he was arrested and sent back to Lublin. In the spring of 1909 he was allowed to return to Petersburg, where he passed his university examination with high honors. Once more in Lublin, on Lenin's instructions he organized the movement of political emigrants and illegal Party literature across the frontier, which he himself crossed several times for meetings with Lenin.

In summer 1912 he carried on underground work in Petersburg and was correspondent for the Bolshevik newspapers *Pravda* and *Zvezda*. Realizing the importance of legal knowledge to the Bolsheviks in their parliamentary fight, he enrolled in the university law faculty. In the fall of 1912 he volunteered to do his military service in the Sixty-ninth Riazan Infantry Regiment. A year later he had risen to the rank of ensign and once more joined Lenin, who sent him to Petersburg to work with the Bolshevik fraction in the Duma; but he was denounced by an *agent provocateur* and again arrested. In summer 1914 he emigrated to Switzerland, where he took part in the Bern conference of foreign sections of the RSDWP. In 1915 the CC of the RSDWP assigned him to illegal work in Russia. He was again arrested; this time he was sent straight from prison to the front, where he was at the time of the bourgeois-democratic February revolution. He had quickly become a favorite of the soldiers, who loved and trusted him thanks to his simple and friendly attitude, uprightness and martial courage, and above all his resolute opposition to the imperialist war. They elected him chairman of the regimental committee of the Thirteenth Finnish Rifle Regiment, and later of the division and army committees of the Eleventh Army on the southwestern front.

In May 1917, as a delegate of [The Eleventh Army] he attended the congress of front-line soldiers in Petrograd, and on behalf of his fellow fighters demanded the cessation of war. With other Bolsheviks then in Petersburg, including Mekhanoshin, Podvoisky, Nevsky, and Sulimov, he took an active part in the work of the Military Organization of the CC of the RSDWP(B). In June he traveled once more to Petrograd for the first all-Russian congress of soviets. Before leaving the front he issued a statement to the troops entitled "Why I Am Going to Petrograd," which was highly praised by Lenin....

After the events of July 3-5 repressions were carried out against the Bolsheviks; and among their arrested leaders was Krylenko, whom Kerensky thought so dangerous that he gave the order: "Even if no civil charges can be brought, Ensign Krylenko is to be placed under guard on my personal responsibility." The arrests of Bolsheviks called forth loud protests among the masses, and resolutions demanding their release were passed at many meetings and rallies....

By a decision of the CC of the RSDWP(B), Krylenko was proposed as a member of the constituent assembly. The upsurge of revolutionary feeling obliged the Provisional Government to free the arrested men, and Krylenko was once more in the thick of revolutionary events. During October the Party worked hard preparing for the armed uprising. Krylenko was elected to the Petrograd RMC and was chairman at the congress of soviets of the Northern oblast, at which a seventeen-member committee was formed including the Bolsheviks Antonov-Ovseenko, Krylenko, Dashkevich, Dybenko, Stuchka, Raskol'nikov, Sergeev, and others. The committee was charged with the duty of fighting for the convocation of a second congress of soviets and "uniting around itself all soviets and military revolutionary organizations."

On October 16 Krylenko, as representative of the Central Bureau of Military Organizations, addressed a meeting of the CC of the RSDWP(B), at which he warmly supported Lenin's resolution on the necessity of immediate preparation for an armed uprising. "The troops," he declared, "are wholly on our side, and we must take the initiative for an uprising." When the historic event took place he was one of its main organizers. "On October 25," he later recalled, "we had to ... visit every sector of the city where 'battles' were likely to be taking place, as well as the line of 'siege' of the Winter Palace where the remnants of the Provisional Government had taken refuge." On the RMC's orders he maintained liaison with the fronts, and on October 26 was able to inform the second congress of soviets that it was supported by the armies of the northern front. This was the congress that adopted the historic decrees on peasants' government in the world, headed by V. I. Lenin. Krylenko joined this government as a member of the committee for military affairs.

In the first days after the victory of the armed uprising the forces of counter-revolution hastily gathered to destroy the soviets. A cadets' revolt broke out in Petrograd as the Kerensky-Krasnov troops were approaching the capital. The Bolshevik Party under Lenin's direction took energetic steps to counter Kerensky's military adventure. It was vital to keep the garrison troops on the side of the revolution, and on the Party's orders Krylenko and others carried on intensive propaganda among the troops and persuaded the hesitant. The cadets had managed to seize the Mikhailovsky riding school building where the armored cars were stationed, and Krylenko hastened there to bring the crews back to their revolutionary allegiance. An eyewitness, Albert Rees Williams, thus describes the scene at a meeting of over 2,000 soldiers: "Krylenko ended his passionate speech ... with the cry: 'Those who are for Kerensky to the right; those who are for the Soviets to the left!' The gray mass of soldiers moved to the left. There were loud cries of delight. The drivers got into their cars, the exhaust pipes spluttered, and soon the great steel devils were rolling through the streets, the blue barrels of their machine guns ready to mow down the counterrevolutionaries."

The headquarters of the military command that directed the defeat of the anti-Soviet revolt was in the Smolnyi building. Podvoisky and Krylenko, both members of the RMC, were here, and on Lenin's orders set about regrouping all the military forces defending Petrograd.... The position was critical, and reinforcements had to be brought up quickly. On October 28 Krylenko tele-graphed in the name of the RMC to the revolutionary committee of the Fifth Army: "There are trains of artillery at Gatchina, where the enemy is giving orders. Bring up loyal revolutionary regiments to catch and punish the traitors."

Thanks to the heroic struggle of the defenders of the Red capital, the Kerensky-Krasnov counterrevolutionary revolt was suppressed. But there remained a center of counterrevolution in the headquarters (Stavka) of the su-preme commander at Mogilev, which ignored the decision of the second congress of soviets regarding the offer of an armistice to all belligerents and refused to obey the Soviet authority. Lenin's retort, on the night of November 8-9, was to appoint Ensign Krylenko commander in chief, by the authority of the government and CPC of the Russian Republic. On the morning of the November 9 the CPC broadcast as follows to all soldiers of the revolutionary army and sailors of the revolutionary fleet:

> Soldiers! The cause of peace is in your hands. Do not allow counterrevolutionary
> generals to thwart the great cause of peace.... Preserve the strictest revolutionary and
> military order.... V. Ul'ianov (Lenin), Chairman of the CPC; N. Krylenko,
> People's Commissar of Military Affairs and Commander in Chief.

Lenin's choice of Krylenko was no accident. He whom Lenin had described as "one of the keenest Bolsheviks and among those closest to the army" was well fitted to carry out the Party's orders by reason of his revolutionary back-ground and the tireless, self-denying work which had won him the soldiers' love and admiration. On November 11 he left for the front, and on the same day a further message of the CPC was addressed to the army. This ran:

> Soldiers: Continue the fight for an immediate armistice. Elect your delegates

for negotiations. Your Supreme Commander in Chief, Ensign Krylenko, is leaving
for the front today to take personal charge of the fight for an armistice.

In accordance with the CPC's decision, Krylenko sent envoys to the German
command to propose negotiations for an armistice. The enemy's official reply
was received on November 14. Having returned to Petrograd and reported the
position to the CC and CPC, Krylenko set out for Mogilev to liquidate the
rebellious headquarters. As his train approached the city, the counterrevolutionaries fell into increasing confusion. The "shock companies" formed
to defend the Stavka quickly left the city together with members of the SR-
Menshevik army committee. On November 19 the Mogilev RMC issued an
order stating that it "recognized Ensign Krylenko, commissar of the existing
government, as the only legal and national commander in chief of the Russian
Army, deriving his authority from the revolution itself." On November 20
Krylenko arrived at Mogilev with units of the revolutionary forces, and was
joined by revolutionary units from the western front under Berzin's command.
The Stavka, surrounded on all sides, surrendered without a fight, and the last
obstacle to peace was thus removed.*

On December 2, 1917, the armistice agreement was signed at Brest Litovsk
by Russia on the one hand and Austria-Hungary, Bulgaria, and Turkey on
the other. That day, Krylenko addressed the troops as follows:

> Comrades: Today, December 2, at Brest Litovsk an agreement was signed for
> an armistice on all fronts on which the Russian army is engaged.... The armistice
> will be followed by peace. The cherished dream of millions of workers and
> peasants and of the nations who inhabit Russia is close to fulfillment.... This
> peace has been bestowed on the Russian people by the revolution of October
> 25. It is brought to the people by the CPC.

In order to achieve and defend peace, the Soviet Republic had at once
to create armed forces of the revolution. The Party took decisions accordingly,
and in an order of December 25, 1917, the supreme commander called on
the revolutionary soldiers of the army to begin to form a new army to defend
the revolution. The creation of the armed forces of the Soviet Republic was
directed from start to finish by the CC headed by Lenin. The organization
and formation of the Red Army was the work of an all-Russian collegium
headed by Krylenko and Podvoisky.

---

*Ensign N. Krylenko was sent by Lenin to replace General N. Dukhonin (1876-1917) as acting
commander in chief of the Russian armies. After the Bolshevik seizure of power Dukhonin had
refused Lenin's order to begin negotiations for peace with the German high command. When
Krylenko arrived in Mogilev, General Dukhonin was arrested and brought to Krylenko's railroad
car at the station. A mob of sailors wanted to kill the general on the spot, but Krylenko spoke
against it. As soon as Krylenko left the scene, however, Dukhonin was dragged out of the car
and beaten to death. This episode climaxed the breakup of the old Russian Army.—ED.

After the conclusion of the Brest Litovsk treaty in March 1918, the Party assigned Krylenko to a new field of work: for the next twenty years he was concerned with the administration of Soviet justice. He was one of the organizers of the first revolutionary tribunals, the judicial organs and procurator's office, and the PC of Justice. Up to the beginning of the 1930s he was public prosecutor at all the main political trials which the proletarian dictatorship conducted against its class enemies. In this capacity he displayed in full measure both Leninist implacability toward enemies of the revolution, and socialist humanity. His indictments, with their brilliant oratory and subtle legal analysis of all the circumstances of guilt, are not only of technical but of high political interest, breathing as they do the spirit of the time and of the class struggles in which our country was engaged.

He was at all times a bold and ardent defender of socialist legality. "Our laws," he declared at the Sixteenth Party Congress, "are the forms in which the Party clothes its will." ... He did much to create and develop the study of Soviet law, the theory and practice of the Soviet political and legal structure. He published more than eighty books and pamphlets and many articles on the theory and practice of Soviet jurisprudence. He took an active part in drafting the most important legislative acts, such as the constitutions of the U.S.S.R. and RSFSR, and various codes and laws. He was also a member of the editorial boards of the History of the Civil War in the U.S.S.R., the Great Soviet Encyclopedia, and other works. On May 5, 1931, by a decree of the Presidium of the All-Union CEC, he was appointed PC of justice of the RSFSR and was relieved of his functions as procurator. In 1936 he became PC of justice of the U.S.S.R.

He was active as a teacher in senior juridical schools: for several years he held the chair of criminal law at the Moscow Institute of Soviet Law and taught at the Institute of Red Professors and other institutes of Soviet construction and law. In 1934 the presidium of the Communist Academy conferred on him the degree of Doctor of Political and Legal Sciences "for his work on the theory of Soviet law, the boldness and freshness of his thinking, his opposition to routine, his fight for the general Party line and class principles in theory and practice, the exceptional variety and range of his scientific works."

At the Fifteenth and Sixteenth CPSU congresses he was elected to the Central Control Commission; he was several times a member of the All-Union CEC, and in 1935 a member of its Presidium. His services to the Soviet state were rewarded with the Order of Lenin and the Order of the Red Banner. He was a revolutionary and a man of the Leninist school. Both before and after the revolution, the first Soviet as commander in chief and in the administration of Soviet justice he fought unsparingly for the people's interests and the realization of Lenin's ideas and principles. In the early days of the pre-1917 emigration, N. K. Krupskaia, who was a severe judge of people, wrote of him: "He is an excellent man and a good comrade." Today all who remember him speak of him warmly as a noble and enlightened soul. E. D. Stasova, who saw much of him in Party work, describes him as "an eminent statesman, a man in love with life, a character of many aspects, profoundly learned and with the most varied interests."

In 1938 his career was tragically cut short. He was slandered and became a victim of arbitrary rule as a result of the cult of Stalin's personality. Today the Party has restored the good name of its son, and Nikolai Vasil'evich Krylenko occupies his due place among the fighters who devoted their lives to the noble ideals of communism.[14]

NESTOR APOLLONOVICH LAKOBA

Biographical data

Born 1893, died 1936. Soviet political leader. Joined the CP in 1912. Born at Lykhny village, Abkhazia, the son of a peasant. Entered the Tiflis seminary in 1910; expelled in 1911. Joined the RSDWP and carried on Party work in Adzharia, Abkhazia, and later at Groznyi. In 1918 he was a leader of the uprising against the Menshevik government in Abkhazia, was deputy chairman of the Sukhum revolutionary military committee and organized a partisan unit. At the end of 1918 the Menshevik government imprisoned him at Sukhum, and in the spring of 1919 he was expelled from Georgia. In 1920, on the orders of the Caucasian bureau of the CC of the RCP(B) he directed the underground Bolshevik organization at Batumi. From March 1921 he was deputy chairman of the Abkhazian revolutionary committee; from February 1922 chairman of the CPC, and in 1930-36 chairman of the CEC of the Abkhazian ASSR. Was a member of the CECs of the Georgian SSR, the Transcaucasian SFSR, and the U.S.S.R., and a member of the bureau of the CC of the Georgian CP. During the cult of Stalin's personality he perished as a result of Beria's machinations. Posthumously rehabilitated.[15]

MIKHAIL MOISEEVICH MAIOROV

Biographical data

Born 1890, died 1940. Party and political leader; joined the CP in 1906. Born at Skorodnoe village, Minsk gubernia, the son of a handicraftsman. Carried on Party work at Kiev, Ekaterinoslav, Saratov, and Moscow. He spent three years in prison and ten in exile. In 1917 he was in charge of the Kiev organization of the RSDWP(B) and the Bolshevik group in the soviet of workers' and soldiers' deputies. Was a delegate to the seventh (April) conference of the RSDWP(B). At the second all-Russian congress of soviets he was elected a member of the All-Russian CEC. In 1918 he was chairman of the all-Ukrainian revolutionary committee. Took part in underground and partisan operations in the Ukraine. Served with the Red Army in 1919–20. Was secretary of the Odessa (1922-23, 1931-32) and Tomsk (1924-27) gubernia committees and chairman of the Astrakhan (1923-24) and Tomsk (1924-27) gubernia CECs. In 1927-30, deputy chairman of the central control commission of the Ukraine CP, and in 1930-31 PC of supplies of the Ukrainian SSR. In 1933-37, secretary of the Central Asian bureau of the CC of the CPSU. Was a delegate to the Tenth, Twelfth, and Fourteenth through Seventeenth Party congresses and the twelfth and fourteenth through sixteenth party conferences. In 1938 he was slandered, subjected to illegal repressions and perished. Posthumously rehabilitated.[16]

VARDAN ALEKSANDROVICH MAMIKONIAN

Biographical data

Born 1898, died 1938. Joined the CP in 1919. In 1920, while studying at the Sverdlov Party School, he was called up by the Party to serve in workers' and peasants' inspection under the RMC of the southeastern front. He also worked as head of the food department and was concerned with the reorganization of industry and agriculture at Piatigorsk. In December 1920 the Caucasian bureau of the CC of the RCP(B) sent him to Armenia with the first group of Communists, which also included D. Ter-Simonian, V. Eremian, and Khashutogian. Soon thereafter the Dashnaks launched their February adventure and all the Party members left for the front. Mamikonian, together with G. A. Atarbetian, served on the Elenovka front; later in 1921 he was for a short time a member of the revolutionary committee and head of workers' and peasants' inspection at Dilizhan. In 1922 he was chairman of the revolutionary committee and the executive committee at Karakilis, spent a year at Stepanavan, and then returned to Karakilis until 1926. As chairman of the executive committee of the Erevan city soviet and deputy PC of finance of Armenia, he was responsible for the building of the first hydroelectric power station at Erevan (Dzorages), also the Leninakan station and for the achievement of the [First] Five Year Plan of national economic development. In 1934 he was PC of supply of Transcaucasia. During his career he was elected a member of uezd committees of the Armenian CP, also of the Armenian and Transcaucasian CECs and the CC of the Armenian CP, and was a delegate to the latter party's first ten congresses. His life was tragically cut short in his fortieth year.[17]

PAVEL NIKOLAEVICH MOSTOVENKO

Biographical data

Born 1881, died 1939. Party and political leader; joined the CP in 1901. Son of a chief forester. Studied at the Petersburg Polytechnical Institute, and while in Petersburg joined the Union of Fighters for the Emancipation of the Working Class. Was a member of the Nizhnii Novgorod, Northern, Tver, and Moscow committees of the RSDWP, and was arrested several times. In 1905 he was chief organizer of the Blagushe-Lefortovsky district of Moscow and took part in the party conference at Tammerfors. Was a delegate to the Fifth Party Congress [London] in 1907. In 1917 he was a member of the Petrograd soviet, delegate to the Sixth Congress of the RSDWP(B) and representative of the Petrograd executive committee on the Rumanian front. Elected as a Bolshevik member of the Constituent Assembly. During the October Revolution he was a member of the Moscow RMC and a leader of the armed uprising in Moscow. At the end of 1917 he was chairman of the Moscow soviet of soldiers' deputies and a member of the presidium of the Moscow soviet. In 1918 he was engaged in underground work in the Ukraine; in 1919 he was secretary of the Ufa gubernia committee of the RCP(B) and helped to organize the Bashkir Republic. In 1921-22 he was the RSFSR diplomatic representative in Lithuania and Czechoslovakia. From 1923 he was engaged in important economic tasks. From 1929 he was rector of the Moscow Higher Technical School and later agent of the Supreme Council of the National Economy in Berlin. In 1934-37 he was director of senior academic courses of the PC of Heavy Industry. Slandered and subjected to repression as a result of the cult of Stalin's personality; rehabilitated posthumously.[18]

ALEKSANDR IVANOVICH MURALOV

Biographical data

Born 1886, died 1937. From 1907 to 1917 he was Party organizer of the sub-raikon of the Rogozhsky district of Moscow. Was arrested and imprisoned, and after his release carried on active underground work. In 1917-19 he was chairman of the uezd committee of the CP and the uezd CEC at Aleksin in the Tula gubernia. In 1919-23, gubernia military commissar and commander of the Tula Fortified Area. After the Civil War he was chairman of the Moscow and Rostov-on-Don councils of national economy and at the same time a member of the bureau of the Donets committee (Donkom) and Donets CEC of the RCP(B). From 1923 to 1938 he was chairman of the Nizhnii Novgorod (Gorki) gubernia executive committee and a member of the bureau of the gubernia committee of the CPSU. During 1928-30 deputy PC, and in 1930-33 PC of agriculture of the RSFSR; in 1933-35, deputy PC of agriculture of the U.S.S.R. In 1935-37, president of the All-Union Lenin Academy of Agriculture. In 1937 he became a victim of the cult of Stalin's personality.[19]

A fighter in Lenin's guard

Communists of the older generation well remember the name of Aleksandr Ivanovich Muralov, a staunch and selfless Leninist. From his youth onward he was in the thick of the revolutionary struggle. In 1905, as a youth of nineteen, he joined the Bolshevik organization of the town of Serpukhov near Moscow and took part in the formation of Marxist groups, the conduct of strikes, and the publication of the Bolshevik newspaper *Vpered* (Forward). As a student at Moscow University he was active as a Bolshevik within the students' organization, and in 1907 he was Party organizer of the underground committee of the Rogozhsky district of Moscow. For this illegal work he was arrested and imprisoned by the Tsarist authorities, but repression could not break his spirit. After his release he continued to be active in the Bolshevik underground in various parts of Russia.

After the October Revolution, he was in the front rank of those engaged in building up the young socialist state. He was chairman of the CP uezd committee and uezd executive committee at Aleksin in the Tula gubernia, and it would be hard to name any sector in which his active influence was not felt. As a Party worker he molded the cadres of the local Bolshevik organization which grew up at the beginning of 1918. Thanks to his skill in choosing able and devoted individuals and creating a constructive atmosphere of mutual confidence and strict discipline, he and the Communists achieved much in the city and uezd in a comparatively short time. Schools, kindergartens, and peasants' reading rooms were opened, and in 1919 Aleksin saw its first congress of peasant women. At the end of that year, when General Denikin's troops were approaching Tula, Muralov became gubernia military commissar and commander of the Tula Fortified Area. After the Civil War he was chairman of the Moscow and Rostov-on-Don councils of national economy and was at the same time a member of the bureau of the Donets committee of the RCP(B) and of the Donets executive committee. From 1923 to February 1928 he was chairman of the Nizhnii Novgorod (Gorki) gubernia executive committee and a member of the bureau of the gubernia committee of the CPSU.

Muralov belonged to the type that Lenin called "practical" workers—that is to say, men of high organizing ability, capable of setting about the solution of any concrete problem in a sober and sensible manner. In addition, he possessed a solid education and a wide political outlook.... As chairman of the Nizhnii Novgorod gubernia executive committee he showed high statesmanship qualities, and in March 1928 the Party promoted him to the post of deputy

PC of agriculture of the RSFSR. He became PC in January 1930, and in March 1933 became deputy PC of agriculture of the U.S.S.R. From June 1935 he was president of the All-Union Lenin Academy of Agricultural Sciences, where he encouraged specialists to concentrate on the practical development of agricultural science throughout the country.

An eminent statesman, staunch Bolshevik, and a member of the glorious cohort which fought through three revolutions, he was elected a delegate to many Party congresses and conferences; he was a member of the All-Russian CEC from 1919 and of the All-Union CEC at all convocations. His brilliant career was cut short in 1937.[20]

GAZANFAR MAKHMUD-OGLY MUSABEKOV

Biographical data

Born 1888, died 1938. Political and Party leader; joined the CP in 1918. Born at Pirebedil' village, Baku gubernia, the son of a peasant. During 1912-17 he studied at the medical faculty of Kiev University, and from 1917 practiced as a physician in the Kuba uezd of Azerbaidzhan. After the February revolution he was chairman of the executive committee of the Kuba soviet, and from December 1917 deputy chairman of the Baku gubernia food committee. From August 1918 he worked as a doctor in an Astrakhan hospital; he was chairman of the Astrakhan Moslem section of the RCP(B) and a leader of the Astrakhan department of the Gummet party. From April 1920 he was a member of the Azerbaidzhan revolutionary committee and PC of food. In 1922-28, chairman of the Azerbaidzhan CPC; in 1929-31, chairman of the CEC of the Azerbaidzhan SSR; and in 1931-36, chairman of the CPC of the Transcaucasian SFSR. From 1925 to 1937 he was a chairman of the CEC of the U.S.S.R. He was also a member of the Executive Committee of the Comintern and a delegate to the Fourteenth through Seventeenth CPSU congresses, at which he was elected a candidate member of the CC of the CPSU. In 1937 he was slandered and illegally condemned, and soon thereafter perished. Posthumously rehabilitated.[21]

ALEKSANDR VASIL'EVICH ODINTSOV

Biographical data

Born 1895, died 19—. Joined the CP in 1917. Born at Vypolzovo village, Ostersk uezd, Chernigov gubernia; son of a priest. Joined the revolutionary movement while attending the Chernigov seminary; after passing through four classes of general education there, he entered the Kiev Commercial Institute and afterward the law faculty of Kiev University. In 1917 he took an active part in restoring Soviet power in the Chernigov and Kiev areas and was a member of the RMC. In 1918 he was commissar of internal affairs of the Ostersk uezd soviet of workers' and peasants' deputies, volunteered for the Red Army and as a political officer in a cavalry regiment and took part in combating Petliura's forces. In June 1919 he was a member of the Party's Chernigov gubernia committee, and was later president of the Extraordinary Revolutionary Tribunal. Commanded an operational sector of the front during the White Polish advance, but was soon recalled for Party work. In 1920-21 he was first secretary of the Party's Kiev gubernia committee, and in 1921-22 secretary of the Odessa committe. From 1923 to 1934 he occupied government posts, was chairman of *Sel'sky gospodar'* (the Farmers' Union) and deputy PC of agriculture of the Ukrainian SSR and U.S.S.R., member of the collegium of the PC of Agriculture of the U.S.S.R., and PC of agriculture of the Ukrainian SSR. From 1934 he was head of agricultural administration of the Azov-Black Sea region and a member of the Party's Azov-Black Sea regional committee. In October 1932 he was elected a member of the CC of the Ukraine CP. Perished during the cult of Stalin's personality.[22]

OVSEP AMBARTSUMOVICH POGOSIAN

Biographical data

Born 1887, died 1938. Born in the village of Verin Karmir-Akhpiur, in the present Shamshadin raion. After attending village school he entered the Nersisian seminary at Tiflis, whence he graduated in 1907. Joined the CP in 1906, and received political training direct from S. Shaumian, A. Zurabian, S. Kas'ian, and others. In 1905-7 he took an active part in the revolutionary struggle of the Transcaucasian proletariat. In summer 1906 he organized a hand-written newspaper, *Bednyikrest'ianin* (The Poor Peasant), at Shamshadin. He was more than once pursued by the police for revolutionary work and was sentenced to death by Dashnak terrorists.

From 1907 he studied at the Moscow Commerical Institute, whence he graduated with an economics degree. Called up during the imperialist war, he carried on active work among the soldiers at Elisavetpol. Before and during the February revolution he and other Bolsheviks and revolutionary soldiers fought stubbornly against the bourgeois Provisional Government, the SR-Mensheviks, and Dashnak "conciliators." At the first elections to soldiers' committees he became chairman of a regimental, and later of a corps committee. Was arrested in August 1917.

During the October Revolution Pogosian was at Tiflis, and was soon sent to Ekaterinodar in the northern Caucasus, where he and some comrades organized the underground newspaper *Problesk*; he wrote articles and features under the pseudonyms I. Shakhmadinsky and I. P. Took an active part in the fight to establish Soviet power in the northern Caucasus. In 1918 he helped to organize the Tamansk Army, and later the Red Eleventh Army. When the Red Army temporarily withdrew from Novorossiisk, on Party orders he directed the evacuation of the city, a high point in the annals of the Civil War. [He also directed] the scuttling of what remained of the fleet, after which he got away to Transcaucasia via Tuapse. In Armenia he made contact with prominent Bolsheviks working at Erevan and elsewhere: S. Alaverdian, A. Mravian, S. Kas'ian, D. Shakhverdian, S. Martikian, and others. In January 1920, at the first conference of Armenian Communist organizations, he was elected to the Armenian committee of the RCP(B). Shortly afterward he was arrested by the Dashnaks and expelled from Armenia. In summer 1920, when the Armenian Bolshevik Party was being organized, he became a member of the foreign bureau of its CC. In January 1921 he was back in Armenia, and in February he was appointed a member of the revolutionary committee of the Dilizhan uezd; later he was sent to Karaklis and the Lori uezd as food procurement agent and member of the Karaklis uezd food commission. In January 1922 he was appointed Armenian PC of food, and from 1923, when the PCs of food of the Transcaucasian republics were unified, food agent for Armenia. In 1925-28 he was chairman of Gosplan and deputy chairman of the CPC of the Armenian Republic.

In 1928 Pogosian was transferred to Moscow, first as head of a department of Gosplan (U.S.S.R.) and later, on Ordzonikidze's recommendation, to work in the PC of Heavy Industry. He occupied other important posts in high economic organs of the state and in the CC apparatus of the Party. He lectured in political economy at the Institute of Eastern Peoples and carried on literary and journalistic activity. At different times he was elected to the CC of the Armenian CP and to its bureau, to the Party's Transcaucasian regional commission, and to the CECs of Armenia, Transcaucasia, and the U.S.S.R. Under the pseudonyms Iosif, I. Shamshadinsky, Sheg, and I. P. he published articles in the legal and clandestine press about economic questions and the life and struggles of workers, peasants, and soldiers. His life was tragically cut short in 1938.[23]

K. SARYMULDAEV

Biographical data

Born 1898, died 1938. Joined the CP in 1918; took an active part in establishing and strengthening Soviet power in the Aulie-Ata (Dzhambul) uezd. In 1919-20 he was chairman of the uezd executive committee and secretary of the uezd and city committee of the Turkestan CP; in 1920-22 chairman of the uezd revolutionary committee, head of the Agitprop department of the Party's Syr-Dar'ia oblast committee, and deputy PC of internal affairs of the Kazakh ASSR. In 1925-28 he was chairman of the supreme council of national economy of Kazakhstan; in 1928-31 chairman of the republic's Gosplan; in 1931-33 PC of agriculture; in 1934-36 chairman of the East Kazakhstan oblast executive committee; and in 1936-37 deputy PC of the food industry of the republic. Was a delegate to several regional Party conferences and to the seventeenth all-Union conference.[24]

VASILII IVANOVICH TOKSIN

Biographical data

Born 1889, died 1942. An eminent Party and state official of the Chuvash Republic. Born at Ianshikhovo-Norvashi village, Tsivilsk uezd, Kazan gubernia, the son of a peasant. Served in the Red Army, 1919-21; took part in Civil War operations against the White Guardists. Studied at the Sverdlov Communist University, 1921-24. From 1925 to 1937 he was continuously engaged on Party and government work in Chuvashia, serving as an instructor, deputy head of organization department, head of press department, and head of cultural and educational propaganda of the Chuvash oblast committee of the CPSU; then deputy PC of agriculture and PC of finance of the Chuvash ASSR. In 1932-37 he was chairman of the CPC of the Chuvash ASSR. In 1937 he was unjustly expelled from the Party and subjected to repression. Rehabilitated posthumously in 1956.[25]

VI. CAPTAINS OF INDUSTRY

GENERAL COMMENTS ON THE PURGE OF ECONOMIC
EXECUTIVES AND ITS EFFECTS ON INDUSTRIALIZATION

The success of industrialization would have been...greater but for the dire consequences of the cult of Stalin's personality and especially the loss of cadres inflicted on industry. Many deserving leaders of industry and skilled organizers of production were slandered and subjected to repression: the names include G. P. Butenko, G. V. Gvakhariia, G. I. Lomov [-Oppokov], S. S. Lobov, I. E. Liubimov, V. I. Mezhlauk, K. M. Ots, M. L. Rukhimovich, and many others. Matters reached a point where, in 1937, Stalin, Molotov, and Kaganovich began to assert that sabotage had infected "all or nearly all our economic, administrative, and Party organizations." The wave of repressions brought about an atmosphere of suspicion that hampered initiative and the technical creative powers of the masses. Stalin and his immediate entourage often disregarded practical possibilities in their unreasoning demand for overfulfillment of the already high norms of industrial construction. This meant that the nation's strength was overtaxed and that many detailed plans were unrealistic or inexpedient. The subjectivist errors fostered by the cult of Stalin's personality compounded the effect of miscalculations that were an inevitable feature of the first long-range national economic plans in history. Nevertheless, the huge resources and advantages of socialism, the system of planned economy and the energies of the people, inspired by the CP, made it possible successfully to complete the industrialization of the country.[1]

The heavy loss

In 1937-38 Soviet industry suffered a heavy blow as a result of mass repressions. The loss thus inflicted was difficult to make good. A large number of young engineers who had graduated from technical college as late as 1933 or 1934 became directors of enterprises, and many gifted organizers of production arose from their ranks as the new commanders gradually gained experience. The outstanding industrial organizers who became prominent during the Third Five Year Plan have become part of the history of our industry and our country. Almost all of them received higher technical education and became acquainted with their chosen fields not only from the point of view of theory but by actual experience as foremen, shop superintendents, chief engineers, and managers.

421

These were the cadres that ran our industry during the war and the postwar reconstruction.[2]

Chemical industry cadres

In 1937-38 the chemical industry suffered a loss of leading cadres that was difficult to repair. The victims of illegal repression included many experienced organizers, able managers of works and projects, engineers, and Party workers. Among those who perished were P. G. Arutuniants, the director of the Bobriki combine; I. S. Enov, former secretary of the Bobriki city committee of the Party; M. Granovsky, director of the Berezniki combine; V. E. Tsifrinovich, director of the Solikamsk combine; E. L. Brodov, director of the chief administration of the nitrogen industry; L. Strezh, manager of the SK-I works; O. P. Osipov-Shmidt, deputy PC of heavy industry; I. I. Todorsky, head of the chief administration of the basic chemical industry; and Professor N. F. Iushkevich....[3]

Railroad personnel

Kaganovich's appointment as PC of transport was marked from the outset by mass arrests of railroad personnel. He himself drew up unfounded political charges against innocent people and insisted on their arrest. He impressed on the Party's economic cadres that disguised enemies of the people were at work in all sectors and that the most thorough and extensive detection methods were necessary. Addressing a meeting of railroad activists on March 10, 1937, he said: "I cannot name a single railroad or region in which Trotskyist-Japanese sabotage has not been at work.... More: there is not a single aspect of rail transport which has not been a prey to saboteurs...."

Under Kaganovich's regime, railroad personnel were arrested in batches according to lists drawn up in advance. Those arrested without cause included his own deputies, almost all managers of individual lines, heads of political departments, and other key personnel who have now been rehabilitated, many of them posthumously. The Commission of Party Control has in its possession thirty-two personal letters from Kaganovich to the NKVD demanding the arrest of eighty-three senior railroad officials. One of these, dated August 10, 1937, is an outstanding example of the criminal irresponsibility with which he concocted baseless accusations. In this letter he demanded the arrest of ten senior members of the PC of Transport for no reason whatsoever except that he, Kaganovich, thought their behavior suspicious. On this ground alone they were branded as spies and saboteurs and suffered the same tragic fate as many others. This was not an isolated case, but an example of his method of operation as PC of transport and of heavy industry and on his tours of oblast Party organizations.[4]

Kharkov economic leaders

The Party archives contain documents which give a picture of the harsh conditions under which the Party organization had to work during the cult of

Stalin's personality. Many of the chief Party and economic leaders in the Kharkov area were slandered and made to suffer unjustly on the pretext of combating enemies of the people. One such was N. N. Demenko, a noted Party worker whose membership dated from 1916, a member of the politburo of the CC of the Ukraine CP and first secretary of that Party's Kharkov oblast committee. Another was N. F. Gikalo, likewise a member of the politburo and first secretary of the Kharkov oblast committee, who had been a Party member since June 1917. Others were N. [sic] I. Svistun, a manager of the Kharkov tractor plant and a member of the Party since 1909; I. P. Bondarenko, a manager of the same plant and a Communist since November 1917; and I. I. Lisin, a Party member since 1913 and director of a cement plant. The cult of personality dealt a severe blow to the whole Party and wrought inconceivable hardship; but it could not prevent our country's forward movement toward socialism. The CP and its organizations at Kharkov and elsewhere succeeded in solving the problem of building socialism in our country.[5]

TEIMUR MAKHMUD-OGLY ALIEV

Biographical data

Born 1896, died 1937. Joined the Bolshevik Party in 1916. In 1916-20 he was chairman of the soviet of peasants' deputies in the Geokchai uezd, served on the district military committee and later on the city soviet of Workers' deputies at Kazan, and carried on underground work at Geokchai, Agdash, and Shusha. After the establishment of Soviet power in Azerbaidzhan he was president of the supreme revolutionary tribunal of the republic and at the same time PC of foreign trade and a member of the presidium of the supreme economic council of the Azerbaidzhan SSR. In 1920-32 he was PC of justice of the Azerbaidzhan SSR, a member of the collegium of the PC of foreign trade of the Transcaucasian SSR, and chairman of the CPC of the Nakhichevan Autonomous Republic. In 1932-37 he was chairman of planning administration of the CEC of the U.S.S.R., deputy chairman of the CPC of the Kazakh SSR, and a member of the Kazakhstan regional commission of the CPSU and also of the Party's Alma-Ata city committee and the Kazakhstan CEC. In July 1937 he was arrested and became a victim of the cult of Stalin's personality.[6]

Loyal to the Party's banner

Azerbaidzhan's first five-year plan—what would it be like, how many new plants would have to be built in Baku and the rest of Azerbaidzhan, and what would be the increase in oil refining capacity? What expansion would take place at the plants of Bibi-Eibat, Ramany, and Kala, and in what directions would the irrigation canals run? Scientists, economists, key workers and all zealous Communists were engaged in working out the great plan. Their work was marked by exact calculation, boldness, and true revolutionary impetus. Inspired by faith in the triumph of a noble ideal, they were sustained by the great works already accomplished by the proletariat and peasants of Azerbaidzhan under the guidance of the Communist Party.

The Communist Teimur Makhmud-ogly Aliev was in direct charge of the group working on the five-year plans. He was PC of finance of the Azerbaidzhan SSR and later chairman of the republic's Gosplan. The plans were indeed within the bounds of reality, as was shown by the fact that the Baku workers fulfilled the oil plan in two and a half years. Aliev's statesmanlike approach and initiative were shown in the efficient distribution of productive resources in the republic. Like the other leading communists of Azerbaidzhan, he could see beyond the forest of oil derricks and factory chimneys to the needs of the workers, taking equal care to develop the republic's economy and to promote the welfare and culture of the population....

While still a youth, he took part in the revolutionary movement. As a student at the law faculty of Kazan University he attended student gatherings, frequented the society of progressive workers, and carried on organizing and propaganda work among the masses. He was arrested, but the police had little evidence and were obliged to release the unruly student. In October 1916 he joined the CP and was thenceforth a professional revolutionary. Returning to his home country of Azerbaidzhan, he was elected chairman of the soviet of peasants' deputies of the Geokchai uezd. From the end of 1917 until the middle of 1918 he was again at Kazan.... During the temporary eclipse of Soviet power in Azerbaidzhan he never doubted the final victory of Bolshevism. He carried on underground work among the peasants and, on the instructions of the Party organization, helped the Shusha uezd underground committee to conduct organizational and propaganda work. Thanks to him, local Party cells were strengthened in Geokchai and Agdash. In the Karabakh region, together with local Communists, he carried on explanatory work among the population of Shusha and neighboring villages, exposing the antinational policy of the counterrevolutionaries and encouraging the workers to unite in brotherly friendship. This was dangerous work, but Teimur did not know what it was to shirk difficulties: he boldly made contact with the operational troops of the Musavatist army and urged them to come over to the people's side.

His revolutionary work prevented him from finishing his university law course, but his knowledge in [the legal] field was of value to the young Soviet republic. Soon after the victory of Soviet power in Azerbaidzhan he was appointed president of the [republic's] supreme revolutionary tribunal. At the same time he was PC of foreign trade and a member of the republic's supreme economic council. The Party entrusted him with responsible office, and he in turn devoted all his power to strengthening revolutionary legality and order, to restoring the republic's economy and developing its economic ties. It is hard to mention any important event in Azerbaidzhan in the early twenties with which he was not in some way connected. In September 1920 he was among the organizers of the Congress of Eastern Peoples.... The revolution had triumphed, but it had many open and secret enemies who were ready to raise their heads at any moment. Counterrevolutionary revolts broke out in various parts of Azerbaidzhan and an uprising against Soviet power took place at Zakataly. Aliev, accompanied by Narimanov, went to the spot and initiated energetic and decisive measures that soon put an end to the revolt....

The Party assigned its faithful son to many types of work. He was a member of the foreign trade collegium of the Transcaucasian SFSR and chairman of the CPC of the Nakhichevan Autonomous Republic. In Nakhichevan he devoted all his rich experience and knowledge to the cause of economic revival, training national cadres and improving the workers' cultural and living conditions. A teachers' seminary was set up in Nakhichevan on his initiative, and he took part in the construction of the Dzhulfa-Baku railroad and in planning new electric power stations in the republic.

In February 1932 he was recalled by the CC of the CPSU and appointed chairman of planning administration of the CEC of the U.S.S.R. In 1933 the CC sent him to Kazakhstan, where he was deputy chairman of the republic's CPC. He was also a member of the Kazakhstan regional committee of the CPSU, the Party's Alma-Ata city committee, and the Kazakhstan CEC. He worked in Kazakhstan until July 1937.

He was several times elected a member of the CC of the Azerbaidzhan CP, the Azerbaidzhan CEC, and the Transcaucasian CEC. He devoted his whole life to fighting for the happiness of the working people and the triumph of communism in our country.[7]

MIKHAIL VASIL'EVICH BARINOV

Biographical data

Born 1888, died 19—. Joined the Bolshevik Party in 1904. Born on Durnovo estate, Saratov gubernia. In 1901 he was a mechanic's apprentice, then a mechanic, lathe operator, and foreman at the Kavkaz works owned by the Mirzoev brothers. In 1911-18 he was secretary of the local Bolshevik Party organization and member of the revolutionary committee of the town of Poti. In 1918-21 he was at Krasnodar, and in 1921-26 worked in the oil industry at Baku, being deputy director and, from 1926 to 1933, director of the State Association of the Azerbaidzhan Petroleum Industry. From 1933 he was director of the main administration of the petroleum industry. He was elected several times to the Baku soviet, the Transcaucasian CEC, and the CEC of the U.S.S.R.; was a member of the CC and Baku city party committee of the Azerbaidzhan CP, the Party's Transcaucasian regional committee, and the presidium of the CEC of the Azerbaidzhan SSR. He became a victim of the cult of Stalin's personality.[8]

A true soldier of the revolution

"A Party member devoted to the revolutionary cause"—such was Kirov's description of M. V. Barinov, who joined the CP in 1904 and became a prominent Soviet statesman, organizer, and director of the country's oil industry. It is a concise but complete and exact account of Barinov's whole life and activity. Devotion to the revolution, the selfless struggle for its victory and the building of socialism—such was the keynote of the career of this outstanding man and thoroughly honest Communist. His name is well known to all workers in the country's oil industry, and is especially close and dear to the workers of Baku and all Azerbaidzhan. He was indeed a son of the Baku working class, among whom he spent thirty-three years of his life.

He was born on October 14, 1888, on Durnovo estate in the Saratov gubernia, a descendant of generations of working men. His grandfather, father, and brothers were workers: his father was a mechanic and threshing-machine operator. In 1889 the family moved to Baku, where Mikhail worked for more than thirty years in the oil industry. Despite [his family's] humble circumstances he received an education at the Russo-Tatar school at Sabunchi and the engineering faculty of the Baku Technical School. He began to work at only thirteen years of age as an apprentice to a mechanic and then became a mechanic, lathe operator, and foreman at the Kavkaz works owned by the Mirzoev brothers. In 1904 he joined the Party through its Balakhany organization. Prominent Baku Bolsheviks often met at the Barinovs' home, where his uncles also lived, and such men as S. Shaumian, P. Dzhaparidze, and I. Fioletov exercised a strong influence on young Mikhail. After the celebrated strike of Baku workers in December 1904, he took part for the next fourteen years in many strikes and revolutionary demonstrations of the Baku oil workers.

After leaving the Baku Technical School in 1911 he went to Batumi and then to Poti, where he was living at the outbreak of the revolution. During these years he carried on active Party work and was secretary of the local Bolshevik organization and a member of the Poti city revolutionary committee. In 1918-21 he lived at Krasnodar, where he went to escape persecution at the hands of the Menshevik government of Georgia. In 1921 he returned to Baku, which had become his second home. At this time economic disaster had overtaken the whole area, turning Baku into an "oil cemetery." In 1920 oil production stood at 30 percent of its prewar level, and the number of wells in operation had fallen from 3,500 to 960.

Under the leadership of the CP and together with the whole Soviet people, the Baku oil workers fought for the victory of socialist construction according to the course mapped out by the great Lenin. Guided by such true Leninists as S. M. Kirov, N. Narimanov, and others, the Azerbaidzhan Party organization conducted a heroic struggle and inspired the Baku oil workers to strive with the utmost enthusiasm for the revival of their industry. The problems and difficulties of this industry were always in the forefront of Lenin's attention. In a telegram to G. K. Ordzhonikidze the great leader wrote: "I have been disturbed at the state of Baku.... Please keep me frequently and exactly informed of progress in improving the oil industry there."

In 1923 Barinov became deputy director of the Azerbaidzhan petroleum industry, and devoted all his efforts to reviving it, together with A. P. Serebrovsky, I. M. Gubkin, and others. [To this end also] the Baku workers displayed prodigies of heroism; in August 1922 the All-Russian CEC conferred on them the Red Banner of Labor as a reward for their exemplary performance in restoring the national economy. In 1926 Barinov became director of the Azerbaidzhan petroleum industry, a post which he held until December 1933. During those years the industry achieved great successes. On March 31, 1931, the Baku workers were among the first in the country to fulfill the First Five Year Plan in two and one-half years, for which the industry and Barinov himself were awarded the Order of Lenin.

Early in December 1933 Barinov became director of the chief administration of the petroleum industry. Working with G. K. Ordzhonikidze, N. V. Kuibyshev, and others, he devoted all his strength and knowledge to building up the socialist society and its economy. In particular he directed the technical reconstruction of the oil industry of our country.

While at Baku he was several times elected to the local soviet, the Transcaucasian CEC, and the CEC of the U.S.S.R.; he was a member of the CC and Baku city committee of the Azerbaidzhan CP, of the Transcaucasian regional committee of the Party, and of the presidium of the CEC of the Azerbaidzhan SSR.

A victim of the cult of Stalin's personality, he was basely slandered, arrested, and perished at the height of his powers. The workers of Azerbaidzhan and the whole Soviet people cherish the noble memory of this true son of the Party and people, the Communist M. V. Barinov.[9]

KARL MIKELEVICH BEGGE

Biographical data

Born 1884, died 19—. Joined the CP in 1902. Born at Libava (Libau). After being arrested for the first time he moved in 1904 to Riga, where he carried on underground work. Was arrested again, and after his release in 1906 became a member of the city committee of the LSDWP (Lettish Social Democratic Workers' Party). In 1907-9 he was a member of the Riga city committee of the Social Democratic Party of the Lettish Region. In 1909 he was sentenced by a military court to four years hard labor, and after serving this sentence was exiled to Siberia. In 1913-17 he was in France, and in 1917-25 in Petrograd, where he was representative of the PC of Foreign Trade, member of the presidium of the Petrograd soviet, and deputy chairman of the Baltic Steamship Administration. In 1925-30 he was chairman of the Soviet trade delegation in Germany, and from 1931 a member of the presidium of the All-Russian Council of the National Economy and of the collegium of the PC of Heavy Industry of the U.S.S.R. He became a victim of the cult of Stalin's personality.[10]

A distinguished career

I should like to say a word in praise of a man whom I consider my teacher and mentor—a staunch Bolshevik who went through the fire of three revolutions and did much to build up the Soviet socialist state. I refer to Karl Mikelevich Begge, who would be eighty years old at about this time. The son of a Libau stevedore, he became a worker and revolutionary at an early age. He helped his father to distribute literature among the workers, and in 1902 was admitted to the Latvian Social Democratic Workers' Party. He was arrested for the first time on March 1, 1904, but managed to trick his captors and escape to Riga, where he threw himself into underground work. He was arrested for the second time in January 1906, and after his release was elected by the Libau Bolsheviks to the city committee of the LSDWP. But the gendarmerie were again on his trail and he had once more to leave his native city. In 1907 he was a member of the Riga city committee of the Social Democratic Party of the Lettish Region, where he worked in the propaganda section. Less than a year later he was arrested again, and in 1909 was sentenced by a military court to four years hard labor. After serving this sentence he was exiled to Siberia, but soon ran away; in the fall of 1913 his Libau comrades secretly put him on board a ship sailing for France.

In August 1917 he came to Petrograd, and after the October Revolution the Party assigned him to the important posts of representative of the PC of Foreign Trade, member of the presidium of the Petrograd soviet, etc. In those difficult and anxious times the port of Petrograd—the only one which the Soviets possessed on the Baltic—had fallen into decay, and Begge devoted all his strength to restoring it. I remember that during the famine which engulfed the young Soviet Republic as a result of the crop failures of 1921-22, the government bought large supplies of foreign grain, and Lenin gave orders that it should be transshipped through the port of Petrograd as rapidly as possible. I was then deputy chairman of the Baltic Steamship Administration and admired the tireless energy with which Comrade Begge tackled his difficult task. In the cold and hungry year of 1921 we handled about 150 ships laden with food cargoes, at a time when the port was navigable for less than seven months in the year. For the rest of the time it was icebound, and our exports and imports had to go through the warmwater ports of bourgeois Latvia and Estonia. The governments of these countries seized the opportunity to impose heavy duties and rail freight charges on our goods in transit. Icebreakers were needed to prolong the period of navigation at Petrograd, and I remember Begge's joy when, together with the Baltic shipyard workers, he reported by telegram to Lenin that the first Soviet icebreaking campaign had begun, with a vessel named the *Ermak*.

He also devoted much strength and energy to developing trade with the U.S.A., Japan, and China. At his suggestion our largest merchant ship at that time, the *Dekabrist*, was sent on a long voyage to the East. During a period of seven months this vessel carried many cargoes for the Soviet Union and sailed over 30,000 miles. Thousands of workers of different nationalities trod its decks in foreign ports and welcomed its crew as representatives of the first workers' and peasants' state in the history of the world.

In 1925-30 Begge was head of the Soviet trade delegation in Germany and took steps for the broad development of Soviet-German trade. A year later he became a member of the presidium of the All-Russian Council of the National Economy. After its reorganization he was a member of the collegium of the PC of Heavy Industry, where he worked directly under the eminent Party and political leader Sergo Ordzhonikidze.

During the cult of Stalin's personality this scrupulously honest Bolshevik was slandered and arrested, and perished. Our Party has restored his good name, and I suggest that the executive committee of the Libava city soviet of workers' deputies would do well to name one of the city's streets after this distinguished son of Latvia, the Communist and Leninist Comrade Begge.[11]

DAVID SAMUELOVICH BEIKA

Biographical data

Born 1885, died 19—. Joined the CP in 1903. Became a teacher in 1905, and in 1906 commanded a partisan detachment at Dobele. In 1915-17 he carried on revolutionary work at Boston, U.S.A., and was secretary of the CC of the General Organization of Lettish Workers. In 1917-19, having returned to Latvia, he carried on underground work in German-occupied Riga. In 1919 he was PC of industry in the Soviet Latvian government. In 1932-37 he was representative of the PC of Heavy Industry of the U.S.S.R. and a member of the CPC of the RSFSR; also secretary of the Smolensk and Arkhangelsk gubernia committees and chairman of the All-Russian Union of Industrial Co-operatives. In 1937 he was a member of the RMC at Madrid, and was later sent by the Party CC to the U.S.A. to strengthen ties with the CP there. Perished during the cult of Stalin's personality.[12]

David Beika's career

David Samuelovich Beika was one of the most outstanding members of the CP, which he joined in 1903. His life is indissolubly connected with the struggle of the Russian, Latvian, and international proletariat for socialism and democracy.

In 1905...the socialists of Dobele, headed by the young teacher David Beika, threw the pastor Zeberg out of the local church; and the people who had been listening to his unctuous words flocked to the main square at the call of those who were proclaiming a new life. Here Beika made his first speech to the excited townsfolk.... Together with farm laborers he took part in organizing the revolutionary distribution committees, confiscating landowners' estates and property, and setting up a people's militia. On a damp, chilly night in November he led the people of Dobele to establish revolutionary power at Yelgava (Mitau)....

In 1906...a punitive detachment had just left Dobele, when at night, under cover of darkness, the young teacher and a few companions stole back into [Beika's] parents' house—a humble dwelling which can still be seen on Imanta Sudmalis Street. His mother embraced her son, pressing her wet cheek to his shoulder and saying: "There's nothing but death all around, David—death and fires. Your teacher Felldman was killed before my eyes. Some ruffian gave a signal with a glove and he was done for—such a man, too.".... The first fires of revenge burned in the German pastor's garden: the revolutionaries set fire to the property of the reactionary who betrayed Bilenshtein.

This was the first exploit of the Dobele group of "forest brothers," as the organized revolutionary detachment was called. It operated under the orders of the Yelgava Party committee, and Beika was elected its first commander. The Black Hundred gangs were filled with confusion and fear, as the newspapers almost every day reported fresh outrages:

> On January 9 the forest between Zhagara and Mezhamuizha was full of armed men. Some of them stormed the water-mill and opened the locks so as to stop its operation. The laborers then held a political meeting in the forest.

                    *   *   *

> At Ila, Biksti, and Sniker the rebels seized equipment which had been consigned to the volost authorities for dispatch to Yelgava.

                    *   *   *

> Yesterday, in broad daylight, a revolutionary band took possession of the town of Sloka, which was in their hands for more than half an hour.

Many years later, Beika described these anxious and difficult days in his interesting "Memoirs of a Forest Brother" *(Memuary lesnogo brata).* These tell of the loss of his best friends, gatherings of outlaws in the mists, fires blazing in baronial castles, open-air discussions, and the short shrift meted out to traitors.

In 1915 the "forest brothers" fled abroad to escape the Tsarist secret police. They scattered all over the world, and Beika after many wanderings arrived at Boston, where he found himself still in the thick of the struggle for the proletariat's rights. The textile workers were on strike at Lawrence—he hastened there with the workers of Boston and Redville, led by the legendary industrial worker Bill Haywood. After the strike had lasted several days and after sharp clashes with the police, 20,000 workers met in a park and were told by the strike committee's representative that the owner of the works had agreed to raise their wages. To celebrate their victory they lustily sang the *Internationale.* The Latvian revolutionary joined in with delight, for it was his victory too.

Beika was Secretary of the CC of the General Organization of Lettish Workers, which unanimously supported the Bolsheviks' appeal to turn the imperialist war into a civil one. Together with Fritsis Rozin', he carried on an implacable struggle against opportunism and helped to bring Lenin's works to the Latvian people. A keen publicist, he was an editor of the newspaper *Stradneks.*

By their work in organizing the left wing of the American Social Democratic Party, Beika, Rozin', Ianis Berzin'-Ziemelis, and other Latvian revolutionaries showed their loyalty to the internationalist cause, placing their knowledge, energy, fighting spirit, and experience of the revolutionary struggle at the disposal of the working class of the country in which they had found refuge as émigrés.

In 1917...the February revolution took place. Russia was on the eve of great events, and Beika hastened home with his friends. His voice was raised in passionate appeal at meetings before the elections to the Riga city duma and the Vidzeme soviet, where he pleaded the cause of the Bolsheviks and "List No. 1." When the Germans entered Riga, on the orders of the CC of the Lettish Social Democratic Party he remained in the occupied city and carried on illegal work. The underground workers' first appeal was devoted to the victory of the Great October Socialist Revolution. It contained the words:

> During twenty-five years of revolutionary struggle, the Riga workers in particular and those of all Latvia have become united heart and soul with the Russian proletariat. Their dream is to continue fighting alongside the Russian workers in the vanguard of the social revolution.

In 1919 ... Beika was PC of industry in the Soviet government of Latvia. Under his direction one factory after another arose from its ruins: woodworking, the manufacture of bricks and paper, food and textiles. The Feniks railroad car works began to operate, and by the end of April unemployment had been wiped out as far as the male population was concerned.

An unusual standard made its appearance at the [1919] May Day demonstration at Riga. The staff was of bamboo and the red cloth had faded in the sun. Beika and his comrades were delighted at the sight of this emblem. The cloth had been bought in Chicago, the bamboo cut in Yokohama, and the words "Workers of the World, Unite!" embroidered in gold when the banner was brought to Harbin.

In 1932...Beika was appointed to the responsible duties of agent of the PC of Heavy Industry of the U.S.S.R. and member of the CPC of the RSFSR. He had behind him years of energetic and brilliant work. He had been wherever the need was greatest, wherever the Party had sent him: secretary of the Smolensk and Arkhangelsk gubernia committees, chairman of the All-Russian Union of Industrial Cooperatives. He had fought famine and destruction, sabotage and banditry, and had set up the first communes and cooperatives.

Literature and books were a lifelong passion with him. During his life he amassed a library of 9,000 volumes in Russian, German, English, French, Italian, and Latvian, all of which languages he could read and write fluently.

In 1937 ... Spain was aflame with civil war. The best of mankind, faithful to the duty of proletarian internationalism, hastened to help the republic. Beika was among them; he set out for the front with his friend Mate Zalka. In Spain he was a member of the RMC. From Madrid he set out for America, the CC having instructed him to strengthen brotherly ties with the CP of the U.S.A. He informed the American comrades of the organizational experience of the CPSU and urged them to fight with all their might against fascism. In those days when Europe was overshadowed by the threat of a new and terrible war, he thought of the fate of all peoples of the world and especially of his Latvian countrymen. In a pamphlet entitled *Latvia's Catastrophe*, published in Boston, he fiercely attacked the Ulmanis regime. "Destroy fascism in Latvia's towns and villages," he wrote. "Strengthen the united front of the Latvian people! Organize yourselves for a great, decisive battle! Only by the destruction of fascism can Latvia's freedom be reborn.".....

The life of this great Latvian revolutionary was tragically cut short during the cult of Stalin's personality. The Soviet people piously revere the memory of this great son of the Party and motherland.[13]

NIKOLAI PAVLOVICH BRIUKHANOV

Biographical data

Born 1878, died 1943. Party names Andrei, Andrei Simbirsky; literary pseudonym N. Pavlov. Soviet political and Party leader. Joined the CP in

1902. Born at Simbirsk, a surveyor's son. Joined the revolutionary movement in 1896. Studied at Moscow University; was active in the student movement at Moscow and Kazan. Arrested and exiled several times. In 1903 he was a member of the Kazan committee of the RSDWP, and in 1906 of the Party's Ufa committee. Was a delegate to the Fifth RSDWP congress in 1907. From the end of 1907 he did Party work at Ufa; was a member of the Ural oblast committee of the RSDWP and helped to edit the newspaper *Ufimskii rabochii*. After the February revolution in 1917 he was a member of the Ufa united committee of the RSDWP, chairman of the Ufa soviet, and a delegate to the seventh (April) all-Russian conference of the RSDWP(B). From October 26, 1917, he was a member of the Ufa gubernia revolutionary committee. From February 1918 he worked in the PC of food as a member of its collegium and deputy PC. From December 1921 he was PC of food of the RSFSR and at the same time head of the chief supply administration of the Red Army and a member of the Council for Labor and Defense. From 1923 he was PC of food of the U.S.S.R.; from 1924 deputy PC of finance, and in 1926-30 PC of finance, of the U.S.S.R. In 1931-33 he was deputy PC of supply of the U.S.S.R. and from 1933 deputy chairman of the central commission of the CPC of the U.S.S.R. on agricultural productivity. At the Fifteenth and Sixteenth congresses of the CPSU he was elected a candidate member of the CC. Subjected to illegal repression during the cult of Stalin's personality; rehabilitated posthumously.[14]

KARL IULII KHRISTIANOVICH DANISHEVSKY

Biographical data

Born 1884, died 1941. Party name "German." Soviet political and Party leader. Born in a family of Latvian gentry. Joined the CP in 1900. At the end of 1906 he became a member of the CC of the RSDWP, representing the Latvian Social Democrats. At the Fifth Congress of the RSDWP in 1907 he was elected to the CC. In 1907-14 he carried on Party work in Petersburg, Baku, Tiflis, Warsaw, Riga, and Moscow. Was arrested several times. In January 1917 he escaped from exile and came illegally to Moscow. After the revolution of February 1917 he was a member of the Moscow committee of the RSDWP(B) and the Moscow soviet. From May 1917 he was an editor of the Social Democratic newspaper *Tsinia* (The Fight) and the Bolshevik newspaper *Okopnaia pravda* (Pravda of the Trenches). In July 1917, at the fifth congress of the Social Democratic Party of the Lettish Region, he was again elected a member of its CC. In 1918, until June, he carried on underground work in Riga; in January-May 1919 he was deputy chairman of the Soviet government of Latvia. During the Civil War he was a member of the RMC of the republic and of the eastern front and president of the revolutionary tribunal

of the RSFSR. From 1921 he was secretary of the Siberian bureau of the
CC of the RCP(B) and chairman of the administrations of the Northern Forests
and Timber Export associations and the Foreign Trade Bank. From 1932 till
1937 he was deputy PC of forest industry of the U.S.S.R. Was a delegate
to the Fifth, Eighth, and Tenth CP congresses. Author of *Nakanune sotsial'noi
revolutsii* (On the Eve of the Social Revolution), 3 vols.; *Professional'nye
soiuzy* (Trade Unions); *Bor'ba za Sovetskuiu Latviiu* (The Fight for Soviet
Latvia), and other works. Subjected to illegal repression during the cult of
Stalin's personality; posthumously rehabilitated.[15]

GABIB PIRDZHAN-OGLY DZHABIEV

Biographical data

Born 1899, died 19——. Joined the Bolshevik Party in 1918. In 1917-19
he carried on underground work in Baku and other Azerbaidzhan towns, was
secretary of the Gummet organization at Balakhany and later carried on underground work in the Dendzhin gubernia. In 1919-20 he was secretary of the
Revolutionary Staff and directed the armed uprising in Baku; then joined the
Red Army on the instructions of the Party organization. In 1920-22 he was
special plenipotentiary of the Azerbaidzhan revolutionary committee and the
CC of the Azerbaidzhan CP in the Shamkhor, Tauz, and Kakh uezds. From
the end of 1920 he was engaged in political work for the army. In 1922-23
he was editor of the journal *Kyzyl Sharg* (Red East) in Moscow. He returned
to Baku and from 1923 to 1930 edited the newspaper *Kommunist*. From 1930
he served in a number of important posts in Moscow in the All-Union Council
of Collective Farms and the PC of Food Industry of the U.S.S.R. He was
a victim of the cult of Stalin's personality.[16]

An ardent revolutionary

Balakhany is famous not only for its mineral resources but for the glorious
revolutionary traditions of its working class. In the fight to overthrow autocracy
and capitalism and establish Soviet power, the Balakhany workers produced
from their midst a galaxy of proletarian leaders devoted heart and soul to the
cause of the Party and the people. One of these was Gabib Pirdzhan-ogly
Dzhabiev, an eminent Bolshevik and fearless revolutionary.

Born and reared in Balakhany, he received there his first revolutionary training and became an active fighter for the happiness of the working masses.
His well-to-do parents dreamed of their son becoming a merchant, but his own
dream was to be a fighter. From his early years he witnessed the pitiless exploitation of the workers and the hard, thankless lot of the laboring population. There
was much that he had still to learn and understand, but he saw clearly one
thing—that the working people's lot was a miserable one.

The development of events in the country after the February revolution of 1917 had a decisive effect on Dzhabiev's career. He left the commercial school and became a worker, and his new surroundings began to form his view of life. He became a fighter for the interests of the working people, linking his fate with the revolutionary struggle of the Baku proletariat.

At the end of 1918 a great event took place in his life: he was admitted into the Bolshevik Party. When he began his tense and dangerous career as a Bolshevik underground worker, Azerbaidzhan was enveloped in the dark clouds of Musavatist reaction. A stranger to fear and fatigue, he devoted himself to reviving Party organizations and cells in Baku and other parts of Azerbaidzhan. Until the spring of 1918 he worked at Balakhany, where he was secretary of the Gummet organization and did much to consolidate the Party's forces. Soon the Party organization entrusted the young Bolshevik with an important task: he went to the Giandzha gubernia and, in the greatest secrecy, helped to form Party groups and cells and carried on revolutionary propaganda among the peasants.

In the fall of 1919 the antinational Musavatist regime underwent a profound crisis. The Azerbaidzhan Communists were preparing for a showdown with the counterrevolutionary forces. Combat units were being formed everywhere, and the workers' detachments were acquiring arms and ammunition. A Revolutionary Staff was created to direct the uprising, and Dzhabiev became its secretary. He performed this difficult and dangerous task with every care for secrecy, but danger was close at hand. In March 1920 the Musavatist police suddenly raided the apartment where he was living. He was not at home, but they found secret Party documents and began wholesale searches and arrests. A large sum of money was placed on Dzhabiev's head.... Soon the police were on his track: he was hiding at the home of a well-known Bolshevik and member of Parliament named Aligeidar Karaev. The latter's house was ringed with troops and the governor-general of the town made his appearance; but the authorities were dilatory, and Dzhabiev escaped. The days of the antinational regime were numbered; Baku prepared for an armed uprising. Red Army units came to aid the revolutionary workers. The Azerbaidzhan Communists and the command of the Eleventh Army worked out a plan of joint action. Before the uprising broke out Dzhabiev, on the instructions of the Party organization, visited the Red Army units. On the morning of April 28, 1920, a group of armored trains of the Eleventh Army under the command of M. G. Efremov entered Baku to aid the insurgent workers. Besides A. I. Mikoyan, G. Musabekov, and other leading members of the Azerbaidzhan Party organization, they were accompanied by G. Dzhabiev.

From the beginning of the establishment of Soviet power in Azerbaidzhan, Dzhabiev with his usual energy threw himself into the task of consolidating the workers' conquests. As special plenipotentiary of the Azerbaidzhan revolutionary committee and the CC of the Azerbaidzhan CP, he carried on indefatigable work in the Shamkhor, Tauz, and Kakh uezds. In October 1920 he attended the regional conference of Communist organizations of the Don and Caucasus, held at Vladikavkaz by the Caucasian bureau of the CC of the RCP(B).

From the end of 1920 he performed political work in the army. In 1922 he was in Moscow, where he edited the journal *Kyzyl Sharg* devoted to the propagation of Marxist-Leninist ideas in the East and concerned especially with problems of socialist construction in the Soviet Eastern republics. He himself often contributed articles to it. Returning to Baku in 1923, he was for many years editor of the newspaper *Kommunist*. The older generation of journalists still remember this bold organizer of the Party press. Besides learned accounts of the history of the Azerbaidzhan revolutionary movement, he wrote fiery articles denouncing the machinations of the enemies of Soviet Azerbaidzhan.

From 1930 he worked in Moscow, where he held a number of important posts in the All-Union Council of Collective Farms and the PC of Food Industry of the U.S.S.R. He was several times elected to ruling Party organs of the republic and took part in the Sixteenth Congress of the CPSU. A fiery revolutionary and passionate fighter for the people's happiness, he became a victim of arbitrary rule during the cult of personality. The toilers of Azerbaidzhan revere the memory of G. Dzhabiev, a true son of the Party and people.[17]

SHALVA ZURABOVICH ELIAVA

Biographical data

Born 1883, died 1937. Joined the Bolshevik Party in 1904. Born at Ganiri village, Kutaisi uezd, Kutaisi gubernia. In 1903 he left high school and entered the law faculty at Petersburg, where he began revolutionary activity. In the 1905 revolution he was a leader of the revolutionary movement in Georgia. In 1906-10 he continued his studies at Petersburg. Was in jail from 1910 to 1913. In 1913-15 he worked on Lenin's *Pravda* and was secretary of the hospital fund of the Treugol'nik (Triangle) factory. In 1916-17 he was in exile in the Astrakhan gubernia and then at Vologda. In 1917, after the February revolution, he was chairman of the Vologda soviet of workers' and soldiers' deputies. In 1919-20 he was chairman of the Special Commission of the CPC of the RSFSR and the All-Russian CEC in Turkestan, then a member of the RMCs of the First Army and of the southern group and the southeastern front. In 1920-23 he was diplomatic representative of the RSFSR in Turkey and Persia, then a member of the RMC of the Eleventh Army and PC of military and naval affairs for the Georgian SSR. In 1923-27, chairman of the CPC of the Georgian SSR; 1927-31, chairman of the CPC of the Transcaucasian SFSR; 1931-35, deputy PC of foreign trade of the U.S.S.R., and 1936-37, deputy PC of light industry of the U.S.S.R. In 1937 he became a victim of the cult of Stalin's personality.[18]

A true son of the Party

Shalva Zurabovich Eliava was born on September 30, 1883, in Ganiri village, Kutaisi uezd, Kutaisi gubernia. He was an outstanding CP leader and government worker, who took an active part in the revolutionary movement and the Civil War and in the socialist development of Georgia and Transcaucasia.

He became a fighter against autocracy and the bourgeois landowners' regime at an early age, when still a pupil at the Kutaisi classical high school. Leaving there in 1903, he entered the law faculty of Petersburg University, where he made contact with revolutionary student groups and took an active part in the students' political demonstration of February 1904. In summer of that year he went to Tbilisi and engaged in active revolutionary work. He joined the RSDWP, and from the outset adhered to the Bolshevik position. During the first Russian revolution he was one of the leaders of the movement in Georgia. In the fall of 1906, pursued by the police, he left Georgia and returned to Petersburg University, but was soon expelled from the capital for his part in student revolutionary activity....

In April 1915 he was again arrested and exiled, first to the Astrakhan gubernia and then to Vologda. After the bourgeois-democratic February revolution he was released and elected chairman of the Vologda soviet of workers' and soldiers' deputies. In the memorable days of the October armed uprising he represented the Vologda gubernia at the second congress of soviets. In February 1919 the CC appointed him chairman of the Special Commission of the CPC of the RSFSR and of the All-Russian CEC in Turkestan. Owing to the advance of Kolchak's bands, the commission could not at first reach Turkestan and was held up at Orenburg. Here Eliava was temporarily mobilized for military work and was appointed a member of the RMC of the First Army commanded by Tukhachevsky, then of the southern group of the eastern front commanded by Frunze. He established direct touch with Lenin, corresponding with him on military and other questions and carrying out important orders of the great leader.

After the defeat of the Kolchak bands, contact with Soviet Turkestan was restored and the special commission went on to its destination. Besides Eliava its members included Frunze, Kuibyshev, Rudzutak, and others. Guided by Lenin's directives, it did much to eradicate the serious mistakes of local Party and government leaders in regard to the execution of Lenin's nationalities policy.

Returning from Turkestan in summer 1920, Eliava was appointed RSFSR diplomatic representative in Turkey and Persia. He also took a leading part in the decisive struggle for the establishment of Soviet power in Georgia, and from the end of 1920 was a member of the RMC of the Eleventh Army. Thereafter he was in the front rank of those building a new life in Georgia, first as PC of military and naval affairs of the new republic, in which post he devoted all his powers to improving its defenses in accordance with Lenin's directives. In 1921-27 he was chairman of the CPC of the Georgian SSR, and in April 1927 he was promoted to the position of chairman of the CPC of the Transcaucasian SFSR. Unswervingly devoted to Lenin's nationalities policy, he did much to restore the national economy, industrialize the country, collectivize agriculture, and accomplish the cultural revolution.

In January 1931 the Party transferred him to important government work in Moscow. In 1931-35 he was deputy PC of foreign trade, and from the beginning of 1936 deputy PC of light industry of the U.S.S.R. In 1937 he became a victim of arbitrary rule and illegality due to the cult of personality. His family suffered along with him.

Commemorating the eightieth anniversary of his birth, the working people of Georgia revere the memory of their faithful son, who devoted all his energy to the great struggle for a brighter future for his people.[19]

NIKOLAI PAVLOVICH GLEBOV-AVILOV

Biographical data

Born 1887, died 1942. Party names Gleb, N. Glebov; real name Avilov. Soviet Party and political leader. Born at Kaluga, a shoemaker's son. Joined the CP in 1904. Carried on Party work in Kaluga, Moscow, Petrograd, and the Urals. Arrested and exiled several times. Studied at Party school at Bologna, where he opposed the Vperedovtsy. In 1913-14 he worked on the staff of *Pravda* and in the former year attended the "summer" conference of the CC of the RSDWP with Party workers at Poronino. After the February revolution of 1917 he was a member of the executive committee of the CC of the RSDWP(B) and worked in the Petrograd trade unions bureau, and subsequently he was a member of the executive committee of the All-Union Central Council of Trade Unions. At the April 1917 conference of the RSDWP(B) he was elected a candidate member of the CC. After the October Revolution he was PC of posts and telegraphs in the first Soviet government. In May 1919 he was commissar of the Black Sea Fleet; later a member of the presidium and secretary of the All-Union Central Council of Trade Unions and PC of labor of the Ukraine. From 1922 he was engaged in Party work in Petrograd. Joined the "new opposition" in 1925, but acknowledged his mistakes after the Fifteenth Party Congress in 1927. From 1928 he was in charge of building, and later director, of the agricultural engineering works at Rostov-on-Don. Subjected to illegal repression during the cult of Stalin's personality; rehabilitated posthumously.[20]

NIKOLAI AFANAS'EVICH KUBIAK

Biographical data

Born 1881, died 1942. Party and government leader; joined the CP in 1898. Born at Meshchevsk, the son of a worker. Began revolutionary activity while working at a Briansk factory. From 1902 he was a member of the Briansk committee of the RSDWP. Took part in the revolution of 1905-7. Represented the Briansk Party organization at the Fifth Congress of the RSDWP in 1907. Was arrested after the congress and in jail from 1908 to 1912, then spent three years in exile. In 1917 he took an active part in the October Revolution; was a deputy in the Petrograd soviet, representing the workers of the Sestroretsk factory, also chairman of the Sestroretsk district council and the Sestroretsk raion committee of the RSDWP(B). In 1918-19 and again in 1920 he was chairman of the Petrograd gubernia executive committee. Was a delegate to the fifth all-Russian congress of soviets. During the Civil War he was a member of the RMC of the Petrograd front. For a time in 1920 he joined the "workers' opposition," but then abandoned it. From 1922 to 1926 he was secretary of the Far Eastern bureau of the CC of the CPSU, and in 1927 secretary of the CC. From 1928 he was PC of agriculture of the RSFSR, and from 1931 chairman of the Ivanovo oblast executive committee. In 1934-37 he was chairman of the all-Union council of the CEC of the U.S.S.R. for municipal economy questions. At the Twelfth through the Sixteenth Party congresses he was elected to the CC of the CPSU. Was a member of the All-Union CEC. Slandered and subjected to repression during the cult of Stalin's personality; posthumously rehabilitated.[21]

GEORGII IPPOLITOVICH LOMOV-OPPOKOV

Biographical data

Born 1888, died 1938. Party names Afanasii, Zhorzh; literary pseudonym A. Lomov. Soviet Party and political leader. Joined the CP in 1903. Born at Saratov, the son of a progressive nobleman. In 1905 he was a member of the Saratov committee of the RSDWP and head of a detachment of armed workers at Saratov. In 1906, while a student at Petersburg University, he was Party organizer of the Zheleznodorozhnyi district. In 1907 he was a member of the Ivanovo-Voznesensk committee and later the Moscow district committee of the RSDWP. In 1909, member and secretary of the Party's Petersburg committee. In 1910-13 he was in exile in the Arkhangelsk gubernia and took part in Polar expeditions. After the termination of his exile and university studies he carried on Party work in Moscow and helped to set up the metal workers' trade union. In 1914 he was exiled to Saratov and in 1916 to eastern Siberia. After the February revolution in 1917 he was a member of the Moscow oblast bureau and the Moscow committee of the RSDWP(B), deputy chairman of the Moscow soviet, and delegate to the Sixth Congress of the RSDWP(B), at which he was elected a candidate member of the CC. He was one of the leaders of the October Revolution in Moscow and a member of the Moscow RMC. Was PC of justice in the first CPC. Took a "left-wing Communist" line in the discussion of the Brest Litovsk treaty, 1918. In 1918-21 he was a member of the presidium and deputy chairman of the Supreme Council of the National Economy; in 1921-23 member of the Siberian bureau of the CC of the RCP(B), member of the Siberian revolutionary committee, chairman of the Siberian industrial bureau of the Supreme Council of the National Economy; member of the Ural bureau of the CC of the RCP(B); and chairman of the Ural Economic Council. From the end of 1923 he was chairman of the All-Russian Petroleum Trade Syndicate; was a member of the presidium of the Supreme Council of the National Economy of the U.S.S.R., a member of the Moscow committee of the RCP(B) and of the Moscow soviet. In the fall of 1926 he was appointed chairman of the administration of Donugal' [the Donets state trust for the production and sale of coal and anthracite]. Was a member of the CC and politburo of the Ukraine CP. From 1929, chairman of the state trust for the petroleum and gas industry. In 1931-33, deputy chairman of Gosplan of the U.S.S.R. Member of the CEC at all convocations. Delegate to the Sixth through the Twelfth and Fourteenth through the Seventeenth Party congresses. At the Sixth, Seventh, and Fourteenth congresses he was elected a candidate member of the Party CC; at the Fifteenth and Sixteenth a full member; and at the Seventeenth a member of the Commission of Soviet Control. In 1934-37 he was a member of the commission's bureau. Wrote articles and pamphlets on economic and political subjects. Subjected to illegal repression and perished during the cult of Stalin's personality; posthumously rehabilitated.[22]

A life devoted to the Party

On February 10 it will be seventy-five years since the birth of Georgii Ippolitovich Lomov (Oppokov)—outstanding Bolshevik and Leninist, a Party and government leader whose whole life was devoted to the Party's cause.

He joined the revolutionary movement as a thirteen-year-old schoolboy. This was not in itself remarkable in those days before the storm, when the events of 1905 were approaching and many quite young people were swept away by the romantic aspects of discussion circles, leaflets, and illegal meetings. What was remarkable was the sense of purpose and strong political instinct that Lomov displayed from his early youth.

When the split took place in the RSDWP he at once and irrevocably joined its Bolshevik wing. He devoted himself to everyday revolutionary work with youthful fervor and exceptional determination. Soon his father's home (the latter was manager of the Saratov branch of the State Bank) became a secret Bolshevik meeting place.... Thus began a revolutionary career that was to be full of hardship and privation, leading through exile at Arkhangelsk, the Miasnitsky police headquarters, and the cells of the Taganksk prison in Moscow. Nevertheless it was the sort of career that men like Lomov would not change for any other. Every new step along this road brought them indescribable happiness—the happiness of fighting for the worldwide triumph of Leninist truth.

For twelve years after the 1905 revolution Lomov was constantly in the most critical areas of the battle. It is sufficient to say that at different times he was elected a member of the Party's Ivanovo-Voznesensk and Moscow committees (the latter more than once); in 1909 he was secretary of the RSDWP committee for Petersburg (where at the same time he graduated in law from the university); and in 1915, after being arrested for the second time, he became the virtual leader of the Bolshevik center at Saratov. During the darkest hours of triumphant reaction he devoted all his strength to preserving and consolidating the Party. Comrades who knew him during his last exile in the Verkholensk uezd of the Irkutsk gubernia (1916-17) remember how, together with Stanislav Kosior and Innokentii Stukov, he passionately defended Leninist views on the war and the prospects of revolution in arguments with Mensheviks and SRs.

There is no space here to enumerate all the details of his career, but it is certainly not necessary to do so. The facts of history bear eloquent witness to his authority within the Party and its profound confidence in him. At the Sixth Party Congress of July 1917, which placed the armed uprising on the revolutionary agenda, he was elected to the CC. As he laconically puts it in his autobiography, "I took part in all decisive meetings of the CC before October. During the October insurrection I was at Petrograd with the CC." Immediately after the October turmoil he became PC of justice in the first CPC, headed by Lenin. The CC was then sent to Moscow to "take part in the struggle for power."... Lomov was a member of the "Seven"—the Moscow RMC. His talents as a true revolutionary had never been so clearly displayed as now. Many matters were settled thanks to his boldness, initiative, and power to size up the most complicated political situation.... After the victorious uprising in Moscow he superintended the nationalization of banks and industry and the reorganization of the whole apparatus of power.

During the Brest peace negotiations he favored the point of view of the "left-wing Communists"; but severe and honest Leninist criticism enabled him to realize his mistakes and in the end to overcome them.

From 1918 to 1921 he was deputy chairman of the Supreme Council of the National Economy, with responsibility for the supply of fuel to the republic, which was cut off from the Donets coal and the oil of Baku and Groznyi. Lenin's short, businesslike memoranda to the chief members of the CPC, the Council of Labor and Defense, and the Supreme Council of the National Economy, and particularly to Lomov himself, show clearly the great importance which the leader of the revolution attached to the battle for fuel, which was a question of life and death for the young Soviet Republic....

Whatever high post Lomov occupied, he remained a true revolutionary—a vivid, impetuous, searching personality.... He was a man of great knowledge, with wide and varied interests and a passion for books, music and the theater. The old hands of the Vakhtangov theater, with whom he was friendly for many years, still remember his exact and subtle critical judgments. In short, he was a complete model of the type of Communist and revolutionary with whom, as Maiakovsky put it, "a whole life could be made." This is not surprising, since he worked with Lenin himself, who knew and valued him.

It is seventy-five years since he was born, and he might easily still be with us.... But in 1938 he became a victim of unjust repression. The memory of this great Bolshevik and Leninist will never vanish from people's hearts.[23]

"Have the swine arrested at once."

It is a good thing that Comrade Voroshilov realized his mistakes in time! In June 1937 a member of Gosplan wrote a letter to Stalin saying that G. I. Lomov (Oppokov), a member of the bureau of the Commission of Soviet Control under the CPC of the U.S.S.R., was on friendly terms with Rykov and Bukharin. Stalin thereupon wrote to Molotov "What shall we do?" and the latter replied "I would have the swine arrested at once." A few days later Lomov was arrested, accused of belonging to a right-wing opportunist organization, and subjected to repression. Today he has been rehabilitated. And who was this Lomov? A member of the Party from as far back as 1903, PC of justice in the first CPC, and afterward deputy chairman of the Supreme Council of the National Economy and deputy chairman of Gosplan; a man who was elected to the CC of the CPSU at its Eleventh, Twelfth, Fourteenth, Fifteenth and Sixteenth congresses.[24]

VALERII IVANOVICH MEZHLAUK

Biographical data

Born 1893, died 1938. Party and government leader. Joined the CP in July 1917. Born at Kharkov, the son of a teacher. Graduated from the historico-literary and law faculties at Kharkov University. Joined the revolutionary movement in 1907. In 1917 he was a member of the Kharkov Bolshevik committee and the Kharkov soviet and was one of the organizers of the Red Guard in the Ukraine. In 1918 he was PC of finance of the Donets-Krivoi Rog Republic, a member of the Donbass oblast committee of the Ukraine CP and of the Donetsk military staff. In 1918-20 he was military commissar of the Kazan gubernia and a member of the RMCs of the Fifth, Tenth, Fourteenth, and Second armies; member of the RMC of the southern front, PC of the Army of the Ukraine, and member of the RMC of the Tula Fortified Area. In 1920-24 he held important railroad posts. In 1924-26 he was a member of the presidium of the Supreme Council of the National Economy and deputy chairman of the chief administration of the metalworking industry (Glavmetall). In 1926-31 he was director of Glavmetall and deputy chairman of the Supreme Council of the National Economy of the U.S.S.R. In 1931-34 he was first deputy chairman of Gosplan of the U.S.S.R.; in 1934-37, deputy chairman of the CPC of the U.S.S.R. From February 1937 he was PC of heavy industry of the U.S.S.R., and from October, deputy chairman of the CPC of the U.S.S.R. and chairman of Gosplan of the U.S.S.R. He was elected to the All-Ukrainian CEC in (1919), the All-Russian CEC (1927-29), and the All-Union CEC (1927-37). From 1927 he was a candidate member of the CC of the CPSU, and from 1934 a full member. Wrote pamphlets and articles on questions of industrialization and the socialist economy. Was chief editor of the newspaper *Za industrializatsiiu*. He was a victim of unjustified repression during the cult of Stalin's personality. While in prison he wrote *O planovoi rabote i merakh ee uluchsheniia* (Planned Work and Methods of Improving It). Posthumously rehabilitated.[25]

A true son of the Party

The name of Valerii Ivanovich Mezhlauk occupies an outstanding place among the chief leaders of the CP and the Soviet State. He was in the front rank of the struggle for Soviet power in the Ukraine, for victory in the Civil War, for the elimination of economic chaos, for industrialization and the fulfillment of the First Five Year Plan. The Party always appointed him to key sectors of the battle for the construction of a new society.

The son of a teacher, he was born at Kharkov on February 20, 1893. From the age of fourteen he took part in the revolutionary movement, organizing circles of pupils and workers, working for an underground press and transporting illegal literature. After the February revolution he was head of the propaganda commission of the Kharkov soviet, distributing political literature and organizing uezd and volost soviets in the Kharkov area and the Donbass.... In July 1917 he joined the Bolshevik Party, and in September 1917 became a member of the Kharkov Bolshevik committee. During the Kornilov revolt, as a member of the RMC he organized Red Guard detachments and supplied them with equipment. On November 10, 1917, after the victory of the October armed uprising in Petrograd, he presided at the stormy session of the Kharkov soviet which proclaimed Soviet power in the city.

In April 1918 the Soviet troops were obliged to evacuate Kharkov. With a detachment of local Red Guardists, Mezhlauk succeeded in transporting money and valuables to Lugansk and thence to Moscow. He risked his life, several times performing prodigies of bravery and heroism. The Whites were determined to capture him. On May 17, 1918, the morning edition of their newspaper *Kievskaia mysl'*, mistaking wishful thinking for reality, actually reported that "V. Mezhlauk, formerly PC of finance of the Donets Republic, was executed in accordance with a sentence of the Military Court."...

In 1919 he was in charge of the PC of army affairs of the Ukraine, and on Lenin's orders organized detachments of Donets workers to defend the Donbass. At this time Lenin wrote to him and other leaders that "the collapse of the Revolution is absolutely inevitable unless we secure a rapid victory in the Donbass."

Mezhlauk took part in innumerable battles in the Ukraine, suppressing the Grigor'ev revolt and wiping out the Makhno bands. When Denikin was marching on Moscow in the fall of 1919, the CC of the RCP(B) ordered Mezhlauk to strengthen the approaches to Tula. After the Whites had been driven far away from the Tula Fortified Area, he was appointed a member of the RMC of the Second Army on the north Caucasian front.

During the celebration of the tenth anniversary of the Red Army, the RMC of the U.S.S.R. announced a decree of the Presidium of the CEC of the U.S.S.R. conferring the Order of the Red Banner on seven military and political leaders for their services in organizing and taking part in military operations during the difficult days of the Civil War. Among these were S. M. Kirov, A. I. Mikoyan, and V. I. Mezhlauk.

After the Civil War was over, the chief front was that of economic construction. The Party declared the mobilization of all Communists for transport work, in which Mezhlauk duly took part.... Later he was put in charge of metalworking and mechanical engineering, being from 1921 to 1931 a member of the presidium and deputy chairman of the Supreme Council of the National Economy of the U.S.S.R. Together with F. E. Dzerzhinsky he directed the complicated work of creating such new branches of Soviet industry as the production of internal combustion engines and boiler-making, as well as strengthening the nation's defense capacity. These were also the years in which the first steps were taken to create the powerful Soviet aviation industry. In November 1925, Dzerzhinsky, drawing up a program for the development of the aviation industry, wrote to Mezhlauk of the necessity of "giving to work on aviation and its ancillary services, long-term though it be, the character of military priority as far as the mass production of aircraft and engines is concerned." And he concluded: "If we succeed in this we shall have earned a page in the history of the nation's defense."

After the Fourteenth Party Congress Dzerzhinsky wrote to Mezhlauk that the metalworking industry must be so organized as to ensure "a progressive transition to full independence of the equipment-producing capitalist countries." It was to comply with this directive of the Party that the major socialist industrial plants were created. In the Civil War Days, Lenin had twice sent Mezhlauk to Tsaritsyn, and in 1926 he was there again—once more in accordance with Lenin's ideas, for the purpose of setting up a national tractor factory. One day—it was July 12, 1926—a large crowd was to be seen between the "Barricades" factory and the village of Portianovka. Thousands of town workers and peasants from nearby villages had gathered to watch the solemn founding of the first large-scale tractor plant in the U.S.S.R. The *Internationale* was sung, and the first stone was laid by Valerii Ivanovich Mezhlauk.

Defending the Leninist line as regards the country's industrialization, Mezhlauk firmly combated the Trotskyist-Zinovievite opposition, mercilessly denouncing its attempts to denigrate the "Party leadership in the field of national economy."...

From 1931 he was first deputy to Kuibyshev as chairman of the U.S.S.R. Gosplan, and subsequently became chairman. From 1933 he was a member of the Council of Labor and Defense, and from 1934 deputy chairman of the CPC of the U.S.S.R. and the Council of Labor and Defense. Under him, the whole work of Gosplan was dedicated to the Party's intention of carrying out Lenin's commands in the construction of a socialist society.

In 1936, on the fifteenth anniversary of Gosplan, the Soviet government awarded the Order of Lenin to Mezhlauk for his services in planning the nation's economy.... At the Fifteenth through the Seventeenth Party congresses he was elected to the CC. For many years he was a member of the All-Russian and the All-Union CEC.

In February 1937 Ordzonikidze was no more, and the Party entrusted Mezhlauk with the direction of heavy industry. In December 1937 he was arrested on a trumped-up charge. He perished on July 29, 1938. So ended the life of an outstanding Communist and fighter for the cause of Lenin's Party, the construction of socialism and communism in our country.[26]

VLADIMIR PAVLOVICH MILIUTIN

Biographical data

Born 1884, died 1938. Soviet Party and political leader, writer and economist. Joined the social-democratic movement in 1903, and became a Menshevik after the Second Congress of the RSDWP. Carried on Party work at Kursk, Moscow, Orel, Petersburg, and Tula. Arrested eight times for revolutionary activity; spent about five years in jail and two in exile. After the February revolution of 1917 he was a member of the Saratov committee of the RSDWP(B) and chairman of the Saratov soviet. At the seventh (April) all-Russian conference of the RSDWP(B) he was elected a member of the Party's CC. Was PC of agriculture in the first Soviet government. In November 1917 he advocated a government coalition with the Mensheviks and SRs, declared his disagreement with the policy of the CC, and left that body and the CPC. Later he acknowledged his error. In 1918-21 he was deputy chairman of the Supreme Council of the National Economy. At the Ninth and Tenth Party congresses he was elected a candidate member of the CC of the RCP(B), and at the Thirteenth through the Sixteenth congresses a member of the Central Control Commission of the CPSU. From 1924 he was a member of the collegium of the PC of workers' and peasants' inspection. From 1928 he was director of the Central Statistical Administration and deputy chairman of Gosplan of the U.S.S.R. Was a member of the Council of Labor and Defense of the U.S.S.R., also of the CPC and CEC, deputy chairman of the Communist Academy and member of the editorial board of the Great Soviet Encyclopedia. Wrote many works on economic questions, including *Agrarnaia politika v SSR* (Agrarian Policy in the U.S.S.R.), 1926; *Istoriia ekonomicheskogo razvitiia SSSR* (History of the Economic Development of the U.S.S.R.), 1928. Slandered and subjected to repression during the cult of Stalin's personality. Posthumously rehabilitated.[27]

Lenin's school of management

Anyone who has read Lenin's works and the post-October Lenin anthologies will have met with the name of V. P. Miliutin. Lenin was constantly writing: "Entrust this to Miliutin"; "Ask Miliutin's opinion"; "Have Miliutin serve on the commission", and so forth.

Miliutin was indeed an eminent member of our Party, concerned above all with the theoretical aspect of problems of the socialist economy. He devoted much energy and time to academic work, and has left us some thirty scientific works and articles. The day after Lenin's death he wrote an interesting memoir entitled "Lenin and Economics". The following is an extract from these unpublished reminiscences:

> Comrade Lenin united in himself the characteristics of a profound theoretician and a great man of action in the fullest sense of this term. In this difficult time of transition we had as the head of the world proletarian movement, the captain of the world-wide social revolution, a man with a unique command of contemporary knowledge and a complete mastery of Marxist method, who could at the same time lead, guide, and direct the masses in their millions—expressing every question in practical terms and bringing it to life with resolute persistence and determination.... At the same time, his theoretical works impress us with their wealth of factual material. He never ceased to collect detailed statistics to support his views and conclusions. Comrades who worked with him know well the care he took to amass necessary data. As a result, everything he did was based on principle, well founded and well sustained. He was truly able to apply Marxism in practice.
>
> He was also notable for his broad presentation of problems. He could perceive the theoretical issue in every detail and tackle every problem in the light of general development. His approach to national and international questions, to

problems of land tenure or of the New Economic Policy, is a classic example of this.

His second great quality as a practical man was his businesslike approach to reality. He could be cruelly ironical about the "fantasies" of comrades whose proposals did not take account of practical conditions. In this respect he was helped by his keen sense of what the masses were feeling and thinking. He always spoke with enthusiasm of the masses, the man on the spot, whom he insisted on seeing from time to time.

His third great quality was that of decision and determination once a problem had been posed and identified. He was an enemy of indecision, hesitation and indulgence.

His fourth quality was his ability to choose, organize, and train those who worked with him. He always took care to know who was carrying out a piece of work and how. Despite his exceptional powers, he was eminently a team worker, who knew how to encourage others and make them work for him.

Finally, his fifth quality was his complete sincerity about his own work and his readiness to confess mistakes. This was characteristic of him throughout his career.

Such were Lenin's main qualities as a practical man. The list is not complete, but it contains the main points.

He attached great importance to the Party apparatus, emphasizing that without it the country could not be efficiently governed. While criticizing the apparatus, he recognized its immense importance and took careful note of its composition and achievements, endeavoring to promote the ablest and most active workers and peasants to leading posts within it.

He not only directed our economic policy and laid the basis for the country's economic administration, but also took a direct hand in this field. Only his extraordinary capacity for work could enable him to accomplish all he did. As chairman of the CPC and the Council of Labor and Defense he was constantly concerned with questions of internal and foreign policy, but at the same time he succeeded in devoting much attention and energy to strictly practical questions. He was notable for a complete absence of bureaucratism, to which he was opposed in principle and of which he showed no trace in practice. What counted with him was direct action and the practical result: he strove for this with all his might, and taught those around him not to be satisfied with paper decrees and decisions. Thanks to his direct and practical participation, the work of the CPC and the Council of Labor and Defense showed brilliant results not only at the center but in the field. Lenin thus showed us how a leader and a theoretician can also be an outstanding practical worker, performing accurately and efficiently all of the day-to-day tasks of life.[28]

N. OSINSKY

Biographical data

Born April 6, 1887; died September 1, 1938. Real name Valerian Valerianovich Obolensky. Soviet political and Party leader and economist. Joined the CP in 1907. Born at Byki village, Kursk gubernia, son of a small landowner. Attended high school from 1897; entered Moscow University in 1905, then studied until 1907 at Munich and Berlin. Carried on Party work in Moscow, Tver, and Kharkov. Was several times subjected to repression by Tsarist authorities. After the February revolution of 1917 he was a member of the Moscow oblast bureau of the RSDWP(B) and on the editorial board of the newspaper *Sotsial-Demokrat*. Was a delegate to the Sixth Congress of the RSDWP(B). After the October Revolution he was manager of the RSFSR State Bank and first chairman of the [RSFSR] Supreme Council of the National Economy (until March 1918). During the debate on the Brest Litovsk treaty in 1918 he was one of those who drew up the "left-wing communist" platform. In 1918 he worked on the staff of *Pravda* and in the Soviet propaganda department of the SCNE. In 1920 he was chairman of the Tula gubernia executive committee and a member of the collegium of the PC of Food. In 1920-21 he was an active member of the anti-Party group for democratic centralism, and in 1923 joined the Trotskyist opposition. In 1921-23 he was deputy PC of agriculture and deputy chairman of the SCNE, and in 1925 a member of the presidium of the U.S.S.R. Gosplan. In 1926-28 he was head of the Central Statistical Administration, and from 1929 deputy chairman of the SCNE of the U.S.S.R. At the Tenth and the Fourteenth through the Seventeenth Party congresses he was elected a candidate member of the CC of the CPSU. Wrote *Amerikanskoe sel'skoe khoziaistvo po noveishim issledovaniiam* (American Agriculture in the Light of Recent Research [Moscow, 1925]) and other works. Subjected to illegal repression during the cult of Stalin's personality; posthumously rehabilitated.[29]

ANDREI FEDOROVICH RADCHENKO

Biographical data

Born 1887, died 1939. Born at Parafievka village, Chernigov gubernia. Was a Menshevik from 1904 to 1912, then a Bolshevik. Arrested several times. In 1917-18 he was chairman of the Druzhkov soviet of workers' and soldiers' deputies (Donbass). In 1918-19 he was engaged in political work for the Red Army. From 1920 he carried on important Party and trade union work in the Donbass. In 1924-25 he was secretary of the Donets gubernia committee of the Ukraine CP. In 1925-28, chairman of the All-Ukraine Trade Union Council and subsequently engaged in important economic work at Vladimir and Ivanovo-Voznesensk; deputy chairman of the All-Union Central Council of Trade Unions. From December 1925 to March 1928 he was a member of the politburo of the CC of the Ukraine CP. He later became a victim to the cult of Stalin's personality.[30]

Ian Ernestovich Rudzutak

IAN ERNESTOVICH RUDZUTAK

Biographical data

Born 1887, died 1938. Joined the Bolshevik Party in 1905. Born in Latvia, the son of a farm laborer. Worked on farms until 1917, then became a wage earner in Riga. Spent ten years in Tsarist prisons. In 1917-19 he was an instructor in the provincial section of the Moscow soviet; later a leading member of the provisional all-Russian central committee of the Textile Trade Union, secretary of the CC of the RCP(B) and a candidate member of the Politburo, chairman of the control commission of the central administration of the Textile Trade Union, chairman of the Council of the All-Russian Textile Union. He was also a member of the All-Union Central Council of Trade Unions, a member of the presidium of the Supreme Council of the National Economy, and chairman of the central committee of the textile industry. From 1922 he was chairman of the supreme collegium of the main administration of water transport of the SCNE, and secretary of the AUCCTU. In 1922-26, secretary-general of the AUCCTU, member of the presidium of the All-Union CEC, and chairman of the Central Asia bureau of the CC of the RCP(B). At the Twelfth Party Congress he was elected a candidate member of the Politburo, a member of the Organization Bureau and secretary of the CC of the RCP(B), PC of transport, and chairman of the Central Control Commission of the CPSU and PC of workers' and peasants' inspection. In 1926-37 he was deputy chairman of the CPC of the U.S.S.R. In 1938 he became a victim of the cult of Stalin's personality.[31]

A true Leninist

Delegates to the Twenty-second Party Congress spoke with sorrow of the eminent Party and government leaders who had fallen victims to arbitrary rule during the cult of personality. Among other names dear to the Soviet people was that of Ian Ernestovich Rudzutak.

A leading member of the old guard of Leninist revolutionaries, he was born in 1887, the son of a Latvian farm laborer. He followed the same calling for some years and then became a factory worker in Riga, where he joined the Bolshevik Party. His whole life was devoted to serving the cause of the working class. A "most dangerous political criminal," as he was called in police records, he spent ten years in Tsarist jails and was released by the February revolution, after which he worked as a traveling instructor for the provincial section of the Moscow soviet. At the same time, with other Bolsheviks he took an active part in reviving the textile trade union, which had been destroyed by the Tsarist authorities. Under Bolshevik leadership the textile workers were the first to unite their trade unions on an all-Russian scale, which played an important part in the fight with the bourgeoisie. Much of the credit for this was due to Rudzutak, who from September 1917 was a leading member of the provisional all-Russian central committee of the Textile Trade Union.

After the October Revolution, when the construction of the Soviet State began, the Party placed him in the most responsible sectors. During the life of Lenin, who greatly valued his qualities as a man and a worker, he was elected secretary of the CC of the RCP(B) and a candidate member of the Politburo. Working under Lenin's direct guidance, he became a Party and political leader of the first rank.

During the cult of personality he was slandered and unjustly condemned, and he perished tragically in 1938. For a long time his name was erased from history. New documents have come to light in the archives which complete our knowledge of his life and deepen our understanding of certain important historical events in which he took a major part. These documents, which cover events of the first years of Soviet power, form the basis of the present article.

The fight for the introduction of workers' control.   Immediately after the victory of the October armed uprising, the Party was confronted with the task of radically reorganizing the national economy on a socialist basis. An important step in this direction was the implementation of Lenin's decree on workers' control, adopted by the All-Russian CEC on November 27, 1917. Representatives of trade unions and factory and plant workers' committees began to form organs of workers' control in the factories, and the All-Russian Council of Workers' Control was set up in Petrograd. Rudzutak devoted much energy to organizing the control system: he was a member of the commission which drafted instructions on the introduction of control into textile enterprises, and from November 29, 1917, was head of the control commission of the central administration of the Textile Trade Union. At one of the commission's first sessions he reported that the decree had been accepted everywhere by the workers of textile enterprises. In face of the factory owners' resistance, the trade union organized the financing of undertakings and the marketing of existing production. Workers' control was turned into a means of preparing for the expropriation of bourgeois property.

Not all members of the trade union administration believed in the victory of the working class. Would the inexperienced workers be able to organize production without the capitalists' help? In reply to the faint-hearted, Ian Ernestovich declared: "Discipline and organization will enable us to get production going." He developed this thought in articles entitled: "The control of production" and "Urgent Business," published in 1917 in the journal *Tekstil'nyi rabochii*.

The first all-Russian congress of textile workers' trade unions and factory and works committees opened at the Trade Union Building in Moscow on January 29, 1918. Rudzutak, in an introductory speech, called on the delegates to concentrate their attention on the administration of the textile industry. Reporting on the work of the provisional all-Russian central committee of the Textile

Trade Union, and basing his remarks on Lenin's instructions, he drew attention to the main problems of trade union work under the new conditions and emphasized that the center of gravity must be shifted to the domain of organization and management. The congress adopted a proposal for the merger of the various trade unions and factory and works committees, thus avoiding overlapping in the work of these bodies. Rudzutak was elected chairman of the Council of the All-Russian Union of Textile Workers and a member of the AUCCTU.

Work on the SCNE.   The Supreme Council of the National Economy (SCNE) was set up in December 1917 to administer the country's economy. The Party appointed to it men who had proven themselves in the fight against disorder, lockouts, and capitalistic sabotage. The following were confirmed as members of its presidium: G. I. Lomov (Oppokov), A. V. Shotman, G. D. Weinberg, and V. Ia. Chubar'. Rudzutak joined their number in May 1918. Lenin took a keen interest in the work of the SCNE and helped it to solve difficult problems. Work under his direct guidance was a valuable education in politics for the presidium members. Each of them was responsible for a different branch of industry, and Rudzutak was put in charge of textile enterprises. In a country where millions of workers were without clothing or footwear, the uninterrupted production of the textile industry was of special importance; but large supplies of cloth were still in the possession of textile magnates. In order to remove this economic lever from the hands of the bourgeoisie, the Soviet government at first proposed to buy cloth from private owners. But the situation which had developed by the summer of 1918 required stronger measures. With the onset of civil war and foreign intervention it was vital to concentrate all material resources in government hands. At a session of the SCNE, Rudzutak proposed that instead of purchasing cloth it should be requisitioned. Despite the protests of some members of the central committee for the textile industry, the presidium approved this proposal and so informed the CPC. At the latter's session of July 16, Lenin put forward a report by himself and Rudzutak on "Methods of Nationalizing All Textile Materials in the RSFSR." In this he made it clear that the only way to nationalize textiles was to requisition them from the wholesalers. Rudzutak warmly supported this view, pointing out: "There is no reason why the state should spend thousands of millions of rubles when the ownership of the textiles would be fully safeguarded if all stores are sealed and an exact inventory is made of their contents." He proposed that the requisition be carried out by the workers and trade union organizations. The CPC approved Lenin's proposal and ordered the central committee for the textile industry to put it into effect within two weeks. Soon the workers had taken over more than 2,000 stores, and huge quantities of material to the value of 2,500 million rubles became the property of the nation. Rudzutak, who was in charge of the operation, reported on it to the CPC....

At this period the Soviet State was nationalizing factories and works. The nationalization of the textile industry was carried out by the central committee of the industry, which had merged with the textile department of SCNE, Rudzutak being elected chairman of the joint body. Much effort was needed to complete the nationalization of a majority of the big and medium-sized concerns, but it was still more difficult to get them operating properly. Rudzutak and two members of the presidium of the committee—V. P. Nogin and F. I. Ozol—paid many visits to the factories to explain to the workers what was required, helping them to overcome their difficulties and master the techniques of operation.

In February 1919 Rudzutak was appointed chairman of the supreme collegium of the chief administration of water transport. This body had the difficult and important task of organizing the sea and river fleets and ensuring the uninterrupted arrival of vitally needed cargoes. At the suggestion of its new chairman, the collegium dispatched special commissions to the Volga, the Mariinsk Canal System, and the Northern and Baltic areas to tighten labor discipline and expedite the repair of vessels and fuel procurement. Rudzutak devoted special attention to navigation on the Volga, which was almost the sole artery of supply for Moscow and Petrograd, and where large stocks of grain and petroleum were waiting at the landing stages. He demanded detailed and verified information about the vessels capable of moving these cargoes. It turned out that the Volga fleet could transport some five and one-half tons of cargo during the navigation season, but that it had fuel for only a few days. On February 20 Rudzutak called a special meeting of the collegium, which appointed members of the water transport administration to supervise the collection of timber so that the fleet received the necessary fuel. The administration also declared the mobilization of specialized workers, carpenters and calkers to repair the wooden ships. Military regulations were brought into effect throughout the commercial fleet. As a result of the exceptional measures that were promptly and decisively introduced under Rudzutak's direction, the ships and barges were available for use when the navigation season opened.

In May 1919 the CPC discussed the report of the water transport administration and instructed Tsurupe, the PC of supply, and Rudzutak to ensure the best possible use of the river fleet for the transport of food supplies. A few days later Rudzutak visited the Volga area to organize the fulfillment of this decision on the spot. Ships, tugs, and barges plied day and night under enemy fire, bringing the Republic vital cargoes of grain, oil, and other supplies.

Discussions concerning trade unions.   "The fronts are quiet." More and more often, this phrase concluded the operational RMC reports published in *Pravda* at the end of 1920. The Soviet people, having defeated the White Guardists and interventionists, were able to turn to peaceful labor. It was the Party's task to stir up the workers and peasants to restore the nation's economy. Rudzutak, as a member of the presidium of the AUCCTU, reported to the fifth all-Russian trade union conference in November 1920 on the unions' tasks in the field of production. In preparing his report he was guided by Lenin's principle of the necessity of active labor force participation in economic construction. In order to strengthen the unions and enhance their role in the building of socialism it was necessary, he declared at the conference, to embark on a wider form of democracy. "Anyone who thinks that our work can be based on compulsion shows a bureaucratic attitude and complete ignorance of what is going on around us." In order to inculcate responsible labor discipline and raise productivity, he proposed a wide system of rewards for outstanding workers, and also the introduction of comradely disciplinary courts to deal with infringements of labor discipline. A majority of delegates thought these proposals useful and timely, but Trotsky disagreed. At a meeting of Party members who were attending the conference he developed a theory of turning the trade unions into an appendage to the state, and spoke of "tightening the screw" and "shaking up" the unions. The conference, however, adopted Rudzutak's proposals. His firmness was much appreciated by Lenin, who said: "All of us on the CC who have not worked in the trade union movement for many years can learn from Comrade Rudzutak."

Trotsky and his followers were not silenced, however. He repeated his demand for a "shake-up" of the unions at the all-Russian conference of the CC of railroad workers' unions, and Bumazhnyi, a leading member of this body, actually stated that democracy was an essentially reactionary concept. The discussion on trade unions in which the Trotskyists involved the Party was basically a discussion of how to associate the working masses with socialist construction, how to lead and direct them. In the debate which now took place, Rudzutak's views, which Lenin supported, proved a sharp weapon against the fractionalists. "This platform is a hundred times better than what Comrade Trotsky wrote after much thought and what Comrade Rudzutak wrote (the resolution of the plenum of December 7) after no thought at all"—such was Lenin's appraisal of Rudzutak's theses.

At a meeting of Communist delegates to the eighth congress of soviets together with members of the AUCCTU and the Moscow city council of trade unions, Lenin argued that the Trotskyist slogan of "shaking up" the unions and turning them into state bodies would mean their liquidation as bodies linking the masses with the Party. Only by persuasion, Lenin declared, could the unions be made to fulfill their function as a driving belt. Without this it would be impossible to harness millions of workers to the building of socialism and communism.

On January 18 *Pravda* published a "Draft Decree of the Tenth Congress of the RCP(B) on the Role and Problems of Trade Unions." This document, known as the "Platform of the Ten", was based on Lenin's views and embodied important points from Rudzutak's theses. It emphasized that the trade unions were schools of communism and that their work should be based on methods of persuasion, while directed in all respects by the CP. Lenin's platform was a decisive blow to the Trotskyists, the workers' opposition, the Democratic Centralists, the Bukharinites, and other factions.* On January 21 *Pravda* printed an article by Lenin entitled "Crisis in the Party" and a letter in which Lenin requested the editor to "publish Rudzutak's theses adopted November 2-6, 1920, by the All-Russian Conference of Trade Unions as a basis for discussion—they are extremely necessary." The theses were duly published below Lenin's letter. The Party assembly within the AUCCTU accepted the "Platform of the Ten", and Rudzutak, who had shown himself a staunch Leninist at this difficult time for the Party, was elected secretary of the AUCCTU. The ensuing discussion of the platform by all Party organizations showed that the mass of Communists understood which side was in the right. An overwhelming majority of these bodies voted in favor of the "Ten's views, and the Party was able to present a united and monolithic front at its Tenth Congress.

At the Genoa conference.   Rudzutak's name is linked with one of the major events in the external history of the young Soviet State. In its tenacious pursuit of peace and businesslike relations with capitalistic countries, the Soviet government in the fall of 1921 addressed a note to the governments of Britain, France, Italy, Japan, and the U.S.A. expressing its agreement to recognize prewar Tsarist debts on condition that payment was to be deferred, credits were to be made available for the restoration of the nation's economy, and the capitalist powers were to agree to recognize the Soviet government. The note proposed an international conference to discuss these questions. The Entente powers at a conference at the beginning of 1922 agreed to call an economic conference of European states at Genoa, to which the Soviet government should be invited.

The Soviet delegation was selected at a special meeting of the All-Russian CEC in January 1922. Lenin was designated as chairman, but was unable to go and was represented by the PC of foreign affairs, G. V. Chicherin. The delegation included the most prominent Soviet diplomats—Krasin, Litvinov, and Vorovsky—and representatives of the Soviet republics, as well as by Rudzutak, who was a member of the Presidium of the All-Russian CEC and secretary-general of the AUCCTU.

The conference opened at the San Giorgio palace on April 10, 1922. The delegates of the first socialist state in the world took their seats along with others in the crowded conference hall. Representatives of Italy, France, Britain, and Germany spoke in turn from the rostrum. The Soviet delegates listened attentively. Many of them did not need an interpreter, and Rudzutak was among these: the years he had spent learning foreign languages in jail had not been in vain. When Chicherin's turn came, he spoke of the Soviet government's inflexible determination to adhere to the principle of peaceful coexistence with all states.

The work of the Genoa conference has been described in detail in many

---

*On the eve of the Tenth Congress of the RCP(B) in 1921, the controversy over trade union control and management of industry threatened to split the Party. Lenin branded the "workers' opposition" "anarcho-syndicalist," and at the opening of the congress the factional groups within the party were outlawed and dissolved.—ED.

historical works; but the part played by Rudzutak, among others, was unjustly suppressed during the period of the personality cult. This gap is largely filled by the verbatim record of a meeting of the RCP(B) fraction at the third session of the All-Russian CEC on May 12, 1922, which is preserved in the Central Party Archives at the Institute of Marxism-Leninism of the CC of the CPSU. From this document it appears that the meeting was discussing its order of business when Kalinin announced that Rudzutak had arrived from Genoa. His appearance at the rostrum was greeted with applause. Someone called out jokingly: "Why aren't you in a tailcoat like a proper diplomat?" to which Rudzutak replied in the same vein: "All our tailcoats were pawned to pay off prewar debts." He went on to say that the delegation had worked under difficulties, as the Italian authorities were determined to "protect" their people from Communist influence. The villa at Santa Margherita, where they were housed, was surrounded by police and plainclothesmen; all the exits were watched, and only those with special passes were allowed in.

Much interest attaches to the passages of his report which show how our delegation, in accordance with Lenin's instructions, combated the imperialists' attempts to force their rapacious demands on Soviet Russia. Lloyd George, the head of the British delegation, indicated in a private conversation that the unyielding Soviet attitude over debts threatened the conference with a breakdown. On April 20 Chicherin wrote a letter to him promising on certain conditions to allow former property holders in Russia the use of their enterprises, and where possible to grant them just compensation. This was departure from the CC's clear and precise instructions, and Rudzutak at once telegraphed a protest to Moscow. On receiving this, Lenin wrote on April 24 to the Politburo: "I fully agree with Rudzutak's opinion in his telegram of the Twenty-second." The Politburo instructed the delegation to adhere strictly to the line prescribed by the CC.

Rudzutak emphasized in his report that the British, French, and other delegates were profuse in their appeals to make peace and put an end to wars, but that their love of peace evaporated as soon as our delegation pointed out that in order to achieve these humane ideals there should be a general reduction of armaments. Then the cry of the "Russian menace" was raised, and the French delegate even stated that the Soviet proposal amounted to a "campaign against France." How like the bourgeois diplomats of 1922 were to present-day imperialist circles in the West! Both are distinguished by their hypocrisy and their efforts to deceive the public by conjuring up the "Communist bogy."

The upright yet flexible policy of the Soviet delegation thwarted the Entente's imperialist plan to isolate our country at Genoa. By a treaty concluded at Rapallo, Soviet Russia and Germany agreed to develop mutually advantageous economic relations. This treaty, as Rudzutak said in his report, "made a definite breach in the united capitalist front against us which had formed at Genoa." The strongest capitalistic state was the first to recognize us *de jure*. Italy and various small states began to talk of concluding their own agreements with Soviet Russia.

At the time of Rudzutak's report the conference was still in session; but thanks to his deep insight into international conditions he was able to assess the situation correctly. However the conference might end, he said, it had already given us a definite advantage: the fact that we had been in conference with thirty-three capitalist powers was in itself a pronounced success. We had convinced the West, he emphasized, that Soviet Russia was a strong power that could stand up for itself.

A few days later, on May 16, Rudzutak's report on the conference was discussed at a plenum of the CC of the RCP(B). The resolution submitted to the Politburo said: "Having heard Comrade Rudzutak's report, the Politburo recognizes that our delegation at Genoa has so far correctly carried out its duties."

Chairman of the Central Asia bureau of the CC of the RCP(B).   During the period of peaceful socialist construction, our Party was confronted with new problems in regard to the nationalities question. The Tenth Congress of the RCP(B) mapped out a broad program of social-economic and cultural transformation of the former national border regions of Tsarist Russia. Central Asia presented particular difficulties, with its huge area inhabited by many peoples at different levels of cultural, economic, and political development. Agriculture, the mainstay of the economy, was in disarray as a result of the war. The area sown with cotton was only 8 to 10 percent of what it had been in 1914. The imperialist powers inspired and supported counterrevolutionary attempts by the property-owning minority; the Basmachi were devastating the land and terrorizing its population. The political and economic difficulties were made more acute by the weakness of many Party organizations. A decree of the CC of the RCP(B) dated August 9, 1922, noted that "Party work is at a low level in the Turkestan CP, and the Party committees are in a state of disorganization." The principles of collective leadership were often neglected, factions arose, and the embers of nationalism were still alive. The CC of the RCP(B) took steps to improve Party work, renewing the composition of the principal organs of the Turkestan ASSR and the Central Asia bureau of the CC of the RCP(B). Rudzutak was appointed chairman of this bureau, whose task was to ensure united leadership of the Party organizations of Turkestan, Bukhara, and Khorezm. The CC's directive to the bureau, drafted by him, emphasized the need to carry out propaganda and organizational measures and, with due care, gradually engage the working masses of the local population in the construction of a new society.

The situation called for prompt execution of the CC's instructions, which were discussed by the bureau under Rudzutak's chairmanship on September 9. Together with measures to improve the work of the PCs concerned with economic affairs and to restore agriculture and industry, a reorganization of the Party apparatus was decided on. The plan for this was confirmed the same day at a joint session of the Central Asia bureau and the plenum of the CC of the Turkestan CP.

At the seventh regional conference at Tashkent in October 1922 Rudzutak reported on "Immediate Tasks of the CP and the Soviet Authorities in Turkestan." In this report he urged the strengthening of Party work and the need to close the Party's ranks and extirpate the remnants of great-power and nationalist tendencies. A resolution was adopted pointing out that the main task for the Turkestan CP was to improve day-to-day conditions of life for the broad masses of the people.

The struggle against economic difficulties was complicated by the weakness of economic ties among the three Central Asian republics. In January 1923, after discussing a report by Rudzutak on the work of the Central Asia bureau, the CC of the RCP(B) decided upon an economic union of the three republics. Rudzutak well understood the importance of this measure and the difficulties it entailed. Guided by Lenin's instructions, the decisions of the CC of the RCP(B) and the state of the Central Asian economy, he refrained from insisting on the unification of all economic activity in the republics. "We must decide about a unified tax system and a single administration of railroads, posts and telegraphs, irrigation and agriculture," he declared when opening the January 1923 plenary session of the Central Asia bureau. The discussions went on for three days. The Bukhara representatives objected to the idea of strengthening economic ties with Turkestan, fearing to be "deprived of sovereignty." Lobimov of the Central Asia bureau, on the other hand, favored rapid unification in the administrative sphere. Rudzutak had to intervene several times, pointing out the errors in both views and patiently explaining the Leninist line, followed by the bureau, of strengthening economic cooperation among the Central Asian republics while preserving and reinforcing their respective sovereignties. "It has been shown in practice," he said, "that no single important economic question can be solved in Turkestan if it is not also solved in Bukhara and Khorezm. This, however, does not mean that the economic organs of the republics must be merged together, but that there must be a coordinating body which can decide matters involving joint economic policy." The CC line, thus expounded and defended by Rudzutak, won the day.

In March 1923 the first economic conference of Turkestan, Bukhara, and Khorezm opened at Tashkent. It entrusted the general direction of economic construction in all the Central Asian republics to the newly created Central Asian Economic Council. It also formulated measures for the unification of the monetary systems of the Bukhara and Khorezm People's Soviet republics with that of the RSFSR. All this facilitated further socialist transformation in the republics, including a unified transport, postal, and telegraph system.

At the Twelfth Party Congress Rudzutak was elected a candidate member of the Politburo, a member of the Organization Bureau, and secretary of the

CC of the RCP(B). He was among those who accepted at once and without reserve the conclusions of Lenin's last articles: "On Cooperation"; "Better Fewer, but Better"; and "Our Revolution." The CC plenum of July 1923 appointed him to a commission to work out practical measures "in connection with the new presentation of the question in Comrade Lenin's articles." In spite of his many important duties in the central organs of the Party and state, he had a thorough understanding of all aspects of life in the Central Asian republics. He drafted written directives, telephoned instructions, held discussions with comrades, and often spent long periods in Tashkent.

In July 1923 the bureau under his chairmanship was considering a program of economic and political development in the Dzhetysui (Semirechensk) oblast—the most remote and backward part of the Turkestan Republic. The draft prepared by the CC of the Turkestan CP was in many respects a good one but needed important amendments, as it did not take into account some of the main provisions of Lenin's cooperative plan. These were put forward by Rudzutak and accepted by the Turkestan CC....

Rudzutak insisted on the importance of strengthening Party organizations, in particular by bringing into the Party the best members of the working class of local nationality. The creation of "sound and healthy Communist cells, an enduring kernel composed of representatives of the local nationalities," was in his view an important basis for the solution of the nationalities question. The correct attitude adopted by the Central Asian bureau fostered the growth of local cadres. By April 1, 1924, of 180 members of the CC and the oblast and uezd committees of the Turkestan CP, 128 were Communists of local nationalities.

Rudzutak pursued firmly and consistently the Party's policy in regard to the national sovereignty of the peoples of Soviet Central Asia. As he pointed out to the eighth congress of the Turkestan CP in 1924, the old administrative boundaries drawn by the Tsarist government were a source of national enmity. Their removal must serve to bring about the complete elimination of survivals of national discord, to strengthen national sovereignty and the unity of our country. In 1924 a commission of the Central Asia bureau set about drafting a plan for the national delimitation of the Central Asian republics. The Politburo of the CC of the RCP(B) discussed the question and on September 25 approved the bureau's plan for the delimitation of republics and oblasts. The new Turkmen and Uzbek Soviet republics were formed, and a few years later the Tadzhik. Lenin's nationalities policy had scored another outstanding victory.

*   *   *

In subsequent years Rudzutak was PC of transport, chairman of the Central Control Commission of the CPSU, and PC of workers' and peasants' inspection. For many years he was a member of the Politburo. In the battle against Trotskyists,

Zinovievites, and the right-wing opposition he invariably maintained the Leninist line based on principle. From 1926 to 1937 he was deputy chairman of the CPC of the U.S.S.R. He fully justified the immense confidence which the Party and people reposed in him. To his last breath he never lost faith in the CP and remained its faithful champion.[32]

M. S. SAMATOV

Biographical data

Born 1894, died 1938. Joined the CP in 1920. Before becoming an adherent of the Soviets he was active in the bourgeois-nationalist Alash party. From 1921 to 1937 he was PC of food of the Kazakh ASSR, director of the Kazakh State Publishing House, chairman of the Semipalatinsk gubernia executive committee, head of administration of the Kazakh national statistical office, etc. Was elected delegate to several regional party conferences, the second and third congresses of soviets of Kazakhstan, and the Third Comintern Congress. Was a member of the presidium of the Kirgiz oblast committee of the RCP(B) and the Kazakh regional committee of the CPSU, also of the presidium of the CEC of the Kazakh ASSR. He permitted occasional practical and theoretical mistakes in the execution of the nationalities policy.[33]

ALEKSANDR PAVLOVICH SEREBROVSKY

Biographical data

Born 1884, died 1943. Joined the CP in 1903. Born at Ufa, the son of a teacher. In 1905 he was a member of the executive committee of the Petersburg soviet of workers' deputies. In 1907, at the time of the mutiny on the torpedo boat *Groziashchii*, he was arrested at Vladivostok and condemned to fifteen years hard labor. In 1908 he escaped to Belgium, where he graduated from technical high school. Returned to Russia in 1912 and carried on active work in Nizhnii Novgorod, Moscow, and Rostov. During the October Revolution he commanded a Red Guard company against Kerensky's forces. In 1919 he was deputy chairman of the Special Supply Commission of the Red Army, later deputy PC of transport and chief of military supply of the Ukrainian front. In 1920-26 he was chairman of administration for the Azerbaidzhan petroleum industry, and in 1926 deputy chairman of the SCNE of the U.S.S.R. In 1932-37, deputy PC of heavy industry of the U.S.S.R. At the Fourteenth through the Seventeenth congresses of the CPSU he was elected a candidate member of the CC of the CPSU. He was arrested in 1937 and perished on April 14, 1943.[34]

An underground worker, engineer and scientist

One day in July 1903, a boy of eighteen slipped out of the gates of the Ufa prison. Two months later the gendarmes, who had sought him in vain, were obliged to report that Aleksandr Serebrovsky, a teacher's son and member of the Bolshevik Party who had been exiled to the Ural region for revolutionary activity, was no longer at Ufa. Meanwhile, a young worker named Osip Loginov ("Grisha") had turned up at the Putilov works in Petersburg. It was under this name that Serebrovsky received his true proletariat schooling and became a professional revolutionary.

In 1905, the year of the barricades, he was elected a member of the executive committee of the Petersburg soviet of workers' deputies. It was here that he first met Lenin. Then came stormy days in revolutionary Baku and Odessa, arrest and escape. He carried on Party work among the sailors at Vladivostok and took part in the mutiny on the torpedo boat *Groziashchii*. Again arrested, he was sentenced to fifteen years penal servitude. But once again the gendarmes had to report that Loginov-Serebrovsky had disappeared. This time he had escaped abroad. In Paris he again met Lenin and on his instructions went to Brussels to study at the higher technical college: the Party needed legal cadres [*sic*]. Three years later, furnished with a degree, A. P. Serebrovsky returned to Russia. At Revel, Moscow, Rostov, Nizhnii Novgorod, and Baku he never ceased, while working as a mechanical engineer, to carry on revolutionary activity. He was arrested seven times by Tsarist agents and once by those of the Provisional Government, but nothing could daunt this brave Leninist. In October 1917 he led a company of workers in the assault on the Winter Palace.

The time came when the victorious proletariat needed its own working-class managers and engineers. A new, unprecedented battle was developing, this time against economic disruption. The Party sent Serebrovsky to various sectors of the new front: he was a member of the administration of the Putilov works, deputy chairman of the Red Army's Special Supply Commission, and deputy PC of transport....

The oil-producing area at that time, as academician I. M. Gubkin has described it, was a veritable cemetery. Serebrovsky's task as chairman of the Azerbaidzhan petroleum industry was to see that the country got its oil as quickly as possible, and this task was carried out....

A Party worker and organizer of the first rank, he was also a gifted engineer and scientist. A legendary episode took place when, in 1921, it was urgently necessary to repair the bridge across the Kura River at Poili, which the Whites had destroyed. The French engineers who had been called in had undertaken to get traffic moving within three months at earliest. Then Serebrovsky stepped in and made his own calculations, with the result that trains were crossing the river four days later.

His gifts as an organizer and engineer were displayed with equal brilliance in a new field when the Party assigned him to restore and develop the gold-mining industry, which was then being carried on in a haphazard and amateurish way in various parts of the Urals, Siberia, the Far East, and Kazakhstan. For many years he directed this industry and that of nonferrous metals, being chairman of the all-Union office and head of the chief administration of the gold and platinum industries, head of the chief administration for the mining and processing of nonferrous metals, deputy chairman of the SCNE, and deputy PC of heavy industry of the U.S.S.R. During this period he visited the U.S.A. three times to study gold-mining methods. These visits resulted in a new scientific work describing the best methods of prospecting and carrying out preparatory, extractive and other works. His book *Zolotaia promyshlennost'* (The Gold Industry) sold four editions in six years and played a great part in the industrialization of gold extraction and that of nonferrous metals.

Occupied though he was with organizational questions, he managed during these years to carry on important research work. He was a professor at the Azerbaidzhan Polytechnic Institute and the Moscow Mining Academy and did much to train scientific and technical cadres. The Party greatly valued his services. From the Fourteenth to the Seventeenth congresses [of the CPSU] he was elected a candidate member of the CC, and he received more than one Order of the Soviet Union. To the end of his life he remained an active, fervent and convinced Leninist, a true comrade and valiant fighter. The repressions of the period of the personality cult cut short the life of a man who could have done much more for the good of the Soviet people and of our socialist state.[35]

ASHOT SARKISOVICH SHAKHMURADOV

Biographical data

Born 1899, died 19—. Joined the Bolshevik Party in 1917. Born at Baian village, Elisavetpol (Giandzha) uezd. Began revolutionary activity in 1915. In 1917-21 he took an active part in establishing Soviet power in Azerbaidzhan, was chairman of the Giandzha uezd land committee, secretary of a raion committee, and then performed important duties in the gubernia Cheka. In 1921-22 he was deputy chairman of the Zangezur revolutionary committee, later that of Aleksandropol; was deputy political officer and acting military commissar of the Armenian Composite Division. In 1922-29 he studied at the chemical faculty of the Moscow (Bauman) Higher Technical School, after which he became shop manager at a Moscow copper-smelting and copper-electrolyte works, then senior engineer of the chief administrations of the metalworking and nonferrous metal industries. In 1929-30 he was deputy chairman of the All-Union Association for the Mining, Processing and Marketing of Nonferrous Metals, Gold, and Platinum (Tsvetmetzoloto). In 1929 and 1935 he went to America to study methods of nonferrous metallurgy. After his first trip to the

U.S.A. he was appointed chief engineer of the Kazakhstan Med'stroi (Copper Works Construction), then director of the northern Caucasus zinc trust, the all-Union association known as Northern Tsvetmetzoloto, and the chief administration for the mining and processing of nonferrous metals. He was also a member of the collegium of the PC of Heavy Industry. At the beginning of 1937 he was appointed director of the Chimkent lead plant. Soon thereafter he became a victim of the cult of Stalin's personality.[36]

A prominent organizer of Soviet industry

Ashot Sarkisovich Shakhmuradov was an active member of the revolutionary movement at Baku and a devoted fighter for the victory of the proletarian revolution in Transcaucasia. After the triumph of Soviet power he became a tireless organizer and builder of the nonferrous metallurgical industry. His brilliant career brought him from the rank of shop manager to the top position in the chief administration of this industry.

He was born in May 1899, the son of a peasant huntsman in Baian village, Elisavetpol (Giandzha) uezd. He attended a city school until 1915 and then entered college at Baku, where his revolutionary career began. In November 1917, while still a youth, he joined the Party and carried a gun in the fight for the Baku Commune. After the victory of the Soviet regime in Azerbaidzhan, he was sent by the CC of the Azerbaidzhan CP to the first legal Party conference at Giandzha (now Kirovabad), where he took part in the suppression of the counterrevolutionary revolt of the Beys and Khans. Soon after, he was head of the Giandzha uezd land committee, directing the distribution to the peasants of landowners' and religious (Christian and Moslem) estates. Later he was elected secretary of the raion committee, and then promoted to important work in the gubernia Cheka. In summer 1921, at the request of the Armenian CP, he was sent with a group of communists to Armenia....

In the fall of 1922 he was sent as one of a large group of Communists to study in Moscow. He attended the chemical faculty of the Bauman Higher Technical School and graduated with honors in 1925. He then became first a shop manager at a Moscow copper-smelting and copper-electrolyte works, then senior engineer for the chief administration of the metalworking and nonferrous metal industries, and finally, in 1929-30, a member of the administration and deputy chairman of the All-Union Association for the Mining, Processing and Marketing of Nonferrous Metals, Gold and Platinum (Tsvetmetzoloto). He was an able and progressive leader of the nonferrous metal industry and worked unceasingly for the adoption of up-to-date methods and techniques. For instance, he himself worked out a process for refining lead and introduced it at a factory operated by the North Caucasian Zinc Trust. Twice, in 1929 and 1935, he visited the U.S.A. to study methods of nonferrous metallurgy. He visited some sixty American plants and on returning home wrote two books:

Tsvetnaia metallurgiia SShA za poslednie gody: Otchet o zagranichnoi komandirovki (Nonferrous Metallurgy in the U.S.A. in Recent Years: Report on a Foreign Tour) (1930), and *Tsvetnaia metallurgiia SShA: Itogi komandirovki* (Nonferrous Metallurgy in the U.S.A.: Results of a Tour) (1935). In these works he gave a detailed description of the technical innovations and methods of extracting and processing nonferrous metals in the U.S.A., and also of the equipment used at American plants.... By an order of April 27, 1933, the PC of heavy industry, G. K. Ordzhonikidze, appointed the young metallurgist director of the chief administration for the mining and processing of nonferrous metals (Glavtsvetmet) and a member of the collegium of the PC of Heavy Industry.

Wherever Shakhmuradov worked, whether as a shop foreman or as head of a central board, he always brought to his duties a spirit of innovation and creative zeal, striving for the adoption of the best methods of extracting and refining ore and producing and processing nonferrous and rare metals.... He was in charge of Glavtsvetmet for four years, and was responsible for speeding up the exploitation of the richest deposits in the world, those at Dzhezkazgan and Almalyk. He advocated the establishment of large enterprises and new centers of nonferrous metallurgy in the eastern parts of the country—Kazakhstan, the Urals, and Bashkiria—and also in the northern Caucasus, Azerbaidzhan, Armenia, etc. Great efforts by the Party and government were needed to transform this formerly backward branch of the economy into one of the most progressive sectors of Soviet heavy industry. Shakhmuradov strove with all his energy and determination for the fulfillment of this honorable task. Unfortunately, many of his plans and intentions were destined to remain unrealized. At the beginning of 1937 he was sent to Kazakhstan as director of the Chimkent lead plant, and soon afterward became a victim of unjustified repression owing to the cult of Stalin. After its Twentieth Congress the Party restored the good name of this devoted and patriotic Bolshevik, an eminent leader who spent all his talents and energy in the service of Soviet industry.[37]

KIRILL VASIL'EVICH SUKHOMLIN

Biographical data

Born 1886, died 1938. Joined the CP in 1905. Political and Party leader. Born in Krasnopol'e village (now Bakhmach raion, Chernigov oblast), the son of a worker. In 1904 he settled in Transbaikal and worked in depots at the stations of Borza, and Manchouli. In August 1905 he joined the RSDWP and carried on revolutionary work among railroad workers. During the October Revolution he took an active part in the establishment of Soviet power at Irkutsk, Manchouli, and other stations of the Transbaikal railroad; was a member of the RMC of the district bureau of the East Siberian soviet of workers', soldiers', and peasants' deputies. During the Civil War he was active in the partisan movement in the Far East. From 1920 he was engaged in trade union work: was a member of the CC of the Railroad Workers' Union, then head of the southern bureau of the CC of the Railroad Workers' Union at Kharkov. In 1925-27 he was deputy PC of workers' and peasants' inspection, then PC of labor of the Ukrainian SSR. In 1927-32, chairman of the SCNE of the Ukrainian SSR. In 1923-33, deputy chairman of the CPC of the Ukraine. In 1933-35, chairman of the central control commission of the Ukraine CP and PC of workers' and peasants' inspection of the Ukraine. In 1935-38, PC of local industry of the Ukraine, chairman of Gosplan, and at the same time deputy chairman of the CPC of the Ukraine. Delegate to the Fourteenth through the Seventeenth congresses of the CPSU. At the Fifteenth and Sixteenth congresses he was elected a candidate member of the CC of the CPSU. He was a delegate to the sixth through the eighth conferences and the ninth through the thirteenth congresses of the Ukraine CP. At the eighth conference he was elected a member of the central control commission of the Ukraine CP, and at the ninth through the thirteenth congresses he was elected a member of the CC of the Ukraine CP. In 1926-29 he was a candidate member, and in 1930-37 a full member, of the politburo of the Ukraine CP. He was several times elected to the all-Ukrainian CEC and the presidium of the CEC of the Ukrainian SSR. Awarded the Order of Lenin. He became a victim of the cult of Stalin's personality.[38]

PANTELEIMON IVANOVICH SVISTUN

Biographical data

Born 1890, died 1938. Born on Man'ki farm, Kremenchug uezd, Poltava gubernia, the son of a poor Ukrainian peasant. Educated at parish school, after which his brother, a railroad worker, got him a job in 1905 as apprentice mechanic at the Kriukov repair works. In 1909 he joined the RSDWP and became a Bolshevik. After the Kriukov Bolshevik organization was broken up in 1913 he moved to Kharkov and worked at the Osnov railroad depot. In 1915, because of his membership in the RSDWP, he was forced to live under police supervision at Poltava, where he was a machinist in a stocking factory. During the October Revolution and Civil War he took an active part in the armed struggle for Soviet power and the building of the Soviet State. In 1921-24 he was chairman of the Kremenchug gubernia Party organization; in 1924-25 deputy chairman of the Kiev gubernia executive committee; and in 1927-30 secretary of the Sumsk oblast committee of the Party. In 1930 he was appointed head of construction of the Kharkov tractor plant. When the plant began operation on October 1, 1931, he was appointed director. In July 1938 he was arrested and became a victim of the cult of Stalin's personality.[39]

S. I. SYRTSOV

Biographical data

Born 1893, died 1938. Delegate to the Eleventh Party Congress with delibera-
tive vote as member of the credentials committee. Joined the CP in 1913.
After the February revolution of 1917 he was a member of the Rostov-
Nakhichevan committee of the RSDWP(B); in 1918-19, military commissar
of a division; from the end of 1919, chairman of the Rostov soviet. In 1921-26
he worked in the CC of the RCP(B), in charge of the agitation and propaganda
department. In 1929 he was chairman of the CPC of the RSFSR. During
the trade union discussions of 1920-21 he defended Trotsky's views, but changed
his position on becoming acquainted with Lenin's platform on the eve of the
Tenth Congress of the RCP(B). In 1930 he was deprived of membership in
the CC for participation in the "left"-right bloc [*sic*]. From 1936 he was director
of the Nogin war chemical works.[40]

VALENTIN ANDREEVICH TRIFONOV

Biographical data

Born 1888, died 1937. Joined the Bolshevik Party in 1904. A Don Cossack,
workman and mechanic. In 1905 he took part in the armed uprising at Rostov-
on-Don. Exiled to the Tobolsk gubernia in 1906; escaped to the Urals, where
he trained workers' detachments. Was secretary of the Ekaterinburg committee.
Exiled to Berezov in 1908. In 1915 he helped to set up an underground press
in Petersburg. After the February revolution he was secretary of the Bolshevik
faction of the Petrograd soviet until June 1917, then a Red Guard organizer.
After the October Revolution he was a member of the collegium of the PC
of Army Affairs and of the RMC. In 1918 he was an organizer of the Ural
Army, member of the Third Army RMC, etc. In 1919-20, member of the
RMC of the southern and southeastern fronts. From 1921, deputy head of
chief fuel administration and chairman of administration of the All-Russian
Petroleum Trade Syndicate. In 1923, chairman of the military collegium of
the Supreme Court of the U.S.S.R. In 1926, Soviet trade representative in
Finland. In 1928, member of the presidium of the All-Union Lenin Agricultural
Academy. For five years ending June 1937 he was chairman of the chief concession committee of the CPC of the U.S.S.R. In 1937 he became a victim of
the cult of Stalin's personality.

An outstanding Party and war leader

Among the old Bolsheviks to whom the Party, after the October victory,
entrusted the vital task of creating the first workers' and peasants' army in

the world, not the least eminent was Valentin Andreevich Trifonov, who devoted all his energy and revolutionary experience to the task of defending the young Soviet State.

His career was a long and varied one. He was born seventy-five years ago, the son of a teacher in the Cossack settlement of Novocherkassk in the Don oblast. He was orphaned in early life and educated in the handicraft school at Maikov, where he was arrested for the first time for organizing a strike. He joined the RSDWP(B) in 1904. Later he worked as a mechanic in the Rostov railroad works, took an active part in the 1905 revolution, and commanded a workers' militia platoon in the Rostov armed uprising. In 1905 he became a professional revolutionary. He was arrested six times, exiled to Siberia four times, escaped three times and resumed active work in the revolutionary struggle.

When the February revolution broke out, he became first secretary of the Bolshevik faction of the Petrograd soviet of workers' and soldiers' deputies, and commissar of the soviet for the Vasilievski Ostrov district. In August 1917 he was elected a member of the so-called Five—the city headquarters of the Petrograd Red Guard. He was coauthor of the draft regulations for the workers' Red Guard, which were approved by a city conference of Red Guardists shortly before the October uprising. He became secretary of the central command and a member of the general staff of the Petrograd Red Guard. He took an active part in preparing the October armed uprising and in operations for the seizure of arms. During the uprising he led armed workers' detachments.

After the revolution he was one of the initial members of the All-Russian Cheka. After the adoption of the decree on forming the army of the socialist state, he became a member of the all-Russian collegium of the PC of Army Affairs.

From April 1918 he was active on the Civil War fronts, organizing resistance to the Germans at Rostov, Krasnodar, and the approaches to Tsaristsyn. From Tsaritsyn he came to Moscow to report personally to Lenin on the situation in the southeast. There exists a telegram from Ordzhonikidze to Lenin [which requests that Lenin] make no decision concerning questions of southeastern defense before seeing Trifonov.

During the White Guard rebellion Trifonov was sent to the Urals, where he worked actively at forming the regular Third Army, was commander of the Kama military flotilla, and served as a member of the RMC of the Third Army and of the RSFSR. In 1919 he was again sent to the south, where he commanded the Don Expeditionary Corps and then became a member of the RMC of the southeastern and Caucasian fronts. He actively helped Ordzhonikidze and Kirov in the fight to liberate the northern Caucasus and Transcaucasia from White Guard and bourgeois nationalist elements.

He was a serious student of military affairs, used his experience to the full, and was a shrewd analyst of military situations. This enabled him to show valuable initiative in battle. Thus, even at the outset of his military career he initiated such important measures as the creation of a system of fortified points in the Urals, the construction of armored trains at the Motovilikhi works, and the adaptation of ships of the river commercial fleet for the equipment of the Kama military flotilla.

He consistently followed the Party's policy in matters of military development, fighting against the "partisan spirit" and in favor of strict discipline and the proper use of military specialists. His thoughts on military problems were expressed in a series of articles entitled "Front and Rear," published in *Pravda* in 1919. Later, in civilian life, he continued to study defense questions and wrote a large work, *Kontury griadushchei voiny* ("Shape of the Next War"), which he finished in 1937 but which unfortunately was not published.

During the acute fuel crisis after the Civil War, the Party also made use of him on other fronts: he was appointed chairman of the All-Russian Petroleum Trade Syndicate and deputy head of the chief fuel administration. Later he was chairman of the military collegium of the Supreme Court of the U.S.S.R. After doing important work abroad he was for five years, ending in June 1937, chairman of the chief concession committee of the CPC of the U.S.S.R.

He was a man of great charm, and we particularly remember his warm, sympathetic attitude toward his colleagues and subordinates. In 1937 he became a victim of unjustified repression. Today the good name of this old Bolshevik and outstanding military and political leader has been restored to the people, and we remember him with deep gratitude for his services to the Party and the revolution.[42]

IL'IA VENIDIKTOVICH TSIVTSIVADZE

Biographical data

Born 1881, died 1937. Joined the Bolshevik Party in 1903. Born at Khoni village, Kutaisi gubernia, the son of a poor peasant. In 1903 he worked as an agitator and propagandist and was a member of the Batumi committee of the RSDWP. In 1904-11 he was at Tiflis, organizing an illegal press; was arrested, and after his release carried on Party work at Kutaisi, Tiflis, Chiatura, and in the northern Caucasus; edited the Bolshevik newspaper *Dro* (Time). In 1911-14 he attended the Shaniavsky People's University in Moscow and carried on revolutionary work in a students' organization and in workers' groups. In 1914-17 he worked in the "Tver group" of the RSDWP, was arrested and exiled to the Irkutsk gubernia. After the February 1917 revolution he was a member of the bureau of the Moscow committee of the RSDWP(B); after the October Revolution, a member of the presidium of the Moscow soviet, chairman of the investigating commission of the Moscow revolutionary tribunal, and deputy chairman of the tribunal, then a member of the Central Auditing

Commission. In 1921-33 he was in Georgia as administrator for the CPC and deputy chairman of the Tiflis soviet. Returned to Moscow in 1923 and was engaged in economic, Party and government work; director of the Special Technical Bureau and of an armament works. In 1937 he fell victim to the cult of Stalin's personality.[43]

A true son of the Party

Maksim Gorky wrote in one of his articles: "All my life I have seen as true heroes only those people who understand work and love it—who make it their aim to set free all human powers for creative purposes, in order to organize life and create conditions worthy of human beings." Just such a man was Il'ia Venidiktovich Tsivtsivadze, whom Lenin and his colleagues affectionately called "Comrade Il'ia." Every line of his biography is connected with great historical events, and his noble life was that of a man in the fullest possible sense.

He was born on March 20, 1881, in the village of Khoni, Kutaisi gubernia, the son of a poor peasant. He went from village school to a church seminary, but was expelled in 1902 for "taking part in disorders" and returned under police escort to his home village. In 1903, at Batumi, he joined the RSDWP. As a fervent agitator and propagandist, he acquired great prestige among the Bolsheviks and was soon elected a member of the Batumi committee of the RSDWP. In the spring of 1904 he went to Tiflis to avoid arrest, and on the Party's orders set up an illegal press; he was arrested and confined in the Metekh jail, whence he was moved to a jail at Kutaisi. After his release he continued Party work in Kutaisi, Chiatura, and the northern Caucasus. In 1907 he edited the Bolshevik newspaper *Dro* and carried out missions for the militant group headed by "Kamo" (S.A. Ter-Petrosian).

In 1911, to hide from the police, he went to Moscow, where he attended the Shaniavsky People's University. There he joined a Bolshevik students' organization, carried on revolutionary activity in workers' groups, and was active in organizing the illegal press. In November 1914, as a member of the "Tver group" of the RSDWP, he posted May Day pamphlets in 1915 and took an active part in preparing the city-wide conference of Bolsheviks. That year he was denounced by a provocateur, arrested, and exiled to the Irkutsk gubernia.

After the February revolution he returned to Moscow, and in April 1917 he was elected to the bureau of the Moscow committee of the RSDWP(B) and became chief organizer of the Zamoskvorech'e district committee of Bolsheviks. A man of great energy and a superb organizer, he often spoke at factories in defense of Lenin's slogans. As a bold revolutionary, he took a prominent part in organizing and leading the strike of 400,000 Moscow workers on the day of the convocation of the counterrevolutionary State Conference. This strike was a harbinger of the October storm.

At one session of the Moscow committee he proposed, in connection with preparations for the uprising of September 1, a general arming of the workers and the formation of detachments among those who already possessed arms. The committee set up a triumvirate consisting of Tsivtsivadze, P. K. Shternberg, and A. S. Verdernikov to direct the organization of the workers' militia. At this time Tsivtsivadze gave much attention to organizing and training detachments of the Red Guard. He paid many visits to enterprises to supervise the guardsmen's training. As soon as a directive was received from the center to organize district (raion) RMCs, he recalls, "We at once summoned the raion committee and, in the presence of [two] Moscow committee members, Comrades R. S. Zemliachka and I. A. Piatnitsky, decided on the composition of the Zamoskvorech'e RMC."

In December 1917, after the victory of the October Revolution, the Party co-opted him onto the presidium of the Moscow soviet. From April 1918 he was chairman of the investigating commission of the Moscow revolutionary tribunal and deputy chairman of the tribunal. In 1917-20 he was elected a delegate to all Moscow Party conferences and to the fifth through the seventh congresses of soviets of the RSFSR and the Eighth and Ninth congresses of the RCP(B). He was elected to the All-Russian CEC at the seventh convocation, and at the Eighth Congress of the RCP(B) he became a member of the Central Auditing Commission.

Lenin knew Tsivtsivadze well and met and talked with him several times. The latter has written interesting accounts of these meetings, which belong to the golden store of Leniniana.

In 1921 the CC of the Party sent him to Georgia, where he was administrator for the CPC and later deputy chairman of the Tiflis soviet. In 1923 he returned to Moscow, where he was engaged first in economic work and later held important Party and government posts. In 1934 the Party CC appointed him director of the Special Technical Bureau, and later of an armaments factory. His life was tragically cut short in 1937. He was a true son of Lenin's Party, a pupil and counselor of Lenin himself. His whole life was a shining example of unselfish service to the cause of the CP, of his motherland and his fellow countrymen.[44]

I. I. ZHELTOV

Biographical data

Born 1890, died 1939. Joined the CP in 1917. Took part in the October armed uprising in Moscow. After the October Revolution he held political, trade union, and economic posts; was chairman of the Bauman district soviet in Moscow, director of a factory at Bezhitsa, chairman of the Moscow gubernia trade union council, deputy chairman of the CPC of Uzbekistan, and member of the collegium of the PC of Labor of the U.S.S.R. From 1931 he was in charge of construction works at Cheliabinsk and Ufa and director of the state trust for the iron ore industry of the central part of the Union.[45]

VII. DIPLOMATS

LEV MIKHAILOVICH KARAKHAN

Biographical data

Born 1889, died 1937. Soviet statesman and diplomat. Joined the RSDWP in 1904, became a Bolshevik in July 1917. Born in Kutaisi gubernia, the son of a petty bourgeois. In 1910-15, studied at the law faculty of Petersburg University. Took part in the trade union movement from 1912; from 1913, belonged to the Mezhraiontsy group. For taking part in the revolutionary movement of 1915 he was arrested and exiled to Tomsk. After the February revolution of 1917 he returned to Petrograd and was elected a member of the Duma for the Petrograd raion, then a member of the Petrograd soviet. After the July events he joined the RSDWP(B). In August 1917 he was elected a member of the presidium of the Petrograd soviet. From November 1917 to the beginning of 1918 he was secretary to the Soviet delegation at the Brest Litovsk peace negotiations. In 1918-20 he was a member of the Foreign Affairs Collegium and deputy PC of foreign affairs. In 1921 he was RSFSR diplomatic representative in Poland, and from August 1923 represented the U.S.S.R. in China. Subjected to illegal repression during the cult of Stalin's personality. Posthumously rehabilitated.[1]

NIKOLAI NIKOLAEVICH KRESTINSKY

Biographical data

Born 1883, died 1938. Soviet Party leader, statesman and diplomat. Joined the CP in 1903. Born at Mogilev, the son of a high school teacher. Graduated from the law faculty of Petersburg University in 1907, and practiced at the bar until 1917. Joined the revolutionary movement in 1901, and in 1903 entered

the Vilna organization of the RSDWP. From 1907 he belonged to the social-
democratic faction of the State Duma and worked for the Bolshevik press at
Petersburg. Arrested several times, in 1904, 1905, 1906, and 1912; exiled
in 1914 to Ekaterinburg, then to Kungur. After the February revolution of
1917 he was a member of the Ural oblast and Ekaterinburg committees of
the RSDWP(B). Elected to the Constituent Assembly on the Bolshevik list
for Perm gubernia. During October 1917 he was chairman of the Ekaterinburg
RMC, then moved to Petrograd; was a member of the collegium of the PC
of Finance of the RSFSR and chief commissar of the National Bank. From
March 1918 he was vice-chairman of the National Bank and at the same
time commissar of justice of the Petrograd labor commune and the union of
communes of the Northern oblast. From August 1918 to October 1922, PC
of finance of the RSFSR. From December 1919 to March 1921, secretary
of the CC of the RCP(B). During the debate on the Brest Litovsk peace treaty
in 1918 he took the "leftwing Communist" view, and during debate on the
trade unions in 1921 he sided with Trotsky. Was counselor for the Soviet
embassy in Germany, 1921-30, and attended the Genoa conference, in 1922.
He was deputy PC of foreign affairs of the U.S.S.R. from 1930. At the Sixth
through the Ninth congresses he was elected a member of the CC. Subjected
to illegal repression in 1937. Posthumously rehabilitated.[2]

VIII. CHEKISTS

IVAN ALEKSEEVICH AKULOV

Biographical data

Born 1888, died 1939. Soviet Party and state leader. Born at Petersburg into an impoverished petty-bourgeois family. Joined the CP in 1907. Carried on Party work at Petersburg and Samara. Arrested and exiled several times. In 1917 he worked in the Party's military organization at Vyborg. In 1918-22 he was secretary of the Ural oblast, Kirgiz region, and Crimea oblast committees of the RCP(B). Played an active part in the Civil War. From 1922 he was engaged in trade union work, and in 1929 was secretary of the AUCCTU. In 1930-37 he was deputy PC of workers' and peasants' inspection of the U.S.S.R. and a member of the presidium of the Central Control Commission of the CPSU. In 1931-32 he was first deputy chairman of the OGPU, and in 1932-33 secretary of the CC of the Ukraine CP for the Donbass. In 1933-35 he was procurator of the U.S.S.R., then secretary of the CEC of the U.S.S.R. Perished in 1939.[1]

TERENTII DIMITRIEVICH DERIBAS

Biographical data

Born 1883, died 19—. Joined the CP in 1903. Engaged in propaganda work, 1903-29; served in the All-Russian Cheka after the Civil War. In 1929-34 he was OGPU plenipotentiary in the Far East, and from 1934 chief of administration of the NKVD in the Far Eastern region. He became a victim of the cult of Stalin's personality.[2]

A fighter of Lenin's old guard

The older generation of Communists well remember the name of Terentii Dimitrievich Deribas, a member of Lenin's intrepid old guard.

Work in social-democratic groups, the study of Marxist literature and the reading of Lenin's *Iskra*—all these enabled this peasant's son and technical high school pupil to realize the depth of the irreconcilable conflict between the exploiters and the toiling masses, and to take the side of the working class. Joining the Party's ranks in 1903, he devoted himself heart and soul to its service. He worked as a propagandist in a study group, distributed Bolshevik proclamations to the workers, and organized strikes at a tobacco factory. He was arrested for the first time in 1904, but escaped and went underground. This was the beginning of his hazardous life as a professional revolutionary. Twice he again boldly escaped the clutches of the police. The outbreak of the October Revolution found him at Troitsk, where he ran the Bolshevik Party organization and took part in the suppression of the first kulak uprisings and in fighting the White Guards.

After the Civil War and the expulsion of the interventionist troops, the Party assigned him to work in the All-Russian Cheka, where he was well schooled under Dzerzhinsky's guidance. As a member of a Chekist group he took an active part in the suppression of the Kronshtadt mutiny and the Antonov revolt. During a fight with the mutineers on the frozen Gulf of Finland he was seriously wounded. At the time of the Party's battle with Trotskyism he adhered firmly to the Party line and trounced the Trotskyists at workers' meetings.

At the end of 1929 the Party sent him as OGPU plenipotentiary to the Far East, and in 1934 he became chief of administration of the NKVD for the Far Eastern region. The sector thus entrusted to him was of great importance. The threat of war was looming in the Far East, and firm measures were necessary to secure our frontiers and thwart Japanese espionage. The Chekists under Deribas's direction, in cooperation with the frontier guards, successfully coped with the danger. His services to the Soviet people were rewarded with the Order of Lenin and twice with the Red Banner. The Khabarovsk Party organization elected him to represent it at the Sixteenth Party Congress, and at the Seventeenth Congress he was elected a candidate member of the CC of the CPSU.

His work in the security organs was marked by integrity, strict adherence to principle, and socialist legality. He resolutely opposed the unjustified arrests that were carried out on the direct orders of Ezhov. Soon he also became a victim of arbitrary power.

The CP has put an end to the unhappy consequences of the cult of personality. The good name of many innocent sufferers has been restored, including that of T. D. Deribas, who would have been eighty years old this year. Remembering the noble figure of this intrepid fighter of Lenin's old guard, we recognize his brilliant services to the people and to the CP.[3]

TARICHAN MIKHAILOVICH D'IAKOV

Biographical data

Born 1897, died 19—. Joined the CP in 1917. Educated at Tver and the polytechnical institute at Tomsk, whence he was called up for the army in his third year. From 1917 to 1922 he was commander of a Red Guard detachment and commissar of internal affairs of the Ukraine. Later he served in the All-Russian Cheka, commanded a frontier defense unit in the Pamirs, represented a frontier detachment and the CEC of the Turkestan ASSR in the Pamir political triumvirate. From 1922 he served in Tashkent in the OGPU (later NKVD). Was arrested during the cult of personality and died in captivity.[4]

His memory lives

In the summer of 1921 a conference was called by the CEC of soviets of the Turkestan ASSR to discuss the position in the Pamirs. Measures were necessary to improve the defenses of the state frontier and help the working people of this remote mountain area to wipe out the remnants of counterrevolutionary forces and strengthen Soviet power. It was decided to send a revolutionary detachment headed by a Communist, aged twenty-four, named Tarichan Mikhailovich D'iakov, whose name is linked with one of the most arduous and glorious pages of the history of the Soviet Pamirs. His life was short, but brilliant and full of activity. It was wholly devoted to the strengthening of Soviet power and the fight against internal and external enemies of our country.

A doctor's son and a member of the RSDWP from the first years of its existence, he finished school at Tver (now Kalinin) and then entered the Tomsk Polytechnic Institute. However, he did not complete his course because the First World War broke out and he was called up for the army in his third year of study.

The days of the autocracy were numbered, and it was swept away by the bourgeois-democratic February revolution. Like other revolution-minded soldiers and officers, D'iakov welcomed the fall of the Tsarist regime. In the stormy months of 1917 he was more than once elected a delegate representing military units at the congresses of soviets of various areas. After the October Revolution he took an active part in the execution of the Leninist decrees adopted by the second all-Russian congress of soviets. In December 1917 he joined the Bolshevik Party. He was actively engaged in fighting the enemies of the Young Soviet State, and at the end of 1917 commanded a Red Guard detachment against anarchists at Samara (now Kuibyshev). Later he was commissar of internal affairs of the Ukraine for a short time.

In 1920 the Party directed him to Central Asia to serve in the All-Russian Cheka—first at Mary in Turkmenistan, where he was active in combating the Basmachi. In the summer of 1921 the Turkestan CEC appointed him commander of a detachment which was sent to the Pamirs to defend the state frontier and help the working people of this distant area to create and strengthen the organs of Soviet power. The detachment encountered many obstacles on its way, as Basmachi bands were rife in southern Kirgizia, so that it did not reach the eastern Pamirs until September. When it did so, a military-political triumvirate

(MPT) was set up, consisting of a representative of the population of the western Pamirs, Shirinsho Shotemore (subsequently one of the leaders of the Tadzhik Republic); an eastern Pamir representative, T. Khusembaev; and T. M. D'iakov, representing both the frontier detachment and the Turkestan CEC. This body, of which D'iakov was virtually the head, was in full charge of strengthening Soviet power on the "roof of the world." It began by organizing revolutionary committees, of which over twenty were in existence in the western Pamirs alone by the end of 1921. During the following year committees were set up throughout the Pamirs, and Party work was also intensified. The Party cells were active in the work of agitation and propaganda, explaining to the rural population the nature of Soviet power and the reasons for measures taken. The committees did all that was possible to establish order and self-government, to restore handicrafts, and so on. At the same time the MPT and the committees were responsible for repelling incessant Basmachi raids, detecting hidden enemies of Soviet power and connecting links between the different nationalities. The Pamir Party organization selected and trained cadres for Party, government, and economic work.

The MPT's work in strengthening Soviet power and organizing peaceful life in the Pamirs gave tangible results. In December 1921 a congress of national representatives of the eastern Pamirs approved the measures taken by the MPT and the eastern Pamir revolutionary committees. D'iakov himself made a great contribution to all this work. A leader who demanded much of himself and his subordinates, he was quick to analyze a complicated situation and draw the right conclusions. His simplicity and the patient, attentive, and unbiased way in which he examined questions put before him won the respect and love of the peasantry. He spared no effort to solve the problems with which he was confronted. He devoted particular care to the training and promotion of members of the Tadzhik people, many of whom later became Party and state leaders of Tadzhikistan.

In the fall of 1922 he was recalled to work in Tashkent, where he served in the OGPU for some months. Then he was transferred to Moscow, where for many years he occupied senior posts in the OGPU and NKVD, showing himself at all times a true Leninist and a Chekist of Dzerzhinsky's school. In 1923 he received the Chekist's Badge of Distinction, and later the government of the Takzhik SSR conferred on him its Order of the Red Banner. He could have done much more useful work for our country and people; but during the period of unjustified repressions due to the personality cult he was slandered, arrested, and died in captivity. Today his good name is restored. In celebrating the fortieth anniversary of the Soviet Pamirs, the workers of the Gorno-Badakhshanskaia Autonomous Oblast and of all Tadzhikistan remember him with deep gratitude as their faithful friend, an active fighter for the strengthening of Soviet power in the Pamirs and a new, happy life for the working people.[5]

SERIKGALI DZHAKUPOV

Biographical data

Born 1892, died 1939. Joined the CP in 1918. From 1918 to 1921 he served as a commissar and then secretary of the Komsomol organization at Urda; then studied at the Sverdlov Communist University in Moscow and was chief secretary of the sections of communist organizations of peoples of the East under the CC of the RCP(B). In 1921-35 he served in the All-Russian Cheka, and in 1935-37 was a leading member of the central apparatus of the NKVD of the Kazakh SSR. Arrested in August 1937; died in captivity in January 1939.[6]

A Chekist's loyalty

A party of men were led out to be shot at the early morning hour when the stars pale in the rosy sky and mists roll over steppe-grass still heavy with dew. The previous evening, a White Cossack band, shouting and firing rifles, had raided Talovka village. Now a dozen men, cruelly beaten and bound with thongs, were being led under guard to a nearby ravine. Panchenko, the commander of a Red Guard detachment, had suffered most cruelly from the Cossack whips. He stumbled along, reeling with unendurable pain, and drops of his blood, like red tulips, clotted in the roadside dust.

A tall, slim youth with a dark aquiline face walked beside the commander, supporting him and gazing stealthily around. He noticed a thicket of reeds rustling in the distance, and also the puffy, bearded faces of the half-drunk Cossacks. At the same time his hands were busily untying the cords that held them both prisoner. When they drew close to the ravine he crouched down, pulled the cords loose and, without a sound, threw himself on the guards. Thus it was that, in May 1918, Serikgali Dzhakupov saved himself, his commander, and his comrades from death by shooting. He was then commissar of the Red Guard detachment, and one of the first Communists to set foot on the Kazakh steppes....

The youthful ardor of the twenty-year-old commissar bore him through the trials of civil war. On the march, under fire, and in savage saber fights he came to understand the inexorable logic of the class struggle, the source of the bestial hatred of the White Cossacks and the insidious nationalist slogans of the Alash-orda. Having escaped being shot at Talovka, Serikgali was once more at the head of a Red Guard unit which routed the White bandits and nationalists in the Bukeev gubernia and the Novouzensk uezd. His warlike exploits were rewarded by the young Soviet Republic with the gift of an inscribed sword of honor....

In September 1918 he was elected secretary of the Komsomol organization at Urda. Soon afterward he went to Moscow to study at the Sverdlov Communist University. For a time he worked as chief organizer of the sections of communist organizations of peoples of the East under the CC of the RCP(B), and in 1921 the Party assigned him to the All-Russian Cheka.

Did he know Dzerzhinsky? This is not an idle question, though it is impossible to be sure of the answer from the scanty evidence at our disposal. Throughout his life Dzhakupov proved that he was worthy to be called a pupil of the Iron Feliks. Absolute devotion to the Party's ideals, a high sense of responsibility, and true humanity—this was what Dzerzhinsky demanded of those who worked with him, saying that they must be people with cool heads, warm hearts, and clean hands. All these qualities Dzhakupov possessed to the full.

In 1924 he worked for a time as secretary of the Party's uezd committee at Gur'ev, and wrote articles for the newspaper *Enbekshi kazakh* which have been preserved. In them we hear the passionate voice of a Communist defending Leninist international principles with equal firmness against great-power chauvinism and the errors of national deviationism.

Returning to Cheka work, he served at Kustanai and was then sent to Central Asia, where he took an active part in fighting the Basmachi. He worked for several years in Tataria, and in 1935 became one of the chief officials of the central apparatus of the NKVD in the Kazakh SSR. These were the years of the unclean spirit of the personality cult, which bred an atmosphere of universal suspicion and spy mania. The complicated international situation of the time combined with many other causes to produce the fatal outbreak of internecine killing. What were Dzhakupov's thoughts at this time? How did this man of courage and scrupulous honesty conduct himself at the time of trial? His superiors demanded blind obedience, ordered him to carry out repressions and obligingly indicated the victims. Among these was the Kazakh poet Saken Seifullin.* Dzhakupov knew this man and loved his poems—the fiery "Young Kazakhs' Marseillaise," steeped in revolutionary feeling, and the proud, sonorous "Sovietstan." How could he raise his hand against one whose escape from Kolchak's death car so strikingly recalled the way in which he himself had cheated the Cossack soldiery? How could he see an enemy of the people in one who had uttered from the depths of his heart such verses as this:

> Soviet Union, home of the brave!
> I am rightly proud of your sons and daughters,
> For there is no stronger link than youth,
> The pride of a great land.
> Soviet Union—the land of the brave!

So, at an operational conference, Dzhakupov declared for all to hear: "I will not put Saken in jail. Dzerzhinsky taught us to punish only our real enemies,

*Saken Seifullin (1894-1939) was a Kazakh poet and political leader who at one time headed the Kazakhstan council of people's commissars. —ED.

and only on solid grounds." He repeated this more than once, frankly and openly, knowing by virtue of his position that all the charges against the poet and tribune of the people were based on nothing but vile slander.

In August 1937 he himself was arrested. At his interrogation he spoke no word that would implicate innocent people, and while in captivity he remained a true Chekist, a man of exemplary fortitude. He wrote letters to Stalin, Ezhov, and Vyshinsky which cannot be read today without emotion. In them he spoke least of all of himself, but defended Saken Seifullin, Seitkali Mendeshev, Nigmet Nurmakov, and other prominent figures in the cultural life of Kazakhstan, laying bare with compelling arguments the absurdity of the charges against them. When he received no reply to his letters he was not daunted, but continued the fight. He wrote again and again, well realizing that he was beating the air, but impelled by loyalty to Dzerzhinsky's precepts and to socialist legality, which was being trampled underfoot. His last letter was written in January 1939, a day or two before he perished.

His personal life does not seem to have been very happy. He was married, but had no children. His wife disappeared from view immediately after his arrest: she is said to have married again hastily to get rid of her "tainted" surname. But the memory of Sarikgali Dzhakupov lives! It has lived in the hearts of his Civil War comrades and Chekist colleagues, and above all those who witnessed his unequal and lonely struggle with the political adventurers who had worked their way to the top of the NKVD. These friends of his shared his views but were not strong enough to stem the tragic course of events.

Some years later, first anonymously and then by name, he began to be held up to young Chekists as an example of unqualified devotion to duty. His story is yet another proof that despite the criminal practices introduced by Beria and his monstrous gang, the Cheka never wholly lost the Dzerzhinsky tradition and the will to fight for the great cause of Lenin's Party. We must remember this, not only for the sake of historical objectivity but because there are some who, in the context of the liquidation of the personality cult, do not shrink from casting a slur on the Chekist cadres as a whole. They do so despite the fact that the Twentieth Congress of the CPSU threw a flood of light on the part played by many true sons of the Party and people who, while serving in the security apparatus, spoke out courageously against the Ezhov-Beria policy of unjustified repressions, and paid dearly for their attempts to reach the deaf ears of Stalin. Among those who remained faithful to the last and died proudly without bowing to the malignity of fate, an honorable place belongs to the Kazakhstan Chekist Serikgali Dzhakupov.[7]

IONAS GRUODIS

Biographical data

Born 1897, died 1937. Born at Salakas, Zarasai uezd, Lithuania, the son of a peasant. Left village school in 1912 and entered a private college at Vilna (Vilnius). Owing to the outbreak of war he moved to Mogilev and then Voronezh, where he met the Lithuanian proletarian poet Iulius Ianonis and came into contact with revolutionary youth. In 1917 he entered the law faculty of Petrograd University, and in August joined the ranks of those fighting for the revolution. In June 1918 he returned to Salakas, where he carried on propaganda among the peasantry. The German forces of occupation tried to arrest him, but without success. In December 1918 he was admitted into the Party and became a member of the Zarasai uezd committee and revolutionary committee. Until the fall of Zarasai, which was the last bastion of Soviet power in Lithuania, he remained at his post there; later he fought in the Civil War and was then assigned by the Party to Cheka work. For about ten years he occupied high posts in the Belorussian OGPU. He was known and highly valued by Feliks Dzerzhinsky, and was awarded the Order of the Red Banner, the Distinguished Chekist's badge, and a gold watch. In 1931-37 he held high office in the administration of the Transcaucasian and Southeastern railroads.[8]

IVAN DIMITRIEVICH KASHIRIN

Biographical data

Born 1890, died 1937. Was a junior captain of Cossacks; joined the Bolshevik Party in 1919 and the Red Army in 1918. In the Civil War he commanded an upper Ural detachment and a separate cavalry brigade. After the war he served in the All-Russian Cheka.[9]

A Soviet commander and Chekist

Ivan Dimitrievich Kashirin was born on January 15, 1890, the son of a Cossack teacher, one of whose ancestors took part in the Pugachev rebellion. The boy's father was the first to instill in him a spirit of resistance to tyranny and violence. Later, his view of life was profoundly affected by the hateful Tsarist gendarmerie and the First World War, in which he served after leaving the Orenburg cadets' school. While he was at the front, the ideas of the Bolshevik Party came to dominate his life. After the February revolution, it was not surprising that he was elected, on the Rumanian front, chairman of the Cossack committee of the First Orenburg Division, which soon became a genuine revolutionary committee. In May 1917, when the corps command attempted to disarm the Bolshevized division, the committee removed the reactionary officers and placed Kashirin in command of the formation. In July, on the orders of the supreme commander, Kornilov, Kashirin was arrested and sent under escort to Orenburg. The reactionary leaders of the Cossack group of the Orenburg army resolved to "publicly disgrace" him by excluding him from the division command. The front-line Cossacks, thus deprived of their "elder brother and guide," wrote to him sorrowfully: "We have lost a true fighter for freedom, a champion of the interests of the working people."

The October Revolution broke out, and at Orenburg the Ataman Dutov raised the standard of anti-Soviet revolt. A White terror raged, and 600 men and women of Bolshevik tendencies were thrown into jail together with all of the local soviet. In order to mobilize the Cossacks, Dutov summoned a meeting of the Second Special Group of the Orenburg Army. The Cossacks of the Verkhneuralsk settlement adopted Kashirin as their representative, and he voiced the demand that "the hirelings of capitalism, White Guard bandits and followers of Dutov should immediately leave the area." In March 1918 Nikolai (his elder brother) and Ivan Kashirin formed the first Soviet Cossack voluntary squadron of Verkhneuralsk, which played no small part in the campaign against Dutov. In April Ivan joined the Bolshevik Party and was elected chairman of the first Verkhneuralsk volost soviet. At the beginning of June he was appointed commander of the newly formed Verkhneuralsk regiments of the Red Army, which withstood the onslaught of many thousands of White Czechs and counter-revolutionary Cossacks in the Zlatoust-Miass area. Shortly thereafter a large formation of six regiments, services, and commands was organized at Verkhneuralsk, and I. Kashirin was elected its commander in chief. In July these regiments were joined by Nikolai Kashirin's detachment from Orenburg and the First Ural Regiment under V. K. Bliukher. Thus the South Ural Composite Partisan Force was formed in the Verkhneuralsk uezd under the supreme command of Ivan Kashirin, and of Bliukher after Kashirin was wounded.

The Kashirin brothers were the guiding spirit for the legendary raid of partisan troops behind the White lines, and the forces under their command were among the best trained and most effective. More than once the fate of the whole army depended on their steadfastness. In the first victorious battle for Verkhneuralsk they put a large enemy army to flight. At Avzian, I. Kashirin's men repulsed an enemy attack in extremely difficult conditions. "At the Belaia river," Bliukher recalls, "our men had decided to stop for a while and bathe, when suddenly the Whites fell upon us. Our fellows leaped out of the water naked, jumped on their horses in the same state, and went straight into the attack. It was an unforgettable scene. After that, Kashirin's troops routed the Whites at Petrovskoe village, so that our units could safely advance from Bogoiavlensk to Arkhangelskoe."... V.A. Zubov, the commander of the First Ural Regiment, recorded that "we owed our success in these battles to Kashirin's cavalry regiments."... The newspaper *Uralskii rabochii* wrote rapturously about the Kashirins, heroes of the Urals, and particularly about Ivan, who "selflessly devoted himself to the people's cause." Their exploits were also recognized by foreign observers. Harris, the U.S. Consul-General in Russia, reported to the [American] president that "the position on the Volga front is critical, and the difficulties are due to the Bolshevik forces led by the Kashirins."

In April 1919 I. Kashirin was attached to the southern group of armies

under M. V. Frunze, in command of a separate Orenburg Cossack cavalry
brigade which bore his name...and which marched victoriously from Buzuluk
to Verkhneuralsk via Buguruslan, Sarai-Gir, Belebei, Ufa, Sim, and Troitsk.
At the end of 1919, in the Buguruslan operation, the Kashirin Brigade, together
with V. I. Chapaev's division, defeated three of Kappel's regiments, captured
a White regiment near the villages of Timoshkino and Kuzminovskoe, and
took more than a thousand prisoners at Sarai-Gir and Filipovskaia. On May
4, 1920, Kashirin's cavalry by a sudden stroke took possession of the Samara-
Zlatoust railroad, disrupting the Whites' battle order. Soon I. Kashirin was
ordered by Frunze to attack the enemy's rear and cut off his communications
with Ufa. The Soviet cavalry, headed by its intrepid commander, swept like
a whirlwind through the enemy positions, broke the Whites' resistance and
on May 17 in a bold raid took possession of Belebei. The brigade's heroism
was rewarded with a Revolutionary Red Banner of Honor, and its brilliant
commander later received the Order of the Red Banner.

On May 28 the Turkestan Army under Frunze began its advance on Ufa.
Kashirin led his regiments behind the enemy lines, and while Chapaev was
crossing the Belaia, he captured the railroad and cut off Ufa. This caused
panic in the enemy camp, and while his forces were attacking Kashirin, Chapaev's
division was able to take the town.

In July the Kashirin Brigade, as part of the Fifth Army, advanced in the
direction of Sim-Zlatoust-Satka-Bakal-Verkhneuralsk. It fought many skirmishes
on the way, operating both as cavalry and on foot. At Sim, the men took
off their boots in order better to pursue the enemy and cut them down. At
Troitsk, they routed a White Cossack brigade.

Kashirin was not only a war hero but a good comrade, who shared with
his men all the hardships of life at the front. They loved him for this, regarding
him as one of themselves and an "old comrade." This man, whose love for
the working people was, as Kalinin and the Cossack department of the All-Russian
CEC expressed it, "proven by his career as a fighter and sealed in blood,"
was appointed by the Party to the All-Russian Cheka: in 1920 he worked in
the Cheka in Soviet Bashkiria, and in 1921 became head of the Orenburg-Turgai
gubernia Cheka. In 1922-27 he was chairman of the Kirgiz Cheka, then OGPU
representative in Kirgizia and deputy chairman of the CEC of the Kirgiz Republic.
In 1928-31 he was OGPU representative in the lower Volga region and a
member of the bureau of the Party's regional committee. "An admirable commander, an upright communist and a man of sterling character"—the words are
those of his former colleague V. A. Odintsov—"he will be remembered as
one of our finest leaders, a true disciple of the great Dzerzhinsky." In 1932-36
he was chief state inspector of the PC of State Farms and a member of the
collegium of the PC of Internal Affairs of the U.S.S.R. He was also a member
of the All-Russian and the All-Union CEC.

His works are not forgotten. In his home territory streets and schools are
named for him, and a bronze bust adorns one of the squares of Verkhneuralsk—a

monument raised by grateful posterity, for whose future he fought unsparingly.[10]

MIKHAIL SERGEEVICH KEDROV

Biographical data

Born 1878, died 1941. State and Party leader. Joined the CP in 1901. Born in Moscow, a notary's son. Entered Moscow University in 1897, but was expelled for revolutionary activity in 1899. Joined the RSDWP when a student at the Yaroslavl Lyceum. Worked in the Nizhnii Novgorod, Yaroslavl, and Simferopol social-democratic organizations; in 1904, in Moscow, took part in digging a tunnel under the Taganska prison for N. E. Bauman's escape. At the beginning of 1905 he took part in organizing the supply of arms to the Moscow workers' detachments. In October 1905 he was a member of the Bolshevik committee at Kostroma and helped to organize the workers' militia. After the defeat of the December uprising (1905) he worked in the Tver and Petersburg Bolshevik organizations and distributed Party literature as an agent of the CC of the RSDWP. In 1908, while in charge of the Zerno publishing concern, he printed a collection of Lenin's articles under the title *During Twelve Years*. He was imprisoned in a fortress from 1908 to 1911 for publishing illegal literature. Emigrated to Switzerland in 1912; returned to Russia on Lenin's orders in 1916, and served as a doctor on the Caucasian front, where he was at the outbreak of the February revolution. In March-April 1917 he was chairman of the Sherifkhane soviet. From May 1917 he was in Petrograd as a member of the military organization of the CC of the RSDWP(B) and the all-Russian bureau of Bolshevik military organizations, also editor of *Soldatskaia pravda* and an organizer of the newspapers *Rabochii i soldat* and *Soldat*. From November 1917 he was a member of the collegium of the PC of Army Affairs, as commissar for the demobilization of the old army. From August 1918 he commanded the troops of the northeastern sector of the western screen, and from September was a member of the RMC of the Sixth Army on the northern front. From March 1919 he was chairman of a special section of the All-Russian Cheka, a member of the collegium of the PC of Internal Affairs, and representative of the CC of the RCP(B) on the southern and western fronts; took part in the defense of Petrograd. In 1921-23 he was agent of the Council of Labor and Defense for the south Caspian fishing industry and a member of the Baku soviet. In 1924-25 he worked in the SCNE and the PC of Health. In 1926-27 he was assistant military procurator to the Supreme Court of the U.S.S.R. In 1931-34 a member of the presidium of Gosplan of the RSFSR, then director of the Military Hygiene Institute. In April 1939 he was subjected to unlawful repression during the cult of Stalin. At the end of 1941 he was treacherously murdered by Beria, who was afraid of being denounced by him. Posthumously rehabilitated in 1953.[11]

A true son of the Party

A document, yellow with time, lies before us:

> This is to certify that Comrade M. S. Kedrov is an agent of the CPC for
> the inspection of the entire war economy and local Soviet institutions of the
> RSFSR, in accordance with the decree of the CPC dated May 18, 1918.
> Chairman of the CPC, Ul'ianov (Lenin).
> Chief Secretary of the CPC, Vlad. Bonch-Bruevich.
> Secretary, L. Fotieva.

These credentials were given to Mikhail Sergeevich Kedrov, a prominent
political figure in the young Soviet Republic who had taken an active part
in all three revolutions, at the time of crisis when the interventionists were
trying to crush the workers' and peasants' state in a fiery ring of fronts. This
first soldier of Lenin's Iron Guard devoted his whole life to the Party and
the people.

He had joined the revolutionary movement in early youth. In 1899, when
he was twenty years old, he was expelled from Moscow University for taking
part in "student disorders." In the Demidov Lyceum of Law Studies at Yaroslavl,
which he then entered, he and N. I. Podvoisky headed the students' committee.
In December 1901 he joined the RSDWP, and from the first days of his
membership showed himself a militant Leninist....

Returning from the south to Moscow, on the Party's instructions he took
up propaganda among the workers. At the beginning of 1903 he was again
arrested and exiled to the Vologda gubernia; he escaped, but was recaptured
at Khotin while on the way to Bessarabia. Having served his sentence in Vologda
he returned to Moscow, where he engaged more actively than ever in the revolutionary struggle. In summer 1905 the Party sent him to Kostroma, where with
Podvoisky and A. M. Stopani he headed the local Bolshevik organization and
organized the workers' militia. In 1906, after a short stay in Moscow, he went
to Petersburg, where he made contact with the underground Bolshevik center
and invested all the money he had inherited from his father in the Party publishing
enterprise Zerno, of which he became official owner early in 1907. He asked
Lenin, who was then abroad, for material for his *Almanac for All* and Lenin
sent an article on the international socialist congress at Stuttgart. He was also
helped in composing the *Almanac* by S. M. Ol'minsky, N. N. Baturin, and
other Bolshevik leaders. The censor banned it, but the bulk of the edition—60,000
copies—was already in the hands of workers, soldiers, and sailors. After the
Almanac was published, it was decided Lenin's works would be collected and
published in three volumes under the general title *During Twelve Years*. The
first volume included "What Is to Be Done?" and "One Step Forward, Two
Steps Back." The edition was confiscated almost immediately, but many copies
were distributed. Owing to the severity of the censorship only the first part

of the second volume appeared, but this was sufficient cause for further police persecution. For publishing Marxist literature, Kedrov was imprisoned in a fortress in solitary confinement from 1908 to 1911.

In 1912 he emigrated to Switzerland, and at Bern he met Lenin for the first time, at a Russian students' evening in 1913. Lenin was delighted by Kedrov's piano playing and said, "How well you play—I had no idea you had such talent." He also took a keen interest in Kedrov's press and the fate of his own works which had fallen into police hands. When they parted, Lenin promised to come and hear Kedrov play on another occasion; this he did several times and heard his favorite works played.

A particularly memorable occasion for Kedrov was when he and Lenin met in Lausanne at the People's Home to hear a lecture by Plekhanov, after whom Lenin spoke. The two returned home together and exchanged impressions of the evening.

While in Lausanne, Kedrov graduated from the medical faculty of the university as a cardiologist. In spring 1916 he returned from Switzerland to Russia, where he made contact with the Bolshevik military organization and carried out various important missions for it. On the Party's orders he took up the post of chief doctor at the military hospital at Kashin in the Tver gubernia. Having organized Party work in the hospital, he was sent to the Persian front. Here, at Sherifkhane, after the February revolution he was elected chairman of the soviet of workers' and soldiers' deputies. In May 1917 the CC of the Bolshevik Party summoned him to Petrograd, where he took part in the all-Russian conference of front and rear military organizations of the RSDWP(B). After the July events he became one of the organizers of the Bolshevik newspaper *Soldatskaia pravda;* when this was suppressed by the authorities he joined the staff of the official Bolshevik organ *Rabochii i soldat.*

In September 1917 he went to western Siberia to establish liaison with Siberian Bolshevik organizations. At the outbreak of the October Revolution he was in the Biisk-Barnaul area and did not get back to Petersburg for two months. There he became head of the PC for Demobilization, with the important and urgent task of demobilizing the old army and navy. Despite great difficulties, the work was completed by April 1918. The government decided to use the same machinery for the purpose Soviet inspection and organizing local economic activity. The PCs of the Republic put forty of their ablest representatives at Kedrov's disposal for his "Soviet inspection" staff, and on May 28, 1918, he and the inspection commission arrived at Arkhangelsk. There was good reason to begin the work in this area, as the interventionists had landed at Murmansk and were hoping to conquer the whole of the north, while the Whites were concentrated in force at Vologda and Arkhangelsk. Accordingly, the first task was to speedily remove all war stores to the interior. At the end of June 1918 martial law was declared at Arkhangelsk and Kedrov took steps to strengthen its seaward defenses with the aid of Red Army units. The weakest link in the city's defense was the military department, which was permeated by hostile elements. Circumstances made it impossible to complete its re-staffing and so prevent treason, and in August 1918 the city fell to the interventionists.

I myself saw Kedrov at this difficult time, when the last train out of Arkhangelsk, which I was driving, reached the station of Tundra. He summoned me to the car he was using as an office and questioned me in detail about conditions in the city. Immediate measures were taken to organize defense and stabilize the front, and on August 8 Kedrov set out for Moscow to obtain the necessary arms, supplies, and military units. On hearing his report, Lenin wrote to the Supreme Military Council:

> We must at once give what is asked. Send everything today from Moscow. Let me have immediately the names and addresses of six former generals and twelve former officers of the general staff who will be responsible for the full and precise execution of this order, and warn them that otherwise they will be shot for sabotage. I require an immediate answer to this message by cyclist from M. D. Bonch-Bruevich.—V. Ul'ianov (Lenin), Chairman of the CPC.

At the beginning of August 1918 Kedrov was put in command of the Sixth Army then being formed in the north. Lenin took an active part in organizing the defense of this sector and in forwarding the necessary supplies. Measures were taken to mobilize local forces to repel the enemy and to send workers', soldiers', and sailors' units from Moscow, Petrograd, Kronshtadt, Ivanovo-Voznesensk, and other cities. In a series of telegrams to Kedrov, Lenin ordered that the bourgeoisie should be mobilized to dig trenches, that fortification work should be speeded up and the defense of Kotlas strengthened at all costs. He also telegraphed: "Is Vologda sufficiently strengthened against the Whites? It would be unpardonable to show any weakness or negligence in this matter."

In accordance with Lenin's orders, the Soviet forces under Kedrov, together with local Party and state organs, worked furiously to make possible active military measures against the invaders, and after nineteen months of hard struggle the north was liberated. Before this date, in September 1918, the CC recalled Kedrov to command the southern and then the western front, where experienced Party cadres were desperately needed, and then assigned him to the Cheka, where he worked as head of a special section and was a member of the collegium. At this time he was elected a member of the All-Russian CEC.

In the Spring of 1921 he went with a group of Chekists to Transcaucasia to inspect the work of the local Cheka. In Baku he often saw Kirov and Ordzhonikidze, with whom he organized the supply of fuel oil to river transport vessels. A few months later he was back in the north, on the Pechora River, organizing trade with a view to the fastest possible economic development of this area. At Ust'-Tsylma, together with Ia. N. Nabatov-Pavlovsk, he also organized the regular appearance of the newspaper *Pechorskaia pravda*.

The Party appointed him to important posts in the SCNE, the Procurator's Office, and the Supreme Court. For four years he was a member of the presidium of the executive committee of the Red Sporting International. Later he worked in the Comintern, being head of its Defense, Scientific, and Technical Section for about five years, and was a member of the presidium of Gosplan of the RSFSR. At the end of his life he was the director of a medical research institute. His appointment caused great excitement within the institute, but after a few months, at the end of 1938, he retired owing to ill health.

Kedrov was a man of great culture, knew four foreign languages, wrote for the Party press, and carried on important historical research. The Soviet government valued his services highly, and he received the Order of the Red Banner and the Chekist's Badge of Honor. In all his fields of activity he devoted much attention to the training of youth. He often lectured and talked to his younger colleagues on political subjects, sharing his rich experience with them.

The life of this true Leninist was tragically cut short during the cult of Stalin's personality. He was arrested in April 1939 and perished in November 1941. Twelve years later he was rehabilitated. The report of the Procurator's Office, published in connection with the unmasking of Beria and his gang, stated that among the latter's crimes was the murder of Kedrov. Kedrov would have been eighty-five years old in February 1963—his birthday is a date which has been piously commemorated by the Soviet people. Streets in Moscow, Arkhangelsk, and Vologda have been named for this glorious veteran of the revolution. The Soviet public honors the memory of this fine man, old Bolshevik, and Chekist, who gave devoted service to the cause of the revolution and the building of socialism in our country.[12]

MARTYN IVANOVICH LATSIS

Biographical data

Born 1888, died 1938. Pseudonym Ian Fridrikhovich Sudrabs. Soviet Party and state leader. Joined the CP in 1905. Born in Latvia, a farm laborer's son. Attended Shaniavsky University in Moscow and became an elementary school-teacher. Took an active part in the 1905-7 revolution in Riga and the October Revolution in Petrograd. Was a delegate to the seventh (April) Party conference and the Sixth Congress of the RSDWP(B). Member of the Petrograd RMC. After the October Revolution he was a member of the collegium of the PC of Internal Affairs, and from May 1918 a member of the collegium of the All-Russian Cheka. In July-November 1918 he was chairman of the Cheka and the military tribunal of the Fifth Army on the eastern front. In 1919-21, chairman of the All-Ukrainian Cheka, after which he again worked in the All-Russian Cheka. Was a delegate to the Eighth and Tenth congresses of the RCP(B). From 1921 he held important economic and Party posts: was chairman of the main administration of the salt industry, deputy head of the main administration of the mining industry, a member of the collegium of the PC of Agriculture of the RSFSR, deputy head of the rural department of the CC of the CPSU, etc. From 1932 he was director of the Plekhanov Institute of National Economy. In 1937 he was slandered as a result of the Stalin cult; illegally condemned and perished. Posthumously rehabilitated.[13]

SERGEI LUK'IANOVICH LUKASHIN (SARKIS SRADIONIAN)

Biographical data

Born 1885, died 1937. Joined the Bolshevik Party in 1905. Born in the Armenian village of Topti in the Don district (now Krym village, Miasnikovsky raion, Rostov oblast), the son of a peasant. Before 1907 he carried on propaganda work among the workers of Chernyigorod, Bibi-Eibat, and other districts of Baku, and also among Petersburg students and workers. In 1907-9 he was a propagandist of the Don committee. In 1910 he was in Germany and Switzerland; in 1910-12 he finished his university studies and carried on underground work in Petersburg. In 1912-16 he organized the Petersburg "Society of Apartment Renters" as a cover for new secret addresses and underground workers' apartments. Was called up in 1916. In 1917-20 he took part in the February and October revolutions, was a member of the CEC of the Soviet Republic of the Don, head of its economic council and PC of justice, a member of the Don bureau and of the RMC of the southern front, head of the investigation department against counterrevolution and member of the control commission of the All-Russian Cheka, secretary of the Party's Rostov city committee, and a member of the presidium of the Don executive committee. In 1920, a member of the CEC of the RSFSR. In 1921-2 secretary of the Don committee of the RCP(B) and secretary of the CC of the Armenian CP as well as chairman of that republic's SCNE. In 1922-25, chairman of the CPC of the Armenian SSR. In 1925-28, deputy chairman of the CPC, chairman of the supreme economic council, and PC of workers' and peasants' inspection of the Transcaucasian SFSR. In 1928-37, chairman of the building committee of the CPC of the U.S.S.R. and chairman of the building section of Gosplan, U.S.S.R. In 1937 he became a victim to the cult of Stalin's personality.[14]

An outstanding member of the CP and the Soviet State

The CP has bred many notable fighters for the freedom of the working class and the people's happiness, who have shown exemplary courage and steadfastness in striving for the great revolutionary ideal. Such was the glorious career of Sergei Luk'ianovich Lukashin (Sarkis Sradionian), an eminent Bolshevik and Leninist and an outstanding leader of the CP and the Soviet State.

He was born on January 13, 1885, in the Armenian village of Topti in the Don district (now Krym village, Miasnikovsky raion, Rostov oblast), the son of a peasant. He attended village school and the Nakhichevan Armenian Diocesan Seminary, and in 1902 continued his schooling at Baku, where he graduated from high school in 1906. He joined the revolutionary struggle in proletarian Baku, and it was there that his Marxist views were formed. The first Russian revolution finally determined the course of his great life, and in 1905 he joined the RSDWP(B).... In 1906 he entered the law faculty of Petersburg University, and later also studied in the economics department of the Polytechnical Institute. In Petersburg he carried on active propaganda work among students and workers. In 1906, in the Finnish town of Terijoki, he saw and heard Lenin for the first time, at a lecture the latter gave for revolutionary students from Petersburg. This was a red-letter event in young Lukashin's life. In summer 1907 he worked as a propagandist for the Don committee: the Tsarist secret police got on his trail, and in the dark days of Stolypin's reaction he was twice arrested. In 1909 he emigrated to Germany and then to Switzerland to avoid arrest, and made contact with Bolshevik groups of émigré students, in whose activities he shared. He paid great attention to social sciences and broadened his Marxist horizon.

In 1910 he returned to Petersburg. A year later he graduated from the university and engaged actively in underground revolutionary activity. In 1912, on the Party's instructions, he and the revolutionary dramatist A. A. Vermishev set up in central Petersburg a "Society of Apartment Renters" as a cover for new secret addresses and underground workers' hideouts. The society was also used for printing and distributing political literature, helping political prisoners to escape, conveying agents across the frontier, and maintaining contact with Bolshevik émigré centers. In 1916 he was called up for army service and continued to carry on propaganda among the soldiers of the Petersburg garrison, explaining to them the antinational character of the imperialist war.

With his unit, he took an active part in the February revolution of 1917. He was elected a member, and then chairman, of the soldiers' committee, and was soon a member of the Bolshevik faction of the Petersburg city duma. After the October struggle, the Party sent him to fight the counterrevolutionary bands of Kaledin, Krasnov, and Kornilov. He was elected a delegate to the first congress of the Don soviets, which which was held at Rostov-on-Don on April 9-14, 1918, and was frequently interrupted by attacks of armed bands of Whites who tried to disrupt its work. The congress elected him a member of the CEC of the Soviet Republic of the Don and head of its economic council. When the counterrevolutionary bands approached Rostov, the CEC moved to the Velikokniazheskaia settlement, where it formed the Don soviet government in which Lukashin was commissar of justice. In September the CC of the RCP(B) set up the Don bureau to direct revolutionary work in the south; Lukashin was a member of this body and also of the RMC of the southern front.

In the fall of 1918 the enemy was advancing from all sides. Counterrevolutionary revolts became more frequent; Comrades Uritsky and Volodarsky were killed, and an attempt was made to assassinate Lenin. Lukashin was transferred to Moscow as head of the investigation department against counterrevolution and a member of the control commission of the All-Russian Cheka. In the same year he was elected a deputy to the Moscow soviet. But the Don committee of the RCP(B) several times requested the CC to release him for work in the Don area, and at the beginning of 1919 he was sent back to the southern front as secretary of the Party's Rostov city committee and a member of the presidium of the Don executive committee. At the end of 1920 the Don working people made him a delegate to the eighth all-Russian congress of soviets, at which he was elected a member of the CEC of the RSFSR.

In March 1921 he was made secretary of the Don committee of the RCP(B), but he did not remain long in this post. At that time the situation in Transcaucasia, and particularly Armenia, was very serious. At the request of the Armenian revolutionary committee, supported by Lenin, the Organization Bureau of the CC of the RCP(B) transferred Lukashin to Armenia, where he was elected secretary of the Party's CC and at the same time became chairman of the republic's council of the national economy. From December 1922 he was chairman of the CPC of the Armenian SSR, where he fully displayed his competence as an organizer and statesman. He mobilized the energies of the republic's workers to solve important economic problems, bearing in mind Lenin's dictum that "irrigation will do more than anything to transform the country, give it a new birth, bury the past, and ensure the transition to socialism," and also his slogan that "communism equals Soviet power plus electrification."

At the end of 1922 Armenia began to build the Shirak Canal. Within two and a half years, thanks to the enthusiastic and selfless toil of workers and peasants, life-giving waters gushed over the Shirak plain. At the beginning of 1923 a start was made on the first big hydroelectric station in Armenia, the Erevan hydroelectric power plant, and a special committee of the CPC under Lukashin's chairmanship was set up to direct the work. In 1924, on his initiative, the State Electrotechnical Trust began to plan the mechanical irrigation of the Karmalin and Echmiadzin raions, and the building of the Aigerlich pumping station was under way in 1925. The Nor-Baiazet hydroelectric plant was begun in 1924, as were those of Kirovakan and Idzhevan. Plants were springing up all over the republic, and Lukashin's planning and firm hand were felt everywhere. He well knew the economic possibilities of our country, especially in Transcaucasia and Armenia. In view of the latter's wealth in textile raw materials, he proposed the construction of a textile factory at Leninakan....

Together with Ordzhonikidze, Kirov, Orakhelashvili, Miasnikian, and Narimanov, he took an active part in setting up the Transcaucasian Federation. He was a member of the "Commission of Four" appointed by the Party CC to draft a treaty of alliance between Azerbaidzhan, Georgia, and Armenia. In 1925 he was transferred to work in the federation itself. At a session of the fourth convocation of the Armenian CEC, A. Ioaninsian, the secretary of the CC of the Armenian CP, warmly thanked him on behalf of all the workers of Armenia for his hard and selfless work for the republic. His field of activity had encompassed industry, agriculture, electrification, irrigation, cooperatives, and state trading.

From 1926 he held important posts in the Transcaucasian SFSR, where he was deputy chairman of the CPC, chairman of the supreme economic council, PC of workers' and peasants' inspection, etc. In 1928 he was transferred to Moscow, where he was chairman of the building committee of the CPC of the U.S.S.R. and chairman of the building section of Gosplan of the U.S.S.R. He was a delegate to the Eleventh through the Fifteenth Party congresses, and at the Fourteenth Congress was elected a candidate member of the CC of the CPSU. On December 2, 1927, when the Fifteenth Congress opened in Moscow, he reported on the First Five Year Plan and was elected to the Commission of the congress, which drafted the final resolution on the plan. On April 4, 1935, on the Fifteenth anniversary of the liberation of Rostov-on-Don from the Whites, he was presented with an address by the Azov-Black Sea regional executive committee and the Rostov city soviet. In 1936 he received the Order of the Red Banner of Labor for his services to the Party and the people. In 1937 he became a victim of arbitrary rule during the cult of Stalin's personality. He is remembered with affection by the people as an outstanding Party and state leader and a true son of the working people.[15]

MAGAZA MASANCHIN

Biographical data

Born 1886, died 1937. Joined the CP in 1918. Served in the Tsarist Army, 1910-17. In 1917-20 he carried on propaganda work at Tashkent, was commander of a special detachment with the staff of the Turkestan front and commanded the battalion named for the Third International on the Semirechensk front. In 1920 he was recalled from the front to Vernyi, then organized a detachment to put down an anti-Soviet revolt at Przhevalsk and organized and commanded the Special Dungan Cavalry Regiment. After the Civil War he held important posts in the NKVD and in state and Party organs at Tashkent and Alma-Ata. In 1937 he became a victim of the cult of Stalin's personality.[16]

A son of the Dungan people

The turmoil of civil war brought forth and hardened many brave revolutionaries and national commanders. One of the true sons of the CP who devoted his whole life to the revolutionary cause was Magaza Masanchin, commander of the Special Dungan Cavalry Regiment.

The son of a farm laborer at Vernyi (Alma-Ata), Masanchin was called up for army service in 1910, at the age of twenty-four. He first became acquainted with revolutionary ideas in the trenches of the imperialist war. After the February revolution he returned to Tashkent, where he carried on propaganda among the population, calling on them to overthrow the emissaries of the Provisional Government and to set up Soviet power. In 1918 he was the first of the Dungan people to join the CP, and soon became commander of a special detachment with the staff of the Turkestan front. Together with a compatriot, the well-known revolutionary Shagabutdinov, he organized Red Army units to fight enemies of the revolution; he also took an active part in suppressing the SR Osipov revolt in Tashkent.*

In November 1919, the bands of the ataman Annenkov and General Shcherbakov had overrun the northern part of the Semirech'e (Dzhetisu) area and were mustering their forces for a fresh attack. The Turkestan commission of the CC of the RCP(B) sent to this front a battalion named for the Third International, under the command of Masanchin and Mansurov. In March 1920 Masanchin was recalled to Vernyi, where I. P. Belov, the commander of the Third Division, ordered him to form a unit of Dungan and Uigur workers to put down an anti-Soviet revolt at Przhevalsk. This body, 160 strong and armed with two machine guns, reached Przhevalsk and with the aid of the uezd Chekists wiped out the White Guard-kulak bands....

The spring of 1921 was especially memorable for Masanchin, as he was then elected a delegate to the Third Congress of the Comintern, and in Moscow met Lenin for the first time.... Soon after returning to Vernyi, he was ordered by the staff of the Turkestan front to lead his regiment to Tashkent to fight the Basmachi, who were giving trouble especially to the inhabitants of the Fergana valley. By summer 1922 the regiment had eliminated the long-standing threat of Maksum's bands, and Soviet power was restored in Fergana.

Masanchin was several times thanked for his services to the motherland by M. V. Frunze, the commander of the Turkestan front. For his success in raising a regiment and his bravery against the Basmachi, he was rewarded with a Sword of Honor and an inscribed silver cigarette case. After the Civil War he held several important posts in the NKVD and other state and Party organs in Tashkent and Alma-Ata. In 1937 he was subjected to unjustified repression. After the Twentieth Party Congress this true son of the people was

---

* In the summer of 1918 Tashkent was in the hands of the Bolsheviks. In July, local railroad workers, headed by a socialist revolutionary, successfully rebelled against the brutal rule of the Bolshevik commissar Frolov. A Transcaspian government was organized with the help of the British general W. Malleson, who was then stationed with troops in Meshed, Persia. This government was liquidated by the Bolsheviks in February 1920.

Meanwhile, in 1919 Osipov, the former "war commissar" of the Provisional Government, rounded up fourteen prominent Communists and had them shot. He then seized Tashkent and proclaimed the convocation of a constituent assembly. He was finally driven from the city by local Communists, and the suppression of the Osipov rebellion was followed by a Bolshevik campaign of terror.—ED.

posthumously rehabilitated and his Party membership restored. His name is inscribed forever in the annals of the Civil War. A street has been named for him at Alma-Ata, and in the Dungan village of Karakunuz in the Kurdai raion of the Dzhambul oblast, the workers of the "Comintern" kolkhoz have erected a monument to their national hero.[17]

ALEKSANDR NESTOROVICH MIKELADZE

Biographical data

Born 1900, died 1937. Born at Tbilisi; joined the CP in 1918. In 1919-22, studied at the medical faculty of Baku University. For revolutionary activity among students he was arrested and sentenced to death by hanging, but escaped to Azerbaidzhan. Was attached to the military triumvirate of the Portovo-Morskoi district, organized the Naval Cheka at Lenkoran, was chairman of the Naval Cheka of Azerbaidzhan, deputy chairman of the Azerbaidzhan CC, and head of the department of the Azerbaidzhan Cheka for the suppression of banditry. In 1922-23 he was head of the administrative department of the Georgian Cheka. In 1923-30, after graduating from the Eastern department of the Moscow Military Academy, he was head of the Karachai-Cherkess oblast department of the GPU. In 1930-37 he was chairman of the GPU in Abkhazia, a member of the presidium of the Abkhaz oblast Committee of Red Partisans, and a member of the collegium of the Georgian GPU. In 1937 he became a victim of the cult of Stalin's personality.[18]

One of an unconquerable band

We have before us a photograph showing a man with a strong face and sharp, watchful eyes. His collar tabs bear an insignia consisting of three diamonds, and he wears on his chest the Military Order of the Red Banner and the badge of membership in the Transcaucasian CEC. The document to which the photograph is attached states that at the request of S. Ordzhonikidze, the Communist Aleksandr Nestorovich, aged twenty-three, is seconded by the CC of the Azerbaidzhan CP to the Caucasian bureau of the CC of the RCP.

Mikeladze was born at Tbilisi in 1900. While still a schoolboy he mastered the rudiments of revolutionary theory and studied the works of Marx, Engels, and Lenin. Under the guidance of the famous revolutionaries Shaumian, Dzhaparidze, Azizbekov, Mikoyan and his own elder brother (a future hero of the Civil War), he began his revolutionary career at a time of alarm and danger.

In October 1917 Soviet power was established in Azerbaidzhan, and in the following March Mikeladze joined Lenin's Bolshevik Party. Soon the Party sent him to the Kuba front to combat the Musavatist bands. Thanks to his courage and coolness, his organizing ability and power of swiftly analyzing a complicated situation, he was able to execute the Party's commands successfully.... But in spite of the efforts and extreme self-sacrifice of the local Bolsheviks, it was not possible to maintain Soviet power in Baku, and the Party had to go underground.

Mikeladze knew Azerbaidzhan and its people well and spoke fluent Azerbaidzhani, Armenian, Turkish, and Persian. All this was a great help to him in carrying on revolutionary work in the difficult conditions of the underground. In 1919 he entered the medical faculty of Baku University, where he formed a cell in which revolutionary students grew acquainted with the Marxist classics under his guidance. He was betrayed and arrested by the Turks, who sentenced him to death by hanging, but with the help of friends he managed to escape. In 1920, after the establishment of Soviet power in Azerbaidzhan, he was attached to the Military Triumvirate of the Portovo-Morskoi district and at the same time commanded a detachment of Communist students. Later he was sent to Lenkoran to organize the Naval Cheka. The Party entrusted him with many other responsible and difficult tasks: he was deputy chairman [*sic*] of the Naval Cheka of Azerbaidzhan, deputy chairman of the Cheka of Azerbaidzhan, head of the department of the Azerbaidzhan Cheka for the suppression of banditry, etc. Whatever the task, he showed the utmost zeal and sense of responsibility, putting forward all his energies in the defense of Leninist principles. At Ordzhonikidze's request the CC of the Azerbaidzhan CP seconded him to Soviet Georgia, where experienced Cheka operatives were urgently needed to combat bourgeois nationalist elements. From October 1922 to 1923 he served as head of the administrative department of the Georgian Cheka.

After completing a course in the Eastern department of the Moscow Military Academy, he was appointed to the northern Caucasus as head of the Karachai-Cherkess oblast department of the GPU. Here, under the direct guidance of A. I. Mikoyan, the secretary of the Party's North Caucasian regional committee, he conducted several major operations against banditry and the despoilers of socialist property. His valor was rewarded by the Military Order of the Red Banner. From 1930 he was chairman of the GPU in Abkhazia, where he was elected a member of the presidium of the oblast Committee of Red Partisans. In February 1932 he joined the collegium of the Georgian GPU.

On the eleventh anniversary of the establishment of Soviet power in Georgia and the tenth anniversary of the Transcaucasian SFSR, he received the latter's Labor Order of the Red Banner for his active participation in most of the principal operations against violators of socialist legality and his exceptional services to socialist development in Transcaucasia. Such eminent Communist leaders as Ordzhonikidze, Mikoyan, Orakhelashvili, Sturua, Atarbekova, Lakoba, Eliava, and many others who worked with him regarded him as one of the staunchest companions of F. Dzerzhinsky, "Knight of the Revolution."

The life of this great Chekist was cut short in 1937. But his brilliant career and his inflexible loyalty to the Leninist and Bolshevik cause are an example of devotion to the interests of the working class and to the great ideals of Marxism-Leninism.[19]

APPENDIX A.

FATE OF LENIN'S FIRST GOVERNMENT
(COUNCIL OF PEOPLE'S COMMISSARS)

Position	Name	Fate
Chairman	V. I. Ulianov – Lenin	Died 1924
PCs of Army and Navy Affairs	V. A. Antonov – Ovseenko	*Liq. 1939
	N. V. Krylenko	Liq. 1938
	P. E. Dybenko	Liq. 1938
PC of Internal Affairs	A. I. Rykov	Liq. 1938
PC of Agriculture	V. P. Miliutin	Liq. 1937
PC of Labor	A. G. Shliapnikov	Arrested in 193-; died in jail, 19--
PC of Trade and Industry	V. P. Nogin	Died 1924
PC of Education	A. V. Lunacharsky	Died 1933
PC of Finance	I. I. Skvortsov – Stepanov	Died 1928
PC of Foreign Affairs	L. D. Bronshtein – Trotsky	Murdered by agent of Stalin 1940
PC of Justice	G. I. Lomov – Oppokov	Liq. 1938
PC of Food	I. A. Teodorovich	—
PC of Posts and Telegraphs	N. P. Glebov – Avilov	Arrested in 193-; died in jail 1942
Chairman for Nationalities	I. V. Dzhugashvili – Stalin	Died 1953

*Liq. — "Liquidated."

Source: Compiled by B. Levytsky from data in Soviet sources.

APPENDIX B.

FATE OF FULL MEMBERS OF THE CC OF THE CPSU ELECTED AT THE SEVENTEENTH CONGRESS (1934)

Name	Date of Birth	Date Joined Party	Last Known Position	Subsequent Fate
Alekseev, P. A.	—	1914	Leningrad Party worker	*liq. 19--
Andreev, A. A.	1895	1914	Until 1962, member of Presidium of Supreme Soviet of the U.S.S.R.	retired
Antipov, N. K.	1894	1912	Chairman of Commission of Soviet Control of the U.S.S.R.	liq. 1941
Badaev, A. E.	1883	1904	Member of collegium of the U.S.S.R. Ministry of Food Industry	died 1951
Balitsky, V. A.	1892	1915	PC of internal affairs of the Ukraine SSR	liq. 19--
Bauman, K. Ia.	1892	1907	Head of department of science of the CC, CPSU	liq. 1937
Beria, L. P.	1899	1917	For many years chief of state security; later vice chairman of CPC, U.S.S.R.	liq. 1953
Bubnov, A. S.	1883	1903	PC of education, RSFSR	liq. 1940
Chernov, M. A.	—	1920		liq. 19--
Chubar', V. Ia.	1891	1907	PC of finance, U.S.S.R.	liq. 1939
Chudov, M. S.	1893	1913	Secretary of Leningrad oblast committee, CPSU	liq. 1937
Chuvyrin, M. E.	1883	1903	Secretary of Donetsk oblast committee, Ukraine CP	liq. 19--
Eikhe, R. I.	1890	1905	PC of agriculture, U.S.S.R.	arrested 1938, liq. 1940
Enukidze, A. S.	1877	1898	Secretary, CEC, U.S.S.R.	liq. 1937
Evdokimov, E. G.	—	1918	Party worker at Stavropol, member of RMC of North Caucasian MD	liq. 1938

*liq. — "liquidated." Date included unless unavailable.

Source: Compiled by B. Levytsky from data in Soviet sources.

501

Ezhov, N. I.	—	1917	From 1936, PC of internal affairs, U.S.S.R.	liq. 1938
Gamarnik, Ia. B.	1894	1916	Deputy PC of defense of U.S.S.R.	suicide 1937
Iagoda, G. G.	1891	1907	PC of internal affairs, U.S.S.R.	liq. 1938
Iakir, I. E.	1896	1917	Commander, Kiev MD	liq. 1937
Iakovlev, Ia. A.	1896	1913	Head of agricultural department, CC, CPSU	liq. 1939
Ikramov, A.	1898	1918	First secretary of CC of Uzbekistan CP	liq. 1938
Ivanov, V. I.	1893	1915	PC of forest industry, U.S.S.R.	liq. 1938
Kabakov, I. D.	—	1914	First secretary of Ural oblast committee, CPSU	liq. 19--
Kadatsky, I. F.	1893	1914	Chairman of Leningrad soviet	liq. 19--
Kaganovich, L. M.	1893	1911	First deputy chairman of Council of Ministers of U.S.S.R. until 1957	retired
Kaganovich, M. M.	1889	1905	In 1956, secretary of CC of Consumer Goods Industry Workers Union	subsequent fate unknown
Kalinin, M. I.	1875	1898	Chairman of Presidium of Supreme Soviet, U.S.S.R.	died 1946
Khataevich, M. M.	1893	1913	Second secretary of CC, Ukraine CP	arrested 1937 liq. 1939
Khrushchev, N. S.	1894	1918	Until October 1964 first secretary of CC, CPSU, and chairman of Council of Ministers, U.S.S.R.	retired
Kirov, S. M.	1886	1904	First secretary of Leningrad oblast and city committees of CPSU	assassinated 1934
Knorin, V. G.	1890	1910	Deputy head of agitation and propaganda, CC, CPSU	arrested 1937 liq. 1939
Kosarev, A. V.	1903	1919	First secretary of CC of U.S.S.R. Komsomol	arrested 1938, liq. 1939
Kosior, I. V.	1893	1908	Far Eastern representative of PC for Heavy Industry	liq. 19--
Kosior, S. V.	1889	1907	Vice chairman of CPC, U.S.S.R. and chairman of Commission of Soviet Control, U.S.S.R.	arrested 1938, liq. 1939
Krinitsky, A. I.	1894	1915	First secretary of Saratov regional committee, CPSU	liq. 1937

Krupskaia, N. K.	1869	1898	Deputy PC of education, RSFSR	died 1939
Krzhizhanovsky, G. M.	1872	1893	Until 1939 vice president of Academy of Sciences, U.S.S.R.	died 1959
Kuibishev, V. V.	1888	1904	First deputy chairman of CPC and Council of Labor and Defense, U.S.S.R.	died 1935
Lavrent'ev, L. I.	—	1910		liq. 19--
Lebed', D. Z.	1893	1909	Vice chairman of CPC, RSFSR	liq. 19--
Litvinov, M. M.	1876	1898	Until 1946, deputy PC of foreign affairs of U.S.S.R.	died 1951
Liubimov, I. E.	1882	1902	PC of light industry, U.S.S.R.	liq. 1939
Lobov, S. S.	1888	1913	PC of food industry of U.S.S.R.	liq. 1939
Manuil'sky, D. Z.	1883	1903	Until 1953 deputy chairman of council of ministers, Ukraine SSR	retired 1953, died 1959
Mezhlauk, V. I.	1893	1917	Deputy chairman of CPC and chairman of Gosplan, U.S.S.R.	arrested 1937, liq. 1938
Mikoyan, A. I.	1895	1915	Until 1965 chairman of Presidium of Supreme Soviet, U.S.S.R.	member of CC, CPSU (1966)
Mirzoian, L. I.	1897	1917	First secretary of CC of Kazakhstan CP	liq. 1938
Molotov, V. M.	1890	1906	Until 1957 minister of foreign affairs of the U.S.S.R.; 1957-60, ambassador to Mongolia	retired
Nikolaeva, K. I.	1893	1909	Secretary, All-Union Central Council of Trade Unions	died 1944
Nosov, I. P.	—	1905		liq. 19--
Ordzhonikidze, G. K.	1886	1903	PC of heavy industry, U.S.S.R.	suicide 1937
Petrovsky, G. I.	1878	1897	Director of Museum of the Revolution, Moscow	died 1958
Piatakov, Iu. L.	1890	1910	Deputy chairman of Supreme Council of National Economy, U.S.S.R.	liq. 1937
Piatnitsky, I. A.	1882	1898	Secretary of Executive Committee of the Comintern	liq. 1939
Postyshev, P. P.	1887	1904	Secretary of Kuibyshev oblast committee, CPSU	liq. 1940

Razumov, M. O.	—	1913	Deputy chairman of CPC,	liq. 19--
Rudzutak, Ia. E.	1887	1905	U.S.S.R.	liq. 1938
Rukhimovich, M. L.	1889	1913	PC of communications, U.S.S.R.	liq. 19--
Rumiantsev, I. P.	—	1905		liq. 19--
Ryndin, K. V.	—	1915	Secretary of Cheliabinsk oblast committee, CPSU	liq. 19--
Sheboldaev, B. P.	1895	1914	Secretary of North Caucasian regional committee, CPSU	liq. 1937
Shvernik, N. M.	1888	1905	Until 1966 chairman of Committee of Party Control, CC, CPSU	member of CC, CPSU (1966)
Stalin, I. V.	1879	1898	First secretary of CC, CPSU, and chairman of Council of Ministers, U.S.S.R.	died 1953
Stetsky, A. I.	—	1915		liq. 19--
Sulimov, D. E.	1890	1905	Chairman of CPC, RSFSR	liq. 1939
Ukhanov, K. B.	1891	1907	PC of local industry, RSFSR	liq. 1939
Vareikis, I. M.	1894	1913	Secretary of Far Eastern regional committee, CPSU	liq. 1939
Voroshilov, K. E.	1881	1903	Member of Presidium of the Supreme Soviet of the U.S.S.R. (chairman until 1960)	in 1966 member of CC of CPSU
Zelensky, I. A.	1890	1906	Chairman of Central Union of Consumers' Cooperatives	liq. 1938
Zhdanov, A. A.	1896	1915	Secretary, CC, CPSU	died 1948
Zhukov, I. P.	1889	1909		liq. 19--

NOTES*

INTRODUCTION

1. See Sarkis Tarossian, *Developments in Armenian Literature* (Munich: Institute for the Study of the U.S.S.R., Studies on the Soviet Union, 1963, no. 3), p. 112.
2. *Trybuna ludu* (Warsaw), February 19, 1956.
3. *Voprosy istorii*, no. 2, 1956, p. 202.
4. To cite only one example: the lead article in the March 4, 1954, issue of *Kommunist* (Moscow) was entitled "Stalin, the Great Legatee of the Leninist Cause."
5. *XIX s"ezd Kommunistichnoi partii Ukraïny* (Nineteenth Congress of the Ukrainian Communist Party), (Kiev, 1956), p. 34.
6. In this trial a special court presided over by Marshal Konev sentenced the following to death by shooting: L. P. Beria, V. N. Merkulov, B. Z. Kobulov, V. G. Dekanozov, S. A. Gogolidze, D. Mierschik, and L. E. Vlodzimirsky.
7. Reported in *Pravda*, December 24, 1954.
8. In the March 1956 issue of *Voprosy istorii* two long-time Ukrainian Bolsheviks from Kiev, Madame I. S. Oslikovskaia and A. V. Suegov, demanded that N. A. Skrypnik be rehabilitated even though at that time he was still considered a "national deviationist." Worth mentioning here also is a letter from veterans of the 1905 revolution that appeared in the March 10, 1956, issue of *Pravda*. This letter was co-signed by some victims of Stalin's mass repressions.
9. Typical of this turn of events is an article by E. M. Burdzhalov in the April 1956 issue of *Voprosy istorii* entitled "O taktike bol'shevikov v marte-aprele 1917 goda" (About the Bolshevik Tactics in March and April 1917), and another article by M. A. Moskalev in the August 1956 issue of the same journal, "Bor'ba za ozdanie marksistskoi rabochei partii b 90-kh godakh XIX veka" (The Struggle for the Creation of the Marxist Workers Party in the 1890s).
10. See *Kommunist Ukrainy* (Kiev), no. 10, 1956.
11. Arguments for a rehabilitation of Dzhadidism, at least in part, are contained in the following publications: *Ocherki istorii partiinoi organizatsii Turkestana. Sotsial demokraticheskiye organizatsii Turkestana v dooktyabrskii (1903-mart 1917)* (Outlines of the History of the Turkestan Party Organization. The Social-Democratic Organizations in Turkestan Prior to the October Revolution [1903-March 1917]), (Tashkent, 1958), pp. 95 ff.; and M. Luldashev, "K istorii Kompartii Uzbekistana" (Contribution to the History of the Uzbek Communist Party), in *Kizil Uzbekiston* (Tashkent), June 17, 1954.
12. *Zaria vostoka* (Tiflis), August 23, 1956.
13. "Kogda utrachivaetsia nauchnyi podkhod" (When the Scientific Approach Is Lost), *Partiinaia zhizn'*, no. 4, 1956.

* See "List of Document Sources" on pp. 519 for full bibliographic data on all sources cited in this section.

14. Quoted from *Geschichte der Kommunistischen Partei der Sowjet-union* (History of the Communist Party of the Soviet Union), (Berlin, 1960), p. 841.
15. Both quotes taken from *Ostprobleme* (Bad Nauheim, Ger.), no. 5 (February 1, 1957), p. 146.
16. *L'Unità* (Rome), July 8, 1957.
17. See *Pravda,* July 7, 1957.
18. *Robitnycha gazeta* (Kiev), November 10, 1961.
19. *XXII s"ezd Kommunisticheskoi partii Sovetskogo Soiuza: Steno-graficheskoi otchet* (Twenty-second Congress of the CPSU: Steno-graphic Account), (Moscow, 1962), vol. 1, pp. 396 ff.
20. *Ibid.*, vol. 2, p. 43.
21. See, for example, *Literaturnaia gazeta,* January 16, 1962.
22. *Prapor* (Kharkov), no. 1, 1963.
23. N. S. Khrushchev and L. F. Ilichev, *Die Kunst gehört dem Volke* (Art Belongs to the People), (Berlin, 1963), pp. 114 ff.
24. *Ibid.*
25. *Voprosy istorii KPSS,* no. 5, 1966, p. 10.
26. Khrushchev's secret speech at the Twentieth Congress, as published by *Amerika-Dienst* (Bonn), June 1956.
27. *Ibid.*
28. *Bol'shaia sovetskaia entsiklopediia,* 2d ed., vol. 5, p. 22.
29. *Ibid.*, 2d ed., vol. 4, pp. 24 ff.
30. Khrushchev and Ilichev, *Die Kunst gehört dem Volke,* p. 119.
31. *Ibid.*, p. 121.
32. *Ukraïns'kyi istorychnyi zhurnal* (Kiev), no. 1, 1962, p. 149.
33. Giuseppe Boffa, *Dopo Krusciov* (Since Khrushchev), (Turin, 1965), p. 152.
34. *Rundschau über Politik, Wirtschaft und Arbeiterbewegung* (Basel), no. 14 (February 8, 1934), p. 525.
35. *Geschichte der Kommunistischen Partei der Sowjetunion,* p. 611.
36. *Istoriia Kommunisticheskoi partii Sovetskogo Soiuza* (History of the Communist Party of the Soviet Union), (2d ed., Moscow, 1962), p. 485. Emphasis in original.
37. *Ibid.*, p. 486.
38. *XXII s"ezd KPSS,* p. 587.
39. According to *Rundschau über Politik, Wirtschaft und Arbeiter-bewegung,* no. 14 (February 8, 1934), p. 515.
40. Khrushchev's secret speech . . . , p. 14.
41. L. M. Shaumian, "Na rubezhe pervykh piatiletok" (At a Milestone of the First Five-Year Plans), *Pravda,* February 7, 1964.
42. Khrushchev's secret speech . . . , as well as *Pravda,* February 7, 1964.
43. *Ocherki istorii Kommunisticheskoi partii Gruzii* (Outlines of the History of the Communist Party of Georgia), (Tiflis, 1962), p. 160.
44. *Marshal Tukhachevskii; Vospominaniia druzei i soratnikov* (Marshal Tukhachevskii; Reminiscences of Friends and Brothers-in-Arms), (Moscow, 1965), p. 230.

45. Iu. P. Petrov, *Partiinoe stroitel'stvo v sovetskoi Armii i Flote . . . 1918-1961* (Party Construction in the Soviet Army and Navy . . . 1918-1961), (Moscow, 1964), p. 229.
46. *Ibid.*, p. 300.
47. *Ibid.*
48. *Ibid.*, p. 301.
49. *Marshal Tukhachevskii; Vospominaniia . . .*, p. 234.
50. Petrov, *Partiinoe stroitel'stvo . . .*, p. 300.
51. *Ocherki istorii Kommunisticheskoi partii Kazakhstana* (Outlines of the History of the Communist Party of Kazakhstan), (Alma-Ata, 1963), p. 202.
52. *Voprosy istorii KPSS*, no. 8, 1965, pp. 105 ff.
53. *Izvestiia*, November 25, 1965.
54. *Trud* (Moscow), January 19, 1964.
55. *Pravda*, December 12, 1963.
56. *Kommunist Tadzhikistana* (Stalinabad), December 25, 1965.
57. *Literaturna Ukrainy* (Kiev), November 6, 1964.
58. *Sovetskaia istoricheskaia entsiklopediia*, vol. 8, p. 379.
59. *Ukrainskii istorichnii zhurnal*, no. 4, 1964, pp. 120 ff.
60. *Pravda*, February 14, 1963.
61. *Marshal Tukhachevskii; Vospominaniia . . .*, p. 244.
62. *Ukraïns'kyi istorychnyi zhurnal*, no. 1, 1963.
63. *Zaria vostoka*, November 18, 1961.
64. Khrushchev's secret speech . . . , p. 22.
65. *Ibid.*, p. 21.
66. *Ibid.*, p. 23.
67. *Ibid.*
68. *Voprosy istorii KPSS*, no. 2, 1963, pp. 96 ff.
69. Khrushchev's secret speech . . . , pp. 22 ff.
70. *Ibid.*, p. 19.
71. *Ibid.*
72. *Plenum Tsentralnogo komiteta Kommunisticheskoi partii Sovetskogo Soiuza (19-23 noiabria 1962)* (Plenum of the CC of the CPSU [November 19-23, 1962]), (Moscow, 1963), p. 369.
73. N. D. Kondrat'ev, *Marshal Bliukher* (Moscow, 1965), p. 292.
74. Lev Nikulin, *Tukhachevskii; Biograficheskii ocherk* (Tukhachevskii; Biographical Sketch), (Moscow, 1964), p. 191.
75. *Pravda*, September 18, 1964.
76. *Voprosy istorii KPSS*, no. 1, 1965, p. 104.
77. *Pravda*, June 10, 1963.
78. *Zaria vostoka*, September 29, 1963.
79. *Pravda*, November 1962.
80. Khrushchev's secret speech . . . , p. 48.
81. See also B. Lewytskyj, "Die Führungskräfte des Sowjetischen Parteiapparates" (The Leading Forces in the Soviet Party Apparatus), *Osteuropa* (Stuttgart), November-December 1965; and "Generations in Conflict," *Problems of Communism* (Washington, D. C.), January-February 1957.

I. LEADERS IN REVOLT AGAINST STALIN: KIROV AND ORDZHONIKIDZE

1. Krasnikov, *Kirov*, pp. 198-201.
2. *Istoriia Kommunisticheskoi partii Sovetskogo Soiuza*, 1st ed. (1959), p. 463.
3. *Istoriia Kommunisticheskoi partii Sovetskogo Soiuza*, 2d ed. (1962), p. 486.
4. Excerpt from N. S. Khrushchev's remarks at the Twenty-second Congress of the CPSU, October 27, 1961, *XXII s"ezd KPSS*, pp. 583-84.
5. *Ocherki istorii Leningrada*, vol. 4, pp. 355 and 381.
6. Excerpt from remarks by Khrushchev, *XXII s"ezd KPSS*, p. 587.
7. *Trud*, December 1, 1964, p. 2.

II. THE DESTRUCTION OF MILITARY CADRES

1. Petrov, *Partiinoe stroitel'stvo v sovetskoi Armii i Flote*, pp. 299-303.
2. Excerpt from remarks by Khrushchev, *XXII s"ezd KPSS*, pp. 585-86.
3. *Marshal Tukhachevskii; Vospominaniia . . .* , pp. 231-34.
4. *Neva*, no. 4, 1966, pp. 104-5 and 107.
5. From preface by Marshal S. Biriuzov, in Tukhachevskii, *Izbrannye proizvedeniia*, vol. 1, pp. 12-15 and 18.
6. Nikulin, *Tukhachevskii*, pp. 189-91.
7. D. V. Pankov, in *Voprosy istorii KPSS*, no. 12, 1964, pp. 93-96.
8. *Ibid.*
9. Pankov, *Komkor Eideman*, pp. 102-3.
10. *Marshal Tukhachevskii; Vospominaniia . . .* , p. 246.
11. Based on *Voenno-istoricheskii zhurnal*, no. 5, 1962, pp. 25-40; and *Marshal Tukhachevskii; Vospominaniia . . .* , p. 247.
12. *Voenno-istoricheskii zhurnal*, no. 5, 1962, pp. 25-40.
13. From speech by A. N. Shelepin, *XXII s"ezd KPSS*, p. 403.
14. From speech by Khrushchev, *XXII s"ezd KPSS*, pp. 186-87.
15. *Sovetskaia istoricheskaia entsiklopediia*, vol. 7, p. 960.
16. *Sovetskaia Estoniia*, no. 170 (7219), July 22, 1967.
17. *Nashe slovo*, October 26 and December 3, 1967.
18. *Sovetskaia istoricheskaia entsiklopediia*, vol. 2, pp. 713-14.
19. *Marshal Tukhachevskii; Vospominaniia . . .* , p. 246.
20. *Voprosy istorii KPSS*, no. 1, 1966, pp. 120-24.
21. *Krasnaia zvezda*, January 27, 1967.
22. Air Marshal S. Krasovskii, *Krasnaia zvezda*, January 17, 1967.
23. Based on *Ukraïns'kyi istorychnyi zhurnal*, no. 6, 1963, pp. 118-20.
24. *Sovetskaia istoricheskaia entsiklopediia*, vol. 1, pp. 634-35.
25. A. Rudenko, in *Krasnaia zvezda*, March 22, 1963.
26. *Marshal Tukhachevskii; Vospominaniia . . .* , p. 235.

27. Lieutenant General (ret.) A. Dobriakov, in *Krasnaia zvezda*, December 1, 1963.
28. *Krasnaia zvezda*, June 15, 1963.
29. *Ibid.*
30. *Marshal Tukhachevskii; Vospominaniia . . .* , p. 235.
31. *Krasnaia zvezda*, November 13, 1964.
32. Korol'kov, *Chelovek dlia kotorogo ne bylo tain*, pp. 17-21.
33. *Marshal Tukhachevskii; Vospominaniia . . .* , p. 238.
34. *Ibid.*, p. 235.
35. *Ibid.*, p. 236.
36. *Sovetskaia istoricheskaia entsiklopediia*, vol. 2, p. 491.
37. Marshal of the Armored Forces R. Rotmistrov, in *Pravda*, November 19, 1964.
38. *Kazakhstanskaia pravda*, November 19, 1964.
39. Kondrat'ev, *Marshal Bliukher*, pp. 288-93.
40. *Marshal Tukhachevskii; Vospominaniia . . .* , p. 236.
41. *Sovetskaia Latviia*, September 20, 1963.
42. General Colonel I. Lebedev, in *ibid.*
43. *Krasnaia zvezda*, February 1, 1964.
44. *Ibid.*
45. *Ukraïns'ka radians'ka entsyklopediia*, vol. 4, p. 360.
46. *Sovetskaia istoricheskaia entsiklopediia*, vol. 5, p. 422.
47. *Pravda*, February 17, 1964.
48. *Sovetskaia istoricheskaia entsiklopediia*, vol. 5, p. 473.
49. *Marshal Tukhachevskii; Vospominaniia . . .* , p. 246.
50. *Ibid.*, p. 238.
51. S. Budennyi, in Airapetian, *Legendarnyi Gai*, pp. 5-6.
52. *Marshal Tukhachevskii; Vospominaniia . . .* , p. 238.
53. *Sovetskaia istoricheskaia entsiklopediia*, vol. 4, p. 71.
54. G. Pukhov, in *Krasnaia zvezda*, June 2, 1964.
55. Based on *Voenno-istoricheskii zhurnal*, no. 10, 1965, pp. 125-27; and *Marshal Tukhachevskii; Vospominaniia . . .* , p. 238.
56. *Voenno-istoricheskii zhurnal*, no. 10, 1965, pp. 125-27.
57. *Marshal Tukhachevskii; Vospominaniia . . .* , p. 238.
58. *Voprosy strategii i operativnogo iskusstva v sovetskikh voennykh trudakh, 1917- 40*, p. 739.
59. *Ibid.*, p. 743.
60. *Krasnaia zvezda*, July 31, 1963.
61. *Ibid.*
62. *Sovetskaia istoricheskaia entsiklopediia*, vol. 7, p. 138.
63. *Voenno-istoricheskii zhurnal*, no. 12, 1965, pp. 120-22.
64. *Ibid.*
65. *Marshal Tukhachevskii; Vospominaniia . . .* , p. 241.
66. *Sovetskaia istoricheskaia entsiklopediia*, vol. 7, p. 459.
67. *Voprosy istorii*, no. 6, 1965, pp. 211-14.
68. *Marshal Tukhachevskii; Vospominaniia . . .* , p. 242.

69. *Sovetskaia istoricheskaia entsiklopediia*, vol. 8, p. 258.
70. Petrov, *Partiinoe stroitel'stvo v sovetskoi Armii i Flote*, p. 303.
71. *Marshal Tukhachevskii; Vospominaniia . . .* , p. 241.
72. *Sovetskaia istoricheskaia entsiklopediia*, vol. 8, p. 338.
73. *Krasnaia zvezda*, April 3, 1963.
74. *Ibid.*
75. *Marshal Tukhachevskii; Vospominaniia . . .* , p. 242.
76. *Ibid.*
77. *Ibid.*
78. *Zaria vostoka*, May 16, 1965.
79. *Marshal Tukhachevskii; Vospominaniia . . .* , p. 242.
80. *Sovetskaia istoricheskaia entsiklopediia*, vol. 9, pp. 413-14.
81. *Voprosy strategii i operativnogo iskusstva v sovetskikh voennykh trudakh, 1917- 40*, p. 746.
82. *Pravda vostoka*, October 7, 1967.
83. *Voprosy strategii i operativnogo iskusstva v sovetskikh voennykh trudakh, 1917- 40*, p. 746.
84. *Voenno-istoricheskii zhurnal*, no. 11, 1965, pp. 122-24.
85. *Ibid.*
86. *Kommunist* (Erevan), April 19, 1966.
87. G. Oganesov, in *ibid.*
88. *Krasnaia zvezda*, August 1, 1964.
89. B. Fonareva, in *ibid.*
90. *Marshal Tukhachevskii; Vospominaniia . . .* , p. 243.
91. *Ibid.*
92. *Ibid.*, p. 244.
93. *Ibid.*
94. *Pravda vostoka*, June 13, 1968.
95. *Sovetskaia istoricheskaia entsiklopediia*, vol. 11, p. 87.
96. *Sovetskaia Latviia*, January 20, 1967.
97. *Sovetskaia istoricheskaia entsiklopediia*, vol. 11, pp. 151-52.
98. *Marshal Tukhachevskii; Vospominaniia . . .* , p. 244.
99. *Voenno-istoricheskii zhurnal*, no. 8, 1965, pp. 33-35, 37-39.
100. *Ibid.*
101. *Marshal Tukhachevskii; Vospominaniia . . .* , p. 245.
102. *Ibid.*
103. *Krasnaia zvezda*, November 21, 1964.
104. Lieutenant General S. Kovalev, in *ibid.*
105. *Marshal Tukhachevskii; Vospominaniia . . .* , p. 245.
106. *Voprosy strategii i operativnogo iskusstva v sovetskikh voennykh trudakh, 1917- 40*, p. 749.
107. *Krasnaia zvezda*, April 19, 1964.
108. *Ibid.*
109. *Voprosy strategii i operativnogo iskusstva v sovetskikh voennykh trudakh, 1917- 40*, p. 749.
110. *Marshal Tukhachevskii; Vospominaniia . . .* , p. 245.

111. *Kommunist* (Erevan), September 4, 1964.
112. *Ibid.*
113. *Krasnaia zvezda,* May 28, 1965.
114. Major General (ret.) T. Govorukhin, in *ibid.*
115. *Marshal Tukhachevskii; Vospominaniia . . . ,* p. 246.
116. *Krasnaia zvezda,* December 19, 1964.
117. *Krasnaia zvezda,* March 2, 1965.
118. *Ibid.*
119. *Marshal Tukhachevskii; Vospominaniia . . . ,* p. 236.
120. *Ibid.,* p. 237.
121. *Ibid.*
122. *Sovetskaia istoricheskaia entsiklopediia,* vol. 3, p. 33.
123. Colonel I. Obertas, in *Krasnaia zvezda,* November 22, 1963.
124. *Marshal Tukhachevskii; Vospominaniia . . . ,* p. 237.
125. *Krasnaia zvezda,* August 21, 1964.
126. *Ibid.*
127. *Voprosy strategii i operativnogo iskusstva v sovetskikh voennykh trudakh, 1917- 40,* p. 741.
128. Based on *Ukraïns'kyi istorychnyi zhurnal,* no. 3, 1962, pp. 148 ff.
129. *Voprosy strategii i operativnogo iskusstva v sovetskikh voennykh trudakh, 1917- 40,* p. 751.

III. PROMINENT LEADERS OF THE CPSU

1. *Kul'turnoe stroitel'stvo v Chuvashskoi ASSR,* vol. 1, p. 368.
2. *Entsiklopedicheskii slovar',* vol. 1, p. 56.
3. *Kommunist* (Erevan), August 31, 1967.
4. *Revoliutsionno-istoricheskii kalendar'-spravochnik 1967 g.,* pp. 270-73.
5. *Sovetskaia istoricheskaia entsiklopediia,* vol. 2, pp. 784-85.
6. Based on *Voprosy istorii KP SSSR,* no. 4, 1963, pp. 109-12.
7. Based on *Voprosy istorii KPSS,* no. 6, 1965, pp. 92-96.
8. *Ibid.*
9. Based on *Ukrains'kyi istorychnyi zhurnal,* no. 12, 1965, pp. 126 ff.
10. *Sovetskaia Rossiia,* January 25, 1967.
11. Iurii Gribov, in *ibid.*
12. Based on *Voprosy istorii KPSS,* no. 7, 1965, pp. 92-97.
13. *Ibid.*
14. *Revoliutsionno-istoricheskii kalendar-spravochnik 1967 g.,* pp. 145-49.
15. *Zaria vostoka,* March 17, 1967.
16. *Ibid.*
17. *Sovetskaia istoricheskaia entsiklopediia,* vol. 4, p. 440.
18. *Ibid.,* p. 481.
19. *Zaria vostoka,* April 17, 1966.
20. *Sovetskaia istoricheskaia entsiklopediia,* vol. 4, pp. 504-5.

21. *Ukrains'kyi radians'kyi entsyklopedychnyi slovnyk*, vol. 1, p. 517.
22. *Sovetskaia istoricheskaia entsiklopediia*, vol. 4, pp. 904-5.
23. *Pravda*, March 11, 1964.
24. *Sovetskaia istoricheskaia entsiklopediia*, vol. 5, p. 785.
25. *Pravda*, April 9, 1964.
26. *Sovetskaia istoricheskaia entsiklopediia*, vol. 5, p. 799.
27. *Istoriia industrializatsii Kazakhskoi SSSR*, vol. 1, p. 441.
28. *Odinnadtsatyi s''ezd RKP (b)*, p. 821.
29. *Kommunist* (Erevan), February 27, 1964.
30. *Ibid.*
31. *Istoriia industrializatsii Kazakhskoi SSR*, vol. 6, p. 860.
32. *Izvestiia*, October 24, 1963.
33. Kalmykov, *Stat'i i rechi*, pp. 4-6.
34. *Bakinskii rabochii*, June 7, 1966.
35. *Ibid.*
36. Based on *Ukraïns'kyi istorychnyi zhurnal*, no. 4, 1962, pp. 151 ff.
37. *Entsiklopedicheskii slovar'*, vol. 2, p. 606.
38. M. D. Bednov, in *Voprosy istorii KPSS*, no. 6, 1963, pp. 98-101.
39. *Sovetskaia istoricheskaia entsiklopediia*, vol. 7, p. 444.
40. *Sovetskaia Belorussiia*, August 29, 1965.
41. *Sovetskaia istoricheskaia entsiklopediia*, vol. 7, p. 989.
42. *Pravda*, November 14, 1963.
43. *Sovetskaia istoricheskaia entsiklopediia*, vol. 7, pp. 990-91.
44. *Pravda*, November 18, 1964.
45. *Kommunist* (Erevan), July 28, 1967.
46. *Ibid.*
47. Based on *Voprosy istorii KPSS*, no. 12, 1964, pp. 96-99.
48. *Sel'skaia zhizn'*, September 9, 1964.
49. Based on *Istoriia SSSR*, no. 3, 1967, pp. 63-68.
50. *Ibid.*
51. *Istoriia industrializatsii Kazakhskoi SSR*, vol. 1, pp. 439-40.
52. *Sovetskaia istoricheskaia entsiklopediia*, vol. 8, p. 292.
53. *Kommunist* (organ of the Armenian CP), January 20, 1966.
54. *Ibid.*
55. *Sovetskaia istoricheskaia entsiklopediia*, vol. 7, p. 149.
56. *Pravda*, September 13, 1963.
57. Based on *Istoriia SSSR*, no. 4, 1967, pp. 56-60.
58. *Ukraïns'kyi istorychnyi zhurnal*, no. 6, 1962, pp. 134-36.
59. *Sovetskaia istoricheskaia entsiklopediia*, vol. 8, pp. 809-10.
60. Based on *Ukraïns'kyi istorychnyi zhurnal*, no. 2, 1964, pp. 113-16.
61. *Zaria vostoka*, August 4, 1965.
62. *Ibid.*
63. Based on *Voprosy istorii KPSS*, no. 1, 1965, pp. 101-4.
64. *Ibid.*, pp. 101-4.
65. *Bakinskii rabochii*, July 22, 1965.

66. *Ibid.*
67. *Zaria vostoka,* November 17, 1964.
68. *Ibid.*
69. *Istoriia industrializatsii Kazakhskoi SSSR,* vol. 1, p. 434.
70. *Pravda,* June 10, 1963.
71. *Ibid.*
72. *Zaria vostoka,* November 17, 1967.
73. *Kul'turnoe stroitel'stvo v Chuvashskoi ASSR,* vol. 1, p. 363.
74. *Bol'shaia sovetskaia entsiklopediia,* vol. 51, p. 239.
75. Based on *Ukrains'kyi istorychnyi zhurnal,* no. 5, 1963, pp. 124-26.
76. *Bakinskii rabochii,* June 19, 1966.
77. *Ibid.*
78. *Bakinskii rabochii,* July 13, 1963.
79. *Ibid.*
80. *Sovetskaia istoricheskaia entsiklopediia,* vol. 11, p. 291.
81. *Turkmenskaia iskra,* September 20, 1964.
82. *Ibid.*
83. Mariagin, *Postyshev,* pp. 299-302.
84. From notes by Barvinets in *ibid.,* pp. 293-98.
85. *Kommunist Tadzhikistana,* November 1, 1967.
86. *Sovetskaia Kirgiziia,* July 7, 1968.
87. Based on *Voprosy istorii KPSS,* no. 2, 1964, pp. 110-13.
88. *Kommunist Tadzhikistana,* April 4, 1964.
89. *Ibid.*
90. *Robitnycha gazeta,* April 12, 1964.
91. *Sel'skaia zhizn',* September 18, 1964.
92. *Ibid.*
93. Based on *Voprosy istorii KPSS,* no. 1, 1965, pp. 94-97.
94. *Ibid.,* pp. 94-97.
95. From speech by N. S. Khrushchev, *XXII s"ezd KPSS,* p. 582.
96. *Zaria vostoka,* March 21, 1965.
97. *Ibid.*
98. *Pravda,* September 18, 1964.
99. *Voprosy istorii KPSS,* no. 2, 1963, pp. 101-6.
100. *Radians'ka Ukraina,* September 20, 1964.
101. *Odinnadtsatyi s"ezd RKP(b),* p. 820.
102. *Sovetskaia istoricheskaia entsiklopediia,* vol. 5, p. 527.
103. *Zaria vostoka,* February 7, 1967.

IV. LEADERS OF THE NATIONAL COMMUNIST PARTIES

1. *Kommunist* (Erevan), November 15, 1961.
2. *Bakinskii rabochii,* November 30, 1961.
3. *Bakinskii rabochii,* January 26, 1938.
4. *KPSS v rezoliutsiiakh i resheniiakh,* vol. 3, p. 308.

5. *Ocherki istorii KP Azerbaidzhana,* pp. 540-42.
6. From a speech by K. T. Mazurov, *XXII s"ezd KPSS,* p. 291.
7. *Kommunist* (Moscow), no. 8, 1964, pp. 76-78.
8. *Ocherki istorii KP Estonii,* pp. 342-43.
9. *Zaria vostoka,* November 19, 1961.
10. *Ocherki istorii KP Gruzii,* pp. 158-59.
11. *Istoriia Iakutskoi ASSR,* vol. 3, p. 285.
12. *Ocherki istorii KP Kazakhstana,* pp. 376-77.
13. *Kommunist* (Moscow), no. 12, 1964, pp. 67-68.
14. *Sovetskaia Litva,* November 19, 1961.
15. *Sovetskaia Moldaviia,* November 17, 1961.
16. *Zaria vostoka,* November 19, 1961.
17. *Ocherki istorii KP Tadzhikistana,* pp. 168-70.
18. *Ocherki istorii KP Turkmenistana,* p. 495.
19. *Ocherki istorii Kommunisticheskoi partii Ukrainy,* p. 466.
20. *Kommunist* (Moscow), no. 10, 1964, pp. 44-45.
21. *Sovetskaia istoricheskaia entsiklopediia,* vol. 1, pp. 491-92.
22. *Ibid.,* pp. 490-91.
23. *Pravda,* April 27, 1964.
24. *Sovetskaia Moldaviia,* September 12, 1964.
25. *Ibid.*
26. Based on *Kommunist Belorussii,* no. 2, 1967, pp. 77-78.
27. *Ibid.,* pp. 77-78.
28. Based on *Ukraïns'kyi istorychnyi zhurnal,* no. 3, 1961, pp. 144 ff.
29. Based on *Ukraïns'kyi istorychnyi zhurnal,* no. 1, 1963, pp. 94-96.
30. *Kommunist Tadzhikistana,* November 29, 1964.
31. S. Ovezova, in *ibid.*
32. *Pravda,* March 12, 1964.
33. *Ibid.*
34. *Entsiklopedicheskii slovar',* vol. 2, p. 732.
35. *Izvestiia,* May 23, 1964.
36. Based on *Ukraïns'kyi istorychnyi zhurnal,* no. 6, 1963, pp. 118-20.
37. *Izvestiia,* May 25, 1966.
38. G. Dimov, in *Pravda vostoka,* May 26, 1966.
39. Based on *Ukraïns'kyi istorychnyi zhurnal,* no. 3, 1961, pp. 145 ff.
40. *Ukrains'ka radians'ka entsyklopediia,* vol. 7, p. 473.
41. *Sovetskaia istoricheskaia entsiklopediia,* vol. 8, p. 584.
42. *Kommunist* (Erevan), December 25, 1966.
43. *Ibid.*
44. *Kazakhstanskaia pravda,* February 23, 1964.
45. *Ibid.*
46. *Bakinskii rabochii,* November 24, 1964.
47. *Ibid.*
48. *Kazakhstanskaia pravda,* December 26, 1964.
49. *Ibid.*

50. *Kommunist* (Erevan), May 30, 1965.
51. *Ibid.*
52. *Ukrains'ka radians'ka entsyklopediia*, vol. 13, p. 228.
53. *Sovetskaia Moldaviia*, December 9, 1965.
54. *Ibid.*
55. *Bakinskii rabochii*, May 26, 1964.
56. *Ibid.*
57. *Kommunist* (Erevan), February 27, 1966.
58. *Ibid.*
59. *Sovetskaia Belorussiia*, April 4, 1965.
60. *Ibid.*
61. *Sovetskaia istoricheskaia entsiklopediia*, vol. 5, p. 632.

V. STATESMEN

1. *Turkmenskaia iskra*, October 26, 1967.
2. *Kazakhstanskaia pravda*, April 24, 1964.
3. *Ibid.*
4. *Kommunist* (Erevan), May 10, 1964.
5. *Ibid.*
6. *Entsiklopedicheskii slovar'*, vol. 2, p. 724.
7. Based on *Voprosy istorii KPSS*, no. 2, 1965, pp. 124-28.
8. *Ibid.*, pp. 124-28.
9. *Kommunist* (Erevan), January 28, 1966.
10. *Ibid.*
11. *Sovetskaia istoricheskaia entsiklopediia*, vol. 7, p. 293.
12. Based on *Ukraïns'kyi istorychnyi zhurnal*, no. 4, 1962, pp. 152 ff.
13. *Sovetskaia istoricheskaia entsiklopediia*, vol. 8, pp. 194-95.
14. *Voprosy istorii KPSS*, no. 5, 1965, pp. 116-20.
15. *Sovetskaia istoricheskaia entsiklopediia*, vol. 8, p. 382.
16. *Ibid.*, p. 913.
17. *Kommunist* (Erevan), February 14, 1968.
18. *Sovetskaia istoricheskaia entsiklopediia*, vol. 9, p. 749.
19. *Sovetskaia Rossiia*, June 21, 1966.
20. *Ibid.*
21. *Sovetskaia istoricheskaia entsiklopediia*, vol. 9, p. 818.
22. Based on *Ukraïns'kyi istorychnyi zhurnal*, no. 8, 1965, pp. 133 ff.
23. *Kommunist* (Erevan), December 12, 1967.
24. *Istoriia industrializatsii Kazakhskoi SSR*, vol. 1, p. 437.
25. *Kul'turnoe stroitel'stvo v Chuvashskoi ASSR*, vol. 1, p. 368.

VI. CAPTAINS OF INDUSTRY

1. *Sovetskaia istoricheskaia entsiklopediia*, vol. 6, pp. 30-31.
2. *Voprosy istorii*, no. 5, 1966, p. 14.

3. Lel'chuk, *Sozdanie khimicheskoi promyshlennosti*, p. 374.
4. *XXII s"ezd KPSS*, p. 215.
5. *Voprosy istorii KPSS*, no. 1, 1965, pp. 122-25.
6. *Bakinskii rabochii*, March 25, 1966.
7. *Ibid*.
8. *Bakinskii rabochii*, October 15, 1963.
9. *Ibid*.
10. *Sovetskaia Latviia*, December 2, 1964.
11. I. Iakovlev, in *ibid*.
12. *Sovetskaia Latviia*, August 31, 1965.
13. *Ibid*.
14. *Sovetskaia istoricheskaia entsiklopediia*, vol. 2, p. 780.
15. *Ibid*., vol. 4, p. 973.
16. *Bakinskii rabochii*, September 8, 1964.
17. *Ibid*.
18. *Zaria vostoka*, September 29, 1963.
19. *Ibid*.
20. *Sovetskaia istoricheskaia entsiklopediia*, vol. 4, p. 468.
21. *Ibid*., vol. 8, p. 249.
22. *Ibid*., pp. 767-68.
23. *Pravda*, February 10, 1963.
24. Speech by A. N. Shelepin, *XXII s"ezd KPSS*, p. 404.
25. *Sovetskaia istoricheskaia entsiklopediia*, vol. 9, pp. 286-87.
26. *Voprosy istorii KPSS*, no. 2, 1963, pp. 99-100.
27. *Sovetskaia istoricheskaia entsiklopediia*, vol. 9, p. 454.
28. *Izvestiia*, December 1, 1964.
29. *Sovetskaia istoricheskaia entsiklopediia*, vol. 10, pp. 642-43.
30. *Ukraïns'ka radians'ka entsyklopediia*, vol. 12, p. 92.
31. Based on *Voprosy istorii KPSS*, no. 4, 1963, pp. 102-8.
32. *Ibid*.
33. *Istoriia industrializatsii Kazakhskoi SSR*, vol. 1, p. 435.
34. *Ukraïns'ka radians'ka entsyklopediia*, vol. 13, p. 81.
35. *Sovetskaia Rossiia*, December 25, 1964.
36. *Bakinskii rabochii*, May 21, 1964.
37. *Ibid*.
38. *Ukraïns'ka radians'ka entsyklopediia*, vol. 4, p. 200.
39. *Voprosy istorii*, no. 2, 1966, pp. 207-9.
40. *Odinnadtsatyi s"ezd RKP(b)*, p. 852.
41. *Malaia sovetskaia entsiklopediia*, vol. 8, p. 945; and *Krasnaia zvezda*, December 18, 1963.
42. *Krasnaia zvezda*, December 18, 1963.
43. *Zaria vostoka*, March 20, 1966.
44. *Ibid*.
45. *Odinnadtsatyi s"ezd RKP(b)*, p. 820.

VII. DIPLOMATS

1. *Sovetskaia istoricheskaia entsiklopediia,* vol. 7, p. 22.
2. *Ibid.,* vol. 8, pp. 75-76.

VIII. CHEKISTS

1. *Sovetskaia istoricheskaia entsiklopediia,* vol. 2, p. 321.
2. *Krasnaia zvezda,* October 11, 1963.
3. *Ibid.*
4. *Kommunist Tadzhikistana,* August 17, 1965.
5. *Ibid.*
6. *Kazakhstanskaia pravda,* January 17, 1965.
7. *Ibid.*
8. *Sovetskaia Litva,* December 8, 1967.
9. *Marshal Tukhachevskii; Vospominaniia . . . ,* p. 241.
10. *Voprosy istorii,* no. 9, 1966, pp. 207-9.
11. *Sovetskaia istoricheskaia entsiklopediia,* vol. 7, pp. 150-51.
12. I. V. Viktorov, in *Voprosy istorii KPSS,* no. 11, 1963, pp. 105-7.
13. *Sovetskaia istoricheskaia entsiklopediia,* vol. 8, p. 496.
14. *Kommunist* (Erevan), January 13, 1965.
15. *Ibid.*
16. *Kazakhstanskaia pravda,* July 27, 1965.
17. *Ibid.*
18. *Zaria vostoka,* March 12, 1966.
19. *Ibid.*

LIST OF DOCUMENT SOURCES

BOOKS

Airapetian, G. A. *Legendarnyi Gai*. Moscow, 1965.

Bol'shaia sovetskaia entsiklopediia (Great Soviet Encyclopedia). 51 vols. 2d ed., Moscow, 1950-58.

XXII [Dvadtsat' vtoroi] s''ezd Kommunisticheskoi partii Sovetskogo Soiuza: Stenograficheskoi otchet (Twenty-second Congress of the Communist Party of the Soviet Union: Stenographic Account). Moscow, 1962.

Entsiklopedicheskii slovar' (Encyclopedic Dictionary). 2 vols. Moscow, 1963-64.

Istoriia Iakutskoi ASSR (History of the Iakut ASSR). 3 vols. Moscow, 1955-63.

Istoriia industrializatsii Kazakhskoi SSR, 1926-1941 gg. (History of the Industrialization of the Kazakh SSR, 1926-1941). 2 vols. Alma-Ata, 1967.

Istoriia Kommunisticheskoi partii Sovetskogo Soiuza (History of the Communist Party of the Soviet Union). 1st ed., Moscow, 1959; 2d ed., rev., Moscow, 1962.

Kalmykov, Betal. *Stat'i i rechi* (Articles and Speeches). B. Kh. Tsavkilov, ed.; U. A. Uligov, E. T. Khakuashev, and D. V. Shavaev, comps. Nal'chik, 1961.

Kondrat'ev, Nikolai D. *Marshal Bliukher*. Moscow, 1965.

Kommunisticheskaia partiia Sovetskogo Soiuza v rezoliutsiiakh i resheniiakh s'' e zdov, konferentsii i plenumov TsK, 1898-1960 (The Communist Party of the Soviet Union in Resolutions and Decisions of the Congresses, Conferences and Plenums of the Central Committee, 1898-1960). 4 vols. 7th ed., Moscow, 1954-60.

Korol'kov, Iu. *Chelovek dlia kotorogo ne bylo tain* (The Man for Whom There Were No Secrets). Moscow, 1966.

Krasnikov, S. A. *Sergei Mironovich Kirov: Zhizn'i deiatel'nost* (Sergei Mironovich Kirov: His Life and Activities). Moscow, 1964.

Kul'turnoe stroitel'stvo v Chuvashskoi ASSR (Cultural Construction in the Chuvash ASSR). 2 vols. Cheboksary, 1965-68.

Lel'chuk, V. S. *Sozdanie khimicheskoi promyshlennosti SSSR* (Construction of the Chemical Industry in the U.S.S.R.). Moscow, 1964.

Malaia sovetskaia entsiklopediia (Small Soviet Encyclopedia). 10 vols. Moscow, 1930-31.

Mariagin, G. A. *Postyshev*. Moscow, 1965.

Marshal Tukhachevskii; Vospominaniia druzei i soratnikov (Marshal Tukhachevsky; Reminiscences of Friends and Brothers-in-Arms). N. I. Koritsky, S. M. Mel'nik-Tukhachevskaia, and B. N. Chistov, comps. Moscow, 1965.

Nikulin, Lev. *Tukhachevskii; Biograficheskii ocherk* (Tukhachevsky; Biographical Sketch). Moscow, 1964.

519

Ocherki istorii Kommunisticheskoi partii Azerbaidzhana (Outlines of the History of the Communist Party of Azerbaidzhan). Baku, 1963.

Ocherki istorii Kommunisticheskoi partii Estonii (Outlines of the History of the Communist Party of Estonia). Tallin, 1963.

Ocherki istorii Kommunisticheskoi partii Gruzii (Outlines of the History of the Communist Party of Georgia). Part II, 1921-1963. Tiflis, 1963.

Ocherki istorii Kommunisticheskoi partii Kazakhstana (Outlines of the History of the Communist Party of Kazakhstan). Alma-Ata, 1963.

Ocherki istorii Kommunisticheskoi partii Tadzhikistana (Outlines of the History of the Communist Party of Tadzhikistan). Dushanbe, 1964.

Ocherki istorii Kommunisticheskoi partii Turkmenistana (Outlines of the History of the Communist Party of Turkmenistan). 2d ed., rev. Ashkhabad, 1965.

Ocherki istorii Kommunisticheskoi partii Ukrainy (Outlines of the History of the Communist Party of the Ukraine). 2d ed., rev. Kiev, 1964.

Ocherki istorii Leningrada (Outlines of the History of Leningrad). Moscow, 1955 — .

Ocherki istorii partiinoi organizatsii Turkestana; Sotsial demokraticheskiye organizatsii Turkestana v dooktyabrskii (1903-mart 1917) (Outlines of the History of the Turkestan Party Organization; The Social-Democratic Organizations in Turkestan Prior to the October Revolution [1903-March 1917]). Tashkent, 1958.

Odinnadtsatyi s''ezd RKP(b) (Eleventh Congress of the Russian Communist Party [Bolsheviks]). Moscow, 1961.

Pankov, D. V. *Komkor Eideman* (Corps Commander Eideman). Moscow, 1965.

Petrov, Iu. P. *Partiinoe stroitel'stvo v sovetskoi Armii i Flote . . . 1918-1961* (Party Construction in the Soviet Army and Navy . . . 1918-1961). Moscow, 1964.

Revoliutsionno-istoricheskii kalendar'-spravochnik 1967 g. (Revolutionary-Historical Calendar-Guide 1967). Moscow, 1967.

Sovetskaia istoricheskaia entsiklopediia (Soviet Historical Encyclopedia). Moscow, 1961 — .

Tukhachevskii, M. N. *Izbrannye proizvedeniia* (Selected Works). 2 vols., with Preface by Marshal S. Biriuzov. Moscow, 1964.

Ukraïns'ka radians'ka entsyklopediia (Ukrainian Soviet Encyclopedia). 17 vols. Kiev, 1959-65.

Ukraïns'kyi radians'kyi entsyklopedychnyi slovnyk (Ukrainian Soviet Encyclopedic Dictionary). 3 vols. Kiev, 1966-68.

Voprosy strategii i operativnogo iskusstva v sovetskikh voennykh trudakh, 1917-40 (Problems of Strategy and Tactical Skill in Soviet Military Studies, 1917-40). Moscow, 1965.

PERIODICALS

Bakinskii rabochii (Baku Worker). Baku.

Istoriia SSSR (History of the U.S.S.R.). Moscow.

Izvestiia (News). Moscow.

Kazakhstanskaia pravda (Kazakhstan Truth). Alma-Ata.
Kizil Uzbekiston (Red Uzbekistan). Tashkent.
Kommunist (Communist; organ of the Armenian CP). Erevan.
Kommunist (Communist; organ of the CC of the CPSU). Moscow.
Kommunist Belorussii (Communist of Belorussia). Minsk.
Kommunist Tadzhikistana (Communist of Tadzhikistan). Stalinabad.
Kommunist Ukrainy (Communist of the Ukraine). Kiev.
Krasnaia zvezda (Red Star). Moscow.
Literaturna Ukraïna (Literary Ukraine). Kiev.
Molodoi kommunist (Young Communist). Moscow.
Nashe slovo (Our Word). Moscow.
Neva (Neva). Leningrad.
Partiinaia zhizn' (Party Life). Moscow.
Prapor (Banner). Kharkov.
Pravda (Truth). Moscow.
Pravda vostoka (Truth of the East). Tashkent.
Rabochaia gazeta (Workers' Newspaper). Moscow.
Radians'ka Ukraïna (Soviet Ukraine). Kiev.
Robitnycha gazeta (Workers' Newspaper). Kiev.
Sel'skaia zhizn' (Village Life). Moscow.
Sovetskaia Belorussiia (Soviet Belorussia). Minsk.
Sovetskaia Estoniia (Soviet Estonia). Tallin.
Sovetskaia Kirgiziia (Soviet Kirgiz). Frunze.
Sovetskaia Latviia (Soviet Latvia). Riga.
Sovetskaia Litva (Soviet Lithuania). Wilnius.
Sovetskaia Moldaviia (Soviet Moldavia). Kishinev.
Sovetskaia Rossiia (Soviet Russia). Moscow.
Trud (Labor). Moscow.
Turkemskaia iskra (Turkmenian Spark). Ashkhabad.
Ukraïns'kyi istorychnyi zhurnal (Ukrainian Historical Journal). Kiev.
Voenno-istoricheskii zhurnal (Military and Historical Journal). Moscow.
Voprosy istorii (Problems of History). Moscow.
Voprosy istorii KPSS (Problems of the History of the CPSU). Moscow.
Zaria vostoka (Dawn of the East). Tiflis.